Deepening Communion

INTERNATIONAL ECUMENICAL

DOCUMENTS WITH

ROMAN CATHOLIC PARTICIPATION

∞

To
Paul A. Crow Jr. and
Günther Gassman
in appreciation and recognition of
their many contributions to the
efforts for Christian unity.

Deepening Communion

INTERNATIONAL ECUMENICAL

DOCUMENTS WITH

ROMAN CATHOLIC PARTICIPATION

∞

Edited by
WILLIAM G. RUSCH AND JEFFREY GROS

with Preface by
CARDINAL EDWARD CASSIDY

and Foreword by
MARY TANNER

UNITED STATES CATHOLIC CONFERENCE
WASHINGTON, D.C.

The National Conference of Catholic Bishops' Committee on Ecumenical and Interreligious Affairs recommended this publication. The texts have been reviewed by Archbishop Alexander Brunett, chair of the NCCB Committee for Ecumenical and Interreligious Affairs, and it is authorized for publication by the undersigned.

Monsignor Dennis M. Schnurr
General Secretary
NCCB/USCC

Text from *Information Service* used with permission of Bishop Pierre Duprey, Secretary of the Pontifical Council for Promoting Christian Unity.

Text from *The Evangelical Roman Catholic Dialogue on Mission 1977-1984*. Copyright © by Basil Meeking and John Stott 1986. Published by Paternoster Press, Carlisle, UK. Used with permission.

First Printing, June 1998

ISBN 1-57455-164-7

Table of Contents

PART THREE METHODIST–ROMAN CATHOLIC

PART FOUR CHRISTIAN CHURCH/DISCIPLES OF CHRIST–ROMAN CATHOLIC

PART FIVE BAPTIST–ROMAN CATHOLIC

PART SIX PENTECOSTAL–ROMAN CATHOLIC

PART SEVEN EVANGELICAL–ROMAN CATHOLIC

PART EIGHT JOINT WORKING GROUP, WORLD COUNCIL OF CHURCHES–ROMAN CATHOLIC

Preface

✠ Cardinal Edward Idris Cassidy
President, Pontifical Council for Promoting Christian Unity

As the twentieth century winds down, it becomes more and more apparent to separated Christians that a major responsibility shared by all who are involved in the search for Christian unity is to foster together an ecumenical momentum that will promote fresh hopes for ecumenical progress in the new millennium. This collection of international ecumenical documents resulting from dialogues with Roman Catholic participation represents a contribution to that momentum.

The reports included in this collection cover the period from the early 1980s to 1996. Momentous world events have taken place during that period, bringing changes that have had impact also on ecumenical relations. Some have claimed that the movement toward Christian unity has stagnated during this period. This volume illustrates clearly, however, that during these years solid theological work has continued to produce important results.

One can see reflected in these reports some of the general trends in the ecumenical movement today or hints of new levels of relationship that have been reached. For example, the reports reflect the fact that ecclesiology has become more and more a central focus in dialogue today (nos. 3, 4, 5, 8, 12, 16). The problems of mission and witness when Christians are divided continue to be explored (e.g., nos. 9, 13, 19). The challenges of reaching the goal of unity have been taken up (nos. 2, 17). In addition to questions having to do specifically with faith, dialogue has begun to take up matters relating to moral issues (no. 20). These observations illustrate that in regard to theological dialogue, which is one of the vital aspects of the ecumenical movement, creative work in the last two decades of the twentieth century has set the stage for an ecumenical entry into the next millennium.

Progress in dialogue should, however, have an impact on other aspects of ecumenism as well, such as prayer, education, and common witness, which in their turn support the dialogue. If progress is made toward theological convergence or consensus on issues that have long divided Christians, how much more necessary for reception of these results are the spiritual aspects of ecumenism, such as prayer and personal *metanoia*, leading to "change of heart," "newness of attitudes" without which "there can be no ecumenism worthy of the name" (*Unitatis Redintegratio*, no. 7). The new insights produced by the dialogue may require a re-evaluation of one's attitudes towards others or their views, or of practices long held in one's own church. When Christians of two communities are asked to agree—for example, to state together a common view of the doctrine of justification—enabled by years of dialogue, they may each, within their respective communities, have to place greater emphasis than they had done previously on some aspect of the doctrine, or put in deeper perspective some other doctrinal insight that had not been previously emphasized. Such challenges make clear that a spiritual preparation leading to or allowing "change of heart" and "newness of attitudes" will be necessary for the faithful of both communities if reception of dialogue insights is to take place.

Insights gained in theological dialogue need also to be supported and matched by educational opportunities within the churches. Theological advances and other moments of grace require ecumenical formation, for all the people of God, in order that the whole church "makes its own the fruits of a dialogue, in a process of listening, of testing, of judging and of living" (*Directory for the Application of Principles and Norms on Ecumenism*, no. 180).

The Catholic Church has put additional emphasis on ecumenical formation in recent years. The revised and updated ecumenical *Directory* (1993) to which I have just referred,[1] treats it at length (nos. 55-91). The Pontifical Council for Promoting Christian Unity has just published an additional document, "The Ecumenical Dimension in the Formation of Those Engaged in Pastoral Work."[2] Its purpose is to make even more explicit what is in the *Directory*. This new document addresses, among other things, the question of a specific course of study in ecumenism as required by the *Directory*. Among the various ecumenical materials and textbooks, described as *basic* for such a course, are documents, reports, and agreed statements produced by bilateral and multilateral ecumenical dialogue, the very materials found in this volume.

The reports published in this collection, and the volumes of dialogue reports published previously, are indicative of a growing body of ecumenical literature directed towards the rapprochement of divided Christians. It is a literature of reconciliation. In the encyclical *Ut Unum Sint*, Pope John Paul II reminds us of the profound theological significance of ecumenical dialogue for reconciliation.

Ecumenical dialogue, he says, "becomes a dialogue of conversion," and thus in the words of Pope Paul VI, an authentic "dialogue of salvation."

> Dialogue cannot take place merely on a horizontal level. . . . It has also a primarily vertical thrust, directed towards the One who, as the Redeemer of the world and the Lord of history, is himself our Reconciliation. This vertical aspect of dialogue lies in our acknowledgement, jointly and to each other, that we are men and women who have sinned. It is precisely this acknowledgement which creates in brothers and sisters living in Communities not in full communion with one another that interior space where Christ, the source of the Church's unity, can effectively act, with all the power of his Spirit, the Paraclete. (no. 35)

That which fosters reconciliation between divided Christians draws them together towards God. How seriously then we need to take these results of dialogue: to study them, to see their implications, prayerfully to consider the reception of their insights. Seeking, as they do, to overcome theological divergencies that have existed in some cases over the centuries, the dialogues and their results are also a reminder to us of how incumbent on us is the need to avoid further church-dividing acts that would make all the more difficult the ultimate task to which dialogue is directed, of tearing down the walls of separation that have afflicted Christians for so many centuries.

It is my pleasure, then, to commend this volume to the reader. It is my hope that the reports herein, fashioned within the context of international dialogue, will be used as sources for ecumenical study in regional, national, and local areas. It is my prayer that these reports will help divided Christians to respond to the prayer of Christ for his followers, "that they may all be one . . . so that the world may believe" (Jn 17:21).

NOTES

1. Pontificium Consilium ad Christianorum Unitatem Fovendam, *Directory for the Application of Principles and Norms on Ecumenism* (Vatican City, 1993).

2. Pontifical Council for Promoting Christian Unity, "The Ecumenical Dimension in the Formation of Those Engaged in Pastoral Work," *Information Service* 96 (1997): IV.

Foreword

Mary Tanner

Moderator, Faith and Order Commission, World Council of Churches

It was at the Missionary Conference in Edinburgh, 1910, that Bishop Charles Brent, an American Episcopalian, saw with overwhelming clarity that the divisions of churches were an insurmountable obstacle to the mission of the Church. This convinced him of the need for theological dialogue to bring about better understanding and to contribute towards overcoming issues that divide churches, without which, Brent was convinced, there would be no lasting unity. The Faith and Order Commission of the World Council of Churches has worked patiently to help churches understand those areas of faith and order that were causes of division and that continue to be reasons for separation today. Vatican II led to the full participation of the Roman Catholic Church within the Faith and Order Commission and to an intensification of the search for agreement in faith through the establishment of bilateral theological dialogues at national and international levels. A complex network of conversations exists today in which it seems everyone is talking to everyone else. The collection brought together in this volume is testimony to the significant achievements of some of the dialogues in which the Roman Catholic Church has been engaged between 1980 and 1996. Set side by side with other volumes, we can only marvel at the advance in understanding and the promise of reconciliation these reports contain.

Earlier fears that the bilateral dialogues would be set over against the multilateral work of the Faith and Order Commission have proved unfounded. Instead, there has been a fruitful inter-relation between the bilaterals and the multilateral work. *Baptism, Eucharist and Ministry*, the most well known and influential of all ecumenical reports, registers a high degree of consensus among many Christian traditions in areas once subjects of painful disagreement and causes of division.[1] The commentaries point to areas where further convergence is required. The achievement of this multilateral statement would hardly have been possible without the work of the bilateral agreements from whose insights it drew. In its turn, *Baptism, Eucharist and Ministry* has become a standard of reference; its consensus and convergences are used in many bilateral reports and church-to-church agreements. The Faith and Order Commission's other work on apostolic faith, on Church and world, together with the renewal studies and, more recently, the work on ecclesiology and ethics, provide an over-arching context in which to situate the achievements of bilateral reports such as those collected in this volume.[2]

Emerging from the impressive results of the theological conversations of this century, whether bilateral or multilateral, are two particular issues that any reader of this volume would do well to consider. The first concerns the nature of the unity that God invites us to make visible to those around us. What is the goal of unity that these reports are aimed at bringing about? Some of the conversations are directed towards overcoming misunderstandings, to destroying false stereotypes that those separated perpetuate of one another and to open up new and creative partnerships and ways ahead. Others look beyond this, seeing the overcoming of differences and the discovery of a deep unity in faith as a step on the way towards the restoration of full visible unity. The question that must be asked is whether there is, at least in outline, an emerging portrait of visible unity or are the dialogues each going in different directions.

It was this theme that lay behind the Fifth World Conference on Faith and Order in Santiago de Compostela, Spain, in 1993. The conference provided a unique opportunity to not only take stock of the convergences of the multilateral and bilateral dialogues, but also to pose the question of where we are going in the ecumenical pilgrimage. The answer came in the theme of the conference, Towards *Koinonia* (communion) in Faith, Life, and Witness. The separate studies, each in its own way, put content into that overall framework. The message of the conference was clear: "There is no turning back, either from the goal of visible unity or from the single ecumenical movement that unites concern for the unity of the Church and concern for engagements with struggles in the world." The unity God calls Christians to make visible in this world is the gift of God's own life, a participation in that personal love that flows between the Father, Son, and Holy Spirit. This is the gift God offers, through the Church, to all people. The notion of *koinonia* is renewing and reshaping a common understanding of visible unity as a diverse and dynamic communion in faith, life, and witness. It is helping divided Christians understand in fresh ways the gifts of faith, baptism, eucharist, ministry, and conciliar communion as God's gracious gifts for sustaining a rich life with diversity, a common life of service and mission. This theme of *koinonia* is central to many of the reports collected in *Deepening Communion*. It enables churches to see that they are not "out of communion" with one another, but already share the profound gift of divine communion. Theological dialogue is one way of assuring ourselves that this is so, and at the same time of providing one of the essential and firm foundations for moving churches onwards with confidence to a communion in faith, life, and witness.

A second issue posed by this important collection is the question of how the insights of these reports are to be received into the everyday lives of churches. Theological dialogue is not an end in itself. The transformation that takes place in those around the table has to extend into the lives of the churches they are chosen to represent. The aim of theological dialogue is to draw together those whose lives are lived in separation for the sake of more faithful, credible, and effective Christian witness. Every church needs to ask itself directly and sharply in the face of these documents what changes are required in its own life and what new relationships are now made possible with its partners through the insights of the theological reports. There will always be new issues to be faced as Christians travel through life in this world. The churches need to take bold steps, confident in the theological agreement already reached, so that they can face together those new challenges to Christian faith and life. Without this, new divisions will appear and separations become further entrenched.

The challenge to receive agreements and convergences reached in dialogues, like those gathered in this volume, is urgent. Many of these agreements could contribute towards formal mutual acknowledgments and binding commitments, which, celebrated symbolically, would mark new stages of relationship. The value of drawing the theological agreements into a statement of mutual acknowledgement and binding commitments, appropriate to the degree of agreement in faith achieved between parties in dialogue, is that churches would formally recognize what has been achieved, declare a firm basis for a degree of shared life, and set down the foundations for future growth together. Without deliberate and official acts of reception of the convergences of the theological dialogues, the next generations may have to repeat many of the marvelous achievements of the twentieth century.

The collection of documents in *Deepening Communion* is an affirmation of the achievement of ecumenical theological conversation. At the same time, it is a challenge to the churches involved to refuse to let these agreements remain on library shelves and to take steps now on the basis of the convergence towards a visible communion in faith, life, and witness.

NOTES

1. *Baptism, Eucharist and Ministry*, Faith and Order, no. 111, Geneva, WCC, 1982.
2. *Confessing the One Faith*, Faith and Order paper, no. 153, Geneva, WCC, 1991.

   Church and World: The Unity of the Church and the Renewal of Human Community, Faith and Order paper, no. 152, Geneva, WCC, 1990.

   Unity in Today's World: Faith and Order Studies on: Unity of the Church–Unity of Humankind, Faith and Order paper, no. 88, Geneva, WCC, 1975.

   The Community of Women and Men in the Church, ed. C. Pavey, Geneva, WCC, 1983.

Introduction

G. Rusch and Jeffrey Gros, Coeditors

The gospel call to the full unity of the church has generated rich energy among the Christian people, church leaders, and theologians, each according to their own calling. Pope John Paul recalls to us the centrality of this call to every dimension of Christian life:

> Concern for restoring unity pertains to the whole church, faithful and clergy alike. It extends to everyone, according to the ability of each, whether it be exercised in daily Christian living or in theological and historical studies. . . . To believe in Christ means to desire unity; to desire unity means to desire the church; to desire the church means to desire the communion of grace which corresponds to the Father's plan from all eternity. Such is the meaning of Christ's prayer: "Ut Unum Sint."[1]

Among the rich harvest of results the Holy Spirit has provided the church in response to the call to unity are these and other texts helping to deepen the communion among those already united in baptism, the Scripture, and a common commitment to God's will for the church. The path toward unity, as it has come to expression in the twentieth century following the foundation of the World Council of Churches (1948) and the Second Vatican Council (1962-1965), can be characterized by three phases: (1) the initial opening to other Christians and their churches, a period of mutual sharing and putting aside historical stereotypes; (2) the engagement in serious theological dialogue with the intent of deepening communion, toward the day when full communion can be celebrated; and (3) the movement, in stages, toward full communion in faith, sacramental life, and witness in the world, on the basis of theological agreement.[2] In this volume of documents, texts are included that represent two of these stages and have implications for the third.

Of course, in any believer, community, or church there are individuals and groups at quite different stages in their own understanding of the ecumenical imperative of the Gospel. They are at different moments in their own conversion to Christ's will for the unity of the church and in their ecumenical formation as to what the Holy Spirit has done among Christians over the decades of dialogue.

Many of the texts in this volume are the result of dialogues engaging Christians, Pentecostals, Baptists, and Evangelicals with Catholics, who are seeking to understand one another and clarify their commonalities and differences (nos. 9-14). Others are dedicated to laying the groundwork for full communion by deepening the communion in faith that will allow for eventual sacramental communion and common means of deciding and acting together (nos. 1-8). There exists a draft Joint Declaration on *Justification by Faith* which, if adopted by the participating churches, will be a necessary step toward full communion. Although it is not included in this volume because it awaits final acceptance by the churches, it is very closely related to two of the Lutheran–Catholic texts, as one stage along the path laid out in *Facing Unity* (no. 2) and embodying common commitments explicated in *The Church and Justification* (no. 3). These three types of documents illustrate the three stages of the ecumenical movement.

A fourth set of documents provides a wider context for the pilgrimage toward full communion by bringing together the multilateral discussion of member churches of the World Council of Churches and the Roman Catholic Church into a Joint Working Group addressing theological and pastoral questions that serve the unity of all of these churches (nos. 15-20). As the World Council of Churches moves beyond its fiftieth year, these documents illustrate its importance to the churches and the investment of the Roman Catholic Church in its mission and vision.

The stage in which the churches are now engaged, including theological dialogue and action together to incarnate in their lives the proposals of years of dialogue, is the *reception* phase of the ecumenical movement. During this phase the theological formulations of the dialogues begin to be internalized into the worship, spiritual, educational, and institutional lives of the churches. As with the other stages of the ecumenical movement, reception is a gradual and multifaceted process, touching every dimension of church life.[3]

These texts should assist the evaluation, reception, and research necessary if their ecumenical content is to make their appropriate contribution at every level of church life. As Pope John Paul has noted: ". . . a new task lies before us: that of receiving the results already achieved" which "must involve the whole people of

God." Results are not to remain "statements of bilateral commissions but must become a common heritage."[4]

These texts are to be seen in the context of a growing tradition of theological agreement. The Roman Catholic Church has been a member of the Faith and Order movement since 1968, a movement that had its first World Conference in 1927. The convergence texts produced by representatives of Orthodox, Anglican, Protestant, and Roman Catholic representatives provide the widest multilateral context for ecumenical discussion. Faith and Order has produced dramatic breakthroughs on the churches' understanding together of the common Christian faith and what is necessary for the full unity of the church to be realized.[5]

Also important are international bilateral texts in which the Catholic Church has participated. A series is available also from the U.S. Catholic Conference on Anglican,[6] Eastern Orthodox,[7] and Oriental Orthodox[8] dialogues with the Catholic Church. Paulist Press has also produced reference volumes of international texts, including those in which the Catholic Church has participated.[9] An extensive volume of international texts exists in German, covering all of the dialogues, ones in which the Catholic Church is involved included.[10] It is hoped that this volume will eventually be available in English, since many of those texts are the background for full communion proposals in various national contexts and also are related to the texts in this volume.

In addition to these important international texts, many national churches have been in dialogue with their national conferences of Catholic bishops and have made important contributions to the pilgrimage toward full communion.[11] There is a rich secondary literature that cannot be taken adequately into account in a resource volume of texts like this one.[12]

While these texts are of different types and with different purposes, they exhibit some common themes. Brief introductions are provided for the Lutheran, Methodist, Pentecostal, Evangelical, and Joint Working Group texts. The Reformed–Catholic text is the second in a series and builds on the previous ecumenical work.[13] The Disciples international text emerges from a national dialogue in the United States[14] and continues to deepen the common ground toward full communion.[15]

The Baptist text is the only international dialogue between these two bodies, the Baptist World Alliance and the Pontifical Council for Promoting Christian Unity. However, within the context of Faith and Order, and in some national bilateral contexts, there is much more extensive Baptist–Catholic interaction than has yet to come to be embodied in international bilateral dialogue.[16] The reader will note that the groups that are pursuing the dialogue of understanding rather than the dialogue toward full communion—the Baptists, Pentecostals, and Evangelicals—share some common concerns: mission, proselytism, religious liberty, salvation, the role of Mary, and the centrality of Scripture.

Other themes are common in the ecumenical discussions, even with their varied styles and purposes. The theology of communion (*koinonia*) is foundational, not only in the dialogues committed to full communion, but also in some of the dialogues building mutual understanding.[17] Within this context, themes of justification, stages toward full communion, tradition and faith, bonds of communion, healing of memories, common witness, and common ethical dialogue characterize these texts.

In the pilgrimage toward full communion in faith, sacramental life, and common witness, the churches are in early stages of their movement into theological dialogue, reception, and decision making based on these agreements. These texts should provide a rich resource for study, prayer, reflection, and deepened research, helping Christians in all dimensions of church life to deepen that communion for which Christ prayed.

NOTES

1. John Paul II, *That They May Be One (Ut Unum Sint)* (Washington, D.C.: United States Catholic Conference, 1995).

2. John Hotchkin, "The Ecumenical Movement's Third Stage," *Origins* 25:21 (November 9, 1995): 353-361. Jeffrey Gros, "Reception and Roman Catholicism for the 1990's," *One in Christ* 31:4 (1995): 295-328.

3. William G. Rusch, *Reception: An Ecumenical Challenge* (Philadelphia: Fortress Press, 1987). Frederick M. Bliss, *Understanding Reception: A Backdrop to Its Ecumenical Use* (Milwaukee: Marquette University Press, 1993). Thomas P. Rausch, SJ, "Reception Past and Present," *Theological Studies* 47:3 (September 1986): 497-508.

4. UUS, no. 80.

5. Lukas Vischer, ed., *A Documentary History of the Faith and Order Movement: 1927-1963* (St. Louis: The Bethany Press, 1963). Günther Gassmann, ed., *Documentary History of Faith and Order: 1963-1993* (Geneva: World Council of Churches, 1993).

6. Robert Wright, Joseph Witmer, eds., *Called to Full Unity: Documents on Anglican–Roman Catholic Relations, 1966-1983* (Cincinnati: Forward Movement Publications/Washington: United States Catholic Conference, 1985). Rozanne Elder, Ellen Wondra, Jeffrey Gros, eds., *Common Witness to the Gospel: Anglican–Roman Catholic Documents (1983-1995)* (Washington, D.C.: United States Catholic Conference, 1997).

7. John Borelli, John Erickson, *Orthodox and Catholic in Dialogue* (Crestwood: St. Vladimir Seminary Press/Washington, D.C.: United States Catholic Conference, 1996).

8. Ronald G. Roberson, ed., *Oriental Orthodox–Roman Catholic Interchurch Marriages and Other Pastoral Relationships* (Washington, D.C.: United States Catholic Conference, 1995).

9. E. J. Stormon, SJ, ed., *Towards the Healing of Schism: The Sees of Rome and Constantinople* (New York: Paulist Press, 1987). Lukas Vischer, Harding Meyer, eds., *Growth in Agreement: Reports and Agreed Statements of Ecumenical Conversations on a World Level* (GA) (New York: Paulist Press, 1984).

10. Harding Meyer, Damaskinos Papandreou, Hans Jörg Urban, Lukas Vischer, eds., *Dokumente Wachsender Übereinstimmung, Band 2 (1982-1990)* (Paderborn: Bonifatius Druck/Frankfurt: Verlag Otto Lembeck, 1992).

11. For example: Joseph Burgess, Jeffrey Gros, eds., *Growing Consensus* (GC) (New York: Paulist Press, 1995); Jeffrey Gros, Joseph Burgess, eds., *Building Unity* (BU) (New York: Paulist Press, 1989).

12. Cf. J. F. Puglisi, S. J. Voicu, eds., *A Bibliography of Interchurch and Interconfessional Theological Dialogues* (Rome: Centro Pro Unione, 1984). The regular bibliographical section of the *Centro Pro Unione Bulletin* is an important resource.

13. GA, 433-464.

14. GA, 153-166.

15. "Disciples of Christ–Roman Catholic International Dialogue," *Midstream* 34, 35 (January 1995, October 1996).

16. Cf. Jeffrey Gros, "Southern Baptists Affirm the Future of Dialogue with the Roman Catholic Church," *Ecumenical Trends* 24:2 (February 1995): 4-6.

17. Cf. Thomas Best, Günther Gassmann, eds., *On the Way to Fuller Koinonia* (Geneva: World Council of Churches, 1993).

Abbreviations

AAS	*Acta Apostolicae Sedis*
AA	*Apostolicam Actuositatem, The Decree on the Apostolate of the Laity*
AG	*Ad Gentes, The Decree on the Church's Missionary Activity*
Apol	Apology of the Augsburg Confession (1531)
ARCIC	Anglican Roman Catholic International Commission
ARCUSA	Anglican Roman Catholic Dialogue in the USA
Balamand	"Uniatism: Method of Union of the Past, and the Present Search for Full Communion. Report of the Joint International Commission for the Theological Dialogue Between the Roman Catholic Church and the Orthodox Church" (Balamand, June 17-24, 1993)
BC	*The Book of Concord. The Confessions of the Evangelical Lutheran Church* (tr. and ed. T. Tappert; Philadelphia: Fortress, 1959)
BEM	*Baptism, Eucharist, and Ministry* (World Council of Churches)
BU	*Building Unity*
BWA	Baptist World Alliance
CA	*Confessio Augustana,* Augsburg Confession
CCIA	Commission of the Churches on International Affairs
CD	*Christus Dominus, The Decree on the Pastoral Office of Bishops in the Church*
CDF	Congregation for the Doctrine of the Faith

CEC	European Conference of Churches
CIC	*The Code of Canon Law* (1983)
CICARWS	Commission of the Churches on Inter-Church Aid, Refugee, and World Service
CICO	*The Code of Canon Law for the Eastern Churches* (1991)
CMC	Church Medical Commission
COCU	The Consultation on Church Union
CW	*Common Witness, A Study Document of the Joint Working Group of the Roman Catholic Church and the World Council of Churches*
CWC	Church World Communion
CWP	"Common Witness and Proselytism: A Study Document," *Ecumenical Review* 23 (1971)
Directory	*Directory for the Application of Principles and Norms on Ecumenism* (1993)
DH	*Dignitatis Humanae, The Declaration on Religious Liberty*
DS	H. Denzinger and A. Schönmetzer, *Enchiridion Symbolorum* (33rd ed.)
DV	*Dei Verbum, The Dogmatic Constitution on Divine Revelation*
ELCA	The Evangelical Lutheran Chruch in America
EN	*Evangelii Nuntiandi, On Evangelization in the Modern World* (1975)
ERCDOM	*Evangelical–Roman Catholic Dialogue on Mission*
FC Ep	Formula of Concord (1577), Epitome
FC SD	Formula of Concord (1577), Solid Declaration
FU	*Facing Unity*
GA	*Growth in Agreement*
GC	*Growing Consensus*
GS	*Gaudium et Spes, Pastoral Constitution on the Church in the Modern World*
JCG	Joint Consultative Group
JPIC	Justice, Peace, and Integrity of Creation
JWG	Joint Working Group, World Council of Churches and Catholic Church

Kinnamon	*The Ecumenical Movement: An Anthology of Key Texts and Voices*
LA	The Leuenberg Agreement
LC	The Large Catechism of Martin Luther (1529)
LCWE	The Lausanne Committee on World Evangelization
LG	*Lumen Gentium, The Dogmatic Constitution on the Church*
LW	*Luther's Works*
LWF	Lutheran World Federation
NA	*Nostra Aetate, The Declaration on the Church's Relations with Non-Christian Religions*
NADEO	National Association of Diocesan Ecumenical Officers
NAE	National Association of Evangelicals
NCCB	National Conference of Catholic Bishops
NCC	National Council of Churches of Christ in the USA
OE	*Orientalium Ecclesiarum, The Decree on the Catholic Eastern Churches*
OL	*Orientale Lumen, The Light of the East*
PCPCU	Pontifical Council for Promoting Christian Unity
PCFNA	Pentecostal Charismatic Fellowship of North America
PCR	Program to Combat Racism
PCID	Pontifical Council for Interreligious Dialogue
PCCW	*The Presence of Christ in the Church and World*
PL	*Patrologia Latina*
PO	*Presbyterorum Ordinis, The Decree on the Life and Ministry of Priests*
SA	The Smalcald Articles (1537)
Santiago	*On the Way to Fuller Koinonia, Official Report of the Fifth World Conference on Faith and Order.* Thomas F. Best and Günther Gassmann, eds. Geneva: WCC, 1994.
SC	*Sacrosanctum Concilium, The Constitution on the Sacred Liturgy*
SBC	Southern Baptist Convention
SODEPAX	Committee on Society, Development, and Peace
TMA	*Tertio Millennio Adveniente, On the Coming of the Third Millennium*

UR	*Unitatis Redintegratio, The Decree on Ecumenism*
USCC	United States Catholic Conference
UUS	*Ut Unum Sint, That They May Be One*
WA	Martin Luther, *Werke*, Weimarer Ausgabe
WADB	WA Die Deutsche Bibel
WARC	World Alliance of Reformed Churches
WC	*Ways to Community* (Roman Catholic–Lutheran Commission, 1981)
WCC	World Council of Churches
WEF	World Evangelical Fellowship

Lutheran–Roman Catholic

Introductory Note

William G. Rusch

The international dialogue between Lutherans and Roman Catholics can trace its origins back to 1965 when a Roman Catholic–Lutheran working group was authorized by the Secretariat for Promoting Christian Unity (now the Pontifical Council for Promoting Christian Unity) of the Vatican and the Lutheran World Federation. The dialogue itself began in 1967 with its main concerns of unity in the truth, the elimination of divisive differences, and therefore the achievement of the full realization of the unity given in Christ.

Over the years this dialogue has produced a number of significant reports that merit careful consideration by the sponsoring churches, i.e., the Roman Catholic Church and the member churches of the Lutheran World Federation. Certainly to be included among these notable documents are *The Gospel and the Church, The Eucharist, Ways to Community,* and *The Ministry of the Church.* These reports from the 1970s and the 1980s can be found in the volume *Growth in Agreement,* edited by Harding Meyer and Lucas Vischer.

These texts form the context and the sequence for the three reports that are included in this volume. There is a sense in which the three documents published here cannot be understood apart from this wider context and sequence.

The first two of these reports come from the initial two decades of international Lutheran–Roman Catholic dialogue, a period of dialogue that disclosed that it was possible for a responsible group of theologians from both church traditions to produce significant reports on key issues that had kept Lutheran and Roman Catholic churches separated.

The third report comes from the period after the Seventh Assembly of the Lutheran World Federation in Budapest in 1984.

Martin Luther—Witness to Jesus Christ was released on May 6, 1983 to mark the 500th anniversary of Luther's birth (1483-1983). Among dialogue reports it is a rather unusual text since it focuses on a historical figure. It has some precedence in the fact that on the occasion of the 450th anniversary of the *Confessio Augustana* the dialogue issued a statement affirming that Catholics and Lutherans are "all under one Christ."

The birth anniversary of Luther offered the occasion to reflect on him as a person and on his work. The joint statement had as its goal to assist in Catholic–Lutheran reconciliation and understanding. The text seeks to stress some of Luther's main concerns and his ecumenical importance. It obviously draws on recent scholarship on Luther, much of it Roman Catholic, to portray a Luther who in former times was often distorted by the Catholics and Lutherans alike, although in different ways.

Facing Unity was issued by the dialogue on March 3, 1984. Its purpose was to provide clarity about the nature of church unity and a model for that goal. The model sought to avoid both absorption or return and gives a pattern of structured fellowship for the churches. Part I explores the critical term "models of unity," and in light of the general agreement about the nature of unity examines the forms or models of unity both in the history of the church and in recent ecumenical discussion. Part II takes up the topic of the forms and phases of Catholic–Lutheran church fellowship. It suggests a process leading to a common office of oversight for the two communions. This text has had considerable influences on other dialogues, most obviously Anglican–Lutheran in Europe and Episcopal–Lutheran in the United States.

Church and Justification is the most recent text from this dialogue, completed on September 11, 1993. It addresses a mandate given to the third phase of the dialogue, after 1984, to deal with the topic of the church in the light of sacramentality and justification. In one sense this discussion brought back an issue from the earliest days of the dialogue: justification. Yet the challenge now was to test the claim of the "far-reaching consensus" on this subject. Between 1986 and 1993 as the dialogue worked, it took into consideration two ecumenical texts of relevance not available earlier: the statement from the U.S. Lutheran–Roman Catholic dialogue, *Justification by Faith* of 1985, and the material on justification from the *Condemnations of the Reformation Era—Do They Still Divide?* of 1986 (Karl Lehmann, Wolfhart Pannenberg, eds. [Minneapolis: Fortress Press, 1990]). By the time of the completion of their work, the participants had produced the most extensive report to date from the Lutheran–Roman Catholic international bilateral on ecclesiology.

Further background on the maturing agreement on justification is provided in Karl Lehmann, Michael Root, William Rusch, eds., *Justification by Faith: Do the Sixteenth-Century Condemnations Still Apply?* (New York: Continuum, 1997). A treatment of these dialogues in the context of other Lutheran World Federation dialogues can be found in Harding Meyer, "To Serve Christian Unity," in Jens Holger Schjørring, Prasanna Kumari, Norman Hjelm, eds., *From-Federation to Communion: The History of the Lutheran World Federation* (Minneapolis: Fortress Press, 1997), 216-285.

Martin Luther— Witness to Jesus Christ

May 6, 1983

The following is a statement by the Joint Roman Catholic–Lutheran Commission, appointed in 1973 by the Secretariat for Promoting Christian Unity in Rome and the Lutheran World Federation, on the occasion of Martin Luther's 500th birthday, as signed by commission cochairmen Bishop Hans L. Martensen, Denmark, and Professor George A. Lindbeck, Yale University, USA.

I. From Conflict to Reconciliation

1. This year our churches celebrate the 500th anniversary of the birth of Martin Luther. Christians, whether Protestant or Catholic, cannot disregard the person and the message of this man. Standing on the threshold of modern times, he has had, and still has, a crucial influence on the history of the church, of society, and of thought.

2. For centuries opinions about Luther were diametrically opposed to one another. Catholics saw him as the personification of heresy and blamed him as the fundamental cause of schism between the western churches. Already in the sixteenth century the Protestants began to glorify Luther as a religious hero and not

infrequently also as a national hero. Above all, however, Luther was often regarded as the founder of a new church.

3. The judgment of Luther was closely connected with each church's view of the other: they accused one another of abandoning the true faith and the true church.

4. In the churches of the Reformation and in theology, the rediscovery of Luther began in the early days of this century. Soon afterwards, intensive study of the person of Luther and his work started on the Catholic side. This study has made notable scholarly contributions to Reformation and Luther research and, together with the growing ecumenical understanding, has paved the way toward a more positive Catholic attitude to Luther. We see on both sides a lessening of outdated, polemically colored images of Luther. He is beginning to be honored in common as a witness to the Gospel, a teacher in the faith, and a herald of spiritual renewal.

5. The recent celebrations of the 450th anniversary of the Augsburg Confession (1980) have made an essential contribution to this perspective. This confession of faith is inconceivable without the person and theology of Luther. Furthermore, the insight that the Augsburg Confession reflects "a full accord on fundamental and central truths" (Pope John Paul II, November 17, 1980) between Catholics and Lutherans facilitates the common affirmation of fundamental perceptions of Luther.

6. Luther's call for church reform, a call to repentance, is still relevant for us. He summons us to listen anew to the Gospel, to recognize our own unfaithfulness to the Gospel, and to witness credibly to it. This cannot happen today without attention to the other church and to its witness and without the surrender of polemical stereotypes and the search for reconciliation.

II. Witness to the Gospel

7. In criticizing various aspects of the theological tradition and church life of his time, Luther considered himself a witness to the Gospel—an "unworthy evangelist of our Lord Jesus Christ." He appealed to the biblical apostolic testimony which, as a "doctor of Holy Scripture," he was committed to interpret and proclaim. He took his stand consciously on the confession of the early church to the triune God and to Christ's person and work, and saw in this confession an authoritative expression of the biblical message. In his striving for reformation, which brought him external persecution and inner tribulation, he found assurance and comfort in his call by the church to study and teach the Scriptures. In this conviction he felt himself supported by the Lord of the church himself.

8. Knowing his responsibility as a teacher and pastor, and at the same time personally experiencing the anguished need for faith, he was led by his intense study

of the Scriptures to a renewed discovery of God's mercy in the midst of the fears and uncertainties of his time. According to his own testimony, this "Reformation discovery" consisted in recognizing that God's righteousness is, in the light of Romans 1:17, a bestowal of righteousness, not a demand that condemns the sinner. "He who through faith is righteous shall live," i.e., he lives by the mercy granted by God through Christ. In this discovery, confirmed for Luther by the church father Augustine, the message of the Bible became a joyful message, that is, "Gospel." It opened for him, as he said, "the gate of paradise."

9. In his writings, as in his preaching and teaching, Luther became a witness to this liberating message. As the "doctrine of the justification of the sinner through faith alone," it was the central point of his theological thinking and of his exegesis of Scripture. Those whose consciences suffered under the dominion of the law and human ordinances and who were tormented by their failures and by concern for eternal salvation could gain assurance through faith in the Gospel of the liberating promise of God's grace.

10. Historical research has shown that the beginnings of an agreement on this fundamental concern of Luther's were already apparent in the theological discussions at the time of the Reformation. But this agreement was not effectively accepted by either side and was obscured and nullified by later polemics.

11. In our time, Luther research and biblical studies on both sides have again opened the way for a mutual understanding of the central concerns of the Lutheran Reformation. Awareness of the historical conditionedness of all forms of expression and thought has contributed to the widespread recognition among Catholics that Luther's ideas, particularly on justification, are a legitimate form of Christian theology. Thus in summarizing what had already been jointly affirmed by Catholic and Lutheran theologians in 1972 ("The Gospel and the Church"), the Catholic–Lutheran statement on the Augsburg Confession says that: "A broad consensus emerges in the doctrine of justification, which was decisively important for the Reformation: it is solely by grace and by faith in Christ's saving work and not because of any merit in us that we are accepted by God and receive the Holy Spirit who renews our hearts and equips us for and calls us to good works" (*All Under One Christ*, 1980).

12. As witness to the Gospel, Luther proclaimed the biblical message of God's judgment and grace, of the scandal and the power of the cross, of the lostness of human beings, and of God's act of salvation. As an "unworthy evangelist of our Lord Jesus Christ," Luther points beyond his own person in order to confront us all the more inescapably with the promise and the claim of the Gospel he confessed.

III. Conflict and the Schism in the Church

13. Luther's interpretation and preaching of justification by faith alone came into conflict with the prevailing forms of piety which obscured God's gift of righteousness. Luther believed that his protests were in conformity with the teaching of the church and, indeed, even defended that teaching. Any thought of dividing the church was far from his mind and was strongly rejected by him. But there was no understanding for his concerns among the ecclesiastical and theological authorities either in Germany or in Rome. The years following the famous "Ninety-five Theses" of 1517 were marked by increasing polemics. As the disputes intensified, Luther's primarily religious concerns were increasingly intertwined with questions of church authority and were also submerged by questions of political power. It was not Luther's understanding of the Gospel considered by itself which brought about conflict and schism in the church, but rather the ecclesial and political concomitants of the Reformation movement.

14. When Luther was threatened with excommunication and summoned to revoke what for him were essential theological convictions, he saw in this the refusal of the secular and church authorities to discuss his theological reasoning. The conflict turned more and more on the question of final authority in matters of faith. Luther appealed to Scripture in this dispute, and came to doubt that all doctrinal decisions of the popes and councils were binding in conscience. Yet his emphasis on the *sola scriptura* and on the clarity of Scripture included acceptance of the creeds of the early church and respect for traditions which were in accordance with Scripture. He maintained throughout all conflicts his trust in God's promise to keep his church in the truth.

15. As the hostility of the church authorities increased, so did Luther's polemical attitude. The pope was rejected as "Antichrist," the Mass condemned as idolatry. In turn, Luther and his followers were categorized as heretics and sometimes even accused of apostasy. The hope that agreement could be reached at the Diet in Augsburg in 1530 was not fulfilled. Luther considered the rejection he met with as a sign of the approaching apocalypse. He could see no way back from the attitude of reciprocal condemnation.

16. Luther was claimed by a great variety of groups and tendencies in church and society in pursuit of their special interests (anticlerical, revolutionary, or enthusiast). He himself fought against these pressures, but his image suffered from distortions which still persist to this day.

17. These historical events cannot be reversed or undone. We can, however, seek to remove their negative consequences by investigating their origins and admitting culpable failures. Ultimately, however, they will only be healed when the

positive aims of the Reformation become the joint concern of Lutherans and Roman Catholics.

IV. Reception of Reformation Concerns

18. The Lutheran churches have tried over the centuries to conserve Luther's theological and spiritual insights. Not all his writings, however, have influenced the Lutheran churches to the same degree. There has often been a tendency to give more importance to his polemical works than to his pastoral and theological writings. Those writings which were given the status of confessional documents are of special ecclesial significance. Among these, his two catechisms occupy a special position in the life of the churches. Together with the *Confessio Augustana*, they form an appropriate basis for an ecumenical dialogue.

19. Nevertheless, Luther's heritage has suffered various losses and distortions in the course of history:

- The Bible was increasingly isolated from its church context, and its authority was legalistically misunderstood because of the doctrine of verbal inspiration
- Luther's high estimate of sacramental life was largely lost during the Enlightenment and in pietism
- Luther's concept of human beings as persons before God was misinterpreted as individualism
- The message of justification was at times displaced by moralism
- His reservations about the role of political authorities in church leadership were silenced for long periods of time and
- His doctrine of the twofold nature of God's rule (the doctrine of "the Two Kingdoms") was misused to legitimate the church's denial of responsibility for social and political life

20. Together with their gratitude for Luther's contributions, Lutheran churches are in our day aware of his limitations in person and work and of certain negative effects of his actions. They cannot approve his polemical excesses; they are aghast at the anti-Jewish writings of his old age; they see that his apocalyptic outlook led him to judgments which they cannot approve, e.g., on the papacy, the Anabaptist movement, and the Peasants' War. In addition, certain structural weaknesses in Lutheran churches have become obvious, especially in the way in which their administration was taken over by princes or the state—which Luther himself wanted to think of as simply an emergency arrangement.

21. A defensive attitude toward Luther and his thinking was in some respect determinative for the Roman Catholic Church and its development since the Reformation. Fear of the distribution of editions of the Bible unauthorized by the church, a centralizing overemphasis on the papacy, and a onesidedness in sacramental theology and practice were deliberately developed features of Counter-Reformation Catholicism. On the other hand, some of Luther's concerns are taken into account in such Tridentine reforming efforts as, for example, the renewal of preaching, the intensification of religious instruction, and the emphasis on the Augustinian doctrine of grace.

22. There has developed in our century—first of all in German-speaking areas—an intensive Catholic reevaluation of Luther the man and of his Reformation concerns. It is widely recognized that he was justified in attempting to reform the theology and the abuses in the church of his time and that his fundamental belief—justification given to us by Christ without any merit of our own—does not in any way contradict genuine Catholic tradition, such as is found, for example, in St. Augustine and Thomas Aquinas.

23. This new attitude to Luther is reflected in what Cardinal Willebrands said at the Lutheran World Federation's Fifth Assembly: "Who . . . would still deny that Martin Luther was a deeply religious person who with honesty and dedication sought for the message of the Gospel? Who would deny that in spite of the fact that he fought against the Roman Catholic Church and the Apostolic See—and for the sake of truth one must not remain silent about this—he retained a considerable part of the old Catholic faith? Indeed, is it not true that the Second Vatican Council has even implemented requests that were first expressed by Martin Luther, among others, and as a result of which many aspects of Christian faith and life now find better expression than they did before? To be able to say this in spite of all the differences is a reason for great joy and much hope."

24. Among the insights of the Second Vatican Council which reflect elements of Luther's concerns may be numbered:

- An emphasis on the decisive importance of Holy Scripture for the life and teaching of the church (DV)
- The description of the church as "the people of God" (LG, chapter II)
- The affirmation of the need for continued renewal of the church in its historical existence (LG, no. 8; UR, no. 6)
- The stress on the confession of faith in the cross of Jesus Christ and of its importance for the life of the individual Christian and of the church as a whole (LG, no. 8; UR, no. 4; GS, no. 37)
- The understanding of church ministries as service (CD, no. 16; PO)

- The emphasis on the priesthood of all believers (LG, nos. 10-11; AA, no. 24)
- Commitment to the right of the individual to liberty in religious matters (DH)

25. There are also other requests of Luther's that can be regarded as fulfilled in the light of contemporary Catholic theology and church practice: the use of the vernacular in the liturgy, the possibility of communion in both kinds, and the renewal of the theology and celebration of the eucharist.

V. Luther's Legacy and Our Common Task

26. It is possible for us today to learn from Luther together. "In this we could all learn from him that God must always remain the Lord, and that our most important human answer must always remain absolute confidence in God and our adoration of him" (Cardinal Willebrands).

- As a theologian, preacher, pastor, hymn writer, and man of prayer, Luther has, with extraordinary spiritual force, witnessed anew to the biblical message of God's gift of liberating righteousness and made it shine forth.
- Luther directs us to the priority of God's word in the life, teaching, and service of the church.
- He calls us to a faith which is absolute trust in the God who in the life, death, and resurrection of his son has shown himself to be gracious to us.
- He teaches us to understand grace as a personal relationship of God to human beings, which is unconditional and frees from fear of God's wrath and for service of one another.
- He testifies that God's forgiveness is the only basis and hope for human life.
- He calls the churches to constant renewal by the word of God.
- He teaches us that unity in essentials allows for differences in customs, order, and theology.
- He shows us as a theologian how knowledge of God's mercy reveals itself only in prayer and meditation. It is the Holy Spirit who persuades us of the truth of the Gospel and keeps and strengthens us in that truth in spite of all temptations.
- He exhorts us to remember that reconciliation and Christian community can only exist where not only "the rule of faith" is followed, but also the "rule of love," "which always thinks well of everyone, is not suspicious,

believes the best about its neighbors and calls anyone who is baptized a saint" (Martin Luther).

27. Trust and reverent humility before the mystery of God's mercy are expressed in Luther's last confession which, as his spiritual and theological last will and testament, can serve as a guide in our common search for unifying truth: "We are beggars. This is true."

Kloster Kirchberg, *Württemberg*
Hans L. Martensen, *Bishop of Copenhagen*
George A. Lindbeck, *Professor of Theology, Yale University*

Facing Unity: Models, Forms, and Phases of Catholic–Lutheran Church Fellowship

March 3, 1984

Preface

Unity in the truth, the elimination of divisive differences, and thus the achievement of church fellowship—these have been and are the main concerns in the dialogue initiated in 1967 between the Lutheran World Federation and the Roman Catholic Church.

With the publication of the Malta Report "The Gospel and the Church" in 1972, a first round of discussions was completed. This established an extensive consensus in the interpretation of justification and also a convergence of views in the controversial question of the relationship between Scripture and Tradition.

With a view to settling problems which it had been impossible to deal with adequately in the Malta Report, a new stage of the dialogue was launched. In 1978, the Roman Catholic–Lutheran Joint Commission was able to adopt the statement on *The Eucharist*, in which serious differences were eliminated and a common witness formulated in fundamental questions. In 1981, the document *The Ministry in the Church* was published, which shows convergences and agreements in the understanding of the common priesthood, the ordained ministry, ordination, and the apostolic succession.

A year earlier, in 1980, there had been the common statement on the *Confessio Augustana*—the basic confession of all Lutheran churches. On the basis of an evaluation of careful studies, the commission was able to affirm that we are "all under one Christ." For it was not only the declared intention of the Augsburg Confession of 1530 to remain in accord with the faith of the early church and the Roman Church: its statements in great measure realize this intention. The "newly discovered agreement in central Christian truths" gave "good ground for the hope that in the light of this basic consensus answers will also be forthcoming to the still unsettled questions and problems, answers which will achieve the degree of unanimity required if our churches are to make a decisive advance from their present state of division to that of sister churches" (*All Under One Christ*, no. 25).

In 1983, the 500th anniversary of the birth of Martin Luther provided the opportunity for a joint statement, *Martin Luther—Witness to Jesus Christ.*

The documents and statements just mentioned served indirectly the goal of church fellowship. The latter was dealt with directly and explicitly in a document, *Ways to Community*, no. 8, published in 1980. "Christian Unity is a blessing of the triune God, a work which he accomplishes, by means he chooses, in ways he determines" (*Ways to Community*, no. 8). These considerations proceed from the unity already given in Christ, focus attention on the barriers which still remain, and point out what is already now possible and necessary; they encourage us to take those steps together which can bring us nearer to the goal.

Finally, in 1984 the commission completed its work on a document on which it had worked for many years: *Facing Unity—Models, Forms, and Phases of Catholic–Lutheran Church Fellowship.* This document strives for clarity regarding the nature of church unity and a concept of that goal which implies neither absorption nor return, but rather a structured fellowship of churches. The prerequisite is community in confessing the one faith and in sacramental life. A solution must be found for still existing divisive differences. The dialogue documents require to be examined, perhaps corrected and supplemented, and finally given authority in the churches. This is a condition for complete church fellowship in word, sacrament, and ministry. The document presented here seeks to outline step by step how such church fellowship could become a reality. The commission is conscious that the latter part of its considerations, in particular, is venturesome and provisional in character. We have always to remain open for God's ways and dispensations. All our reflections are, in the end, "a prayer to the Lord who knows ways which surpass our vision and are beyond our power," as the document says in conclusion.

COCHAIRMEN

Hans L. Martensen, *Bishop of Copenhagen, Denmark*

George A. Lindbeck, *Professor, Yale University, USA*

Introduction

1. The full realization of unity given in Christ and promised by him calls for concrete forms of ecclesial life in common. Of what sort could and should these be? What is their relationship to our present ecclesial realities? What challenges are connected with this? What concrete steps have to be taken? We pose these questions by considering in Part I the key term "models of unity," and in the light of our substantially common understanding of the nature of unity, we examine the forms or models of church unity found in the history of the church, particularly the recent ecumenical discussions. In Part II we deal specifically with the relationship between the Roman Catholic Church and the Lutheran churches and with the question of forms and phases of Catholic–Lutheran church fellowship.

Part I. Concept of Unity and Models of Union

2. For us "models of union" are not arbitrary constructions. We see in them realizable forms of the fundamental understanding of unity described in our document *Ways to Community* (Roman Catholic–Lutheran Joint Commission, Geneva, 1981).

3. The unity of the church given in Christ and rooted in the triune God is realized in our unity in the proclaimed word, the sacraments, and the ministry instituted by God and conferred through ordination. It is lived both in the unity of the faith to which we jointly witness, and which together we confess and teach, and in the unity of hope and love which leads us to unite in fully committed fellowship. Unity needs a visible outward form which is able to encompass the element of inner differentiation and spiritual diversity as well as the element of historical change and development. This is the unity of a fellowship which covers all times and places and is summoned to witness and serve the world.[1]

4. It is our conviction that in its essential aspects, this view of unity corresponds with the formulation adopted by the Third Assembly of the World Council of Churches at New Delhi in 1961: "We believe that the unity which is both God's will and his gift to his Church is being made visible as all in each place who are baptized into Jesus Christ and confess him as Lord and Savior are brought by the Holy Spirit into one fully committed fellowship, holding the one apostolic faith, preach-

ing the one Gospel, breaking the one bread, joining in common prayer, and having a corporate life reaching out in witness and service to all and who at the same time are united with the whole Christian fellowship in all places and all ages in such wise that ministry and members are accepted by all, and that all can act and speak together as occasion requires for the tasks to which God calls his people."[2]

A. The Church as Fellowship

5. The one church of Jesus Christ assumes concrete form in local churches which participate in the diversity of historical, cultural, and racial situations in which the people live to whom the Gospel is proclaimed in word and sacrament. The church is therefore a communion (communio) subsisting in a network of local churches. "This Church of Christ is truly present in all legitimate local congregations of the faithful which, united with their pastors, are themselves called churches in the New Testament. For in their own locality these are the new people called by God, in the Holy Spirit and in much fullness (cf. 1 Thes 1:5). In them the faithful are gathered together by the preaching of the gospel of Christ, and the mystery of the Lord's Supper is celebrated. . . . In these communities, though frequently small and poor, or living far from any other, Christ is present. By virtue of Him the one, holy, catholic, and apostolic Church gathers together."[3]

6. This view of church unity as communion (communio) goes back to the early days of Christianity. It is determinative for the early church as well as for the life and ecclesiology of the Orthodox churches. In recent times it has been particularly stressed in Catholic ecclesiology. Part of the fundamental stress of the Second Vatican Council is that the one church exists in and consists of particular churches.[4] "By divine Providence it has come about that various churches established in diverse places by the apostles and their successors have in the course of time coalesced into several groups, organically united, which, preserving the unity of faith and the unique divine constitution of the universal Church, enjoy their own discipline, their own liturgical usage, and their own theological and spiritual heritage. . . . This variety of local churches with one common aspiration is particularly splendid evidence of the catholicity of the undivided Church."[5] This view is regarded as both giving rise to and determining the reestablishment of unity. "The deepening . . . of an ecclesiology of communion is . . . perhaps the greatest possibility for tomorrow's ecumenism. . . . So far as the reintegration of the Churches into unity is concerned, we have to follow the line of this ecclesiology, which . . . is both very ancient and yet very modern."[6]

7. This view of the church and of ecclesial unity is also in accord with Lutheran ecclesiology.[7] The local communities gathered around word and sacrament do not remain isolated as visible forms of the church of Jesus Christ, but rather

live in such larger and organically united communities as regional churches, national churches, folk churches, etc. The worldwide Lutheran community, which has the Lutheran World Federation as an instrument, is made up of churches that are bound together by a common understanding of the Gospel and by participation in the sacraments which that includes.

B. Models of Partial Union

8. On the basis of our understanding of the nature of unity, those models appear inadequate which are determined only by concepts of church unity which are only partial. In the opinion of some, however, they can play an important transitional role in certain situations if they are understood either as "steps" on the way to unity or as "partial" expressions of unity; moreover, they can also draw attention to important components of unity.

9. (1) For instance, one can wish to achieve mere *"spiritual"* unity by deliberately dispensing with common ecclesial structures and visible organization. Since the visible manifestations of unity—understood as an essentially spiritual, inward possession—are not expected until the end of time, external features and structures are considered not only superfluous but even as false and harmful. Although such a posture may well remind us of the essential and irrevocable spiritual dimension of all ecumenical efforts,[8] and also of the provisional nature of our expressions of church unity, it nevertheless fails to see the essential visible character of the church and of its unity to such an extent that it cannot be considered as a valid model of unity.

10. (2) This also applies when the unity of the church is expressed in the form of a mere *fellowship-in-dialogue*, where formerly separate communities, delimited and mutually condemnatory, engaged in lively questioning of each other, in listening and speaking. Although dialogue is an essential phase in efforts toward church unity, and although the dialogue momentum must not disappear even in a united church, a mere fellowship-in-dialogue falls short of being a full expression of church unity.

11. (3) Furthermore, a form of union which understands itself essentially as *fellowship-of-action* takes seriously the element of common service that is indispensable for a Christian concept of unity, but at the same time (measured by the understanding of unity in no. 3 above) lacks certain essential elements that do not permit it to be seen as a fully valid model of unity. This is true not only of ad hoc fellowship-of-action, but also of such structured church unions as Christian "councils" or "study groups," and church "federations" or "alliances," whose purpose is primarily to facilitate practical cooperation.

12. (4) The practice of *intercommunion* or the proffering of eucharistic hospitality between divided churches must also be seen as only a partial way of express-

ing unity. The ecumenical and pastoral value of intercommunion or eucharistic hospitality is assessed differently. Some people see in them a step on the way to unity, others regard them as a problematical attempt to realize unity. But it is clear to all that, at the very most, we are here concerned with a provisional expression of unity that will be endangered time and time again, and that it is essential to go further.

C. Models of Comprehensive Union

13. In recent ecumenical discussions a series of models of union has been developed and partly practiced in the life of the churches. These models correspond more closely to our understanding of unity than the ones mentioned above. They go beyond partial aspects and bring the whole of unity into view. Endeavors to give concrete shape to Catholic–Lutheran church fellowship cannot ignore such discussion and experiences; they are fulfilled in the framework of these discussions, are codetermined by them, and can receive from them important directives and impulses. Below we describe and briefly analyze the most important and best known of these models. The order in which they are here treated follows a historical rather than systematic sequence.

14. A description of these models must allow for a particular difficulty. Although individual models can be clearly distinguished from each other or can be related to each other, there is often considerable confusion on the level of terminology. This confusion is partly because in some cases a different meaning may be given to the model than is inherent in it. This can be noted, for example, in the case of the model of "conciliar fellowship" and the model of "church fellowship." Therefore, when giving a detailed account of each particular model one should seek to avoid private interpretations. One should always refer to those texts which may be regarded as the most original, representative, or official in character (for example, reports of the Commission on Faith and Order of the World Council of Churches, the Conference of Secretaries of Christian World Communions, the Assemblies of the World Council of Churches, or individual Christian world communions).

15. The terminological confusion, however, has sometimes found its way even into these more representative texts—for example, concepts of "organic union" or "organic unity" and "corporate fellowship." In each particular instance one should explain how the same concept can refer to differing realities. It helps to clarify the situation and the concepts if a sketch—at least in outline—is given of the motivation and context which have contributed to the development of a model.

1. Organic Union

16. The concept "organic union" or "organic unity" is one of the oldest ecumenical concepts, and it can refer either to a specific understanding of unity or to a

particular model of union. The concept which refers to the unity of the church as the "body of Christ" was taken over by the church union movements at the beginning of the century in order to describe their ecumenical goal. In the course of time, it received a specific meaning that it had not had originally and, as far as many are concerned, still does not yet have (see also nos. 19-22 below).

17. According to this specific meaning—which has become increasingly common in the terminology of the Faith and Order movement and then in the World Council of Churches—the model of "organic union" reflects a thinking which regards the existence of different confessional churches as a decisive obstacle to attaining true Christian unity and therefore takes the view that unity can be realized only by surrendering traditional ecclesial and confessional allegiance and identity. "Organic union," which generally comprises the working out of a common confession of faith, agreement about sacraments and ministry, and a homogeneous organizational structure, therefore arises out of the union of existing churches and ecclesial identities to form a "new fellowship with its own new name" and an "identity of its own."[9] It is "costly" and involves "surrender of the denominational identities" through merging "to form one body," "a kind of death" of the denominations which existed before; but it is nevertheless regarded as the way "to receive a fuller life."[10]

18. The use of this model of "organic union" has hitherto been concentrated mainly on the local, national, and regional levels.

2. Corporate Union

19. Like the concept of "organic union" or "organic unity," the concept of "corporate union" has a long history. In addition, both concepts seem to have been at first identical in content and therefore interchangeable,[11] and indeed many today still regard them as such. At any rate, one must take care to note that "corporate" or "organic" unity or union do not mean here the same thing as the concept of "organic union" in the sense just described (cf. nos. 16-18 above). The danger here of terminological confusion and factual misunderstanding is particularly great.

20. The concept "corporate union" and the corresponding concept "organic union" confront us, inter alia, in Catholic theologians and the Anglican–Catholic dialogue. There they precisely do not mean realizing unity by surrendering existing ecclesial tradition. Rather, different church communities form in "corporate union"—on the basis of an essential consensus on questions of faith and a joint episcopal constitution as in the early church—a fellowship of faith and life in which they as relatively independent corporate members retain a permanent place. They have thereby the possibility and the duty of preserving what in view of the apostolic witness they consider to be of permanent value in their theology and piety, placing it in the service of the fellowship as a whole.

21. A merger or mutual absorption of existing ecclesial traditions is rejected because "every church fellowship would lose its character in a fusion of this kind."[12] "Corporate union" is therefore "union in diversity"[13] or, as is said, a unity of churches "which remain churches and nevertheless become one church."[14]

22. This model of "corporate union" has now become the declared aim of the Anglican–Catholic dialogue, though with the label "organic unity."[15] In this sense Paul VI, in an address on the occasion of the visit of the archbishop of Canterbury and referring to the Anglican–Catholic conversations at Malines, said, "The pace of this movement [Anglican–Catholic rapprochement] has quickened marvelously in recent years, so that these words of hope 'the Anglican Church united not absorbed' are no longer a mere dream."[16]

3. Church Fellowship Through Agreement (Concord)

23. A model of union has been developed and become operative among the Lutheran, Reformed, and United churches in Europe which is described as "church fellowship." Substantially it is based on a doctrinal agreement (the Leuenberg Agreement, 1973) jointly drawn up and ratified by these churches.

24. In this context church fellowship means: "On the basis of the consensus they have reached in their understanding of the gospel" and on the basis of having determined that "the doctrinal condemnations expressed in the confessional documents no longer apply to the contemporary doctrinal position of the assenting churches," the various churches accord each other "fellowship in Word and sacrament" ("table and pulpit fellowship") and also fellowship in the ecclesial ministry ("mutual recognition of ordination and the freedom to provide for intercelebration").[17] The doctrinal agreement here involved does not imply a "new confession of faith."[18] Rather, the church fellowship made possible by this agreement is a fellowship among "churches with different confessional positions" in continuing "loyalty to the confessions of faith which bind them, or with due respect for their traditions."[19]

25. Although such a church fellowship understands itself as the realization of church unity in the full sense, it does not consider itself as something sealed and static. Rather, it contains a dynamic element inasmuch as the churches constituting the fellowship pledge themselves to "strive for the fullest possible cooperation in witness and service to the world."[20] Furthermore, this orientation towards a continual confirmation and deepening of the fellowship is expressed in the fact that the churches "pledge themselves to their common doctrinal discussions."[21]

26. Although this model of a church fellowship through agreement (concord) was first developed and practiced in the context of the Lutheran, Reformed, and United churches in Europe, it is fundamentally open and applicable also to other churches and other geographical regions. Indeed, it is no longer limited to Europe.

4. Conciliar Fellowship

27. By taking up and purposely elaborating the statements made at New Delhi and Uppsala, the Commission on Faith and Order developed the concept of "conciliar fellowship," which was received by the WCC Assembly in Nairobi, 1975. Although "conciliar fellowship" can also "refer to a quality of life within each local church,"[22] in the true sense this concept denotes a detailed model of union.

28. This "conciliar fellowship" model finds its application not so much at the level of the local churches but "in the first place it expresses the unity of church separated by distance, culture, and time."[23] It intends to be, therefore, a model of union on a wider level, ultimately on the level of the universal church. The definition says: "The one Church is to be envisioned as a conciliar fellowship of local churches which are themselves truly united."[24]

29. In this "conciliar fellowship" the various local churches "recognize the others as belonging to the same Church of Christ," confess the same apostolic faith, have full communion with one another in baptism and eucharist, recognize each other's members and ministries, and are one in witness and service in and before the world. The structural bond necessary for the "conciliar fellowship" is provided primarily by "conciliar gatherings,"[25] i.e., by means of "representative gatherings."[26] Both Catholics and Orthodox stress thereby that "conciliar fellowship" necessarily encompasses also the ministry transmitted in apostolic succession.

30. "Conciliar fellowship" does not mean a monolithic unity,[27] but rather a "diversity" which must "not only be admitted but actively desired."[28] For a long time it was not at all clear what place amid these diversities would be accorded the individual church or confessional traditions, especially since the "conciliar fellowship" model seemed to be very closely connected with the model of "organic union" (see nos. 16-18 above).[29] Indeed, it seemed to presuppose "organic union."[30] In the meantime these considerations have been further developed by the Commission on Faith and Order[31] and also by other bodies[32] in such a way that confessional traditions can undoubtedly retain an identifiable life in this "conciliar fellowship," provided that this will not call into question the basic elements of "conciliar fellowship."

5. Unity in Reconciled Diversity

31. There have always been tendencies within the ecumenical movement that aimed at an ecumenical fellowship in which the existing ecclesial traditions with their particularity and diversity would remain in integrity and authenticity. The above described models of "corporate union" (see nos. 19-22 above) and of "church fellowship by means of agreement" (see nos. 23-26 above) are examples of this.

32. In this sense, and against the background of intensified ecumenical commitment on the part of the churches and Christian world communions, the model of "unity in reconciled diversity" has recently been developed.[33] It is based on the

idea that "the variety of denominational heritages [is] legitimate" and forms part of "the richness of life in the church universal." When "in the open encounter with other heritages" the existing traditions and denominations lose their "exclusive" and "divisive character, there emerges a vision of unity that has the character of a 'reconciled diversity.' "[34]

33. The idea of "unity in reconciled diversity" means that "expression would be given to the abiding value of the confessional forms of the Christian faith in all their variety" and that these diversities, "when related to the central message of salvation and Christian faith" and when they "ring out, [are] transformed and renewed" in the process of ecumenical encounter and theological dialogue; they "lose their divisive character and are reconciled to each other . . . into a binding ecumenical fellowship in which even the confessional elements" are preserved.[35] "Unity in reconciled diversity" therefore does not mean "mere coexistence." It means "genuine church fellowship, including as essential elements the recognition of baptism, the establishing of eucharistic fellowship, the mutual recognition of church ministries, and a binding common purpose of witness and service."[36]

34. The model of "unity in reconciled diversity" comes "very close to the concept of 'conciliar fellowship'. . . and cannot be put forward as a rival to this concept." The tension felt occasionally in the beginning *vis-a-vis* the model of "conciliar fellowship"—"that the latter seems to take insufficiently into account the legitimacy of the confessional differences and therefore the need to preserve them,"[37]—seems to have been largely overcome in the meantime.[38]

D. The Example of the Union of Florence

35. For possible church union without merger or absorption, the example of Florence is important.

36. The union between the Latin and Byzantine churches formed at the Council of Florence did not represent a merger. Without prejudicing the unity of faith basic to the fellowship, each church preserved its own liturgical, canonical, and theological tradition. This common faith could be expressed in various formulations (for example, as regards the "procession" of the Holy Spirit) and tolerate diversities of discipline (for example, the toleration of remarriage of divorced Christians of the Greek but not of the Latin rites, a differentiation still operative at Trent).

37. Even though this attempt failed, impulses from Florence did not remain without effect. It is due to them that the Roman Catholic Church can no longer be identified by its Latinism. Following Vatican II, however, the model of sister churches applies, a model that is inspired by the relationships that existed during the first millennium.[39]

38. Moreover, several statements made by Vatican II about the united Eastern churches are of great importance in the search for a model of unity in diversity. There we read: "That Church, Holy and Catholic, which is the Mystical Body of Christ, is made up of the faithful who are organically united in the Holy Spirit through the same faith, the same sacraments, and the same government and who, combining into various groups held together by a hierarchy, form separate Churches or rites."[40]

"Such individual Churches, whether of the East or of the West . . . differ somewhat among themselves in what are called rites (that is, in liturgy, ecclesiastical discipline and spiritual heritage). . . ."[41] "Therefore, attention should everywhere be given to the preservation and growth of each individual Church. For this purpose, parishes and a special hierarchy should be established for each where the spiritual good of the faithful so demands. The Ordinaries of the various individual Churches which have jurisdiction in the same territory should, by taking common counsel in regular meetings, strive to promote unity of action."[42]

39. Vatican II, therefore, does not call for a single jurisdiction or a single bishop in each particular case. Moreover, the council considers it to be legitimate for the church of one particular rite, i.e., a church with its own spiritual, theological, and canonical tradition, to reach out everywhere, even beyond its original geographical limits. Admittedly, it is a question here of provisional measures in the expectation of the restoration of unity between the Roman Catholic Church and the Eastern churches which are not yet in full fellowship with it.[43]

40. The example of Florence shows that it is possible for the Roman Catholic Church to unite with another church without merger if that church confesses the same faith and if the mutual recognition of ministries can be achieved. For this example shows

- The possibility, at least temporarily, of the presence of two bishops at the same place and
- The justification of different theological, canonical, and spiritual traditions carried by these different episcopal jurisdictions

E. Fellowship of Sister Churches

41. Without being able to refer to them as "models" of union in the strict sense, two concepts merit particular attention, which have proved to be important and useful in endeavors to conceive of and practice models of union. Both concepts, each in its own way, express and underscore the idea of unity in diversity as emphasized particularly by some of the models of union described above ("corporate

union," see nos. 19-22 above; "church fellowship through agreement," see nos. 23-26 above).

1. Ecclesial "Types"

42. The view was taken repeatedly in the past that the ecumenical problem derives from the fact that, ever since the early days, distinct basic types and archetypes of the faith have existed within Christianity; these types, though fundamentally interconnected, differ distinctively from each other with regard to specific characteristics of piety, doctrine ethos, ecclesial structures, etc., and manifest themselves to some extent in the existing churches. The ecumenical task, then, would not consist of eliminating these different basic types or of merging them, but rather of making visible their legitimacy and of preserving and keeping them together in the fellowship of the one church for which we strive.

43. The view that within Christianity there exist different ecclesial types (typoi) has also been presented in more recent times. The term typos, for example, has been defined as follows: "Where there is a long coherent tradition, commanding men's love and loyalty, creating and sustaining a harmonious and organic whole of complementary elements, each of which supports and strengthens the other, you have the reality of a typos." The elements that constitute each ecclesial typos are a "characteristic theological method and approach," "a characteristic liturgical expression," a specific "spiritual and devotional tradition," a "characteristic canonical discipline." "The life of the Church needs a variety of typoi which would manifest the full catholic and apostolic character of the one and holy Church."[44]

2. Sister Churches

44. Recently the concept of "sister churches" has become even more important. As an expression of the fellowship between individual local churches, it has a long tradition that goes right back to the early church and was used in this sense by the Second Vatican Council.[45] For some time this concept has also been used to describe fellowship that has been regained or aspired to between separated churches, especially in the ecumenical relations between the Roman Catholic Church and the Orthodox churches.

45. This new usage goes back above all to the message that Pope Paul VI sent to the Ecumenical Patriarch Athenagoras I. It reads as follows: "Now, after a long period of division and reciprocal incomprehension the Lord grants us that we rediscover ourselves as sister churches despite the obstacles which were then raised between us. In the light of Christ, we see how urgent is the necessity of surmounting these obstacles in order to succeed in bringing to its fullness and perfection that unity—already so rich—which exists between us." This fellowship between "sister churches" is a fellowship in diversity. "It is a matter of knowing and of respecting

each other in the legitimate diversity of liturgical, spiritual, disciplinary and theological traditions (cf. UR, nos. 14, 17) by means of a frank theological dialogue, made possible by the reestablishment of brotherly charity in order to attain accord in the sincere confession of all revealed truths."[46]

Part II. Forms and Phases of Catholic–Lutheran Fellowship

On the Way to Church Fellowship

46. All the models of union described above undoubtedly contain valuable pointers for shaping Catholic–Lutheran church fellowship. Nevertheless, none of these models was worked out in a specifically Catholic–Lutheran context. One must therefore ask whether, in envisioning a promising form of Catholic–Lutheran fellowship, one should not consider more closely the particularities of that relationship. One should by no means assume, however, that there exists one single model which can lead us to fellowship.

47. What is significant and useful in the foregoing description and analysis of the various models of union for the shaping of the Catholic–Lutheran fellowship is: The unity we seek will be a unity in diversity. Particularities developed within the two traditions will not merely be fused, nor their differences completely given up.

> This is underscored by the models of "unity in reconciled diversity," "corporate union," and "church fellowship through agreement," as well as by the concepts of *typos* and "sister churches."

What is really at stake is that a theologically based agreement of the type that already exists in the Catholic–Lutheran dialogue should work through divergences to the point where they lose their church-divisive character. At the same time it should both clarify and make certain that remaining differences are based on a fundamental consensus in understanding the apostolic faith and therefore are legitimate.

> This aspect is particularly stressed by the models of "unity in reconciled diversity" and "church fellowship through agreement."

Once the divergences of both traditions have lost their divisive force, they can no longer be the subject of mutual condemnation. It should be publicly declared that they are now groundless.

> This is emphasized, above all, by the model of "church fellowship through agreement."

The unity we seek must be rooted in common sacramental life.

> This is implied by all models, but is particularly implicit in the understanding of unity as *communio*.

The unity we seek must assume concrete form in suitable structures that would enable our hitherto separated communities to lead a truly common life and to make joint action possible both at the level of the local churches and at the universal level.

> This is stressed particularly by the models of "organic union" and "conciliar fellowship."

In our endeavors to find the appropriate structures needed for full and binding fellowship, we shall have to face up to the question of jointly exercising the ministry of church leadership, present in the office of bishop in the early church.

> This is one of the presuppositions of the model of "corporate union."

48. Christian reconciliation plays an important part in all the forms and phases of the unity we seek. We jointly confess that we have been reconciled with God through Christ. As we acknowledge this with thanksgiving and praise, we must also confess our sins and errors and know ourselves to be called to be reconciled with others.

The mutual reconciliation which we seek as Christians of different churches, and which stands entirely under the reconciliation that occurred in Christ, does not simply eliminate our differences. There are differences that stem from error and weakness of faith and which cannot therefore be overcome without repentance, self-criticism, and renewal. Here reconciliation has its price. But there are also differences between us that derive from the fact that the one church of Christ exists in various places, and that one and the same faith can be expressed and lived in different ways. We can recognize such differences as legitimate, yes, even accept them with joy, as far as they enable us to learn from each other, correct, stimulate, or enrich us.

This mutual recognition, which can be achieved step by step, is decisive for the process of reconciliation. Reconciliation cannot happen without the freedom, given us through Christ's reconciliation, from our instinctive fear of the other as stranger and our anxious concern for our own identity.

Reconciliation is not possible without dialogue and constant communication. It is a process of discerning the spirits and of searching for steps along a pathway known only to God. Reconciliation is thus a dynamic process, even where church unity exists or has been reestablished. For as long as sin and conflict remain and as long as Christians and churches live in changing times and in a diverse world, this process will not be completed.

49. The dynamic inherent in the process of reconciliation and the realizing of church fellowship unfolds itself more clearly in the efforts for

    a.   Fellowship in confessing the one apostolic faith (community of faith)

    b.   Fellowship in sacramental life (community in sacraments)

    c.   Fellowship as a structured fellowship in which community of faith and community in sacraments find adequate ecclesial form and in which common life, common decisions, and common action are not only possible; they are required (community of service)

During this process of realizing church fellowship, there is no sequential or gradational relationship between the achievement of community of faith, community in sacraments, and community of service. According to our understanding of unity (see no. 3 above), the concretization of church fellowship rather constitutes an integral process in which each of these three elements achieves full realization only together with the others. This process is characterized by the two interrelated aims of "recognition" and "reception."[47]

Growth of Church Fellowship Through Mutual Recognition and Reception

50. The stage of full mutual recognition has not yet been attained between our churches, although it is beginning to reveal itself.

In recent years a broad process of comprehension and rapprochement embracing all levels of church life has led to the fact that our churches see each other in a completely different way than before. Likewise, recent decades have seen positive changes, with regard to forms of thought and life of our churches, which shaped them and greatly influenced their relationship with each other.

51. True to the spirit of Vatican II (see no. 53 below), the Roman Catholic Church has changed its view *vis-a-vis* the Lutheran churches. A reassessment both of the common past and of the Lutheran heritage has taken place. This is clearly expressed by the words of Pope John Paul II on the occasion of his visit to the land of Luther in 1980.

With regard to the history of our separation, the pope said: " 'Let us no more pass judgment on one another' (Rom 14:13). Let us rather recognize our guilt. 'All have sinned' (Rom 3:23) applies also with regard to the grace of unity. We must see and say this in all earnestness and draw our conclusions from it." "If we do not evade the facts we realize that the faults of men led to the unhappy division of Christians, and that our faults again hinder the possible and necessary steps towards unity. I emphatically make my own what my predecessor Hadrian VI said in 1523 at the Diet of Nuremberg: 'Certainly the Lord's hand has not been shortened so much that he cannot save us, but sin separates us from him. . . . All of us, prelates and priests, have strayed from the right path and there is not anyone who does good (cf. Ps 14:3). Therefore must all render honor to God and humble ourselves before him. Each of us must consider why he has fallen and judge himself rather than be judged by God on the day of wrath."[48]

On the occasion of Martin Luther's 500th anniversary, the pope wrote: "In fact, the scientific researches of Evangelical and Catholic scholars, researches whose results have already reached notable points of convergence, have led to the delineation of a more complete and more differentiated picture of Luther's personality and of the complex texture of the social, political and ecclesial historical realities of the first half of the sixteenth century. Consequently there is clearly outlined the deep religious feeling of Luther who was driven with burning passion by the question of eternal salvation."[49]

Concerning the Catholic–Lutheran dialogue, particularly the conversation on the Augsburg Confession, the pope took up the statement of the German Catholic bishops: "Let us rejoice to discover not only partial consent on some truths, but also agreement on the fundamental and central truths. That lets us hope for unity also in the areas of our faith and our life in which we are still divided up to now."[50]

52. In the Lutheran churches, likewise, there has been a profound change of attitude vis-a- vis the Catholic Church. With reference to the plea for forgiveness of Pope Paul VI and in answer to it, the Fifth LWF Assembly (1970) stated: "It is . . . in accordance with this commandment of truth and love that we as Lutheran Christians and congregations be prepared to acknowledge that the judgment of the Reformers upon the Roman Catholic Church and its theology was not entirely free of polemical distortions, which in part have been perpetuated to the present day. We are truly sorry for the offense and misunderstanding which these polemic elements have caused our Roman Catholic brethren. We remember with gratitude the statement of Pope Paul VI to the Second Vatican Council in which he communicates his plea for forgiveness for any offense caused by the Roman Catholic Church. . . . Together with all Christians [we] pray for forgiveness in the prayer our Lord has taught us."[51]

The presence of official Lutheran observers at all the sessions of the Second Vatican Council, the subsequent beginning of bilateral dialogues both at the world level and in many countries, closer life together and increased cooperation with local Catholic churches, parishes, and Catholic Christians have led Lutherans to a new understanding of Catholic piety, church life, and teaching. The Roman Catholic Church is no longer regarded as "false church." Many differences have lost their former unfamiliarity and divisive rigor as far as Lutheran sensitivity is concerned. One now encounters a general readiness to abandon long-standing negative prejudices and to examine doctrinal condemnations pronounced in the past to see whether they are still valid today. Thus, for example, the papal office and its holders appear in a new light that makes former condemnations and the hostile images of the past untenable. In view of common theological understandings and liturgical developments in both churches, the sharp condemnation of Catholic Mass is considered to belong to the past, as is shown, for example, by the decisions of some Lutheran churches in favor of reciprocal eucharistic hospitality.[52]

53. The Roman Catholic Church has not only changed its attitude *vis-a-vis* the Lutheran churches but with Vatican II has also renewed its forms of thought and life.

- Vatican II adopted an understanding of church that does not exclusively identify the Roman Catholic Church with the church of Jesus Christ, but also recognizes the church of Jesus Christ outside its bounds in other churches and ecclesial communities.[53]
- Attention to the "hierarchy of truths," as called for by the *Decree on Ecumenism*,[54] implies that every theological statement must be related to the foundation of the Christian faith. Lutherans have similar concerns.[55]
- Moreover, in its forms of piety, its liturgical life (celebration of Mass, for example), and its government (for example, by the general development of synodal elements at all levels of church life), the Catholic Church is reflecting on its origins, thereby showing concretely that in each of these areas it understands itself as a church in need of "continual reformation."[56]

54. A renewal of the forms of theological thinking and ecclesial life is also taking place in the Lutheran churches.

- The renewed orientation in the early decades of this century to the Reformation and Reformation theology, accompanied by a historical examination of developments in the early church and the Middle Ages, has led in recent decades to a deepened understanding of church, ecclesial ministry, and worship.
- The sacramental dimension of worship, preserved during the Reformation but often diminished later, is again emphasized without weakening the stress on the word. In many respects this emphasis has reshaped the liturgical life of the Lutheran churches.

- The normative function of Scripture in the life, teaching, and proclamation of the church continues to be maintained; an exclusivistic understanding of Scripture, detached from the transmission process and church tradition, seems to have been overcome.
- Continuity with the early church, which was preserved and indeed stressed by the Reformers, is again seen more clearly and is creating an enhanced awareness of the ecumenicity and catholicity of the Lutheran confession.

A. Community of Faith

55. For Catholics and Lutherans alike the common confession of the one apostolic faith means (1) bearing joint witness to this faith, (2) taking account of legitimate differences, and (3) overcoming the obstacles raised by earlier mutual condemnations.

1. Joint Witness to the Apostolic Faith

56. For the unity of our churches and especially for our task of preaching, common witness to the apostolic faith is of fundamental importance. If we apply the principle of the "hierarchy of truths," the christological and trinitarian center or "foundation of the Christian faith" is primarily at stake.[57] It is from there that the full catholicity of the faith is again to be mutually comprehended. Such an endeavor will bring about shifts of emphasis and changes in the self-understanding of our churches: overcoming of onesidedness, loosening of constraints, correction of certain exaggerations.

57. This process is already underway:

- The starting point is the common affirmation of the faith of the early church, formulated by the early councils in obedience to Holy Scripture and witnessed to in the creeds of the early church (Apostles' Creed, Nicene Creed, Athanasian Creed).[58]

  > "Together we confess the faith in the Triune God and the saving work of God through Jesus Christ in the Holy Spirit. . . . Through all the disputes and differences of the sixteenth century, Lutheran and Catholic Christians remained one in this central and most important truth of the Christian faith."[59]

- The process of growth in common witness is advanced by a new consensus regarding the relationship between *Holy Scripture and tradition,* long the subject of controversy: "

> This poses the old controversial question regarding the relationship of Scripture and tradition in a new way. The Scripture can no longer be exclusively contrasted with tradition, because the New Testament itself is the product of primitive tradition. Yet as the witness to the fundamental tradition, Scripture has a normative role for the entire later tradition of the church."[60]

- It extends to our understanding of the Gospel expressed during the Reformation, particularly in the doctrine of justification:

> "Today, however, a far-reaching consensus is developing in the interpretation of justification. Catholic theologians also emphasize in reference to justification that God's gift of salvation for the believer is unconditional as far as human accomplishments are concerned. Lutheran theologians emphasize that the event of justification is not limited to individual forgiveness of sins, and they do not see in it a purely external declaration of the justification of the sinner. Rather the righteousness of God actualized in the Christ event is conveyed to the sinner through the message of justification as an encompassing reality basic to the new life of the believer."[61] "It is solely by grace and by faith in Christ's saving work and not because of any merit in us that we are accepted by God and receive the Holy Spirit who renews our hearts and equips us for and calls us to good works."[62]

- It entails a far-reaching consensus regarding the understanding and the celebration of the eucharist (see no. 76 below).[63]
- It has led to a basic, though not yet complete, consensus in the understanding of church:

> "By church we mean the communion of those whom God gathers together through Christ in the Holy Spirit, by the proclamation of the gospel and the administra-

tion of the sacraments, and the ministry instituted by him for his purpose. Though it always includes sinners, yet in virtue of the promise and fidelity of God it is the one, holy, catholic, and apostolic church which is to continue forever."[64] "It stands under the gospel and has the gospel as its superordinate criterion"; its "authority . . . can only be service of the word and . . . it is not master of the word of the Lord."[65]

• It extends also to the understanding and exercise of the ordained ministry in the church:

> The special ecclesial ministry, which is transmitted by ordination (see no. 71 below), "is instituted by Jesus Christ"[66] and as such "is constitutive for the church."[67] Its specific function is "to assemble and build up the Christian community by proclaiming the word of God, celebrating the sacraments and presiding over the liturgical, missionary and diaconal life of the community."[68] In performing this function the ministry stands "in the midst of the whole people and for the people of God," but "inasmuch as the ministry is exercised on behalf of Jesus Christ and makes him present, it has authority over against the community."[69]

58. Even though efforts toward consensus regarding the apostolic faith must be continued, as was shown particularly clearly in our common reflection on the Augsburg Confession, one may already say that we can "discover not simply a partial consensus on some truths, but rather a full accord on fundamental and central truths,"[70] to put it in the words of Pope John Paul II and of the German Catholic bishops.

59. The Executive Committee of the Lutheran World Federation took this up and announced: "We . . . agree that . . . Roman Catholics and Lutherans 'have discovered that they have a common mind on basic doctrinal truths which points to Jesus Christ, the living center of our faith' (All Under One Christ, no. 17) and that therefore with regard to the Augsburg Confession one may and should speak of 'a full accord on fundamental and central truths' . . . or respectively of a 'basic consensus' of faith (ibid., nos. 18, 25)."[71]

60. To reach the goal in this effort towards consensus in the apostolic faith, one must take account of how our two churches understand and practice doctri-

nally authoritative teaching, and which office holders may therefore in the name of our churches pronounce an official judgment about the theological consensus attained in our dialogue.

In the Roman Catholic Church the function of authoritative teaching is in a special manner the task of the bishops, who discharge this task "in a many-sided exchange regarding faith with believers, priests, and theologians."[72] Doctrinal decisions of the church are ultimately binding when "the bishops interpret the revealed faith in universal agreement with each other and in communion with the Bishop of Rome."[73]

In the Lutheran interpretation, too, "the holders of the episcopal office are . . . entrusted in a special manner with the task of watching over the purity of the Gospel."[74] But in most Lutheran churches authoritative teaching is effected more in a process of consensus-building in which church leaders or bishops, teachers of theology, pastors, and nonordained members of the congregation participate with basically equal rights. Usually this process has synodal forms.[75]

Authoritative teaching in both churches is subject to the norm of the Gospel[76] and is oriented to past doctrinal decisions recognized as binding. In both churches doctrinal decisions, if they are to become fruitful and develop their full situational force, depend on far-reaching reception in the consciousness and life of the local churches, congregations, and believers.[77]

It can therefore be seen that both churches can and do teach in an authoritative way, and that in spite of existing differences, there are important parallels in achieving authoritative teaching. Thus, it is possible for both churches, each in its own way, to accord authoritative character to the agreements in their understanding of the apostolic faith which they have attained. It would be important to ensure that this process, going on within the two churches, even now proceeds with a certain degree of synchronization and as much commonality as possible.

2. Unity of Faith in the Diversity of Its Forms of Expression

61. Unity in the same faith does not mean uniformity in the way it is articulated and expressed. This is one of the basic presuppositions of the ecumenical movement of our century.[78]

Whenever the reference is to doctrine and life, Reformation theology reiterates the conviction that complete conformity is not a condition for church unity.[79]

62. Vatican II states: "While preserving unity in essentials, let all members of the Church, according to the office entrusted to each, preserve a proper freedom in the various forms of spiritual life and discipline, in the variety of liturgical rites, and even in the theological elaborations of revealed truths."[80]

In this sense Pope Paul VI expressed himself repeatedly and, in doing so, gave even more concrete shape to the idea of unity of faith in the diversity of its forms of expression. In his speech in the Cathedral of Phanar (1967) he said: "In the light of our love for Christ and of our brotherly love, we perceive even more clearly the profound identity of our faith, and the points on which we still differ must not prevent us from seeing this profound unity. And here, too, charity must come to our aid, as it helped Hilary and Athanasius to recognize the sameness of the faith underlying the differences of vocabulary at a time when serious disagreements were creating divisions among Christian bishops. Did not pastoral love prompt St. Basil, in his defense of the true faith in the Holy Spirit, to refrain from using certain terms which, accurate though they were, could have given rise to scandal in one part of the Christian people? And did not St. Cyril of Alexandria consent in 433 to abandon his beautiful formulation of theology in the interest of making peace with John of Antioch, once he had satisfied himself that in spite of divergent modes of expression, their faith was identical?"[81]

Somewhat similarly, on the occasion of the 1600th anniversary of the death of St. Athanasius (1973), Pope Paul VI said in an address to Patriarch Shenouda: "He [Athanasius] in turn recognized in the Church of the West a secure identity of faith despite differences in vocabulary and in the theological approach to a deeper understanding of the mystery of the Triune God."[82]

63. Diversities—be they diversities of church traditions or diversities caused by specific historic, ethnic, and cultural contexts—can be understood and lived as different forms of expressing the one and the same faith when they are "related to the central message of salvation and Christian faith" and do not endanger this center,[83] and when they are therefore sustained by one and the same Gospel. It is not necessary that each church adopt the specific forms of belief, piety, or ethics of the other church and make them its own. But each church must recognize them as specific and legitimate forms of the one, common Christian faith. Then it is "justified to recognize a legitimate diversity in the plurality of traditions and to assess them positively."[84]

64. In this sense, for example, the Catholic–Lutheran dialogue on the eucharist has led to the result that the existing differences in the statements about the manner in which Christ is present in the eucharist "must no longer be regarded as opposed in a way that leads to separation," but that in common, albeit in different ways, "the reality of the eucharistic presence" is testified to.[85] Similarly, the Catholic–Lutheran dialogue document on the ministry in the church, with a view to the different interpretations and statements regarding "sacramentality" and "uniqueness" of ordination, was of the opinion that it could speak of a "consensus on the reality" as follows: "Wherever it is taught that through the act of ordination the Holy Spirit gives grace strengthening the ordained person for the lifetime ministry of word and sacrament, it must be asked whether differences which previously divided the churches on this question have not been overcome."[86]

65. In the area of ethical decisions it appears important that the Catholic Church right up to and including the Council of Trent[87] did not condemn the practice of divorced persons remarrying in the Eastern Orthodox churches, although it did reject this practice for itself.

66. The joint Catholic–Lutheran reflection on the Augsburg Confession must be seen in this context, as it proceeded during recent years and when it had become clear that as far as this confession is concerned—including its diverse expressions and approaches—one could note "full accord on fundamental and central truths."[88] Likewise, quite a few dogmatic decisions of the Catholic Church need a common and, if possible, binding interpretation that would bring out more clearly the common ground of our faith. This would be particularly true for the more recent dogmas relating to Mary and to the papacy, because for Lutheran churches and Christians to accept that they are in accordance with Scripture and Gospel represents a serious problem.[89]

3. Removal of Doctrinal Condemnations

67. Our ecclesial awareness has been traumatized by mutual condemnations. These may have been uttered as formal, reciprocal, doctrinal condemnations, but they can also be seen as general prejudices that have taken root in the consciousness of the members of our churches. It is precisely in this form that they have had particularly widespread and fateful repercussions. In order to return to a common confession of the one faith and a true communal relationship, it is necessary that each of our churches declare officially, in all points where this is possible in view of the current teaching of the other church, that these condemnations have become meaningless.

68. Past doctrinal condemnations cannot be rendered ineffectual through a relativizing of truth. Rather, it is the duty to be truthful which calls us to act.

Theological-historical research and more recent ecclesial developments lead us even now to the insight that in important questions those reciprocal doctrinal condemnations are not or are no longer applicable. Thus, for example the necessary rejection by the Reformation of the "Pelagians and others who teach that, without the Holy Spirit and by the power of nature alone, we are able to love God above all things and can also keep the commandments of God in so far as the substance of the acts is concerned,"[90] does not affect the official teaching of the Catholic Church.[91] Vice versa, the equally necessary Catholic rejection of those who hold that "Christians are not concerned with the Ten Commandments"[92] or that "anyone who has become justified once can no longer sin or lose his state of grace"[93] is not applicable to the position of the Lutheran confessions.[94] Similarly, the Reformation condemnation of "those who teach that the sacraments justify by the outward acts" and "without the proper attitude in the recipient"[95] is not applicable to Catholic teaching,[96] and vice versa, the Catholic rejection of those who say that "the sacraments of the New Covenant do not communicate grace *ex opere operato*, but that the faith alone is sufficient to obtain the grace of divine promise"[97] does not apply to the Lutheran confessions.[98] Moreover, the Reformation's condemnation of the sacrifice of the Mass as a denial of the once-for-all sacrifice of the cross[99] does not touch the teaching of the Catholic Church[100] any more than Catholic condemnation of those who deny the real presence of Christ in the eucharist[101] or call it into question by rejecting the doctrine of transubstantiation[102] need apply to the Lutheran church and its teaching.[103]

69. To be sure, agreement that earlier doctrinal condemnations are no longer applicable cannot be achieved by mere statements of consensus issued by theologians. What is really needed are official declarations by the chief teaching authorities of each of the churches concerned, each according to its own procedures. In the Catholic Church this falls within the competence of the Holy See in agreement with the episcopate as a whole. In the Lutheran churches the most appropriate procedure would be one analogous to what was done in accepting the Leuenberg Agreement, i.e., a form of synodal process in the individual churches (see nos. 23-26 above). Official declarations of this type, however, will gain their true ecclesial importance and find their way into the life of the people of God only if they happen in the framework of liturgical celebrations that give expression to both penitence and thanksgiving.

B. Community in Sacraments

70. Community with Christ and community of Christians with each other are mediated through word and sacrament in the Holy Spirit. Where Christians and churches desire full community with each other, it follows that their joint understanding of the apostolic witness and their common testimony to the Christian faith (see no. 55ff. above) must go hand in hand with a common sacramental life.[104] We can note gratefully that in this respect important things have happened recently. (1) Our churches have a more intensive sacramental life. (2) With regard to understanding and celebration of the sacraments, a growing agreement can be noted. The requirements for a common sacramental life have, however, not yet been fully met. (3) Within the fundamental consensus, open questions remain.

1. Growth of Sacramental Life in our Churches

71. In both the consciousness of Lutheran and Roman Catholic churches, the sacramental dimension of the Christian life has in recent times once again come to the fore. Growing out of the sacrament of baptism (Rom 6:3ff.), Christian life in its deepest sense is the gift of sharing in the death and resurrection of Jesus Christ. This sharing is mediated through proclamation of the word and celebration of the sacra-

ments equally.[105] In the sacraments it occurs in a manner which accents the corporeality, the personal character, and the community dimension of this sharing, whereby it should be noted that for Lutherans as well as for Catholics the word belongs to the nature of the sacraments themselves.[106]

72. The deepened consciousness of the sacramental dimension of Christian existence has also reshaped the life and practice of our churches.

In several respects the last few centuries have seen a renewal of sacramental life in the Roman Catholic Church.

- New emphasis has been placed on the interrelatedness of *sacrament, proclaimed word and faith* that the Reformers felt necessary to stress again.[107] This has influenced the reform of the liturgical orders for the celebration of the sacraments.
- The primary importance of baptism[108] and of the eucharist[109] has been stressed, especially by reshaping their celebration.
- A comprehensive view of the sacramental life of the church has been given precedence over an isolated approach to individual sacraments, by understanding the church in Christ as the universal sacrament of salvation,[110] as the sacrament of unity.[111]

These tendencies have led to liturgical developments which parallel many Lutheran concerns: greater space for the proclamation of the word of God, use of the vernacular, more frequent communion under both kinds, curtailing of Masses without the participation of the people, to mention only the most important reforms.

73. Paralleling this, an intensification of sacramental life in the Lutheran churches has developed.

- Regarding baptism, which in the Lutheran tradition has always been considered fully a sacrament and a fundamental and permanent point of reference of Christian existence, there is renewed appreciation of its place in the Sunday gathering for worship.
- The eucharist is today being celebrated more frequently at the regular Sunday worship service than was the case in the past. The Reformation had stressed that Lutheran communities celebrated it with particular devotion and reverence, expressly urging believers to communicate.[112]
- It is stressed that as far as the Lutheran tradition is concerned, the sacramental dimension of Christian life was never called into question and, indeed, was expressly defended in inter-Reformation disputes. It was thus possible for the Lutheran Reformers—following the Scriptures (Col 1:27; 1 Tm 3:16)—to speak of Christ as the one sacrament[113] or to attribute

"sacramental" character to the word of the Scripture and the proclaimed word as bearers of the presence of Christ and as efficacious word.[114]

74. The linkages of the sacraments and their liturgical celebrations both with the world and with all humanity have again been discovered by Lutheran and Catholic traditions together.[115]

2. Increasing Agreement in Understanding and Celebration of the Sacraments

75. Lutherans and Catholics are conscious that they participate in one and the same baptism.[116] In keeping with the statement BEM, we jointly confess that "Christian baptism is rooted in the ministry of Jesus of Nazareth, in his death and in his resurrection. It is incorporation into Christ, who is the crucified and risen Lord; it is entry into the New Covenant between God and God's people."[117] This common understanding of baptism is expressed in the manner in which baptism is administered, and is confirmed by the fact that almost everywhere our churches have officially recognized each other's baptism. Moreover, our churches are faced by common or similar pastoral tasks concerning the understanding of baptism and how it is expressed and concretized in baptismal practice, faith-life, and the piety of congregations and the faithful.

76. A great deal of progress towards a common understanding and celebration of the eucharist has been made in recent years as a result of numerous dialogues between our churches at various levels. In the course of these dialogues, it proved possible to reconcile positions with regard to the understanding of the eucharist that had previously been thought to be in conflict and were therefore seen as divisive (sacrifice of the Mass, eucharistic presence); many of the remaining differences are within the common sphere, thus depriving them of their divisive force.[118] Regarding liturgical form, both churches are moving towards growing consensus in the basic elements of eucharistic celebration.[119]

77. Theological endeavors have also led to a better reciprocal understanding regarding the other sacraments in the Catholic Church, whose sacramental character has hitherto been admitted only hesitantly or not at all by the Lutheran churches.

78. Various Catholic–Lutheran dialogues on the ordained ministry in the church have shown that, even though Lutherans do not speak of ordination as a sacrament, there is yet "substantial convergence" between the Catholic and Lutheran understanding and practice wherever ordination is celebrated through the laying on of hands and prayer (epiklesis) as act of blessing, and wherever it is taught "that through the act of ordination the Holy Spirit gives grace strengthening the ordained person for the lifetime ministry of word and sacrament."[120] Lutheran tradition has taken account of this even though it does not include ordination among

the sacraments in the strict sense. "In principle . . . [it does] not reject" the sacramental understanding of ordination.[121]

79. The Augsburg Confession and both of Luther's catechisms treat confession (of sin) in close connection with the baptismal and eucharistic sacraments. In the Apology of the Augsburg Confession, they are even expressly included among the sacraments.[122] Present-day Catholic–Lutheran research with regard to the understanding of confession in the Augsburg Confession, moreover, has brought to light misunderstandings of each other's position that existed on both sides in the sixteenth century.[123] The Roman Catholic liturgy of penitence, which places the accent on the remission of sins and on personal guidance, together with the more frequent celebration of penitence, foreseen in the new Catholic liturgy, help to promote understanding between our two churches. The difficulties encountered today by the practice of personal confession in certain areas of the Catholic Church and the widespread lack of understanding among many Lutherans make confession a common pastoral task for both churches.

80. Our dialogue about marriage and mixed marriages has revealed a "view of marriage which is in a profound sense a common one." We affirm together that the event of salvation in Christ affects Christians also in their conjugal life which can never be without reference to it. The relationship is nothing other than the grace "as a lasting promise," which Christ grants people in their married life, a grace that "is not simply an idea" but "reality." This means, however, attributing to marriage a "sacramental" aspect, a "sacramental power," even though the Reformation churches do not consider it "to be a sacrament in the full sense of the word."[124]

81. Confirmation and the anointing of the sick have received hardly any consideration in the Catholic–Lutheran dialogue.

Since in the western churches confirmation developed into a rite distinct from baptism, the questions regarding the necessary age for its administration and its precise function have been discussed again and again. In the Lutheran Reformation confirmation disappeared completely. Later it was reintroduced as a rite of admission to the Lord's Supper and/or the celebration of coming of age. As such it was closely linked with previous catechetical instruction. In the Catholic Church confirmation is understood to be an integral part of sacramental initiation into the church, although here, too, it is not devoid of catechetical aspects. In both churches the promise of the gifts of the Holy Spirit is central. Even in the Lutheran understanding confirmation is an act of blessing performed through the prayer of the congregation, and in which grace is promised and granted to the confirmand. Catholics and Lutherans both participate in the ecumenical discussion of the questions about a proper relationship of confirmation to baptism and Christian witness.[125]

82. In the course of postconciliar reforms in the Catholic Church, the anointing of the sick was emphasized more strongly than before as a special help for the

sick and the dying, and it was linked with the proclamation of the word. Lutherans have seldom practiced the anointing of the sick. They have, however, attributed great importance to the pastoral care of sick people. In some Lutheran churches this has recently led to attempts to reintroduce anointing of the sick.[126] This could therefore become the subject of a promising dialogue between Catholics and Lutherans, if one bears in mind the common pastoral tasks and the emerging rapprochement. Both Catholics and Lutherans are now finding a point of encounter inasmuch as the former are gradually getting away from an isolated understanding of the individual sacraments, and the latter are more and more abandoning a narrow use of the concept of sacrament. This, in order to understand and live together the sacramental dimension of Christian existence in a new and better way. Particularly in the present situation where people experience social isolation and personal loneliness, both traditions have a special pastoral task towards the sick and the dying.

3. Open Questions, Remaining Differences, Basic Agreements

83. In spite of an enhanced common awareness of the sacramental dimension of Christian and ecclesial life, and in spite of a deepened consensus in the understanding and praxis of the sacraments, there remain open questions that must be answered with a view to the common sacramental life that belongs to full church fellowship. Clarification of these questions must be brought about in joint dialogue and in the life and praxis of each of the two churches. In this connection the agreements which already exist, or which we have now reached, give us the freedom to challenge each other and to ask reciprocally critical questions regarding teaching and praxis.

84. Nevertheless, even here we must not strive after a questionable homogeneity. Just as in the case of the understanding of faith, the common sacramental life needed for unity must not be mistaken for uniformity. Room must be left for legitimate diversities. This is true not only in relation to the understanding and shaping of the individual sacraments or sacramental ecclesial acts, but also in relation to the concept of sacrament as such. The open questions remaining, especially regarding the number of sacraments, are ultimately rooted in an open concept of sacrament. Not only between our two churches, but also within our churches, the concept of sacrament is not fixed in every last detail. A certain fluctuation historically in determining the number of sacraments—as well as the differentiation between or "ranking" of the sacraments[127] (and a conjunctive "analogue-use" of the sacramental concept)—all point in this direction.

85. For an understanding and the celebration of the individual sacraments and therefore also for the common sacramental life of our two churches, it has to be taken into account that the sacraments are part of God's trinitarian act of salvation: the

work that God performed in Christ once for all for the salvation of the world is mediated by the Holy Spirit, who works through word and sacrament so that *communio sanctorum* is formed, i.e., church as participation in the gifts of salvation and as communion of the faithful.

This makes it clear once more how important it is for a proper understanding and conservation of the sacramental dimension of Christian existence and church life when both our traditions are able to speak of Christ as the one sacrament and therefore as the source of the individual sacraments (see nos. 72 and 73 above). At the same time it becomes clear why on the Catholic side one speaks today of the church as the "sacrament."[128] The Lutheran tradition is not yet very familiar with this thought, and it is often inclined to criticize it. But its intention should be acceptable for Lutherans: as the body of Christ and *"koinonia"* of the Holy Spirit, the church is the sign and instrument of God's grace, an instrument that of itself can do nothing. The church lives by the word as it lives by the sacraments, and at the same time stands in their service.

C. Community of Service

86. The church lives by word and sacrament and also stands in their service. It has therefore a structured form in which the service of the whole people of God and the service of those who have been entrusted with the special ordained ministry can act together. Consequently, in our search for church fellowship, it is not possible to separate the efforts for community of faith (II.A.) and sacramental life (II.B.) from efforts for a structured church fellowship (community of service) that would permit and ensure common life, common decisions, and common action (see no. 49 above).

1. Commitment to a Structured Fellowship (Community of Service)

87. If in the present process of growing reciprocal recognition and reception, our two churches affirm increasingly that they confess the same faith and share a common understanding of the sacraments, then they are also entitled and obliged to enter into structured fellowship with each other. With the New Testament we confess the church as "people of God," as "body of Christ," and as "temple of the Holy Spirit." This confession does not permit us to limit the relationship between our churches to be a mere reciprocally respectful coexistence or internalization. This confession calls us to live out the existing community of faith and sacrament also in a structured ecclesial fellowship. Each of these images of the church, found in the New Testament, confronts us with this commitment.

88. The church as people of God is called to live in unity, for God does not lead Christians to himself and to salvation in isolation or independently of each other. Faith, without ceasing to be personal faith, is always a faith that lives in the

community and is transmitted, preserved, and renewed in it. Just as the people of the old covenant encompassed different tribes and yet was one single people of God, the new people of God has been called together from all nations of the earth, embraces all the diversity of the human world, lives in many places, and listens to God's calling in many languages and in many different ways. It is nevertheless a single undivided people, called by the one Lord, in the one Spirit, to one faith, to solidarity and love for each other, and to common witness and service in the world.

89. The church, the new "people of God," is the body of Christ. "For by one Spirit we were all baptized into one body" (1 Cor 12:13). Elsewhere, speaking of the eucharist, St. Paul says: "The bread which we break, is it not a participation in the body of Christ? Because there is one bread, we who are many are one body" (1 Cor 10:16ff.). Just as the eucharist is not a part of the body of Christ but the whole Christ, so also the local church is not only a part of the whole, but a realization of the church of God.[129] If therefore according to the New Testament the individual local church is church of God in the full sense, it is yet not the whole church of God. This limited nature of the individual churches and their necessary solidarity with each other calls for a concrete and lived out fellowship which embraces all aspects of ecclesial life. It corresponds to the nature of the church which as "body of Christ" is an organic whole.

90. Just as the church is called to be "people of God" and "body of Christ," it is also called to be temple of the Holy Spirit. Since the plenitude of the gifts of the Spirit is given only in the fellowship of all local churches, no church can claim the Holy Spirit for itself alone.[130] Such a claim would contradict the fellowship instituted by the Holy Spirit. The same would be true if one single church wanted to live a life independent of the other churches, if it wanted to dominate them, or even if it were indifferent towards the faith of these churches. Confessing the church as "temple of the Holy Spirit" and recognizing the other church as "temple of the Holy Spirit" means therefore entering into active fellowship with this church. If one and the same spirit of love and unity lives in the churches, all are obliged to pray for each other, to work together, and to care for each other.

91. The growing reciprocal recognition as church thus leads us to binding common life, to active exchange, and to mutual acceptance in witness, service, and solidarity according to the nature of the church as "people of God," "body of Christ," and "temple of the Holy Spirit." It commits our churches at both the local and the universal levels not only to an occasional fellowship, practiced from time to time, but to a fully lived-out fellowship that requires for its realization a structured form.

2. Structured Church Fellowship and a Common Ordained Ministry

92. The dialogue between our churches and, in general, ecumenical efforts for visible unity of the church have shown that the structured form needed for full and

binding fellowship between churches can be manifold and variable. It is not limited to the hierarchical dimension of the church but rather embraces the service of the whole people of God, includes the charisma of all the faithful, and expresses itself in synodal structures and processes. At the same time, fellowship in the ordained ministry forms an essential part of the structured church fellowship.

This fellowship in the ordained ministry, though not yet fully realized, is nevertheless basically present in the mutual recognition of ministries as forms of the ministry instituted by Christ.[131] The coexistence of ministries mutually recognized must be transformed into a common exercise of ordained ministry appropriate to its nature, whereby particular importance is attached to the common exercise of the "ministry of leadership and of pastoral supervision *(episkope)*."[132]

Only in a church fellowship so structured is it possible to take joint decisions to preserve and further the apostolicity, catholicity, and unity of the church and to act jointly in witness and service.

93. There already exists today a broad area in which a partial common exercise of ordained ministry and also of ecclesial *episkope* is possible, desirable, and even necessary. It is carried out between our two churches, for example, in the area of social responsibility, in the ethical, diaconal, and charitable fields, or in evangelization.

94. But yet these forms of cooperation between ordained ministries are far from a comprehensive fully common exercise of the ordained ministry. In order to have progress one must look at three factors:

1. The statement of Vatican II which, regarding the ordained ministry of the Reformation churches, speaks of a "lack of the sacrament of orders"[133]
2. A certain "asymmetry" in the more precise definition of the theological value assigned to the ministry, particularly of the historic episcopacy in the understanding of the church
3. The close bond that exists in the Catholic Church between the bishops and the pope

95. (1) While according to the Lutheran understanding of church the existence of the ministry in the Catholic Church is not to be called into question,[134] Catholics cannot yet fully recognize the ordained ministry in Lutheran churches because according to their view, these churches lack the fullness of the ordained ministry since they "lack of the sacrament of orders."[135] This would only be possible through a process of "acceptance of full church communion"[136] of which fellowship in the historical episcopacy is an essential part.

96. (2) Catholics and Lutherans share the conviction that the ordained ministry of the church, which because it is "instituted by Jesus Christ"[137] "stands over

against the community as well as within the community,"[138] is "essential" for the church.[139] Nevertheless it is possible for Lutherans—and in this they differ from Catholics—to give a theological description of the church without making explicit mention of the ministry because it is either "presupposed"[140] or implied by the proclamation of the word and the administration of the sacraments.

97. Lutherans, like Catholics, can recognize as "the action of the Spirit"[141] the historical differentiation of the one apostolic ministry into more local ministry and more regional forms, and they can consider "the function of *episkope* . . . as necessary for the church."[142] Likewise Lutherans feel free "to face up to the call for communion with the historic episcopal office"[143] (i.e., the historically evolved pattern of episcopal ministry in the form of the office of bishop standing in apostolic succession). Nevertheless Lutherans and Catholics place different accents on the significance of that historic episcopal office for the church.[144]

98. The two problems are closely related. The "lack of the sacrament of orders" that the Catholic side claims to be inherent in the ministry of the Lutheran churches cannot, because of its very nature, be annulled solely by theological insights and agreements or by ecclesiastical or canonical declarations and decisions, as, for example, by the theological and canonical act of recognizing these ministries. What is needed rather is acceptance of the fellowship in ecclesial ministry, and this, ultimately, means acceptance of the fellowship in episcopal ministry which stands in apostolic succession. Lutherans are fundamentally free and open to accept such fellowship in the episcopal office. Yet within this understanding of the importance or significance of the episcopal office for the catholicity, apostolicity, and unity of the church, Lutherans are inclined to place the accent differently from Catholics.

99. The problems mentioned here need not block the road to fellowship in the church ministry and therefore to a fully structured ecclesial fellowship. But it does call for renewal and deepening of the understanding of the ordained ministry, particularly the ministry serving the unity and governance *(episkope)* of the church.

100. (3) In connection with the above mentioned, it has to be borne in mind that as far as Catholics are concerned, fellowship in the ordained ministry is expressed by the college of all bishops with the pope at its head.

101. A Roman Catholic bishop or a group of Catholic bishops do not exercise their *episkope* without involving the whole of the episcopate.[145] When bishops intend to take a decision committing them and their church to a process which has as its goal full church fellowship with Lutheran churches, they can only do this in community with the whole of the Catholic episcopate. The same is true if within their own church they wish to concretize a common exercise of *episkope* with their Lutheran partners.

102. In concrete terms this means that the bishops exercise *episkope* in the fellowship collegially with the first among them, the pope. They recognize the

supreme jurisdictional authority of the pope over the universal church and all the faithful, an authority that—according to Vatican I—is of an episcopal, ordinary, and direct nature.[146]

103. The process that is to lead to a common ordained ministry via the joint exercise of the *episkope* therefore necessarily requires the participation of the pope. He can, in the face of the entire Roman Catholic Church, guarantee the propriety of this process. He can help assure that the unity reestablished in one place will not lead to new divisions in another. Thus, according to its mission, the Petrine ministry cannot only protect fellowship but further it.

3. Joint Reflection on the Early Church

104. The understanding of a ministry serving the unity of the church and *episkope*, on which Catholics and Lutherans diverge to some extent, can be deepened and gain in commonality, if the two sides reflect together about how this ministry was seen and practiced in the early church. Both sides have good reasons for participating in such a reflection.

105. According to the statements of Vatican II on the sacramentality and collegiality of the episcopal office,[147] Catholics no longer follow the view that prevailed in the Middle Ages. Taking the presbyterate (*sacerdotium*) as point of departure, it differentiated the episcopate only by virtue of its greater dignity and jurisdictional authority. One indication of this is the fact that in the 1968 edition of the *Pontificale Romanum*, the former prayer accompanying the imposition of hands is replaced by the prayer taken from Hippolytus's *Apostolic Tradition*. Within Catholic theology this return to the early church fathers is also a call to emphasize more strongly the collegiality of the bishops as an expression of the fellowship of local churches.

106. The Lutheran Reformation basically affirmed the episcopal office of the early church.[148] There was readiness to retain the episcopal office in its traditional form, even though there was criticism of the manner in which the office was exercised at that time. To some extent this criticism was explicitly associated with and legitimated by references to the early church.[149] Thus it is clear that also on the Lutheran side, the question of episcopal ministry is dealt with in reference to the early church.

107. The understanding of the nature of episcopal ministry which then prevailed becomes obvious in the rite of ordination of a bishop. Essential aspects of this are also significant for us today:

108. (a) Ordination is at the same time a charismatic, liturgical, and ecclesial event.

The early church did not separate the charismatic event (gift of the Spirit) from the liturgical ceremony (imposition of hands as part of the eucharistic service on Sundays) nor from its ecclesial context (commissioning and jurisdiction). In the worshiping community and by the imposition of hands of the bishops, the new bishop receives the gift of the Spirit.[150] This gift contains a special charism of presiding over his church.[151]

109. The bishop is a baptized member of the local *koinonia*.[152] In the ordination he, as one who is baptized, receives the call of the church and induction into an office. These two aspects are linked by the action of the Holy Spirit, through which the new bishop receives a gift of grace, which is not intended for his own well-being and does not separate him from the congregation, but which is rather for the benefit of the congregation and which places him in its service.[153]

At the local level bishops stand in their churches and serve them as a personal responsibility. The particular responsibility of one bishop is thus linked with the responsibility of all, as is also shown by the ordination liturgy.

110. (b) The vigilance with regard to the apostolicity of the faith that belongs to the bishop's duty is bound up with the responsibility for the faith borne by the whole Christian people.

Members of the church participate in the election of their bishop and receive the person who is to exercise the apostolic ministry. In addition, when the candidate answers the ordination questions and confesses his faith in the presence of the congregation, the congregation is witness that the bishop represents the authentic apostolic faith. All this shows that the apostolic succession is not really to be understood as a succession of one individual to another,[154] but rather as a succession in the church, to an episcopal see and to membership of the episcopal college,[155] as shown by the lists of bishops.[156]

The responsibility of the congregation is not limited to the moment of ordination. Its full scope is illustrated by the exception "that one must deny one's consent even to bishops when it happens that they err and speak in a manner that contradicts the canonical texts."[157] This means that the *episkope* is not exercised in isolation but normally in concert with the community of the believers, i.e., within a diversity of ministries and services and in the synodal life of the local church.

111. (c) The bishops are servants of unity and of the fellowship among churches. Even though the Christians in a given place must give their consent in the election of their bishop, they do not impose their hands at his ordination. That is done by the leaders of the neighboring churches.

Bishops thus both represent the universal church in their own church and represent their own church among all other churches.[158] This mediating position corresponds to the task of the new bishop in the realm of faith, which is expressly emphasized by the confession-like structure of his ordination. As leader of his own church together with the other bishops (collegiality), he is to bear witness to the faith received from the apostles and to watch over it.

Furthermore, the bishops are those who primarily, though not exclusively, ensure regular communication between the churches. This is done formally in regional or even universal conciliar life that serves to further or reestablish fellowship among the churches.

Finally, bishops are obliged to promote the common action and common witness of the churches. All this indicates that the episcopal office, as understood in the light of ordination, must be exercised collegially if it is to serve the fellowship of the churches.

4. The Significance of Reflection on the Early Church for Church Fellowship Between Catholics and Lutherans

112. This understanding by the early church of the episcopal office as a service to the *koinonia* can stimulate, correct, and enlarge the view of Catholics and Lutherans in their endeavors for a commonly exercised *episkope*. It becomes particularly clear that *episkope* is exercised in concert with the church as a whole in a personal, collegial, and communal way. Consequently, the exercise of the *episkope* cannot be separated from the responsibility of the laity or from "synodality" or conciliarity.

113. In the sense of the early church, the episcopal office is to serve the *koinonia* of the local church in a threefold manner:

- *Personal:* Christ "came not to be served but to serve" (Mk 10:45). This is the duty of all Christians. It is particularly applicable to bishops in an office for which they have received grace, authority, and responsibility. This personal dimension of *episkope* excludes any purely administrative or functional interpretation of this ministry. Since it serves the diversity of gifts granted to Christians and the mission of the people of God, the incumbents themselves are not in the center. Accordingly the linkage between the person of the incumbent and the commission of the office is properly balanced, and former misunderstandings can be eliminated.[159]

- *Collegial,* in the sense that one is never bishop for oneself, but in collegiality with the priests and deacons and in a college with the fellow bishops. On the basis of ordination a bishop becomes bishop of the church over which he presides, and at the same time is recognized as bishop by the whole church and shares responsibility for it. When churches are in communion, ordination and full ecclesial recognition go hand in hand. From this follows the fully sanctioned participation of the bishops in the conciliar life of the church of God at both its regional and universal levels.

- *In cooperation with the congregation,* inasmuch as the bishop's ministry, even though it is not exercised in the name of the people, is generally exercised in fellowship with the people and respects the diversity of the ministries and charisma given by the Spirit.[160] Thus absolute sovereignty either on the part of the congregation or the bishop is excluded.

114. These three ways of exercising the bishop's ministry correspond to what the New Testament teaches us about the manner in which the apostles themselves exercised their ministry.[161] They have also been underscored repeatedly in the wider ecumenical endeavors.[162] Also within our churches corresponding new deliberations are taking place.

115. Since the Second Vatican Council the Catholic Church has been introducing institutional changes which stress the coresponsibility of parishioners in the local churches. Various councils have been set up to bring together the local pastors and members (parish councils), the bishop and the faithful in his diocese (pastoral councils), and the bishop and the presbyters (presbyteral councils). Likewise, diocesan and regional synods have been held with the participation of laity. The functions of the bishops are thus being combined in a structured manner with the responsibility of the whole people of God and its various members.

116. The realization of a true communal life which corresponds to the nature of the church as a fellowship (koinonia) is an important current concern of the Lutheran churches. Efforts are thus being made—partly by referring to the insights of the Reformation, which stress again the early church's concept of the priesthood of all the baptized—to meet the dangers of a "clerical church" by trying to further the participation and active responsibility of all parish members. In the emphasis on the local congregation assembled by God through word and sacrament, which is characteristic of the Lutheran understanding of church, evidences of a congregational narrowness are today seen with a more critical eye than in former times, and efforts are being made to counteract them theologically and practically. The enhanced awareness of the importance of the episkope, clearly to be seen among Lutherans, must be noted in this connection. It is understood, however, not as a mere administrative office but as a ministry of word and sacrament, and particularly as ministry of the pastor pastorum, which serves the wider ecclesial fellowship and becomes its effective representative.

5. Approach to a Jointly Exercised Ministry of Fellowship

117. Common reflection about the early church brings to light a way to a jointly exercised ministry which requires careful examination. The following considerations may be of help. The proposed process is not necessarily the only possible one, though it does seem to avoid obstacles which have, up to now, impeded the way to church fellowship. The description here given may be modified in many of its details. It is neither a rigid nor a final plan. Preserving its central intention, however, is what is important.

118. The process leading to full realization of church fellowship as a structured community is, strictly speaking, a correlated and integral process involving reciprocally recognized ministries and the joint exercise of ministries, especially of the ministry of the *episkope*.[163] Fully spelled out, it has the following structure:

An officially declared mutual recognition of ordained ministries opens the way by means of an initial act to the joint exercise of *episkope*, including ordaining. A series of such ordinations would eventually lead to a common ordained ministry. The process could function at the universal level, but could also be set in motion at local, regional, or national ecclesial levels.

The process would thus have the following phases:

- Preliminary forms of a joint exercise of *episkope* (chapter 6)
- Initial act of recognition (chapter 7)
- Collegial exercise of *episkope* (chapter 8)
- Transition to a common ordained ministry (chapter 9)

119. It is of decisive importance for understanding and implementing this process that one attend to and preserve its integral and correlative character. It is not a matter of isolated acts or of phases in a gradual process. Rather the reciprocal recognition of ministries means essentially enabling and initiating the joint exercise of *episkope* out of which then the ordained ministry arises. And therefore a mutual recognition of ministries which does not initiate the joint exercise of *episkope* and the common ordained ministry growing out of it is insufficient for the realization of structured church fellowship. Furthermore, a joint exercise of *episkope*, including ordaining, is inconceivable without the act of mutual recognition of the ministries, an act which by its nature enables and initiates the joint exercise of *episkope*.

6. Preliminary Forms of the Joint Exercise of Episkope

120. As a rule a preparatory process will be needed before the above described correlative and integral process of mutual recognition of ministries[164] and joint exercise of *episkope* begins in its strict sense, a process during which a gradual recognition of ministries and the appropriate prototypical forms of a joint exercise of ministries, especially the ministry of *episkope*, are developed.

121. Such preliminary forms are, for example:

- Working groups or Christian councils which already exist in many countries
- Mutual invitation of church leaders, pastors, and laity to synods of the two churches, with a right to speak

- Development of more solid forms of working relationship, at the local or regional levels, between those who exercise *episkope* in the two churches so that even now they can speak and act jointly where conscience does not require them to speak and act separately
- Creation, in a country or a region, of conciliar organs for the exchange of experiences and for common consultation in order to arrive at common decisions in such matters as evangelization, social service, public responsibility

122. Also in these preliminary forms or steps on the way to joint exercise of the *episkope*, the main point will always be interrelating of both dimensions of the process, i.e., mutual recognition and joint exercise of the ministries, in which the participation and active cooperation of the entire ecclesial community should also be ensured.

7. Initial Act of Recognition

123. If a fundamental consensus is reached on faith, sacramental life, and ordained ministry such that remaining differences between Catholics and Lutherans no longer can appear as church-dividing, and reciprocal doctrinal condemnations no longer have any basis, then a mutual act of recognition should certainly follow.

124. This act entails a recognition of the fundamental consensus which is ecclesially binding and, at the same time, a mutual recognition that in the other church, the church of Jesus Christ is actualized. It declares and confirms the will of both churches to relate to each other as churches of Jesus Christ and to live in full fellowship *(communio ecclesiarum)*. Concerning the common ministry needed for full church fellowship, this means:

- On the Catholic side, affirmation of the existence in the Lutheran churches of the ministry instituted by Christ in his church, while at the same time pointing to a lack of fullness of the ordained ministry as a *defectus* which, for the sake of church fellowship, has jointly to be overcome;
- An enabling and concurrent authoritative beginning of a joint exercise of *episkope* which progressively brings about and implies fellowship in the fully structured ordained ministry.

125. The act of recognition should be appropriate to the binding, ecclesial, and integral character of the process of realizing church fellowship. To it belong a binding confessional declaration and an appropriate liturgical celebration in which, if possible, the first joint ordination should be held, thus marking the beginning of the joint exercise of *episkope*.

Church fellowship begun in this manner opens possibilities of sacramental and particularly eucharistic fellowship, the modalities of which have to be clarified on the Catholic side according to the existing canon law.[165]

126. Church fellowship between Catholics and Lutherans is ultimately sought as a fellowship between the whole Catholic Church and the totality of the Lutheran churches. Any act of initial recognition—whether it involves the churches at the local, regional, national, or international levels—must have this as its goal.

On the Lutheran side, in view of these considerations, the relevant decisions would be taken by the independent churches (for example, *Landeskirchen* or national churches, or their associations). In this respect forms must be found which ensure that action is being taken in solidarity with the other churches of the Lutheran communion.

On the Catholic side, note must be taken of the requirements of the episcopate as a whole. Depending on the circumstances at any given time, local bishops, bishops of a church province, or an episcopal conference would have to take primary responsibility. If a positive judgment is arrived at, the act of initial recognition must occur in cooperation with the pope, because such an act concerns the whole Catholic Church. On the basis of his particular responsibility for the unity of Christians and the fellowship of the churches, it is the task of the pope to approve or encourage such a local act in the name of the Catholic Church.

8. A Single Episkope in Collegial Form

127. The common exercise of *episkope*, including ordaining—made possible by the recognition of ministries—through which community of faith and sacraments between Lutherans and Catholics becomes structured church fellowship, will initially take the shape of a *single* episkope *exercised in collegial form*.

In places where they exist together, the churches would provide for themselves a single episcopate in collegial form. It would go beyond all preliminary forms of parallel or partial joint exercise of *episkope*, but without merging the two episcopates. This single episcopate would at the same time ensure necessary unity and legitimate diversity. What is foreseen is a form of local church in which our churches would truly be one without having been absorbed. This is the case, for example, with the united churches of the East (see nos. 35-40 above) and is the intention of the model of "unity in reconciled diversity" (see nos. 31-34 above).[166] In such a situation, the Catholic or Lutheran congregations would preserve their existing links with their bishop. Moreover, the collegial exercise of *episkope* in a region or a country can be furthered by the presence of a regional primate to whom his episcopal colleagues grant certain privileges, as for example, convening and chairing of an assembly, or under certain conditions, representation of the church of the region or country *vis-a-vis* civil authorities.[167]

128. Such a form of jointly exercised *episkope* is most readily derived from the *ductus* of the preceding considerations, commends itself on the basis of the nature of the growing understanding and convergence between Catholics and Lutherans, and corresponds most clearly and honestly to the mutual recognition of ministries already set forth. This form of jointly exercised *episkope* is also in basic agreement with the understanding of the unity of the local church as it was held and practiced in the early church.

The unity of the local church found expression in the early church through a single bishop exercising jurisdiction in one and the same territory.[168] The catholicity and apostolicity of the church as well as its unity was thus to be demonstrated and preserved.

Neither race nor language nor class nor any other human condition can be the principle of church unity. The "localness" of the church, linked with a single bishop, makes clear that thereby Christians are one with each other and that, on the basis of one faith and one baptism, they gather around one eucharist. This eucharist is always celebrated in unity with the bishop.

129. There are, therefore, multiple reasons for the traditional principle of a single bishop in one local church. However in a situation in which—as in ours—the concern is the realization of church fellowship between hitherto separated churches, forms of local church structure seem possible which ensure and testify to the unity, catholicity, and apostolicity of these churches without in each case being presided over by only one single bishop.

130. That does not exclude the question whether, following the creation of the common ministry to which the jointly exercised *episkope* would lead (see chapter 9 below), there can or shall be also other forms of jointly exercised *episkope* than the collegial one (see chapter 10 below).

131. Whatever the precise procedures for the common exercise of *episkope* may be, the nature and the content of the decisions to be taken must be subject to an evaluation process which could extend over several years. On the Catholic side, churches engaged in such a process must account before the whole Catholic Church for their initiatives, the difficulties encountered, and their positive experiences. Other Catholic churches, in contact with Lutheran churches somewhere in the world, will listen to them attentively. The indispensable discussion partner for them will be the Roman See because of its special role within the Catholic Church.

9. Transition from Joint Exercise of Episkope to a Common Ordained Ministry

132. The joint exercise of the ministry of *episkope*, which includes ordaining, leads to the gradual establishment of a common ordained ministry.

133. The formation of the ordained church ministry would be the result of individual ordinations which would take place whenever there is a candidate to ordain. All neighboring bishops, Lutherans and Catholics, on the basis of the jointly exercised *episkope* would ordain the new minister together. At the end of this process—within a reasonable space of time—the common ordained ministry would be realized.

134. Each of these ordinations must be understood and undertaken as an event which is at the same time (a) confessional, (b) epicletic, (c) communal, and (d) juridical:

a. At the moment of taking up his ministry, the new minister confesses the apostolic faith before the entire worshiping community which, together with the Catholic and Lutheran bishops (or other ministers exercising *episkope*) present on that occasion, witnesses to the correctness of his faith.

b. The entire action of ordination is embraced by the invocation of the Holy Spirit by the whole worshiping community.[169] Within this liturgical action the gift of the Spirit, necessary for the exercise of the ministry, is imparted through the imposition of hands by the Catholic and Lutheran bishops.

c. Not everything, however, can depend on the common imposition of hands. The whole congregation is also involved. It could in one way or another participate in the election of the ordinand. As a rule, members of the church or congregation testify to the faith and morals of the candidate. The church or congregation for which the minister is being ordained engages in an act of acceptance (reception). Finally, ordination also concerns the fellowship among the churches, since it is one of the tasks of those ordained to further this fellowship.

d. Ordination sets one immediately into the service of the church and confers the authority inherent in such service. In the Catholic Church, a new bishop has to be appointed or confirmed by the pope. As various current concordats indicate, or as in the election of the patriarchs of the united churches of the East, the Catholic Church can adopt various procedures that do not necessarily eventuate in direct appointment.

135. It must be clearly understood that at stake in joint ordinations by Catholic and Lutheran bishops is a gift of grace of the Holy Spirit received in common by Catholics and Lutherans. In a confession of gratitude the two partners recognize together that the common and collegial ordained ministry is a gift of the Spirit to the apostolic church. At this juncture it would therefore be wrong to pose the question of what the one partner has given to the other.

136. A common ordained ministry would thus grow out of the jointly exercised *episkope*. This transition would be a process which is so irrevocably rooted in a truly joint exercise of *episkope* that, should it not take place or be discontinued, one could no longer really speak of a jointly exercised *episkope*. Ordination constitutes one of the most important functions of *episkope*.[170]

137. This transition to a common ordained ministry is preeminently a *gift of God*. Understood as epicletic and confessional events, the ordinations through which our churches receive the ministry show that this common ordained ministry also is not the result of human efforts, but God's gift given through God's Spirit.

138. The *dimension of ecclesial reconciliation* inherent in this event should be expressed in all local congregations through preparation marked not only by joy and gratitude, but also by penitence, both sides confessing their sins against *koinonia*.

139. In this act of reconciliation and penitence, as is generally characteristic of the path we have proposed, our churches turn resolutely towards the future and leave it to God to judge the past. This implies that the time elapsing between the reciprocal recognition of ministries and the beginning of the jointly exercised episkope on the one hand, and the establishing of the common ministry on the other, be considered or declared a time of real but growing and deepening church fellowship. It is a *period of transition vouchsafed by God*.[171]

140. The form described here for realizing a common ordained ministry is not intended to exclude other forms. Rather, it appears to us to be the most appropriate one for the relationship between Lutheran churches and the Roman Catholic Church. In filling vacant posts by new ordinations, one avoids problems which could encumber other procedures which have been discussed or could allow for misinterpretations:

a. *Reordination:* Its problems are not only terminological: one would properly speak of "ordination" in the case of an ordination considered null and void. Reordination is primarily a problem because the church whose ministers were newly ordained would have to admit the invalidity of all previous ordinations.

b. *Supplementary Ordination:* In view of the fact that previous ordinations were intended for a particular church and not for the universal church, a "supplementary ordination" has been considered. The problem here is that existing ordinations are not then taken seriously. For the Catholic Church, therefore, a "supplementary ordination" is inconceivable when it recognizes the ordination of a previously separated church, as, for example, the Orthodox Church.

c. *Act of "Reconciliation of Ministries":* What is meant here is a comprehensive act of worship during which, by mutual imposition of hands, forgiveness is asked and the Holy Spirit is invoked in prayer that it would grant to all the gifts they need. The problematic of such a broad act of "reconciliation of ministries" derives from its ambiguity and, consequently, from its unclarity. Is there implicitly an ordination or a supplementary ordination? Is the validity of previous ordinations taken seriously?

d. *Mutual Commissioning:* If previous ordinations in the other church are considered valid, a mutual commissioning of ordained ministers would be conceivable in order to achieve a common church ministry. The problematic here is that this would be a mere administrative act, while the establishment of a ministerial fellowship cannot be reduced to a legal action. Moreover, mutual commissioning would be an act among ordained ministers with no attention to the role of the people of God.

141. For the transition period, the way proposed makes it imperative to determine precisely the juridical status of the jointly ordained as well as of those bishops and ministers (presbyters) not yet jointly ordained.

10. Exercise of the Common Ordained Ministry

142. After the realization of a common ordained ministry, the exercise of the episcopate need not be uniform for each place. Specific historical, social, and cultural situations, as well as the diversity of spiritual traditions, can speak in favor of exercising that ministry in different ways. According to local circumstances, one can imagine at least three forms of the exercise of the episcopate and, consequently, of a truly united local church:

143. First Form: A Single *Episkope* in Collegial Form. In this case the mode of exercising the *episkope* already practiced during the transition period would be continued (see nos. 119-122 above).

144. Second Form: A Single Bishop for Differently Structured Parishes. Parishes which differ on the basis of their spiritual and theological traditions live under one bishop who cares for the fellowship among them and also protects their legitimate differences. Thus in the united evangelical *Landeskirchen* of Germany, for example, there are Reformed and Lutheran parishes which have a common bishop or church president and are subject to a common church authority. Also, Catholic Armenians or Maronites living under a bishop of the Latin rite have the possibility of maintaining their religious identity outside their native country by having their own parishes. In the framework of church fellowship, a similar practice would be conceivable between Catholics and Lutherans.

145. Third Form: Merger. The churches unite into a single church in which the parishes are also merged. The merged church would have only a single bishop. This form which is foreseen, for example, by the model of "organic union" (see nos.

16-18 above) seems legitimate and feasible—if it is desired— especially in the case of churches which live in a non-Christian environment.[172]

11. Indivisibility of the Koinonia

146. The realization of church fellowship in which community of faith and community in the sacraments attain ecclesial shape confronts both Lutherans and Catholics with the question of the indivisibility of the *koinonia*, even though the problem does not present itself in a completely symmetrical manner for the two sides.

147. From the Lutheran point of view, if a Lutheran church enters into full fellowship with the Catholic Church, it does not mean:

    a.   That this church enters *ipso facto* into fellowship with those churches which are already in fellowship with the Catholic Church

    b.   That this Lutheran church forgoes *ipso facto* its fellowship with the other Lutheran churches and with other churches not in fellowship with the Catholic Church

    c.   That the remaining Lutheran churches, in fellowship with this church but not with the Catholic Church, enter *ipso facto* into fellowship with the Catholic Church or renounce their fellowship with this church[173]

But it does mean:

    a.   That for this church the question of fellowship with those churches which are in fellowship with the Catholic Church is raised on a new level, under new presuppositions, and with greater urgency than previously

    b.   That this church affirms as its task and responsibility working towards fellowship of all other Lutheran churches with the Catholic Church

    c.   That the remaining Lutheran churches also consider and affirm the possibility of a fellowship with the Catholic Church as their own possibility to a greater extent than previously

148. On the Catholic side this question arises: Is it possible for the Catholic Church to be in full fellowship with a church which is itself in fellowship with another church with which the Catholic Church is not in fellowship?

Only a few insignificant historical precedents can be cited: in the early church, for example, perhaps the schism of Meletius of Antioch and the special position of St. Basil; in more recent times (seventeenth/eighteenth century), fellowship with Orthodox church groups of the Greek islands without these churches becoming united churches. A remote analogy is the mutual admission to the eucharist in emergency situations by the Patriarchate of Moscow and the Catholic Church without this agreement being extended to the whole Orthodox Church.

Whatever historical precedents there may be, it is especially necessary to answer authoritatively the questions raised above. In doing so, it is assumed:

a. That the third church holds no doctrines which clearly contradict central truths of faith

b. That even if there is agreement in the central truths of faith, this church and its members are not admitted *ipso facto* to the eucharist in the whole Catholic Church

Future Perspective

149. At the end of our description of how to achieve Catholic–Lutheran church fellowship, many questions still remain open. The origins and the history of our ecclesial separation are too complex for us to be able to describe clearly and without ambiguity the process of overcoming it. Only as we continue along the road which we have started together will the obscurity disappear and answers be found to still-open questions. We are sure to find in our churches many partners who will accompany us on this road with additions and corrections, encouragement, and reassurance.

We hope to find also in other churches people who accompany us on this road. It could be that our reflections will help them, just as we have received and continue to expect valuable impulses from them. Even as our efforts have their presuppositions in specific Catholic–Lutheran realities and have their goal in Catholic–Lutheran church fellowship, still we must not lose sight of the task and the aim of wider Christian unity. It is our deep conviction that each individual step towards unity must be understood as a step taken towards the unity of all churches. This unity remains always "a blessing of the Triune God, a work which he accomplishes, by means he chooses, in ways he determines."[174] Consciousness of that has been strengthened and deepened in us in the course of efforts to describe our common path. Seen in this way, all our reflections are a prayer to the Lord who knows ways which surpass our vision and are beyond our power.

List of Signatories

This document was signed by all members of the joint commission:

Roman Catholic Members

Rt. Rev. H. L. Martensen (chairman)
Rt. Rev. P. W. Scheele
Dr. J. Hoffmann
Rev. J. F. Hotchkin
Rev. Chr. Mhagama
Dr. St. Napiorkowski
Dr. V. Pfnür

Lutheran Members

Dr. G. A. Lindbeck (chairman)
Rt. Rev. D. H. Dietzfelbinger (unable to attend)
Rev. K. Hafenscher
Dr. P. Nasution
Rev. I. K. Nsibu
Dr. L. Thunberg
Dr. Bertoldo Weber

Consultants

Dr. H. Legrand, OP (Roman Catholic)
Dr. H. Meyer (Lutheran)
Dr. H. Schütte (Roman Catholic)

Staff Members

Rev. E. L. Brand (Lutheran World Federation)
Dr. P. Duprey (Secretariat for Promoting Christian Unity)
Msgr. A. Klein (Secretariat for Promoting Christian Unity)
Rev. C. H. Mau Jr. (Lutheran World Federation)

NOTES

1. *Ways to Community*, Roman Catholic–Lutheran Joint Commission (Geneva, 1981), especially nos. 4-52.

2. *The New Delhi Report* (London, 1962), report of section III, no. 2, p. 116.

3. LG, no. 26.

4. Ibid., no. 23; cf. CIC, can. 368f.

5. LG, no. 23.

6. J. Willebrands, "The Future of Ecumenism," in *One in Christ*, 1975, 4, p. 323.

7. Cf. W. Elert, *Abendmahl und Kirchengemeinschaft in der alten Kirche hauptsächlich des Ostens* (Berlin, 1954); *Koinonia—Arbeilen des Ökumenischen Ausschusses der Vereinigten Evangelisch-Lutherischen Kirche Deutschlands zur Frage der Kirchen- und Abendmahlsgemeinschaft* (Berlin, 1957).

8. UR, no. 8.

9. "Concepts of Unity and Models of Union," A Preliminary Study Document of the Faith and Order Commission (October 1972); FO/72:20, IIId and IVb.

10. *Breaking Barriers* (Nairobi, 1975; London/Grand Rapids, 1976), report of section II, pp. 65 and 63, nos. 14 and 10.

11. *The Second World Conference on Faith and Order* (Edinburgh, 1937; London, 1938), pp. 252f.

12. H. Tenhumberg, "Kirchliche Union bzw. korporative Wiedervereinigung" in *Kirche und Gemeinde*, ed. W. Danielsmeyer and C. H. Ratschow (Witten, 1974), pp. 24f.

13. J. Ratzinger, *Theologische Prinzipienlehre. Bausteine zur Fundamentaltheologie* (Munich, 1981), p. 121.

14. J. Ratzinger, "Die Kirche und die Kirchen" in *Reformatio*, 1964, p. 105.

15. *The Final Report* of the Anglican Roman Catholic International Commission, 1981, conclusion in GA, p. 116.

16. AAS 5 (1977): 284.

17. Leuenberg Agreement, nos. 29-33.

18. Ibid., no. 37.

19. Ibid., nos. 29 and 30.

20. Ibid., no. 29.

21. Ibid., no. 37.

22. Nairobi, op. cit., p. 60, no. 4.

23. Ibid.

24. Ibid., no. 3; cf. definition of "local church," "The Unity of the Church—Next Steps," in *What Kind of Unity?* Faith and Order Paper No. 69 (Geneva, 1974), p. 123.

25. Nairobi, op. cit., p. 60, no. 3.

26. "The Unity of the Church—Next Steps," op. cit., A.III.3, p. 122.

27. Nairobi, op. cit., p. 60, no. 4.

28. Ibid., p. 61, no. 7.

29. "The Unity of the Church—Next Steps," op. cit., A.IV, pp. 123ff.

30. Accra Report, "The Unity of the Church: The Goal and the Way," in *Uniting in Hope* (Accra, 1974), Faith and Order Paper No. 72, p. 114.

31. *Sharing in One Hope*, Commission on Faith and Order (Bangalore, 1978), Faith and Order Paper No. 92, Geneva, pp. 235-242.

32. For example, at the First Forum on Bilateral Conversations (April 1978) or at the Consultation Between the World Council of Churches and the World Confessional Families (Geneva, October 1978), see *LWF Report*, 15 (June 1983), Günther Gassmann, Harding Meyer, "The Unity of the Church—Requirements and Structure," pp. 33-39, 50-54.

33. "The Ecumenical Role of the World Confessional Families in the One Ecumenical Movement," discussion paper from two consultations with representatives from world confessional families (Geneva, 1974), nos. 17-21, *LWF Report*, 15 (June 1983): 27f.

34. Ibid., no. 30, p. 31.

35. *In Christ—A New Community*, The Proceedings of the Sixth Assembly of the Lutheran World Federation (Dar-es-Salaam, 1977; Geneva, 1977), Statement on Models of Unity, p. 174.

36. Ibid., p. 174; cf. *Ecumenical Relations of the Lutheran World Federation*, Report of the Working Group on the Interrelations Between the Various Bilateral Dialogues (Geneva, 1977), no. 154.

37. *In Christ—A New Community*, op. cit, p. 174.

38. See above, no. 30; cf. G. Gassmann, H. Meyer; "The Unity of the Church," op. cit., pp. 15ff.

39. *Tomos Agapis*. Dokumentation zum Dialog der Liebe zwischen dem Hl. Stuhl und dem Ökumenischen Patriarchat 1958-1976, edited on behalf of the Stiftungsfonds PRO ORIENTE, Vienna (Innsbruck/Vienna/Munich, 1978), passim.

40. OE, no. 2.

41. Ibid., no. 3.

42. Ibid., no. 4.

43. Cf. ibid., no. 30.

44. Jan Cardinal Willebrands, in an address given to representatives of the Anglican Communion in Cambridge, England, January 1970; text published in *Documents on Anglican–Roman Catholic Relations* (Washington, 1972), pp. 39ff.

45. UR, no. 14.

46. Message of Pope Paul VI to Patriarch Athenagoras I on July 25, 1967, *Information Service*, The Secretariat for Promoting Christian Unity, 1967/3, pp. 12f.; AAS 59 (1967): 852-854.

47. The two concepts must be distinguished from each other. Each of them has a distinct meaning and conceptual history. Cf. in the vast literature, for example: A. Grillmeier, "Konzil und Rezeption. Methodische Bemerkungen zu einem Thema der ökumenischen Diskussion der Gegenwart," *Theologie und Philosophie* 45(1970): 321-352;

Y. Congar, "La 'réception' comme réalité ecclésiologique," *Revue des Sciences Philosophiques et Théologiques* 56 (1972): 369-403; G. Gassmann, "Rezeption im ökumenischen Kontext," *Ökumenische Rundschau* 26 (1977): 314-327; H. Meyer, "'Anerkennung'—Ein ökumenischer Schlüsselbegriff," *Dialog und Anerkennung. Beiheft zur Ökumenischen Rundschau* no. 37 (Frankfurt, 1978), pp. 25-41; M. Garijo, "Der Begriff der 'Rezeption' und sein Ort im Kern der katholischen Ekkiesiologie," *Theologischer Konsens und Kirchenspaltung,* edited by P. Lengsfeld and H. G. Stobbe (Stuttgart, 1981), pp. 97-109, and Anmerkungen, pp. 167-172; E. Lanne, "La 'réception,'" *Irénikon* LV(1982): 199-213.

The term "reception" is often used with regard to accepting specific statements or documents, but here we intend both terms, "reception" and "recognition," to be designations of interchurch relations and actions:

"Recognition" means basically a theological and spiritual affirmation of the other church in its special emphases, which confers on this church—as a whole or in individual elements of its belief, life, or structure—legitimacy and authenticity. "Reception" means basically a theological and spiritual affirmation of the other church—as a whole or in individual elements of its belief, life, or structure—which accepts and appropriates the special emphases of the other church either as its own or as contributions (in the sense of correction or complement). Therefore "recognition" and "reception" each involve a specific emphasis: "Recognition" stresses more strongly the special character of the other in its independence, an independence capable of fellowship. "Reception" emphasizes more strongly the special character of the other as containing elements to be adopted and integrated into a church's own life and thinking and into its fellowship with the other church. "Recognition" and "reception" must go hand in hand and complement each other in efforts for church fellowship. There can be no "reception" without recognition of the legitimacy and authenticity of the other. "Recognition" calls for beginning the process of accepting and adopting the particular features of the other inasmuch as they represent a contribution to the life and thinking of the partner and are considered as necessary for realizing the fellowship.

48. Pope John Paul II in Germany, *Information Service,* The Secretariat for Promoting Christian Unity, no. 45, 1981/I, pp. 5f.; p. 7.

49. Pope John Paul II's Letter on Fifth Centenary of Birth of Martin Luther to Cardinal Willebrands, President of the Secretariat for Promoting Christian Unity, *Information Service,* op. cit., no. 52, 1983/III, p. 83.

50. Pope John Paul II in Germany, *Information Service,* op. cit., no. 45, 1981/I, p. 6.; cf. Pastoral Letter of German Bishops "Thy Kingdom Come" (20 January 1980), *KNADokumentation* no. 5, 23 January 1980; and Lutheran–Roman Catholic Discussion on the Augsburg Confession, Documents 1977-1981, edited by Harding Meyer, *LWF Report* 10 (August 1980): 55 and 64.

51. *Sent into the World,* The Proceedings of the Fifth Assembly of the Lutheran World Federation (Evian, 1970; Minneapolis, 1971), pp. 156f.

52. Cf. the recommendations regarding eucharistic hospitality by the church of the Augsburg Confession of Alsace and Lorraine, December 1973, *Lutheran World* 22 (1975): 152ff. and the "Pastoraltheologische Handreichung der Vereinigten Evangelisch-Lutherischen Kirche Deutschlands" regarding the question of the participation of Lutheran Christians in the celebration of the eucharist by other confessions,

1975. Cf. also A *Statement on Communion Practices*, ALC/LCA, 1978, p. 7, "Intercommunion."

53. The affirmations that the church of Christ "subsists in the Catholic Church" (LG, no. 8) and that the Spirit of Christ has not refrained from using "these separated Churches and Communities . . . as means of salvation" (UR, no. 3) show that the Catholic Church does not identify the church of God with its own visible boundaries. This constitutes a considerable change in attitude. It indicates a recognition that "some, even very many, of the most significant elements or endowments which together go to build up and give life to the Church herself can exist outside the visible boundaries of the Catholic Church" (ibid.) and an awareness "that whatever is wrought by the grace of the Holy Spirit in the hearts of our separated brethren can contribute to our own edification" (ibid., no. 4).

54. UR, no. 11.

55. Cf. "The Gospel and the Church" (Malta Report), no. 25.

56. UR, no. 6; cf. also LG, no. 8.

57. UR, no. 11; cf. Malta Report, nos. 24f.

58. Cf. BC, pp. 17ff.

59. *All Under One Christ*, no. 13; cf. *Lutherans and Catholics in Dialogue* I, "The Status of the Nicene Creed as Dogma of the Church" (Washington, D.C., 1965); and "Erklärung zur 1600-Jahr-Feier des Glaubensbekenntnisses von Nizäa-Konstanlinopel" of the Joint Commission of representatives from the Evangelical Church in Germany and the Catholic Church, *KNA Dokumentation* 16 (3 June 1981).

60. Malta Report, no. 17.

61. Ibid., no. 26.

62. *All Under One Christ*, no. 14.

63. Cf. *The Eucharist*, nos. 1-45 and 76; cf. also "The Liturgical Celebration of the Eucharist," ibid., pp. 29ff.

64. *All Under One Christ*, no. 16.

65. Malta Report, nos. 48 and 21.

66. *The Ministry in the Church*, no. 20.

67. *All Under One Christ*, no. 18; cf. *The Ministry in the Church*, no. 17.

68. *The Ministry in the Church*, no. 31.

69. Ibid., nos. 14 and 23.

70. See footnote 50 above.

71. "Lutheran–Roman Catholic Discussion on the Augsburg Confession Documents 1977- 1981," op. cit., p. 76.

72. *The Ministry in the Church*, no. 51.

73. Ibid., no. 52.

74. Ibid., no. 53.

75. Cf. ibid., no. 55.

76. Ibid., no. 57.

77. Cf. ibid., nos. 52 and 54.

78. Already during the First World Conference on Faith and Order it was said that "unity . . . does not mean uniformity." Reports of the World Conference on Faith and Order (Lausanne, August 1927; Boston, 1928), Report on Subject VII, p. 20.

79. AC, VII; BC, p. 32; cf. Luther's comment to the confession of the Bohemian Brethren, WA 50, p. 380; Confessio Helvetica Posterior, XVII; 39 Articles, art. 19.

80. UR, no. 4; cf. LG, no. 23.

81. *Information Service,* Secretariat for Promoting Christian Unity, 1967/3, p. 10. Similarly it is reported in the message of the Holy Father to the Ecumenical Patriarch that "it is a matter of knowing and of respecting each other in the legitimate diversity of liturgical, spiritual, disciplinary, and theological traditions (cf. UR, nos. 14 and 17) by means of a frank theological dialogue, made possible by the reestablishment of brotherly charity in order to attain accord in the sincere confession of all revealed truths. In order to restore and preserve communion and unity, care must indeed be taken to 'impose no burden beyond what is indispensable' (Acts 15:28; UR, no. 18)."

82. *Information Service,* Secretariat for Promoting Christian Unity, no. 22, October 1973/IV, p. 7.

83. Statement on "Models of Unity," *In Christ—A New Community,* op. cit., p. 174.

84. Gemeinsame Synode der Bistümer der BRD, 1974, no. 4.33. The Assembly of the Lutheran World Federation (1977) spoke in this connection of "a way of living encounter, spiritual experience together, theological dialogue and mutual correction, a way on which the distinctiveness of each partner is not lost sight of but rings out, is transformed and renewed, and in this way becomes visible and palpable to the other partners as a legitimate form of Christian existence and of the one Christian faith." *In Christ—A New Community,* p. 174. Cf. no. 33 above.

85. *The Eucharist,* no. 51; cf. nos. 48-51 and 16.

86. *The Ministry in the Church,* no. 33; cf. nos. 32 and 39.

87. Cf. Tridentinum, Sess. XXIV, canon 7; DS, 1807 and note 1.

88. Cf. no. 51 above; cf. *All Under One Christ,* particularly nos. 14f.

89. With a view to Eastern Orthodox churches, Joseph Cardinal Ratzinger says regarding the doctrine of primacy: "Rome does not have to require of the East more regarding the primacy doctrine than was formulated and practiced during the first thousand years." Basically it can be said "that what was possible for a thousand years, cannot be impossible for Christians today" ("Die Frage der Wiedervereinigung zwischen Ost und West," *Theologische Prinzipienlehre,* op. cit., 209).

90. CA XVIII, ed. 1531; BC, p. 40.

91. Cf. DS, 1551-1553.

92. DS, 1569.

93. DS, 1573.

94. Cf. CA XX, 1f., BC, p. 41; CA XII, 7, BC, p. 35; SA, part III, III, 42-45, BC, pp. 309f.

95. CA XIII, ed. 1531, BC, p. 36; Apol IV, 63, BC, p. 115.

96. Cf. *The Eucharist,* no. 61; pp. 69-75.

97. DS, 1608.

98. Cf. CA V, 2; VIII, 2; XIII; BC, pp. 31, 33, 35f.; *The Eucharist,* pp. 70-73.

99. SA, part II, II, BC, pp. 293ff.

100. Cf. *The Eucharist,* nos. 56-61.

101. DS, 1651.

102. Cf. DS, 1652.

103. Cf. *The Eucharist,* nos. 14-17, 50-51.

104. Cf. *Ways to Community,* nos. 14ff.

105. Cf. Apol XII, 5, BC, pp. 211f.; DV, no. 2; PO, nos. 2 and 4; SC, no. 7.

106. Cf. SC, no. 35; on the Lutheran side the reception of the sentence of St. Augustine: *"Accedat verbum ad elementum et fit sacramentum"* ("when the Word is added to the element or the natural substance, it becomes a sacrament"), for example in the Large Catechism IV, 18, BC, p. 438, and in the Smalcald Articles, part III, V, 1, BC, p. 310.

107. SC, nos. 24, 35, 51, 52; *The Eucharist,* nos. 7 and 61.

108. LG, no. 15; UR, no. 22.

109. AG, no. 9; PO, no. 5.

110. LG, no. 48, cf. nos. 1 and 9.

111. SC, no. 26. In this respect present-day theology can speak of the church as the "primordial sacrament" and of Christ as the "proto-sacrament" in whom and through whom the church is the universal sacrament of salvation (LG, nos. 1 and 48).

112. CA XXIV, I and 4, BC, p. 56.

113. WA 6, 86; WA 6, 501, LW, vol. 36, p. 18; cf. Melanchthon's Loci communes theologici, *The Library of Christian Classics,* Melanchthon and Bucer (London, 1969), vol. XIX, p. 135.

114. WA 9, 440-442.

115. Cf. for example *The Eucharist,* nos. 38-41.

116. Cf. LG, no. 15; UR, nos. 3, 4, and 22.

117. *Baptism, Eucharist, and Ministry,* Faith and Order Paper No. 111 (Geneva, 1982), Baptism, I, 1.

118. Cf. *The Eucharist,* and the document of the Catholic–Lutheran dialogue in the USA: "The Eucharist: A Lutheran-Roman Catholic Statement," *Lutherans and Catholics in Dialogue,* III, "The Eucharist as Sacrifice" (Washington/New York, 1967).

119. Cf. *The Eucharist,* nos. 75 and 76; "The Liturgical Celebration of the Eucharist," ibid., pp. 29ff.

120. *The Ministry in the Church,* no. 33; cf. no. 32; also Malta Report, no. 59; and the document of the Catholic–Lutheran dialogue in the USA: "Eucharist and Ministry: A Lutheran–Roman Catholic Statement," *Lutherans and Catholics in Dialogue,* IV (Washington/New York, 1970), no. 16.

121. *The Ministry in the Church,* no. 33.

122. Apol XIII, 4; BC, p. 211.

123. H. Fagerberg, H. Jorissen, "Busse und Beichte," *Confessio Augustana—Bekenntnis des einen Glaubens*, edited by H. Meyer, H. Schütte (Paderborn/Frankfurt, 1980), pp. 228ff.

124. *Theology of Marriage and the Problems of Mixed Marriages* (Geneva, 1977), nos. 16-21 and 29.

125. BEM, op cit., Baptism, no. 14.

126. *Occasional Services*, A Companion to Lutheran Book of Worship (Minneapolis/Philadelphia, 1982), "Service of the Word for Healing," pp. 89-102.

127 Baptism and eucharist as "chief basic sacraments," *Ways to Community*, no. 18; cf. Tridentinum, DS, 1603; LG, no. 7; and the concept of *potissima sacramenta* of Thomas Aquinas (S.Th. III q. 62, a. 5) or the *sacramenta maiora*.

128. Cf. LG, nos. 1, 9, 48; SC, no. 26.

129. This theological principle describes the relationship among the local churches in New Testament times and also the relationship of the local churches within the Catholic Church according to the understanding of Vatican II: "This Church of Christ is truly present in all legitimate local congregations of the faithful, which, united with their pastors, are themselves called churches" (LG, no. 26). "In and from such individual churches there comes into being the one and only Catholic Church" (ibid., no. 23; cf. CD, no. 11). The application of this principle to the Catholic Church and the Lutheran churches must be regarded as legitimate from the moment—but only from the moment—they have found their way back to community in faith and sacramental life universally or locally.

130. LG, no. 13 interprets the words (1 Pt 4:10): "As each has received a gift, employ it for one another as good stewards of God's varied grace" pneumatologically and applies them to the local churches. In the spirit of this theological principle, LG, no. 13, adds that in the people of God "each individual part of the Church contributes through its special gifts to the good of the other parts and of the whole Church. Thus through the common sharing of gifts and through the common effort to attain fullness in unity, the whole and each of the parts receive increase."

Such a theological principle can be applied to the relationship between the Catholic Church and the Lutheran churches. Reestablished unity in faith and in the sacraments enables them jointly to share in the dynamic which LG, no. 13, describes as follows: "Moreover, within the Church particular Churches hold a rightful place. These Churches retain their own traditions without in any way lessening the primacy of the Chair of Peter. This Chair presides over the whole assembly of charity and protects legitimate differences, while at the same time it sees that such differences do not hinder unity but rather contribute toward it. Finally, between all the parts of the Church there remains a bond of close communion with respect to spiritual riches, apostolic workers, and temporal resources."

131. Cf. *The Ministry in the Church*, no. 85.

132. Ibid., nos. 42, 43, and 44.

133. UR, no. 22.

134. *The Ministry in the Church*, no. 79.

135. Ibid., nos. 75-78.

136. Ibid., no. 82.

137. Ibid., no. 20.

138. Ibid., no. 23.

139. Ibid., no. 17.

140. Ibid., no. 30.

141. Ibid., no. 45.

142. Ibid., no. 43.

143. Ibid., no. 80.

144. Cf. ibid., nos. 43 and 66.

145. Cyprian said: "The episcopate is one, each part of which is held by each one for the whole," "The Treatises of Cyprian," I, 5, *The Writings of the Ante-Nicene Fathers,* vol. 5 (Grand Rapids, 1965), p. 423.

146. With respect to Catholic ecclesiology these terms have to be understood as follows:

    - They do not mean that the pope became the bishop of the Catholic Church as a result of the First Vatican Council. The signature of Paul VI under the documents of Vatican II identifies him as the bishop of the Catholic Church in Rome (cf. H. Marot, "Note sur l'expression 'episcolus ecclesiae catholicae,'" *Irénikon* 37(1964): 221-226; again mentioned in Y. Congar (editor), "La collégialité épiscopale. Histoire et théologie," *Unam Sanctam* 37(1965): 94-98.

    - Nor do they mean that the pope can take the place of the local bishops daily and permanently because, like the primacy, the episcopate exists by "the same divine institution" (cf. the collective declaration of the German episcopate regarding the circular letter of the German chancellor concerning the future election of the pope, DS, 3112-3116, and the letter of approval by Pius IX).

    - Finally they do not mean that there is no distinction between his commission as primate of the Catholic Church and his task as patriarch of the West. Thus, for example, the code *Juris Canonici* promulgated in 1983 is valid only for the Latin church. The bilateral dialogue between the Catholic Church and the Orthodox churches will probably induce the Holy See to determine which of its present functions belong to the primacy and which to the patriarchate of the West.

    And yet these expressions confirm the fact that the Catholic bishops always exercise their ministries in fellowship with the bishop of Rome and that the pope, in turn, exercises his ministry of unity and leadership within the college of bishops and the community of the churches thanks to the universal jurisdictional authority that is associated with his commission. This authority is defined as "ordinary" not in the sense of "daily" but in the sense of "not delegated," because it is part of his commission. The point of the primacy is not the day-to-day government of the church but to serve its unity.

147. LG, nos. 21f.

148. Apol XIV, 1, BC, p. 214; SA, part III, X, BC, p. 314; FC SD, X, 19, BC, p. 614; cf. *The Ministry in the Church*, no. 42.

149. CA XXVIII, 28, BC, p. 85; SA, part II, IV, BC, pp. 298ff.; Treatise on the Power and Primacy of the Pope, 13-15, 62f., 70f., BC, pp. 322, 330f., 331f.

150. That all may be "praying in their heart for the descent of the Spirit," *The Apostolic Tradition of Hippolytus.* (Ann Arbor, Mich.: Archon Books, 1962), no. 2, p. 33.

151. *"Pneuma hegemonikon,"* ibid., no. 3, pp. 34f.

152. Cf. Augustine: *"Pro vobis episcopus, vobiscum christianus"* (PL, 38, 1483).

153. Cf. the continuation of the quotation of Augustine: *"Illud est nomen suscepti officii, illud gratiae"* (PL, 38, 1483).

154. The canons do not permit a bishop to ordain his successor (cf. canon 75 of the so-called Apostolic Canons, Bruns I, 11; Synod of Antioch, 341, canon 23, Bruns I, 86; Synod of Caesarea, 393, see E. W. Brooks, *The Sixth Book of the Letters of Severus Patriarch of Antioch* (London: Oxford, 1903), vol. II, pp. 223-224; Roman Synod, 465, canon 5, Bruns II, pp. 283-284). See also the statement made by Augustine who found himself in an embarrassing situation, since his bishop Valerian had asked him to be not "his successor, but . . . be associated with him as coadjutor," and he had been ordained by Megalius, Primate of Numidia. Augustine excuses Valerian on the grounds that canon 8 of Nicea, which does not allow the coexistence of two Catholic bishops in the same town, was not known in Hippo (*The Fathers of the Church, Early Christian Biographies* [Washington, D.C., 1952], "The Life of St. Augustine by Bishop Possidius," chap. 8, p. 82; PL, 32, 39-40).

155. Cf. *The Ministry in the Church*, no. 62.

156. Episcopal lists are lists of those who preside over a church (cf. L. Koep, *Bischofslisten*, RAC 2, pp. 410-415). This connection between succession and tradition *within* a church has always been stressed jointly by Catholics and Orthodox (cf. the second session of the Joint International Commission for Theological Dialogue between the Roman Catholic Church and the Orthodox Church, Munich 1982: "The minister is also the one who 'receives' from his church, which is faithful to tradition, the word he transmits" (*Information Service*, op. cit., no. 49, 1982, II/III, p. 110).

157. Augustine, *De unitate ecclesiae* 11, 28; PL, 43, 410-411. Cf. also Thomas Aquinas, *De veritate quaestio*, q. 14, a. 10 ad 11: "And we believe the successors of the apostles and the prophets only insofar as they tell us those things which the apostles and prophets have left in their writings" (*Truth*, Chicago, 1952/4, vol. 2, p. 258).

158. Vatican II says: "Each individual bishop represents his own church, but all of them together in union with the Pope represent the entire Church" (LG, no. 23).

159. Approaches in this direction can be found in P. E. Persson, *Kyrkans ämbete som Kristusrepresentation* (Lund, 1961) (shortened German version: *Representatio Christi. Der Amtsbegriff in der neueren römisch–katholischen Theologie* [Göttingen, 1966]) and in L. M. Dewailly, "La personne du ministre et l'objet du ministère" (about Persson's book), *RSPhTh* 46(1962): 650-657.

160. Note how Cyprian wanted to exercise his authority together with the Christians of his community, priests and deacons, and the college of bishops, i.e., in a synodal and collegial manner: "From the beginning of my episcopate, I decided to do nothing of my own opinion privately without your advice and the consent of the people" (St. Cyprian, *Letters 1-81* [Washington D.C., 1964], Letter 14,4, p. 43). "I think that I alone ought not to give a decision in this matter . . . since this examination of each one must be discussed and investigated more fully, not only with my colleagues, but with the whole people themselves" (ibid., Letter 34,4, p. 89; cf. Letter 19,2, pp. 52f.). Regarding the relationship between the bishop and his congregation in a number of large episcopal sees in the time of the early church, see L. Scipioni, *Vescovo e popolo*, Milano, Vita e

Pensiero, 1977; regarding the Middle Ages, see Y. Congar, "Quod omnes tangit ab omnibus tractari ac approbari debet," *RHDFE* 4e série, 36, 1958, pp. 210-259, reprinted in *Droit ancien et structures ecclésiales, Variorum Reprints,* London, 1982.

161. Their ministry can be exercised in *a personal* manner, which is shown very clearly in the letters of St. Paul. Behind the statements and instructions of Paul lie the grace and function given to him personally (cf. the expression "by the grace given to me" in Rom 12:3 and 15:15; 1 Cor 3:10; Gal 2:9; see also Col 1:25; Eph 3:2, 7f., and from the greetings Rom 1:1; 1 Cor 1:1; 2 Cor 1:1; Gal 1:1 [cf. also Col 1:1; Eph 1:11]; regarding the topic, cf. Gal 1). Paul also needs the *koinonia* of the other apostles if his preaching is to be not in vain (cf. Gal 2:1-10, especially verse 9; 1 Cor 15:7f.).

This *collegiality* of the (twelve) apostles appears particularly in the Acts of the Apostles which speaks stereotypically of "the apostles" (in plural—twenty-six times) and where they are often presented as a body acting homogeneously (cf. Acts 2:42f.; 4:33, 35, 36f.; 5:12; 6:6; 8:14, 18; 11:1. Occasionally Peter appears as protagonist of the apostles: cf. Acts 2:14, 37; 5:2f., 29). It is noteworthy that the exercise of authority by the apostles by no means excludes the cooperation of the *presbyters* and the *congregation,* but proceeds in "concerted action," as is expressly the case at the election of the "seven" (Acts 6:2-6) and is shown even more clearly in connection with the so-called Council of Apostles (cf. Acts 15:2, 4, 22f., 16:4). Note also the justification of Peter before "the apostles and the brethren who were in Judea" (Acts 11:1-18). This *koinonia* with the congregation in the exercise of the ministry is less directly expressed but is substantially present in a more nuanced way in the letters of Paul. These letters give evidence of great respect for the responsibility of the congregation in spite of their stress on the authority of the apostle. Paul (usually) does not decree, but argues (indicative—imperative!) and thus takes the congregation at their word regarding their own Christian freedom. It is striking that apart from specific questions of faith, Paul hardly ever gives his *own* instructions regarding the concrete ordering of the practical life of the congregation, but only intervenes when the praxis of the congregation errs. That in this respect Paul understands his authority as subsidiary to the authority of the congregation is expressed clearly in 1 Corinthians 5 and 6:1-12, where he does not appeal to the "offenders," but to the congregation which should really have acted on its own.

162. The BEM statement on the Ministry (1982) notes: "The ordained ministry should be exercised in a personal, collegial and communal way" (no. 26). This is developed by stressing the complementarity of these three aspects, and it is added: "An appreciation of these three dimensions lies behind a recommendation made by the First World Conference on Faith and Order at Lausanne in 1927: 'In view of (i) the place which the episcopate, the council of presbyters and the congregation of the faithful, respectively, had in the constitution of the early church, and (ii) the fact that episcopal, presbyteral and congregational systems of government are each today, and have been for centuries, accepted by great communions of Christendom, and (iii) the fact that episcopal, presbyteral, and congregational systems are each believed by many to be essential to the good order of the Church, we therefore recognize that these several elements must all, under conditions which require further study, have an appropriate place in the order of life of a reunited Church. . .'" (Commentary, no. 26).

163. Cf. remarks on "recognition" and "reception" as "interrelated aims" (no. 49 above and note 47).

164. *The Ministry in the Church*, nos. 74-86; especially nos. 83-85.

165. Cf. particularly CIC, can. 844, nos. 1-3, pp. 156f.

> "1. Catholic ministers may lawfully administer the sacraments only to catholic members of Christ's faithful, who equally may lawfully receive them only from catholic ministers, except as provided in paras. 2, 3 and 4 of this canon and in can. 861, para. 2.
>
> "2. Whenever necessity requires or a genuine spiritual advantage commends it, and provided the danger of error or indifferentism is avoided, Christ's faithful for whom it is physically or morally impossible to approach a catholic minister, may lawfully receive the sacraments of penance, the Eucharist and anointing of the sick from non-catholic ministers in whose Churches these sacraments are valid.
>
> "3. Catholic ministers may lawfully administer the sacraments of penance, the Eucharist and anointing of the sick to members of the eastern Churches not in full communion with the catholic Church, if they spontaneously ask for them and are properly disposed. The same applies to members of other Churches which the Apostolic See judges to be in the same position as the aforesaid eastern Churches so far as the sacraments are concerned."

166. In connection with such a situation Pierre Duprey writes: "It is possible that what the Council of Chalcedon and tradition as a whole regarded as essential, that is that there should be one bishop in a single place, may be impossible to realize, at least in the first stage—a stage which may be very long. But . . . it is of capital importance to achieve the unity of *episkope*: if it cannot be personal, it can be collegial" (*Midstream* XVII:4 [October 1978]: 384).

167. Some Lutheran churches, for example in Sweden and Finland, have an episcopal primate by established custom and consider this order as helpful. A resident bishop acting in concert with suffragans is a manner of exercising *episkope* often encountered in the Catholic Church.

168. Nicaea, c. 8 (COD, 9); Constantinople I, c. 2 (COD, 27-28); Lateran IV, c. 9 (COD, 215).

169. Hippolytus, op. cit., no. 2, p. 33.

170. Cf. *The Ministry in the Church*, nos. 29, 43-44.

171. Hesitations expressed in the BEM statement on the Ministry lose their point: Churches that are willing "to accept episcopal succession as a sign of the apostolicity of the life of the whole Church . . . yet . . . cannot accept any suggestion that the ministry exercised in their own tradition should be invalid until the moment that it enters into an existing line of episcopal succession" (no. 38).

172. Cf. the statement concerning the attitude of the LWF to churches in Union Negotiations, *Sent into the World*, op. cit., pp. 142f.

173. Compare, for example, the situation that has been created by the establishment of church fellowship between Lutheran, United, and Reformed churches in Europe—Leuenberg Agreement, 1973.

174. *Ways to Community*, no. 8.

Church and Justification

September 11, 1993

Foreword

Visible unity has always been and continues to be the ultimate goal of the international dialogue between the Roman Catholic Church and the Lutheran Communion. In 1992 this dialogue, sponsored by the Lutheran World Federation and the Pontifical Council for Promoting Christian Unity, celebrated its twenty-fifth anniversary, having begun its work in Zurich in 1967, just after the close of the Second Vatican Council.

With this document the dialogue completes the third phase of its work, a phase which has addressed an issue at the heart of Lutheran–Roman Catholic relations: the role of the church in salvation. This theme grew organically out of the reports of the first two phases.

The Malta Report, *The Gospel and the Church* (1972), marked the end of the initial phase of dialogue. It ascertained a "far-reaching consensus" in the doctrine of justification and demonstrated a convergence of views in the area of Scripture and Tradition. The Malta Report became the foundation for further dialogue, establishing its direction and demonstrating its feasibility. The breadth of its scope led naturally to a series of documents in the second phase dealing with more particular dogmatic issues seen as church-dividing since the sixteenth-century Reformation.

Having before it not only the confessional documents of the Reformation era, but also the documents of Vatican II, and benefiting from the labors of theologians in biblical, liturgical, dogmatic, and historical studies, the Lutheran–Roman Catholic Joint Commission was able, in its second phase, to transmit to the churches common documents on *The Eucharist* (1978) and *The Ministry in the Church* (1981). It also produced statements marking two Reformation anniversaries: *All Under One Christ* was a common statement on the *Confessio Augustana* in observance of the 450th anniversary of its presentation in 1530, and *Martin Luther—Witness to Jesus Christ* was issued in 1983, the 500th anniversary of the reformer's birth. Both documents and the many other articles and addresses that these anniversaries also occasioned are important contributions toward the goal of Catholic–Lutheran unity.

Two further documents from the second phase of dialogue addressed themselves to how visible unity might be realized in concrete ways: *Ways to Community* (1980) and *Facing Unity—Models, Forms, and Phases of Catholic–Lutheran Church Fellowship* (1984).

When in 1985 the question of how to proceed to a third phase was addressed, a joint memorandum began with this judgment:

> The dialogue has brought us to a point from which it is no longer possible to go back. Thus the question about the actualization of Catholic–Lutheran church fellowship should be the framework for the further dialogue. . . .

A statement from the Seventh Assembly of the Lutheran World Federation (1984) was then quoted with approval:

> In the third phase of the continuing theological dialogue, the themes must be so formulated that the implications for church fellowship of the consensus expressed or the convergence achieved are clearly sought.

After a reference to the doctrinal condemnations of the Reformation era, the joint memorandum concludes:

> It can be observed that . . . Catholics and Lutherans keep coming back to the question about the understanding of the church, more precisely to the central question of the church and the nature of its instrumentality in the divine plan of salvation (church as sign and instrument; "sacramentality" of the church). . . . This

question immediately raises again, especially for the Lutheran side, the question of the doctrine of justification. It is less a matter of the understanding of justification as such . . . rather it is a matter of the implications of the mutual relationship of justification and the church.

It was noted how this brings the discussion back to an issue present already in the first phase of dialogue. Almost two decades later, however, the new Joint Commission had to take account of how the issue of justification had surfaced again in its documents on eucharist and ministry and be aware of the growing intensity of a new debate as to whether a "fundamental difference" between Protestantism and Catholicism really exists.

The third phase of dialogue was instructed to deal with the question of the church in light of sacramentality and justification. It began its work in the spring of 1986, completing it in 1993. Plenary sessions were held annually. In most years there was a drafting meeting scheduled between plenary sessions.

Once the work had begun it was the responsibility of the Joint Commission to shape, clarify, and determine its own course. Though the joint statement here presented clearly follows the original mandate in the joint memorandum of 1985, two developments should be noted which may assist the reader in understanding our work. First, because of the developments between 1972 (Malta Report) and 1986, the Joint Commission found itself compelled to test the claim of a "far-reaching consensus" on justification. In so doing they relied heavily on the comprehensive American dialogue statement, *Justification by Faith* (1985), and on the justification chapter of *The Condemnations of the Reformation Era—Do They Still Divide?* (1986).

Second, as work progressed on what has become *Church and Justification*, ecclesiological themes not originally part of the schema required attention. The scope of the project had to grow if the result was to be persuasive. Thus it has become the most extensive statement to be presented by the international dialogue to date.

In submitting its work the Joint Commission asks that this report be seen together with the documents from the second phase, *The Eucharist* and *The Ministry in the Church*, as well as *Ways to Community* and *Facing Unity*. It asks whether, taken together, these documents constitute the sufficient consensus which would enable our churches to embark upon concrete steps toward visible unity which have become more and more urgent.

COCHAIRMEN
Paul-Werner Scheele, *Bishop of Würzburg, Germany*
James R. Crumley, Jr., Bishop (retired), *Lutheran Church in America, USA*

1. Justification and the Church

1. Catholics and Lutherans in common believe in the triune God who for Christ's sake justifies sinners by grace through faith and makes them members of the church in baptism. Thus faith and baptism link justification and the church; the justified sinner is incorporated into the community of the faithful, the church, and becomes a member of it. Justification and the church thus stand in a vital relationship and are fruits of the saving activity of God.

2. According to Lutheran tradition the justification of sinners is the article of faith by which the church stands or falls.[1] Thus Luther says in the exposition of Psalm 130:4, which for him is the epitome of the doctrine of justification: "for if this article stands, the Church stands; if it falls, the Church falls."[2] This is the background against which the Catholic–Lutheran dialogue has as its theme the relation between justification and the church. A consensus in the doctrine of justification—even if it is nuanced—must prove itself ecclesiologically. Everything that is believed and taught about the nature of the church, the means of salvation, and the church's ministry must be founded in the salvation event itself and must be marked by justification-faith as the way in which the salvation event is received and appropriated. Correspondingly, everything that is believed and taught about the nature and effect of justification must be understood in the overall context of statements about the church, the means of salvation, and the church's ministry. This is the necessary precondition by which all the life and activity of the church must constantly be checked, as was stressed in the USA dialogue, *Justification by Faith*. "Catholics as well as Lutherans can acknowledge the need to test the practices, structures, and theologies of the church by the extent to which they help or hinder 'the proclamation of God's free and merciful promises in Christ Jesus which can be rightly received only through faith.'"[3]

3. At the beginning of this dialogue document on the church in the light of justification-faith, it should be emphasized that justification and the church are truths of faith (1.1) because both are grounded in faith in Christ and the Trinity (1.2) and are an unmerited gift of grace which becomes at the same time a challenge in our world (1.3).

1.1. Justification and the Church as Truths of Faith

4. Catholics and Lutherans together testify to the salvation that is bestowed only in Christ and by grace alone and is received in faith. They recite in common the creed, confessing "one, holy, catholic, and apostolic church." Both the justification of sinners and the church are fundamental articles of faith. In faith in the triune God, we confess that this God justifies us by grace without our meriting it and

gathers us together in his church. His mercy is and remains the source of our life. "Solely by grace and by faith in Christ's saving work and not because of any merit in us . . . we are accepted by God and receive the Holy Spirit who renews our hearts and equips us for and calls us to good works."[4] It is by God's incomprehensible "glorious grace" that we have access through Christ in one Spirit to the Father, "are citizens with the saints and also members of the household of God," and "are built together spiritually into a dwelling place for God" (Eph 2:18-22; cf. Eph 1:5f.).

5. Strictly and properly speaking, we do not believe in justification and in the church but in the Father who has mercy on us and who gathers us in the church as his people; and in Christ who justifies us and whose body the church is; and in the Holy Spirit who sanctifies us and dwells in the church. Our faith encompasses justification and the church as works of the triune God which can be properly accepted only in faith in him. We believe in justification and the church as a *mysterium*, a mystery of faith, because we believe solely in God, to whom alone we may completely consign our lives in freedom and love and in whose word alone, which promises salvation, we can establish our whole life with complete trust. Consequently we can say in common that justification and the church both guide us into the mystery of the triune God and are therefore *mysterium*, the mystery of faith, hope, and love.

1.2. Justification and the Church Founded in the Mystery of Christ and of the Trinity

6. According to the witness of the New Testament, our salvation, the justification of sinners, and the existence of the church are indissolubly linked with the triune God and are founded in him alone. This is attested in various but consistent ways. "God . . . proves his love for us in that while we still were sinners Christ died for us. . . . Now that we have been justified by his blood, will we be saved through him from the wrath of God. For if while we were enemies, we were reconciled to God through the death of his Son, much more surely, having been reconciled, will we be saved by his life" (Rom 5:8-10). "For God so loved the world that he gave his only Son, so that everyone who believes in him may not perish but may have eternal life" (Jn 3:16). "In this is love, not that we loved God but that he loved us and sent his Son to be the atoning sacrifice for our sins" (1 Jn 4:10). In short, God "first loved us" (1 Jn 4:19). Our salvation in the triune God is founded in the sending of the Son and of the Holy Spirit (cf. Gal 4:4-6; Jn 14:16f., 26; 16:7-15).

7. Accordingly, the church has its foundation in the sacrifice of the Son and the sending of the Spirit. God "obtained" his church "with the blood of his own Son" (Acts 20:28). Christ has saved the church for it is his body (cf. Eph 5:23). Christ "loved the church and gave himself up for her, in order to make her holy by cleansing her with the washing of water by the word" (Eph 5:25f.). By virtue of the

sending of the Holy Spirit the young church appears publicly on the day of Pentecost (cf. Acts 2). Especially in Paul's letters, the relation of the church to the triune God becomes clear, when he describes it as the pilgrim people of God the Father, as the body of Christ, the Son, and as the temple of the Holy Spirit.

1.3. Justification and the Church as Unmerited Gift of Grace and Challenge

8. When Paul describes God's church in Corinth as "those who are sanctified in Christ Jesus, called to be saints" he shows by this that the church and its members live entirely by the unmerited gift of Christ's grace, for which he expressly gives thanks (1 Cor 1:2-4). In the Letter to the Ephesians the unmerited gift of grace which constitutes both Christian existence and the church becomes an occasion for the praise of God's majesty and grace (cf. Eph 1:3-14). "For by grace you have been saved through faith, and this is not your own doing; it is the gift of God—not the result of works, so that no one may boast" (Eph 2:8f.). The mystery of Christ and of the Trinity is the foundation for this unmerited gracious gift of justification and the church: "But when the goodness and loving kindness of God our Savior appeared, he saved us, not because of any works of righteousness that we had done, but according to his mercy, through the water of rebirth and renewal by the Holy Spirit. This Spirit he poured out on us richly through Jesus Christ our Savior, so that, having been justified by his grace, we might become heirs according to the hope of eternal life" (Ti 3:4-7). It corresponds to the graciousness of this gift that human beings contribute nothing but can only receive it in faith: "For by grace you have been saved through faith" (Eph 2:8; cf. Rom 3:28).

9. Lutherans and Catholics together acknowledge the biblical witness on justification and the church as an unmerited gift of grace; they see in this witness a tremendous challenge in our world. God "desires everyone to be saved and to come to the knowledge of the truth" (1 Tm 2:4). The message of justification is an expression of God's universal saving will. It promises salvation and the right to life without regard to merit and worthiness. God accepts the sinful creature in pure mercy and thus cancels out the law of works and achievement as the basis for life. God thus opens up a way of life, which most profoundly contradicts that which prevails in the world: the life of love. This love arises out of faith and passes on the boundless mercy which it has received. It suffers from the distress and injustice that others experience and meets it with self-sacrifice and renunciation. And it urges the members of the church to promote justice, peace, and the integrity of creation together with all people of goodwill, amid the glaring contrast between poor and rich, and in the conflicts between ideologies and interests, races, nations, and sexes. Thus the church is both a contradiction and a challenge in our world—as the place where merciful justifica-

tion is proclaimed, as the locus for community and love, as coshaper of a more just and humane world.

2. The Abiding Origin of the Church

2.1. Jesus Christ as the Only Foundation of the Church

10. "No one can lay any foundation other than the one that has been laid; that foundation is Jesus Christ" (1 Cor 3:11). In all its trenchancy this statement is to be evaluated and heeded as the fundamental principle of ecclesiology. "The one and only foundation of the church is the saving work of God in Jesus Christ which has taken place once for all."[5] Everything that is to be said on the origin, nature, and purpose of the church must be understood as an explanation of this principle. As an essential mark of the church, its unity—which since the very beginning of church history has existed only as a unity under threat, challenged by fragmentation (cf. 1 Cor 1:10ff.)—is to be understood solely in the light of this principle.

11. "Jesus the Christ" or "Jesus is Lord" is the original form of the Christian confession of faith. The author of this confession, through which the church as community becomes heard in this world, is the Holy Spirit, in whose power Christ is known as the Lord (1 Cor 12:3), and God the Father, who by his revelation gives us faith in the Messiah and Son (cf. Mt 16:17). The church owes its origin "not to a single, isolated act by which it was established" but is "founded in the totality of the Christ-event . . . starting from the election of the people of God of the Old Testament, in the work of Jesus, in his proclamation of the kingdom and in the gathering of the disciples through his call to conversion and discipleship, . . . in the institution of the Lord's Supper, in the cross and resurrection of Christ, in the outpouring of the Holy Spirit and in the fact that this whole path is directed towards eschatological consummation in the *parousia* of the Lord."[6] In this comprehensive sense, the term "founding or institution of the church by Jesus Christ" is a meaningful explication of the ecclesiological principle in 1 Corinthians 3:11, which cannot be abandoned.

12. Jesus' whole work is determined and permeated by the mystery of the Trinity. It was always in obedience to the Father who sent him (cf. Jn 5:19); it was also filled with the authority and power of the Holy Spirit through whom Jesus had his existence (cf. Lk 1:35), who showed him to be the Son of God from his baptism onwards (cf. Lk 3:22), and who revealed him with power by resurrection from the dead (cf. Rom 1:4). Thus the trinitarian confession was already included in the original form of the confession of Christ, as a doxology of the work of salvation which has taken place once for all.

2.2. The Election of Israel as the Abiding Presupposition of the Church

13. The church of the New Testament was always aware that the history of the people of God did not begin with itself. The God who raised Jesus from the dead is the same God who called Abraham to be the father of all who believe, who elected Israel from among all the nations to be his treasured possession, and who entered into an enduring covenant with it (cf. Rom 9:6). In salvation history the church thus presupposes the history of Israel (cf. Acts 13:16ff.; Heb 1:1f.). "The Church ever keeps in mind the words of the Apostle about his kinsmen, 'who have the adoption as sons, and the glory and the covenant and the legislation and the worship and the promises; who have the fathers, and from whom is Christ according to the flesh' (Rom 9:4-5), the son of the Virgin Mary."[7] The church must always remain conscious of the fact that "she received the revelation of the Old Testament through the people with whom God in his inexpressible mercy deigned to establish the Ancient Covenant. Nor can she forget that she draws sustenance from the root of that good olive tree onto which have been grafted the wild olive branches of the Gentiles (cf. Rom 11:17-24)."[8]

2.2.1. God's Grace as the Continuum of Israel's History

14. God communicated to Israel the mystery of his name and assured them "I am the Lord your God" (Ex 20:2). "You only have I known of all the families of the earth" (Am 3:2; cf. Dt 7:6). For that purpose God already called Abraham from his father's house and his homeland (cf. Gn 12:1) into a path of obedient faith in him who called him (cf. Gn 15:6; 17:1). Israel's faithfulness was not to be divided: "You must remain completely loyal to the Lord your God" (Dt 18:13). Israel shall therefore not have any other gods but serve only the one and only true God (cf. Ex 20:3-5). "Hear, O Israel: The Lord is our God, the Lord alone. You shall love the Lord your God with all your heart, and with all your soul, and with all your might" (Dt 6:4f.). This was and is Israel's fundamental confession.

15. God's choice of Israel from among all the nations as his own people is not based on its merits or outstanding achievements. "It was not because you were more numerous than any other people that the Lord set his heart on you and chose you— for you were the fewest of all peoples. It was because the Lord loved you . . . that the Lord has brought you out with a mighty hand" (Dt 7:7f.). This love remains steadfast. Though Israel often broke its covenant faith with God, God remained open to its conversion. Where God might have rightly terminated the covenant or said to Israel, as to an adulterer, "You are not my people," he called them to himself with the loving words, "Children of the living God" (Hos 1:10; cf. Rom 9:25f.). Thus the miracle of the forgiveness of sins belongs to the gifts of God's love for his people

(cf. Is 44:2). From the start God's covenant faithfulness includes the forgiveness of sins. Many psalms testify to this, just as the prophets not only proclaim judgment but repeatedly testify also to grace and return. God's grace is the origin and foundation of the old and the new covenants and the basis for the expectation of eternal glory.

2.2.2. *The Election of Israel for the Nations*

16. Although God's saving concern was repeatedly rejected and the covenant broken, God himself preserved the continuity of his gracious care by ever-renewed saving initiatives. And just as the covenant with Noah established a new start in humanity's history with God, so too the election of Israel from the beginning aimed at the inclusion of all nations in God's salvation history.

17. The blessing God promised Abraham is not limited to making his descendants a great nation but has its climax in the promise, ". . . in you all the families of the earth shall be blessed" (Gn 12:3; cf. Gal 3:8). The prophets see as the final act of salvation history the nations of the earth moving to Jerusalem like a star-shaped pilgrimage from every direction, to receive a common salvation in God's universal kingdom of peace (cf. Is 2:1-5; Mi 4:1-4). Zion as the center of Israel is to become the center of the messianic kingdom of peace for the whole world of nations, and a descendant of David, the great king of Israel, is to be the king of peace ruling over all the nations (cf. Is 9:5f.). As the chosen Servant of God, he himself will bring the justice of God to the peoples of the whole earth (cf. Is 42:1-12; 49:6).

2.3. The Foundation of the Church in the Christ-Event

18. "But when the fullness of time had come, God sent his Son, born of a woman, born under the law, in order to redeem those who were under the law, so that we might receive adoption as children. And because you are children, God has sent the Spirit of his Son into our hearts, crying, 'Abba! Father!'" (Gal 4:4-6). Jesus' mother was a Jewish woman. As the Messiah of Israel, Jesus is descended from the family of David (cf. Lk 1:32f.; Rom 1:3f.). The God whose rule Jesus proclaimed is the God of Abraham, Isaac, and Jacob. It was to the people of Israel that Jesus directed this proclamation (cf. Mt 15:24; 10:6). Jesus proclaimed God's love in an unheard-of radical way: "I have come to call not the righteous but sinners" (Mk 2:17). In line with this he taught love for this God whose kingly rule is consummated in mercy and the love of one's neighbor, including enemies (cf. Mt 5:44). On these two fundamental commandments "hang" all the law and the prophets (Mt 22:40; cf. Dt 6:5; Lv 19:18).

19. That Jesus as Son of God is the Messiah and that in him the eschatological rule of God has dawned is the unique saving event which effects a definitive sal-

vation for all the nations, going beyond all the saving gifts in the history of his people. All the promises of the prophets are fulfilled in him: he is the light that illumines all darkness, the life that overcomes all the power of death, the righteousness that cancels out all sin. According to the witness of the New Testament the "new covenant" (Jer 31:31-34) has been inaugurated in his "blood" (1 Cor 11:25; Lk 22:20), and his blood is the "blood of the covenant" (Ex 24:8) which was poured out for all "for the forgiveness of sins" (Mt 26:28; cf. Mk 14:24). In Jesus is perfected God's faithfulness to the covenant. From the beginning God has held fast to his will to save, against all human unfaithfulness: ". . . God has imprisoned all in disobedience so that he may be merciful to all" (Rom 11:32).

2.3.1. The Proclamation of the Reign of God in Word and Deed

20. What Jesus proclaimed was the dawn of the exclusive reign of God (cf. Ps 97), which was looked for by Israel, sung in the "new song" (Ps 96), but effected in an entirely unexpected way. In many parables Jesus speaks pointedly of its nearness in figures of speech. It is like a tiny seed out of which a great tree will grow (cf. Mt 13:31f.). It is like a "treasure hidden in a field" or an incomparably beautiful pearl, which should be acquired here and now and for which one will spend no less than everything one has (Mt 13:44-46). It comes up and grows "of itself"; human effort can neither aid it in any way (Mk 4:26-29) nor prevent what it does (cf. Mt 13:24-26). It is God's action alone. But all those who accept it from Jesus' words and deeds must allow themselves to be wholly taken into service by it and must subordinate everything else to it (cf. Lk 9:57-62).

21. The reign of God is present in Jesus' words and deeds. By virtue of "the Spirit of God" he expels demons (Mt 12:28) and frees human beings from their power (cf. Mk 5:1ff.). It is the saving power of God's eschatological reign that Jesus promises to sinners (cf. Mk 2:10f.). "I have come to call not the righteous but sinners" (Mk 2:17; cf. Lk 18:9ff.). In common meals in which eschatological joy of salvation prevails, he celebrates the miracle of the presence of the kingdom of God with "tax collectors and sinners" (Mk 2:15f.). These meals are also harbingers of the eucharistic community of the church after Easter.

22. What Jesus proclaims as the power of God's reign is his justifying love, which creates salvation: his unlimited mercy, with which he receives the lost into his Father's house and bestows rich gifts on them (cf. Lk 15:11ff.); forgives sinners their guilt (cf. Mt 18:23ff.); promises salvation to the poor, the hungry, and the suffering (cf. Lk 6:20-23); and gives the last the same share in his salvation as the first (cf. Mt 20:1ff.). Correspondingly, the unlimited love of one's neighbor is the real meaning of the righteousness that God calls for from his elect (cf. Lk 10:25-37). Thus, in the Sermon on the Mount Jesus shows us the actual intention of God's law in its individual commandments. Just as the reign of God redeems the lost, so too it

lays on those who are saved the duty of solidarity with the lost as "peacemakers" (Mt 5:9), and prepares them to accept persecutions, slanders, and sufferings "for righteousness' sake" (Mt 5:10-12).

23. Jesus called specific persons to follow him as his disciples. Thus, they became personal witnesses to the nearness of the reign of God. That reign is to be accepted at once, without delay and apprehensiveness (cf. Lk 14:15ff.; 17:28ff.). The disciples are to leave everything (cf. Mk 1:16ff.; 10:29f.) in order to be fully with Jesus (cf. Mk 3:14) and follow him wherever he goes. Self-denial is as much a mark of citizenship in the kingdom of God (cf. Mt 18:3f.) as following Jesus (cf. Mk 8:34).

24. Jesus called twelve disciples as his particular followers. He sent them out and empowered them as his messengers (apostles) to proclaim his message of the kingdom of God to the whole people of Israel and, as a sign of its nearness, to heal the sick and free the possessed from the power of the demons just as he had done (cf. Mk 3:14f.; 6:7; Mt 10:7f.). That the apostles numbered twelve corresponds to the full complement of the tribes of Israel. Thus, their ministry has a meaning in terms of salvation history: in the proclamation of Jesus the kingdom of God has definitively dawned, that kingdom which is the consummation of God's history with his chosen people, however much its ultimate manifestation on the last day is still pending. But at the same time, the ministry of the twelve apostles also has a fundamental ecclesial significance. The apostles are to preach the Gospel after Easter so that their witness is foundational and normative for the whole church. According to Luke 10:1, Jesus also sent out seventy (or seventy-two) other disciples with the same mission. Their number matches that of "the elders of Israel" (Ex 24:1; Nm 11:16f.) and relates likewise to the people of Israel as a whole and to the full complement of the nations (cf. Gn 10).

25. The kingdom of God is the eschatological saving reality that affects the whole world. In earthly terms it is unattainable. Nevertheless, because it is there in Jesus, it is present among his disciples (cf. Lk 17:20f.). The same is also true of the church: it is not identical with the kingdom of God, which even after Easter remains hidden in the eschatological future. The kingdom is entirely God's affair, not that of any human being, nor is it at the disposal of anyone in the church. And yet its eschatological saving reality can already be experienced in the church in the "righteousness and peace and joy" which, imparted by word and sacrament, take effect in the common life of Christians "in the Holy Spirit" (Rom 14:17). In this sense it can be said that the church is the kingdom of God already present but "hidden"[9] "in mystery."[10]

2.3.2. Cross and Resurrection

26. Jesus, who taught his disciples to pray for protection from eschatological sufferings (cf. Mt 6:13; Lk 11:4), who was aware of the provocation of his message (cf. Mt 10:34-39), and who proclaimed the reign of God in weakness (cf. Mt 11:12;

Mk 4:30-32 para.), was himself willing to accept the consequences arising from his preaching. He himself lived out the willingness to serve to the end and the readiness for martyrdom which he demanded from his disciples (cf. Lk 22:27; Mk 9:35 para.; Mk 8:34f.). When he journeyed up to Jerusalem, he knew what had befallen John the Baptist and was aware of the fate of the prophets (cf. Mk 6:14-29; 9:13; Mt 23:34-39). In regard to the aim of his mission he was able to say: "For the Son of Man came not to be served but to serve, and to give his life as a ransom for many"(Mk 10:45; cf. 1 Tm 2:5).[11] In unwavering confidence that the reign of God was coming (cf. Mk 14:25), he voluntarily took upon himself (cf. Mt 26:39, 42) his death on the cross as a necessity (cf. Mk 8:31; 9:31; 10:32f.) laid upon him in accordance with God's saving will and suffered the distress of being forsaken by God (cf. Mk 15:34; Mt 27:46). In this he fulfilled the prophecy of the Servant of God who "bore the sin of many" (Is 53:12): "But he was wounded for our transgressions, crushed for our iniquities; upon him was the punishment that made us whole, and by his bruises we are healed" (Is 53:5; cf. 1 Pt 2:24; Rom 4:25).

27. In the night before his death, at supper together with the Twelve, Jesus "took a loaf of bread and after blessing it he broke it, gave it to them, and said, 'Take, this is my body.' Then he took a cup, and after giving thanks he gave it to them, and all of them drank from it. He said to them, 'This is my blood of the covenant, which is poured out for many'" (Mk 14:22-24). Thus, with effective signs Jesus gave his disciples an anticipatory share in the saving event of his atoning death as a once-for-all sacrifice, through which all who believe in him have been redeemed from sin (cf. Mt 26:28) and freed for life in the Spirit. According to the formulations in Mark and Matthew, that which happened for Israel in the action of the covenant made at Sinai (Ex 24:8) now happens "for many." According to the formulations in Luke and Paul (cf. 1 Cor 11:25), the prophetic promise of the new covenant (cf. Jer 31:31-34) is realized. The meaning is the same: the eschatological miracle of a universal "eternal redemption" (Heb 9:12) takes place in Jesus' sacrificial death on the cross. With the command, "Do this in remembrance of me" (1 Cor 11:24f.; Lk 22:19), Jesus promises his church that in every celebration of the Lord's Supper he himself will be present as the one who was sacrificed for us, in the same way as in this meal with the apostles on the Passover Eve before his death: "For as often as you eat this bread and drink the cup, you proclaim the Lord's death until he comes" (1 Cor 11:26).

28. For the disciples the story of Jesus' passion becomes the story of their denial. They fell asleep while Jesus, in his prayer that night, struggled with the will of his heavenly Father (cf. Mk 14:37-41). Upon his arrest they all fled (cf. Mk 14:50). Even Simon, the "Rock," goes back on his word: having just been willing to share death and prison with his Master (cf. Lk 22:23), he denies him three times (cf. Mk 14:66ff.). Only Jesus' prayer for him keeps him from falling into Satan's control

and brings him back to faith, thereafter to strengthen his brothers (cf. Lk 22:31ff.; Jn 21:15ff.). Abandoned by everyone in Gethsemane, Jesus accepted his own death, surrendering in complete faith to his Father, so that "he became the source of eternal salvation for all who obey him" as "a high priest according to the order of Melchizedek" (Heb 5:7-10). Thus, in every act of worship Christ's congregation goes to that cross "outside the gate" that there they may bear his shame (Heb 13:10-12) and have that communion with the crucified, which takes us beyond earthly time into the "city that is to come" (Heb 13:14).

29. Jesus' mother stands below the cross with two other women and the "disciple whom he loved" (Jn 19:25-27). Jesus commends them to each other: the disciple to Mary as her son in his stead and Mary to the disciple as his mother. Thus, in the form of these two a small community stands under Jesus' cross as archetype of the church whose permanent place is the cross of its Lord whence it has its life. After Jesus' death a soldier pierced his side "and at once blood and water came out" (Jn 19:34)—a sign that the saving effect of his death would benefit his church through the sacraments of baptism and the Lord's Supper (cf. 1 Jn 5:5-8).

30. In the early hours of Easter morning three women disciples find Jesus' grave empty, and an angel announces his resurrection (cf. Mk 16:1ff.). The risen Christ himself "appeared to Cephas, then to the twelve" (1 Cor 15:5) and frequently to still others, men and women. The resurrection of the crucified is God's central eschatological miracle, the breakthrough of the eschaton: Jesus is "the first fruits of those who have died," the first to experience resurrection (1 Cor 15:20; cf. Col 1:18): he is God's act of new creation, through which he has procured victory for the love with which his Son gave himself to us (cf. 1 Cor 15:57; Rom 8:31-39; Col 2:13f.). By this act of God's power, the death of Christ has acquired saving power: as the justification of sinners (cf. Rom 4:25) and as reconciliation with God (cf. 2 Cor 5:18-21) as well as a new creation—life in the power of the Spirit (cf. 2 Cor 5:17; Rom 8:9-11; Eph 2:5f.; 1 Pt 1:2). In his exaltation above "every name" (Phil 2:9-11) the risen Lord has become "head of the body, the church" (Col 1:18) and has become lord over the entire universe, a lordship which will last till he hands over the universe—reconciled and at peace—to his Father, and God becomes "all in all" (1 Cor 15:25-28).

31. Before his exaltation to the Father, for his disciples Jesus opened up the understanding of Scripture as witness to Christ, its center being his suffering on the cross and his resurrection (cf. Lk 24:45f.). He gave the apostles the commission and authority to preach the Gospel of repentance for "the forgiveness of sins . . . to all nations" (Lk 24:47): "Go therefore and make disciples of all nations, baptizing them in the name of the Father and of the Son and of the Holy Spirit, and teaching them to obey everything that I have commanded you. And remember, I am with you always, to the end of the age" (Mt 28:19f.). As a legacy he gave his church the Holy

Spirit which was to "guide" them "into all the truth" (Jn 16:13), empower them to forgive sins (cf. Jn 20:23), and enable them to preach and bear witness among all the nations (cf. Acts 1:8). In the power of the Spirit of God the church was to abide in the love of Christ as he abides in his Father's love (cf. Jn 14:16f.; 15:10)—"that they may all be one" so that the world may know that Jesus Christ is the Son sent by the Father who loves his own as the Father loves him (Jn 17:21-23).

2.3.3. The Church as the People of God from All Nations

32. The wonderful plan of God's salvation history is that in Jesus' mission that purpose is also fulfilled which from the beginning God had linked to the election of Israel: the inclusion of all nations in the promised salvation and the foundation of the church as God's eschatological community of salvation. Just as at the beginning God recognized Abraham's righteousness without merit or worthiness but on the basis of faith alone (cf. Gn 15:6; Rom 4:3-8), so too he has made the same justification "by faith apart from works prescribed by the law" (Rom 3:28) the entrance into his church for everyone (cf. Rom 4:16f.; Gal 3:6-9). Jesus Christ is the one Lord of the one church from among all the nations (cf. Acts 10:34-36), the one foundation and cornerstone of what God has built (cf. Eph 2:20f.). Abraham's faith in the God who justifies sinners is fulfilled in the faith of Christians in Jesus Christ (cf. Rom 4:3).

33. In the outpouring of the Spirit on the day of Pentecost, God confirms that the assembly of those who believe in Jesus as the Christ is God's messianic people of the last days (cf. Acts 2; 1 Cor 12–14; Jn 14:15-31; 16:4-15; 20:19-23). Therefore the apostle's proclamation of the Gospel "concerning his Son" (Rom 1:3) serves to "bring about the obedience of faith among all . . ." (Rom 1:5). Paul is not ashamed of the Gospel, which "is the power of God for salvation to everyone who has faith, to the Jew first and also to the Greek. For in it the righteousness of God is revealed through faith for faith; as it is written, 'The one who is righteous will live by faith'" (Rom 1:16f.). In this way Paul unfolds the Gospel concerning the Son, identifying it with the Gospel of the righteousness of God.

2.4. The Church as "Creature of the Gospel"

2.4.1. The Proclamation of the Gospel as Foundation of the Church

34. As on earth the Lord called and gathered people by the proclamation of the "good news of the kingdom" (Mt 4:23; 9:35; 24:14; Mk 1:14), so too after Pentecost the calling and the fresh gathering of God's people is continued by the proclamation of the "good news of Christ" (Rom 15:19; cf. 1:16; 1:1-9). For this purpose the risen Lord chooses his witnesses and sends them into the world (cf. Mt 28:19; Mk 16:15; Acts 1:8; Jn 20:21). When they proclaim the Gospel of "Jesus as the Messiah" (Acts 5:42) and people hear that Gospel and accept it in faith as a

promise of salvation, congregations are constituted from Jerusalem as far as Rome. The commission laid upon the apostles is "to proclaim the gospel" (Rom 1:15; 1 Cor 1:17; 9:16). This Gospel, as "God's word" (1 Thes 2:13) or the "word of the Lord" calls people to be "imitators of . . . the Lord" (1 Thes 1:5-8), and brings the church into being (cf. 1 Cor 15:1f.).

35. At the side of the audible word of gospel proclamation stand baptism and the Lord's Supper as visible means of God's saving acts and of the gathering of his people (cf. 1 Cor 10:1-13). Just as a rescued Israel emerges out of the Red Sea, so the Christian community emerges out of baptism; as the manna was for Israel in the desert, so now the Lord's Supper is the pilgrim food for God's new people. Through baptism all are bound together with Christ (cf. Rom 6:3ff.) and form the one "body of Christ" (1 Cor 12:27). The Lord's Supper is par excellence the visible and effectual expression of the congregation as a "sharing in the body of Christ" (1 Cor 10:16f.).

36. The sixteenth-century Reformation highlighted with utmost emphasis the fact that the church lives on the basis of the proclamation of the Gospel. It reproached the church of that time for not corresponding to that fundamental dependence on the Gospel in its life and doctrine, and for having to a great extent withdrawn itself from subordination to the Gospel. Consequently the main ecclesiological concern of the Reformation was perpetual dependence on the Gospel and subordination to it. This was concentrated in the formula that the church is *creatura evangelii*.[12] Already in 1517 the sixty-second of Luther's Ninety-five Theses spoke of "the most holy gospel"[13] as "the true treasure of the church"[14] and one of the key principles of Lutheran ecclesiology takes this up: "The entire life and nature of the church is in the word of God."[15] Article seven of the Augsburg Confession corresponds to this, describing the church as "the assembly of all believers among whom the Gospel is preached in its purity and the holy sacraments are administered according to the Gospel."[16]

37. The conviction that the church lives out of the Gospel also determines the Roman Catholic understanding of the church. In Vatican II's *Dogmatic Constitution on the Church* we read, ". . . the gospel . . . is for all time the source of all life for the Church";[17] and the *Decree on the Church's Missionary Activity* says that the "chief means of this implantation [i.e., of the church] is the preaching of the gospel of Jesus Christ."[18] The apostolic exhortation of Pope Paul VI, *Evangelization in the Modern World*, states, "The Church is born of the evangelizing activity of Jesus and the Twelve. . . . Having been born consequently out of being sent, the Church in her turn is sent by Jesus. . . . Having been sent and evangelized, the Church herself sends out evangelizers. [They are] to preach not their own selves or their personal ideas, but a Gospel of which neither she nor they are the absolute masters and

owners, to dispose of it as they wish, but a Gospel of which they are the ministers, in order to pass it on with complete fidelity."[19]

38. In the Malta Report Catholics and Lutherans together said that the church "as creatura et ministra verbi . . . stands under the gospel and has the gospel as its superordinate criterion."[20] There was agreement that "the authority of the church can only be service of the word and . . . it is not master of the word of the Lord."[21] This primacy of the Gospel over the church was also attested jointly in regard to church order and the ministry.[22]

39. For the Reformation it was self-evident that the proclamation of the Gospel as the imparting of grace and salvation does not take place only in the preached word. Even when the Reformers were particularly stressing the importance of proclaiming the word, they held fast to the idea that the Gospel is also communicated through the sacraments and that the preached word and administered sacraments belong together. The Smalcald Articles state that the "Gospel" is not proclaimed "in . . . one way" but "through the spoken word," "through baptism," "through the holy sacrament of the altar," and "through the power of the keys."[23] The definition of the church as creatura evangelii therefore means that the church lives on the basis of the Gospel that is communicated in word and sacrament and accepted through faith.

40. Imparting the Gospel in word and sacrament implies the ministry of proclaiming the word and administering the sacraments. This corresponds to the biblical witness according to which the message of reconciliation implies the "ministry of reconciliation" (2 Cor 5:18ff.). Proclaiming the word and administering the sacraments are therefore not merely momentary acts but fundamental realities which permanently define the church. While all believers are to communicate the Gospel in their own spheres of life, the proclamation of the word and the administration of the sacraments as public acts are perpetually assigned to the ministry instituted by God. A basic agreement exists here between Catholic and Lutheran teaching, notwithstanding the existing differences in how this ministry is understood and organized. This has been repeatedly ascertained by the Catholic–Lutheran dialogue: "By church we mean the communion of those whom God gathers together through Christ in the Holy Spirit, by the proclamation of the gospel and the administration of the sacraments, and the ministry instituted by him for this purpose."[24]

2.4.2. The Proclamation of the Gospel in the Holy Spirit

41. We share the belief that the Holy Spirit creates the church as the communion of believers through faith in the Gospel and works through this communion. The proclamation of the Gospel takes place in the power of the Holy Spirit (cf. Acts 1:8). It comes "in power and in the Holy Spirit and with full conviction" and makes those who accept the word themselves messengers of the Gospel (1 Thes

1:5-8). The Holy Spirit who is promised and given to those who bear witness to the Gospel (cf. Jn 20:22) empowers them for their witness (cf. 2 Cor 4:13), keeps them with Christ (cf. Jn 14:26; 15:26f.), and gives them the certainty of acting not in their own strength but "for Christ" (2 Cor 5:20) and with his authority (cf. Jn 20:23).

42. The Holy Spirit who calls and empowers witnesses for gospel testimony also awakens and sustains the faith which responds to the proclaimed Gospel, faith which accepts it as the promise of salvation (cf. 1 Thes 1:5f.; 1 Tm 1:14). It is the Spirit who enables those who hear the message to confess Christ as Lord (cf. 1 Cor 12:3; Rom 10:9f.). In this "Spirit of adoption," they have access to God through Christ and call him "Father" (Rom 8:14-16; Eph 2:18).

43. In awakening faith through the proclaimed Gospel, the Holy Spirit brings the church into being (cf. Acts 2) as congregations who are known and commended for their faith (cf. Rom 1:8; 1 Thes 1:8). Through the Spirit all are "baptized into one body" (1 Cor 12:13). In the variety of gifts the Spirit binds the individual believers together as living members (cf. 1 Cor 12:4ff.). The unity of the Spirit is also the principle of the unity of this body that is the church (cf. 1 Cor 12:13; Eph 4:3f.), which as a whole is a "dwelling place for God" in the Spirit (Eph 2:22).

2.4.3. The Proclamation of the Gospel by the Apostles

44. That Jesus Christ is the church's "foundation" (1 Cor 3:11) and that the church lives on the basis of the Gospel of Christ is concretized in the fact that the apostles called by Christ are also the church's "foundation" (Eph 2:20). This they are not of themselves but by the power of the Gospel which they have received and to which they are primary witnesses—the Gospel transmitted in word and sacrament that creates, sustains, and governs the church. This has permanent eschatological validity. The twelve apostles of Jesus will "sit on twelve thrones, judging the twelve tribes of Israel" (Mt 19:28 para.), and the "twelve foundations" bear "the twelve names of the twelve apostles of the Lamb" (Rv 21:14).

45. In the ancient church, appealing to the apostles and their testimony was the decisive defense against false doctrine. "We have learned from none others the plan of our salvation, than from those [i.e., the apostles] through whom the Gospel has come down to us."[25] As the apostles received the revelation from Christ, so too the church receives it through the apostles,[26] and the "rule of faith" acquires its binding nature through its faithful reflection of this apostolic tradition.[27] Augustine sums up: "What the whole church believes is wholly rightly believed, even if it has not been directly decided by councils, but has been transmitted only on apostolic authority as belonging to the unquestioned substance of the faith."[28] The title of the creed as the "Apostles' Creed"[29] expresses this conviction of the abiding, binding nature of the apostolic witness.

46. This apostolic testimony—according to the common conviction of our churches—has its normative expression in the New Testament canon. All subsequent church proclamation, doctrine, and tradition is interpretation. As apostolic writings the scriptures of the New Testament, together with those of the Old Testament, are "the only rule and norm according to which all doctrines and teachers alike must be appraised and judged" say the Lutheran Confessions.[30] The *Dogmatic Constitution on Divine Revelation* of Vatican II states that the apostles had the commission to "preach to all men the gospel" as "the source of all saving truth and moral teaching."[31] Hence "apostolic preaching, which is expressed in a special way in the inspired books" must be "preserved by a continuous succession of preachers until the end of time."[32] Though Lutherans and Catholics think differently in many respects about the way in which the apostolic norm is safeguarded, the shared conviction nevertheless is that "apostolicity" is an essential attribute of the church and the criterion par excellence of its faith, its proclamation, its teaching, and its life.

47. In the Lutheran–Roman Catholic dialogue to date, this common conviction that the apostolic witness is the normative origin of the church has repeatedly been expressed and confirmed: The church stands for all time on the foundation of the apostles; it is in "all historical changes in its proclamation and structures . . . at all time referred back to its apostolic origin."[33]

3. The Church of the Triune God

3.1. The Trinitarian Dimension of the Church

48. It is our common confession that the church is rooted in God's election of Israel as well as being founded in the Christ-event and the proclamation of the Gospel by the apostles in the Holy Spirit. So long, however, as this confession does not recognize the profound relationship of the church to God as Holy Trinity it remains inadequate and open to misunderstandings. This relationship of the church to the triune God is both causal and substantive, involving the differentiated yet reciprocal unity of Father, Son, and Holy Spirit.

49. The church is the communion of believers called into existence by the triune God. As such it is a divinely created, human reality. That the church is anchored in the divine life of the triune God does not thereby negate its human dimension nor open the way to ecclesial presumptuousness. But it does preclude an understanding of the church which tends to regard it merely or even primarily as a human societal phenomenon. God allows the church to share in the triune divine life: the church is God's own people, the body of the risen Christ himself, the temple of the Holy Spirit (3.2). The church's unity or communion (*koinonia, communio*) partakes of and reflects the unity of the triune God (3.3).

50. This biblical view of the substantive relation of the church to the triune God, which is developed in what follows, was profoundly familiar to the ancient church. It is alive in the more recent Roman Catholic understanding of the church, as is shown for instance by Vatican II's *Dogmatic Constitution on the Church*,[34] and the Orthodox-Roman Catholic dialogue.[35] But this trinitarian view is also at home in the Reformation view of the church. The Catholic–Lutheran dialogue to date has repeatedly shown this,[36] as has the statement of the Lutheran World Federation Assembly in 1984, *The Unity We Seek*: the church and its unity "participates in the unity of the Father, Son, and Holy Spirit."[37]

3.2. The Church as God's Pilgrim People, Body of Christ, and Temple of the Holy Spirit

3.2.1. The Church as God's Pilgrim People

51. When the church of the New Testament applies to itself the honorific title of Israel, "people of God," it is not using merely comparative language, nor is it simply referring to the sum of individual believers. Neither does "people of God" mean only that it is God who summons and holds this "people" together. Besides all these things it means that this people has its "holiness" and its fundamental character as a "chosen race" of God the Father by really belonging to God (1 Pt 2:9; cf. Ex 19:5f.). As such, this "people," in its historical-terrestrial existence, is by no means immune to temptation, error, and sin. It is the "pilgrim" people of God standing under God's judgment for the duration of its earthly pilgrimage and depending upon God's daily renewal of grace and fidelity. Therefore, it needs confession of sin and constant renewal. Nevertheless and precisely because of this, it is and remains the people who belong to God the Father.

52. Since the coming of Jesus Christ, the community of those who have been baptized in his name, who confess Christ and call upon him, has been the chosen people of God, a title hitherto applied only to the people of Israel. Two things are therein expressed simultaneously: the church's continuity with Israel and the dawn of a new stage of salvation history in which faith in the one God takes shape as faith in the triune God, and the community of God's elect expands to include believers in Christ from all peoples. The invitation to Israel remains open to join the chorus of faith in God's eschatological saving action in the proclamation, passion, and resurrection of Jesus, the Messiah and the Son of God, and thus to belong to the communion of the church. In the picture of the old covenant pilgrim people of God, the church may recognize itself as the people of the new covenant moving towards entry into the kingdom of God, the aim of its earthly pilgrimage. "People of God" thus expresses the intimate relationship of the church with Israel and of Israel with the church in the history of salvation.

53. People from all nations belong together as Christians in the one universal church. As the people of God in the midst of all peoples, the church embraces all the diversity of the human world. It lives in many places and hears God's call in many languages and in a multiplicity of ways. Nevertheless, it is a single undivided people, called by the one Lord, in one Spirit, to one faith, to solidarity and mutual love, to common witness and service in the world, and to be for people of all races and social classes. Thus, in its being and its mission the church is a sign for the future unity of humanity.

54. Through baptism the people of God is called to be a priestly people: "But you are a chosen race, a royal priesthood, a holy nation, God's own people, in order that you may proclaim the mighty acts of him who called you out of darkness into his marvelous light" (1 Pt 2:9). In both the Lutheran and the Catholic traditions, therefore, we rightly speak of the "priesthood of all the baptized" or the "priesthood of all believers."[38] What constitutes this priesthood is that all the baptized have access to God through Christ, the "one mediator" (1 Tm 2:5) and "high priest" (Heb 4:14), that all confess their faith in the one Lord, call upon him in prayer, serve him with their whole life, and witness to all people everywhere (cf. 1 Pt 3:15).[39]

55. Within the church as people of the new covenant, all social, racial, and sexual divisions have in principle been overcome (cf. Gal 3:26-28). There are no privileges nor any precedence of some over the others (cf. Mt 23:8; Mk 9:35). In the world with its struggles for power, racial conflicts, and social tensions, Christians are therefore in duty bound together with all people of goodwill to contribute to reconciliation and peace. Like their Lord they are to care for the poor and the oppressed, to seek fellowship with them and to intervene publicly on their behalf. As witnesses to their Lord who is "the resurrection and the life" (Jn 11:25) Christians should everywhere be a light of hope for all "who have no hope" (1 Thes 4:13).

3.2.2. The Church as Body of Christ

56. Also the New Testament references to the church as a "body" go far beyond the limits of a mere comparison. As a result of baptism all Christians become one body in the one faith through the one Spirit. The many members of that body do indeed have different tasks but they are nonetheless "individually . . . members one of another" (Rom 12:4-5). This social reality of the church as a spiritual organism (cf. 1 Cor 12:14-26) has its actual basis in the sacramental reality of real participation in Christ and the linking of the lives of all Christian believers in and with Christ, the crucified and risen Lord: "Do you not know that all of us who have been baptized into Christ Jesus were baptized into his death? Therefore we have been buried with him by baptism into death, so that, just as Christ was raised from the dead by the glory of the Father, so we too might walk in newness of life" (Rom 6:3f.). Consequently all are together not only "one body" (1 Cor 12:12) but also "the body

of Christ" (1 Cor 12:27). Christ himself "is the head . . . from whom the whole body, joined and knit together by every ligament . . . promotes the body's growth in building itself up in love" (Eph 4:15f.). Thus, baptism is the entry into the Christian life in the sense of participation in Christ himself. It is the abiding foundation of all life and of all common life in the church.

57. Rooted in baptism, this reality of the church as "Christ's body" finds ever new expression in the Lord's Supper. When the Lord says: "This is my body that is for you" (1 Cor 11:24), the broken bread becomes for us all a "sharing in the body of Christ. Because there is one bread, we who are many are one body, for we all partake of the one bread" (1 Cor 10:16f.). The designation of the church as "body of Christ" indicates, therefore, the elementary and vital bond between Christ, the Lord's Supper, and the church: "Baptized by the one Spirit into the one body (cf. 1 Cor 12:13) believers—nourished by the body of Christ—become ever more one body through the Holy Spirit."[40] Christ who is himself really present in the celebration of the Lord's Supper, "nourishes and tenderly cares for" his church as his body (Eph 5:29f.), after making "her holy by cleansing her with the washing of water by the word" (Eph 5:26). Just as in anticipation the people in the wilderness "all ate the same spiritual food and all drank the same spiritual drink . . . Christ" (1 Cor 10:3f.), so the church lives through its Lord, present in the Holy Supper as the "bread of life" (Jn 6:35), "the living bread that came down from heaven" so that the promise holds: "Whoever eats of this bread will live forever" (Jn 6:51). "Those who eat my flesh and drink my blood have eternal life . . . [they] abide in me, and I in them" (Jn 6:54-56).

58. It is from this sacramental reality of the church as "Christ's body" that the spiritual-diaconal reality of its common life flows. As Paul describes it, all Christians are equipped and called by God's Spirit to fulfill the membership given to them in the body of Christ in a distinctive way (cf. 1 Cor 12:4-6; Rom 12:6-8). Each one is needed and all need each other (cf. 1 Cor 12:14ff.). "Like good stewards of the manifold grace of God, serve one another with whatever gift each of you has received" (1 Pt 4:10; cf. Eph 4:7). All are to serve "the building up" of the church and its unity (Eph 4:12) with their gifts and are to contribute to peace (cf. Eph 4:3), which means concretely "for the common good" of all (1 Cor 12:7). Thus, the principle of all living together in the church is love (cf. 1 Cor 13:13–14:1). This finds expression in the structures of the church's life.

3.2.3. The Church as Temple of the Holy Spirit

59. Reference to the constitutive relation between church and Holy Spirit runs through the whole New Testament witness concerning the church. Here too the question is not only that of a causal relation—in the sense that the Holy Spirit makes the church of the New covenant come into existence, that the proclamation

of the Gospel takes place in the power of the Spirit, that it is the Spirit who awakens faith in those who hear the Gospel, and that the Spirit bestows on the church his manifold gifts. The Holy Spirit does all that by remaining in the church and entering into a close and substantive relation with the church. It is part of the mystery of the church that the Spirit of God is its spirit. This finds expression in the image of the church as "temple of the Holy Spirit." Even if the direct application of this concept to the church is not found in the New Testament, it is nevertheless quite clear that the New Testament statements regarding the Holy Spirit and his relation to the church have this intention.

60. The Holy Spirit is "poured out" on the disciples and on all who accept the message of Christ in faith (Acts 2:17f.; 10:45); the Spirit is "distributed"[41] (Heb 2:4) and "given" (e.g., 2 Cor 1:22; Eph 1:17), and they "receive" (e.g., Acts 1:8; 2:38; 1 Cor 2:12; Gal 3:14) and "have" (Rom 8:9) the Spirit. Believers are "filled" with the Holy Spirit (e.g., Acts 2:4; 9:17; Eph 5:18), so that they are now in "the spirit" and live, walk, and serve (e.g., 1 Cor 14:16; Gal 5:16; 5:25; 1 Pt 4:6) "in" the Spirit—i.e., "in the new life of the Spirit" (Rom 7:6). So it can then be said that the Holy Spirit "dwells" (1 Cor 3:16; Jas 4:5) in the believers and that they are "the temple of the living God" (2 Cor 6:16; cf. 1 Cor 3:16), "a temple of the Holy Spirit" (1 Cor 6:19).

61. That which is true of believers as individuals is also true of the community of believers as a whole, the church: they are to be "built together spiritually into a dwelling place for God" (Eph 2:22), into a "spiritual house" (1 Pt 2:5), and they are to grow "into a holy temple in the Lord" (Eph 2:21). The greeting and the blessing of the Apostle is addressed to the community as a whole: "the communion of the Holy Spirit be with all of you" (2 Cor 13:13). This Holy Spirit, with whom the community has "communion" and who dwells in the church as in a holy temple, leads men and women to faith by the proclamation of the Gospel (cf. 1 Thes 1:5), acts in baptism (cf. Acts 2:38; 1 Cor 6:11), and in the Lord's Supper (cf. 1 Cor 10:1-4; 12:13) for their salvation, supports them in their prayer (cf. Rom 8:26), and through Christ gives them access to God the Father (cf. Rom 8:14-16; Eph 2:18). The Spirit strengthens the witnesses of the Gospel (cf. 1 Thes 1:5-7), maintains the church in truth (cf. Jn 14:26), and bestows upon it the manifold riches of his gifts (cf. 1 Cor 12:4-6). The one Spirit is the principle of the church's unity (cf. 1 Cor 12:13; Eph 4:3f.). As God's power, through which Jesus was raised from the dead (cf. Rom 1:4), the Spirit is, amidst the earthly life of the church, the "first installment" of the future fullness of salvation (2 Cor 1:22), in which the faithful already participate and which is the goal of their earthly pilgrimage.

62. Catholics and Lutherans both teach that the church as a community of believers is called and gathered together by the Holy Spirit through the proclamation of the Gospel in word and sacrament, and is empowered by the Holy Spirit who works in and through it. The statements contained in Luther's Small and Large

Catechisms[42] here coincide with those of the *Dogmatic Constitution on the Church*[43] of Vatican II.

3.3. The Church as *Koinonia/Communio* Founded in the Trinity

3.3.1. The Unity of the Church Sustained and Formed by the Triune God

63. Participation in the communion of the three divine persons is constitutive for the being and life of the church as expressed in the three New Testament descriptions of it as "people of God," "body of Christ," and "temple of the Holy Spirit." Thus the church also shares in the communion of the Father with the Son and of both with the Holy Spirit. The unity of the church as communion of the faithful has its roots in the trinitarian communion itself, as this is expressed in the greeting of the First Letter of John: ". . . so that you also may have fellowship with us; and truly our fellowship is with the Father and with his Son Jesus Christ" (1 Jn 1:3; cf. Jn 17:21).

64. This can already be seen in the fact that the three designations of the church are not simply interchangeable, while being intimately linked together and referring to each other. This corresponds to the inseparable but at the same time differentiated unity of the three divine persons and their activity.

- The church as "people of God" of the new covenant is the communion of those who have been baptized in Christ's name and have received the Holy Spirit.
- As "body of Christ," the faithful and the church have a share in Christ who was raised from the dead "by the glory of the Father" (Rom 6:3f.); and through the Holy Spirit the faithful are incorporated into the body of Christ, and they receive their gifts for the building up of the body.
- In the church as "temple of the Holy Spirit," it is the Spirit who as "the Spirit of Christ" (Rom 8:9; cf. 2 Cor 3:17) binds the faithful to Christ, the mediator of all salvific gifts, and who through him gives them access to the Father, whom they may invoke as "Abba, Father" in the same Spirit.

65. However one looks at the church, whether as "people of God" or "body of Christ" or "temple of the Holy Spirit," it is rooted in the inseparable communion or *koinonia* of the three divine persons and is thereby itself constituted as *koinonia*. It is not primarily the communion of believers with each other which makes the church *koinonia*; it is primarily and fundamentally the communion of believers with God, the triune God whose innermost being is *koinonia*. And yet the communion of believers with the triune God is inseparable from their communion with each other.

3.3.2. Koinonia/Communio *Through Preaching, Baptism, and the Lord's Supper*

66. That the church as *koinonia* is based in the trinitarian *koinonia* is shown and realized in the proclamation of the Gospel, baptism, and the Lord's Supper.

67. The preaching of the Gospel, from which the church as fellowship of believers lives, can be rightly understood only in its trinitarian frame of reference. But it also links the individual believer and all believers with God in the divine trinitarian *koinonia*. The church's preaching proclaims the "good news of Christ" (Rom 15:19; cf. 1:16). In their preaching the apostles and with them all witnesses to the Gospel are "ambassadors for Christ" (2 Cor 5:20). They "teach" what Jesus Christ—who will remain with them "always, to the end of the age"—has "commanded" them (Mt 28:20). The preaching of the Gospel of Christ takes place in the "power" of the "Holy Spirit" (Acts 1:8). The Spirit calls and empowers the witnesses for their ministry (cf. Jn 20:22f.; 2 Cor 4:13). The Spirit awakens and sustains the faith which accepts the Gospel that is preached as the promise of salvation (cf. 1 Thes 1:5f.; 1 Tm 1:14) and which responds to it in confession (cf. 1 Cor 12:3). In this proclamation by the apostles and all the witnesses—a proclamation which is sustained by the Holy Spirit—Jesus' preaching of the "good news of the kingdom of God," by which he called people to him and gathered them around him, is continued after Easter and Pentecost. Jesus' preaching in word and deed acquired its authority solely from the fact that his words and deeds were identical with those of the Father who had sent him (cf. Jn 14:10, 24; Jn 8:28; 10:15). Of Jesus as "beloved" Son of the Father can it be said, "listen to him!" (Mt 17:5 para.).

68. Baptism in the name of the Father, Son, and Holy Spirit (Mt 28:19) leads us into communion with the triune God and into sharing in his blessings and thus also knits believers together into a communion. Baptism is calling and election by God and makes us God's possession: thus also creating the community of those who are called and chosen, "God's own people" (1 Pt 2:9). In baptism we are baptized into Christ's body, partaking of his death and resurrection, and putting on Christ: consequently the baptized also constitute "one body . . . one with another" (Rom 12:4f.) and are one communion in which creaturely and social divisions no longer count for anything (cf. Gal 3:26-28). The baptized receive the Holy Spirit: they are thus also bound together into one communion "in the one Spirit" (1 Cor 12:12f.; Eph 4:3f.).

69. The celebration of the Lord's Supper draws believers into the presence and communion of the triune God through thanksgiving (*eucharistia*) to the Father, remembrance (*anamnesis*) of Christ, and invocation (*epiklesis*) of the Holy Spirit. In a special way the celebration is the *koinonia* of believers with the crucified and risen Lord present in the Supper, and for that very reason it also creates and strengthens the *koinonia* of the faithful among and with each other. Paul says: "The cup of bless-

ing that we bless, is it not a sharing in the blood of Christ? The bread that we break, is it not a sharing in the body of Christ? Because there is one bread, we who are many are one body, for we all partake of the one bread" (1 Cor 10:16f.). His rebuke of the Corinthians follows this dialectic precisely; when their practice of the Lord's Supper violates their *koinonia*, they profane their eucharistic communion with the Lord (cf. 1 Cor 11:20-29).

70. It is the common conviction of our churches that in and through the eucharistic *koinonia* with Christ, ecclesial *koinonia* is established and strengthened. On the Catholic side one can point, for instance, to Vatican II, especially to its *Dogmatic Constitution on the Church*,[44] or to Thomas Aquinas, for whom the reality (*res*) of the Lord's Supper is "the mystical body of Christ" in which we are strengthened "through unity with Christ and with his members."[45] On the Lutheran side this conviction is expressed, for instance, in Luther's sermon on "The Blessed Sacrament of the Holy and True Body of Christ and the Brotherhoods 1519,"[46] which is important for his ecclesiology, or in Martin Chemnitz's commentary on 1 Corinthians 10 in which, adopting the trinitarian standpoint, he says, "In the Lord's Supper . . . we all receive one and the same body of Christ . . . and because in this way the members of the church are fused into one body of Christ, they are also bound up with each other and become one body whose head Christ is. Thus when we receive the body and blood of Christ in the Lord's Supper, we are closely bound up with Christ . . . and through Christ we are united with the Father. . . . Thus we become partakers (*koinonia*) of the Father, the Son and the Holy Spirit. This all comes about from the saving communion (*koinonia*) of the body and blood of the Lord. . . ."[47]

71. In these explanations based on the New Testament witness, both our traditions understand themselves to be in agreement with the ancient church for which the Pauline statements on *koinonia* in Christ were decisive. St. John of Damascus summarizes this patristic theological tradition as follows: "If [the eucharist] is also called communion, and truly is so, because of our having communion through it with Christ and partaking both of His flesh and His divinity, and because through it we have communion with and are united to one another. For, since we partake of one bread, we all become one body of Christ and one blood and members of one another and are accounted of the same body with Christ."[48]

3.3.3. Koinonia/Communio *as Anticipatory Reality*

72. The three biblical designations of the church as "people of God," "body of Christ," and "temple of the Holy Spirit" all interpret its trinitarian basis in anticipatory fashion:

- The universal people of God will first gather in its entirety on the last day; only in anticipation of that ultimate gathering can the church be the people of God today who live already on the basis of what God will make of them.
- The church is the body of the crucified and risen Christ for whose return in glory we still wait.
- The church is the temple of the Holy Spirit whose reality among us is "down payment" (*arrabón*) of eschatological reality.

Thus, the church is already everything the biblical designations of it say it is—but in such a way that it awaits in anticipation what is most profoundly its being and the source of its life.

73. This also holds good for the church as *koinonia*. It is already a partaking in the *koinonia* of the Father, Son, and Holy Spirit; but as the pilgrim church it is such provisionally and in fragmentary fashion; and this means in anticipation and expectation of its final destination, which is still pending: consummation in the kingdom of God, in which the triune God will be "all in all" (1 Cor 15:24-28).

3.4. Ecclesial Communion—Communion of Churches

3.4.1. *Common Witness*

74. On both the Catholic and the Lutheran side, the concept of *koinonia/communio* has once more become important ecclesiologically; indeed, it has become central. In Lutheranism this becomes clear in the increasing use, and above all theological deepening, of the term "church fellowship/communion," which it has been possible to observe more or less since the 1950s. The term is understood as an acceptance of the concept of *koinonia/communio* in the early New Testament church as described above, and it can also claim the support of the Reformation view of the church and incorporate specific aspects of it. Especially since Vatican II, the idea of *koinonia/communio* and the term itself have become determinative for the Catholic view of the church. In this we see "the central and fundamental idea" of the ecclesiology developed by the council.[49]

75. On the basis of a concept of *koinonia* derived from the New Testament and the early church, Lutherans and Catholics agree that the church is a *koinonia/communio* rooted in the mystery of the holy Trinity. Proof of that assertion is found both in the Lutheran Confessions and documents of Vatican II.

76. According to the teaching of the council, "human dignity lies in man's call to communion with God."[50] The council refers to 1 John 1:2f., according to which believers are to attain *koinonia* with the Father and the Son, for God has revealed himself so that "through Christ . . . man has access to the Father in the Holy Spirit

and comes to share in the divine nature."[51] God thus seeks "to establish peace or communion between sinful human beings and Himself, as well as to fashion them into a fraternal community."[52] In this way the mystery of the church is indicated, for according to the council the communion with God in the body of Christ effected through the Holy Spirit is the foundation for the *koinonia* of the church. The Spirit dwells in the faithful, guiding and governing the church. It establishes the "communion of the faithful and joins them together . . . in Christ."[53]

77. The Lutheran Confessions indicate the chief meaning of church fellowship by designating the nature of the church as the communion of the faithful[54] which originates in communion with Christ through the Holy Spirit, and which lives from faithful hearing of the word and receiving of the sacraments. When CA 7 describes the "one holy Christian church" as the "assembly of all believers,"[55] it means that "communion of saints"[56] of which the Apostles' Creed speaks.[57] The fact that "communio" is understood and translated as "assembly" or "congregation" and not, for linguistic reasons, rendered "community" in German, should not cause the term to lose any of its New Testament or early church content or meaning. There is no sociological reductionism involved. Instead, the fellowship (*communio*) is an assembly or congregation "under one head, Christ, called together by the Holy Spirit," in which "I also am a part and member, a participant and co-partner in all the blessings [*Güter*] it possesses. I was brought to it by the Holy Spirit and incorporated into it through the fact that I have heard and still hear God's Word, which is the first step in entering it."[58] "To have communion or fellowship" therefore does not simply mean "having some relationship with another person" but rather that "many persons share or eat or partake of one common thing."[59] Just as the communion of Christians with each other is grounded in their common sharing in Christ, so it is for them a communion of mutual sharing and mutual help and service: "This fellowship is twofold: on the one hand we partake of Christ and all saints; on the other hand we permit all Christians to be partakers of us, in whatever way they and we are able."[60]

78. According to the Second Vatican Council, it is through the word of preaching and the celebration of the sacraments, of which the eucharist is the "center and summit," that Christ, the author of our salvation, becomes present in the church.[61] "From the table of both the word of God and of the body of Christ" the "bread of life" is offered the faithful.[62] In the breaking of the eucharistic bread they actually gain a share in the Lord's body and are raised to communion with him and among one another, for communion in the body of Christ makes those who receive the one bread into the body of the Lord.[63] The eucharist is therefore the summit of ecclesial *communio*[64] and "the very heartbeat of the congregation of the faithful."[65]

79. Catholics and Lutherans together understand that the communion with God mediated through word and sacrament leads to communion of the faithful

among themselves. This takes concrete shape in the communion of the churches: the one, holy, catholic, and apostolic church, the *una sancta* of the creed, is realized in the *communio ecclesiarum* as local, regional, and universal communion, and so as church fellowship.

80. There is only one church of God. In the New Testament the same word *ecclesia* signifies both the whole church (e.g., Mt 16:18; Gal 1:13) and the church of a region (e.g., Gal 1:2), the church of a city (e.g., Acts 8:1; 1 Cor 11:18) or of a house (e.g., Rom 16:5). Accordingly, Lutherans and Catholics see the church of God in local, regional, and universal terms, but these different ways in which the church becomes a reality must be understood on the basis of the one, holy, catholic, and apostolic church, the *una sancta* of the creed.

81. Because the church, as communion of the faithful, is based in communion with Christ, the one Lord, there is only one single church. According to the Lutheran Confessions the promise that it will "remain forever" applies only to that *una sancta ecclesia*.[66] That church is "a holy Christian people,"[67] persons "scattered throughout the world who agree on the Gospel and have the same Christ, the same Holy Spirit, and the same sacraments."[68] The church "is mainly an association of faith and of the Holy Spirit in men's hearts."[69]

82. According to the Second Vatican Council, "God has gathered together as one all those who in faith look upon Jesus as the author of salvation and the source of unity and peace, and has established them as the church, that for each and all she may be the visible sacrament of this saving unity. While she transcends all limits of time and of race, the church is destined to extend to all regions of the earth, and so to enter into the history of mankind."[70] "The church, then, God's only flock, like a standard lifted high for the nations to see, ministers the Gospel of peace to all mankind, as she makes her pilgrim way in hope toward her goal, the fatherland above."[71]

83. Looked at diachronically—through all time—the *una sancta* as an eschatological reality pervades the whole of history, from the first days (*ecclesia ab Abel*) to the last, the time of Christ's return in glory. It has taken shape especially since the elect people of God has become the body of Christ and the temple of the Holy Spirit, and hence represents for the faithful the place of new life and of that *communio* with God which finds expression in communion with each other.

3.4.2. The Lutheran Understanding of Local Church

84. Differences between the Catholic and Lutheran position appear when the question is posed about the realization of the church from a synchronic—here and now—point of view. For Lutherans the local congregation is church in the full sense; for Catholics it is the local church led by its bishop.

85. Lutherans understand the *una sancta ecclesia* to find outward and visible expression wherever people assemble around the Gospel proclaimed in sermon and sacrament. Assembled for worship the local congregation therefore is to be seen, according to the Lutheran view, as the visible church, *communio sanctorum*, in the full sense. Nothing is missing which makes a human assembly church: the preached word and the sacramental gifts through which the faithful participate in Christ through the Holy Spirit, but also the minister who preaches the word and administers the sacraments in obedience to Christ and on his behalf, thus leading the congregation.

86. The understanding of the church as communion of persons based on communion with the one Lord includes the communion of separate congregations bound together in true communion with Christ. Therefore congregations may not distance themselves nor isolate themselves from one another. The communion they have in Christ must be visible.

87. Lutheran congregations are part of larger fellowships which are themselves constitutionally structured. According to geographical, historical, national, or political realities they form dioceses or juridically autonomous provincial or national churches. These larger communities are held together by communion in Christ, and that shows itself in their common understanding of the apostolic faith (confessional communion), in word and sacrament (pulpit and altar fellowship), and in a mutually recognized ministry.

88. In the second half of the nineteenth century, consciousness of the global dimension of ecclesial communion grew stronger among the Lutheran churches. First came regional[72] and finally worldwide Lutheran associations.[73] For decades the Lutheran World Federation understood itself as "free association of churches"—having common confessions but without having declared pulpit and altar fellowship. The concept of "church fellowship" played an increasingly important role as the federation responded to repeated questions about its ecclesial character. "Church fellowship" combined the New Testament/patristic concept of *koinonia/communio* with the Lutheran understanding of church.[74] More recently it was the concept of communion itself which became the leitmotif of efforts toward the clarification and new definition of the nature of the Lutheran World Federation, efforts which came to their conclusion in the decision of the federation's 1990 assembly. Now the constitution states: "The Lutheran World Federation is a communion of churches which confess the triune God, agree in the proclamation of the Word of God and are united in pulpit and altar fellowship."[75]

89. It therefore becomes clear what, according to Lutheran understanding of the church as *koinonia*, is constitutive, irrespective of whether the expression is congregational, territorial/national, or global: the common understanding and confession of the apostolic faith (confessional communion) and communion in preaching and the sacraments (pulpit and altar fellowship), including by implica-

tion the ministry of proclamation and the administration of the sacraments (recognition of ministries).

90. This understanding of church as *koinonia* was and is determinative for ecumenical efforts of the Lutheran churches. The sought-for visible unity of the church is, in this sense, understood as ecclesial communion.[76] The statement of the 1984 Lutheran World Federation Assembly, *The Unity We Seek*, is developed by explicit use of the concept of communion.[77]

3.4.3. The Roman Catholic Understanding of Local Church

91. When Catholics view the church synchronically and spatially, they understand that it expresses itself throughout the earth as local church, regional church, and universal church, but that none of these expressions can be exclusively identified with the *una sancta*. Rather the *una sancta* is for each expression the criterion for unity in the truth.[78]

92. In Catholic ecclesiology the local church is essentially neither a part of the universal church nor an administrative or canonical district of it. According to the teaching several times stated at Vatican II, the church of God is truly present and effective in the local church, i.e., diocese.[79] The decree on the bishops' pastoral office states, "A diocese is that portion of God's people which is entrusted to a bishop to be shepherded by him with the cooperation of the presbytery. Adhering thus to its pastor and gathered together by him in the Holy Spirit through the gospel and the eucharist, this portion constitutes a particular church in which the one, holy, catholic, and apostolic church of Christ is truly present and operative."[80] The theology of the local church here presented coheres with the conciliar theology of the people of God.[81] The expression "portion" *(portio)* was deliberately preferred to "part" *(pars)*, because a "portion" contains all the essential features of the whole— which is not the case with "part." In other words the local church has all the qualities of the church of God, and one must not therefore look upon it as a branch office of the universal church. The mention of the bishop points to the structural fellowship of the local churches with each other, for as a result of his ordination the bishop functions as a connecting link of the church, both as the representative of the whole church in his church and as the representative of his church in relation to all the others.[82] The reference to the presbytery points to the collegial nature of the ministry in the local church.

93. On the level of the diocese one finds a full presence of the church of God. Moving out from this level, the fundamental conciliarity of the church is expressed in the participation of the bishop in a council. Since however parishes also have the structural characteristics of the church of God ("portion" of the people of God, Holy Spirit, Gospel, eucharist, and ministry), the Second Vatican Council recognizes: "Parishes set up locally under a pastor who takes the place of the bishop . . . in a cer-

tain way represent the visible Church as it is established throughout the world."[83] In actual fact it is the parish, even more than the diocese, which is familiar to Christians as the place where the church is to be experienced.

94. Each of the constitutive elements of the local church ("portion" of the people of God, Holy Spirit, Gospel, and eucharist, presidency of the bishop) and their presence together show that the local church is indeed the church of God in the full sense, but that cannot be regarded as the whole church of God. "The local church is not a free-standing, self-sufficient reality. As part of a network of communion, the local church maintains its reality as church by relating to other local churches."[84] Part of its nature is to be in real fellowship with other local churches and with the church as a whole.

95. This fellowship of the local church with the church universal is not an abstract, purely theoretical reality. In the local church one encounters the essential mystery of the church; in the local church one is instructed in the faith and led to a confession of the apostolic faith and only there can one be baptized, confirmed, ordained, married, and receive the Lord's body at his table. Only through the local church is one a member of the Catholic Church. Nor can one conceive of the universal church apart from the local churches, as if the whole church could exist apart from the local churches. In actuality, "in and from such individual churches there comes into being the one and only Catholic Church."[85] In both terms—"in these" and "out of them"—the reciprocal nature of the relationship is expressed, not the priority of one over the other. If "out of them" is deleted, the universal church would disintegrate into separate particular churches; if one removes "in these," the local church is degraded into nothing but an administrative unit of the universal church.

96. The relation of "reciprocal inherence"[86] or "mutual indwelling"[87] which exists between the local and the universal church neither dissolves the independence of the local church nor its essential inclusion in the universal church but consolidates both, in the same way as the ultimate responsibility of each bishop to God for his local church and for his faithful does not call in question his inclusion in the college of bishops with the pope. According to the teaching of the council the bishop is the "visible source and foundation" for the unity of the local church and the "Roman Pontiff . . . is the visible source and foundation of the unity of the bishops and of the multitude of the faithful," while the local churches are fashioned after the model of the universal church.[88] Thus the church is a unity in and out of diversity, it is a body of churches,[89] or a *communio* of churches.

97. The fellowship of local churches, that is to say the church universal, is therefore not a platonic entity. It is what supports each individual church. Only for the church universal does the promise hold good of remaining in the truth. That cannot be said of any local church. In periods of great crisis where the specific expression of faith was at stake, only the fellowship of all the churches, and especially the

ecumenical councils, succeeded in working out answers in spite of the well-known communication difficulties. The contributions and initiatives which single local churches made toward resolving disputed questions had their full impact only in the framework of reception by the communion of churches. Generally it is true that "mutual solicitude, support, recognition, and communication are essential qualities among local churches. Even from earliest times, the local churches felt themselves linked to one another. This *koinonia* was expressed in a variety of ways: exchange of confessions of faith; letters of communion as a kind of 'ecclesiastical passport'; hospitality; reciprocal visits; mutual material help; councils; and synods."[90]

98. A consequence of the universal character of the great commission in the New Testament (cf. Mt 28:19; Acts 1:8; 2:1-12) is the pluriformity of the local churches within the church catholic. It is also a matter of experience that effective evangelization has been possible only through the formation of regional churches strong enough to influence a whole culture. An image in the *Decree on the Church's Missionary Activity* of Vatican II makes it plain how the universality of mission calls for the involvement of human cultures in the faith and thus requires as well the specific characteristics of the particular churches as conditioned by their cultural context: it is the church which after Pentecost "speaks all tongues, which lovingly understands and accepts all tongues, and thus overcomes the divisiveness of Babel."[91] This church is entrusted with a universal yet unique message. Consequently, it must avoid the danger of particularism; that is, it must be ready to understand and respect as valid the language of the other. At the same time, the church's missionary task is to follow Christ who committed himself "in virtue of His Incarnation, to the definite social and cultural conditions of those human beings among whom He dwelt."[92] In this sense the "congregation of the faithful, endowed with the riches of its own nation's culture, should be deeply rooted in the people."[93]

99. Thus the particular churches are catholic in the full sense only if they have gone through a process of critical inculturation which requires them, within the culture and society in which they live, to examine what has to be affirmed, purified, and integrated.[94] In "each major sociocultural area" the emergence of particular churches presupposes that "every appearance of syncretism" be excluded and that "particular traditions, together with the individual patrimony of each family of nations, can be illumined by the light of the gospel, and then be taken up into Catholic unity. Finally, the individual young Churches, adorned with their own traditions, will have their own place in the ecclesiastical communion. . . ."[95] Thus, the catholicity of the whole church will be enriched by the catholicity of the particular churches. Accordingly, the *Dogmatic Constitution on the Church* sketches this ideal: "In virtue of this catholicity each individual part of the church contributes through its special gifts to the good of the other parts and of the whole church. Thus through

the common sharing of gifts and through the common effort to attain fullness in unity, the whole and each of the parts receive increase."[96]

100. As a result of taking seriously the special character of particular churches, Vatican II also hopes for a stimulus for the restoration of unity among the separated Christians. The *Constitution on the Church* states that "this variety of local churches with one common aspiration is particularly splendid evidence of the catholicity of the undivided Church,"[97] and the *Decree on Ecumenism* says: "Let all members of the Church, according to the office entrusted to each, preserve a proper freedom in the various forms of spiritual life and discipline, in the variety of liturgical rites, and even in the theological elaborations of revealed truth. In all things let charity be exercised. If the faithful are true to this course of action, they will be giving ever richer expression to the authentic catholicity of the Church, and, at the same time, to her apostolicity."[98]

101. Because cultural units are usually more comprehensive than a diocese, it is necessary that this definition of particular churches be actualized by associations of local churches, for example in the classical form of patriarchates, or in the modern form of churches *sui iuris* and by conferences of bishops of the same or several nations, or on the level of a whole continent, e.g., CELAM.[99] One must further note patriarchal, provincial, and plenary synods as well as the declarations of the bishops' conferences. It is also the task of the papal primate to protect proper diversity. "Moreover, within the Church particular Churches hold a rightful place. These Churches retain their own traditions without in any way lessening the primacy of the Chair of Peter. This Chair presides over the whole assembly of charity and protects legitimate differences, while at the same time it sees that such differences do not hinder unity but rather contribute toward it."[100]

102. The Gospel of salvation is directed to the whole of humanity: God created the church with a view to universal reconciliation and unity, and Jesus promised to remain with his church to the end of the age (cf. Mt 16:18; 18:20; 28:20; Eph 4:1-13). In this sense the *una sancta* and the church universal will always have precedence over the local churches. At the same time it is true that the church of God has always assumed a local shape; for Christians receive baptism, celebrate the eucharist, and give a socially identifiable witness always in a particular place. In this sense there will always be a priority of the local churches over the church as a whole, but not over the eschatological *una sancta*. Consequently, we may speak of a reciprocity in the relations between the local and the universal church. But it is different with the *una sancta*, which permeates the whole of history as an eschatological reality and with which no realization of the church of God as a local, regional, or universal church can be exclusively identified.

103. The eucharist best expresses the reciprocal relation between the local churches, the universal church, and the eschatological church. "Since Pentecost

the church celebrates the eucharist as the one, holy, catholic, and apostolic church. The eucharistic celebration, therefore, embraces the church both in its local and universal dimension. It thus affirms a mutual presence of all the churches in Christ and in the Spirit for the salvation of the world."[101]

104. In the documents of Vatican II the designation "mother church" is not applied to any local church nor even to the church of Rome, but is strictly reserved for the *una sancta*. This demonstrates that the fellowship of all the churches makes them sisters in its bosom. As the *Decree on Ecumenism* puts it, there is that "communion of faith and charity . . . which ought to thrive between local Churches, as between sisters."[102]

3.4.4. Tasks of Further Dialogue

105. The Catholic view of the church as *koinonia/communio* may be made fruitful for ecumenical endeavor,[103] and it too—like the Lutheran view of a "church fellowship"—has its specific emphases and configurations. However, the fundamental idea in both cases is the same and is ecclesiologically determinative in the same way. It is part of the nature of every local church to be open towards the other local churches. Catholicity requires that.

106. According to the belief of the Catholic Church, of course, the primatial function of the bishop of Rome is an essential element of the church, with the consequence that each local church must be related to the primacy of the church of Rome and its bishop in order to be in the full communion of churches. But on the other hand it must not be forgotten that the Roman primacy is also related to the *koinonia* of the local churches. The Catholic–Lutheran dialogue must deal with the question of the ministry of oversight in the whole church in the context of ecclesial *koinonia* in general, but also in the particular context of the Roman Catholic understanding of the relationship between the episcopal college and the papal office. To be sure a problem thereby arises in regard to the Catholic ecclesiology of communion to which the ecumenical dialogue has, in various ways, called attention. In spite of Catholic adherence to the principle of a ministry of unity in the universal church, the challenge to self-criticism cannot be ignored. The doctrine of primacy must be further developed, and primatial practice must be shaped accordingly. One hopes, therefore, that in its further work the Catholic–Lutheran dialogue on ecclesiology will take up the theme of a ministry of leadership for the universal church within the framework of communion ecclesiology.

4. The Church as Recipient and Mediator of Salvation

107. In the summary of the biblical witness on the abiding origin of the church, it was stressed that the proclamation of the Gospel by the apostles in the

Holy Spirit is the foundation of the church, and that as *creatura evangelii* the church is committed to serving the Gospel.[104] Thus the church is the recipient and mediator of salvation. In the great biblical images of the people of God, the body of Christ, and the temple of the Holy Spirit, the church shows itself to be a *koinonia* founded in the life of the triune God from whom it receives life and salvation, and the church imparts life and salvation in faithfulness to its task of mission, which it has received from God.[105]

4.1. The Church as *Congregatio Fidelium*

108. A comparison of Lutheran and Catholic views of the church cannot disregard the fact that there are two fundamentally inseparable aspects of being church: on the one hand, the church is the place of God's saving activity (the church as an assembly, as the recipient of salvation) and on the other it is God's instrument (the church as ambassador, as mediator of salvation). But it is one and the same church which we speak of as the recipient and mediator of salvation. In the course of the history of theology, the emphases have been variously placed. While Lutherans see the church mainly as the recipient of salvation, as the "congregation of the faithful," *congregatio fidelium*, contemporary Catholic theology emphasizes more the church as the mediator of salvation, as "sacrament" of salvation.[106]

4.1.1. The Lutheran View

109. "The Creed calls the holy Christian church a *communio sanctorum*, 'a communion of saints.'"[107] Luther thus repeats in the Large Catechism what he had already set out in *A Brief Explanation . . . of the Creed*: "I believe that there is on earth, through the whole wide world, no more than one holy, common Christian Church, which is nothing else than the congregation, or assembly of the saints, i.e., the pious, believing men on earth, which is gathered, preserved, and ruled by the Holy Ghost, and daily increased by means of the sacraments of the Word of God."[108] Thus, the church is not simply the sum of its individual members, for it is founded on the very word of God that faith receives, and individuals belong to it by receiving the word and sacrament in faith. The power of the Holy Spirit is what produces and sustains this assembly of believers among whom the individual is reckoned.

110. According to the Augsburg Confession the church is "the assembly of all believers among whom the Gospel is preached in its purity and the holy sacraments are administered according to the Gospel."[109] The Apology explains this: "The church is . . . mainly[110] an association of faith and of the Holy Spirit in men's hearts. To make it recognizable, this association has outward marks, the pure teaching of the Gospel[111] and the administration of the sacraments in harmony with the Gospel of Christ."[112] The context makes clear that "pure doctrine and conformity to the

Gospel" indicates the message of justification by which the church's life must be evaluated and to which the church as a whole is subordinated. In this the Augsburg Confession restates the teaching of the ancient, but also the medieval church.[113] The church receives its whole life and being from Christ, whose body it is, and who "renews, consecrates and governs [it] by his Spirit."[114] It can live only on the basis of this promise of the forgiveness of sins and the fellowship of salvation which has been bestowed on it. The church is gift in every respect because it lives by the Spirit of God and from the Lord present in it.

111. The proclamation of the Gospel and the celebration of the sacraments characterize the church as communion of salvation where Christ is present and where we can find him: "Those who are to find Christ must first find the church. . . . But the church is not wood and stone but the mass of people who believe in Christ; one must hold to it and see how they believe and pray and teach; they assuredly have Christ with them."[115] Luther emphasizes the necessity of the church for the salvation of individuals so strongly that he can say, "I believe that no one can be saved who is not found in this congregation, holding with it to one faith, word, sacraments, hope and love."[116] Similarly the church is highlighted in the Apology as the place of the promise of salvation for children. They are to be baptized, so that they will share Christ's promise, which "does not apply to those who are outside of Christ's church, where there is neither Word nor sacrament, because Christ regenerates through Word and sacrament."[117] "For the kingdom of Christ is only where the Word of God and the sacraments are to be found."[118] Faith and listening to the voice of the good shepherd, Jesus Christ, distinguish the church as God's people from every other people; for, "thank God, a seven-year-old child knows what the church is, namely, holy believers and sheep who hear the voice of their Shepherd."[119] The church is therefore the *congregatio fidelium*, the congregation of salvation as a faith-congregation, founded by God's word and bound to it: "God's Word cannot be present without God's people, and God's people cannot be without God's Word."[120]

112. Faith in the Gospel allows believers to place their salvation entirely in God's hands and makes them free to serve God and humanity. The gift of the faith-community becomes the task of acting in line with *koinonia*; everything is common to everyone in the congregation of salvation. Luther says: "I believe that in this congregation or Church, all things are common [cf. Acts 2:44], that everyone's possessions belong to the others and no one has anything of his own; therefore, all the prayers and good works of the whole congregation must help, assist and strengthen me and every believer at all times, in life and death, and thus each bear the other's burden, as St. Paul teaches" (cf. Gal 6:2).[121] The "communion of believers," *communio credentium*, finds concrete expression in the general priesthood of all believers. By baptism all believers receive a share in the priesthood of Christ. They

can and should therefore witness to the Gospel and intercede for each other before God. "Therefore because he [a Christian] is a priest and we are his brothers, all Christians have power and authority and must so act that they preach, and come before God each asking for the other and offering themselves up to God."[122] In the general priesthood a representational authority is given; for one is always a priest for others. Understood in this way, being a Christian is a social charisma, a service before God for and to others.

4.1.2. The Catholic View

113. *Congregatio fidelium* was the predominant definition for the church in the late medieval theology. The *Catechism of the Council of Trent (Catechismus Romanus)* too speaks of the church as "the congregation of the faithful."[123] To it belong all "who were called by faith to the light of truth and the knowledge of God, that . . . they may worship the living and true God piously and holily, and serve him from their whole heart."[124] The catechism also refers to Augustine's words with regard to Psalm 140: "The Church . . . consists of the faithful people, dispersed throughout the world."[125] In reference to the Apostles' Creed, the catechism sees a statement about the church[126] in the words, "communion of saints."[127] As communion on the basis of the confession of faith and the sacraments as well as the communion of life, this "communion of saints" is described as mutual love and mutual helping in sorrow and need. For this view the catechism has recourse above all to the Pauline statements on the church as the body of Christ; the gifts of God are given for the use of the whole church and should benefit everyone.[128]

114. The church is the assembly of those who believe in Christ. Vatican II describes the whole church as "all those, who in faith look upon Jesus as the author of salvation"[129] and calls the individual congregation the "congregation of the faithful";[130] it thus appropriates the terminology of Augustine, who describes the church as redeemed community,[131] the "community and society of the saints."[132] *Communio* is the fundamental ecclesiological concept of the council even if it uses the idea of *communio* on many levels and nowhere defines it. The church was established by Christ as "fellowship of life, charity and truth"[133] and the Holy Spirit "gives her a unity of fellowship and service."[134] The entire saving work of Jesus Christ and therefore the church is founded in the mystery of the triune God; "in order to establish peace or communion between sinful human beings and Himself, as well as to fashion them into a fraternal community, God determined to intervene in human history in a way both new and definitive."[135] This communion with God and of human beings among themselves is brought about by God's word and the sacraments. "For those who believe in Christ, who are reborn not from a perishable but from an imperishable seed through the Word of the living God (cf. 1 Pt 1:23), not from flesh but from water and the Holy Spirit (cf. Jn 3:5-6), are finally established

as 'a chosen race, a royal priesthood.'. . . (1 Pt 2:9-10)."[136] The council states that in Christ "all the faithful are made a holy and royal priesthood. They offer spiritual sacrifices to God through Jesus Christ, and they proclaim the perfections of Him who has called them out of darkness into His marvelous light. Hence, there is no member who does not have a part in the mission of the whole Body."[137] The council calls this priesthood the "common priesthood"[138] to distinguish it from the "ministerial priesthood."[139] The eucharist is preeminent among the sacraments; "the eucharistic action is the very heartbeat of the congregation of the faithful over which the priest presides."[140] "Truly partaking of the body of the Lord in the breaking of the eucharistic bread, we are taken up into communion with Him and with one another."[141]

115. The council states equally clearly that "the People of God finds its unity first of all through the Word of the living God. . . . For through the saving Word the spark of faith is struck in the hearts of unbelievers, and fed in the hearts of the faithful."[142] The proclamation of the word is essential for the right administration of the sacraments; "for these are sacraments of faith, and faith is born of the Word and nourished by it."[143]

116. The *Decree on the Church's Missionary Activity* describes pointedly the power of God's word to justify and awaken faith: "The Holy Spirit, who calls all men to Christ by the seeds of the word and by the preaching of the gospel, stirs up in their hearts the obedience of faith. When in the womb of the baptismal font He begets to a new life those who believe in Christ, He gathers them into the one People of God."[144] Nor is the judging power of God's word in any way ignored. "The words of Christ are at one and the same time words of judgment and grace, of death and life. For it is only by putting to death what is old that we are able to come to a newness of life. . . . By himself and by his own power, no one is freed from sin or raised above himself, or completely rid of his sickness or his solitude or his servitude. On the contrary all stand in need of Christ, their Model, their Mentor, their Liberator, their Savior, their Source of life."[145] Thus, the church lives as a communion of believers, not by its own strength but entirely from God's gift. This of course becomes its task in passing on the faith and mediating salvation.

4.1.3. Common Witness

117. Both Lutherans and Catholics understand the church as the assembly of the faithful or saints which lives from God's word and the sacraments. Seen thus, the church is the fruit of God's saving activity, the community of his truth, his life, and his love. Christ who acts in his saving word and sacrament confronts the church, which is the recipient of his and the Holy Spirit's activity. The presence of Christ marks the church as the place where salvation takes place. The gift of salvation however becomes the task and mission of the church as the community which has

received salvation. Thus, the church is taken by its Lord into the ministry of mediating salvation. That holds good in association and mutual support within the congregation of the faithful itself but also particularly in confronting the world, especially all who still do not believe and still do not belong to the assembly of the faithful.

4.2. The Church as "Sacrament" of Salvation

4.2.1. The Church Under the Gospel and the Twofold Salvific Mediation of the Gospel

118. The Lutheran–Roman Catholic dialogue has stated that the church "stands under the gospel and has the gospel as its superordinate criterion."[146] For this one can appeal both to Luther, who sees the church as "creature of the gospel"[147] and to Vatican II according to which "the gospel . . . is for all time the source of all life for the Church."[148] The Gospel by which the church was created and lives is mediated externally and corporally in dual form: by word and by sacrament. Both modes of mediation however are connected in fundamentally indissoluble fashion without doing away with their specific characteristics. The word proclaimed is an audible sign, the sacraments are a visible word. These are the two modes in which the transmission of the Gospel is saving in its effect. Thus, not only is attention drawn to salvation or information given about it, but the Gospel thus confronts people in their inmost selves as effectual externally and corporally by its presence, bringing them to faith, justifying and sanctifying them.

119. Because in this way the church lives from the Gospel and is taken into the service of the dual mediation of the Gospel that effects salvation, Catholic talk of the church as "sacrament" can be described in terms of its purpose: "As the body of Christ and *koinonia* of the Holy Spirit, the church is the sign and instrument of God's grace, an instrument that of itself can do nothing. The church lives by the word as it lives by the sacraments and at the same time stands in their service."[149] The meaning of what is said about the church as the "sacrament" of salvation will be worked out below with reference to the Catholic and Lutheran traditions and their common foundation in the Bible.

4.2.2. The Catholic View

120. In the documents of Vatican II the church is referred to as "sacrament"—a sign and instrument of salvation—especially where the nature of the church and its universal mission are explained in considerable detail. At the beginning of the *Constitution on the Church* there is a programmatic statement, "Christ is the light of all nations."[150] By the church's proclamation of the Gospel to all creatures (cf. Mk 16:15), all people are to be illumined by the radiance of Christ, which "brightens the countenance of the Church"; for "by her relationship with Christ, the

Church is a kind of sacrament of intimate union with God, and of the unity of all mankind, that is, she is a sign and an instrument of such union and unity."[151] The council underlines very distinctly the church as centered in Christ, when it sees its "sacramentality" to be completely "in Christ." Catholic theology therefore speaks also of the "primal sacrament" *(Ursakrament)* which Jesus Christ himself is. The council takes this direction when it speaks in the *Constitution on the Sacred Liturgy* of the "Mediator between God and man: . . . for His humanity, united with the person of the Word, was the instrument of our salvation. Thus in Christ there came forth the perfect satisfaction needed for our reconciliation, and we received the means for giving worthy worship to God.'"[152]

121. Of the church as the "messianic people" we also read: "Established by Christ as a fellowship of life, charity, and truth, it is also used by Him as an instrument for the redemption of all, and is sent forth into the whole world as the light of the world and the salt of the earth (cf. Mt 5:13-16)."[153] The council sees the establishment of the church as rooted in the whole mystery of Christ[154] but links the statement of the church as "sacrament" in a special way with the resurrection of Christ and the sending of the Spirit: "Rising from the dead (cf. Rom 6:9), He sent His life-giving Spirit upon His disciples and through this Spirit has established His body, the Church, as the universal sacrament of salvation. Sitting at the right hand of the Father, He is continually active in the world, leading men to the Church, and through her joining them more closely to Himself. . . ."[155]

122. The term "sacrament," as a sign and instrument of salvation, gives expression to the universal mission of the church and its radical dependence on Christ. It thus becomes clear that neither the foundation of the church nor its goal lies in the church itself, and that it therefore does not exist by itself or for itself. Only in and through Christ, only in and through the Holy Spirit is the church effectual as a mediator of salvation. That is especially important when theologians speak of the sacraments as self-actualizations of the church, in order to prevent a purely outward understanding of the church as simply the steward of sacraments as means of grace, and instead to set forth an inner affinity, which though is not an identity, between the church and the sacraments, both being signs and instruments of salvation. As a "communion of life, love, and truth" on the one hand and as an "instrument for the salvation of everyone" and as "universal sacrament of salvation" on the other hand, the church is the actual place and instrument of the universal saving will of God "who desires everyone to be saved and to come to the knowledge of the truth" (1 Tm 2:4). God's will that all should be saved becomes for the individual a gracious promise when the church testifies to the truth of Christ and celebrates and proffers the sacraments, i.e., when Christ's salvation is present in the witness and sacramental celebration of the church done in and through Christ and thus in and

through the Holy Spirit. In the church—his body and his bride—Christ himself remains thus present for all people of the world through his saving acts.

123. In Catholic thought the concept of "sacrament" is constantly applied to the church analogically.[156] Church is not "sacrament" in the same sense as the sacraments of baptism and the eucharist. That is already clear in reference to how they function: the individual sacraments develop their saving efficacy "on the basis of their being celebrated";[157] their efficacy is not dependent on the worthiness of the minister or the recipient, because it is Christ who effects salvation in the sacraments. That cannot be said about the church as "sacrament" in the same way. Rather, one applies the concept of sacrament to the church to aid in theological reflection, for it clarifies the inner connection between outward, visible structure and hidden, spiritual reality. Just as the sacraments in scholastic thinking are described as visible signs and instruments of invisible grace, Vatican II sees the church as "one interlocked reality which is comprised of a divine and a human element" in which "the communal structure of the Church serves Christ's Spirit, who vivifies it by way of building up the body (cf. Eph 4:16)."[158] But this view of the church as "sacrament" also stands in the context of the effective imparting of salvation to all people: "The one Mediator . . . communicates truth and grace to all" through the church.[159] Speaking of the church as "sacrament" in the context of salvation for all people and of mission theology shows especially that Vatican II did not simply take over such earlier theories as "primal sacrament." Rather, the council's own theological point of departure is a further development of earlier considerations.

124. Here again we see that although it is his body, the church cannot be simply identified with Christ absolutely. It is taken into his service to mediate salvation to all people and needs the constant vivifying power of the Holy Spirit. In influencing its own members, it is Christ who as head grants participation in his Spirit and who thus causes the life and growth of the body.[160] It is part of the logic of such a sacramental concept of the church that the church in its human weakness must "incessantly pursue the path of penance and renewal"[161] and be called to "continual reformation."[162] Even outside the "visible structure" of the church, "many elements of sanctification and of truth can be found"[163] and God's saving activity is visibly and latently at work at the same time among "those who have not yet received the gospel."[164]

4.2.3. The Lutheran View

125. For Lutheran theology it is of fundamental and crucial importance that God bestows forgiveness, life, and the bliss of salvation on every believer through word and sacraments as means of grace[165] and that the church as the "assembly of all believers" is the place "in" which these means of grace are effectual.[166] This means that preaching as "the living voice of the gospel"[167] itself has "sacramental"

character, given that within the audible word lies the power to impart to the faithful that reality of salvation to which the words of the proclamation point. "When I preach, Christ himself preaches in me."[168] Thus, the "external word,"[169] as an "effectual word,"[170] stands alongside the sacraments as means of grace. We "must constantly maintain that God will not deal with us except through his external Word and sacrament."[171] The teaching of the Anabaptists "that the Holy Spirit comes to us . . . without the external word of the Gospel"[172] is therefore expressly condemned as such. The condemnation of the Donatists—for whom the sacraments become useless and ineffectual when administered by "wicked priests"—likewise points to the objective efficacy of word and sacrament, which remain "efficacious even if the priests who administer them are wicked men,"[173] because they are instituted and enjoined by Christ.

126. But if the church is the place where these means of grace become effectual, it follows that the church itself is in a derivative sense an instrument of salvation. On the one hand it is called into being as a *congregatio fidelium*, a church, through the event of the "means of grace" so that it is itself a *creatura evangelii*; on the other, it is the place where people participate in salvation—there is no alternative. In this sense it is true for Reformation theology too that there is no salvation outside the church.[174]

127. As mediator of word and sacrament the church is the instrument through which the Holy Spirit sanctifies; "it is the mother that begets and bears every Christian through the Word of God,"[175] but in such a way that Jesus Christ himself is working and becomes salvifically present in its preaching and administration of the sacraments. In other words, however much the mediating activity of the church and the saving activity of God coincide in what happens there, they are nevertheless plainly different in this: while it is true that the church imparts participation in salvation to believers, nevertheless it is Christ alone and not the church who has gained salvation for the world and who bestows on believers participation in this salvation through word and sacrament. In what it does, the church is totally the servant of Christ, its Lord, being called to this service and given authority for it by Christ, its Lord.

128. Against this background, Lutherans note affinities but also questions regarding the new Catholic understanding of the church as "sacrament." Lutheran thought corresponds more closely to the designation of Jesus Christ as "sacrament" found in Augustine[176] and later Roman Catholic theology. Christ is the "single sacrament"[177] of God, because he himself is the means par excellence of salvation. The individual sacraments are means of salvation because through them Jesus Christ accomplishes salvation and thus establishes and preserves the church. This means that the church does not actualize its own existence in the sacraments; rather the church receives salvation and its very being from Christ and only as recip-

ient does it mediate salvation. In this perspective, the individual sacraments are linked with Christ as he faces the church. One should be reticent about language which blurs this distinction. Talk about the church actualizing itself in the sacraments is open to serious misunderstanding and is better avoided. Lutheran theology points to the fact that calling the church "sacrament" must be clearly distinguished from the way "sacrament" is applied to baptism and the Lord's Supper.

129. The first Lutheran query entails a second: how does the understanding of the church as "sacrament" relate to that of the church as holy and sinful? Differently from baptism and the Lord's Supper, which exist wholly in their instrumentality and sign-character, the church is instrument and sign of salvation as the community of those who receive salvation. In other words, the church is instrument and sign as the community of believers, who as people justified by God are at the same time holy and sinful. Lutherans point out that Catholic references to the church as "sacrament" must not contradict the fact that the church is at the same time holy and sinful.[178]

130. There are certainly Lutheran theologians who apply "sacrament" to the church. Yet reservations about references to the church as "sacrament" remain in Lutheran theology, since such references can lead to misunderstandings on both the points just explained. Therefore many confine themselves to speaking of the church as sign and instrument of salvation in the sense already outlined.

4.2.4. The Unity and Distinctness of Christ and the Church

131. We can leave it to further theological reflections to determine how Christ and the church are one in sacramental activity without thereby being identified, and how a possible sacramental view of the church therefore has its roots in the fundamental description of Christ as the "primal sacrament" and is limited by that statement. Talk of the church as "sacrament" is in fact foreign to the Lutheran ecclesiological tradition and is acceptable only under the reservations just set forth—reservations which Catholic theologians also take seriously. Nevertheless, harking back to the biblical witness we can together state the following.

132. The New Testament sees the mystery of the relationship between Christ and the church in unity and diversity. The unity is highlighted in a series of statements, for instance, when Paul not only sees baptized believers as "one in Christ" but addresses them as such (Gal 3:28). According to Paul, the community is "one body in Christ" (Rom 12:5), and as "body of Christ" (1 Cor 12:27) is in fact "Christ" (1 Cor 12:12). It becomes clear that this unity in Christ does not imply an undifferentiated identity when Christ is described as "head of the body, the church" (Col 1:18; cf. Eph 1:22f.; 4:14ff.; 5:23). We are to distinguish head from body but on no account to separate them, for the "building up [of] the body of Christ" (Eph 4:12-16) proceeds from Christ, the head, who has saved the church as his body (cf. Eph 5:23). "The church

is subject to Christ" always (Eph 5:24) and linked to him in love (cf. Eph 4:16). The interlinking of unity and diversity becomes clear especially in the image of the bride and bridegroom (cf. 2 Cor 11:2; Eph 5:22ff.; Rv 19:7f.; 21:2; 22:17).

133. Of course the personal relation between Christ and church must not obscure the different quality of relations between the two; for from the start the church is the redeemed, receiving church and remains so forever. Precisely in the light of the doctrine of justification it becomes plain that the church owes its existence and activity solely to the mercy of God in Jesus Christ and to the breath of the Spirit. Only so is Christ able to make salvation effectual through the church in proclamation and the sacraments. Both the Lutheran and Catholic understandings of the church's salvific service through word and sacrament are based on this biblical foundation. We can leave it to theological reflection to explain in greater detail how this works, if only it becomes and remains clear that God's eschatological promise of grace really determines the church's activity and guides it from within, and that salvation thus appears palpably in history. Nevertheless it must be evident that salvation can never be effected by human beings or be at their disposal, but even in the activity of the church it remains the gift of God.

134. On the basis of the stipulations mentioned, there is agreement among Lutherans and Catholics that the church is instrument and sign of salvation and, in this sense, "sacrament" of salvation. To be sure, the reservations are taken seriously by both sides, and one must strive for a theological language that is unambiguous.

4.3. The Church Visible and Hidden

135. The view has often been advanced that the terms "visible church" and "invisible church" point to a disagreement between Roman Catholic and Lutheran ecclesiologies. Often one appeals to Luther's saying, the holy church "is invisible, dwelling in the Spirit, in an 'unapproachable' place."[179] Post-Reformation Catholic ecclesiology reacted polemically to such an understanding of the church and focused almost exclusively on the church as an external, visible entity marked out by creed, sacramental structure, and hierarchical leadership. Thus, Bellarmine stressed that as an "association"[180] the church was "just as visible and palpable as the Republic of Venice."[181] In the nineteenth century especially, Lutherans and Catholics both thought that this was the essential difference in their ecclesiologies.

136. But the assumed disagreement often lost its sharp contours, since each side repeatedly denied that it taught what the other side condemned. Thus, Melanchthon in the Apology of the Augsburg Confession utterly rejected the reproach that the church was, in the Lutheran Reformation view, only a kind of "Platonic republic."[182] Nor—in the light of the pronouncements of Vatican II—can the reproach be sustained that the one holy church is equated undialectically on the

Catholic side with its empirical historical form. For there it is said of the church that while "the visible assembly and the spiritual community" are indeed "not to be considered as two realities," they are nevertheless linked together asymmetrically: ". . . the communal structure of the Church serves Christ's Spirit, who vivifies it by way of building up the body (cf. Eph 4:16)."[183]

137. It seems that oversimplified formulations have led, wrongly, to the view that here the two churches are at odds. In what follows the aim is to examine whether there is ultimately a conflict between the two positions.

138. On the Lutheran side the Augsburg Confession by no means describes the church as an invisible entity. Rather it describes the church as an "assembly"[184] to which a "ministry" constitutively belongs.[185] Also, regarding the words of Luther quoted above[186] one must note that they continue, ". . . therefore its [the church's] holiness cannot be seen."[187] For Luther the word "church" here does not denote an invisible entity. His point is that the church does not display visibly the essential marks that qualify it as church—in this instance "holiness." That the word "church" nevertheless means a visible assembly becomes evident in the fact that there are "marks" of the church, "that is, Word, confession, and sacraments,"[188] all of which represent extremely visible realities.

139. The Lutheran view of the church is of course marked by a tension which may easily evoke misunderstanding of the "invisibility" of the church. According to the Apology, "hypocrites and evil men are . . . members of the church according to the outward associations of the church's marks . . . especially if they have not been excommunicated."[189] Thus, it might seem as if there were on the one hand the invisible "association of the faith" and on the other the "outward association" which is recognizable by "marks." But Lutherans have rejected that view ever since the Apology.[190]

140. Lutheranism sees the church as an "assembly." An assembly is not as such invisible. Invisible rather is the fact that this assembly really is church, i.e., that this visible body is the "body of Christ," that God really is at work in the word and in the sacraments that are its visible marks, and that its ministers are servants of the Holy Spirit. The predicate "invisible" is appropriate for the church insofar as it is an object of faith. This is also shown by the statement of Luther which has been quoted, in which he says "anyone who thinks this way turns the article of the Creed 'I believe a holy church' upside down; he replaces 'I believe' with 'I see.'"[191] The same purpose is clearly revealed where Luther dissociates himself polemically from abuses of the ambiguous word "church" in ecclesiastical politics. "If these words had been used in the Creed: 'I believe that there is a holy Christian people,' it would have been easy to avoid all the misery that has come in with this blind, obscure word 'church.'"[192]

141. In the Lutheran view, certain aspects of the church's visibility are what it makes invisible: only to the eye of faith is an assembly recognizable as the assembly of the people of God, and yet—between the times—the church has to be visible. In this world what makes it a hidden church is the same as what made Christ on the cross a hidden God, i.e., that he was only all too visible in and for this world. The passage often quoted from Luther's Large Commentary on Galatians makes this clear. The crucial section reads: "God conceals and covers [the church] with weaknesses, sins, errors, and various offenses and forms of the cross in such a way that it is not evident to the senses anywhere."[193]

142. The tension characteristic of the Lutheran understanding of the hiddenness of the church manifests a recurring problematic which all traditions have wrestled with in understanding the church and which they must continue to deal with. That is why Vatican II says that "possessing the Spirit of Christ" is fundamental to being "fully incorporated into the society of the Church." Those are not saved, however, who do "not persevere in charity," though they remain "indeed in the bosom of the Church" but "only in a 'bodily' manner and not 'in their hearts.'"[194] In its *Constitution on the Church* the council does not solve the problem. The difficulty of the relationship between church membership "according to the heart" and membership only "according to the body," and thus between the church as spiritual and as visible corporeal entity is for us a common difficulty. To be sure, the Lutheran emphasis that the hiddenness of the church corresponds to a specific characteristic of the Christian faith, namely recognizing God at work in that which seems opposed to him, introduces a dimension which goes beyond the problem of the recognition of church membership.

143. In statements quoted from Vatican II's *Dogmatic Constitution on the Church*, Lutherans discern important convergences in the way the church is understood. The constitution sees the church unambiguously in the context of the mystery of the universal bestowal of the saving love of God the Father, as that is revealed in the history of Jesus as the Christ[195] and made effective by the Holy Spirit in election, reconciliation, and communion, so that "all believers would have access to the Father through Christ in the one Spirit."[196] The constitution resolutely maintains that the church is the "body of Christ." In so doing it follows the Pauline statements, but it avoids precise definition of membership in this body.[197]

144. The *Constitution on the Church* produces a synthesis, which is new for Catholic theology, between the spiritual or transcendent reality of the church and its visible social reality. The spiritual community of faith, hope, and love lives on the basis of the Father's gift. Through the one bread which Christ proffers, believers are made into one body, and as temple of the Holy Spirit, the church is above all a mystery of communion with the triune God himself.[198] At the same time the church is also a historical reality. It began with Jesus' proclamation of the reign of God and

the founding of the messianic people of the new covenant, and this community of disciples has had unmistakable elements of social organization since the apostolic age.[199] The visible congregation stands in a complex relation to the mystery of the *koinonia* in which it has its origin and to which it seeks to give credible shape. Because the council posits an indissoluble link between the church as a visible assembly and the mystery of life shared in communion with God, it is possible to speak of the church as a "sacrament."[200]

145. Crucial here is the analogy between the visible communal structure serving the life-giving Spirit, by which it is vivified, and the assumed human nature of Christ serving the eternal Word.[201] By the very fact of its service, the social community is involved in a constant struggle as it journeys through history. Again and again it is in need of cleansing and renewal;[202] and this continuous reform encompasses all the moral, disciplinary, and doctrinal witness of the church to God's grace.[203]

146. A simple identification of the salvation-community with the empirical church, such as would place the empirical church beyond reform, is clearly labeled by Vatican II as an error which Catholic teaching should avoid.

147. Catholics and Lutherans are in agreement that the saving activity of the triune God calls and sanctifies believers through audible and visible means of grace which are mediated in an audible and visible ecclesial community. They also agree that in this world the salvation-community of Christ is hidden, because as a spiritual work of God it is unrecognizable by earthly standards, and because sin, which is also present in the church, makes ascertaining its membership uncertain.

4.4. Holy Church/Sinful Church

148. With the creeds of the early church we confess in common that the church is "holy." This holiness essentially consists in the fact that the church participates in the triune God, who alone is holy (cf. Rv 15:4), from whom it derives and to whom it is journeying:

- The church is holy through the gracious election and faithfulness of God. Just as the people of the old covenant were a "holy nation" because they had been chosen to be God's "treasured possession" (Ex 19:5f.; cf. Lv 11:44f.; Dt 7:6), so too by virtue of the new covenant of grace the church is God's "holy nation," the people who became his special possession (1 Pt 2:9).
- The church is holy through the saving work of Christ. Christ sanctified himself for his own, "so that they also may be sanctified in truth" (Jn 17:19); he sacrificed himself for the church, his "bride," "in order to make her holy" (Eph 5:25f.).

- The church is holy through the presence of the Holy Spirit. The Holy Spirit dwells in believers as in a temple (cf. 1 Cor 3:16; 6:19; Eph 2:22); they are "sanctified by the Holy Spirit" (Rom 15:16; cf. 1 Cor 6:11); the Holy Spirit builds up the church and equips it by means of the gifts of the Spirit (cf. 1 Cor 12; Eph 4:11f.); the Holy Spirit gives life to the church and strengthens it through spiritual fruits (cf. Gal 5:22).

149. Insofar as the holiness of the church continues to be rooted in the holiness of the triune God, we make common confession that the church in its holiness is indestructible. Christ has promised his presence to his disciples "to the end of the age" (Mt 28:20) and has promised his church that "the gates of Hades will not prevail against it" (Mt 16:18).

150. Vatican II's *Dogmatic Constitution on the Church* states: "The Church . . . is holy in a way which can never fail. For Christ, the Son of God, . . . loved the Church as His Bride, delivering Himself up for her. This He did that He might sanctify her (cf. Eph 5:25-26). He united her to Himself as His own body and crowned her with the gift of the Holy Spirit, for God's glory."[204]

151. This belief in the indestructibility and abiding existence of the church as the one holy people of God is an essential element in Luther's ecclesiology and is fundamental for a correct understanding of his struggle for reform. "The Children's Creed [Catechism] teaches us (as was said) that a Christian holy people is to be and to remain on earth until the end of the world. This is an article of faith that cannot be terminated until that which it believes comes, as Christ promises, 'I am with you always, to the close of the age.'"[205] In this sense the Augsburg Confession says, "It is also taught . . . that one holy Christian church will be and remain forever."[206]

152. This belief in the indestructibility of the one holy church includes the idea that in the ultimate sense the church cannot apostatize from the truth and fall into error. In this conviction the Reformation understands itself to be in continuity with the prior theological and ecclesiastical tradition; thus, it has always understood the biblical promises in this way (cf. Mt 16:18; 28:20; Jn 16:13). So "the church cannot err"[207] repeatedly occurs in the Reformers in this or a similar form,[208] and the Catholic–Lutheran dialogue has also referred to this shared conviction.[209]

153. Of course, the confession of the church's holiness has always gone hand in hand with the knowledge that the power of evil and sin, although it will not overcome the church, is nevertheless at work in it. The church "without a spot or wrinkle or anything of the kind" (Eph 5:27) will appear only at the end of its earthly pilgrimage, when "Christ will present her to Himself in all her glory."[210] The holiness of the church therefore exists both "already" and "not yet." It is a "genuine though imperfect holiness."[211]

154. It is part of the theological tradition of our churches to apply the biblical pictures and parables of the weeds among the wheat (cf. Mt 13:38), the wise and foolish bridesmaids (cf. Mt 25:1ff.) or the net and the fish (cf. Mt 13:47f.), to the church in its visible and temporal reality: the church in its concrete form always includes good and evil people, believers and unbelievers, true and false teachers. The ancient church's condemnation of the Novatian and Donatist views of the church was adopted by the Reformation. The statement in Article 8 of the Augsburg Confession, that in the church, which is "properly speaking nothing else than the assembly of all believers and saints," there are nevertheless still "many false Christians, hypocrites and even open sinners . . . among the godly,"[212] expresses a conviction shared equally by Catholics and Lutherans.

155. As especially the Lutheran–Roman Catholic dialogue on justification has shown, there is also agreement that all believers as members of the church are involved in a relentless struggle against sin and are in need of daily repentance and the forgiveness of sins. They depend constantly on justifying grace and rely on the promise which is given them in the struggle against evil.

156. With this in mind, it is not in dispute between us that the church is "holy" and "sinful" at the same time and that the imperative calling to holiness is always a concomitant of the indicative that holiness has been bestowed (cf. 1 Thes 4:3f., 7; 2 Cor 7:1). Thus, the church is in constant need of repentance and the forgiveness of sins, and of cleansing and renewal. Vatican II stated this repeatedly, even if it does not use the term "sinful" of the church. The *Dogmatic Constitution on the Church* says: "While Christ, 'holy, innocent, undefiled' (Heb 7:26) knew nothing of sin (2 Cor 5:21), but came to expiate only the sins of the people (cf. Heb 2:17), the Church, embracing sinners in her bosom, is at the same time holy and always in need of being purified, and incessantly pursues the path of penance and renewal."[213] And the *Decree on Ecumenism* states, "Christ summons the Church, as she goes her pilgrim way, to that continual reformation of which she always has need, insofar as she is an institution of men here on earth."[214]

157. Differences between our churches emerge in answering the question, Where does the idea of church's need for renewal or of its sinfulness find its necessary limit, by reason of the divine pledge that the church abides in the truth and that error and sin will not overcome it?

158. The Lutheran Reformation no less emphatically than Roman Catholic theology stresses the fact that there is and must be such a limit. Thus, Luther is able to distinguish between "erring" and "remaining in error." By this he wishes to show how abiding in the truth, which is promised to the church, is not a reality in peaceful possession but under the faithfulness and forgiveness of God is realized in ongoing struggle against error.[215] Even more important is the distinction he makes between the teaching and the life of the church. Whereas in regard to its life the

"holy church is not without sin, as it confesses in the Lord's Prayer 'Forgive us our sins,'"[216] the opposite is true of its teaching, i.e., of its obedient proclamation of the Gospel, insofar as the Gospel is preached, the sacraments are administered, and absolution is given "on behalf of Christ" (2 Cor 5:20)[217] and by his authority. "The teaching must be neither sinful nor reprehensible and it does not have its place in the Lord's Prayer in which we say 'Forgive us our sins.' For it is not our doing, but God's own Word which cannot sin or do wrong."[218]

159. In this conception the Lutheran Reformation lies wholly in the realm of what is also maintained on the Catholic side. The conviction that the church's abiding in the truth—its indefectibility—is not a reality held in peaceful possession is also shared on the Catholic side. Therefore, Catholics and Lutherans can say in common that "the church's abiding in the truth should not be understood in a static way but as a dynamic event which takes place with the aid of the Holy Spirit in ceaseless battle against error and sin in the church as well as in the world."[219] Luther's distinction between the life and the teaching of the church corresponds to the Catholic distinction between the "members" of the church, who in their constancy in faith, their life, and their deeds are always in need of the forgiveness of sins and of renewal,[220] and the church itself, which in teaching and proclamation expounds the unalterable "deposit of faith";[221] between the church as an "institution of men here on earth," which "Christ summons . . . to . . . continual reformation,"[222] and the church as "enriched with heavenly things," as a divine creation with the "elements of sanctification and of truth" given to it by Christ.[223]

160. From the Lutheran standpoint serious questions to the Catholic view first present themselves where the God-given indestructible holiness of the church and God's promise that the church will abide in the truth are so objectivized in specific ecclesial components that they appear to be exempt from critical questioning. Above all this, Lutheran query is directed at ecclesial offices and decisions which serve people's salvation and sanctification. The question arises when the Holy Spirit's aid is attributed to them in such a way that as such they appear to be immune from the human capacity for error and sinfulness and therefore from needing to be examined. That will be dealt with in what follows.[224] Similar questions are also directed at the institution of the canonization of saints.

161. These Lutheran questions cannot be regarded as superfluous, even in the light of the fact that in the Catholic view these ecclesial offices and decisions have their historically variable forms and are carried out by sinful human beings. For that reason they continue to be imperfect, can obscure the indestructible holiness of the church,[225] and therefore are in need of reform.[226]

162. In fact these Lutheran queries touch directly on the self-understanding of the Roman Catholic Church at a decisive point; but they suggest conclusions which as such were not there from the beginning.

163. The Lord's promise that it will abide in the truth is the basis for the Catholic Church's belief that the truth can be articulated in propositions and can lead to forms of expressing the Gospel which are inerrant and infallible.[227] Further, it believes that there are abiding, established ecclesial offices which are willed by God's providence.[228] Also that the saints perfected by God are not all anonymous but are named by canonization as those who may be addressed as the perfected of God.[229]

164. Thereby very diverse areas are addressed of which the first, inerrant truth, and the last, perfected holiness, have one thing in common: they express the fact that God's activity in this world—in its decisive and definitive quality—is incarnational and anticipates the eschaton. They of course represent such diverse levels that they should not simply be mentioned in one breath. Catholic thinking finds it hard to see why the effects of divine decisiveness should be intrinsically open to criticism and why it is not enough to distinguish between human sinfulness and the divine saving activity in such a way that, although they remain exposed to human inadequacy and sinfulness, God's works are inherently good and cannot be rendered ineffectual.

165. In spite of the above questions one may, regarding the overarching problematic of the holiness of the church and its need for renewal, speak of common Lutheran–Roman Catholic basic convictions. Taken together they constitute a broad consensus within which remaining differences are neither abolished nor denied. Still only in discussing each of the relevant ecclesiological points in question is it possible to discover their theological and ecumenical importance.

4.5. The Significance of the Doctrine of Justification for the Understanding of the Church

4.5.1. The Problem and the Original Consensus

166. Many of the questions which Catholics and Lutherans address to one another regarding the relation between the doctrine of justification and the understanding of the church emerge from two different concerns, which may be summarized as follows: Catholics ask whether the Lutheran understanding of justification does not diminish the reality of the church; Lutherans ask whether the Catholic understanding of church does not obscure the Gospel as the doctrine of justification explicates it. Neither concern is unfounded, but needs to be clarified, especially because the New Testament knows of no opposition between Gospel and church.

167. In dealing with the relationship between the doctrine of justification and the understanding of the church, it is important to note which perspective on justification is employed. It is not primarily a matter of how the saving event can be rightly described and how God communicates his righteousness to the sinner. This indeed stands at the center of Reformation arguments but, as such, has no immedi-

ate critical implications for ecclesiology. These emerge only when—as happened especially in the Lutheran Reformation—justification is seen both as center and criterion of all theology. Therefore the doctrine of the church must correspond to justification as criterion. The reciprocal questions of Catholics and Lutherans mentioned above arise only from such a perspective.

168. The far-reaching consensus in the understanding of justification noted during this and other Lutheran–Roman Catholic dialogues leads to testing the consensus on the critical significance of the doctrine of justification for all church doctrine, order, and practice. Everything which is believed and taught regarding the nature of the church, the means of grace, and the ordained ecclesial ministry must be grounded in the salvation event itself and bear the mark of justification-faith as reception and appropriation of that event. Correspondingly, all that is believed and taught regarding the nature and effects of justification must be understood in the total context of assertions about the church, the means of grace, and the church's ordained ministry. Expressing the Lutheran position, the Malta Report of 1972, *The Gospel and the Church*, stated: ". . . all traditions and institutions of the church are subject to the criterion which asks whether they are enablers of the proper proclamation of the Gospel and do not obscure the unconditional character of the gift of salvation."[230] In the United States, the Lutheran–Roman Catholic dialogue took over this assertion as its common declaration: "Catholics as well as Lutherans can acknowledge the need to test the practices, structures, and theologies of the church by the extent to which they help or hinder 'the proclamation of God's free and merciful promises in Christ Jesus which can be rightly received only through faith.'"[231]

4.5.2. Common Basic Convictions

169. Just as the New Testament does not acknowledge a fundamental contradiction between Gospel and church, so we too must beware lest we see justification and the church as being from the outset in conflict with each other, let alone as being incompatible. Three basic convictions, shared by Catholics and Lutherans, and which lead from the doctrine of justification into ecclesiology, prevent that.

170. First, the Gospel, as the Reformation doctrine of justification understands it, is essentially an "external word." That is to say it is always mediated through one or more individuals addressing one or more other individuals. The Gospel is not a doctrine that can be internalized as one's own in such a way that thereafter no further address from other persons is needed. It remains a message "from outside," and hearers remain dependent on its communication by one who proclaims it. This is expressed, for instance, in Article 7 of the Augsburg Confession, which describes the church not simply as the "assembly of all believers" or *congregatio sanctorum* but also links this "assembly of all believers" constitutively to the "external" witness of the Gospel in preaching and the sacraments, which conversely

can have their place only in the church, "the assembly of all believers."[232] On the one hand, the church lives from the Gospel; on the other, the Gospel sounds forth in the church and summons into the community of the church.

171. Second, the Gospel which is proclaimed in the Holy Spirit is according to its nature a creative word. If belief in the Gospel is our righteousness, then the Gospel does not merely inform us about righteousness but makes us through the Holy Spirit into new, justified persons who already "walk in newness of life" (Rom 6:4). This conviction, common to Catholics and Lutherans, leads into the understanding of church. For if we confess in common that the Gospel that gathers the church really is God's creative word, then we must also confess in common that the church itself really is God's creation and as such is a social reality that unites people.

172. Third, God, who creates the church through his word and has promised that it will abide in the truth and will continue to exist, is faithful to his word and his promise. In the interim, until this promise attains its eschatological goal in the consummation of all things, God effects his faithfulness in the historical form of the church also through structures of historical continuity. Previously, Old Testament Israel was a real historical people which lived from God's promises. To them he gave structures of historical continuity. To be sure, the continuity of the church appears especially to Lutherans to be a constant struggling against the dangers of error and apostasy and finally a victory of God's faithfulness over the constantly recurring unfaithfulness of human beings. This view rests on constitutive ecclesial experiences which are not without their ecclesiological relevance. But Lutherans nonetheless hold that the church will continue in existence and that there are structures which contribute to this continuity, without of course being able to guarantee it.

4.5.3. The Areas of Controversy

173. The questions which arise regarding the relationship between justification and the church may be presented and discussed in four areas: (1) the institutional continuity of the church, (2) the ordained ministry as ecclesial institution, (3) the teaching function of the church's ministry, and (4) the jurisdictional function of the church's ministry. Each of these areas relates to the above-mentioned reciprocal questioning by Catholics and Lutherans: whether the Lutheran doctrine of justification diminishes the reality of the church; whether the Catholic understanding of the church obscures the Gospel as it is explicated by the doctrine of justification.

4.5.3.1. Institutional Continuity of the Church

174. As a creature of the Gospel and its proclamation, which is always "external," creative, and sustained by God's faithfulness, the church exists continuously through the ages: "one holy Christian church will be and remain forever."[233] Just as

everything God creates through his word and sustains in faithfulness to his word has its history, so too the church has its history. It is historical like other creatures, though in a unique way: only the church is promised that it will endure and that the gates of hell will not overcome it.

175. The historicity of the church is most profoundly bound up with that of the Gospel which calls it into being and from which it lives. As the proclaimed and transmitted external word the Gospel mediates the abiding faithfulness of God in the midst of the history of this world.

176. The church created by the Gospel is more than the total sum of persons who belong to it here and now. The church is "assembly" not only as congregation which gathers for worship at a particular time and in a particular place. At the same time it is "assembly" in a sense transcending time and place, as church of all people and generations, as the church founded in the Christ-event and existing in the pre-existent reality of fellowship in the body of Christ. In this sense the church is a communal, social reality of singular character and continuous existence.

177. If God creates the church as a historical community with a continuous existence by means of the external Gospel, this activity of God has its counterpart in the establishment of structural and institutional realities. These serve the continuity of this community, are an expression of it, and therefore themselves have a continuous existence. The founding of the church, i.e., its institution in the Christ-event and the establishment of such structural and institutional realities, are therefore indissolubly linked together.

178. Apostolic preaching, which has its precipitate in the New and the Old Testament canons, together with the sacraments of baptism and the Lord's Supper and the divinely empowered "ministry of reconciliation" (2 Cor 5:18), are such God-appointed means and signs of the continuity of the church, which according to Reformation conviction, too, remain constantly in the church.[234] They are institutions in which God makes his creative grace and sustaining faithfulness visible and effective, and which for their part effect and testify to the permanence of the church by their continuity. Their perpetual continuity and that of the church are inseparable.

179. These realities, which were established along with the foundation of the church, have taken on specific forms in the course of history or have produced other realities which in turn testify to the continuity of the church and serve it, and which therefore likewise have a long-term purpose or have proven themselves to be enduring. This is particularly true regarding the forms which the "ministry of reconciliation" took on very early in the history of the church. But it also holds good for the creeds, dogmas, or confessional writings which have arisen in history as an expression of the apostolic faith, and which have their basis in the biblical writings, especially in the confessions of faith found in the New Testament. Our two churches

give in part different and indeed controversial responses to the question of how far and to what degree these ecclesiastical realities which have arisen in history share in the enduring quality of the realities established when the church was founded. The reasons for the differences are certainly theological and ecclesiological, but very often they also reflect different experiences of the church. But it is not in dispute that (1) these realities arose in the history of the church and were not directly and explicitly established when it was founded; (2) they can certainly give expression to the continuity of the church and be of service to it; and (3) they nevertheless remain capable of renewal and in need of renewal.

180. Above all, however, it is agreed that all institutional or structural elements of church continuity are and remain instruments of the Gospel, which alone creates and sustains the church, not in their own right but only insofar and as long as they testify to the continuity of the church and serve that continuity. Their effectiveness as signs and means of the continuity of the church is limited and called in question when and for as long as their relatedness to and transparency for that Gospel are diminished or obscured.

181. This is true regarding how the church deals with the realities which are integral to its foundation and—according to our common conviction—are indispensable to it, such as the word of God available in the canon of Holy Scripture, the sacraments of baptism and the Lord's Supper, and the ministry of reconciliation. But this is especially true of the signs and means of continuity in the church which have emerged in history. Here the idea of the indispensable nature of these signs and instruments of institutional continuity for the church, as advocated not only but especially on the Catholic side, may itself evoke the concern, and indeed reproach that the Gospel of the radical gratuitousness of the gift of salvation and unconditional nature of the reception of salvation is being obscured. Consequently, special care is needed to see to it that these instruments and signs of institutional continuity in the church do not cease to function as servants of the Gospel, not even when one seems obligated to grant them an ecclesially indispensable and binding character.

4.5.3.2. Ordained Ministry as Institution in the Church

182. It has already been said in common[235] that the "ministry of reconciliation" which proclaims reconciliation with God "on behalf of Christ" (2 Cor 5:18-20) is one of the indispensable institutional realities given to the church from the beginning to express and serve its continuity.[236] It was also said in common that these realities built into the church, and also their further configurations in history, do not in themselves testify to the church's continuity or bring it about, except insofar as they serve the Gospel through which the Holy Spirit creates and sustains the church. The more these institutional realities are thus subordinated to the justifica-

tion criterion, the less we can say that they as such contradict the doctrine of justification and are condemned by it.

183. This is true also of the ordained ministry insofar as it is by its nature, according to our churches' view, that "ministry of reconciliation" (2 Cor 5:18). The critical assertion that the ordained ministry as an institution of continuity by its very existence runs counter to the doctrine of justification is thus repudiated fundamentally.

184. However, the fact that the Reformation doctrine of justification and its emphasis on the unconditionality of the gift of salvation has at times been understood as questioning the necessity of the ordained ministry and the legitimacy of its institutional, ecclesial form calls for an even more pointed rejoinder.

185. First of all it must be stressed, as the previous Roman Catholic–Lutheran dialogue has done, that the Lutheran Reformation knows no such ecclesiological consequence of the doctrine of justification. There is no contradiction between the doctrine of justification and the idea of an ordained ministry instituted by God and necessary for the church. Quite the opposite. The Augsburg Confession already makes this clear, with its characteristic transition from the article on justification[237] to that on the church's ministry.[238] There justifying faith is grounded in the Gospel, which the ordained ministry is to proclaim in word and sacraments. Article 14 of the Augsburg Confession excludes the idea, which only arose in the nineteenth century, that "the church's ministry" or the "preaching ministry" could mean anything other than the ecclesiastical institution of the ordained ministry. For Luther and the Lutheran Confessions, the church's ministry and the Gospel are so closely united that they can both be spoken of in identical terms[239] and can let the church be founded on the ministry.[240] In a similar sense Lutheran orthodoxy taught that the triune God is "the primary efficient cause" of the church and that the church's ministry is the "efficient cause which God uses to gather his church."[241]

186. In agreement with the Reformation, and without contradicting the Reformation doctrine of justification, we can therefore repeat what has already been said in the Lutheran–Roman Catholic dialogue on the ministry: ". . . the existence of a special ministry is abidingly constitutive for the church."[242]

187. These points show that Reformation thought provides no basis for fearing that the very existence of an ordained ministry as necessary institution for the church obscures the Gospel. Above all it must be seen how the institution of the ministry is positively in line with the Gospel and its explication through the doctrine of justification.

188. If the New Testament—and with it the Lutheran Reformation—sees the special character of the ordained ministry in the fact that ministers are called to preach reconciliation publicly "on behalf of Christ" (2 Cor 5:20),[243] and thus stand "over against the community" even while "within the community,"[244] this corre-

sponds directly to the inmost concern of the doctrine of justification itself. At stake is that God in Christ approaches human beings "from outside" for their salvation notwithstanding everything they know, are capable of, and are. Human beings— even believers—cannot say to themselves what God has to say to them and cannot bring themselves to that salvation which God alone has prepared for them. This structural movement "outside us and for us"[245] is constitutive of the saving revelation of God in Christ. It is continued in the proclamation of the Gospel and must continue there if the Gospel is not to be obscured. For this, God establishes the ordained ministry, and consequently, from among his many followers, Jesus calls his emissaries, in whom his mission from the Father is continued (cf. Jn 20:21; 17:18) and of whom it is true to say, "whoever listens to you listens to me" (Lk 10:16) and "whoever welcomes you welcomes me, and whoever welcomes me welcomes the one who sent me" (Mt 10:40).

189. Thus, not only does the institution of the ordained ministry not contradict the Gospel as it is explicated by the doctrine of justification, but corresponds to it and in the last analysis receives its character of indispensability for the church from that correspondence. The Lutheran–Roman Catholic dialogue on the church's ministry had drawn attention to this also when it stated with the Accra document of that time and with the later BEM statement[246] that "the presence of this ministry in the community 'signifies the priority of divine initiative and authority in the Church's existence.'"[247]

190. It is no contradiction of the close connection between the ministry and the Gospel but is rather in line with it, that for the ministry and for ordained ministers the doctrine of justification as explication of the Gospel must be the criterion for their own self-understanding and actions. For although the connection between the ministry and the Gospel certainly exists, it is no guarantee against abuse and false doctrine. Just as the New Testament knows of and warns against "false teachers"[248] and "false apostles"[249] (2 Pt 2:1; 2 Cor 11:13), it is also part of the historical experience of the church that the office, in its bearers and their ministry, may come to contradict the Gospel (cf. Gal 1:6ff.; 2:14). The way this experience registers in the ecclesiology and church law of our two churches differs in part. The possibility of a conflict between the ministry and the Gospel and thus the need for the church to stand guard over the primacy of the Gospel are however seen and affirmed on both sides.

191. The conviction that the doctrine of justification must, as an explication of the Gospel, be the critical yardstick for our understanding and exercise of the ministry is applied in the Lutheran Reformation and the Lutheran churches in a special and for them significant way. It relates to the specific forms which the divinely instituted ministry has assumed in the course of history. This is true above all in regard to the specific formation of the ecclesial ministry of leadership

(episkope). The development of the ministry into an episcopate standing in a historic succession, i.e., the continuity of apostolic succession which occurred already very early in history[250] was fully affirmed by the Lutheran Reformation and emphatically championed,[251] just as other church realities were affirmed and conserved which had come into being in the course of history (e.g., the biblical canon, the creeds of the ancient church). For Lutheran thinking too it is entirely possible to acknowledge that the historical development of an episcopate in a historic succession was not something purely within the sphere of history, set in motion only by sociological and political factors, but that it "has taken place with the help of the Holy Spirit" and that it "constitutes something essential for the church."[252]

192. However, Lutherans cannot agree when something is seen in this historically developed formation of the ministry whose existence plays a part in determining the very being of the church. The reason is not simply the ecclesial experience of the Reformation, namely that, at least in central Europe, the Reformation struggled for the truth of the Gospel not only without the support of the church's episcopate but even against its resistance. The deeper reason is the concern that putting episcopacy on such a level endangers the unconditional nature of the gift of salvation and its reception. And that is precisely what is at stake in the Reformation doctrine of justification. For this unconditionality necessarily implies that only that may be considered necessary for the church to be church which is already given by Jesus Christ himself as means of salvation. If ecclesial structures, which emerged in history, are elevated to that level, they become preconditions for receiving salvation and so, in the Lutheran view, are put illegitimately on the same level with the Gospel proclaimed in word and sacrament, which alone is necessary for salvation and the church.

193. Here a clear difference between Catholics and Lutherans reveals itself in the theological and ecclesiological evaluation of the episcopal office in historic succession, a difference which has been repeatedly noted in the Catholic–Lutheran dialogue up to now.[253]

194. According to Roman Catholic understanding, there is a historic development of the then-permanent form of the ordained ministry. This is especially true of its post-apostolic organization into "bishops, priests, and other ministers."[254] Here of course we have to consider that this post-apostolic organization and identification of distinctions in the ministry is already attested to incipiently in the Bible and was introduced in the transition from the "emerging" to the "developed" church.

195. The shared Catholic–Lutheran conviction that the historical emergence of the ministry's structure is not simply to be traced back to human—sociological and political—factors but "has taken place with the help of the Holy Spirit"[255] is, in the Catholic view, understood and prioritized differently than in Lutheran thought. Unlike the Lutherans, Catholics see a "divine institution" in the organization of the

ministry as it has developed through history, i.e., a development led, willed, and testified to by divine providence.[256] Under the operation of the Holy Spirit within the apostolic tradition, episcopacy and apostolic succession as orderly transmission of the ordained ministry have developed as the expression, means, and criterion of the continuity of the tradition in post-apostolic times. Thus, in the providence of God the bishops "by divine institution"[257] are successors to the apostles. The task of the apostles to tend the church of God continues in the episcopacy, and bishops are to exercise it continually.

196. The episcopate and apostolic succession as the orderly transmission of the ordained ministry in the church are therefore in the Catholic view essential for the church as church, and so are necessary and indispensable. Nevertheless, word and sacrament are the two pillars of the church which are necessary for salvation. The episcopate and apostolic succession stand in service as ministry to what is necessary for salvation, so that the word will be authentically preached and the sacraments rightly celebrated. The episcopate and apostolic succession serve to safeguard the apostolic tradition, the content of which is expressed in the rule of faith. The Spirit of God uses the episcopate in order to identify the church in every historical situation with its apostolic origin, to integrate the faithful in the one universal faith of the church, and just so through the episcopate to make its liberating force effective. In this sense the episcopate is in the Catholic view a necessary service of the Gospel, which is itself necessary for salvation.

197. The difference between the Catholic and Lutheran views on the theological and ecclesiological evaluation of the episcopate is thus not so radical that a Lutheran rejection or even indifference toward this ministry stands in opposition to the Catholic assertion of its ecclesial indispensability. The question is rather one of a clear gradation in the evaluation of this ministry, which can be and has been described on the Catholic side by predicates such as "necessary" or "indispensable," and on the Lutheran side as "important," "meaningful," and thus "desirable."[258]

198. For a proper understanding of this Catholic–Lutheran difference in the evaluation of the episcopate, it is necessary to observe that behind it lie two different correlations of salvation and church.

199. According to the Lutheran doctrine of justification and the Lutheran understanding of the church, it is only through the proclamation of the Gospel in word and sacraments, which ordained ministers are called to do, that the Holy Spirit effects justifying faith[259] and that the church is created and preserved.[260] The church exists in the full sense of the word where this saving gospel proclamation takes place.[261]

200. Following this ecclesiological line, nothing good and "profitable"[262] for ecclesial communion which exists alongside the Gospel proclaimed in word and

sacraments may be considered ecclesially necessary, in the strict sense of that word, lest the one thing necessary for salvation—the Gospel—be endangered.[263]

201. According to the Catholic understanding of faith, there is also a stable correlation of church and salvation which cannot be dissolved. Therefore Vatican II calls the church "the universal sacrament of salvation."[264] It is sign and instrument of salvation for all humanity, so that without the church there is no salvation. Within this context, however, Catholic thinking further differentiates the subjective and personal consideration of human salvation by reason of God's grace and the objective and ecclesiological view of the church as recipient and mediator of salvation. Therefore, the Second Vatican Council maintains with regard to non-Catholic Christians that "many elements of sanctification and of truth can be found outside of her visible structure"[265] and that the non-Catholic churches and communities are used by Christ's Spirit as "means of salvation."[266] In addition, Vatican II says in relation to non-Christians that God's saving activity is at once visibly and invisibly at work among those who have not yet received the Gospel, and that God "can lead those inculpably ignorant of the Gospel to that faith without which it is impossible to please Him."[267] To this extent there is, according to Catholic understanding, a correlation between salvation and church consisting not only in the church membership of those who hear the word in faith and receive the sacraments fruitfully, but there is also an ordination to the church on the basis of the visible and hidden saving work of God's grace outside the church which can lead to saving faith.

202. This differentiation is also expressed regarding the ecclesial necessity of the episcopal office in apostolic succession, something which is not necessary for the salvation of individual persons. Because of such a differentiation it is possible for Catholics to assert the necessity of this office without thereby contradicting the doctrine of justification. Thus the episcopal office is understood in the church as a necessary ministry of the Gospel, which itself is necessary for salvation.

203. Even so, Catholics will have to take seriously and answer the Lutheran question. If Catholics hold that the Lord's Supper celebrated in Lutheran churches has "because of the lack [defectus] of the sacrament of orders . . . not preserved the genuine and total reality [substantia] of the Eucharistic mystery,"[268] does that not, after all, show that they regard the episcopal office in historic succession as the regular transmitter of the ordained ministry in the church, and so indirectly as necessary for salvation? Catholics must answer that an ecclesiology focused on the concept of succession, as held in the Catholic Church, need in no way deny the saving presence of the Lord in a eucharist celebrated by Lutherans.

204. The difference in the theological and ecclesiological evaluation of the episcopal office in historic succession loses its sharpness when Lutherans attribute such a value to the episcopate that regaining full communion in this office seems important and desirable, and when Catholics recognize that "the ministry in the

Lutheran churches exercises essential functions of the ministry that Jesus Christ instituted in his church"[269] and does not contest the point that the Lutheran churches are church.[270] The difference in evaluating the historic episcopate is thereby interpreted in such a way that the doctrine of justification is no longer at stake and consequently it is also possible to advocate theologically the regaining of full communion in the episcopate.[271]

4.5.3.3. Binding Church Doctrine and the Teaching Function of the Ministry

205. The church's abiding in the truth, which is God's promise and also his commission to the church, requires inescapably that the church must distinguish the truth of the Gospel from error. That means, however, the church must teach. This does not at all contradict the Reformation doctrine of justification because its own claim is to promote this very distinction between truth and error in a fundamental way.

206. The commission to continue in the truth, like the promise to bring this about, holds good for the church as a whole. Our churches are agreed on this. We also agree that it is primarily the Spirit of God, promised to the church and dwelling in it,[272] who enables it so to continue and gives it the authority to distinguish truth and error in a binding way, that is, to teach.[273] Finally, we agree that for his activity God in the Holy Spirit makes use of temporal instruments and circumstances which he himself has bestowed upon the church as a temporal and creaturely entity;[274] and that the ministry is one of these instruments and circumstances.[275] There is no tension between this and the doctrine of justification as criterion for the church's life and activity.

207. It is in fact true of the Lutheran as much as of the Roman Catholic Church that like the church in every age, it is a teaching church which sees itself under the continuing commission to preserve the truth of the Gospel and to reject error. Its catechisms, especially Luther's Large Catechism, and most particularly the Confessions with their "teaching" and "rejecting" exemplify this.[276]

208. The difference between our churches only begins to surface where the issue is how the church's responsibility for teaching is exercised. When the Roman Catholic Church attributes a special responsibility and authority for teaching to the ministry and in particular to the episcopate, this in itself still does not imply any essential difference from the Lutheran view and practice. For in the Lutheran view too the ministry, along with its mission and authority to preach the Gospel and inseparably from them, is given a responsibility for the "purity" of the proclaimed Gospel and the "right" administration of the sacraments "according to the Gospel."[277] It was also axiomatic for the Reformation that there are ordered ministries in the church such as the teaching office of theologians and faculties who had the right and duty to distinguish truth and error in a special way. Luther was him-

self able to assert his rights as a theological teacher in face of the ecclesiastical authorities who had themselves appointed him as such.

209. Following the medieval tradition, it was extremely common for the theological faculties in areas of the Lutheran Reformation to exercise something like an ecclesial teaching function. Nor was it contested on the Reformation side that a special responsibility for teaching belongs to the bishops: they are entitled "according to divine right . . . to . . . judge doctrine and condemn doctrine that is contrary to the gospel," and congregations are therefore in duty "bound to be obedient to the bishops according to the saying of Christ in Luke 10:16, 'He who hears you hears me.'"[278] The episcopal structure was however not preserved in most churches of the Reformation.[279] Very early in the German lands (about 1527) there developed within the framework of ecclesial governance by princes an alternative system for supra-parish doctrinal oversight by creating superintendents, visitors, or visitation commissions. They exercised the function of a teaching office by seeing to it that parish preaching and the administration of the sacraments were true to the Gospel. "Also in our day there is interpretation and development of church doctrine in Lutheran churches through the decisions of the appropriate ecclesial authorities" (bishops' synods, church councils) in which office-bearers, church members, and theological teachers together play a part.[280] Nevertheless, significant differences appear here too.

210. The Reformers thought that the promise and responsibility which held good for the whole church was concentrated to such an extent in the teaching ministry exercised by bishops and the pope in the Roman church that the inerrancy promised to the church as a whole had shifted to the bishops and the pope. This, so it was said, revealed the new Roman "definition of the church," which was rejected.[281] Regarding the promise and commission to abide in the truth the following principle held good for the Reformation: "Nor should that be transferred to the popes which is the prerogative of the true church: that they are pillars of the truth and that they do not err."[282]

211. Here, according to Reformation conviction, the critical function of the doctrine of justification comes into play. In this, the primary question is not that the church as the congregation of the faithful (*congregatio fidelium*) might take second place to the church as "supreme outward monarchy";[283] or that the equality of the people of God might be canceled out. And it certainly is not a question of a modern ideal of freedom or the application to the church of the idea of the sovereignty of the people. The issue is, first and foremost, the primacy of the Gospel over the church—the freedom, sovereignty, and ultimate binding nature of the Gospel as God's word of grace.

212. The Reformation conviction is that this Gospel, even if proclaimed in the church and by ministers called to serve "in Christ's place and stead,"[284] cannot without reservations and with no questions asked be consigned to an ecclesiastical

ministry to preserve. For insofar as this ministry, like every church institution, is carried out by human beings who are capable of error, not only would the danger of error be increased thereby, because the error would then take on binding force in the church, but also and above all a sovereignty and ultimate binding force would attach to the decisions and stipulations of this ministry and its representatives which are reserved for the Gospel alone. That is why what people teach in the church must ultimately be measured against the Gospel alone. Only then is it certain that the church relies on God's word and not human words.

213. For the sake of the Gospel, the Reformation doctrine of justification therefore requires that the church's ministry and its decisions should as a matter of principle be open to examination by the whole people of God. As a matter of principle justification debars them from insulating themselves from such an examination. In regard to its decisions the teaching ministry must permit "question or censure,"[285] as the Apology says, by the church as a whole, for which the promise of abiding in the truth holds good, and which is the people of God, the body of Christ, and the temple of the Holy Spirit. Otherwise it seems doubtful from a Reformation perspective that the teaching ministry serves the word of God and is not above it.[286]

214. The binding nature of church teaching is not canceled out by this but is made subject to a reservation. In the Reformation view the teaching of the church or of a teaching ministry must take place precisely in this dialectical tension between the claim of its binding nature and the reservation relating to that binding nature. This will demonstrate that the teaching ministry respects the independence of the Gospel and its ultimate binding nature, which is nothing other than the independence and binding nature of the grace of God. In this, church teaching as such demonstrates its own conformity with the Gospel.

215. It is thus clear that the doctrine of justification certainly does not lead Reformation thinking into a depreciation, far less a rejection, of binding church teaching and of a teaching ministry of the church. The churches of the Lutheran Reformation themselves carry out binding teaching and themselves have organs or ministries for the church's teaching. They even have displayed the willingness and indeed the "deep desire"[287] to recognize for themselves the church's teaching ministry in its traditional form.[288] What they insist on is solely that this teaching and this teaching ministry be in accordance with the Gospel in their self-understanding and exercise and do not contradict the Gospel.[289]

216. The problem of a tension between the claim to and the reservation related to binding teaching arises for Catholics too. Admittedly from their point of view the matter has a different weight and value. According to Catholic teaching the church as a whole is "the pillar and bulwark of the truth" (1 Tm 3:15). "The body of the faithful as a whole . . . cannot err in matters of belief" as it receives the

"supernatural sense of the faith" from the Spirit of truth.[290] Within the people of God, the bishops in communion with the bishop of Rome are the authentic teachers of the faith by virtue of their episcopal ordination as successors in the presiding ministry of a local church.[291] But their teaching office remains anchored in the life of faith of the whole people of God, who share in the discovery of and in witnessing to the truth. Thus "the vigilance with regard to the apostolicity of the faith that belongs to the bishop's duty, is bound up with the responsibility for the faith borne by the whole Christian people,"[292] and thus bishops exercise their teaching ministry "only in community with the whole church" and "in a many-sided exchange regarding faith with believers, priests, and theologians,"[293] for the whole "People of God shares also in Christ's prophetic office."[294]

217. "While it is possible for the individual bishop to fall away from the continuity of the apostolic faith . . . Catholic tradition holds that the episcopate as a whole is nevertheless kept firm in the truth of the gospel."[295] The bishops have to watch over the continuity of the apostolic faith, while being bound to the canon of Scripture and the apostolic tradition: the "teaching office is not above the word of God but serves it, teaching only what has been handed on."[296] It has the task of listening reverently to the word of God, preserving it in holiness, and expounding it faithfully.[297] The same is valid for the priest. "The task of priests is not to teach their own wisdom but God's Word."[298] This submission to the canon of the Scriptures and the apostolic tradition is the basic criterion for the response of faith, especially in borderline cases, so that according to Augustine and Thomas Aquinas it can be said: "One must deny one's consent even to bishops when it happens that they err and speak in a manner that contradicts the canonical texts."[299]

218. The church can make infallible decisions on doctrine, as happened in the early church at ecumenical councils.[300] These decisions explicate the revelation that has taken place once for all, and are made in harmony with the faith of the entire people of God, certainly not against them.[301] These decisions, when made under specific conditions, are valid of themselves and do not need any subsequent formal approval, though they of course "depend on extensive reception in order to have living power and spiritual fruitfulness in the church."[302]

219. Decisions of the church's teaching ministry are indeed binding—as dogma, even definitively binding. But the church knows it is the pilgrim people of God on the march. Hence recognition of the truth in theology and dogma is fragmentary and often one-sided, since it is frequently a response to errors that have taken an extreme position. Dogma is historically conditioned and therefore open to corrections, deeper understanding, and "new expressions."[303] The church nevertheless believes that the Holy Spirit guides it into the truth and preserves it from error when solemn definitions are made. When the teaching ministry appeals to the Holy Spirit (cf. Acts 15:28), this does not run counter to the criterion of the doc-

trine of justification. For the question here is not about conditions for salvation, but the criteria of our knowledge of revelation. The message of the radical gratuity of the gift of salvation, and of the unconditionality of the reception of salvation, is not obscured by the institution of councils, because their role is to witness to the truth of revelation and to protect this truth against erroneous opinions.

220. The Catholic understanding of faith holds that the Gospel is interpreted by the consensus of a council and this can therefore in special cases bring forth a definitively binding statement (a dogma in the Catholic view) on which members of the church can rely as an expression of the Gospel. Even if faith does not rest in the formulation but in the reality, that is, in the truth of the Gospel, it nevertheless needs the formulation in which the Gospel is expressed, the wording of which must be very carefully heeded in a critical situation (cf. 1 Cor 15:2; 4:6).

221. On the other hand, also in Catholic understanding, a dogmatic statement is not simply a given about which no further questions may be asked. "The tradition which comes from the apostles develops in the Church with the help of the Holy Spirit. For there is a growth in the understanding of the realities and the words which have been handed down. This happens through the contemplation and study made by believers, who treasure these things in their hearts . . . , through the intimate understanding of spiritual things they experience, and through the preaching of those who have received through episcopal succession the sure gift of truth. For, as the centuries succeed one another, the Church constantly moves forward toward the fullness of divine truth until the words of God reach their complete fulfillment in her."[304] Looked at in this light, the transmission of faith, official doctrinal proclamation, and the history of dogma are complex hermeneutical processes in which all the faithful, members of the teaching office, and theologians are participants even if in differing ways.[305] Abiding in the truth of the Gospel does not exclude the painstaking quest for the truth. It is not carried out alone by one component of the church but is due in the last analysis to the support and guidance of God's Spirit who exercises control through the fellowship of the whole people of God.

222. This comparison of the Lutheran and Catholic understanding of binding doctrines shows, despite all the different emphases and a fair number of critical questions, that binding teaching need not contradict justification. Catholics and Lutherans agree that binding teaching illuminates the truth of the Gospel, on which truth alone members of the church may and should rely in living and dying and which alone sustains their faith. They agree that, for example, in the councils that confess the faith in the Trinity and in Jesus Christ the truth of the Gospel is explicated. There are considerable differences, to be sure, as to how the truth of the Gospel is affirmed. Even if Catholics cannot in the same way appropriate the Lutheran dialectic in which the claim to a binding character for doctrine contrasts with a reservation as to that binding character, and if they ask whether there is not

a danger here that the opinion of individuals will be identified with the truth of the Gospel, they too are aware of the provisional nature of human knowledge of the truth, even in the ultimately binding decisions of the teaching office. If Lutherans pose the above-mentioned question concerning the Catholic form of binding teaching, they are nevertheless faced with the task of rethinking "the problem of the teaching office and the teaching authority" and of reflecting especially on the council as an institution, that is, as "the locus for the expression of the consensus of all Christendom,"[306] and of its importance to which the Reformation always firmly held.[307]

4.5.3.4. Church Jurisdiction and the Jurisdictional Function of the Ministry

223. The questions of doctrine and the church's teaching office, and of ecclesial jurisdiction and the jurisdictional function of the ministry are very close to each other and show clear parallels. In part the two questions even overlap, insofar as decisions of the church's teaching ministry are juridically binding.

224. Catholics and Lutherans together say that God, who establishes institutional entities in his grace and faithfulness, and who uses them to preserve the church in the truth of the Gospel, also uses church law and legal ordinances for this purpose.

225. Thus, Lutherans cannot say that Gospel and church on one side and ecclesiastical law on the other are mutually exclusive or that the doctrine of justification prohibits the development of binding ecclesial law. The very fact that in Reformation lands legally binding church orders (Kirchenordnungen) came into being at a very early date, and that in their doctrinal sections (corpora doctrinae), which were replaced later by the confessions, the doctrine of justification has a central place, shows that justification itself participated in the juridically binding nature of these church orders. Constitutions of today's Lutheran churches indicate this also.

226. When, however, it comes to the understanding of church law and its binding nature; when the question is raised to what extent and in what sense the church, and especially the ordained ministry, have the authority to make legally binding decisions and regulations; and when it is asked to what extent such decisions, once taken, can be critically examined on the basis of the Gospel—then a difference between Catholics and Lutherans becomes evident, just as it does with the question of doctrine and the teaching ministry.

227. This difference, however, is to be seen in the context of common basic convictions which have already been highlighted in the Lutheran–Roman Catholic dialogue.

- In regard to church law as a whole the principle holds good for both churches that "the salvation of souls . . . must always be the supreme law."[308]
- That in turn means that according to common conviction all church law and all development of ecclesial law are related and subordinated to the service of the Gospel. "The church is permanently bound in its ordering to the gospel which is irrevocably prior to it"; the Gospel is "the criterion for a concrete church order."[309]
- Even where, in line with the traditional view and terminology, the character of "divine law," a *ius divinum*, is attributed to church legislation, it has a historical shape and form, and it is therefore both possible and necessary to renew and reshape it.[310]

228. These common basic convictions show that church law, notwithstanding its claim to be binding, is by its nature and by definition subject to a reservation as to its binding nature. This is of crucial importance, because it is precisely the critical demand raised by the doctrine of justification regarding all church legislation and so also to all church legal authorities. No church legislation can claim to be binding in such a manner that it is necessary for salvation, thus equaling the ultimate binding nature of the Gospel, which is itself the binding nature of grace. Insofar as this demand is not met, church law becomes subject to criticism from the doctrine of justification. On this our churches agree in principle. It is important that this agreement should also be maintained in church practice; but whether, how, and to what extent this happens in our churches must be verified from one case to another.

229. These basic convictions apply also to the question to what extent and in what way a jurisdictional function is appropriate to the ordained ministry. The Reformation too can in fact attribute a jurisdictional function to the ministry, but in so doing it emphasizes the primacy of the Gospel and, essentially, those limitations which are recognized in common by Catholics and Lutherans.[311]

230. This is the overall intention of Article 28 of the Augsburg Confession.[312] It develops a view of the power (*potestas*) of the bishops, which unequivocally includes jurisdictional functions. At the same time it seeks to guarantee the harmony of this ministry and its exercise with the Gospel, doing this essentially in the framework of the basic convictions outlined above.

231. The proper tasks of the bishop, which appertain basically to the pastor also—because of a theological lack of clarity in the differentiation between bishop and pastor—are, according to CA 28, "to preach the Gospel," "to forgive . . . sins," "to administer . . . the sacraments," to "condemn doctrine that is contrary to the Gospel," and to "exclude from the Christian community."[313] They can be summed

up in the terms "power of keys,"[314] "the office of preaching,"[315] or "jurisdiction."[316] These show that according to the Reformation view, the ministry as a pastoral office includes jurisdictional functions, certainly in such a way that these functions do not become autonomous but remain bound up in the total pastoral responsibility of the ministry and so preserve their pastoral character.

232. Over against these functions of the ordained ministry which are "necessary for salvation"[317] and are in this sense by "divine right"[318] but which must be exercised "not by human power but by God's word alone,"[319] the duty of the congregation to obey holds good.[320] It is an obligation, however, which is paired with the duty to refuse obedience should the ministry violate the Gospel in its exercise of these functions.[321]

233. Alongside this the bishops can undoubtedly exercise yet another kind of jurisdiction,[322] from marriage legislation through ceremonial laws and regulations for worship to decrees for fasts and so on. Such regulations in the last analysis serve the orderly common life of the congregation,[323] and they may be changed, replaced, and even abrogated.[324] Here too indeed a duty on the part of the congregation to obey holds good,[325] but it is fundamentally different in kind. It does not end only where these regulations of the ministry which relate to church law violate the Gospel in their content. It already ends where they are imposed as "necessary for salvation"[326] and binding on the conscience,[327] and here changes into a duty to refuse obedience. For these regulations are already contradicting the "teaching concerning faith," that is, of the "righteousness of faith"[328] and "Christian liberty," i.e., the freedom of the Christian from the law,[329] and they thereby become subject to criticism by the doctrine of justification.

234. It is a Lutheran conviction that there is a legitimate jurisdictional function of the ordained ministry in this context which is defined by the doctrine of justification.

235. According to the Catholic view the above-mentioned common basic convictions also mark the jurisdictional authority of the episcopate.[330] The exercise of law and canonical practice is always to be seen in its pastoral intention and within a concern for the salvation of humanity.

236. The authority and power of bishops is part of their being shepherds and presiders over the church. It is founded in the divine mission that Christ entrusted to the apostles,[331] to hand on the Gospel which "is for all time the source of all life for the Church."[332] This power also includes the right and the duty to regulate everything in the church which pertains to the ordering of worship and of the apostolate. But it should be carried out in accordance with the example of the Good Shepherd, Jesus Christ.[333] Bishops exercise their pastoral and jurisdictional authority in the name of Christ and personally, i.e., as their special, regular, and direct power, in communion with the bishop of Rome.[334] In this connection they have

always to take into account the fact that every ordering of the church develops from a permanently given basis, namely, that the church is a community of faith and sacraments. The proclamation of the word of God and the celebration of the sacraments constitute the church and determine its nature, because the Lord of the church effects salvation in them. The binding force of a church law therefore presupposes the conviction that the church is a faith and sacramental community. The aim of the law and canons of the church is to serve the church's order and to express its unity while contributing to the good order of the care of souls. Thus church order, with law and canons, arises out of the nature of the church as a faith and sacramental community.

237. Catholic teaching insists that no one may be coerced into believing nor be "forced to act in a manner contrary to his own beliefs" in religious matters.[335] Even the call of God to serve him in spirit and in truth, though it binds human beings in their conscience to obey that call, does not coerce them into doing so.[336] And while church norms and laws can indeed be binding in conscience on Christians as members of the church, they cannot "release a member of the church from his direct responsibility to God."[337]

238. The Catholic–Lutheran dialogue has stressed that "the church is permanently bound in its ordering to the gospel which is irrevocably prior to it. . . . The gospel, however, can be the criterion for a concrete church order only in living relationship with contemporary social realities. Just as there is a legitimate explication of the gospel in dogmas and confessions, so there also exists a historical actualization of law in the church."[338] In this sense the Codex Iuris Canonici of 1983 also attempts a reordering of Catholic church legislation in the light of Vatican II, in order to correspond better with the church's mission of salvation. In particular the ecclesiological guidelines of the dogmatic constitution Lumen Gentium and the pastoral constitution Gaudium et Spes constitute the hermeneutical framework for this. "Over the course of time, the Catholic Church has been wont to revise and renew the laws of its sacred discipline so that, maintaining always fidelity to the Divine Founder, these laws may be truly in accord with the salvific mission entrusted to the Church. . . . This new Code can be viewed as a great effort to translate the conciliar ecclesiological teaching into canonical terms."[339]

239. Catholic theology draws attention to the fact that it is God's saving activity, not ecclesiastical lawgivers with their legislation, which establishes the fellowship of believers and therefore brings people into a new social situation with obligations: that of the believers' fellowship with each other and with God. This new social situation is expressed by the ecclesiastical lawgiver in legal ordinances. The point of ecclesiastical legislation is to help believers perceive and fulfill their rights and duties as well as possible in the light of the faith, and thus to contribute to the realization of the saving mission of the church.

240. Because church legislation can be seen as a normative function of the tradition of faith, and because the binding force of church laws is ultimately founded in the binding force of faith, church law differs from every other law. Because of the binding force of faith, the church legislator addresses the religious conscience, and thus ecclesiastically binding norms presuppose a free decision of faith. Consequently, it is possible for a discrepancy and thus a case of conflict to arise between the obligation of a church law and the conscience of the individual Christian believer. Catholic theology, of course, does not generally speak of a "reservation" regarding the binding character of church laws, but in individual cases it does take into account the possibility of conflict. The salvation of human beings counts as supreme law. If in a concrete instance the application of the existing canons may prejudice or even endanger a person's salvation, that constitutes a case in which Christian believers who are quite willing to obey church law and have also shown this in practical living may, and even must, nevertheless come to a decision which is against the letter of the law, because on the basis of faith they see themselves entitled or even obliged to make that decision as a matter of conscience.

241. Despite different ecclesiological starting points and a different frame of reference, fundamental common elements and correspondences do exist between Lutherans and Catholics on the matter of the doctrines of justification and salvation and their relation to the jurisdictional authority of the ordained ministry. The task of church laws is to serve the salvation of the individual.

242. We may sum up by saying that in regard to all the problem areas discussed here (4.5.3.1-4), we may not speak of a fundamental conflict or even opposition between justification and the church. This is quite compatible with the role of the doctrine of justification in seeing that all the church's institutions, in their self-understanding and exercise, contribute to the church's abiding in the truth of the Gospel which alone in the Holy Spirit creates and sustains the church.

5. The Mission and Consummation of the Church

243. As the recipient and mediator of salvation the church has its enduring foundation in the triune God. Its ultimate goal is consummation in God's kingdom. God will create his eternal and universal kingdom of righteousness, peace, and love, and himself will bring about his own definitive reign and salvation. God has chosen and established the church by grace in this age and for this age, so that it may proclaim his Gospel to all creatures (cf. Mk 16:15), worship him unceasingly, and praise him for the "riches of his grace" (cf. Eph 1:3-14), and in witness and service make known to all people his loving kindness and goodness of heart (cf. Ti 3:4-6), until he himself dwells ultimately in our midst and makes all things new (cf. Rv 21:3-5). Thus, while in this age the church does indeed have its responsible missionary task

of proclaiming the Gospel (cf. 1 Cor 9:16) and serving God and humanity (cf. Mt 22:37-40), it also goes on its way through this age in the certainty of God's mercy and grace (cf. 2 Cor 12:9) and in joyful confidence in the return of the Lord. Jesus has said to us, "But strive first for the kingdom of God and his righteousness, and all these things will be given to you as well" (Mt 6:33); and he has taught us to pray, saying "Father, hallowed be your name. Your kingdom come" (Lk 11:2).

5.1. The Church's Mission

244. Everywhere Lutherans and Catholics find themselves repeatedly confronted by the same challenges—challenges which vary greatly in the different regions of the world and can also change very quickly (5.1.1). This leads Lutherans and Catholics to address these challenges together and to reflect afresh on the mission of the church in the light of the message of justification (5.1.2). We are agreed that our missionary task represents a true if limited participation in God's own realization of his plans as Creator, Redeemer, and Sanctifier (5.1.3). Regarding the most important elements in our task as churches—evangelization, worship, and service to humanity—no essential differences divide us (5.1.4). Such a broad consensus demands of our churches that we intensify and expand their field of practical cooperation on every level in serving the Gospel of Jesus Christ.

5.1.1. Common Challenges to Our Churches in a Constantly Changing World

245. The challenges facing the churches throughout the world are often quite varied, corresponding to the different regional contexts; but in a given place they confront Lutherans and Catholics and in the same way. In South Africa racist thinking has not stopped at the doors of just one church. In other countries of Africa and in parts of Asia, Christians of all confessions see themselves threatened or even persecuted by a militant Islam. In the southeast part of Europe, the churches face the challenge to overcome extreme ethnic and national allegiances in a situation of flagrant violation of human dignity up to genocide. In the countries of Latin America, the incredible differences between poor and rich cut across all the churches and confessions. Religious alienation in the secular context of many European countries never affects only one church by itself.

246. Many problems arise not only in the one or the other context; they confront our churches worldwide: the reawakening of nationalism, extreme rightist tendencies, increasing readiness for violence, and violence itself. These and similar common challenges make the churches look afresh at their missionary task and confront them with the inescapable question, how far they can and really want to make common cause in the face of such challenges. An example of a common quest for

answers to today's questions in the light of the Gospel and of the various church traditions is the conciliar or ecumenical "process of mutual commitment to justice, peace, and the integrity of creation" to which the Assembly of the World Council of Churches in Vancouver called in 1983. That led to the European Ecumenical Assembly "Peace with Justice" in Basel in 1989 and the "World Convocation" in Seoul in 1990, as well as to activities in many countries and regions of the world.

247. How quickly contexts can change has become very clear in those countries of Eastern Europe that have in virtually bloodless revolutions liberated themselves from many years of one party's and ideology's position of supremacy. The complexity of human living conditions and the speed of social change in our age call for the churches to test constantly the challenges of the changing contexts in the light of the Gospel in order to fulfill their task of mission authentically and contextually. The "signs of the times" are thus a call to the churches to reflect on their own origins and to make appropriate responses. Together they can contribute to perceiving present forms of the enduring struggle between faith and unbelief, sin and justice, the old and the new creation, correctly. In so doing the church must pay particular attention to how people today express both their distress and their hopes.

248. A church which has been called together by Christ to serve his work on earth will therefore always have to make an effort to realize to the utmost its missionary opportunities. The gospel message of grace and reconciliation compels those who have heard and accepted it to bring it to those who have not yet heard it or who have still had no proper opportunity to accept it. We must be alarmed when we think about those who have forgotten or estranged themselves from God's good news. Catholics and Lutherans together must accept their missionary calling as disciples of Jesus Christ. They must in common face the challenges of constant renewal in their churches under the influence of the Holy Spirit, so that they become common instruments for God's saving plan in ever more authentic ways.

249. In reflecting on the common challenges we are fully aware of the inner relationship between church and unity. The existing separations between Lutherans and Catholics are an obstacle for the one ministry of reconciliation to which we are called. Discord among Christians openly contradicts—as Vatican II says—"the will of Christ, provides a stumbling block to the world, and inflicts damage on the most holy cause of proclaiming the good news to every creature."[340] Therefore, the changing world in which we live offers a great challenge to our churches to pursue with new energy our ecumenical pilgrimage towards visible unity.

5.1.2. Reflection on the Church's Mission in Light of the Message of Justification

250. The late prophetic testimonies of Israel already give us an inkling of a fundamental dimension of our life and calling in the church. The Lord God showed

his saving power by gathering his people from the countries to which they had been dispersed and reestablishing them as his chosen servants (cf. Is 41:8-10; 43:1-7). But God's salvation is intended to reach all the ends of the earth (cf. Is 45:22f.), and one day all peoples are to flock into the city of the Lord (cf. Is 60:3f., 10, 14). At the same time those who belong to the people of Israel are described as "witnesses" who are to testify to the mercy of the Lord and the almighty work by which he realizes his plan of salvation (cf. Is 43:10, 12; 44:8). And finally some of those gathered by the Lord from different nations and tongues shall be sent to "the coast lands far away" in order to proclaim the glory of the Lord and bring new worshipers into the house of the Lord (cf. Is 66:18-21).[341]

251. What was already in evidence in Israel in the period after the Exile reached its consummation in Jesus Christ. As church we find our identity in him, especially in his own mission to preach the Gospel (cf. Mk 1:15; 1:28f.), to call not the righteous but sinners (cf. Mk 2:17), and to give his life as a ransom for many (cf. Mk 10:45). Jesus found his own task of mission outlined by the prophets, to "bring good news to the poor" and "to proclaim release to the captives" (Lk 4:18); and this has continuing relevance for us as his disciples, as a guideline for our own decisions and preferences in the service of love.

252. Jesus sent out his disciples to spread his message and healing ministry throughout Galilee (cf. Lk 9:1f.). Thus, at the same time he anticipated what was still to come. After his resurrection Jesus passed on his mission to the disciples, which still today is his legacy for Christians: "As the Father has sent me, so I send you" (Jn 20:21). In all the Gospels we find this commission of the risen Lord, which defines the church. "Go into all the world and proclaim the good news to the whole creation" (Mk 16:15). "Go therefore and make disciples of all nations, baptizing them in the name of the Father and of the Son and of the Holy Spirit, and teaching them to obey everything that I have commanded you" (Mt 28:19f.). "Thus it is written, that the Messiah is to suffer and to rise from the dead on the third day, and that repentance and forgiveness of sins is to be proclaimed in his name to all nations, beginning from Jerusalem" (Lk 24:46f.; cf. Acts 1:8).

253. As individuals and communities we know ourselves to be addressed by these words, and in obedience we accept the commission of our Lord to evangelize, to win new disciples, and to spread his healing presence throughout the world. The full significance of this commission passes our understanding. But we know that we live through him who died "to gather into one the dispersed children of God" (Jn 11:52). The church has received "fellowship . . . with the Father and with his Son Jesus Christ" (1 Jn 1:3), a fellowship which is meant for all people. As the church we are chosen and destined to go out into the world and bear fruit (cf. Jn 15:16) by spreading the knowledge of the one true God and Jesus Christ, who is eternal life (cf. Jn 17:3).

254. This call to service, so emphatically entrusted to us by the Lord, plainly exceeds our human striving and performance. The missionary sending of the church is at all times made possible by the power of the Holy Spirit, just as that power was given to the apostolic community for their witness to the risen Christ (cf. Acts 2:33-36; 3:12-15; 5:30-32; 13:1-4, 30-33). The church knows that it is filled with "power from on high" and that it is thus enabled to proclaim God's own conquest of human wickedness and his call to repentance (cf. Lk 24:47-49; Acts 2:23f.). In the spirit of Pentecost the church summons men and women to baptism and to new life in congregations of apostolic teaching, to the sharing of resources and gifts, to the breaking of bread and to prayer, praise, and intercession (cf. Acts 2:42-47; 4:32-35). Further evangelizing must still be carried out in our world, and our churches are confident that the Holy Spirit which was once poured out will continue to overcome human obstacles (cf. Acts 10:44-48), open hearts to the Gospel (cf. Acts 16:14), and create new congregations which are brought to life by the apostolic witness to Jesus Christ.

255. In faith we look back on these unrepeatable beginnings through which God has deeply impressed the missionary command on the nature of the church. We bear a treasure for the world. We stand together in that ministry of reconciliation which affects the whole world. Although as individuals and communities we are only earthen vessels, we are encouraged by the Spirit of God to accept the missionary task of speaking about him in whom we believe, Jesus Christ. We have the task of preparing the ways by which he can come to human beings as their reconciler, as God's own righteousness, and as the beginning of the new creation (cf. 2 Cor 5:17-21).

5.1.3. Mission as Sharing in God's Activity in the World

256. Catholics and Lutherans are agreed that the mission of the church to proclaim the Gospel and serve humanity is a true—even if also limited—sharing in God's activity in the world toward the realization of his plan as Creator, Redeemer, and Sanctifier. Reflection on the nature of our calling and authority as church has priority, and we are grateful that our dialogue enables us to do this together (5.1.3.1). But God's activity in the world is more comprehensive than what he carries out through the church. And the commission to Christians to let themselves be taken by him into service goes beyond the sphere of the church. Both our traditions have developed their own ideas about this: the Lutheran doctrine of God's two kingdoms and the Catholic doctrine of the rightful autonomy of creation,[342] of earthly spheres and realities (5.1.3.2).

5.1.3.1. Common Understanding

257. We have learned to understand the nature of our missionary task in the church by considering the activity of our God whom Holy Scripture reveals as Creator of heaven and earth, Redeemer of lost humanity, and Sanctifier of those who are brought to the Lord Jesus Christ. Through God's grace and call, the mission of the church shares in the continuing activity of Father, Son, and Holy Spirit. The church serves God's missionary activity in his world. Our ministry is therefore characterized by what we ascribe to the divine persons, i.e., their respective activities in creation, redemption, and sanctification. God graciously accepts our words and deeds by accomplishing his own plan to save and to bless.

258. In effectual and sustaining love God the Creator is devoted to everything he has created, and he shows his special love for human beings, whom he has made in his image (cf. Gn 1:26). Conversely, human beings are called to be God's fellow workers. As stewards they are entrusted with care for creation, and to them is committed the promotion of justice and well-being for all, for which purpose God has given them reason and conscience as well as specific institutional structures as instruments of his creative and sustaining love. We know of course from the teaching of the faith and from our own experience that this love has to operate in the context of the fallen world, which is characterized by sin. Justice and protective measures, which must be established here, can do no more than limit the effects of evil; they cannot uproot it.

259. The call and commitment to serve God's creative and sustaining will applies to everyone, both Christians and non-Christians. They are to strive together for peace, justice, and the integrity of creation. With the aid of their reason they must together look for practical ways and for a mode of organizing the institutional order which in their period of history will best serve to realize those purposes that God has appointed. Here church members have no greater competence than their non-Christian sisters and brothers who are made in the image of God; on the other hand there may be differences of opinion between them regarding the best way to achieve common objectives.

260. In relation to the creative and sustaining will of God, church members have no additional call to obedience and no special competence beyond that of their fellow humans. But in view of the obscuring of the creative and sustaining will of God in this sinful world, they have a special responsibility. Transformed by the Gospel, individual Christians—already a new creation in faith—have, like the church as a whole, a sharpened awareness of the standards and tasks that hold good for all human beings, and advocate them with unprejudiced hearts. Where necessary, vis-a-vis other persons as well as on their behalf, Christians are to step in both by admonition, advice, and action and by their own style of life in the cause of human dignity, fundamental human rights, and for freedom, justice, and the integrity of creation.

They are to alleviate distress and suffering. Thus, as individuals and as a church community they point to God-given values and standards of creation. At the same time they draw the attention of their fellow creatures to the limited objectives and possibilities of their social and political activities and preserve them from excessive ideological demands and from the temptation to totalitarianism.

261. God sent the Son as Redeemer in order to proclaim unconditional divine grace for sinful humanity. In the form of a servant, Jesus took sin upon himself in order to conquer it and make available to all believers a share of his righteousness and of new life and access to the Father in the Holy Spirit. Jesus Christ is the center of the missionary task of the church, which recognizes that he has commissioned it to bring his liberating message and grace to all peoples. Here lies the special mission of the church: to fulfill Jesus' commission, to missionize the world, and to build up communities of disciples who, transformed by faith already here on earth, radiate the firm hope of future fulfillment of the kingdom of God on the day of eschatological consummation. Church members rejoice in their regeneration through baptism, in which they have been anointed in Christ through the Holy Spirit to be members of a priestly, prophetic, and royal people. From baptism they receive their supreme dignity and their responsibility to serve the mission of Jesus Christ in dependence on him and conformed to him. This includes the priestly ministry of praise, self-sacrifice, and intercession. Part of this is the prophetic commission to expose evil, proclaim salvation, and also witness to the hope of glory in the midst of the afflictions of this age. Royal dignity is therein epitomized by living in Christian freedom from sin and from the contrarieties of the world (cf. Rom 8:31-39), and thus serving humanity fearlessly by word and deed, so that the dominion of sin will be overcome, creation will serve human welfare, and preferential love will be shown to our weak and ill-treated brothers and sisters.

262. God sent the Spirit into the world to bring people to faith by means of word and sacrament, to justify sinners, and to call together the church as a *koinonia*, in this way attaining the ends of the mission of the Son. Thus, in the midst of the old world the new creation is already raised up in holiness. In baptism, through the Spirit, men and women are made members of a community which acts as instrument of the Spirit's mission. Through proclamation in different forms, through actions which testify to the new world which has dawned—though still marked by ambiguity and limitation—and, where necessary, through acting representatively and critically for the present world, Christians implement this task and thus minister to the saving rule of God, which has already begun with the death and resurrection of Jesus and with the outpouring of the Holy Spirit.

5.1.3.2. Two Traditions

263. Lutherans and Catholics understand the mission of the church as sharing in God's activity in the world; they also know, however, that God's activity in the world goes beyond the sphere of the church. Even if bounds are set to the God-given task of the church, Christians are aware that they must serve God in all areas of society. How this is understood and practiced is differently expressed in our two traditions.

5.1.3.2.1. The Lutheran Teaching on the Two Kingdoms

264. In order to do justice theologically and pastorally to this situation, the Lutheran tradition developed the doctrine of the "two kingdoms (realms)" of God. This is not a concrete socioethical program, but it does define an ethical locus for Christians who already live their lives as citizens of the new world while also continuing as citizens of the old world. How can Christians, whose rule of life is the Sermon on the Mount, hold responsible positions in politics, administration of justice, law enforcement, economy, or the military? The two kingdoms cannot be equated with the distinction between the church and the world; they are also to be found within the church, because the church is a *corpus permixtum* and every Christian is still a sinner.

265. The real-life context of Christians is the spiritual kingdom of the *communio sanctorum*. Here Christ is head of a spiritual realm, as through word and sacrament in the Holy Spirit he brings people to faith and preserves that faith.[343] The behavior appropriate to this kingdom is the radical love that corresponds to the Sermon on the Mount,[344] a love that arises out of faith and is made possible by the Holy Spirit: unreserved readiness to serve, waiving one's own rights, nonresistance, nonviolence in following Jesus Christ and in his strength. Such love makes visible already in the present world the new world desired by God.

266. Because this love is the fruit of the heart transformed in faith, it cannot be elevated to the status of law nor advocated as a general standard for social life. Indeed, in the context of the fallen world that would mean giving evil the upper hand and handing over human society to the selfishness and arbitrariness of the powerful.[345] Where faith does not prevail, that is, among non-Christians but also in regard to Christians themselves, since they too remain sinners, it is necessary to have a social order which checks evil, and which despite evil guarantees the best possible life. This will be an order which cares for the protection of life and limb and for civic justice.[346] Its instruments are not the word and the Spirit but the law[347] and institutions which are equipped with power and make use of force where there is no other possibility.[348] The social order does not operate through the transformation of hearts but by imposing obligations and calling for obedience, and in the last resort through compulsion.

267. Although this ordering of life does not correspond to God's real intentions for humanity, it is nevertheless also an instrument of his love, as his "worldly kingdom," through which he preserves and forms creation even in its fallen state. Such ordering of life must therefore be affirmed as "instituted and ordained by God for the sake of good order."[349] As distinct from the spiritual kingdom, the instruments of the worldly kingdom are not contingently and particularly effectual; rather, its standards are embedded in the consciences of human beings[350] and established in the institutions of human society.[351] That is to say, they can and must claim universality and prove themselves in human society. Consequently, the actual structuring of political and social life is entrusted in great measure to human reason and expertise, whether of Christians or non-Christians,[352] and may vary according to context and historical perspective.[353] All structuring possibilities aim at and are limited by the contribution they make to the preservation and just ordering of the world.

268. The two kingdoms have to be strictly distinguished with regard to their goals, instruments, and methods.[354] If this does not happen, either the spiritual kingdom is robbed of its uniqueness, as the renewed heart and corresponding ethic of radical love and renunciation are reduced to conventional morality and sociopolitical justice, or conversely the worldly kingdom is ruined. It is ruined because society, thinking its members are already wholly good, dispenses with erecting the barriers of external order, laws, and needed institutional force against evil and thus leaves the field open for it, or because the attempt is made to influence hearts and achieve unselfish, idealistic acts—by whatever criteria one measures these—with the use of compulsion.

269. Nevertheless, distinguishing between the two kingdoms does not mean separating them. They cannot be parceled out between two separate groups, as if the renewed heart and its corresponding ethic were something for only a few, while the mass of Christians could do without them. Rather, they are given with faith itself and are common to all Christians.[355] But all Christians continue to be also citizens of the unredeemed world and as creatures of God together with all other human beings, they have the responsibility of caring for its preservation and organization and of committing themselves to serving God's worldly kingdom. Thus Christians, according to their respective station in society (one's "calling"), will also hold and exercise power, help in promoting and enforcing law, and put down violence—even by the use of disciplined opposing force—instead of renouncing power, law, and force in the spirit of the Sermon on the Mount.[356] Whether they act in the one way or the other depends on whether they are acting on their own behalf or for others. Here the spheres frequently overlap so that Christians can decide which principle they must follow according to their own consciences only. But they can be certain that even where because of societal responsibility they exercise or appeal to power, law, and force they are not contradicting God's will but serving it.[357] Indeed they

have to regard this service as a duty in the practical and disinterested fulfillment of which they demonstrate their Christianity in the world.[358] In such activity, even if they do nothing other than is done by all persons of goodwill, they will do it differently, by bringing into evidence something of the love and readiness to forgive which is a special characteristic of Christian faith.[359] But they will also be aware of working to preserve and order a world in which evil still lurks and sets limits to the good that may be achieved.

270. In contrast to the sixteenth century, the doctrine of the two kingdoms requires modification in many respects today. For historical changes and the unsettled nature of social structures, with the resultant opportunities and difficulties, are more obvious today than before. Also the fact that justice and the ironing out of social inequalities—not only among individuals but also among groups, nations, and continents—is perceived in an entirely different way today, as memoranda and other church statements of the last few decades show. But all this does not change anything in the fundamental assertions of the doctrine of God's two kingdoms itself. It continues to show the way by making it possible to maintain the eschatological existence of believers but at the same time to assert their place and responsibility for the world, which remains God's creation but is still unredeemed, without the two spheres being confused or separated.

271. Thus, on the one hand, the doctrine of the two kingdoms secures that the life of faith has another foundation, other instruments, and another shape than sociopolitical life in the world. Neither are worldly authorities entitled to intervene in spiritual concerns, nor can faith and its ethical fruits become worldly themselves by becoming a social program, whether utopian or of a clerical and theocratic nature. And on the other hand, it makes clear that the conservation and ordering of the world, even in its unredeemed state, are subordinate to the will of God, but that this is to be worked out in ways which are not specifically Christian and comprehensible only to believers, but which claim to apply for everyone. Thus, the doctrine of the two kingdoms makes it possible to allow autonomy in sociopolitical actions over against the Gospel and to endorse the secular character of the ordinances of the world—though this autonomy may not set itself against God's purpose of conserving and properly ordering the world. Those who are aware that ethical standards are based in the will of God must be especially vigilant in insisting on this, in view of the manifold obscuring elements in the life of society. The doctrine of the two kingdoms imposes on Christians a life and activity in tension between two systems of reference, but this is the same tension present in the very nature of the life of faith, that of being in the world and not of the world. This tension will be resolved only with the full and definitive dawn of the kingdom of God.

5.1.3.2.2. The Roman Catholic Teaching on the "Proper Autonomy of
Earthly Affairs"

272. Catholic teaching also recognizes the limits of the church's task, especially by its acknowledgment of the proper "autonomy of earthly affairs."[360] This
autonomy does not leave human activities in the political and economic fields to
arbitrary decisions. But neither can these fields be directly explained or shaped by
the biblical revelation and the Gospel of Jesus Christ. The Catholic view of autonomy rests on the perception that the Creator has endowed all his creatures with
their own specific nature and inner development, with their own structures, values,
and modes of action. Human experience studies and rational reflections are entitled
to explore creation. Moreover, the values which permeate this world impinge on the
human moral conscience on all levels.

273. Reason and conscience operate together in molding the order of this
world. Nevertheless, Christian faith places the realities of the world in a new horizon of meaning and integrates them there. Christian values, such as the dignity and
freedom of each person as well as mercy, kindness, and gentleness in social legislation, are to be integrated into responsibility for the world. Therefore, faith makes it
possible to challenge critically destructive tendencies in society, politics, economics,
and culture, and to strengthen the positive impulses of a secular ethic.

274. "Christ, to be sure, gave His Church no proper mission in the political,
economic or social order. The purpose which he set before her is a religious one."[361]
He commissioned his disciples to spread his Gospel, build up congregations, promote holiness, and guide people to eternal life. These religious priorities free the
church from any essential ties with a particular form of human culture or a specific
political, economic, or social system. The church lays claim to no power over the
secular sphere, no matter how much it strives for the freedom to operate in society,
to serve selflessly, and to testify to Christ's message. Catholic doctrine addresses
Christians as "citizens of two cities" and reminds them of the profusion of their
professional, political, and social duties.[362] Calling people to action in this world is
in fact stimulated by Christ's call to conversion and newness of life. Christian formation stimulates new energies and a new sensitivity, which are discernibly advantageous to the secular world. It promotes, for example, a vision of unity which
transcends all differences of nationality, race, and class, a detachment from possessions as the standard of personal dignity, and a dynamic of love for humanity for
whose salvation Christ died.

275. On the basis of new social, political, and economic challenges in the last
two centuries, challenges which did not previously exist, Catholic theology has
developed a social teaching which to a great extent has been received magisterially.
This teaching of the popes, the Second Vatican Council, and numerous bishops'
conferences is primarily directed towards molding the moral conscience of church

members but is also concerned with persuading all people of goodwill and thus influencing public order. This socioethical doctrine has developed, and will go on developing, in the effort to keep pace with the rapid changes in the modern industrial world and the gap between North and South. By nature it is a doctrine regarding human beings in society, human dignity, human rights, and the moral values that must determine social action. Pope and bishops have not flinched from denouncing systematic exploitation and injustice. The same socioethical doctrine has however refrained from offering ready-made models and promoting the implementation of technical solutions for problems. It has left open the field where rational research and personal values converge as the basis of options for the creation of a social order. It is even officially acknowledged that within the church there can be differences of opinion between honest and faithful Catholics in regard to their individual modes of procedure in the promotion of the common good.[363]

276. This comprehensive body of social teaching, whose individual statements are issued with different degrees of binding character, represents an aspect in contemporary Catholic life and teaching to which, for the theological reasons explained above, nothing in the Lutheran churches corresponds. At a future stage in our dialogue this aspect of asymmetry between our churches must be dealt with in regard to socioethical questions and, more fundamentally, in relation to the extent of the church's competence in moral questions.

5.1.4. The Fundamental Components of the Church's Missionary Task

277. Lutherans and Catholics are agreed on the priority of the task of evangelizing the world (5.1.4.1), on the central significance of proclaiming and celebrating the grace of God in worship (5.1.4.2), and on the commandment to serve humanity as a whole (5.1.4.3). They also agree that "*martyria, leitourgia, and diakonia* (witness, worship, and service to the neighbor) are tasks entrusted to the whole people of God."[364]

5.1.4.1. Commission to Evangelize

278. The essential task which our Lord gave his church is the proclamation of the good news of his saving death and his resurrection. As Christians we share in the Lord's missionary commission and, like the apostolic preaching on the day of Pentecost, our message too contains the invitation to baptism and to sharing in the "promised Spirit of new life and freedom" (cf. Acts 2:38). We are convinced that evangelism brings with it God's unique gift of grace to the world, and we agree with the words of the Apostle Paul, ". . . woe to me if I do not proclaim the gospel!" (1 Cor 9:16).

279. Evangelism lays claim to the whole person for witness to Christ; it demands the witness of a life which corresponds to the Gospel in faith, hope, and

love. Here it is not simply a question of the work done by those sent out as missionaries but also of the witness of each individual Christian and each Christian community. Although the specific objective of evangelizing is bringing people to faith and not creating a new order of society, it nevertheless has a profound effect on the life of society. For Christians today insist on the strict observation of freedom of religion and freedom of conscience, and in common with all people of goodwill, they are especially watchful and zealous in supporting the conservation and humane structuring of the world, and enter the lists against discrimination, oppression, and injustice. By the way in which they do these things, they make evident the love and forgiveness of God that has been bestowed on them.

280. We recognize that it is particularly necessary nowadays to enter into interreligious dialogue, paying respectful heed to those who belong to other religious traditions. It is imperative to respect the convictions of others in order to create a basis for peace in societies where Christians live as neighbors of adherents of other great world religions. We keep ourselves open to the idea that God can be active in hidden ways in non-Christian religions too, and we therefore enter into dialogue with other religions in a trusting readiness to learn. Beyond such dialogue, however, we also see ourselves as obliged by the Gospel to bear credible witness to the grace and truth which have been given to the whole world in a unique way in Jesus Christ, and we hope that this witness encounters faith.

281. In our day a special task is the reevangelizing of traditionally Christian areas where large numbers of the baptized have lapsed into mere nominal Christianity. We are thus commissioned to invite our contemporaries to recognize afresh the glory of God that shines in the face of Jesus and to accept the message of reconciliation (cf. 2 Cor 4:6; 5:19). A precious treasure has been entrusted to us which we should pass on to all people.

5.1.4.2. Centrality of Worship

282. Our dialogue has already expressed a common understanding of our calling to join in the great eucharistic doxology in the presence of our Lord: "through him, with him, in him, in the unity of the Holy Spirit, all honor and glory is yours, almighty Father, now and forever." For our unity with Christ leads to the everlasting Father through the power of the Holy Spirit in preaching, thanksgiving and praise, intercession, and self-offering.[365] Worship is thus central to our mission as a church, for in it we celebrate our justification in Christ and proclaim as a priestly people the marvelous works of him who has called us "out of darkness into his marvelous light" (1 Pt 2:9).

283. Common worship is by its nature not a means to any other end. Worship is rather the most important matrix of faith and an essential expression of it, for in worship our faith is induced and nourished through the proclamation of the Gospel

of Christ and our common sharing with others in the same Gospel and the same sacramental life. In worship we are linked with Christians of every age right back to the apostles and joyfully celebrate the grace of communion with the Father and his Son Jesus Christ (cf. 1 Jn 1:3). Worship may therefore never be made to serve an ideology or be reduced to an educational tool. Services of worship are intended to attract and invite people and to radiate an aura of the kindness and benevolence of our God, who has redeemed us because of his mercy (cf. Ti 3:4-6).

284. In worship our church community, the church at a particular time and in a particular place, becomes concrete and visible in a special way. The annual round of the liturgical seasons and feasts, with their climaxes at Christmas, Good Friday/Easter, and Pentecost, deepens our ecclesial identity as the people of God, the body of Christ, and the temple of the Holy Spirit. When we gather together to confess our sins, to hear God's saving word, to remember his great deeds, and to sing hymns and songs, to intercede for a blessing on everyone, and to celebrate the eucharistic meal, we are a people of faith in the most pregnant sense. This is our proper task as church, and we accept it as such with a sense of responsibility to offer our Creator and Redeemer adoration and praise in the name of all creatures, through our Lord Christ. In worship the existence of the church as an existence for others becomes particularly clear in "supplications, prayers, intercessions, and thanksgivings" (1 Tm 2:1f.) for all people, particularly also for those responsible in government, which the congregation assembled in the Holy Spirit in the presence of Christ offers to God. Here too we must remain aware that as justified sinners we ourselves are constantly in need of repentance and conversion. Since we have been called to such a ministry of reconciliation, we lament all the more the scandal of separation and the divisions among us, which are an obstacle to the full expression of the unity of the one priestly people that comes before God to praise him and be renewed through his word and Spirit.

5.1.4.3. Responsibility of the Church and the Service of Humanity

285. Our task must bear the deep imprint of Jesus' view: "For the Son of Man came not to be served but to serve, and to give his life as a ransom for many" (Mk 10:45). In following him, who in "the form of a slave" (Phil 2:7) became the mediator of the grace we have received, we have been called to an attitude and behavior like his. In obedience to him who affirmed the Creator's will for the world, we must contribute to its preservation and well-being. Thus as Christians and as communities, we are instruments of God in the service of mercy and justice in the world.

286. God's activity in the world is more comprehensive than what he does through the church. Fulfilling the commission of evangelism and worship is the service due to all humanity. By striving in common with all people of goodwill for healing, protection, and promotion of human dignity, for respectful and rational

handling of the resources of creation, for the consolidation of social unity, respect for social diversity, and for deepening of the general sense of responsibility, Christians are servants of the Creator's love for the world. Through their readiness to do without and their unselfish charity, they reflect the light of Christ even where his name is not confessed.

287. Together with their non-Christian brothers and sisters but also where necessary over against them, Christians serve humanity, championing human dignity and inalienable and inviolable human rights. Knowing that these are received by human beings from their Creator, the church interprets them as expressions of an obligation toward God and speaks to others of the transcendent dimension of their lives. If necessary, the church also must address specific political and social problems in the effort to raise consciousness regarding human distress and the demands of civil justice.

288. Christians serve human society by supporting structures in politics, law, administration, education, and economics which promote holistic human development. They contribute towards awareness and the strengthening of ties that bind all human beings in one family despite racial, cultural, national, and socioeconomic differences. They are eager to provide generous aid in situations of special distress, and they work on projects directed towards promoting long-term solutions to overcome misery.

289. The contribution which Christians make in all areas of social life—in politics, education and nurture, health, science, culture, and the mass media—is to work like yeast in dough. Such action, determined by competence and dedication, is an essential part of the task which Christians are to fulfill in order to stop the destructive flood of evil and to promote lives in accord with human dignity and reverence toward God.

5.2. The Eschatological Consummation of the Church

290. Reflection on the church as the recipient and mediator of salvation as well as on its mission would remain incomplete if its eschatological consummation were not also taken into account. It is precisely in the eschatological consummation of the church, as seen by the New Testament and expressed in the creed, that we see the convergence in God of all the paths of the church as God's pilgrim people. God himself definitively causes his rule and his salvation to prevail. Thus, the church's role as recipient and mediator of salvation once again becomes plain in terms of its end and consummation. In what follows, the eschatological consummation of the church will be considered from a twofold standpoint: first, in regard to the communion of saints (sanctorum communio) as it is confessed in the Apostles'

Creed (5.2.1), and second, in regard to the New Testament message of the kingdom and rule of God (5.2.2).

5.2.1. Sanctorum Communio

5.2.1.1. Common Faith

291. Lutherans and Catholics confess "the communion of saints" (sanctorum communionem) in the Apostles' Creed. According to Luther's Large Catechism this means the church: a "Christian congregation or assembly," "a holy Christian people." It is a communion of saints because it lives harmoniously in one faith and in love under one head, Christ, and by the Holy Spirit. Through the Holy Spirit every member of this "holy community" shares in everything and especially in the word of God. The Holy Spirit constantly remains with the church, sanctifies it, strengthens its faith, and produces its fruits.[366]

292. The Catechismus Romanus understands the expression sanctorum communio similarly as the explanation of what the church is, for communion "with the Father and with his Son Jesus Christ" is realized in this community of the saints (1 Jn 1:3). "Communion of saints" means communion on the basis of the confession of faith and the sacraments, especially baptism and the eucharist, and on the basis of the interrelationship of all members of the body of Christ. It is a unity and community brought about by the Spirit, because the Holy Spirit sees to it that whatever gift anyone has belongs to the whole communion.[367]

293. Catholics and Lutherans confess in common that the "communion of saints" is the community of those united in sharing in the word and sacraments (the sancta) in faith through the Holy Spirit, the community of "those who are sanctified in Christ Jesus [and] called to be saints [the sancti]" (1 Cor 1:2).

5.2.1.2. Community of Perfected Saints

294. Beyond the circle of believers in Christ who live on earth, the "communion of saints" is seen as a community of those who have been sanctified, cutting across all the ages and reaching into the eternity of God, a community in which one shares and into which one enters through the church. The patristic church believed "the communion of saints" to the glory of God, honored God himself in the saints, and thus kept alive the longing for the life to come. In the Lutheran Confessions too there is a fundamental adherence to the idea of a living communion with the saints, for despite criticism of invocation of the saints, it is not denied that we should give "honor to the saints": in thanks to God for their gifts of grace, in the strengthening of our faith because of their example, and in "imitation, first of their faith and then of their other virtues, which each should imitate in accordance with his calling."[368] It is granted "that the angels pray for us" and that "the saints in heaven pray for the

church."[369] From ancient times therefore in the preface of the liturgy it is said: "Through him the angels praise your majesty, the heavenly hosts adore you, and the powers tremble; together with the blessed Seraphim all the citizens of heaven praise you in brilliant jubilation. Unite our voices with theirs and let us sing praise in endless adoration: Holy, holy, holy."[370] Vatican II placed the ideas of the fathers and the practice of venerating the saints in an ecclesiological context.[371] It stresses the eschatological character of the church as the pilgrim people of God and speaks of that people's "union with the Church in heaven."[372]

5.2.1.3. Communion of the Church on Earth with the Perfected Saints

295. In confessing the *sanctorum communio*, our common faith in the triune God who will perfect the church finds expression. For the *communio* with God which has already been given and realized on earth through Jesus Christ in the Holy Spirit is the foundation of Christian hope beyond death and of the *communio* between Christ's saints on earth and Christ's saints who have already died. The communion of saints reaches beyond death because it is founded in God himself. Only through death and judgment can individuals and the church as a whole reach consummation (cf. 1 Cor 4:4f.; 2 Cor 5:10; Acts 10:42; Heb 11:6; 9:27; 1 Pt 4:17). Thus, belief in the communion of saints as the consummation of the church in no way makes light of sin, death, and judgment. Because our fellowship with the dead is in God alone, our relations with the dead are in the safekeeping of the mystery of God. Such an unfathomable difference exists between the present temporal and the future eternal life (cf. 1 Cor 15:37-57) that we cannot adequately comprehend eternal life in words. We can express it only in images of hope, as Holy Scripture indicates (cf. 1 Cor 2:9). Nevertheless we believe in the fundamental indestructibility of the life given us in Christ through the power of the Holy Spirit even through the judgment and beyond death.

296. Because of the horror of death we mourn the dead at the grave, but because we are Christians we mourn as those who have hope. Our common Christian hope is the crucified and risen Lord through whom God will also lead the dead to glory with Christ (cf. 1 Thes 4:14). Those who are sanctified in Christ Jesus will be "with the Lord forever" (1 Thes 4:17) even through death and judgment. Christians believe in God, who is not a God of the dead but of the living (cf. Mk 12:27 para.), for "to him all of them are alive" (Lk 20:38b). Paul confesses that we do not live or die to ourselves but that "whether we live or whether we die, we are the Lord's" (Rom 14:7-9), and that nothing, not even death, can separate us "from the love of God in Christ Jesus our Lord" (Rom 8:35-39). Therefore, the pilgrim people of God are aware that they look "for the city that is to come" (Heb 13:14) of the sanctified church, "the heavenly Jerusalem, . . . the assembly of the firstborn who are enrolled in heaven, . . . and to the spirits of the righteous made perfect"

(Heb 12:22f.). The communion of saints, the unity of the pilgrim and heavenly church, is realized especially in worship, in the adoration and praise of the thrice-holy God and the Lamb, our Lord Jesus Christ (cf. Rv 4:2-11; 5:9-14). The pilgrim church reaches its goal and thus its end and consummation when "the last enemy . . . death" is deprived of its power and the Son hands over everything to the rule of God the Father so that "God may be all in all" (1 Cor 15:24-28).

5.2.2. The Church and the Kingdom of God

5.2.2.1. New Testament View

297. According to the witness of the synoptic Gospels, the reign of God is the core of the preaching of Jesus of Nazareth (cf. Mk 1:15; Mt 4:17), the petition for the coming of his Father's kingdom is the center and fulcrum of his prayer (cf. Lk 11:2; Mt 6:9f.), and the reign of God comes to human beings as the reality proclaimed as well by his deeds (cf. Lk 11:20; Mt 12:28). Thus through and in Jesus himself the reign of God becomes present, and thus God's lordship establishes itself among those whom Jesus healed and who were affected by his preaching (cf. Lk 17:20f.).

298. By his preaching and practice of the kingdom of God, Jesus wished to call all Israel and prepare them to be eschatologically renewed and recreated by God. Especially the calling and sending out of the Twelve (cf. Mk 3:14; 6:7; Mt 10:6) is a luminous sign that the reign of God presumes an actual people, in and through whom that kingdom can be established. The coming of the kingdom of God and the eschatological new creation of Israel belong inseparably together. Right up to his death Jesus maintained this, as shown by the eschatological perspective of his eucharistic words (cf. Mk 14:25 para.; Lk 13:29; 14:15; 22:30). Jesus' last meal, as an anticipation and interpretation of his death, becomes a bequest ensuring that God's offer is renewed for all Israel through Jesus' death as an atonement. Without merit or limit, sins are forgiven and new life bestowed (cf. Mk 14:24 para.).

299. Even if God has created for himself in the church an actual people made up of Jews and Gentiles (cf. Eph 2:11-22) who owe their existence to the death and resurrection of Jesus and to the sending of the Spirit, this "new" people of God, which believes in the Messiah as having come, is still fundamentally related to Israel as a whole. The will of Jesus to gather Israel together held good then and still does. Seen in this way, Jesus' will to gather the eschatological people of God in wholeness and fullness, and under the rule of God, already includes the post-Easter church. Paul confirms this in his reflections on Israel in relation to salvation history: in the church consisting of Jews and Gentiles it is specifically the Gentile Christians who must never forget the origin of salvation history. Israel became salvation to the nations and will also be saved (cf. Rom 9–11). For the church this means that it is the actual peo-

ple of God in whom the reign of God is already kindled and through whom it is to extend. The church is the dawning and the sign of the kingdom of God.

5.2.2.2. Lutheran View

300. Though the Lutheran Confessions contain no specific reflections on the theme of the kingdom of God and the church, there are nevertheless enough indications that the church is oriented towards the kingdom of God and taken into service for that kingdom, and that hidden in the church, the kingdom of God or of Christ has already dawned and is at work. In the explanation of the second petition in the Lord's Prayer, the Large Catechism equates the kingdom of God with the saving activity of Jesus Christ who was sent "into the world to redeem and deliver us from the power of the devil and to bring us to himself and rule us as a king of righteousness, life and salvation." This he does in the Holy Spirit through his word. This kingdom is a "kingdom of grace" which is already actively present here on earth but will be consummated in eternity and will bring its citizens to their destination there. Coming to us temporally "through the Word and faith" it will become manifest "in eternity" and definitively on the return of Christ.[373]

301. According to the Apology the church is the kingdom of Christ as the *congregatio sanctorum*, as he rules by the word and by preaching, works through the Holy Spirit, and increases in us faith, the fear of God, love, and patience within the heart.[374] The church is not identical with the ultimate and all-embracing kingdom, which God will introduce at the end of the ages, but in the church it already begins here on earth[375] and is already hiddenly present.[376] In good works as fruit of faith it is already visible before the whole world.[377] In itself, however, the kingdom is "hidden under the cross," like Jesus before he entered his heavenly dominion.[378] Mingled with unbelievers (cf. Mt 13:36ff., 47ff.; 25:1ff.) and still sinners themselves, the holy members of the church cannot yet represent the kingdom of God unambiguously. In spite of the fact that the church is not a "Platonic republic,"[379] the kingdom has already broken in. Only the *notae*, the marks of the church, i.e., the "pure teaching of the Gospel and the sacraments" are unequivocal. This tension will cease only when at the end of the ages Christ himself totally realizes and reveals the kingdom.[380]

5.2.2.3. Catholic View

302. Catholics are also persuaded that the kingdom of God is inseparably linked with the person of Jesus Christ. "In Christ's word, in His works and in His presence this kingdom reveals itself to men."[381] In Jesus the reign of God has dawned, and he himself is the reign of God in person. The council speaks in a more nuanced way about the church. On the one hand it says that it receives from the exalted Lord "the mission to proclaim and to establish among all peoples the king-

dom of Christ and of God," but on the other hand it stresses that despite its gradual growth the church "strains toward the consummation of the kingdom."[382] Its destiny is "the kingdom of God which has been begun by God Himself on earth, and which is to be further extended until it is brought to perfection by Him at the end of time. Then Christ our life (cf. Col 3:4) will appear."[383] In this way the council clearly highlights the church's being taken into service for the kingdom of God and on the other hand keeps open, in the eschatological reservation, the fact that the kingdom of God is not at human disposal. God himself will establish and perfect his reign. The church is only "the kingdom of Christ now present in mystery,"[384] the "initial budding forth of that kingdom" on earth.[385]

303. Thus, taking up the sacramental ecclesiological thinking of the council, one can also speak of the church as the sacramental sign of the kingdom of God through the presence of the Lord in the Holy Spirit.[386] Because the crucified and risen Lord is with his church "always, to the end of the age" (Mt 28:20), it is—with trust in this promise—the sacramental sign of the kingdom of God. The presence of the Lord is made actual in the Holy Spirit and is communicated in the word of God, the celebration of the eucharist and the other sacraments, and in the community of brothers and sisters. The Spirit does indeed "blow where it chooses" (Jn 3:8) but in and through the church this Spirit accomplishes the saving activity of God and his reign. The Spirit works in the world in the witness and service of the church, and in the Spirit the church fulfills its adoration, its intercessions, and its advocacy for everyone before God. Thus, the church serves the reign of God for the world. It is directed towards the kingdom of God as its eschatological salvation.

304. The kingdom of God is therefore the church's constant orientation, abiding motivation, critical court of appeal, and final goal. The power of the coming kingdom is already really present in the church through its Lord in the Holy Spirit. The Holy Spirit effects forgiveness of sins, sanctification, and life in the church. The Spirit supports its mission and perfects its catholicity. In the miracle of tongues at Pentecost the "divisiveness of Babel" is indeed fundamentally overcome.[387] Nevertheless the Spirit makes the church repeatedly cry, Come! so that the dispersed children of God may ultimately be gathered together (cf. Rv 22:17-20; Jn 11:52). Seen in this way, the church is the place where the reign of God has already dawned, and thus it is the recipient of salvation. But at the same time it is also an instrument and sign for the reign which God himself implements, and thus it is the mediator of salvation. At the end the church will be taken up into the kingdom of God, i.e., it will come to an end because it is no longer needed as sign and instrument. But this end is also the consummation of its earthly form as the place of God's reign and the beginning of its new, definitive existence in the eternal kingdom of God.[388]

5.2.2.4. Perspective in Ecumenical Dialogue

305. In ecumenical dialogue too the church is seen in various ways as sign and instrument of the presence of Christ, the mission of Christ, and the kingdom. Thus the Commission on Faith and Order of the World Council of Churches states that "the Church is called to be a visible sign of the presence of Christ, who is both hidden and revealed to faith, reconciling and healing human alienation in the worshiping community."[389] In its report on the meeting in Bangalore the same commission says, "The Church is a sign and instrument of Christ's mission to all humankind."[390] In the message of the 1980 World Conference on Mission and Evangelism in Melbourne, it was said that "the good news of the kingdom must be presented to the world by the church, the Body of Christ, the sacrament of the kingdom in every place and time."[391] Despite all the inadequacies of the churches as they actually exist, the reality of their character as signs of the eschatological rule of God is highlighted and stressed: "Yet there is reality here. The whole church of God, in every place and time, is a sacrament of the kingdom which came in the person of Jesus Christ and will come in its fulness when he returns in glory."[392]

306. Similar pronouncements are to be found in the bilateral ecumenical dialogues. Thus in the Lutheran–Roman Catholic dialogue in the USA the mission of the church is seen "to be an anticipatory and efficacious sign of the full unification of all things when God will be all in all."[393] The Anglican–Lutheran dialogue calls the church "an instrument for proclaiming and manifesting God's sovereign rule and saving grace,"[394] but also indicates that an "authentic fellowship of the reconciled"[395] is a precondition for the proper exercise of the mission and service of the church. Thus, a necessary reservation is pointed out in order to evaluate realistically talk of the church as a sign of the kingdom of God. It is an ongoing task of the church to be a credible sign of the kingdom. Its credibility will repeatedly be distorted by human weakness and sin and become blurred by lack of contrition. Therefore, the church always needs purification through repentance and renewal. The Report of Section III of the World Conference on Mission and Evangelism in Melbourne speaks of a frightening claim, "frightening, because it causes every one of us to examine our personal experience of the empirical church and to confess how often our church life has hidden rather than revealed the sovereignty of God the Father whom Jesus Christ made known."[396]

5.2.2.5. Common Witness

307. Lutherans and Catholics together regard the church as the dawning and the instrument of the kingdom of God. Two things should be maintained together. On the one hand, there is the reality of the powers of the kingdom of God, especially in the proclamation of the word of God and the celebration of the sacraments as the means of salvation, but also in the reconciled community of sisters and broth-

ers as the place of salvation. On the other hand, there is the interim nature of all words and signs in which salvation is imparted but also the inadequacies in preaching, worship, and the serving community as these exist in practice among believers. To this extent the church always lives on the basis of letting itself be lifted up into the coming kingdom, remembering its own provisional nature. The earthly church will find its eschatological consummation only when the kingdom has come. Then when God's kingdom dawns the church will be consummated and all hiddenness fully revealed.

308. The assembly of the faithful as a community of the perfected is the consummation of the church in the unveiled, pure presence and reign of God who is love, with whom and in whom all those made perfect have community and are in constant touch with each other: "God may be all in all" (1 Cor 15:24-28). "And I heard a loud voice from the throne saying, 'See, the home of God is among mortals. He will dwell with them as their God; they will be his people, and God himself will be with them; he will wipe every tear from their eyes. Death will be no more; mourning and crying and pain will be no more, for the first things have passed away.' And the one who was seated on the throne said, 'See, I am making all things new'" (Rv 21:3-5a).

Members of the Lutheran–Roman Catholic Joint Commission

This document was approved unanimously by the members of the Joint Commission, 11 September 1993.

Roman Catholic Members

Most Rev. Paul-Werner Scheele (chair from 1988 to 1993)
Most Rev. Karl Lehmann (chair from 1986 to 1987)
Most Rev. Hans L. Martensen
Dr. Christian Mhagama
Most Rev. Alfons Nossol
Dr. Vinzenz Pfnür
Dr. Lothar Ullrich
Dr. Jared Wicks

Lutheran Members

Rt. Rev. (retired) Dr. James Crumley (chair)
Dr. Johannes P. Boendermaker
Rt. Rev. Gottfried Brakemeier
Rt. Rev. Manas Buthelezi

Dr. Inge Lönning
Dr. Dorothea Wendebourg
Rt. Rev. (emeritus) Ulrich Wilckens

Consultants

Dr. Robert Jenson (Lutheran)
Dr. Aloys Klein (Roman Catholic)
Dr. Hervé Legrand (Roman Catholic)
Dr. Harding Meyer (Lutheran)

Staff Members

Rev. Eugene L. Brand (Lutheran World Federation)
Msgr. Basil Meeking (Secretariat for Promoting Christian Unity, 1986 to 1987)
Msgr. John Radano (Pontifical Council for Promoting Christian Unity)
Rev. Heinz-Albert Raem (Pontifical Council for Promoting Christian Unity, from
    1990)

NOTES

1. *"Articulus stantis et cadentis ecclesiae."*

2. WADB 40,III,352,3: *"quia isto articulo stante stat Ecclesia, ruente ruit Ecclesia."*

3. *Justification by Faith,* Lutherans and Catholics in Dialogue VII (Minneapolis), 1985, 153.

4. *All Under One Christ,* 1980, Statement on the Augsburg Confession by the Roman Catholic–Lutheran Joint Commission, 14, in GA, 241-247.

5. *Kirchengemeinschaft in Wort und Sakrament.* Bilaterale Arbeitsgruppe der Deutschen Bischofskonferenz und der Kirchenleitung der Vereinigten Evangelisch-Lutherischen Kirche Deutschlands, Paderborn/Hannover, 1984, 1 (hereafter: *Kirchengemeinschaft*).

6. Ibid, 2; cf. LG, nos. 3f.

7. NA, no. 4.

8. Ibid.

9. Apol 7,17f.; BC 171.

10. LG, no. 3.

11. *Kirchengemeinschaft,* 2; LG, no. 5.

12. WA 2,430.

13. WA 1,236: *sacrosanctum evangelium;* LW 31, 31.

14. Ibid: *Verus thesaurus ecclesiae;* ibid.

15. WA 7,721.

16. CA 7, BC 32.

17. LG, no. 20.

18. AG, no. 6.

19. EN, no. 15.

20. Report of the Joint Lutheran–Roman Catholic Study Commission on "The Gospel and the Church," 1972, 48 (hereafter: Malta Report), GA, 169-189.

21. Ibid, 21.

22. Ibid, 33, 47, 48, 50; cf. 56.

23. SA III, 4; BC 310.

24. *All Under One Christ,* no. 16.

25. Irenaeus, "Against Heresies," III.1.1 in *Ante-Nicene Father,* (Grand Rapids, Mich., 1967), 1,414.

26. Cf. Tertullian, *De praescr.,* 6, 37.

27. Cf. Tertullian, *Adv. Marc.,* 1, 21; 4, 5.

28. Augustinus, *De bapt.,* 4, 31: *"Quod universa tenet ecclesia, nec conciliis institutum sed semper retentum est nonnisi auctoritate apostolica traditum rectissime creditur."*

29. Cf. for instance Rufinus, *Expositio Symboli apostolorum,* no. 2: CCL, 20, 134f.

30. FC Ep 1; BC 464.

31. DV, no. 7.

32. DV, no. 8.

33. Malta Report, no. 57; cf. *The Ministry in the Church*, Roman Catholic–Lutheran Joint Commission (Geneva, 1982); GA, 248-275.

34. LG, especially no. 1.

35. "The Mystery of the Church and of the Eucharist in the Light of the Mystery of the Holy Trinity," Joint International Commission for Theological Dialogue between the Roman Catholic Church and the Orthodox Church, 1982, especially II, 1 and I, 5/d.

36. Cf. *Ways to Community*, Roman Catholic–Lutheran Joint Commission (Geneva, 1981), 9-13, in GA, 215-240; *The Ministry in the Church*, no. 12; FU, supra.

37. *LWF Report* No. 19/20, 1985, 175.

38. Cf. WA 16,407, 38,247; LG, nos. 9-17; in the ecumenical dialogue cf. BEM, Ministry, nos. 1-6 in GA, 465-503; *The Ministry in the Church*, nos. 12-13; *Kirchengemeinschaft*, 61.

39. See below 5.1.

40. *The Eucharist*, Lutheran–Roman Catholic Joint Commission (Geneva, 1980), 25, in GA, 190-214.

41. "*Merismós pneúmatos agioû.*"

42. Cf. BC 345, 415-420.

43. Cf. LG, no. 4.

44. E.g., LG, no. 7; cf. no. 3.

45. Thomas Aquinas, *Summa Theologiae* III, 73a.1; 79a.5.

46. WA 2, 742-758; LW 35, 45-73.

47. Martin Chemnitz, "*Fundamenta sanae doctrinae de vera et substantiali praesentia . . . corporis et sanguinis Domini in Coena,*" IX.

48. St. John of Damascus, *The Orthodox Faith* IV, 13, *The Fathers of the Church* (Washington, 1958), Vol. 37, 361.

49. Documents of the Extraordinary Synod, *The Final Report* (Rome, 1985), in *The Tablet* (14 December 1985), II,C,1.

50. GS, no. 19.

51. DV, no. 2.

52. AG, no. 3.

53. UR, no. 2.

54. "*Communio/congregatio sanctorum/fidelium.*"

55. CA 7, BC 32.

56. "*Communio sanctorum.*"

57. Apol 7,8; BC 169; cf. translation and interpretation of *communio sanctorum* in Luther's Large Catechism as "a communion of saints," as "a little holy flock or community"; BC 416f.

58. LC II, 3; BC 417; cf. Apol 7,8: "'Church' means, namely, the assembly of saints who share the association of the same Gospel or teaching and of the same Holy Spirit, who renews, consecrates, and governs their hearts." BC 169.

59. Luther to the term *koinonia* in 1 Corinthians 10:16ff.; WA 26,493; LW 37,356.

60. WA 2,754; LW 35, 67.

61. AG, no. 9.

62. DV, no. 21.

63. Cf. LG, no. 7 with reference to 1 Corinthians 10:16f.; cf. LG, no. 3.

64. Cf. LG, no. 11.

65. PO, no. 5: "*congregatio fidelium.*"

66. CA 7; BC 32; cf. Apol 7,9; BC 169f.

67. LC II, 3; BC 417.

68. Apol 7,10; BC 170.

69. Apol 7,5; BC 169.

70. LG, no. 9.

71. UR, no. 2.

72. North America and Europe.

73. Lutheran World Convention, 1923; Lutheran World Federation, 1947.

74. CA 7.

75. LWF Constitution III: Nature and Functions.

76. Cf. *Agreement Between Reformation Churches in Europe* (Leuenberg Agreement), 1973, Frankfurt, 1993, 29 and 33; FU, 23-26.

77. *LWF Report* No. 19/20, Budapest, 1984, 175.

78. The terminology for describing the local church and the church as a whole (all the local churches that are in communion with each other) does not derive from a systematic and critical decision. Even Vatican II did not come to such a decision. Consequently in the council's documents, *ecclesia localis* and *ecclesia particularis* can designate the diocesan church, but with equal frequency the two terms also describe associations of diocesan churches. *Ecclesia universa* (used on twenty-three occasions) and *ecclesia universalis* (used on twenty-five occasions) designates the church as a whole or the universal church. This is never described as the church of Rome.

The *Codex Iuris Canonici* of 1983, which does not have the expressions *ecclesia localis* and *ecclesia universalis*, makes use of the two terms *ecclesia particularis* (diocese) and *ecclesia universa* (the church as a whole). Catholic theologians have not wholly identified themselves with this choice of terms. They prefer to reserve the term "particular church" (*ecclesia particularis*) for associations of churches which are characterized by their special cultural features and to describe the church in one place as the "local church" in order to preserve the catholicity of the church.

In German this leads to preferring the term *Ortskirche* ("local church") to "particular church" and likewise to the term "partial church" (which suggests the false idea that the local church is a part of the universal church).

79. Cf. SC, no. 41; LG, nos. 23 and 26; CD, no. 11.

80. CD, no. 1l.

81. Cf. LG, chapters 2 and 3.

82. Cf. LG, no. 23, and FU, 112.

83. SC, no. 42.

84. *The Church: Local and Universal*, 36. JWG, infra.

85. LG, no. 23.

86. International Commission of Theologians, *Themata Selecta de Ecclesiologia* (Documenta 13). Vaticano 1985, 32: *"mutua interioritas."*

87. John Paul II, Speech to the Roman Curia, 20 December 1990, AAS 83 (1991): 745-747.

88. LG, no. 23.

89. *Corpus ecclesiarum* (LG, no. 23). The reason of the corporeality of the church is the sacramental sharing in the body of Christ; see above 76 and 78.

90. *The Church: Local and Universal*, 37.

91. AG, no. 4.

92. AG, no. 10.

93. AG, no. 15.

94. Cf. LG, no. 13.

95. AG, no. 22.

96. LG, no. 13.

97. LG, no. 23.

98. UR, no. 4.

99. Consejo Episcopal Latinoamericano (Council of Latin American Bishops).

100. LG, no. 13.

101. *The Church: Local and Universal*, no. 24.

102. UR, no. 14; cf. FU, 44f.

103. Cf. FU, 5-7.

104. See above 2.4.

105. See above 3.3.

106. See below 4.2.

107. LC III.47; BC 416.

108. WA 7,219; LW Phil.Ed. II,373.

109. CA 7 (and 8); BC 32; BSLK 61, 1: *"Congregatio sanctorum [et vere credentium], in qua evangelium pure docetur et recte administrantur sacramenta."*

110. *"Principaliter,"* cf. CA 8: *proprie.*

111. *"Pura evangelii doctrina."*

112. Apol 7,5; BC 169.

113. Cf. CA 1 and 3.

114. Apol 7,5; BC 169.
115. WA 10,I/1:140, 8.14.
116. WA 7,219,6; LW Phil.Ed. II,373.
117. Apol 9,2; BC 178.
118. Ibid., German text.
119. SA III,12; BC 315.
120. WA 50,629,34; LW Phil.Ed. II, 271.
121. WA 7,219,11; LW Phil.Ed. II, 373.
122. WA 12,308,4.
123. *Catechism of the Council of Trent* I, 10, 2; *Cat. Rom.* I, 10, 5: "*coetus omnium fidelium.*"
124. Ibid., I, 10, 2.
125. Ibid.
126. Ibid., I, 10, 24.
127. *Communio sanctorum.*
128. *Catechism of the Council of Trent* I, 10, 23-27.
129. LG, no. 9.
130. AG, nos. 15, 19; PO, nos. 4f.
131. "*Civitas redempta.*"
132. PO, no. 2.
133. LG, no. 9.
134. LG, no. 4: "*in communione et ministratione.*"
135. AG, no. 3.
136. LG, no. 9.
137. PO, no. 2.
138. LG, no. 10.
139. Ibid.
140. PO, no. 5.
141. LG, no. 7, referring to 1 Corinthians 10:17.
142. PO, no. 4.
143. Ibid.
144. AG, no. 15.
145. AG, no. 8.
146. Malta Report, no. 48.
147. WA 2,430,6: "*creatura . . . evangelii.*"
148. LG, no. 20.
149. FU, 85.
150. LG, no. 1.

151. Ibid.

152. SC, no. 5.

153. LG, no. 9.

154. Cf. LG, nos. 2-5.

155. LG, no. 48; cf. LG, nos. 7, 59.

156. Thus the term "sacrament" is always placed within quotation marks when related to the church in order to draw attention to the analogous use of language. This is expressly highlighted in the *Dogmatic Constitution on the Church* when talking of the church as "a kind of *[veluti]* sacrament . . . a sign and an instrument. . . ." (LG, no. 1).

157. *"Ex opere operato."*

158. LG, no. 8.

159. Ibid.

160. Cf. LG, no. 7, referring to 1 Corinthians 12, Ephesians 1, and Colossians 2.

161. LG, no. 8; cf. no. 48.

162. UR, no. 6.

163. LG, no. 8; cf. UR, nos. 3f.

164. LG, no. 16; GS, no. 22.

165. Cf. CA 5.

166. CA 7.

167. *"Viva vox evangelii."*

168. WA 20,350,6: *"Quando ego praedico, ipse [sc. Christus] praedicat in me."*

169. *"Verbum externum."*

170. *"Verbum efficax."*

171. SA III, 8; BC 313.

172. CA 5; BC 31.

173. CA 8; BC 33.

174. *"Extra ecclesiam nulla salus";* cf. Apol 9,2; BC 178.

175. LC I,40ff.; BC 416.

176. Augustine, Ep. 187, CSEL 57,113.

177. Cf. WA 6,501,37; 86,7f.; LW Phil.Ed. II,177.

178. See below 4.4.

179. WA 40/II,106,19; LW 27,84.

180. *"Coetus."*

181. Bellarmine, *Disputatio de conciliis et ecclesia,* III.ii.

182. Apol 7,20; BC 171.

183. LG, no. 8.

184. CA 7; BC 32.

185. CA 5 and 14; BC 31 and 36.

186. See above 135.
187. WA 40/II,106,20; LW 27,84.
188. Apol 7,3; BC 169.
189. Ibid.
190. Apol 7,1-22; BC 168ff.
191. WA 40/II,106,29; LW 27,85.
192. WA 50,625,3; LW Phil.Ed. V,265.
193. WA 40/II,106,21; LW 27,84; cf. Apol 7,19.
194. LG, no. 14.
195. LG, nos. 1-8.
196. LG, no. 4.
197. Cf. LG, no. 7.
198. Cf. LG, no. 8.
199. Cf. LG, nos. 5,9.
200. See above 4.2.
201. Cf. LG, no. 8.
202. Ibid.
203. Cf. UR, no. 6.
204. LG, no. 39.
205. WA 50,628,16; LW 41,148.
206. CA 7; BC 32.
207. *"Ecclesia non potest errare."*
208. Cf. WA 18,649f.; 30 III, 408; 51,513 and 515f.; Apol 7,27; BC 173.
209. E.g., Malta Report, nos. 22f.; *The Ministry in the Church*, no. 58.
210. UR, no. 4, cf. Augustine, *Retract.*, lib.II, c. 18.
211. LG, no. 48.
212. CA 8; BC 33.
213. LG, no. 8; cf. no. 40.
214. UR, no. 6.
215. WA 38,215f.
216. WA 51,516,15.
217. Cf. Apol 7:28; BC 173.
218. WA 51,517,19; see also 513ff., especially 516f.; cf. WA 38,216.
219. Malta Report, no. 23.
220. Cf. LG, nos. 8, 40; DS 229 and 1537.
221. UR, no. 6.
222. Ibid.

223. LG, no. 8; cf. UR, no. 3.

224. See 4.5.3.1-4.

225. Cf. GS, no. 43.

226. Cf. UR, no. 6.

227. See below 4.5.3.3.

228. See below 4.5.3.2.

229. See below 5.2.1.

230. Malta Report, no. 29.

231. *Justification by Faith*, no. 153; cf. no. 28.

232. CA 7; BC 32.

233. Ibid.

234. WA 40 I,69; cf. 46,6f.

235. See above 178.

236. Cf. *The Ministry in the Church*, no. 17.

237. CA 4; BC 30.

238. CA 5; BC 31.

239. Apol 7,20; BC 171; WA 30 III, 88.

240. *Tractatus*, 25.

241. Johann Gerhard, *Loci theologici*, XXII,V,37,40.

242. *The Ministry in the Church*, no. 18.

243. Cf. Apol 7,28; BC 173.

244. *The Ministry in the Church*, 23.

245. *"Extra nos pro nobis."*

246. Cf. BEM, Ministry, nos. 8, 12, 42.

247. *The Ministry in the Church*, no. 20.

248. *"Pseudodidaskaloi."*

249. *"Pseudoapostoloi."*

250. Cf. *The Ministry in the Church*, nos. 40-49, 59-66.

251. Cf. Apol 14; BC 214f.

252. *The Ministry in the Church*, no. 49; cf. no. 50.

253. Ibid, no. 46f.; especially FU, 94-98.

254. DS 1776.

255. *The Ministry in the Church*, no. 49.

256. Cf. DS 1776: *"hierarchiam divina ordinatione institutam"*; cf. LG, no. 28: "Thus the divinely established ecclesiastical ministry is exercised on different levels by those who from antiquity have been called bishops, priests, and deacons."

257. LG, no. 20.

258. Cf. Apol 14; BC 214f.; WA 26,195f.; *The Ministry in the Church*, nos. 65f., 49 and 50; FU, 106, 97.

259. Cf. CA 5; BC 31.

260. Cf. CA 7; BC 32; WA 7,721; see above 36.

261. See above 85.

262. Apol 7,34; BC 175.

263. Apol 7,30-37 interprets CA 7: The question in the *nec necesse est* is not whether what is added in the church to proclaim the Gospel is "profitable" and "necessary" for the church. The main question is rather whether it is "necessary for righteousness" (*necessarius ad iustitiam*). BC 173ff.

264. LG, no. 48.

265. LG, no. 8; cf. UR, no. 3.

266. UR, no. 3.

267. AG, no. 7.

268. UR, no. 22.

269. *The Ministry in the Church*, no. 77.

270. Cf. UR, nos. 19-23.

271. Cf. FU, 117-139.

272. See above 3.2.3.

273. Cf. Malta Report, no. 18.

274. See above 4.5.2.

275. See above 4.5.3.1.

276. CA 1: "*Ecclesiae magno consensu apud nos docent . . .*" "Our churches teach with great unanimity . . ." (BC 27); cf. CA 1-21 (BC 27ff.), and the conclusion in the first part of the *Confessio Augustana* which says: "This is just about a summary of the doctrines that are preached and taught in our churches" (BC 47).

277. CA 7; BC 32.

278. CA 28,21f.; BC 84.

279. Cf. *The Ministry in the Church*, 42.

280. Cf. ibid., 55.

281. Apol 7,23-27, especially 23; BC 172f.

282. Apol 7,27; BC 173.

283. Apol 7,23; BC 172.

284. Apol 7,28; BC 173.

285. Apol 7,23; BC 172.

286. Cf. DV, no. 10.

287. Apol 14,1 and 2; BC 214.

288. Cf. Malta Report, no. 66; *The Ministry in the Church*, nos. 65f., 73, 80; FU, 97.

289. Cf. Malta Report, no. 66.

290. LG, no. 12.
291. Cf. LG, no. 25.
292. FU, 110.
293. *The Ministry in the Church*, no. 51.
294. LG, no. 12.
295. *The Ministry in the Church*, no. 62; cf. LG, no. 25.
296. DV, no. 10; cf. *The Ministry in the Church*, no. 50.
297. Cf. ibid., 50 and 62.
298. PO, no. 4.
299. FU, 110 and footnote 157.
300. Cf. among others DS 265.
301. DS 3073f.
302. *The Ministry in the Church*, no. 52.
303. Cf. *Mysterium ecclesiae*, 5, Statement by the Vatican Congregation for the Doctrine of the Faith.
304. DV, no. 8.
305. Cf. DV, no. 10.
306. *The Ministry in the Church*, nos. 56 and 73.
307. See above 211-214.
308. CIC, can. 1752: "*salus animarum semper suprema lex*"; Malta Report, no. 32: For church law, "the final decisive viewpoint must be that of the salvation of the individual believer."
309. Malta Report, no. 33.
310. Cf. ibid., nos. 31 and 33.
311. See above, 227.
312. CA 28: The Power of Bishops; BC 81ff.
313. CA 28,5 and 21; BC 81 and 84.
314. CA 28,5 and 8; BC 81.
315. CA 28,10; BC 82.
316. CA 28,20f. and 29; BC 84f.
317. CA 28,8f.; BC 82.
318. CA 28,21; BC 84.
319. Ibid.
320. CA 28,22; ibid.
321. CA 28,23ff.; ibid.
322. CA 28,29ff.; BC 85f.
323. CA 28,53 and 55; BC 89f.
324. CA 28,66f. and 73f.; BC 92ff.

325. CA 28,55; BC 90.

326. CA 28,43-48; 50; 53 and frequently; BC 88ff.

327. CA 28,42; 49; 53; 64; 77 and frequently; ibid.

328. CA 28,37; 50; 52; 66 and frequently; BC 86ff.

329. CA 28,51; 60; 64 and frequently; BC 89ff.

330. See above 227.

331. LG, no. 27.

332. LG, no. 20.

333. LG, no. 27.

334. LG, no. 27; CD, no. 3.

335. DH, no. 2 (in re religiosa neque aliquis cogatur ad agendum contra suam conscientiam); 12.

336. DH, no. 11.

337. Malta Report, no. 32, referring to DH, nos. 2, 10-12.

338. Malta Report, no. 33.

339. John Paul II, apostolic constitution Sacrae Disciplinae Leges, promulgating the new Code of 1983; CIC, XIff.

340. UR, no. 1.

341. Cf. Redemptoris Missio, no. 12.

342. Cf. GS, no. 41.

343. Apol 16, BC 222ff.; cf. also CA 28,8f; LC III, 53.

344. LC I, 5th Commandment; BC 390f.; WA 6,36f., 43; 15,300f.; 11,245,250; 30/II,111f.

345. WA 15,302; 11,252f.; cf. Apol 16,6.

346. CA 28, 11.

347. "Usus civilis legis."

348. CA 28,11.

349. CA 16; BC 37; cf. Apol 13,15; BC 213.

350. FC SD 5; BC 564ff.

351. LC I,141f.; 150; BC 384ff.

352. WA 40,III,221-223.

353. WA 18,818; 24,6-9.

354. CA 28,12; BC 83; Apol 16,2; BC 222.

355. LC I; BC 390f.; WA 6,37f.; 11,245,249f.; 18,308f.

356. Apol 15,25f.; BC 218f.

357. Apol 16,13; BC 224.

358. CA 27,49; BC 78f.; Apol 27,37; BC 275.

359. Apol 4,121f.; BC 124; cf. also WA 11,279; 7,544f.,600; 15,293.

360. GS, no. 36.

361. GS, no. 42.

362. GS, no. 43.

363. Cf. GS, no. 43.

364. *The Ministry in the Church,* no. 13.

365. *The Eucharist,* no. 12; 29-37.

366. Cf. LC II.3; BC 417ff.

367. Cf. *The Catechism of the Council of Trent,* I:X,23-26.

368. Apol 21,4-7; BC 229f.

369. Apol 21,8f.; BC 230.

370. *The Eucharist,* no. 39.

371. Cf. LG, no. 50f.

372. LG, no. 50.

373. LC III,51ff.; BC 426f.

374. Apol 16,54; BC 222ff.

375. Ibid.

376. Apol 7,17; BC 171.

377. Apol 4,189; BC 133.

378. Apol 7: 18f.; BC 171; see above 142f.

379. Apol 7,20; BC 171; *"civitas platonica."*

380. Apol 7,17-20; BC 171.

381. LG, no. 5.

382. Ibid.

383. LG, no. 9.

384. LG, no. 3.

385. LG, no. 5.

386. See above 121-125.

387. AG, no. 4.

388. Cf. LG, no. 48f.

389. *Uniting in Hope. Accra 1974,* 93, Faith and Order Paper 72.

390. *Sharing in One Hope. Bangalore 1978,* 239, Faith and Order Paper 92.

391. *Your Kingdom Come.* World Council of Churches (Geneva, 1980), 235f.

392. Ibid.

393. "Differing Attitudes Toward Papal Primacy" 1, in *Papal Primacy and the Universal Church* (Minneapolis, 1974).

394. Anglican–Lutheran International Conversations, London, 1973 (Pullach Report), 59 in GA, 13-34.

395. Ibid.

396. *Your Kingdom Come,* 193.

PART TWO

Reformed–Roman Catholic

Towards a Common Understanding of the Church

Second Phase (1984-1990)

Introduction

1. As representatives of the Reformed churches and of the Roman Catholic Church, we have carried on a dialogue whose purpose has been to deepen mutual understanding and to foster the eventual reconciliation of our two communities. Our conversations have been officially sponsored by the World Alliance of Reformed Churches and the Pontifical Council for Promoting Christian Unity. We have met in Rome, Italy (1984), Kappel-am-Albis, Switzerland (1985), Venice, Italy (1986), Cartigny, Switzerland (1981), and Ariccia, Italy (1988). This report emerged out of these encounters. Joint subcommittees met in Geneva (1989 and 1990) to take into account further suggestions of the commission for the report and to prepare it for publication.

2. An earlier phase of this dialogue took place under the same sponsorship between 1970 and 1977. That series of conversations produced a report entitled *The Presence of Christ in Church and World* (PCCW), which gave attention to issues such as the relationship of Christ to the church, the church as a teaching authority, the eucharist, and the ministry. These earlier conversations discovered considerable

common ground but left open questions pertaining to such matters as authority, order, and church discipline. During approximately these same years representatives of the Lutheran World Federation joined Reformed and Roman Catholic participants in a trilateral dialogue to produce a report titled *The Theology of Marriage and the Problem of Mixed Marriages*.

3. In this second phase of dialogue just completed, we have concentrated more directly on the doctrine of the church. Certain ecclesiological issues touched upon in the earlier conversations are further treated. Building on this previous work, we have now gone deeper into the realm of ecclesiology, bringing important aspects of this subject into bilateral conversations for the first time. In this way, we have sought further to clarify the common ground between our communions as well as to identify our remaining differences. We hope these results will encourage further steps toward common testimony and joint ecumenical action.

4. We have discovered anew that the Roman Catholic Church and the Reformed churches are bound by manifold ties. Both communions confess Jesus Christ as Lord and Savior, affirm the trinitarian faith of the apostolic church through the ages, and observe the one baptism into the threefold name. In recent years Reformed and Roman Catholic Christians have begun, in many places and at many different levels, to share the experience of fellowship and to seek fuller communion in truth and love for the sake of our common service of Jesus Christ in the world. Our churches share more common ground than previously we were able to see.

5. Yet we have also realized anew that there remain disagreements and divergences between us. Some of these have emerged in the course of this dialogue and have been tackled head-on. Others have been perceived but left for substantive treatment in future dialogue.

6. Our communions are called to live and witness together to the fullest extent possible now and to work together toward future reconciliation. The common ground we share compels us to be open toward one another and to aspire to that communion into which the Spirit seeks to lead us. Each communion is bound in conscience to bear witness to the way in which it understands the Gospel, the church, and the relationship between them, but at the same time to bear this witness in dialogue and mutual support. As we articulate our differing positions in love, we are challenged to a deeper fidelity to Jesus Christ.

7. This report presents the results of our dialogue in four chapters. Chapter 1 recalls the sixteenth-century Reformation and recounts the path taken by each communion since that time. The new openness of ecumenical relationships has helped us to see our respective histories in new perspectives and to clarify our relationships today. A new assessment of our common ground and of our disagreements is now possible; we are moving closer to being able to write our histories together.

8. The existence of this common ground gives us a context for discussing what remains controversial. Thus its content needs careful consideration. Chapter 2 seeks to accomplish this. This chapter focuses upon two areas of fundamental agreement: that our Lord Jesus Christ is the only mediator between God and humankind and that we receive justification by grace through faith. It follows that together we also confess the church as the community of all who are called, redeemed, and sanctified through the one mediator.

9. A complete ecclesiology was beyond our scope in this phase of dialogue. But it seemed especially important to reconsider the relation between the Gospel and the church in its ministerial and instrumental roles. Chapter 3 takes up this question and carries it through a series of topics: the church as *creatura verbi* and the church as sacrament of grace, continuity and discontinuity in church history, the question of church structure, and the ordering of ministry. Certain convergences are set forth, and the remaining issues noted for future consideration.

10. Finally, Chapter 4 sketches some ways forward. Our churches meet in many settings. In ways appropriate to each situation we may (1) take specific steps to deepen our existing fellowship; (2) address issues in such a way as to come closer to a reconciliation of memories; (3) find arenas for common witness; and (4) consider the nature of the unity we seek.

11. The Dialogue Commission offers this report to its sponsors in the hope that it may encourage us all to work for the unity of Christians which we believe is God's will.

Chapter 1: Toward a Reconciliation of Memories

1.1. Whence Have We Come?

12. Whence have our communions come? What paths have they followed— together and apart, interacting, reacting, and going their separate ways—over 450 years to reach where they are today? This first chapter consists of accounts, written with consultation by each delegation, of our respective histories in relation to one another, as we see them now after five years of annual dialogues.

13. Today, in the late twentieth century, our churches are not the same dialogue partners they were even a generation ago, let alone in the sixteenth century. In the past, we tended to read our histories both selectively and polemically. To some extent, we still do. We see the events through which we have lived through confessionally biased eyes. The present reality of our churches is explained and justified by these readings of the past. Yet we are beginning to be able to transcend these limitations (a) by our common use of the results of objective scholarly inquiry,

and (b) by the dialogue our churches have had with each other in this consultation and elsewhere.

14. Historical scholarship today has not only produced fresh evidence concerning our respective roles in the Reformation and its aftermath. It also brings us together in broad agreement about sources, methods of inquiry, and warrants for drawing conclusions. A new measure of objectivity has become possible. If we still inevitably interpret and select, at least we are aware that we do and what that fact means as we strive for greater objectivity and more balanced judgment.

15. The method used in our present dialogue has also deepened our shared historical understanding. We first drafted our respective parts of this chapter separately. Reading and reviewing these drafts together we learned from each other and modified what we had written. We were reminded that over the centuries our forbears had often misunderstood each other's motives and language. We learned that our histories were sometimes a matter of action and reaction, but that at other times we followed separate paths. We occasionally heard each other speak vehemently and felt some of the passions that dictated the course of historical events and still in some ways drive us today.

16. All this has contributed to a certain reassessment of the past. We have begun to dissolve myths about each other, to clear away misunderstandings. We must go on from here, as our conclusion shows, to a reconciliation of memories, in which we will begin to share one sense of the past rather than two.

1.2. A Reformed Perspective

1.2.1. The Ecclesiological Concerns of the Reformers

17. The sixteenth-century Reformation was a response to a widespread demand for a general renewal of church and society. This demand had begun to be heard long before: it grew more insistent in the fourteenth and fifteenth centuries, led to the emergence of reformed communities such as the earlier Waldensians and the Hussites, and was addressed by several church councils. In the sixteenth century it resulted in the establishment of the major Protestant churches in various parts of Europe. Thus the unity of the medieval western church was shattered not only by the separation between the Protestant churches and the see of Rome, but also by the fact that the Reformation consisted of several reforming movements occurring at different times and places, often in conflict with one another, and leading to the different communions and confessional groups we know today.

18. Although the Reformed churches came to form a movement distinct from the Lutheran Reformation in Germany, they shared the same fundamental concerns: to affirm the sole headship of Jesus Christ over the church; to hear and proclaim the message of the Gospel as the one word of God which alone brings

authentic faith into being; to reorder the life, practice, and institutions of the church in conformity with the word of God revealed in Scripture. In all this there was no intention of setting up a "new" church: the aim was to reform the church in obedience to God's will revealed in his word, to restore "the true face of the church," and, as a necessary part of this process, to depart from ecclesiastical teachings, institutions, and practices which were held to have distorted the message of the Gospel and obscured the proper nature and calling of the church. For many complex reasons, there resulted new forms of church organization with far-reaching social, political, and economic ramifications—forms determined on the one hand by the fresh vision of the church's calling and commission, and on the other hand by rejection of a great deal that had developed in the previous centuries.

19. Among the chief affirmations of early Reformed ecclesiology were:

- The unity and universality of the one true church, to which those belong whom God has called or will call in Jesus Christ
- The authority of Jesus Christ governing the church through the word in the power of his Spirit
- The identification of an authentic "visible church" by reference to the true preaching of the word and the right administration of the two dominical sacraments of baptism and the Lord's Supper
- The importance of a proper church order, central to which was the office of the ministry of word and sacrament and, alongside it, the oversight exercised by elders sharing with the ministers of the word in governing the affairs of the church

20. As a consequence of these affirmations, the Reformers rejected all in the life of the church which, in their understanding, obscured the unique mediatorship of Jesus Christ and seemed to give to the church an excessive role alongside him. The emphasis placed in the ensuing controversy on the authority of the church and its hierarchy led them to question the value of episcopal succession as an expression of the continuity of the church in the apostolic truth through the centuries. In particular, they rejected teachings such as the following:

- The appeal to the church's tradition as an authority equal to Scripture or belonging together with it
- The universal authority of the pope
- The claim that church councils constitute an infallible teaching authority
- The canonical distinction between the office of a bishop and that of any other minister of the word and sacraments

1.2.2. The Emergence and Spread of the Reformed Churches

21. It is conceivable that many if not all of the Reformers' goals might have been realized without dividing the western church into different confessional traditions. Their aims and insights could perhaps eventually have been accepted by the entire church and issued in a comprehensive, unified Reformation. In fact, this did not happen. The established leadership of the western church was not generally prepared to agree to the amendments of doctrine, church order, and practice which the Reformers sought. The Reformers for their part were convinced that nothing less than obedience to God and the truth of the Gospel was at stake and interpreted resistance as unwillingness to undergo conversion and renewal. In addition, the process of reform proceeded at different paces and took different forms in different local and national settings. The result was division and much mutual exclusion even among the Reformation churches.

22. In this and in the subsequent development of the Reformed churches, such factors as geography, politics, social and cultural development played a considerable part. The Reformation took place in a period of radical intellectual, cultural, and political upheaval, which irreversibly altered the face of Europe and paved the way for the emergence of the modern world. The nascent Reformed churches of the sixteenth century both contributed to and were molded by these wider movements. The countries most profoundly influenced by Reformed theology were prominent among those in which, in the sixteenth and seventeenth centuries, for better or for worse, the seeds of modern democracy were fostered, new forms of economic order developed, autonomous natural science came to its first great flowering, and the demand for religious tolerance became increasingly insistent. Where it became influential, the Reformed ethos stimulated commerce, challenged despotisms, encouraged parliamentary government, and enhanced national consciousness.

23. In these developments, however, the Reformed churches showed that they could, in their own ways, fall victim to many of the same faults they criticized in the Roman Catholic Church. They became legitimators of sometimes oppressive political establishments, fell into clericalism, and grew intolerant of minority viewpoints. They were occasionally guilty of condemnations, burnings, and banishment, for example, in regard to the Anabaptists in Switzerland, acts in many cases typical of their times but not to be excused on that account. The Reformed also sometimes lent themselves to various forms of national chauvinism, colonialism, and racism. At times their criticisms of opponents (and especially of the papacy) grew intemperate even by the standards of an age given to vituperative language.

24. It has been claimed that the heritage and influence of Reformed thought contributed significantly alongside that of Renaissance and later humanism to the shaping of modern western culture. There is less agreement concerning the exact nature of this modernizing influence. It has been argued that in many respects the

Reformation was more a medieval than a modern phenomenon, yet it set processes in motion that had far-reaching influence. Even the Enlightenment of the eighteenth century can properly be seen as owing much to these impulses, albeit in largely secularized form. So, too, can the rise of modern biblical criticism in the eighteenth century and its rapid development from the nineteenth onwards.

25. The Reformed churches themselves could not but be affected by all these direct and indirect outworkings of the Renaissance and the Reformation. It must be admitted that they have displayed—especially up to the middle of the nineteenth century, but on occasion also since then as well—a tendency to divide and subdivide on matters of theological or ecclesiological principle. Rationalism, in the guise of a tendency to frame theology in tightly deductive systems, exacerbated this tendency. At times, rationalism gave rise in some Reformed churches to movements which even questioned such fundamental dogmatic convictions as the Trinity and the divinity of Jesus Christ. Another source of diversity lay in varying conceptions of proper church order, e.g., whether the government of the church should be synodal, congregational, or episcopal.

26. The family of Reformed churches has continued to grow and spread up to the present. The expansion of the Reformed family is primarily due to the missionary movement of the last two centuries. In 1875, the Alliance of Reformed Churches was founded as a rallying point for the worldwide Reformed and Presbyterian family. In 1970, it was widened to include the Congregational churches as well. The World Alliance of Reformed Churches counts today about 170 member churches. The majority of the member churches of the Alliance are to be found in Asia, Africa, Latin America, and the Pacific. Moreover, the last century has witnessed major efforts towards reunion within the Reformed family, and since 1918 various Reformed churches have entered transconfessional unions. Among the member churches of the Alliance there are today also some sixteen united churches, from the Evangelical Church of the Czech Brethren (1918) to the United Reformed Church in the United Kingdom (1981). At the same time it has also become increasingly more aware of the challenge to search after a fuller ecumenical unity. It is mindful of the abiding heritage of the Reformation, but at the same time of the common calling of all Christians today to confess and hold aloft that to which all adhere and in which all believe, namely the good news of Jesus Christ, "the one Word of God which we have to hear and obey in life and in death" (Theological Declaration of Barmen, 1934).

27. In pursuing its theological task, the World Alliance of Reformed Churches draws on the resources supplied by the rich tradition of Reformed theology through the centuries from Zwingli and Calvin and their contemporary Reformers to such figures of the recent past as Karl Barth, Josef Hromadka, and Reinhold Niebuhr. It also stands in the heritage of witness reflected in the confessions of the Reformed

churches from the sixteenth century onwards and seeks to continue that witness faithfully today. It does not do so, however, in the spirit of a narrow traditionalist Reformed confessionalism. Rather, it is open ecumenically and concerned to face contemporary and future social, cultural, and ethical challenges. The contribution of Reformed theology to today's churches does not consist merely in the maintenance of theological traditions or in the preservation of ecclesiastical institutions for their own sake, but in being what Karl Barth called "the modest, free, critical and happy science" (*Evangelical Theology*, ch. 1), which enquires into the reality of God in relation to us human beings individually and in community in the light of Jesus Christ, Emmanuel, "God with us."

1.2.3. Contemporary Reformed Attitudes Toward the Roman Catholic Church

28. Before the Second Vatican Council, with notable exceptions, the general Reformed view was that the Roman Catholic Church had not faced the real challenge of the Reformation and remained essentially "unreformed." This conviction was reinforced in the modern era on the doctrinal level by the definitions of the dogmas of papal infallibility (1870), the immaculate conception of the Virgin Mary (1854), and her bodily assumption (1950). In practical terms, the same conviction grew from the experience of Reformed minorities in countries dominated by Roman Catholicism. Up to this day the memory of the persecution of Reformed minorities plays a significant role. The development of the two traditions largely in isolation— even when alongside each other in the same country—increased the inclination of Reformed Christians and churches to view the Roman Catholic Church in terms of its reaction against the Reformation and reinforced negative attitudes toward Roman Catholic teaching, piety, and practice.

29. Signs of a change in perspective began to appear in the nineteenth century, but remained sporadic. Contacts increased and the desire for a new mutual understanding became more apparent in the twentieth century, not least as an offshoot of the active role played by many Reformed churches from the beginnings of the ecumenical movement. But it is really only since the pontificate of John XXIII and the events surrounding the Second Vatican Council that a genuinely new atmosphere has developed between the Reformed and the Roman Catholic churches. The presence of Reformed observers at the council and at other occasions since, the experience of ecumenical contact, shared activity, worship, and dialogue at many different levels from the local congregation to international commissions, and increasing cooperation and collaboration between Reformed and Roman Catholic scholars in work of exegetical, historical, systematic, and practical theology—all this has helped to break down misunderstandings and caricatures of the present-day reality of the Roman Catholic Church. In particular, these develop-

ments have helped the Reformed to appreciate the seriousness with which the Roman Catholic Church has placed the word of God at the center of its life, not least in modern liturgical reforms.

30. In general it can be said today that a process of reassessment and reevaluation of the Roman Catholic Church has been taking place among the Reformed churches in the last decades, though not proceeding at the same pace everywhere. There are within the Reformed family those whose attitude to the Roman Catholic Church remains essentially negative: some because they remain to be convinced that the modern development of the Roman Catholic Church has really addressed the issues of the Reformation, and others because they have been largely untouched by the ecumenical exchanges of recent times and have therefore not been challenged or encouraged to reconsider their traditional stance. But this is only one part of the picture. Others in the Reformed tradition have sought to engage in a fresh constructive and critical evaluation both of the contemporary teaching and practice of the Roman Catholic Church and of the classical controverted issues.

31. There is on the Reformed side an increasing sense that while the Reformation was at the time theologically and historically necessary, the division of the western church should not be accepted as the last word; that it is at best one-sided to read that history as if all the truth lay on the side of the Reformers and none at all on the side of their opponents and critics within the Roman Catholic camp; that there have been both in the more remote and more recent past many positive developments in the Roman Catholic Church itself; that the situation today presents new challenges for Christian witness and service which ought so far as possible to be answered together rather than in separation; and—perhaps most important of all—that Reformed Christians are called to search together with their Roman Catholic separated brothers and sisters for the unity which Christ wills for his church, both in terms of contemporary witness and in terms of reconsidering traditional disagreements. Theological dialogue, joint working groups on doctrinal and ethical issues, and programs of joint action undertaken by some Reformed churches together with the Roman Catholic Church in recent years—all these reflect this new climate, witness to a new and more positive evaluation of the Roman Catholic Church as an ecumenical partner, and hold out hope of further increase in mutual understanding in the future.

32. This is not to say that all problems between Reformed and Roman Catholic churches have already been resolved; it is to say that a search for solutions is underway and being undertaken together by both sides. One question requiring further consideration is whether our two traditions from their separation in the sixteenth century onwards need still to be seen as mutually exclusive. Or can they not rather be seen as reconcilable? Can we not look upon each other as partners in a search for full communion? In that search we may be led to discover complemen-

tary aspects in our two traditions, to combine appreciation for the questions and insights of the Reformers with recognition that the Reformed can also learn from the Roman Catholic Church, and to realize that Reformed and Roman Catholics need each other in their attempt to be more faithful to the Gospel. Those who have begun to think in this way are attempting to reconcile their heritage as heirs of the Reformation with their experience of fellowship with and learning from their sisters and brothers in the Roman Catholic Church. They are asking: Can our common faith set the questions which have divided and in part still divide us in a wider horizon of reconciliation?

1.3. A Roman Catholic Perspective

1.3.1. Ecclesiological and Reforming Concerns of Roman Catholics at the Time of the Reformation

33. What was the condition of the western church on the eve of the Reformation? Contemporaries found much to criticize. So have subsequent historians. Indeed, one of the most striking characteristics of the age was the vehemence of its rhetoric against certain abuses. Efforts were of course being made to change things for the better. Reform within the Catholic Church was undertaken in an urgent and more systematic way, however, only after the Council of Trent (1545-63) began to address it. But by that time the Protestant Reformation was already well established and underway.

34. Especially denounced at that time were the venality and political and military involvements of some of the popes and members of the curia; the absence of bishops from their dioceses; their often ostentatious wealth and neglect of pastoral duties; the ignorance of many of the lower clergy; the often scandalous lives of clergy, including bishops and certain popes; the disedifying rivalry among the religious orders; pastoral malpractice through misleading teaching about the efficacy of certain rites and rituals; the irrelevance and aridity of theological speculation in the universities and the presence of these same defects in the pulpit; the lack of any organized catechesis for the laity; and a popular piety based to a large extent on superstitious practices. Judgment on the church just before the Reformation has, therefore, been severe—and justly so.

35. Efforts at reform remained sporadic, uncoordinated, or confined to restricted segments of society. Among these efforts was the Observantist movement in the mendicant orders, which sought to restore the simplicity of their original inspiration. Furthermore a reform of the diocesan clergy in Spain was well underway by 1517. The Humanist movement encouraged a reform of theology and ministry that would depend more directly on biblical texts; it advocated a reform of education for both clergy and laity and proposed an ideal of piety that insisted upon

greater interiority and simplicity in religious practice. In the early stages of the Reformation the urgency of the situation was reflected also in the attempts of Pope Adrian VI (1522-23) to implement reform in the curia and elsewhere. The very vehemence with which its abuses were denounced in some sectors of the church and society indicates, moreover, a deepened religious sensitivity. In such a perspective the great leaders of both the Reformation and the Catholic Reform must be seen as products of the concerns of the age into which they were born and, to that extent, in continuity with those concerns and, indeed, with each other.

36. How, then, can we explain the resistance met by the proposals of Reformers like Luther, Zwingli, and Calvin? It is at this point that their discontinuity with previous efforts at reform emerges. While those earlier efforts concentrated on discipline, education, pastoral practice, and similar matters, Luther addressed himself first and foremost to doctrine, as later did Zwingli and Calvin. Many people, and not only theologians, were taken by surprise and were unwilling to accept this sudden shift to reform of doctrine and especially Luther's emphasis on the doctrine of justification. They were shocked by the implication that the church had for centuries been in error about the true meaning of the Gospel. Moreover, Luther's case was soon embroiled in a thicket of personal and theological rivalries and of imperial-papal politics, so that fair procedures and the serenity required for docility to the Spirit were tragically and almost irretrievably compromised at the opening moment. At practically that same moment a vituperative rhetoric from both sides began to dominate theological exchanges.

37. In such an atmosphere the demands and proposals of the Reformers were often also misunderstood by Catholics and then just as often distorted into caricatures. Direct access to their writings was at best piecemeal, at worst thought unnecessary. This meant that almost without exception, the centrality and dramatically evangelical nature of the issue of justification for the Reformers was not grasped. Very few Catholics really understood that for the Reformers what was at stake was not simply this or that doctrine, practice, or institution but the very Gospel itself. Thus, for Catholics "reform" continued to be conceived in pre-Reformation terms as addressing disciplinary and pastoral issues in their established form. They understood their engagement with the Reformation as refuting its "doctrinal errors."

38. In Catholic circles attention turned more or less immediately to ecclesiological issues. Up to the time of the Reformation reflection on the church had fallen into two main categories. The first consisted of polemical and apologetical works dealing with church order that arose out of conflicts between popes and either bishops or secular leaders. The argumentation was juridical and political. These works, which provided a ready-made, though theologically and biblically inadequate, defense of certain church institutions, were then utilized against the Reformers.

39. The second consisted of assumptions that were more properly theological in nature, but that had become embedded in writings and practice in a much less systematic way. These assumptions were, however, broadly operative in the minds of many persons, and they must be taken into account if we are to understand Catholic resistance to the Reformation. Some of these assumptions and the conclusions drawn from them were as follows:

- Christ founded the church, establishing it on the apostles, who are the basis of the episcopal order of ministry and authority in the church. In this order the bishop of Rome had more than primacy of honor, though the precise nature, extent, and function of this primacy was much debated.

   Therefore the proposals of the Reformers concerning church order appeared to be an attack on the apostolic foundation of the church.
- Christ promised unity for the church. Consensus in doctrine, extending through the ages, was a hallmark of the Spirit's work and a sign of Christ's unfailing presence in the church.

   Therefore the turmoil accompanying the Reformation and the conflict among some of the Reformers themselves were taken as proof positive that the Spirit of God was not at work among them.
- Although the church lived under Scripture, the church was chronologically prior to the writings of the New Testament and had recognized since earliest times that it itself as a community, especially when assembled in council, was the authoritative interpreter of the divine word.

   In contrast, the Reformers seemed to arrogate to themselves the right to interpret Scripture in a way at variance with the continuing tradition of the community, and they did not seem to provide any warrant for their interpretation that was necessarily grounded in the community.
- Bishops held primary responsibility for church polity.

   In contrast, Luther, Zwingli, and the English reformers appeared to deliver the church into the hands of secular princes and magistrates, thus threatening to reduce the church to a mere instrument of secular politics.

1.3.2. The Council of Trent and the Roman Catholic Reform

40. Within only a few years after the beginning of the Reformation, the seriousness of the crisis had become apparent to many. Less apparent were the means to address it effectively. Particularly from Germany, however, there soon came the cry for a council. Pope Paul III convoked the Council of Trent in December 1645. By that time—a full generation after Luther's Ninety-five Theses—positions had become so hardened and embittered that reconciliation was, humanly speaking, impossible. Responsibility for the long delay in convocation must be ascribed in part

to the complex political situation and to the ambivalent or obstructionist attitudes of some Protestant leaders, but lies principally with the fearful, vacillating, and self-serving policies of Pope Clement VII (1523-34). By the time Trent began its work, Zwingli had died (1531), Luther had less than a year to live, and other Reformers (such as Calvin) were already utterly convinced that Rome was unwilling to undertake the profound reform they wanted.

41. The Council of Trent was destined to last with long periods of interruption, over eighteen years, finally concluding in December 1563. Attempts to have Protestants participate failed for a number of reasons, with the result that membership in the council was restricted to Catholics. This fact indicated that the religious divisions were already deep and widespread. In a situation like this, the course of the council almost perforce helped confirm and sharpen the divisions, just as the various Protestant Confessions of Faith had done and would continue to do.

42. Trent addressed both doctrinal and disciplinary issues. Among its doctrinal decrees, the most fully discussed and the most earnestly researched was the Decree on Justification, approved in 1547. The complaint of Luther and others that the church in its actual practice taught a Pelagian doctrine of justification was taken by the principal authors of the decree with utmost seriousness. Every effort was made to avoid formulations that would fall into that heresy, yet considerable care was also exercised to insist on some measure of human responsibility, under grace, in the process of salvation. In its other doctrinal decrees, Trent gave an extraordinary amount of attention to the sacraments because they were perceived as falling under special attack.

43. The Council of Trent was animated by the conviction that it had the special guidance of the Spirit, and it considered itself to be the special vehicle of the continuing action of Christ in the church. Trent's explicit emphasis on the continuity of the church in practice, doctrine, and structure with the apostolic age was more pronounced than in any previous council. This emphasis prevented serious consideration of most of the changes the Reformers found to be required by their reading of the New Testament. At the council a certain reciprocity of word and church was taken for granted, as given and witnessed in both the early and contemporary church. The council, unlike the Reformers, ascribed apostolic authority to certain "traditions," although it refrained from providing a list of them.

44. Trent was notably concerned not to condemn any doctrinal position held by "Catholic theologians," and, although it never mentioned a single Reformer by name, it condemned what it thought were Protestant errors. Its decrees must, therefore, be interpreted with great caution. For several reasons, including the wide range of opinions in the council, Trent made practically no direct and explicit pronouncements about the ecclesiological disputes then raging. However, the very fact that the council took place was itself an expression of the self-understanding of the church.

45. In its decrees "concerning reform," Trent articulated its presumptions in generally juridical terms. It meant these decrees, however, to serve better ministerial practice and more effective care of souls. In reaffirming traditional structures, Trent at the same time undertook a certain redefinition of some of them. Perhaps the most sweeping, though implicit, ecclesiological redefinition in the council and during that era was that the church was primarily a pastoral institution. Trent sought especially to direct bishops to a properly pastoral appreciation of their office. It assigned to them the preaching of the word as their principal task, an assignment taken with the utmost seriousness by many post-Tridentine bishops, following the example set by Charles Borromeo and others.

46. Although Trent had given the greatest importance to the responsibility of bishops to proclaim the word of God (cf. Sessio XXIV, 11 Nov. 1563, can. IV *De Reformatione;* COD [1973] p. 763), the doctrine of the sacrament of order promulgated a few months sooner in the same year did not provide any place for the ministry of the word, so much was the council worried about defending the doctrine of sacraments (Sessio XXIII, 15 July 1563, *De Ordine,* COD [1973], pp. 742 ss.). This fact masks what was actually happening in Catholicism at the time and for several centuries thereafter. In fact, the ministry of the word was vigorously pursued, not so much because of the criticism of the Reformers as because in this regard the same reforming ideals impelled both Protestants and Catholics, even though much Catholic preaching may not have been biblical in a sense that the Reformed could recognize.

47. This development in the ministry of the word illustrates the fact that Catholic reform in the sixteenth and seventeenth centuries was much broader than the Council of Trent and cannot be simply equated with it. That reform promoted, among many other things, a great flowering of spiritualities and cultivation of religious experience, a vast program of catechesis, extensive systems of schools for laity and clergy, as well as other new forms of ministry and evangelization. Impressive though the reform was in so many ways, however, it was not without its failures and false steps. For instance: many earlier abuses like the nepotistic practices of the papal court and the seignorial style of the episcopacy seemed little affected for the better; the various inquisitions had terribly deleterious effects resulting from repressive measures that included confiscation of goods, banishments, and executions. The reading of the Bible in the vernacular, although not always forbidden to laity (contrary to that which is often asserted), was subject nevertheless to some extremely strict conditions, which in practice discouraged the laity. Those who were educated were able to read in Latin, as did the clergy, but those who would read it in the vernacular were often considered suspect. Moreover, the doctrinal and disciplinary decrees of Trent itself often came to be interpreted with a rigor and a partisanship the council did not intend.

1.3.3. From Trent to the Present

48. Post-Tridentine partisanship was manifested in various ways, not the least of which was the manner of stressing divergent understandings of the church. For example, when Roman Catholic apologists focused on the notes of the church—one, holy, catholic, and apostolic—Catholic positions were presented in ways intended to refute the ecclesiological claims of their Protestant contemporaries as well as to convey what Roman Catholics believed about the church. Thus, in contrast to the diversity of Protestant movements, Roman Catholics were united in one, visible church under the pope; where the Reformers championed justification by faith alone, Roman Catholics maintained also the role of good works in sanctification (in being made holy) and insisted on the grace conveyed by a worthy reception of the sacraments; where the newly formed Protestant churches had broken with the apostolic succession of the universal church, the Roman Catholic Church had retained the threefold apostolic ministry of episcopate, presbyterate, and diaconate; where the Reformers relied on their individual interpretation of Scripture, Roman Catholics claimed to preserve the entirety of catholic doctrine transmitted from Christ through the ages.

49. Such one-sided argumentation (which has generally been abandoned by Roman Catholic theologians since Vatican II) was apologetically successful—if not in convincing Protestants—at least in assuring Roman Catholics that theirs was the one and only true church of Jesus Christ. Moreover, post-Tridentine apologetics capitalized on the divisiveness within Protestantism in contrast to the organic unity of Roman Catholicism. At the same time, post-Tridentine Catholicism became ever more juridical in its approach to a wide range of issues and ecclesiology increasingly institution-oriented and papally centered.

50. This "pyramidal" ecclesiology, which emerged in the context of rising nationalism, received considerable reinforcement in the nineteenth century when both the spiritual prerogatives and the political power of papacy were subject to repeated attacks. Many ecclesiologists hastened to defend both the spiritual independence and the doctrinal authority of the popes. Simultaneously, on the popular level, the pope was considered the symbol of Roman Catholic unity, his slightest command a matter of unquestioning obedience. In the eyes of many, both within and outside the Roman Catholic Church, papal centrism appeared to have been absolutised by the First Vatican Council's teaching on the "primacy and infallible teaching authority of the Roman Pontiff." Due to the adjournment of the council shortly after this definition, Vatican I did not have sufficient opportunity to take up the broader ecclesiological issues in the schema De Ecclesia, which was proposed for consideration but never adopted.

51. In fact, the teaching of the First Vatican Council in this regard is much more nuanced than either its ultramontane proponents or its antipapal opponents

seem to have realized. For example, Vatican I did not teach that "the pope is infallible," as is popularly imagined. Rather it taught that the pope can, under carefully specified and limited circumstances, officially exercise the infallibility divinely given to the church as a whole, in order to decide questions of faith and morals for the universal church.

52. Forces already then at work have had profound effects on the Catholic Church in the twentieth century, influencing ecclesiology as well. Renewal movements relating to biblical studies, liturgy, theology, pastoral concerns, ecumenism, and other factors paved the way for the Second Vatican Council (1962-1965). Influenced also by the ecumenical movement, this council's rich presentation of the church in *Lumen Gentium* differed significantly from apologetical approaches to the past. Concentrating not just on institutional aspects, but on basic biblical and patristic insights on the church, *Lumen Gentium* reemphasized, among other themes, the notion of the church as the people of God and as a communion. All members of the people of God, it said, participate, even if in different ways, in the life of Christ and in his role as prophet, priest, and king (LG, nos. 9-13). The council described the dimensions of collegiality in which the bishops of the whole world live in communion with one another and with the pope, the head of the episcopal college. While reiterating again the primacy of the bishop of Rome, the council made clear that the bishops also "exercise their own proper authority for the good of their faithful, indeed even for the good of the whole Church" (LG, no. 22). In focusing on an ecclesiology of communion, the council was also able to give fresh insights on relations already existing, despite separations, with Christians of other churches and ecclesial communities—a real though imperfect communion that exists because of baptism (UR, no. 22).

53. As already seen, Catholics agree that there was need for reform in the church in the sixteenth century, and acknowledge the fact that church authorities did not undertake the reform which might have prevented the tragic divisions that took place. At the same time the Roman Catholic Church has never agreed with some of the steps taken by the Reformers relating to their separation from the Roman Catholic communion, nor with certain theological positions that developed in Reformed communities, and seeks dialogue with the Reformed on those issues. The various ways in which reform and renewal have taken place within the Catholic Church since the sixteenth century illustrate resources that existed for bringing renewal from within. Thus, while the Council of Trent came too late to avoid divisions, it clarified Catholic doctrine and introduced reforms which have had lasting effects in the church. The birth of new religious orders from the sixteenth century to the twentieth, and the renewal of older religious orders, gave fresh impulses to missionary activity. From the sixteenth century, evangelization has increased. Catholic missionaries, sometimes at the cost of their lives, brought the

Gospel to lands where it had never been heard before. In traditionally Christian countries, other groups emphasized apostolates of service to the poor and of education of the young or the renewal of contemplative life. Movements of lay spirituality and Catholic action have flourished, especially in the twentieth century, along with movements for liturgical, biblical, and pastoral renewal. Such developments and many others paved the way for the significant reform and renewal brought about in the Catholic Church through the Second Vatican Council which continue to be implemented in the church today.

1.3.4. Contemporary Roman Catholic Attitudes Toward the Reformed Churches

54. The ecumenical experience of Roman Catholics also gradually increased, sometimes intentionally through such efforts as the Week of Prayer for Christian Unity, and sometimes circumstantially as in the experiences of World War II, when Christians from different churches suffered and died together as prisoners and refugees. While such shared experiences helped to develop the ecumenical climate in which Vatican II met, even the most prophetic could not have predicted that the council would provide what turned out to be a pervasive reorientation in Roman Catholic liturgy and life, theology and thought.

55. Prior to Vatican II, the attitude of most Roman Catholics towards Protestants in general, and members of Reformed churches in particular, was negative, though the degree of negativity ranged from overt hostility in some places to guarded acceptance in others. Friendship between members of the two traditions tended to be based on family, business, and social relationships, in which religious differences were frequently left undiscussed. Genuine theological dialogue, though not unknown, was comparatively rare; more common were polemical exchanges in which Roman Catholics criticized and sometimes caricatured the history, doctrine, and worship of their Protestant "adversaries."

56. Roman Catholic negativity toward the Reformed churches had a number of intertwined bases. On the ecclesiastical level, the most obvious focus of contention was the Reformed rejection of the episcopacy and the papacy that was also sometimes expressed in terms that Roman Catholics found extremely offensive. Another cause of opposition was the fact that the Reformed principle of *sola scriptura* resulted in a repudiation of many Roman Catholic teachings and practices, such as the sacrifice of the Mass, Marian devotions, and the earning of indulgences.

57. These religious differences were further intensified by social, economic, and political disparities. In areas where Roman Catholics were a minority, they frequently felt themselves oppressed by members of the "Protestant establishment." The separate and frequently antagonistic development of the Reformed and Roman

Catholic communities tended to perpetuate stereotypes and, in some cases, still continues to impede dialogue even today.

58. Although there were some instances of ecumenical dialogue between Reformed and Roman Catholic theologians prior to the Second Vatican Council, it was the council that provided the significant breakthrough for overcoming the long-standing antagonism in Reformed–Roman Catholic relationships. While the council primarily aimed at achieving an *aggiornamento* within the Roman Catholic Church, the presence of observers from other Christian communions, including Reformed churches, was a constant reminder that ecclesial reform and renewal are not only internal concerns, but have ecumenical implications as well.

59. In particular, *Unitatis Redintegratio* noted that the churches and communities coming from the Reformation "are bound to the Catholic Church by an especially close relationship as a result of the long span of earlier centuries when Christian people lived together in ecclesiastical communion" (no. 19). It recognized that the Spirit of Christ has not refrained from using them as a means of salvation (no. 3). The council encouraged Catholics to work for the reunion of all Christians through ecumenical dialogue, a disavowal of prejudices, and cooperation on projects of mutual concern. Instead of repeating the polemical accusations that charged Protestant Christians with the sin of separation, the council acknowledged them as "separated brethren" (*fratres seinucti*), justified by their faith through baptism, who reverence the written word of God, share in the life of grace, receive the gifts of the Holy Spirit, celebrate Christ's death and resurrection when they gather for the Lord's Supper, and witness to Christ through the moral uprightness of their lives, through their works of charity, and their efforts for justice and peace in the world.

60. During the years since Vatican II, this process of reconciliation has been carried on in different ways and at various levels—local, national, regional, international. For example, Reformed and Roman Catholics have prayed together, have been involved in theological dialogue at various levels; they have joined in producing Bible translations; they have collaborated on a variety of projects of social concern, economic justice, and political witness. At the international level, the efforts of the dialogue cosponsored by the Vatican Secretariat for Promoting Christian Unity and the World Alliance of Reformed Churches were recognized by Pope John Paul II in a letter to Dr. James McCord, President of the World Alliance of Reformed Churches, on the occasion of its General Council in Ottawa, in July 1982:

> The way upon which we have embarked together is without return, we can only move forward, that is why we strive to manifest unity more perfectly and more visibly, just as God wants it for all those who believe in him. (Secretariat for Promoting Christian Unity, *Information Service*, 51 [1983], p. 30)

61. In the scholarly world, these efforts at reconciliation have been accompanied by new interpretations of Reformation history and theology. For example, Roman Catholic theologians today generally acknowledge that many of the issues raised by the Reformers urgently needed to be faced and resolved. Similarly, Roman Catholic historians, while not agreeing with all aspects of their thought, have become more sympathetic to Zwingli and to Calvin, no longer seeing them chiefly as rebels against ecclesial authority but as Reformers who felt obliged by their understanding of the Gospel to continue their efforts to reform the church at all costs. The "zeal that animated these two outstanding religious personalities of Swiss history" was favorably noted by Pope John Paul II on the occasion of his pastoral visit to the Catholic Church of Switzerland in 1984:

> The legacy of the thought and ethical convictions particular to each of these two men continues to be forcefully and dynamically present in various parts of Christianity. On the one hand, we cannot forget that the work of their reform remains a permanent challenge among us and makes our ecclesiastical division always present, but on the other hand, no one can deny that elements of the theology and spirituality of each of them maintain deep ties between us. (Secretariat for Promoting Christian Unity, *Information Service* 55 [1984], p. 47)

1.4. Conclusion

62. As mentioned at the beginning of this chapter, these reviews of our respective histories, even when sketched so briefly, have shown us "whence we have come," so that we can better understand where we are—so that we can better understand what yet needs to be done in reassessing our past. We see more clearly how our respective self-understandings have been so largely formed by confessional historiographies of the sixteenth and seventeenth centuries. These differing self-interpretations have, in turn, fostered the establishment of whole sets of different values, symbols, assumptions, and institutions—in a word, different religious and ecclesial cultures. The result is that today, as in the past, the same words, even the same biblical expressions, are sometimes received and understood by us in quite different ways.

63. The very recognition that this is the case marks important progress in our attempt to rid our memories of significant resentments and misconceptions. We need to set ourselves more diligently, however, to the task of reconciling these memories, by writing together the story of what happened in the sixteenth century, with

attention not only to the clash of convictions over doctrine and church order, but with attention also as to how in the aftermath our two churches articulated their respective understandings into institutions, culture, and the daily lives of believers. But, above all, for the ways in which our divisions have caused a scandal and been an obstacle to the preaching of the Gospel, we need to ask forgiveness of Christ and of each other.

Chapter 2: Our Common Confession of Faith

2.1. Our Lord Jesus Christ: The Only Mediator Between God and Humankind

64. Before moving on to matters which are still points of disagreement and divergence between our churches, we as a dialogue commission propose to confess together our faith in Christ. We give this affirmation of faith the title "confession" even though it is neither a confession in the ecclesial sense nor a complete state-ment of faith. We do so because we are convinced that the importance of what we are able to say together merits such a title.

65. We make this confession of faith, wishing to manifest publicly our desire to reexamine the reasons which brought about our separation in the past and to assess whether or not they are still of such a nature as to justify our division. Jesus Christ, in whose name our forbears separated themselves from one another, is also the one who unites us in a community of forgiveness and of kinship. We wish to voice our conviction that what unites us as Christians is more important, more essential, than that which separates us as Roman Catholics and Reformed. Even if full communion is not yet granted us, we cannot define our relations to each other simply in terms of separation and division.

66. We make this confession, moreover, mindful of this world of ours, so as to give common witness before it. With respect for all who seek God, however God is named for them, or even if for them God cannot as yet be named, we wish to speak the good news of salvation brought in Jesus Christ by God seeking out humankind. In that good news we Christians already find our reconciliation and the strength to work for the fuller reconciliation of all with God and with each other.

67. This confession involves on our part the recognition of the authority of the Scriptures, as these have been identified by the early church, to whose teaching we desire to remain obedient. We recall what was said on this subject in the report of the first phase of our dialogue (PCCW, nos. 25-33). In the same way we recog-nize together in the teaching of the ancient church the force of a *norma normata*, i.e., an authority which is subject to the authority of the Scripture, and we desire to maintain that teaching in its purity. The teaching of the church ought to be an

authentic explanation of the trinitarian and christological affirmations of the early confessions of faith and the early councils (cf. on this subject, PCCW, nos. 34-38).

2.1.1. Christ, Mediator and Reconciler

68. Before all humankind, our sisters and brothers, we announce the death of the Lord (cf. 1 Cor 11:26) and proclaim his resurrection from the dead (cf. Rom 10:9; Acts 2:32, 3:15). In that mystery of death and resurrection we confess the event which saves humanity, that is, liberates it from the distress in which it is imprisoned by sin and establishes it in communion of life with God. That event reveals who God is, who Christ is as mediator between God and humankind.

69. a. God is the one who "chose us (in Christ) before the foundation of the world. . . . He destined us in love to be his sons through Jesus Christ" (Eph 1:4-5), a God of tenderness and mercy, who wills not the death of the sinner, but rather that the sinner should be converted and live. God is the one who has loved us unto death: indeed, in the person of Jesus Christ, God himself died on the cross for, "in Christ, God was reconciling the world to himself" (2 Cor 5:19). But this was not the "death of God" proclaimed in recent times: it was the death of the Just One fallen into the hands of evil persons, and faithful to his mission to the end. Jesus died a death which is a victory over the death which touches all. God's omnipotence is revealed in the deepest weakness of human nature, assumed in solidarity with us. If the death of Jesus is the work of sinners, God from all eternity has made it one with the design of salvation, accomplishing that life-giving work by raising Jesus from the dead. Placed at the heart of human violence, Jesus by his love has transformed the work of death into the work of life.

b. The death and resurrection of Jesus also reveal to us who we are: not merely creatures who are object of God's benevolence, but also human beings capable of sin, historically imprisoned in the bonds of a sin which is our curse. From the beginning we hid ourselves from God, and this is why God is hidden from us. It is not that God is distant and inaccessible, but that we reject the God who is too near and too explicit. This awareness of alienation and exile in the midst of faith we call sin. We recognize that there is a betrayal of God's trust in us and that God's heart is saddened by our separation. From this condition we cannot free ourselves by our own strength. This is why the need and expectation of a mediator are central to the old covenant, where the law, sacrifices, prophecies, wisdom are ways of mediating between a living God and a humanity subject to sin and death. But none of these paths fully reach the goal. Because of sin, the law intended for life judges, condemns, and leads to death. Substitute sacrifices are endlessly repeated. Prophecies lag, bide their time, fall silent. Wisdom remains an ideal. In Jesus, the unique mediator, in his death and resurrection we are radically freed from this situation: the way of true life is opened to us anew.

c.　The death and resurrection of Jesus finally reveal who Jesus himself is, the one mediator between God and humanity, that is, the one who comes to reconcile us with God. This is why we accept together the confession of faith of the New Testament. "For there is one God, and there is one Mediator between God and men, the man Christ Jesus, who gave himself as a ransom for all" (1 Tm 2:5-6). We confess that "there is no other name under heaven given among men by which we must be saved" (Acts 4:12).

70. Mediation and reconciliation have been embodied and located, named and personified in Jesus of Nazareth, whence it was thought at that time nothing good could come; condemned and executed at Jerusalem, which God has since David's time identified as the place of God's peace; resurrected by the power of God; and placed at God's right hand. This is the news still surprising and overwhelming, which constitutes the Gospel; of this the church is the beneficiary and the herald.

71. We therefore confess together that Christ, established as mediator, achieves our reconciliation in all its dimensions: God reconciling humanity; human beings reconciled with each other; and humanity reconciled with God.

- On the one hand, indeed, in and through Jesus Christ we have reconciliation with God. For "every good endowment and every perfect gift is from above, coming down from the Father of lights" (Jas 1:17). For "all this is from God, who through Christ reconciled us to himself . . ." (2 Cor 5:18); "In him we have redemption through his blood, the forgiveness of our trespasses" (Eph 1:7).

- On the other hand, in and through Jesus Christ, we have reconciliation among ourselves, "for he is our peace, who has made us both one." In his flesh he "has broken down the dividing wall of hostility . . . that he might create in himself one new man in place of the two, so making peace, and might reconcile us both to God in one body through the cross, thereby bringing the hostility to an end. And he came and preached peace to you who were far off and peace to those who were near" (Eph 2:14-17). The vertical and horizontal dimensions of reconciliation are interdependent: just as hostility is the consequence and sign of separation from God, so reconciliation in peace among human beings is the fruit and sign of reconciliation with God. From Christ we receive the gift of reconciliation which aims to extend to all. To this we witness together in faith.

- Finally, thanks to Jesus Christ, Jews and Gentiles "both have access in one Spirit to the Father" (Eph 2:18). In and through Christ we can offer ourselves "as a living sacrifice, holy and acceptable to God, which is . . . spiritual worship" (Rom 12:1). For he "gave himself up for us, a fragrant offering and sacrifice to God" (Eph 5:2). Jesus, the Christ, marks the end of condemnation by the law, because he is ". . . our righteousness and sanctification and redemption" (1 Cor 1:30); he marks the end of the sacrifices of the law because "he entered once for all into the holy place, taking . . . his own blood, thus securing an eternal redemption" (Heb 9:12); Christ marks the end of waiting on prophecies because he fulfills all that was written of him ". . . in the Law of Moses, and the prophets and the psalms" (cf. Lk 24:44); Christ marks the end of the anonymity of wisdom, for he himself is the "wisdom of God" (1 Cor 1:24).

72. We confess together that just as God is unique, the Mediator and Reconciler between God and humankind is unique and that the fullness of reconciliation is entire and perfect in him. Nothing and nobody could replace or duplicate, complete or in any way add to the unique mediation accomplished "once for all" (Heb 9:12) by Christ, "mediator of a new covenant" (Heb 9:15; cf. 8:6 and 12:24). This mediation is still present and active in the person of the risen Christ who "is able for all time to save those who draw near to God through him, since he always lives to make intercession for them" (Heb 7:25).

2.1.2. The Work of Christ Reveals That He Is the Son Within the Trinity

73. In his life and in his death Jesus is revealed as the Son *par excellence* of God, the one who alone knows the Father and whom the Father alone knows (cf. Mt 11:27), who can address himself to God saying "Abba, Father" (Mk 14:36). Thus in the light of Jesus' resurrection and exaltation, Christians have confessed that he has been made Christ and Lord (cf. Acts 2:36) and that he is the one to whom are applied the words of the Psalm: "Thou art my Son, today I have begotten thee" (Acts 13:33; cf. Heb 1:53). He is, then, this one whom God has sent us (cf. Gal 4:4); he who "though he was in the form of God did not count equality with God a thing to be grasped, but emptied himself, taking the form of a servant, being born in the likeness of men. And being found in human form he humbled himself and became obedient unto death, even death on a cross" (Phil 2:6-8). This is why with the church of every age, we confess Jesus Christ as at once true God and true human being, at once one with God and joined in solidarity with humankind, not an intermediary between God and humanity but a genuine Mediator, able to bring

together God and humanity in immediate communion. His reconciling mediation opens up for us a vision of his mediation in creation: he is "the first-born of all creation; for in him all things were created, in heaven and on earth . . . all things were created through him and for him" (Col 1:15-16). He is the Word and "all things were made through him" (Jn 1:3). The mediation of Christ has thus a cosmic universality: it is directed towards the transformation of our world in God.

74. Finally, the work of Jesus, the Son, reveals to us the role of the Spirit of God who is common to him and to the Father: it reveals to us that God is triune.

75. The Holy Spirit is present and active throughout the history of salvation. In the life of Jesus the Spirit intervenes at all the decisive moments: Jesus was conceived by the Holy Spirit (cf. Lk 1:35; Mt 1:20); the Spirit descended on him at his baptism (Lk 3:22); he was filled with the Holy Spirit (Lk 4:1); he accomplished his ministry with the power of the Spirit (Lk 4:14). He proclaimed that the prophecy of the Book of Isaiah: "The Spirit of the Lord is upon me, because the Lord has anointed me" (61:1) was fulfilled in him (Lk 4:17-21). He rejoiced in the Holy Spirit (Lk 10:21). No one had ever possessed the Spirit as he did, "not by measure" (Jn 3:34). Still more, it is he who promises to send the Spirit (Jn 14:26; 16:7) and invokes the Spirit on his own disciples after the resurrection (Jn 20:22), because his death had been an act of "giving up" the Spirit to God and at the same time an act of "transmission of the Spirit" (Jn 19:30). In turn God raises him up and gives him the Spirit, so that he might spread the Spirit among us (cf. Acts 2:32-33). By the life, death, and resurrection of Jesus, the Holy Spirit becomes the common gift of the Father and the Son to humanity.

76. Just as the Spirit came upon Jesus at the moment of his baptism, so the Spirit descends upon the disciples gathered in the upper room (Acts 2:1-12) and on the Gentiles who listen to the word (Acts 10:44-48). These three closely linked "Pentecosts" belong to the foundation of the church and make it the "temple of the Spirit." Thus the design pursued from the beginning by God the Creator and Savior—to bring into being a people—is accomplished.

2.2. Justification by Grace, Through Faith

77. Because we believe in Christ, the one Mediator between God and humankind, we believe that we are justified by the grace which comes from him, by means of faith which is a living and life-giving faith. We recognize that our justification is a totally gratuitous work accomplished by God in Christ. We confess that the acceptance in faith of justification is itself a gift of grace. By the grace of faith we recognize in Jesus of Nazareth, established Christ and Lord by his resurrection, the one who saves us and brings us into communion of life with God. To rely for sal-

vation on anything other than faith would be to diminish the fullness accomplished and offered in Jesus Christ. Rather than completing the Gospel, it would weaken it.

78. To speak in this way of our justification and reconciliation with God is to say that faith is above all a reception (Rom 5:1-2): it is received and in turn it gives thanks for grace. The raising to life, by God alone, of Jesus Christ, put to death by all, is the eschatological event which defines faith as reception of a gift of God, not as any human work (Eph 2:8-10). We receive from Christ our justification, that is our pardon, our liberation, our life with God. By faith, we are liberated from our presumption that we can somehow save ourselves; by faith, we are comforted in spite of our terror of losing ourselves. We are set at liberty to open ourselves to the sanctification which God wills for us.

79. The person justified by the free gift of faith, i.e., by a faith embraced with a freedom restored to its fullness, can henceforth live according to righteousness. The person who has received grace is called to bear fruits worthy of that grace. Justification makes him or her an "heir of God, co-heir with Christ" (Rom 8:17). The one who has freely received is committed to gratitude and service. This is not a new form of bondage but a new way forward. And so, justification by faith brings with it the gift of sanctification, which can grow continuously as it creates life, justice, and liberty. Jesus Christ, the one mediator between God and humankind, is also the unique way which leads toward pleasing God. Faith receives freely and bears testimony actively, as it works itself out through love (Gal 5:6).

2.3. The Calling of the Church; Its Role in Justification by Grace Through Faith

80. Together we confess the church, for there is no justification in isolation. All justification takes place in the community of believers or is ordered toward the gathering of such a community. Fundamental for us all is the presence of Christ in the church, considered simultaneously as both a reality of grace and a concrete community in time and space. Christ himself acts in the church in the proclamation of the word, in the celebration of the sacraments, in prayer, and in intercession for the world. This presence and this action are enabled and empowered by the Spirit, by whom Christ calls to unite human beings to himself, to express his reality through them, to associate them in the mystery of his self-offering for them.

81. The church's calling is set within the triune God's eternal plan of salvation for humankind. In this sense, the church is already present at creation (Col 1:15-18). It is present in the history of humankind: "the church from Abel," as it was called in the ancient church. It is also present at the covenant declared to Abraham from which the chosen people would come. Even more, the church is present at the establishment of the people of the covenant. Through the law and the

prophets, God calls this people and prepares them for a communion which will be accomplished at the sending of Emmanuel, "God with us" (cf. Mt 1:23). The novelty introduced by the incarnation of the Word does not call into question the continuity of the history of salvation. Nor does it call into question the significance of the interventions of that same Word and Spirit in the course of the Old Testament revelation. For God has not rejected this people (Rom 11:1). The continued existence of the chosen people is an integral part of the history of salvation.

82. Nevertheless we believe that the coming of Christ, the Word incarnate, brings with it a radical change in the situation of the world in the sight of God. Henceforth the divine gift which God has made in Jesus Christ is irreversible and definitive. On God's side, salvation is accomplished and is offered to all. The presence of God has become inward among believers (Jer 31:33; Ez 36:26) in a new fashion, by the Holy Spirit which conforms them to the image of Jesus Christ. At the same time, God's presence becomes universal; it is not limited to one people but is offered to all humanity called to be gathered together by Christ in the Spirit.

83. This is why we believe that the people of God gathered together by the death and resurrection of Christ does not live solely by the promise. Henceforth it lives also by the gift already received through the mystery of the event of Jesus, Christ and Lord, who has sent his Spirit. We therefore confess Jesus Christ as the foundation of the church (1 Cor 3:11).

84. The inauguration of the church takes place in time and in stages related to the unfolding of the Christ-event. These stages, closely related as they are, are three in number:

a.   There is, first, the missionary activity of Jesus "in the days of his flesh" (Heb 5:7): his preaching of the kingdom, which presupposes the promises of the Old Testament, and his mighty works; the invitation to believe in him and the call to conversion addressed to all; the gathering of the disciples, men and women (Lk 8:1-3), and the appointment of the group of Twelve (Mk 3:13-19); the change of Simon's name to Peter (Mt 16:18) and the role which is assigned to him in the circle of the disciples (Lk 22:31-32).

b.   The second stage is Jesus' celebration of the Last Supper with these same disciples as a memorial (Lk 22:14-20) of the giving of his life for all; his death on the cross, by which he accomplished the salvation of all (Jn 12:32); the resurrection of Jesus, which gathers the scattered community of the disciples. The risen Christ for forty days leads his followers into a more profound faith (Acts 1:2-3); in leaving them he gives them the command to baptize (Mt 28:18), to preach repentance and forgiveness, and to bear witness to him (Lk 24:47-48).

c. The third stage is the sending of the Spirit upon the community of one hundred and twenty gathered on the day of Pentecost (Acts 2:2-4). The disciples are sent out to Israelites and to Gentiles, as is shown by the gift of the Spirit to the Gentiles (Acts 10:44), which may be called a "new Pentecost." Thus, the church is founded once for all, fully constituted and equipped for its universal vocation in the world and for its eschatological destiny. This gift of the Spirit is the firstfruits. The Spirit's work of renewal and gathering will be fully achieved and manifested only when Christ returns in glory.

85. The church is called into being as a community of men and women to share in the salvific activity of Christ Jesus. He has reconciled them to God, freed them from sin, and redeemed them from evil. "They are justified by his grace as a gift, through the redemption which is in Christ Jesus" (Rom 3:24).

86. The justification of Jesus' disciples, sinful individuals freely justified by grace without any merit on their part, has been one of the constitutive experiences of the Christian faith since the foundation of the church. Justification by grace through faith is given us in the church. This is not to say that the church exercises a mediation complementary to that of Christ or that it is clothed with a power independent of the gift of grace. The church is at once the place, the instrument, and the minister chosen by God to make heard Christ's word and to celebrate the sacraments in God's name throughout the centuries. When the church faithfully preaches the word of salvation and celebrates the sacraments, obeying the command of the Lord and invoking the power of the Spirit, it is sure of being heard, for it carries out in its ministry the action of Christ himself.

87. The ministerial and instrumental role of the church in the proclamation of the Gospel and in the celebration of the sacraments in no way infringes the sovereign liberty of God. If God chooses to act through the church for the salvation of believers, this does not restrict saving grace to these means. The sovereign freedom of God can always call anyone to salvation independently of such actions. But it is true to say that God's call is always related to the church, in that God's call always has as its purpose the building up of the church, which is the body of Christ (1 Cor 12:27-28; Eph 1:22-23) (cf. no. 101).

88. This common confession of the church, of its vocation and of its role in justification by grace through faith, provides a positive context for a study of some of the questions which still divide us in our respective understandings of the relationship between Christ's Gospel and the church as a community existing in the world.

Chapter 3: The Church We Confess and Our Divisions in History

3.1. Introduction

89. The difficulties which still separate our communions arise largely from our different understandings of the relationship between that which we confess, on the one hand, concerning the origin and the vocation of the one, holy, catholic, and apostolic church in God's plan of salvation and, on the other hand, the forms of its historical existence. Our two communions regard themselves as belonging to the *una sancta* but differ in their understanding of that belonging.

90. In addressing this subject, we must move beyond comparative ecclesiology. Our method requires us both to say what we can together and to recognize without ambiguity that which cannot yet be the object of consensus.

91. This implies a double challenge. There are, first, differences of perspective such that we find in the position of the partner a complementary point of view or a different accent on a single, commonly held truth. In opening ourselves to the partner's critique, we can learn to express our own views in a more balanced way and perhaps find a common frame of reference for understanding each other.

92. Secondly, however, some of our positions seem simply to diverge. They appear mutually incompatible or incommensurable. That leaves us, for the present at least, with no choice but to agree to disagree, while seeking clarity about the nature of our disagreements. We find, among other things, that we disagree about what issues are serious enough to be church-dividing. Questions which, from the Roman Catholic side, are obstacles to full communion are not necessarily so from the perspective of the Reformed, and vice versa. This does not dispense us from the responsibility of searching for reconciliation across even the most apparently insurmountable barriers. In the meantime we respect each other, and we are grateful for the measure of community that is possible between us.

93. In this report we do not treat the whole range of ecclesiological issues. We prefer to highlight three particular arenas of discussion because of what is at stake in them and because of the light they can cast on the way to a fuller consensus. We shall deal, first, with two conceptions of the church which, though different, we consider potentially complementary. We then deal with two areas of apparent divergence or incompatibility: our views of continuity and discontinuity in church history, and of the church's visibility and ministerial order.

3.2. Two Conceptions of the Church

94. We have already affirmed the ministerial and instrumental role of the church in the proclamation of the Gospel and the celebration of the sacraments (nos. 85-86). Word and sacrament alike are of the very nature of the church. They also provide us with two different conceptions for understanding the church and the way in which it fulfills its ministerial and instrumental role: the first, more "Reformed," the second, more "Roman Catholic."

3.2.1. The Church as "Creatura Verbi"

95. The church existing as a community in history has been understood and described in the Reformed tradition as *creatura verbi*, as "the creation of the word." God is eternally word as well as Spirit; by God's word and Spirit all things were created; reconciliation and renewal are the work of the same God, by the same word and Spirit.

96. God's word in history has taken a threefold form. Primarily it is the word made flesh: Jesus Christ, incarnate, crucified, and risen. Then it is the word as spoken in God's history with God's people and recorded in the Scriptures of the Old and New Testaments as testimony to Jesus Christ. Third, it is the word as heard and proclaimed in the preaching, witness, and action of the church. The third form depends upon and is bound to the second, through which it has access to the first, the word incarnate in Jesus Christ. This is why the Reformed tradition has insisted so emphatically that the preaching, teaching, and witness of the church through the centuries—the church's dogma and tradition—are always to be subordinated to the testimony of the Bible, that Scripture rather than Tradition is "the word of God written" and "the only infallible rule of faith and practice." Scripture is the control by which the church's proclamation must be governed if that proclamation is to witness authentically to God's word in Jesus Christ and to be "the word proclaimed." For the word of God is one consistent word: The word of judgment and mercy, the Gospel of reconciliation, the announcing of the reign of God. It is a word alive as Jesus Christ himself is alive: it is a word calling to be heard, answered, and reechoed; it is a word claiming response, obedience, and commitment as the word of grace which evokes and empowers authentic faith.

97. The church depends upon this word—the word incarnate, the word written, the word preached—in at least three ways:

- The church is founded upon the word of God
- The church is kept in being as the church by the word of God
- The church continually depends upon the word of God for its inspiration, strength, and renewal

98. In each of these aspects, the word and Spirit of God work together, for it is the power of the Spirit that enables the hearing of the word and the response of faith. The word and Spirit of God together establish, preserve, and guide the community of the church in and through human history. The church, like faith itself, is brought into being by the hearing of God's word in the power of God's Spirit; it lives *ex auditu*, by hearing.

99. This emphasis upon hearing the word of God has been of central importance in Reformed theology since the sixteenth century. This is why the Reformed have stressed "the true preaching of the word" together with "the right dispensing of the sacraments according to the institution of Jesus Christ" as a decisive "mark of the true church." Behind this emphasis lies a keen awareness of the way in which the Old Testament proclaimed "the word of the Lord," of the New Testament recognition of Jesus Christ as "the word who was in the beginning with God"—and of the new sense in the sixteenth century that the Bible is a living, contemporary word with which the church's teaching and order, as these had come to develop, were by no means always in harmony. Against the appeal to continuity, custom, and institution, the Reformed appealed to the living voice of the living God as the essential and decisive factor by which the church must live, if it will live at all: the church, as *creatura verbi*.

100. Thus far, our exposition has been relatively traditional and familiar. But despite the intended organic relationship between word and church, the Reformed tradition has not always held it steadily in view. It has sometimes inclined to verbalism, to the reduction of the Gospel to doctrine, of the divine word incarnate in Jesus Christ to theological theory. Proclamation of the word has been seen simply as an external mark of the church rather than intrinsic to it, the church itself regarded more as the place where Scripture is interpreted than as a community living from the word. Such understandings fall short of the full meaning of *creatura verbi* as describing the nature and calling of the church.

101. The church is the creation of the word because the word itself is God's creative word of grace by which we are justified and renewed. The church is the human community shaped and ruled by that grace; it is the community of grace, called to let "this mind be among yourselves, which is yours in Christ Jesus . . ." (Phil 2:5). The community of faith is thus not merely the community in which the Gospel is preached; by its hearing and responding to the word of grace, the community itself becomes a medium of confession, its faith a "sign" or "token" to the world; it is itself a part of the world transformed by being addressed and renewed by the word of God.

3.2.2. The Church as "Sacrament of Grace"

102. Even before Vatican II, many Roman Catholic theologians described the church as a "sacrament," because this term is associated with the biblical term "mys-

tery." Such a sacramental description highlights the comparison between what the church is and what is enacted in the celebration of the sacraments. The adoption of this term by the Second Vatican Council (LG, no. 1) for speaking of the church has made this usage almost a commonplace in Roman Catholic thought.

103. The Second Vatican Council described the church, because of its relationship with Christ, as "a kind of sacrament, or sign of intimate union with God, and of the unity of all humankind" (LG, no. 1). The church is described as the "universal sacrament of salvation" (LG, no. 48; GS, no. 45; AG, no. 1), the "visible sacrament of this saving unity" (LG, no. 9), and the "wondrous sacrament" (SC, no. 5). In some cases the conciliar text indicates the deep roots of this conception of the church in patristic thinking by referring to some expressions of Cyprian, who speaks of ecclesial unity as a sacrament (LG, no. 9 and SC, no. 26). It then directly applies these formulas to the church in extending the dynamic of their meaning. At the same time, it refers to a prayer in the Roman Missal before the restoration of Holy Week, which affirms that "from the side of Christ on the cross there came forth the wondrous sacrament which is the whole Church" (SC, no. 5).

104. The application of the category "sacrament" to the church is doubly analogical. On the one hand, it is analogical with regard to its application to Christ. Christ, indeed, is the primordial sacrament of God in that the *logos* became flesh, assuming our humanity. Jesus is the full revelation of grace (cf. Jn 1:14) and "the image of the invisible God" (Col 1:15), the one who has become "the source of eternal salvation to all who obey him" (Heb 5:9). That is why Paul proclaims "the mystery of Christ" (Col 4:3). Later on, Augustine, for whom the terms "mystery" and "sacrament" are practically equivalent, writes: "There is no other mystery of God than Christ" (PL, nos. 33, 845). For St. Thomas the original sacraments of our salvation are the "mysteries of the flesh of Christ"; in particular, the passion and the resurrection of Christ are sacraments by reason of their double character of being exemplary sign as well as instrumental and effective cause (cf. *Comp. Theol.* 239; *S. Theol.* IIIa, q. 62, art. 5 and *primum*). Luther made his own this traditional interpretation of Christ: "The Holy Scriptures know only one sacrament, which is Christ the Lord himself" (*Disputatio de fide infusa et acquisita*, 1520, 18; WA, 6, p. 86). All language concerning the sacramentality of the church, then, must respect the absolute lordship of Christ over the church and the sacraments. Christ is the unique foundational sacrament, that is to say, the active and original power of the whole economy of salvation visibly manifested in our world. The church is a sacrament by the gift of Christ, because it is given to it to be the sign and instrument of Christ.

105. In the New Testament the term "mystery" is not directly applied to the church, although Ephesians 5:32 applies this term to Genesis 2:24 and relates that verse to the relationship between Christ and the church (and the Latin Vulgate translated "*mysterium*" as "*sacramentum*"). The church then is only a sacrament

founded by Christ and entirely dependent on him. Its being and its sacramental acts are the fruit of a free gift received from Christ, a gift in relation to which he remains radically transcendent, but which, however, he commits to the salvation of humankind. That is why, according to the Second Vatican Council, "It is not a vain analogy to compare the church with the mystery of the Word Incarnate," for its one complex reality is "constituted from both a human aspect and a divine aspect" (LG, no. 8). This analogy should not make us forget the radical difference which remains between Christ and the church. In particular, the church is only the spouse and the body of Christ through the gift of the Spirit.

106. On the other hand, the church is called a sacrament by analogy to the liturgies of baptism and the eucharist, which the Greek fathers called "the mysteries," in a sense already analogous to the Pauline *mysterion*. The sacraments are the gestures and the words which Christ has confided to his church and to which he has linked the promise of grace by the gift of his Spirit.

107. In the church as "sacrament," "a bridge is built between the invisible face of creation and the design of God realized in the Covenant" (cf. Groupe des Dombes, *L'Esprit Saint, l'Eglise et les Sacrements*, 23). Or, in a slightly different register, one can also call the church a "living sign." The terms "sacrament" and "sign" imply coherence and continuity between diverse moments of the economy of salvation, they designate the church at once as the place of presence and the place of distance, and they depict the church as instrument and minister of the unique mediation of Christ. Of this unique mediation the church is the servant, but never either its source or its mistress.

108. As Christ's mediation was carried out visibly in the mystery of his incarnation, life, death, and resurrection, so the church has also been established as visible sign and instrument of this unique mediation across time and space. The church is an instrument in Christ's hands because it carries out, through the preaching of the word, the administration of the sacraments, and the oversight of communities, a ministry entirely dependent on the Lord, just like a tool in the hand of a worker. So the New Testament describes the ministry of the church as serving as the ministry of Christ. Ministers are "God's fellow workers" (1 Cor 3:9), "servants of Christ and stewards of the mysteries of God" (1 Cor 4:1), "ministers of a new covenant" (2 Cor 3:6), "ministers of reconciliation" accomplished by Christ (cf. 2 Cor 5:18) and, more generally, "envoys" or "ambassadors for Christ" (2 Cor 5:20).

109. The instrumental ministry of the church is confided to sinful human beings. It can therefore be disfigured or atrophied, mishandled and exaggerated. But the reality of God's gift always transfigures human failure, and God's fidelity to the church continually maintains it, according to the promise (Mt 28:20) which sustains it in its mission of salvation across the ages.

110. The church is thus constituted as a sacrament, an instrument of the unique mediation of Christ, a sign of the efficacious presence of that mediation. The church is such in that it lives out of the word, which has engendered it and which it proclaims, and to the extent that it is open and docile to the Spirit that dwells within it. The Paraclete maintains and continually renews the memory of Christ in the church (Jn 14:26; 16:15) until the Savior comes again. This Paraclete accomplishes in the church the ministry of liberty (2 Cor 3:17), of truth (Jn 16:13), of sanctification (Rom 8:12-13), and of transformation (2 Cor 3:18). In this way, the church is the bearer of the tradition of the word, that is, the sacrament of the word of God; and bearer of transmission of salvation, that is, the sacrament of Christ and of the Spirit.

111. If the church is seen in relation to its source, it may be described as the sacrament of God, of Christ, and of the Spirit—as a sacrament of grace. If it is seen in relation to its mission and calling, it may be called the sacrament of the kingdom, or the sacrament of salvation (LG, no. 48): "like a sacrament, that is a sign and instrument of intimate union with God and of the unity of the entire human species" (ibid., no. 1).

3.2.3. Questions and Reflections

112. We are agreed in recognizing the radical dependence of the church in receiving the transcendent gift which God makes to it, and we recognize that gift as the basis of its activity of service for the salvation of humanity. But we do not yet understand the nature of this salutary activity in the same way. The Reformed commonly allege that Catholics appropriate to the church the role proper to Christ. Roman Catholics, for their part, commonly accuse the Reformed of holding the church apart from the work of salvation and of giving up the assurance that Christ is truly present and acting in his church. Both these views are caricatures, but they can help to focus attention on genuine underlying differences of perspective, of which the themes of *creatura verbi* and *sacramentum gratiae* serve as symbols.

113. The two conceptions, "the creation of the word" and "sacrament of grace," can in fact be seen as expressing the same instrumental reality under different aspects, as complementary to each other or as two sides of the same coin. They can also become the poles of a creative tension between our churches. A particular point at which this tension becomes apparent is reached when it is asked how the questions of the continuity and order of the church through the ages appear in the light of these two concepts.

3.3. The Continuity of the Church Through the Ages

114. In what sense can it be said that the church has remained one from generation to generation? This question is of immediate relevance for relations between the Reformed and Roman Catholic churches because the events leading to the Reformation and resulting in division seem to imply a discontinuity in the life of the one church.

3.3.1. God's Fidelity and Our Sinfulness

115. Together we believe that God remains faithful to God's promise and never abandons the people he has called into being. "God is faithful, by whom you were called into the fellowship of his Son, Jesus Christ our Lord" (1 Cor 1:9). Such is the ground of our conviction that the church continues through the ages to carry out the mission it has received until the end of time, because "the powers of death shall not prevail against it" (Mt 16:18). Through the church, Christ, who is present with us all days until the end of time (cf. Mt 28:20), leads us indefectibly to salvation.

116. The continuity of the church has an origin: it is the sending of the apostles on a mission by Christ, a *sending* which makes them "apostles"; it has a purpose—the *mission*, "apostle," to make disciples of all the nations (cf. Mt 28:19). This is why the church is of its essence apostolic, and its ministry is within an apostolic succession. As was said in our preceding document, this succession "requires at once a historical continuity with the original apostles and a contemporary and graciously renewed action of the Holy Spirit" (PCCW, no. 101). Apostolicity is then a living reality which simultaneously keeps the church in communion with its living source and allows it to renew its youth continually so as to reach the kingdom.

117. God's fidelity is given to men and women who are part of a long history and who, moreover, are sinners. The church's response to God's fidelity must be renewed to meet the challenges of various times and cultures. The church is not worthy of its name if it is not a living and resourceful witness, concretely addressing people's needs. This is also why the church's continuity demands that it recognizes itself as *semper reformanda*. The sinfulness of humanity, which affects not only members of the church but also its institutions, is opposed to fidelity to God. If human sinfulness does not put the church in check, it can nevertheless do grave harm to the church's mission and witness. The constant need for reform in the church is recognized. "Christ summons the Church, as it goes on its pilgrim way, to that continual reformation of which it always has need, insofar as it is an institution of human beings here on earth" (UR, no. 6). The church must then live within a constant dynamic of conversion.

3.3.2. The Need for Reform and Renewal

118. We acknowledge that at the time of the Reformation, the church was in urgent need of reform. We recognize that the various strivings for reform were in their profoundest inspiration signs of the work of the Holy Spirit. In the event of the Reformation, the word of God played a role, that word which is "living and active, sharper than any two-edged sword, piercing to the division of soul and spirit" (Heb 4:12). Not everything that happened can be attributed to the word because in the division of the western church, human sinfulness also played its part. Our common awareness of this summons us to "discern the spirits," i.e., to distinguish in this process the work of human sinfulness from the work of the Spirit. As Roman Catholics and Reformed, we should not seek to justify ourselves here. We must each assume responsibility for our own past and for that part of the sin which was our own.

119. But that is not all. If it is true that "in everything [even sin, one could say] God works for good with those who love him, who are called according to his purpose" (Rom 8:28), we must then recognize the mysterious design of God which moves toward its accomplishment in spite of our division. Our continual conversion to Christ should make us discover and understand the positive meaning of this event in the life of Christ's church. It reminds us of the church's dependence on Christ and the Spirit, who act in it and for it with sovereign liberty. It invites us to recognize new fruits of holiness. It involves us in a Christian striving that impels us to reconcile in our lives complementary aspects of the one Gospel. Reflection on the positive meaning of the Reformation, despite the division, concerns us all, because it is a major event in the history of the church.

3.3.3. Questions and Reflections

120. Nonetheless, as things are at present, divergences persist between us in our understanding of the continuity of the church and its visibility. The Reformed churches give first consideration to continuity in the confession of faith and in the teaching of gospel doctrine. It is in this sense that the church remains apostolic and the ministers raised up in it by the Spirit form part of the apostolic succession. The Catholic Church, for its part, considers that this apostolicity of faith and preaching, as well as that of the administration of the sacraments, are linked to a certain number of visible signs through which the Spirit works, in particular to the apostolic succession of bishops.

121. We both acknowledge the reality of tradition, but we do not give it the same weight. The Reformed see in Holy Scripture the sufficient witness of the Gospel message, a message that "constantly creates the understanding of itself afresh" (PCCW, no. 29) and is the locus of the immediate communication of the truth. This does not imply disregard for tradition as an expression of faithful communion throughout the centuries. Catholics for their part regard Scripture as the

213

norma normans of all doctrine of the faith, but they think that Scripture, the work of the living tradition of the apostolic generation, is in its turn read and interpreted in a living way in an act of uninterrupted transmission which constitutes the tradition of the church throughout its history. The authority of this living tradition and of the magisterial decisions which mark it from time to time is founded on submission to the message of Scripture. In order to help the people of God be obedient to this message, the church is led to make interpretative decisions about the meaning of the Gospel (cf. PCCW, nos. 30, 32).

122. Further, we differ in our understanding of the nature of sin in the church. Undoubtedly, we both recognize that, whatever the effect of sin on persons and institutions, the holiness of the preaching of the word and of the administration of the sacraments endures, because the gift of God to the church is irrevocable. In this sense the church is holy, for it is the instrument of that gift of holiness which comes from God. But the Reformed think that God's fidelity is stronger than our infidelity, than the repeated "errors and resistances to the word on the part of the church" (PCCW, no. 42). Hence the church can experience moments when despite the exemplary witness of individuals its true identity is obscured by sin beyond recognition. This does not mean that God abandons the church, which, for the Reformed, continues in being always and until the end of time. On the Catholic side, it is thought that human sin, even if it goes so far as to mar greatly the signs and institutions of the church, never nullifies its mission of grace and salvation and never falsifies essentially the proclamation of the truth, because God unfailingly guards the church "which he has obtained with the blood of his own Son" (Acts 20:28). The times of the worst abuses were frequently times in which great sanctity flourished. In other words, we do not think in the same way about the relation of the church to the kingdom of God. The Reformed insist more on the promise of a "not yet"; Catholics underline more the reality of a gift "already there."

123. Accordingly, our respective interpretations of the division in the sixteenth century are not the same. The Reformed consider that the Reformation was a rupture with the Catholic "establishment" of the period. This establishment had become greatly corrupted and incapable of responding to an appeal for reform in the sense of a return to the purity of the Gospel and the holiness of the early church. Nevertheless, this does not mean that the resulting division was a substantial rupture in the continuity of the church. For Catholics, however, this break struck at the continuity of the tradition derived from the apostles and lived through many centuries. Insofar as the Reformed had broken with the ministerial structure handed down by tradition, they had deeply wounded the apostolicity of their churches. The severity of this judgment is moderated today because ecumenical contacts have made Catholics more aware of the features of authentic Christian identity preserved in those churches.

124. In the future, our dialogue will need to address such still often divisive questions as the following:

1. Considering the interpretation of our positions given above, what can Reformed and Roman Catholics now say together about the reform movements of the sixteenth century—the reasons behind them, the course they took, and the results that came about?
2. Recognizing (because of baptism and other ecclesial factors) that despite continuing divisions a real though imperfect communion already exists between Reformed and Roman Catholic Christians, what implications does this communion have for our understanding of the continuity of the church?
3. To what extent can we together proclaim the Gospel in an idiom intelligible to our contemporaries, even if we differ in some ways in our understanding of the apostolic faith?
4. How can we reconcile the freedom of the individual Christian in appropriating the Christian message with the responsibility of the church for authoritatively teaching that message?

In the past, we have usually answered such questions from our separate ecclesiological perspectives; in the future, we will need to work out a joint response in dialogue.

3.4. The Visibility and the Ministerial Order of the Church

125. The Reformed and Roman Catholic communions differ in a third way with respect to their understanding of the relation between Gospel and church. Our divergence here has to do with the role of visible structure, particularly in relation to mission and ministry. We will look first at visibility and invisibility in the church as such, and then at mission and ministerial order.

3.4.1. The Church: Visible and Invisible

126. In the past, Reformed churches have sometimes displayed a tendency not only to distinguish, but also to separate the invisible church, known to God alone, and the visible church, manifest in the world as a community gathered by the word and sacrament. In fact, such a distinction is not part of genuine Reformed teaching. We can affirm together the indissoluble link between the invisible and the visible. There exists but one church of God. It is called into being by the risen Christ, forms "one body," is summoned to "one hope," and acknowledges "one Lord, one faith, one baptism, one God and Father of us all . . ." (Eph 4:4-6). Christ,

through his Spirit, has empowered this church for a mission and a ministry in the world and equipped it to call others to the same unity, hope, and faith. From its earliest time, it has been provided through God's grace with ministerial means necessary and sufficient for the fulfillment of its mission.

127. The invisible church is the hidden side of the visible, earthly church. The church is manifest to the world where it is called to share in the kingdom of God as God's chosen people. This visible/invisible church is real as event and institution, wherever and whenever God calls men and women to service.

128. This visible/invisible church lives in the world as a structured community. Gathered around word and sacraments, it is enabled to proclaim God's Gospel of salvation to the world. Its visible structure is intended to enable the community to serve as an instrument of Christ for the salvation of the world. It thus bears witness to all human beings of the saving activity of God in Jesus Christ. This testimony of the visible/invisible church often calls it to a confrontation with the world. In such testimony the church sees itself summoned to praise and glorify God. In all its visible activity, its goal is *soli Deo gloria, ad maiorem Dei gloriam.*

129. We diverge, however, on the matter of the closer identification of the church with its visible aspects and structure. Roman Catholics maintain that the church of Christ "subsists" in the Roman Catholic Church (LG, no. 8), a formulation adopted at the Second Vatican Council to avoid the exclusive identification of Christ's church with it. They admit likewise that many "elements" or "attributes" of great value, by which the church is constituted, are present in the "separated churches and communities" and that these last are "in no way devoid of significance and value in the mystery of salvation" (UR, no. 3). The question is, therefore, to what degree they can recognize that the church of Christ also exists in the Reformed churches. The Reformed for their part do not understand the church as reducible to this or that community, hierarchy, or institution. They claim to belong to the church and recognize that others also do. Their chief difficulty is not in extending this recognition to the Roman Catholic Church, but the view that the Roman Catholic Church has of its special relation to the church of Jesus Christ.

3.4.2. Mission and Ministerial Order

130. Catholics and Reformed agree that the order of the church originates in the Gospel which the risen Christ charged his disciples to proclaim. In this perspective, it is given first in word and sacrament: "Go, therefore and make disciples of all nations, baptizing them in the name of the Father and of the Son and of the Holy Spirit, teaching them to observe all that I have commanded you; and lo, I am with you always, to the close of the age" (Mt 28:19-20; cf. Lk 24:47-48; Jn 20:21b).

131. For those who follow Christ, the word of God contained in Scripture and proclaimed, lived, and interpreted in the church is the fundamental and inalienable

point of reference for the church's order. Scripture bears the word of salvation by which faith is born. Faith leads to baptism, and it is nourished by the celebration of the Lord's Supper, the eucharist.

132. This mission, which the risen Christ committed to the "eleven" (Mt 28:16) and from which the church arose, implies that one should distinguish between those who announce the Gospel ("you") and those to whom it is proclaimed ("make disciples"). It entails, moreover, a ministry of word, sacrament, and oversight given by Christ to the church to be carried out by some of its members for the good of all. This triple function of the ministry equips the church for its mission in the world.

133. This ministerial order manifests itself above all in the ministry of the word, i.e., in the preaching of the Gospel, "the word of God which you heard from us" (1 Thes 2:13; cf. 2 Cor 11:7), the announcing of repentance and forgiveness of sins in the name of Jesus (Lk 24:47-48), and the proclaiming of him as the one anointed with the Spirit "to preach good news to the poor . . . to set at liberty those who are oppressed" (Lk 4:18). He who was the preacher of God's word *par excellence* has thus become the Preached One in the word carried to the "ends of the earth" (Acts 1:8) by his chosen witnesses (Acts 10:41-42).

134. The ministerial order also finds expression in the ecclesial rites, traditionally called sacraments. We believe that in them Christ himself acts through the Spirit among his people. The church is ordered through baptism, in which all who believe in Christ are not only washed and signed by the triune God, but are "built into a spiritual house, to be a holy priesthood" (1 Pt 2:5). Similarly, in the Lord's Supper, or the eucharist, the community of faith, hope, and love finds its rallying point: "Because there is one bread, we who are many are one body, for we all partake of the one bread" (1 Cor 10:17). Such rites along with the word of God are fruitful means of grace for those who believe, and by them the whole people of God is built up and nurtured.

135. This order is further manifest in the ministry of oversight *(episkope)*, exercised by church members for the fidelity, unity, harmony, growth, and discipline of the wayfaring people of God under Christ, who is "the Shepherd and Guardian *(episkopos)*" of all souls (1 Pt 2:25). Various "gifts," "services," and "activities" are inspired by God's Spirit in the church (1 Cor 12:4-6), but all members are called upon to be concerned for that same unity, harmony, and upbuilding of the church.

136. Leadership in the New Testament took different forms at various times and places under diverse names (see, e.g., Acts 1:20-25; 20:17, 28; 1 Cor 12:28; Eph 4:11-13; Phil 1:1; 1 Tm 3:1-13; 4:14; 5:3-22; Ti 1:5-9). Paul often refers to himself as the "servant/slave of Jesus Christ" (Rom 1:1; Gal 1:10; Phil 1:1) and as such writes to churches that he has founded as one exercising authority in virtue of the Gospel that he preaches (1 Thes 2:9, 13; cf. 1 Cor 15:11: "Whether it was I or they,

so we preach and so you believed"). Though we have no direct indication that the communities founded by Paul were presbyterally organized, but only the affirmation of Acts 14:93, where Paul, according to Luke, appoints presbyters "in every church." Paul was at least aware of a structure of leadership in some communities to which he wrote: 1 Thessalonians 5:12: "respect those who labor among you and are over you in the Lord and admonish you"; Philippians 1:1, greetings are sent to "all the saints in . . . Philippi, with the overseers and deacons" (syn episkopois kai diakonois). From the various forms of leadership mentioned in the pastorals there emerged a pattern of episcopoi, presbyters, and deacons, which became established by the end of the second century.

137. This pattern of leadership developed from some New Testament forms, while other (even earlier) New Testament forms did not develop. The spread and theological interpretation of ecclesial leadership in the immediate post-New Testament period must be seen against the background of the wider development of the early church and its articulation of the faith (see 1 Clem 40-44, especially 42, 1-2, 4; 44, 1-2; Ignatius of Antioch, Eph 2, 1-5; Magn 2; Hippolytus, *Apost. Trad.*). In the course of history some of the functions of such leaders underwent change; even so the ministry of bishops, presbyters, and deacons became in the ancient church the universal pattern of church leadership.

3.5. The Mutual Challenge

138. We have now explored and reflected upon three dimensions of the relation between Gospel and church. Despite our agreements, there remain divergences between us which deserve further exploration and offer us new challenges.

139. First, on the question of doctrinal authority in the church, the previous report, *The Presence of Christ in Church and World* (nos. 24-42), described our agreement concerning the view that we in large measure share regarding Scripture and its canon. In this area, formerly contested matters have been substantially clarified. This document likewise has identified the core of what still separates us in the interpretation of Scripture, the authority of confessions of faith and of conciliar decisions, and the question of the infallibility of the church. These divergences still remain to this day. Among the remaining divergences, the following are particularly important. Both sides emphasize the indefectible character of Spirit-guided preaching and teaching that mirrors the Gospel and Holy Scripture. Roman Catholics relate that preaching and teaching to a God-given authority vested in the church, which, in service to the word of God in Scripture and Tradition, has been entrusted with authentically interpreting it, and which in distinct cases is assisted by the Holy Spirit to pronounce infallibly on matters of faith and morals. Reformed Christians

refer such preaching and teaching ultimately to the supreme authority of the word of God in Scripture as illuminated by the Holy Spirit.

140. Second, on the question of the sacraments, in spite of growing convergence, there still exists between us not only a disagreement concerning their number, but also a divergence in our understanding of "sacrament" and of the competence of the one who ministers. Roman Catholics recognize seven sacraments, according to the Council of Trent (DS 1601), though they give a major importance to baptism and eucharist and recognize in the eucharist the center of the sacramental life of the church. The Reformed churches recognize baptism and the Lord's Supper as sacraments in the ordinary sense, though also recognizing in the laying on of hands "an efficacious sign which initiates and confirms the believer in the ministry conferred" (PCCW, no. 98). Calvin himself did not object to calling ordination a sacrament, but he did not count it on a level with baptism and eucharist because it was not intended for all Christians (*Institutes* IV:19, 28).

141. Third, the earlier document (PCCW, no. 98) provides a common description of ordination, putting in relief its double reference to the "historical and present action" of Jesus Christ and to "the continual operation of the Holy Spirit." Nevertheless, the nature of ordination still causes difficulty between us. Is the laying on of hands a sending on a mission, a passing on of a power, or an incorporation into an order? (cf. ibid., no. 108). On the other hand, can a defect in form put in question or invalidate the ministry as such—or can such a defect be remedied "by reference to the faith of the Church" (ibid.)? One further difference concerning the ordained ministry cannot be ignored, especially today. In the Reformed churches, as in many other Protestant communions, it has become increasingly common in recent decades to ordain women without restriction to the ministry of word and sacrament.

142. Fourth, on the question of how the authority of Christ must be exercised in the church, we are in accord that the structure of the ministry is essentially collegial (cf. PCCW, no. 102). We agree on the need for *episkope* in the church, on the local level (for pastoral care in each congregation), on the regional level (for the link of congregations among themselves), and on the universal level (for the guidance of the supranational communion of churches). There is disagreement between us about who is regarded as *episkopos* at these different levels and what is the function or role of the *episkopos*.

a. Catholics insist that the ordained ministry is a gift of God given to persons "set apart" (cf. Rom 1:1) in the community. By the sacrament of ordination the minister is united with Christ, the sole High Priest, in a new way which qualifies him to represent Christ in and for the community. The one ordained can act there *"in persona Christi"*; his ministry is an embassy in the name of Christ in the service of the word of God (cf. 2 Cor 3:5). Ordination to the priesthood qualifies one to represent the church before God, in its offering to the Father through Christ in the Spirit. All of these aspects of this ministry are especially realized in the eucharistic celebration. The ordained ministry thus places the church in total and current dependence on its unique Lord.

b. Likewise, for Catholics, at the heart of the ministry, ordained in the succession of the apostles, stands the bishop, who continues in the community the preaching of the apostolic faith and the celebration of the sacraments, either in his own right or through his collaborators, the priests and deacons. His role is also to develop a life of harmony within the community *(homothymadon)*. The bishop also represents his church before other local churches in the bosom of the universal communion. Charged to maintain and deepen the communion of all the churches among themselves, the bishops, with the bishop of Rome who presides over the universal communion, form a "college." This "college" is seen as the continuation of the "college" of the apostles, among whom Peter was the first. The bishop of Rome, understood as the successor of Peter, is the prime member of this college and has the authority necessary for the fulfillment of his service on behalf of the unity of the whole church in apostolic faith and life.

c. Reformed churches also emphasize the importance of the ordained ministry of word and sacrament for the life of the church (cf. Eph 4:11-16). The Reformed understanding of the ministry is in general more "kerygmatic" than "priestly"; this corresponds to the awareness of the word of God as the power by which the church lives. Within this perspective, however, there is a valid sense in which the Reformed minister acts "in the person of Christ"—e.g., in preaching, in dispensing the sacraments, in pastoral care—and also represents the people, in articulating and leading their worship. For this reason Reformed churches approach the preparation and ordination of ministers with great care, emphasizing the need for a proper order and the laying-on of hands by duly ordained ministers.

d. The Reformed stress the collegial exercise of *episkope*. At the local level the responsibility lies with pastors, elders, and/or deacons, with a very important role often played by the church meeting. At regional and national levels it is exercised collectively by synods. The same applies, in principle, to the universal level. The Reformed have never given up hope for a universal council based on the authority of the Scriptures. That hope has not yet materialized, though ecumenical world assemblies in our century are an important step towards its fulfillment.

e. The Reformed hold that the sixteenth century brought into being a new form of church order based on Scripture and a practice of the ancient church, adapted to the needs of a new situation. Reformed churches today still maintain that pattern and believe it to be legitimate and serviceable in the life of the church. This does not exclude the possibility of further development in the ecumenical future of the church.

143. Finally, we have begun to come to terms with the particularly difficult issue of the structure of ministry required for communion in the universal church. The earlier report (PCCW) made allusion to it. Our discussion of the matter has shown how complex the issues involved are and how different the perspectives in which they are seen on both sides. As we pursue the dialogue on the church's structure and ministry, this theme deserves closer attention.

144. As a program for future dialogue, we suggest the following questions:

• Our interpretations of Scripture are inextricably bound up with our ecclesiological convictions. With what hermeneutical and doctrinal perspectives do we approach the New Testament in the search for guidance on the ordering of the church in the ecumenical future?

• What significance is there for the church today in the role assigned to Peter in several central New Testament passages—and in the way in which that role was interpreted in the ancient church?

• What is the connection between the ministry of leadership described in the New Testament (presidents, leaders, bishops, pastors) and in the ancient church, and (a) Roman Catholic bishops and (b) Reformed ministers of word and sacraments?

Chapter 4: The Way Forward

145. Our five years of dialogue have convinced us that a new situation now exists between the Roman Catholic Church and the Reformed churches. It has become apparent that the two confessions share much in common and can, therefore, enter into a living relationship with each other. Encounters in many parts of the world have led to mutual openness and a new understanding. It has become clear that the two sides have much to say to each other and also much to learn from each other.

146. The common ground that unites our churches is far greater than has usually been assumed. We start from the premise that God has already granted us unity in Christ. It is not for us to create unity, for in Christ it is already given for us. It will become visible in our midst as and when we turn to him in faith and obedi-

ence and we realize fully in our churches what he expects from us. We firmly believe that the unifying power of the Holy Spirit must prove stronger than all the separation that has occurred through our human sinfulness. This confirms our conviction that we must work for the ultimate goal of full communion in one faith and one eucharistic fellowship.

147. At the same time, however, our dialogue has shown that certain disagreements in understanding the relationship between the Gospel and the church have not yet been overcome. It would therefore be unrealistic to suppose that the time has now come for declaring full communion between our churches.

148. But we do believe that the living relationship that has come into being between our churches makes possible a new way of dealing with these divergences. They should not be looked upon primarily as grounds for mutual exclusion but should rather be seen as terrain for mutual challenge. In ecumenical encounter we can deepen our understanding and our obedience. We can discover in the other the gift of God.

149. "Welcome one another, therefore, as Christ has welcomed you, for the glory of God" (Rom 15:7). On the basis of this appeal of the Apostle Paul, we conclude that the Roman Catholic Church and the Reformed churches should no longer oppose each other or even simply live side by side. Rather, despite their divergences, they should live for each other in order to be witnesses to Christ. Guided by this mission, they should open themselves to and for each other.

4.1. The Diversity of Situations

150. In some countries, far-reaching agreement has already been achieved. Official dialogues have taken place and, as a general rule, these have led to results similar to those to be found in the present report. In some other countries the churches maintain close relationships and collaborate regularly, reacting together to important problems of public life. But there are also countries where their relations, even today, hardly go beyond occasional and individual contacts. The mistrust inherited from the past has not yet been overcome. Political situations and sociological factors often play an important part in this mistrust. In some places the Roman Catholic and Reformed churches even find themselves on opposite sides of political conflict. In other places, closer relations are made more difficult by the numerical size of the partners: whenever a large church finds itself faced with a small minority, a great deal of sensitivity and effort are needed if living relationships are to be established. In many places, the diversity of the Reformed churches makes interconfessional dialogue and collaboration more complex.

151. We agree that initiatives should be taken to deepen Christian fellowship in each country. We are grateful for the convergences we have found in the dialogue

at the international level and believe that these results can serve as a stimulus for the churches in each country. But the desired living relationship cannot be created only by an agreement at the international level. First, according to the Reformed under-standing, each member church is responsible for its own confession, its life, and its witness; consequently, the World Alliance of Reformed Churches has no binding authority over its member churches. Secondly, we are convinced that the call for unity must always aim at concrete and lived communion. It is always addressed to "all in each place." But we do believe that the mutual understanding reached in international dialogue should serve as an encouragement to establish more active relations between our churches at the local level.

4.2. Steps Along the Way to Unity

152. We suggest that dialogues between local churches should keep in mind the following steps on the way to unity:

a. Our churches should give expression to mutual recognition of baptism. In some countries, the Roman Catholic and Reformed churches have already agreed to accept each other's baptism fully and without reserve, provided that it has been celebrated in the name of the Father, the Son, and the Holy Spirit and with the use of water. We believe that such agreements can and should be made in all places without delay. Such an agreement implies that under no circumstances can there be a repetition of baptism which took place in the other church. Mutual recognition of baptism is to be understood as an expression of the profound communion that Jesus Christ himself establishes among his disciples and which no human failure can ever destroy.

b. Though mutual recognition of baptism is already possible today, we are not yet in a position to celebrate the eucharist or Lord's Supper together. Our different understandings of the relation between the Gospel and the church also have consequences as regards admission to communion.

The Reformed churches take the view that, precisely because Christ himself is the host at the table, the church must not impose any obstacles. All those who have received baptism and love the Lord Jesus Christ are invited to the Lord's Supper (see the Declaration of the World Alliance, Princeton, 1954).

The Roman Catholic Church, on the other hand, is convinced that the celebration of the eucharist is of itself a profession of faith in which the whole church recognizes and expresses itself. Sharing the eucharist therefore presupposes agreement with the faith of the church which celebrates the eucharist.

This difference in the understanding of eucharistic sharing must be respected by both sides. Still, we recall and reaffirm the progress in our common understanding of the eucharist that has already been made in the first phase of dialogue (PCCW, nos. 67-92). Aspects of the common understanding were summarized in these words, which we repeat again here: ". . . we gratefully acknowledge that both traditions, Reformed and Roman Catholic, hold to the belief in the Real Presence of Christ in the eucharist; and both hold at least that the eucharist is, among other things:

1. A memorial of the death and resurrection of the Lord
2. A source of living communion with him in the power of the Spirit (hence the *epiclesis* in the liturgy) and
3. A source of the eschatological hope for his coming again" (PCCW, no. 91)

c. In many countries there has been a rapid rise in the number of confessionally mixed marriages in recent years. It is not therefore surprising that the problem of a more appropriate way of dealing with this new reality has cropped up time and again in the course of bilateral dialogues. We hold that confessionally mixed marriages could be seen as an opportunity of encounter between the two traditions, even though some difficulties cannot be denied. We deem it to be important that the two churches should jointly exercise pastoral responsibility for those who live or grow up in confessionally mixed marriages in a manner which supports the integrity of the conscience of each person and respects their rights. In this respect see also the report of the dialogue between the Roman Catholic Church, the Lutheran World Federation, and the World Alliance of Reformed Churches (*The Theology of Marriage and the Problem of Mixed Marriages*, cf. no. 2 above).

4.3. Toward the Reconciliation of Memories

153. In Chapter 1 we tried together to understand our separated histories afresh. Beyond this lies a step not yet taken. From understanding each other's memories we must move to a reconciliation of the memories of Roman Catholics with those of Reformed Christians, and vice versa. Shared memories, even if

painful, may in time become a basis for new mutual bonding and a growing sense of shared identity.

154. This proposal has been made time and again by both Reformed and Roman Catholic authorities. Pope John Paul II formulated it in the following terms: "Remembrance of the events of the past must not restrict the freedom of our present efforts to eliminate the harm that has been triggered by these events. Coming to terms with these memories is one of the main elements of ecumenical process. It leads to frank recognition of mutual injury and errors in the way the two communities reacted to each other, even though it was the intention of all concerned to bring the church more into line with the will of the Lord" (Address to the members of the Swiss Evangelical Church Federation, 14 June 1984).

155. Chapter 1 shows how much has been accomplished in this direction. Mention should be made, for example, of the efforts of Roman Catholic historians to produce a new interpretation of the great Reformers, especially John Calvin, or the attempt of the World Alliance to give a new overtone to the memories of the revocation of the Edict of Nantes. But much yet remains to be done.

156. As illustrations we choose the following:

a. The problem of interpreting the rupture caused by the Reformation has already been touched on. In addition to the theological reflections already offered, serious historical research needs to be jointly undertaken.

b. We must tackle the problem of the condemnations that the Roman Catholic Church and the Reformed churches pronounced against each other. The polemics between the churches found expression in mutual anathematizations, and these continue to make themselves felt today. One need only think, for example, of the condemnation of certain Roman Catholic teachings and practices in such Reformed confessions as the Heidelberg Catechism or the Westminster Confession, or the identification of doctrines condemned by the Council of Trent with certain of the teachings of the Reformers. Conscious efforts at theological and historical research will have to be made in order to distinguish the justified concerns of these declarations from the polemical distortions.

c. Particular attention should be paid to the way in which confessional separation was brought to the Americas, Africa, Asia, and Oceania. Churches in these areas had no part in originating the separation. It was only through migration or missionary expansion that European divisions were transplanted to these continents. What in actual fact are the reasons for the separate existence of these churches today? A careful historical analysis might well bring to light new factors of separation which have been added to the inherited confessional differences.

4.4. Common Witness in the World of Today

157. "Living for each other" as churches must also mean "bearing common witness." We take the view that the Roman Catholic Church and the Reformed churches must make every effort to speak jointly to the men and women of today to whom God desires to communicate Christ's message of salvation.

158. Every opportunity for taking common stands with regard to contemporary issues should be taken and used. Our separation must not prevent us from expressing the agreement we have already achieved in our witnessing. For example, the Roman Catholic Church and the World Alliance of Reformed Churches are wholly agreed that every form of racism is contradictory to the Gospel and must therefore be rejected. In particular, they see apartheid as a system that the Christian church must condemn if its evangelical credibility is not to be put into jeopardy.

159. Something very similar applies with regard to the witness of the churches on issues of justice, peace, and the integrity of God's creation. The most profound convictions of their faith oblige both churches to render decisive witness in these fields. They would imperil the integrity of their teaching if they failed to give it.

160. We also know, however, that challenges which call for common confession in our day and age also generate new divergences and divisions. These could stress and endanger our still fragile fellowship. It is therefore all the more important that we should continually listen anew together to what the Spirit is saying to the church today: the Spirit who will lead us to the fullness of the truth.

4.5. What Kind of Unity Do We Seek?

161. Even though we are still far from being able to proclaim full communion, it is important for the relations between our churches that we should have an agreed vision of the ultimate goal that should guide our efforts. This is a question that needs further study. Various concepts of unity have been proposed and deserve attention. But we believe that serious consideration should be given in our Reformed–Roman Catholic relationship, and in the ecumenical movement in general, to the description of the "unity we seek," as expressed by the Assembly of the World Council of Churches in Nairobi (1975). This text describes what is called "conciliar fellowship," and goes as follows:

> The one Church is to be envisioned as a conciliar fellowship of
> local churches which are themselves truly united.
>
> In this conciliar fellowship each local church possesses,
> in communion with the others, the fullness of catholicity, wit-
> nesses to the same apostolic faith, and therefore recognizes the

others as belonging to the same Church of Christ and guided by the same Spirit.

As the New Delhi Assembly pointed out, they are bound together because they have received the same baptism and share in the same eucharist; they recognize each other's members and ministries.

They are one in their common commitment to confess the Gospel of Christ by proclamation and service to the world. To this end, each church aims at maintaining sustained and sustaining relationships with her sister churches, expressed in conciliar gatherings whenever required for the fulfillment of this common calling. (David M. Paton, editor, *Breaking Barriers*, Nairobi, 1975. "The Official Report of the Fifth Assembly of the World Council of Churches, Nairobi, 23 November–10 December, 1975." London: SPCK, and Grand Rapids: Wm. B. Eerdmans, 1976, p. 60)

162. We see in the Nairobi declaration a sketch of the way in which organic unity could be structured even at the universal level. The statement does not describe the present state of relations between the churches, but rather serves the purpose, without reference to conciliarist controversies of the past, of articulating a concept and vision of unity toward which Christians can move to overcome their divisions.

163. Some of the features described in this text have since been given further attention within our dialogue and within the broader ecumenical movement. A crucial factor in the description is that each local church "witnesses to the same apostolic faith." Without this there can be no unity. In this report, for example, the second chapter, "Our Common Confession of Faith," indicates important aspects of the apostolic faith that we can confess together. Basic for unity too is the need to share the same faith in regard to baptism, eucharist, and ministry. An important contribution towards achieving this is the document of the Faith and Order Commission on *Baptism, Eucharist, and Ministry*, to which the churches have given their official responses.

164. If the living relationship between our churches is to grow, we must consciously foster regular contact with each other. If each church is to consider God's gift in the other, each will have to orientate itself towards the other. Inherited problems of doctrine call for further reflection. Newly arising problems (for example, relationships and dialogue with people of other living faiths, or issues raised by the progress of science and technology) must become subjects of frank and open dia-

logue. The road to unity can be traveled more readily if both communions can learn to listen together to the word of God and to the questions raised by each other.

165. We pray God to grant us the Spirit to heal wounds, to gather and edify Christ's people, to purify us, and to send us into the world anew.

Participants

World Alliance of Reformed Churches

Members:
Rev. Dean Lewis S. Mudge (USA) (cochairman)
Rev. Shirley C. Guthrie (USA) (meetings 1984-1987)
Rev. Alaisdair I. C. Heron (FRG)
Rev. Bernard M. Muindi (Kenya) (meetings 1984, 1985, 1987)
Most Rev. Mercuria M. Serina (Philippines) (meetings 1984-1985)

Consultants:
Rev. Lukas Vischer (Switzerland)
Rev. Paolo Ricca (Italy)
Rev. John E. Burkhart (USA) (1986)
Rev. Alan Falconer (Ireland) (1986)
Rev. Alan E. Lewis (Scotland) (1985)

Staff:
Rev. Alan P. F. Sell (Geneva) (1984-1987)
Rev. Henry Dirks-Blatt (Geneva) (1985)
Rev. Christiane Nolting (Geneva) (1988)

Roman Catholic Church

Members:
Rev. Bernard Sesboüé, SJ (France) (cochairman)
Rev. Joseph A. Fitzmyer, SJ (USA)
Rev. John H. Fitzsimmons (Scotland) (meetings 1984, 1985, 1988)
Rev. Francis T. Lysinge (Cameroon)
Rev. Joseph Trütsch (Switzerland) (meetings 1984, 1985, 1988)

Consultants:
Msgr. Dr. Aloys Klein (staff, Rome, 1984) (FRG) (1985, 1986, 1988)
Rev. Emmanuel Lanne, OSB (Belgium) (1986-1988)

Rev. John Ford, CSC (USA) (1987-1988)
Rev. John O'Malley, SJ (USA) (1987-1988)
Rev. Elmar Salmann, OSB (Italy) (1984)
Rev. Heinz Schütte (FRG) (1984)

Staff:
Rev. Pierre Duprey, M. Afr. (Rome)
Msgr. John A. Radano (Rome) (1985-1988)

World Council of Churches Observer

Rev. Günther Wagner (Switzerland) (1985, 1986, 1988)

PART THREE

Methodist–Roman Catholic

Introductory Note

Geoffrey Wainwright

The dialogue between the World Methodist Council and the Roman Catholic Church dates from 1967. Its work has been organized in five-year phases in order to allow its reports—which are addressed simultaneously to the Vatican—to be presented to the World Methodist Council at its quinquennial meetings. The reports have popularly been designated by the place and date of the WMC meetings which received them (Denver, 1971; Dublin, 1976; Honolulu, 1981; Nairobi, 1986; Singapore, 1991; and Rio de Janeiro, 1996). The first two reports engaged in tentative and wide-ranging exploration of commonalities and differences between the Catholic and Methodist traditions, with some emphasis on topics that were at the time occupying other ecumenical and bilateral dialogues, notably eucharist and ministry. The third report, *Towards an Agreed Statement on the Holy Spirit* (Honolulu, 1981), started to find more of a distinctive voice in its discussion of sanctification and Christian experience, even as it also treated in a pneumatological perspective the current question of "authority in the church" ("The papal authority, no less than any other within the church, is a manifestation of the continuing presence of the Spirit of Love in the church or it is nothing.")

The three reports that are printed below mark a deliberate effort to discern, compare, and (if possible) henceforth develop in common the basic presuppositions and perceptions that afford the matter of (what is called in Catholic terminology) "fundamental theology" on its more dogmatic front: ecclesiology (Nairobi, 1986), apostolic tradition (Singapore, 1991), revelation and faith (Rio de Janeiro, 1996).

The Nairobi report begins with some biblically grounded principles concerning the nature of the church and, recognizing that the divisions represented by "denominational churches" are contrary to the unity Christ wills, reflects historically and prospectively on "ways of being one church." Rather too quickly, as it turned out, the report goes on to tackle the particular question of "the Petrine office." Two more general notions are introduced in the Nairobi report that then continued to be reaffirmed in the subsequent work of the joint commission: the trinitarian character and work of God that both enables and models the Christian *koinonia*; and the commitment to "visible unity" in the "full communion in faith, mission, and sacramental life" as the goal of the exercise.

The Singapore report, trying to bridge the gap between the New Testament and the present condition of divided Christians seeking unity, examines the notion of apostolic tradition and seeks to give as common a reading as possible of ecclesial history so that agreed patterns of Christian faith, life, and community may be accepted as normative. Controversial questions regarding ministry are located within the service of the apostolic tradition. Word and Spirit are the trinitarian categories employed in the attempt to overcome old disputes concerning the relation of Scripture and Tradition.

The Rio de Janeiro report places its discussion—most fundamental of all—concerning revelation and faith under the biblical banner of 1 John 1:1-3. One benefit of this is to undercut false oppositions between, say, word and sacrament: "In Christ, in his words, his deeds, his entire existence, God has been revealed in audible, visible, tangible form; God has been received by human ears, eyes, and hands. ... The modes of the announcement [of the gospel] appropriately reflect, echo and hand on what was seen, heard and touched in the embodied manifestation of God in Jesus Christ. Accepted in faith, the words, signs and actions of the gospel . . . become the means of communion with the one true God, Father, Son and Holy Spirit."

The Rio report left some issues that the renewed joint commission will tackle for "Brighton, 2001." In particular, the commission has now begun to face in a more concentrated way the question of the teaching office within the perspectives set by the section of the Rio report devoted to "the discernment of faith" (nos. 53-72). This will inevitably include discussion of the form and importance of "a structure which binds together local churches to testify to the global nature of the gospel and of the church universal" (no. 128).

Further reading may be found in Geoffrey Wainwright, *Methodists in Dialogue* (Nashville: Abingdon Press/Kingwood Books, 1995). As the World Methodist Council–Roman Catholic reports themselves appear in the *Information Service* of the Pontifical Council for Christian Unity, they are accompanied by commentaries from Catholic theologians: Jean-Marie Tillard for Nairobi, 1986; Jared Wicks for Singapore, 1991; and William Henn for Rio de Janeiro, 1996.

Towards a Statement on the Church

Fourth Series (1982-1986)

Preface

Over the past twenty years, successive Joint Commissions between the Roman Catholic Church and the World Methodist Council have reported to their respective churches at five-year intervals through the Vatican Secretariat for Promoting Christian Unity and the World Methodist Council. A significant body of material has been considered by Methodists and Roman Catholics meeting annually since the commencement of these bilateral discussions in 1967.

The first report issued by a joint commission was known as the *Denver Report* (so named for the city where the World Methodist Council met in 1971). Covering the period of 1967-1970, the report addressed the following subjects: Christianity and the contemporary world, spirituality, Christian home and family, eucharist, ministry, and authority.

As will be readily understood, some of these areas were only examined in a cursory way and were taken up by the *Dublin Report* (1972-1975). Taking the Denver document as a point of departure, the commission advanced joint exploration in the areas of spirituality and some moral issues, while pressing on to consider in greater depth the doctrines of the eucharist and the ordained ministry.

During the next quinquennium, a significant agreed statement on the Holy Spirit was issued in the *Honolulu Report* (1977-1981). This was written in a more popular style. It was during this time that another change was introduced—the periodic publication of parts of the report, for study and comment, as they were developed in the course of the five years. Sections on Christian experience and Christian moral decisions covered new ground, and discussions begun on authority were reported as requiring fuller development.

The text of the *Nairobi Report*, which follows, represents the work of the present 1982-1985 Joint Commission, which met on four occasions. The first session at Reuti-Hasliberg, Switzerland, in 1982, established "The Nature of the Church" as the theme for the quinquennium. Building upon a careful outline, preparations were made for research and the writing of papers to explore the various subthemes. Subsequent meetings in Milan, Lake Junaluska, and Venice explored the nature of the church, sacraments, episcopacy, and "ways of being one church"; Peter in the New Testament and the Petrine ministry; and authority in the church, under the heads of jurisdiction and the teaching office. In the light of the work done at the final meeting in Venice, a proposal at the conclusion of the text suggests that the next commission proceed to address the general theme of the apostolic tradition.

In Venice tribute was paid the late Msgr. Richard Stewart for his faithful and effective service as the Roman Catholic cosecretary of the commission for the past seven years. Msgr. Stewart died unexpectedly at age fifty-eight in July 1985 while on holiday in England. He was for seven years a member of the Vatican Secretariat. The Joint Commission, recognizing his theological acumen, his careful concern for every detail of the work, his boundless energy, and profound commitment to the cause of Christian unity, wishes to dedicate this report to him.

The *Nairobi Report* deals with some of the most difficult questions Roman Catholics and Methodists have faced together. Although there are similarities in the order and structure of the two churches, Methodists and Catholics at present differ in their doctrine of the ministry and of the teaching office. The commission has started to address these divergences, exploring their origins in history and seeking perspectives for agreement. It has reaffirmed those things already held in common with regard to the role of leadership in the church and the quest for Christian unity.

We now make this report available in the hope that it will stimulate wide study, discussion, and reactions among both Catholics and Methodists. Such discussion and reaction at this stage of our dialogue will be invaluable for our continued progress on the path towards that fullness of fellowship and communion which is our aim and objective.

COCHAIRMEN

Bishop William R. Cannon, *World Methodist Council*
Bishop J. Francis Stafford, *Roman Catholic Church*

1. Because God so loved the world, he sent his Son and the Holy Spirit to draw us into communion with himself. This sharing in God's life, which resulted from the mission of the Son and the Holy Spirit, found expression in a visible koinonia1 of Christ's disciples, the church.

I. The Nature of the Church

2. Christianity arose because of the life, death, and resurrection of Jesus. Although it is possible to speak of a "people of God" from the time of Abraham, the expression "Christian church" designates the assembly of the Christian faithful. The ministry of Jesus himself was addressed to a people, so that the first persons who heard and accepted the proclamation of the kingdom were already oriented to one another by their relationship within Israel. As is shown by this gathering of those who walked with him and shared a common life with him, especially the Twelve, the ministry of Jesus created a community. After the resurrection this community shared the new life conferred by the Spirit, and very soon came to be called the church. Baptized into the faith and proclaiming the crucified and risen Lord, the members were united to one another by the Spirit in a life marked by the apostolic teaching, common prayer, the breaking of bread, and often by some community of goods; and those who were converted and drawn to them became part of this *koinonia*.

3. As the assembly of God's people gathered in Christ by the Holy Spirit, the church is not a self-appointed, self-initiated community. It originated in the redemptive act of God in Christ; and it lives in union with Christ's death and resurrection, comforted, guided, and empowered by the Holy Spirit (see further in the *Honolulu Report*, 1981, nos. 19-21, "The Holy Spirit in the Christian Community").

4. The church is a complex reality. The New Testament provides a great variety of images for the church (body of Christ, people of God, bride of Christ, temple, flock or sheepfold, royal priesthood, etc.—many of these reflecting Old Testament imagery), and theologians have offered other images and models. None of these can express exhaustively or even adequately exactly what the church is, the whole of its mystery. Nevertheless, each has purpose since different images illustrate different aspects of the church. For instance, as the Second Vatican Council exemplifies, it is easier to think of reform, change, and repentance if one speaks of the church as the people of God (cf. Vatican Council II, LG, chap. 3), because this connotes among other things a pilgrim people still full of imperfections and liable to sin. Notwithstanding our sinfulness, the risen Christ unites us with himself as his body, and some of the other images we have listed illustrate the holiness of the church as the people he has made his own.

5. In the New Testament period, diversity of time, place, and circumstances produced diversity among groups of believers—diversity of community structures, diverse formulations of the faith, diverse traditions shaped by different histories and problems, diverse house meeting places within the same city, diverse Christian centers. Nevertheless, passages in the New Testament, such as the account in Acts 15 of the Council of Jerusalem, attest to *koinonia* among such diversities, and to a sense of *the* church to which all Christians belong. There are also passages, such as 1 John 2:19, that suggest the breaking of the *koinonia* because certain diversities were deemed intolerable distortions of what was from the beginning.

6. Just as the Old Testament represents the tradition of the people of Israel, so the New Testament Scriptures, which have become normative and corrective for all Christian traditions in every age, themselves arose from the life and tradition of the apostolic and early church. They should be read with reverence and prayer. Yet an important task of scholarship in all Christian churches is to examine critically the biblical material in order to hear the Scriptures in their own terms and to help the church discern the word of God for its life today. (See also the *Honolulu Report*, no. 34.)

7. The church is judged, transformed, and empowered for mission by the word of God as appropriated through the Spirit. The reforming power of the word is evident in such instances as some of the medieval reforms (monastic, papal, mendicant), the Reformation and the Catholic renewal of the sixteenth and seventeenth centuries, the evangelical revival of the eighteenth century, the ecumenical movement of the twentieth, and many other movements of renewal.

8. The church lives between the times of the life, death, resurrection, and exaltation of Jesus Christ and his future coming in glory. The Spirit fills the church, empowering it to preach the word, celebrate the eucharist, experience fellowship and prayer, and carry out its mission to the world: thus the church is enabled to serve as sign, sacrament, and harbinger of the kingdom of God in the time between the times.

9. Christ works through his church, and it is for this reason that Vatican II speaks of the church as a kind of sacrament, both as an outward manifestation of God's grace among us and as signifying in some way the grace and call to salvation addressed by God to the whole human race (cf. LG, no. 1). This is a perspective that many Methodists also find helpful.

10. The mystery of the word made flesh and the sacramental mystery of the eucharist point towards a view of the church based upon the sacramental idea, i.e., the church takes its shape from the incarnation from which it originated and the eucharistic action by which its life is constantly being renewed.

II. Church and Sacraments

11. Being a Christian has necessarily both a personal and a communal aspect. It is a vital relationship to God in and through Jesus Christ in which faith, conversion of life, and membership in the church are essential. Individual believers are joined in a family of disciples, so that belonging to Christ means also belonging to the church which is his body.

12. Both the personal and communal aspects of the Christian life are present in the two sacraments that Methodists and Roman Catholics consider basic. Baptism initiates the individual into the *koinonia* of the church; in the eucharist, Christ is really present to the believer (cf. *Dublin Report*, 1976, no. 54), who is thus bound together in *koinonia* both with the Lord and with others who share the sacramental meal.[2]

13. It is by divine institution that the church has received baptism and the eucharist, outward signs of inward grace consisting of actions and words by which God encounters his people; these signs are recognized as sacraments by both churches. The church has authority to institute other rites and ordinances, which are valued as sacred actions and signs of God's redeeming love in Christ (cf. *Honolulu Report*, no. 49, concerning marriage). Some of these the Roman Catholic Church recognizes as sacraments, since it sees them as ultimately derived from the will of Christ. Methodists, while using the term "sacrament" only of the two rites for which the Gospels explicitly record Christ's institution, do not thereby deny sacramental character to other rites.

14. Sacraments are to be seen in the wider context of God's action in salvation history, in the church, and in individual human lives. The grace which comes through the sacraments is the grace of Christ, the visible image of the unseen God, in whom divine and human natures are united in one person; the church proclaims the action of the same Christ at work within us; and the individual sacraments likewise convey the reality of his action into our lives.

15. The sacraments are effective signs by which God gives grace through faith. Their efficacy should not be conceived in any merely mechanical way. God works through his Spirit in a mysterious way beyond human comprehension, but he invites a full and free human response.

16. Salvation is ultimately a matter of our reconciliation and communion with God—a sharing in God's life which is effected through real union with Christ. Those actions of the church that we call sacraments are effective signs of grace because they are not merely human acts. By the power of the Holy Spirit, they bring into our lives the life-giving action and even the self-giving of Christ himself. It is Christ's action that is embodied and made manifest in the church's actions which, responded to in faith, amount to a real encounter with the risen Jesus. And so, when

the church baptizes, it is Christ who baptizes. Likewise it is Christ who says: "This is my body . . . this is my blood" and who truly gives himself to us. The fruit of such encounters is our sanctification and the building up of the body of Christ.

III. Called to Unity

17. Already in the New Testament the term *ekklesia* is used for the community of those who accepted Jesus' proclamation of the kingdom, transmitted by apostles and disciples. In this church their response of faith was sealed in baptism, as they confessed their sins and were forgiven, received the Holy Spirit, and were joined together in Christ.

18. More specifically, *ekklesia* or church is applied in the New Testament to Christians meeting together in a house or living in the same city. We also find the term "the church" used in a more universal way for the body of Christ which is the fullness of him who fills all in all, the communion of the saints on earth and in heaven.

19. All these usages of the word "church" have continued throughout Christian tradition. In addition, as a result of further factors, geographical and historical, the term came to be used in other ways. Some of these usages arose because of diversities of language or rite, such as Syrian church, Coptic church, or Latin church. Others came about because of fundamental differences in doctrine, faith, or ecclesial polity, such as Lutheran Church, Methodist Church, or Roman Catholic Church.

20. As Methodists and Roman Catholics, we recognize that the divisions underlying this last usage are contrary to the unity Christ wills for his church. In obedience to him who will bring about this unity, we are committed to a vision that includes the goal of full communion in faith, mission, and sacramental life.

21. Such communion, which is the gift of the Spirit, must be expressed visibly. This visible unity need not imply uniformity, nor the suppression of the gifts with which God has graced each of our communities.

IV. Ways of Being One Church

22. As we reflect on a reunited church, we cannot expect to find an ecclesiology shaped in a time of division to be entirely satisfactory. Our explorations towards a more adequate ecclesiology have begun and are helping us to give proper recognition to each other's ecclesial or churchly character. They will also assist in overcoming our present state of division.

23. We have found that *koinonia*, both as a concept and an experience, is more important than any particular model of church union that we are yet able to

propose. *Koinonia* is so rich a term that it is better to keep its original Greek form than bring together several English words to convey its meaning. For believers it involves both communion and community. It includes participation in God through Christ in the Spirit, by which believers become adopted children of the same Father and members of the one body of Christ sharing in the same Spirit. And it includes deep fellowship among participants, a fellowship which is both visible and invisible, finding expression in faith and order, in prayer and sacrament, in mission and service. Many different gifts have been developed in our traditions, even in separation. Although we already share some of our riches with one another, we look forward to a greater sharing as we come closer together in full unity (cf. UR, no. 4).

24. In our discussion we found that the following, each in its own way, offered elements for a model of organic unity in the *koinonia* of the one body of Christ:

a. Considerable value was found in the notion of what have come to be called *typoi*. This implies that within the one church in which there is basic agreement in faith, doctrine, and structure essential for mission, there is room for various "ecclesial traditions," each characterized by a particular style of theology, worship, spirituality, and discipline.

b. From one perspective the history of John Wesley has suggested an analogy between his movement and the religious orders within the one church. Figures such as Benedict of Nursia and Francis of Assisi, whose divine calling was similarly to a spiritual reform, gave rise to religious orders, characterized by special forms of life and prayer, work, evangelization, and their own internal organization. The different religious orders in the Roman Catholic Church, while fully in communion with the pope and the bishops, relate in different ways to the authority of pope and bishops. Such relative autonomy has a recognized place within the unity of the church.

c. A third train of ideas is suggested by the term "sister churches." In its original usage, the expression contained a strong geographical component (e.g., church of Rome, church of Constantinople). But more recent usage, as when Paul VI looked forward to the Roman Catholic Church embracing "the Anglican Church" as an "ever-beloved sister," hints that it may be possible to envisage reunion among divided traditions as a family reconciliation (cf. Pope Paul VI's letter to Patriarch Athenagoras, Anno Ineunte, July 25, 1967. In *Tomos Agapis* [1958-1982], English translation, E. J. Stormon, SJ [New York: Paulist Press, 1986], no. 176).

d. The relations between churches of the Roman (Latin) rite and those of various oriental rites also in communion with the bishop of Rome afford a further possible model for the retention of different styles of devotion and church life within a single communion.

25. In trying to take these ideas further, we began to explore the acceptable range of variety and uniformity in the church.

26. Christians, sharing the same faith, relate to God in a great variety of ways, often helped by spiritual traditions which have developed, under the providence of God, in the course of history. Some of these traditions are embodied in and furthered by religious societies, renewal movements, and pious associations or institutes. The church should protect legitimate variety both by ensuring room for its free development and by directly promoting new forms of it.

27. We broached the question whether such varying needs can be provided for within the framework of the local congregation and how far a particular tradition or form of prayer and worship may require special provisions (parishes, ministries, other organizations). How far would the pastoral care of such groups require separate, possibly overlapping jurisdictions, or could it be provided by one, single, local form of *episkope* (supervision or oversight)?

28. There have to be limits to variety; some arise from the need to promote cohesion and cooperation, but the basic structures of the church also set limits that exclude whatever would disrupt communion in faith, order, and sacramental life.

V. Structures of Ministry

29. We have reflected on the structure of ministry in the church. An examination of the New Testament evidence and of subsequent history shows that the church has always needed a God-given ministry. From the written data alone it cannot be ascertained with certainty whether the threefold ministry of bishop, presbyter, and deacon, which developed from the New Testament (cf. *Dublin Report*, no. 83) was established in the first century. It is acknowledged that it became generally established in the second and third centuries and was clearly universal in the same post-New Testament period in which the Scriptural canon was established and the classical creeds were formed. Roman Catholics and some Methodists would see a similarity in these three developments under the guidance of the Holy Spirit. But we are not agreed on how far this development of the ministry is now unchangeable and how far loyalty to the Holy Spirit requires us to recognize other forms of oversight and leadership that have developed, often at times of crisis or new opportunity in Christian history. Practically, however, the majority of Methodists already accept the office of bishop, and some Methodist churches that do not have expressed their willingness to accept this for the sake of unity.

30. A stable pattern of ordained ministry (e.g., the threefold one) has never prevented a variation of the ways pastoral care has actively been exercised, and there is no reason to suppose that such flexibility will cease when Methodists and Catholics are united in faith, mission, and sacramental life.

31. Unity in faith, mission, and sacramental life can be achieved only on an apostolic basis. As the *Dublin Report* already recognized, "We all agree that the Church's apostolicity involves continuous faithfulness in doctrine, ministry, sacrament and life to the teaching of the New Testament" (no. 84). At present, however, we differ in the account we give of the apostolic succession. For Roman Catholics, the graded threefold ministry is derived from the teaching of the New Testament through the living tradition of the church. The succession in ministry is guaranteed by episcopal laying on of hands in historical succession and authentic transmission of the whole faith within the apostolic college and the communion of the whole church (cf. *Dublin Report*, no. 85). "Methodists . . . preserve a form of ministerial succession in practice and can regard a succession of ordination from the earliest times as a valuable symbol of the church's continuity with the church of the New Testament, though they would not use it as a criterion" (*Dublin Report*, no. 87).

32. In Roman Catholic teaching (see LG, nos. 18-29), bishops are ordained to the fullness of the sacrament of order for a pastoral and priestly ministry which is responsible for the authentic teaching of the truths of salvation and for the rule of the churches entrusted to them. Therefore, as successors of the apostles, they preach the Gospel and preside at the celebration of the sacraments, fostering the unity of the people of God in a given place, that the church may increase to the glory of God. In collegial communion with fellow bishops and with the bishop of Rome, they cement and express the bond of the universal fellowship.

33. Broadly speaking, there are in World Methodism two basic patterns of church government, one deriving from North America and one from Britain. From its inception, American Methodism has been episcopal in constitution, not claiming apostolic succession in the sense of the Roman Catholic Church but laying stress on the teaching, preaching, pastoral, sacramental, and governing aspects of the episcopal office. British Methodism has a single order of ordained ministry and in those churches which have followed the British pattern, *episkope* (pastoral oversight) is exercised through the conference and, by authority of the conference, is shared among chairmen of districts and superintendent ministers. The British Methodist Church did not in its origin reject episcopacy but developed without it because of the historical circumstances of its origin. In recent years it has expressed the willingness in principle to embrace episcopacy, for it has done so in certain reunion schemes outside Britain and was willing to do so in England in certain schemes which did not eventually succeed.

34. Both Roman Catholics and Methodists believe that *episkope* of the churches is a divinely given function. The Roman Catholic Church and many Methodist churches express *episkope* through bishops. It is the belief of the Roman Catholic Church and these Methodist churches that for the exercise of their ministry the bishops receive special gifts from the Holy Spirit through prayer and the laying on of hands.

35. Methodist churches which have an ordained ministry but do not have bishops, believing them not to be essential to a church, have considered adopting them as an enrichment of their own life and to promote the unity of Christians; such bishops would be a focus of unity and a sign of the historic continuity of the church.

36. It is Roman Catholic teaching that "to ensure the indivisible unity of the episcopate, [Jesus Christ] set St. Peter over the other apostles" (LG, no. 18) as a "fundamental principle of unity of faith and communion." This is basic to Catholic belief in the primacy of the bishop of Rome. This primacy is exercised in a collegial relation with the other bishops of the church and finds a privileged expression in councils of the church.

37. For Methodists the concept of primacy is unfamiliar, even if historically John Wesley exercised a kind of primacy in the origins of the Methodist Church. In his day this was carried out in the context of his conference of preachers; today's conference continues to embody certain elements of this function.

38. Since Catholics and Methodists have committed themselves to seeking full unity in faith, mission, and sacramental life, we now have to turn to questions of the Petrine office and the primacy of the bishop of Rome.

VI. The Petrine Office

39. We begin with the New Testament, in which the Twelve, and also Paul and other apostles, fulfilled important functions. But in the light of the questions which subsequently arose, we naturally concentrate on Peter even though we do not wish to isolate him from the other apostles, seeking to give a factual account of the relevant New Testament material.

40. With this background in mind, we shall then turn to consider subsequent history by starting from the nature of leadership and primacy in the church. Discernment of the various factors in Scripture and history might contribute to an agreed perception of what functions the see of Rome might properly exercise in a ministry of universal unity, by what authority, and on what conditions.

A. Peter in the New Testament

41. Simon Peter had a special position among the Twelve: he is named first in the lists and is called "first" (Mt 10:2); he is described as among the first called; he is among the three or four associated with Jesus on special occasions; at times he is portrayed as spokesman for the others, either answering or asking questions; he is named as the first of the apostolic witnesses to the risen Jesus; he is remembered as having confessed Jesus during the ministry (even if the Gospels differ in their presentation of that confession); he is renamed by Jesus. However, his misunderstanding of Jesus, his failure to heed warnings, and his denials are also narrated.

42. Special sayings in the Gospels point to a distinctive church-oriented role for Peter (Mt 16:18-19; Lk 22:31-32; Jn 21:15-17). In Acts, chapters 1–15, after the resurrection, Peter exercises a certain leadership in the affairs of the early church. In the scene of Acts 10 it is revealed to him that the church must be open to the Gentiles, a position he had to defend in Jerusalem (Acts 11:2ff.). Paul's Letter to the Galatians shows Peter as an important figure at Jerusalem, as having an apostolate to the circumcised, and as agreeing with Paul that Gentile converts need not be compelled to conform to Jewish circumcision. However, it also shows Peter as yielding to the "men who came from James" on the issue of not eating with the Gentiles—a concession that Paul describes as not being straightforward about the truth of the Gospel (2:14).

43. Acts 15 shows Peter, Barnabas, Paul, and James as all speaking to the issue of the admission of Gentile converts without circumcision, but indicates that James insisted on their observance of specific purity laws. Galatians 2 and Acts 15 have led many to suspect that Peter's position in relation to Judaism stood in between that of James on the one side and of Paul on the other. Some would regard the failure to mention Peter in the second half of the Book of Acts as a sign that his authority had declined; others would regard the fact that Luke concentrates on Peter first and then on Paul as reflecting the author's purpose to show how Christianity gradually moved from Jerusalem and the mission to the Jews, towards Rome and the Gentile mission.

44. 1 Corinthians shows a party loyal to Peter (Cephas) in a Greek city in the 50s (1 Cor 1:12; 3:22); it also raises the *possibility* that Peter's activities had brought him to Corinth (9:5). After mentioning the appearances of the risen Jesus to Peter and to others (1 Cor 15:5-8), Paul says, "Whether then it was I or they so we preach and so you believed." This is seen as an indication of basic elements shared by Peter's and Paul's preaching, in spite of the disagreement described in Galatians 2:14.

45. 1 Peter portrays Peter as an apostle writing from Babylon (by which is meant Rome), instructing Christians in Asia Minor, and as a presbyter exhorting fel-

low presbyters to be good shepherds (5:1-3). 2 Peter 3:15-16 portrays Peter as advising people how to interpret the letters of "our beloved brother Paul."

46. Many scholars think the Petrine letters were written after Peter's lifetime; some or all of the special gospel sayings about Peter referred to in no. 42 may also have been committed to writing after Peter's death. Therefore an evaluation of the New Testament evidence concerning Peter must take into account not only Peter's relationship to Jesus before the resurrection, and Peter's career in the early church, but also how Peter was regarded after his death.

47. The New Testament depicts Peter in a plurality of images and roles: missionary fisherman (Lk 5; Jn 21); pastoral shepherd (Jn 21; Lk 22:32; 1 Pt 5); witness and martyr (1 Cor 15:5; cf. Jn 21:15-17; 1 Pt 5:1); recipient of special revelation (Mt 16:17; Acts 10:9-11; 2 Pt 1:16-17); the "rock" named by Jesus (Mt 16:18; Jn 1:24; Mk 1:42); recipient of the keys of the kingdom of heaven (Mt 16:18); confessor and preacher of the true faith (Mt 16:16; Acts 2); guardian against false teaching (2 Pt 1:20-21; 3:15-16; Acts 8:20-23); and weak human being and repentant sinner, rebuked by Christ and withstood by Paul (Mk 8:33; Mt 16:23; Mk 14:31, 66-72; Jn 21:15-17; Gal 2:5). Most of these images persist through two or more strands of the New Testament tradition, and several recur in subsequent church history.

B. Primacy and the Petrine Ministry

48. In looking at the question of universal primacy one may begin with the desirability of unity focused around leadership.

49. All local churches need a ministry of leadership. In early church development such leadership came to be exercised by the bishop, who was a focus of unity. Eventually churches were grouped in provinces, regions, and patriarchates, in which archbishops, primates, and patriarchs exercised a similar unifying role in service to the *koinonia*.

50. Analogously the question arises whether the whole church needs a leader to exercise a similar unifying role in service to the worldwide *koinonia*.

51. Given this context, one then has to face the claim that the Roman see already exercises such a ministry of universal unity. As the Roman claim was essentially complete by the fifth century, it may be helpful to examine the lines of development which led in that direction. The special position and role of the Roman see in the early church depended on the convergence of several factors. Some of these factors had to do with the particular city in which the church was located, some with the development of the episcopate (cf. no. 29), and others with the relation of the bishop of Rome to Peter and Paul. For Roman Catholics the decisive factor for the special position and role of the Roman see is the relation of the bishop of Rome to Peter.

52. As the capital city of the empire, Rome's strategic importance for the worldwide mission of Christianity was recognized already in New Testament times (cf. Acts). Paul looked for the support of the Roman church in his preaching of the Gospel, and Peter, as we have seen, is portrayed as writing from Rome to Christians in Asia Minor. In the second century Rome was already recognized as an apostolic church. Both I Clement, written from Rome, and Ignatius, writing to Rome, mention Peter and Paul. Irenaeus of Lyons acknowledged the outstanding force of Rome's testimony to the apostolic tradition on account of its dual foundation (*fundata et constituta*) upon Peter and Paul (cf. *Adv. Haereses* III, iii). That both of them suffered martyrdom there no doubt gave Rome an advantage over Antioch or Corinth, churches which also rejoiced in the same twofold apostolic connection. By the latter half of the second century, the lists of the bishops of Rome mention Peter first, although from I Clement and the Shepherd of Hermas it is not clear precisely when a sole bishop was recognized as a figure distinct from the other presbyters.

53. By the middle of the third century (cf. Cyprian, *De catholicae ecclesiae unitate*, no. 4), "Petrine" texts from the Gospels had begun to be applied, *mutatis mutandis*, to the bishop of Rome. The fact that Peter's ministry in the life of the church is emphasized even in New Testament passages written after his death indicates that images of Peter had continued importance for the church. The application of the Petrine texts in the third century could be seen as reflecting this ongoing importance. Luke 22 has Jesus, with his own death in view, charging Peter to strengthen the brethren. In John 21, the risen Lord commands Peter to tend and feed the flock. In Matthew 16, Peter, who confessed his faith in Jesus as "the Christ, the Son of the living God," is named the rock on which Christ will build his church, and he is given the power to bind and loose, and the very keys of the kingdom. In Acts, Peter at Pentecost correspondingly takes the lead in proclaiming the lordship of the crucified and risen Jesus. Peter's mediating position in New Testament controversies between the positions of Paul and James (cf. no. 43) made him a figure for fostering unity in the essentials of the faith. The Petrine role of enunciating the faith, sometimes at points of conflict, was illustrated at the Council of Chalcedon when the bishops approved the doctrine of Leo I of Rome: "This is the faith of the fathers; this is the faith of the apostles; this is the faith of us all; Peter has spoken through Leo."[3]

54. In the early centuries many had been willing, more or less spontaneously, to accord to the Roman church a respect of the kind reflected in the phrase of Ignatius of Antioch, "presiding in love" (*Ad Rom.*, Introd.). In the second century Rome's repudiation of Marcion and Valentinus helped to establish orthodoxy for the whole church. On the other hand, Roman involvement in controversies was not always appreciated nor the Roman solution accepted (e.g., the response of the Asian churches to Victor over the date of Easter). In the fourth and fifth centuries, with Christianity established as the religion of the Empire, the popes began to make

more frequent use of the language of Roman law in their interventions, supported by the bishops in closest geographical proximity (i.e., within the western patriarchate). This more juridical turn sharpened the issue of authority. On the one hand the authority of the Roman church promoted missionary activity, monastic life, and doctrinal and liturgical cohesiveness, and after the collapse of the western empire helped to preserve and shape European civilization. On the other hand, increasingly developed formulation and application of the Roman claims, and more vigorous resistance to them, alike contributed to the origin and continuation of divisions in Christianity, first in the East and eventually in the West.

55. From this survey it will be seen that the primacy of the bishop of Rome is not established from the Scriptures in isolation from the living tradition. When an institution cannot be established from Scripture alone, Methodists, in common with other churches which stem from the Reformation, consider it on its intrinsic merits, as indeed do Roman Catholics; but Methodists give less doctrinal weight than Roman Catholics to long and widespread tradition.

56. The Roman Catholic members are agreed that being in communion with the see of Rome has served as the touchstone of belonging to the church in its fullest sense. This commission is agreed that not being in communion with the bishop of Rome does not necessarily disqualify a Christian community from belonging to the church of God (cf. "The Roman Catholic Church has continued to recognize the Orthodox Churches as Churches in spite of divisions concerning the primacy," Anglican–Roman Catholic International Commission, *Authority* II, no. 12). Likewise, Methodist members are agreed that Catholic acceptance of the Roman primacy is not an impediment to churchly character.

57. The positions stated in the previous paragraph, however, do not justify acquiescence in our present division. For Roman Catholics reconciliation with the see of Rome is a necessary step towards the restoration of Christian unity. Others see the claim of the bishop of Rome as an obstacle to Christian unity. It is now necessary to reexamine these claims in the hope of furthering unity. In a period when Christians of all communions frequently meet and cooperate and are often highly critical of divisions in the church, such an examination has fresh urgency.

58. Methodists accept that whatever is properly required for the unity of the whole of Christ's church must by that very fact be God's will for his church. A universal primacy might well serve as focus of and ministry for the unity of the whole church.

59. From history it can be shown that some of the current functions carried out by the bishop of Rome pertain to his diocesan see or to his office as patriarch of the Latin church and do not pertain to the essence of his universal ministry of unity. A clearer recognition of this today would make it easier for Methodists to reconsider

whether the bishop of Rome might yet exercise this ministry for other Christians as well as for those who already accept it.

60. In considering the possible exercise of the ministry of the bishop of Rome among Christians who do not at present accept it, questions about jurisdiction and infallibility are both understood by Roman Catholics as aspects of the primacy which the bishop of Rome has among other bishops in virtue of his special relation to Peter and the special position of the church in Rome deriving from the witness of Peter and Paul.

C. Jurisdiction[4]

61. It is within an understanding of the episcopal office, as outlined above (nos. 31-38), that Roman Catholics see the special role of the bishop of Rome. Just as each bishop is a focus of unity in his own diocese, so the bishop of Rome is such a focus in the communion of dioceses of the whole church. In regard to the diocese of Rome, the pope has the authority or jurisdiction that the bishops have in their dioceses. Roman Catholics believe that he also has ordinary jurisdiction throughout the church in the sense that he acts by virtue of his office and not by delegation. This is an immediate episcopal jurisdiction in all dioceses, in the exercise of which he is required to respect each local church and the authority of each bishop. Catholics recognize that theological exploration of the relation between the authority of the pope and that of the local bishop remains unfinished. The authority of the pope should not in any case, they say, be described exclusively or primarily in jurisdictional terms. Just as many images are used of Peter in the New Testament (see no. 47), so a variety of images may be used of the pope. It may be said that he is called to be an effective symbol of the unity of the church in faith and life. He is a reminder of the apostles witnessing to the resurrection, of Paul preaching to the Gentiles, and of Peter professing faith in Christ and being sent to feed the sheep. In a particular way the pope is a sign of Peter. "Vicar of Peter" is an ancient title that indicates that Peter, a saint in heaven, is present in the church on earth and is, as it were, made visible in the pope. As the papal legate said at the Council of Ephesus (A.D. 431), "Peter . . . lives, presides and judges . . . in his successors."[5]

62. It would not be inconceivable that at some future date in a restored unity, Roman Catholic and Methodist bishops might be linked in one episcopal college and that the whole body would recognize some kind of effective leadership and primacy in the bishop of Rome. In that case Methodists might justify such an acceptance on different grounds from those that now prevail in the Roman Catholic Church. Moreover, as said above, some of the current functions carried out by the bishop of Rome pertain to his diocesan see or to his office as patriarch of the Latin church rather than to his universal ministry of unity. Further joint study would need

to be done on the nature of episcopacy and on the precise nature and extent of the authority which properly belongs to the pope's universal ministry.

D. Authoritative Teaching

63. Because God wills the salvation of all men and women, he enables the church, by the Holy Spirit, so to declare the truth of the divine revelation in Jesus Christ that his people may know the way of salvation.

64. The Scriptures bear permanent witness to the divine revelation in Christ and are normative for all subsequent tradition.

65. At different moments of history it is sometimes necessary to clarify the contents of Christian faith, and even to define the limits of orthodoxy. For this reason the Christian church convenes in councils, whose purpose it is to bring into sharper focus various aspects of Christian belief. Properly understood, the decisions of the ecumenical councils which met in the first centuries command assent throughout the whole church, and there is no reason to think that at the end of the patristic era God stopped enabling his church to speak in such a way. Other occasions have called and may still call for such authoritative guidance.

66. According to Catholic belief, the authority of such councils derives from the charisma of teaching and discernment which the Spirit gives for the building up of the body. The episcopal college exercises this teaching ministry through discerning the faith of Christians, present and past, and always with reference to the supreme norm of the Scriptures. To the extent that the church in any era teaches the truths of salvation that were originally taught in the Scriptures, that teaching is binding. To definitions of a council "the assent of the Church can never be wanting, on account of the action of the Holy Spirit, by which the universal flock of Christ is kept and makes progress in the oneness of faith" (LG, no. 25).

67. It is acknowledged that a general council would take on new and greater significance if convened in a situation in which all Christians were united and represented. It is also acknowledged that many councils of the early church were not recognized as genuine councils and their teaching did not have the guarantee of truth (e.g., Robber Synod of Ephesus in 449).

68. Roman Catholics believe that the bishops of the church enjoy the special assistance of the Holy Spirit when, by a collegial act with the bishop of Rome in an ecumenical council, they define doctrine to be held irrevocably.

69. As understood by Roman Catholics, papal infallibility is another embodiment of the infallibility with which the church has been endowed. Christ's promise of sure guidance and the gift of the Spirit were to the whole church and result in the church's capacity to formulate the faith in a manner that is beyond

doubt. In carefully defined and limited circumstances, the pope exercises this capacity in and for the whole church.

70. Catholics understand that he does this when, as teacher and pastor of all the faithful, he is to be understood as teaching that some particular matter of faith or morals is part of divine revelation requiring the assent of believers. In this case reception of the doctrine by the assent of the faithful cannot be lacking.

71. When the pope teaches infallibly, infallibility is, properly speaking, not attributed to the pope, nor to the teaching, but rather to this particular act of teaching. It means that he has been prevented by God from teaching error on matters relating to salvation. It does not mean that a particular teaching has been presented in the best possible way, nor does it mean that every time he teaches he does so infallibly.

72. Methodists have problems with this Roman Catholic understanding of infallibility, especially as it seems to imply a discernment of truth which exceeds the capacity of sinful human beings. Methodists are accustomed to see the guidance of the Holy Spirit in more general ways: through reformers, prophetic figures, church leaders, and Methodist Conferences for example, as well as through general councils. Methodist Conferences, exercising their teaching office, formulate doctrinal statements as they are needed, but do not ascribe to them guaranteed freedom from error. Nevertheless Methodists always accept what can clearly be shown to be in agreement with the Scriptures. The final judge of this agreement must be the assent of the whole people of God, and therefore Methodists, in considering the claims made for councils and for the pope, welcome the attention which Roman Catholic theologians are giving to the understanding of the reception of doctrine.

73. Methodists have further difficulty with the idea that the bishop of Rome can act in this process on behalf of the whole church. We have not yet discussed together the content of the doctrines of the immaculate conception and assumption of the blessed virgin Mary, but from the Methodist point of view, whether they are true or not, they are not regarded as essential to the faith. It therefore seems to Methodists that these dogmas lack assent and reception by all Christian people. In any case, it can be expected that further study on the reception of doctrine will throw more light on the subject of infallibility.

74. An approach towards convergence in thinking about infallibility may perhaps be reached by considering the Methodist doctrine of assurance. It is the typical Methodist teaching that believers can receive from the Holy Spirit an assurance of their redemption through the atoning death of Christ and can be guided by the Spirit who enables them to cry "Abba, Father" in the way of holiness to future glory.

75. Starting from Wesley's claim that the evidence for what God has done and is doing for our salvation, as described above, can be "heightened to exclude

all doubt," Methodists might ask whether the church, like individuals, might by the working of the Holy Spirit receive as a gift from God in its living, teaching, preaching, and mission an assurance concerning its grasp of the fundamental doctrines of the faith such as to exclude all doubt, and whether the teaching ministry of the church has a special and divinely guided part to play in this. In any case, Catholics and Methodists are agreed on the need for an authoritative way of being sure, beyond doubt, concerning God's action insofar as it is crucial for our salvation.

Proposals for Future Work

76. In light of the work done so far we make the following proposal for the topics of the next quinquennium. Grouped under the general heading "The Apostolic Tradition," they could include the apostolic faith; its teaching, transmission, and reception; the sacramental ministry, ordination, and apostolic succession; Mary; and the church.

Participants in the Dialogue

Methodists

Most Rev. William R. Cannon, Atlanta, Georgia, USA, Chairman, World Methodist Council (cochairman)

Sr. Cynthia A. Clare, United Theological College of the West Indies, Kingston, Jamaica

Rev. Ira Gallaway, First United Methodist Church, Peoria, Illinois, USA

Rev. A. Raymond George, Bristol, England

Dr. Thomas Hoyt Jr., Hartford Seminary, Hartford, Connecticut, USA (1982 meeting)

Rev. Geoffrey Wainwright, Duke University, Durham, North Carolina, USA

Rev. Norman Young, Queen's College, Melbourne, Australia

Rev. Joe Hale, General Secretary of the World Methodist Council (secretary)

Catholics

Most Rev. J. Francis Stafford, Bishop of Memphis, USA (cochairman)

Rt. Rev. Peter Cullinane, Bishop of Palmerston North, New Zealand

Most Rev. John Onaiyekan, Bishop of Ilorin, Nigeria

Rev. Raymond E. Brown, Union Theological Seminary, New York, USA

Rev. Basil Meeking, Under-Secretary, Secretariat for Promoting Christian Unity (1985 meeting)

Rev. Cuthbert Rand, Ushaw College, Durham, England

Rev. George Tavard, AA, Methodist Theological School, Delaware, Ohio, USA

Msgr. Richard Stewart, Secretariat for Promoting Christian Unity (secretary 1982-1984)

Rev. Kevin McDonald, Secretariat for Promoting Christian Unity (secretary, 1985)

NOTES

1. Cf. no. 23.

2. Our discussions revealed that we must still examine and resolve persisting differences concerning the efficacy of baptism, particularly of infants. Neither of us believes that a nonbaptized person is by that very fact excluded from salvation, nor that baptism automatically ensures perseverance unto salvation. Both in this paragraph and the succeeding one the references to the eucharist emphasize only certain communal and personal aspects which are immediately relevant to this discussion of the church. In the *Dublin Report,* nos. 47-74, the commission has given a much fuller account of the present areas of agreement and of remaining disagreement concerning this sacrament.

3. See E. Schwartz, ed., *Acta Conciliorum Oecumenicorum,* II/I, ii, 81(277); cf. Leo, *Epistle* 98 (Migne, PL 54, 951).

4. For an explanation of this item, cf. ARCIC I, *Authority* II, no. 16.

5. Cf. Schwartz, op. cit., I/I, iii, 60.

The Apostolic Tradition

Fifth Series (1986-1991)

Preface

The theological dialogue between the Roman Catholic Church and the World Methodist Council has now been going on for twenty-five years. The early years of this dialogue dealt with a wide range of issues, doctrinal, ethical, and pastoral. In the last fifteen years, the dialogue has focused on a series of interrelated doctrinal issues which have also been the subject of attention in other ecumenical dialogues. In 1981 we produced a report on *The Holy Spirit* and in 1986 *Towards a Statement on the Church*. To these documents we now add our text on *The Apostolic Tradition*. In it we seek to address some of the questions that are outstanding, following on previous studies.

It is important to note that this report has deliberately not addressed all the differences of doctrine or practice that exist between us in respect of the questions it deals with. For example, there is no detailed examination of the question of apostolic succession; we do not investigate the different ways in which Catholics and Methodists actually teach and hand on the faith. Nor do we evaluate the ecclesiological self-understanding that is specific to either Catholics or Methodists. Our concern, rather, has been to set out theological perspectives within which such more specific questions may be viewed. We propose these perspectives as consistent with the doctrinal positions of both churches but not as full expositions of them. What we hope is that a careful reading of this report may enable Catholics and Methodists to see their own and each other's doctrine and practice in a wide theological and historical perspective, and to discern convergences between them.

This approach is consistent with our conviction that we already share a certain though as yet imperfect communion. It is a staging post at which we are aware of much that we hold in common and respect the gifts that have been bestowed on one another in our time of separation. But we are also "committed to a vision that includes the goal of full communion in faith, mission, and sacramental life" (*Towards a Statement on the Church*, no. 21). The gradual realization of that vision requires us to explore critically and constructively the theological bases which underpin our present positions. This report is a contribution to that process.

This document was completed at a plenary meeting of the commission which took place at the house of the "Filles du Coeur de Marie" at the Rue Notre Dame des Champs in Paris. The members of the commission wish to express their appreciation of the hospitality they received from the sisters there.

COCHAIRMEN
Bishop James W. Malone, *Roman Catholic Church*
Dr. Geoffrey Wainwright, *World Methodist Council*

Because God so loved the world, he sent his Son and the Holy Spirit to draw us into communion with himself. This sharing in God's life, which resulted from the mission of the Son and the Holy Spirit, found expression in a visible *koinonia* [communion, community] of Christ's disciples, the church.
—Report of the Joint Commission between the Roman Catholic Church and World Methodist Council, 1982-1986, Fourth Series

Introduction

1. Jesus Christ was sent among us by God the Father to make known and to bring to completion the divine purpose of salvation, the "mystery of Christ" hitherto hidden and "now revealed in the Spirit" (Col 1:26 and Eph 3:5). In the power of the Holy Spirit, this mission continues in and through the church, the family Christ gathers together in common obedience to the Father's will. As Christ's servant, the church proclaims to the world the message of his victory over sin and death, provides a living sign of that victory, and summons everyone to repent and believe the Gospel and so receive the promised Spirit.

2. It is Christ's will that his disciples should live at peace with one another; he binds them together through the gift of divine grace. The New Testament documents do not present us with an unattainable ideal but describe the actual life of a real society brought into being by Christ.

This society is not a closed fellowship of perfect observance: its members have not already attained all that God intends, and it is open to all the world. It acknowledges that by his grace true followers of Christ may be found everywhere and welcomes them into its company as they affirm their Christian discipleship.

3. This Roman Catholic–Methodist dialogue, and the whole movement for unity in the faith, follows the path Christ set for his church in obedience to the mission he himself received from God the Father and transmitted to us (Mt 28:18-20). It is a movement that breaks down the barriers sin has set up between Christians, drawing all believers into a single fellowship of praise and forming lifelong enemies into friends for eternity. Today as Catholics and Methodists we both face the urgent task of evangelizing a world deeply affected by superstition and secularism, by indifference and injustice; we must look together to the one Lord who sends the Spirit upon us all that we may go out and witness in his name. Doing this with credibility entails a common understanding of the Gospel and the ability to recognize in each other's lives and confessions an authentic witness to the faith.

4. In order to build on previous work in the dialogue, the commission pursued a theme which has proved increasingly important throughout the whole ecumenical movement, namely the *Apostolic Tradition*, understood as the teaching, transmission, and reception of the apostolic faith. It is hoped that this approach may set the difficult problem of ministry in a new light, since this topic has hitherto been predominantly considered in its relationship to the administrative and sacramental life of the church rather than in relation to its teaching.

5. In the overall title of this report, *The Apostolic Tradition*, the word "Tradition" signifies the living transmission of the Gospel of Christ, by manifold means, for the constant renewal of every generation. Christians do not order the life of the church by the fixed repetition of rigid routine laid down in the past. Rather, by recalling and holding fast to the treasured memory of the events of our salvation, we receive light and strength for our present faith as, under God, we seek to meet the needs of our own time. It is Christian hope that makes possible our wholehearted and active contribution to the continued handing on of the transforming power contained in the Gospel.

6. Our knowledge of the past life of the people of God, witnessing to their experience of God's action among them, enables us to recognize and to comprehend the risen Christ as he speaks to us today. We learn to express ourselves in his language in the midst of the people he has made; he sends the Spirit to us to open our understanding and to guide our words and actions in the service of his loving pur-

pose for the extension and completion of God's kingdom. We enter into his loving purpose as, by God's grace, we receive in faith the benefits of Christ's saving death on the cross and with him, dying to self, are raised to new life (Rom 6:3-4). This is the mystery that constitutes the true life of every believer and gives meaning and effect to all preaching and teaching of the church, to every practice, ministry, and ordinance.

Part One: The Apostolic Faith—Its Teaching, Transmission, and Reception

7. In the New Testament description of the birth of the church, a role is attributed to each of the three persons of the Trinity, which is both distinct and inseparable from the role of the other two. To the Father is attributed the gracious purpose by which we were chosen for filial adoption in union with the Eternal Word before the foundation of the world. The actual work of founding the church is attributed to the Son and to the Holy Spirit. The Son founds the church by his act of redemption. The Spirit is cofounder of the church with the Son, by being the church's principle of sanctification. The two divine missions—the sending of the Son and of the Spirit by the Father—are extensions in our world of time of the two eternal processions in the Trinity. The new relationship, both individual and corporate, which they bring about in human beings towards God, is none other than what the New Testament calls the church.

8. The indivisible relationship between these two divine missions is everywhere present in the patterns which govern every aspect of the life of the church: its confession of faith, the discipleship of its members, and their communion with one another. It is the Holy Spirit who enables us to confess the truth revealed in the Son, to be united to him in a relationship as adopted children of the Father, and to live in charity in the one body of Christ.

I. Word and Church

9. "In many and various ways God spoke of old to our ancestors by the prophets; but in these last days he has spoken to us by the Son, whom he appointed the heir of all things, through whom also he created the world" (Heb 1:1-2). The church of God has been brought into being by the same creative and self-revealing activity of God. In the Son, God has spoken definitively to us: the Son who is so completely the expression of his heavenly Father that he is called God's Word (Jn 1:1-18). He makes known God's purpose and carries it out. For the Word of God, now made flesh, speech and action are intrinsically connected; his words take effect and his deeds have meaning.

10. It is the cross and resurrection of Christ that supremely reveal him to us, achieving his purpose and making him our Savior. When the apostles preached Christ, they proclaimed Christ crucified and risen. When the church preaches Christ today, it is the same proclamation that is made. Christ, the Word of God incarnate, still has the same message for us and the same gifts of grace by which he saves us.

11. The apostolic mission, the charge laid on the apostles to transmit the message of Jesus Christ to their own and to all successive generations, is precisely the service of the Word. The person of Christ, his teaching and his work for us: it was to all this that the apostles bore witness, for all this is God's Word.

12. As the Gospel was preached by the apostles, the church was called together and built up. Service of the Word was their overriding responsibility (Acts 6:2-4), a service of Christ himself and of the community that by faith came to be identified with him (Acts 6:7; 12:24; 19:20).

13. A profound understanding of the church must begin with a reflection on the Word of God, who brings the church into being and continues to make the church what it is. The Word spoken to us in Christ calls forth our response. Thus, the church is sustained by a conversation, initiated by the Lord. God, who called all worlds into being by the power of his Word, speaks to us kindly and with sternness, gently and with thunderous warnings, with laws and with love, in proclamation to his people and heart-to-heart to each and every one. By calling together a messianic community in which the promises were fulfilled, Christ made himself known as Messiah. As he called his flock to follow him, he showed himself to be the Good Shepherd.

14. That which the church was to become as a consequence of the apostolic mission is discernible in its first coming to birth, and to discern that coming to birth, one must be aware of the extent to which Christ by deed and by word engaged his followers in communication with himself.

15. Christ was content to speak with other audiences and with later generations through those who became his first disciples. Only this degree of confidence invested by Christ in his followers could match the free self-communication of God to the world and to those whom he had made in his own image. To draw all to himself, the Son died upon the cross. He gave us his words and his very self and waits patiently for us to understand. Any other way would have frustrated his own purpose: to draw us to love him. In order to fulfill this saving purpose, he called into being the church where the Word's recreating power is evident, remaking people into a community that could share his life and live in harmonious relationships with one another. Thus the church is the place where the Word of God is spoken, heard, responded to, and confessed (Rom 10:8-17). The law of God, so the prophets said, was to become a law not written externally on tablets of stone but written on our

hearts, taken in, and made heart-knowledge: it was to be our second nature (Jer 31:31-34).

16. The Tradition received by the apostles itself continues an unbroken process of communication between God and human beings. Every possible human resource is employed to sustain and deepen this process: linguistic, ritual, artistic, social, and constitutional. The written word of Scripture is its permanent norm. Through the sacraments of baptism and the eucharist, the memory of the events whereby the church came into being is preserved. The living Word has made a living community in which men and women converse with God and speak their faith to one another. Guided by its pastors and teachers, the church continues to communicate with all generations, preserves its own identity and message, and is daily renewed in its obedience.

17. Through the living Word, recalling and renewing the acts of Christ's life for us, his history becomes our history. We celebrate our new birth; we are forgiven, strengthened, and healed; we are united with one another; we find our vocation for ministry; and we give thanks to God through the power of Christ's death and living victory. In his life on earth, the Word confirmed his words by his actions for us; the same is true today.

18. The growth of the church comes about through a continued hearing and assimilation of the Word of God. To be sure that we are hearing the Word, we maintain communion with those who have heard and obeyed the Word before us. But we will not be saved simply by repeating what other generations have said and done. We must express for ourselves, act for ourselves, and ourselves be transformed through the renewal of our minds and hearts, if the living Tradition of Christ and his apostles is to be continued. The faith must be handed on.

19. In every time and in every place, the church lives and moves by calling to mind all that it has seen and heard of the marvels of God's Word in his created world and in the history he is making with us. But we do not live in the past. Memory enables us to recognize the Lord as he comes to us today. His presence in the events of our lives proves to us that his words are true. His deeds for us today make possible our own words of praise and our own acts of service by which God is glorified.

20. But the Word of God, with us today, does not tell us, any more than the apostles were told, what comes next in our story. Since the gospel tradition looks to the future, we live in hope. And Christian hope is the strength that enables us, claiming his promises, to be totally committed to the present. We know that we are traveling towards the one whose memory we cherish and whose presence we know. By confessing our faith in living words, we learn how to die with Christ, to hide our life in him, so that when he appears we too will be made known in glory.

21. In conclusion, we recall that the search for ecumenical reconciliation has revealed only too clearly the difficulty of reuniting Scripture and Tradition once they have been notionally separated. Scripture was written within Tradition, yet Scripture is normative for Tradition.

The one is only intelligible in terms of the other. We do not claim to have resolved here all the ecumenical problems that arise in relation to this issue. What we have sought to do is to ask ourselves how the Christian of today can confess with Christians of all time the one true faith in Jesus Christ, the same yesterday, today, and forever.

II. Spirit and Church

22. In the New Testament the action of the sovereign and life-giving Spirit is closely related to the action of the Word. What God does through the Word is done in the Spirit, so that the same effect can often be attributed to the Word, or to the Spirit, or to both. It is God's action that is perceived in all cases.

23. Thus the Spirit appears in the New Testament narrative as early as the annunciation: the angel assures Mary that "the Holy Spirit will come" upon her and "the power of the Most High will overshadow" her (Lk 1:35). Therefore her Son will be called Son of the Most High and will be recognized by the prophet Simeon, inspired by the Holy Spirit, as the one through whom God has prepared his salvation (2:30).

24. As Jesus' ministry begins at his baptism by John, the Spirit descends upon him in the form of a dove, and leads him to the desert where he rejects the temptation from the evil one to carry out this ministry in ways disobedient to the will of the Father (Mk 1:10; Mt 3:16). At Nazareth, Jesus affirms that the prophecy of Isaiah 61:1-2 ("The Spirit of the Lord is upon me . . .") is now fulfilled in him (Lk 4:18-21). At the heart of Jesus' ministry, Luke places the promise of an outpouring of the Spirit (Lk 11:13).

25. The Gospel of John emphasizes particularly the promise and presence of the Spirit. The Baptist identifies Jesus as one who "baptizes in the Holy Spirit" (Jn 1:33). True worship will be "in Spirit and in truth" (Jn 4:23). The promised Spirit is the Paraclete (Advocate) and the Spirit of truth (14:15-17; 15:26). This promise is fulfilled when Jesus is glorified on the cross (7:37-39).

26. The outpouring of the Spirit is presented in several ways in the New Testament. For John, the Spirit is given by the risen Christ on the evening of the resurrection and empowers the disciples to forgive and to retain sins (20:22-23). For Luke in Acts (2:1-11), the Spirit is given on the day of Pentecost, and the Spirit's presence is manifested in extraordinary ways. In Acts, the manifestation of the Spirit is seen as a proof that baptism has been received: those who have been bap-

tized must receive the Spirit (the sealing). The Spirit is received by all those who "hear the Word," both Jews and gentiles (Acts 10:45). The Spirit leads Paul in his missionary journeys (Acts 13:2-5).

27. The Spirit distributes gifts to all for the good of the *koinonia* (1 Cor 12:1-11). The Spirit is the inner power of the new life in Christ. Because the faithful are in Christ and with Christ, they receive the Spirit and are in the Spirit. There is a diversity of gifts, yet these are united in their source, the one Spirit, and in their purpose, the *koinonia*. Yet the Spirit "blows where it wills," and the faithful cannot put limits to the Spirit's action in humankind.

28. The Holy Spirit, the third person of the Trinity, acts not as an impersonal force but personally inspires and guides those who come to believe. The Spirit seeks the unbelievers and reaches them in ways that are often mysterious, transforming their hearts. The Holy Spirit prepares the way for the preaching of the word to those who do not believe, enabling them to respond in faith and to know the saving grace of God. The Spirit thus creates and maintains the oneness of the church, bringing the many into unity and joining to their head the members of the body of Christ. Believers recognize one another as members of the body, share in one ministry of word and sacrament, and partake of the eucharistic meal, where through and with Christ, in the Spirit, they offer a sacrifice of praise and thanksgiving to the Father.

29. As the Spirit abides in the community where the faith is confessed in fidelity to Christ, the Spirit makes the faithful aware of the presence among them and within them of Christ and of the Father. God dwells in the faithful, and they dwell in God, in whom they "live and move and have their being." This spiritual presence is pure, unmerited gift. It calls the faithful to holiness, brings them to and keeps them in the justice that is of Christ, sets them on the way to perfection, and empowers them to act through the Spirit's many gifts. As the faithful use their gifts of the Spirit for the good of the community and the spread of the Gospel, they also receive the fruits of the Spirit (Gal 5:22-23), which build up the life of the church in peace and joy.

30. Yet the gifts can be neglected and abused. In their sinfulness, the believers can resist and grieve the Spirit. But the Holy Spirit is also the Paraclete or Advocate who pleads for them and brings about repentance, forgiveness, and reconciliation.

31. The Holy Spirit reminds the disciples of the message and words of the Lord and enables them to participate in the saving events of the life, death, and rising of Christ. The Holy Spirit is invoked in the Supper of the Lord; and, in preaching and proclamation, it is the Spirit, moving the hearts and minds of the hearers, who leads them into the fullness of truth. The Spirit's abiding presence in the church through the ages is enlivened by moments of abundant outpouring, times when the faithful have the impression of living through "a new Pentecost." Thus the Spirit guides the church in recognizing the word in the Scriptures, so that they

become the document and charter of its life. The Spirit enables the people of God and their ministers to understand and interpret the Word in the Scriptures, to transmit and explain it verbally, to hear it and receive it with faith. When it becomes necessary, the same Spirit leads the church to self-criticism and so to reform and renewal, in greater fidelity to its memory of Christ. The Spirit thus writes the Gospel in the hearts of the faithful, and this Gospel in the heart inspires the members of the *koinonia* to let the word which they believe give form to their prayer of praise and thanksgiving. In all these ways the Spirit continues to shape and enrich the memory of the community.

32. The power and presence of the Spirit lead the faithful from grace to grace. As the Holy Spirit leads them to reflect on their memory of Christ, to partake of his memorial, and to experience Christ as a present reality, they are opened to God's purpose both for themselves and for the whole of creation. The Spirit inspires them to pray and strive for the welfare of all of God's creatures, and so to protect and promote the habitat that God has given them. In ways that are known to God alone, the Spirit is also present and active among those who have not heard the Gospel or have not believed it. The Christian believers trust in God's hidden action transforming the world according to God's ultimate purpose. They seek to discern God's saving power at work. The Spirit makes them eager to see the fulfillment of all of God's promises and to pray for the coming of God's kingdom. The same Spirit gives them the certainty that the obstacles and evils that are symbolized in "the world, the flesh, and the Devil" will be overcome by God's power in God's own time. But the Christian hope that is nurtured by the Spirit also looks further than this earth and the present life. It looks forward to the eternal kingdom, where God reigns among the saints of all ages and nations and tongues. In this final transformation the Spirit will bring to an end the trials of the church on earth, the sufferings of the saints, and will bring the elect into the glory that the Father has reserved for those who love him (1 Cor 2:9).

III. The Pattern of Christian Faith

33. In John's Gospel, Jesus says, "I am the way, the truth, and the life," and goes on to affirm that though he is to go away, he leaves his Spirit who will witness to him. The Spirit will convince us of sin and lead us into the truth. Since the truth is always Christ's, there is a continuum of faith with the past. Thus, the Holy Spirit has enabled the faithful to confess Christ in every generation, and the church continues in this communion of saints. It is this permanence in Christ and in the Spirit which gives the church its identity and self-understanding and keeps it in the Gospel which it has to proclaim to the world.

34. In each generation the church inherits a history in which earlier Christians have sought to express the truth of God in their own time and place, and in that history an important place is given to those theologians who provided the earliest elucidations of the faith. The church also knows that God will provide witnesses to the faith in the future, but the present church has its own particular responsibility to the word and the Spirit now.

35. We know from past history and present experience that Christ's Spirit of truth works in a dynamic of continuity and change. The Holy Spirit brings home to us the truth of the Gospel in a variety of ways. For while the Spirit never changes, the manner of the Spirit's operation may vary with each group of believers. The Spirit moves in a gracious and positive manner, even when demanding costly discipleship. And we have the injunction laid on us not to grieve the Spirit; rather, we must cooperate with the Spirit.

36. What cooperation is thus demanded? Referring to the Holy Spirit's role in binding us to Christ, St. Irenaeus maintained that through God alone can God be known. Developing the same theme, St. Athanasius asserts that the divine Word became human so that we, in some sense, might become divine. Thus, we cooperate with the Spirit as we take to ourselves this self-giving of God in the mystery of the incarnation. This, according to biblical witness, is the way God has chosen from all eternity for the salvation of humankind. Therefore, every ordered expression of the Gospel is an attempt to proclaim this mystery—the love of God who saves in Christ—and all our efforts to discern and describe Christian belief must find their focus here. Since the heart of the Gospel and the core of the faith is the love of God revealed in redemption, then all our credal statements must derive from faith in Christ, who is our salvation and the foundation of our faith. Thus, as Vatican II recognized, "there exists an order or 'hierarchy' of truths since they vary in their relation to the foundation of the Christian faith" (UR, no. 11). Likewise Methodists, following Wesley, recognize an "analogy of faith" among the major doctrines of the church.

37. The faith which is believed is believed within particular settings. The expression of the faith has been shaped by cultures before us, and we in turn seek to speak it in the language of our time and place. Inculturation conveys the faith authentically only when what is contextual, be it language or any other form of cultural expression, is itself transformed by the transcendent truth of the Gospel. It then in turn becomes an effective means of transforming the lives of those who belong to this culture. Affirmations about God made by the believing community are active symbols, calling for realization in the lives of its members. Therefore, when Christians recite the creed within a liturgical setting, they do more than list a set of beliefs—they identify themselves with that great company "whose lives are hid with Christ in God" (Col 3:4). Because the Spirit provides in the church such

abundant gifts of perception and understanding, the recitation of the creed engenders in every age a great diversity and richness of faith. We say "we believe," and the life of the church is deepened and renewed.

38. The Nicene Creed, used by both Catholics and Methodists in their liturgy and teaching, is a comprehensive and authoritative statement of Christian faith. It was the text upon which John Wesley based his explication when, in his *Letter to a Roman Catholic*, he summarized "the faith of a true Protestant." We include the text of the creed, known as the Nicene Creed, since it constrains us to take very seriously the degree of communion that Catholics and Methodists already share. In a world deeply affected by superstition and by unbelief, our proclamation of this common faith must be an occasion for giving thanks and a stimulus to deepen our unity in Christ:

> We believe in one God, the Father, the Almighty, maker of heaven and earth, of all that is seen and unseen. We believe in one Lord, Jesus Christ, the only Son of God, eternally begotten of the Father, God from God, Light from Light, true God from true God, begotten, not made, of one Being with the Father. Through him all things were made. For us men and for our salvation he came down from heaven: by the power of the Holy Spirit he became incarnate from the Virgin Mary, and was made man. For our sake he was crucified under Pontius Pilate; he suffered death and was buried. On the third day he rose again in accordance with the Scriptures; he ascended into heaven and is seated at the right hand of the Father. He will come again in glory to judge the living and the dead, and his kingdom will have no end. We believe in the Holy Spirit, the Lord, the giver of life, who proceeds from the Father and the Son. With the Father and Son he is worshiped and glorified. He has spoken through the prophets. We believe in one, holy, catholic, and apostolic church. We acknowledge one baptism for the forgiveness of sins. We look for the resurrection of the dead, and the life of the world to come. Amen.

IV. The Pattern of Christian Life

1. The Gift of New Life

39. Faith in Jesus Christ involves assent to the truths of the Gospel. In confessing these truths we likewise confess our new identity as sons and daughters of God. As our minds are filled with the truths of the Gospel, they are transformed,

and that transformation brings about a new life. St. Paul tells his converts to be "transformed by the renewing of their minds" (Rom 12:2). Through the hearing of and response to the Gospel a crucial change of both heart and mind takes place. So it is that Paul prays to God for his new converts "that you may be filled with knowledge of God's will in all spiritual wisdom and understanding, so that you may lead lives worthy of the Lord, fully pleasing to him, as you bear fruit in every good work and as you grow in knowledge of God" (Col 1:9-10).

40. Through Christ's death and resurrection the way is opened for reconciliation to the Father in the Holy Spirit. Baptism, the sacrament of faith, is the sign of that new life which the Father gives us through Christ in the Spirit. Christ's death has put to death sin in our lives; it has freed us from the bondage of sin and death. The new life that replaces the old is a life of love: it is a sharing in the inner life of God that is communicated to us by the Holy Spirit: "God's love has been poured into our hearts through the Holy Spirit that has been given to us" (Rom 5:5). This love is pure gift, and in virtue of it we are drawn ever more deeply into the inner life of God and are able to cry "Abba, Father" (Gal 4:6). It is other-centered and boundless in its range and scope, directed to the whole world. In particular, it pushes us out to the poor, the weak, and the unloved. It is love without preference and without distinction, since because of the work of Christ, there is no longer Jew or Greek, slave or free, male or female (Gal 3:28).

2. The Challenge of New Life

41. This gift is also call and responsibility. Paul tells the Colossians that it is precisely because they have died and been raised to new life that they must put to death those features of their old way of life which still persist. They must put away their old garments and "put on the garment of God's chosen people" (cf. Col 3:12). The obligation of Christians to change their lives is rooted and grounded in what God has done for them. For a few, the transformation comes quickly, as John Wesley noted in his "Plain Account of Christian Perfection." But for most the putting to death of the old way of life and the taking on of the new involves Christians in a long and painful process of maturing in love. It is a costly journey and inevitably involves suffering, since the pattern of Christian life will reflect the pattern of Christ's dying and rising. It was the constant concern of Paul to foster and nurture this growth. Individuals, then, are changed by the saving action of God in Christ that is appropriated through the power of the Holy Spirit. But the bestowal of the gift of new life on individuals constitutes a new principle of unity. The baptized share together in the life of love, and this sharing is a vital dimension of the *koinonia* which is the church.

3. The Communion of New Life

42. By allegiance to Christ the believer becomes part of the community in which Christ is remembered (*anamnesis*). Christ's words to his disciples are relevant here. The Christian is brother, sister, mother to Christ in community with others (Mk 3:31-35; Mt 12:46-60; Lk 8:19-21).

43. The early Christian believers were part of a community where life was lived in common with others, the disunity of Babel being reversed by the events of and after Pentecost (Acts 2:44; 4:32). In Acts 2:42 we read of the four fundamental elements in their life together: hearing the teaching of the apostles, communion (*koinonia*), breaking of bread, and the prayers.

44. In their worship on the Lord's day they experienced his presence and renewing grace as they celebrated the eucharist together. In the service itself, the profound nature of their relation to each other was manifested in the giving of the peace and preeminently in the holy communion: "The bread which we break, is it not a sharing in the body of Christ? Because there is one bread, we who are many are one body, for we all partake of the one bread" (1 Cor 10:16-17). The eucharist remains the focus where the pattern of life specific to Christians is shown forth.

45. It has been customary to state that Methodists regard the preaching of the word as the central act of worship, while for Catholics the eucharist is "the center and culmination" of Christian life (PO, no. 5). This contrast should not be put too strongly. In the beginnings of Methodism, the Wesleys encouraged and practiced a much more frequent observance of the Lord's Supper than was customary in the Anglican Church of the time, and in recent decades Methodists are increasingly appreciating the centrality of the eucharist and Catholics the fundamental importance of the preaching of the word.

4. The Source of New Life

46. By baptism we are received into the community of belief and are nurtured there as the faith is passed on to us ("traditioned" to us) through the family and the church. Unless this "traditioning" takes place, we receive little of the Christian faith. Each generation and each person must claim for themselves the life of faith. We receive the faith in more explicit terms through hearing the preached word, Sunday schools, catechism classes, first communion classes, confirmation classes, and church-sponsored schools. Sustained growth in the Christian faith requires time spent in study of the Scriptures and in prayer based on the Scriptures. The faith is nourished in both our traditions by devotional life that plays a significant part in its growth. There are also many ways in which the spiritual life has been nurtured among us, e.g., Christian family life, Methodist class meetings, various lay apostolates, and renewal movements in the Catholic Church, the practice of retreats, ecu-

menical house groups, and marriage enrichment courses. In all these situations "heart speaks to heart" (cor ad cor loquitur).

5. The Practice of New Life

47. The Christian hope is that humanity will one day be gathered into Christ when the Gospel has been preached to all nations (Mt 24:14; 28:19). In the widest sense of the mission of the church, there is the mandate to feed the hungry, clothe the naked, visit the sick and the prisoners, welcome the stranger (Mt 25:31-46). These "works of mercy" belong to the Christian mission in the widest sense, and Catholic-Methodist cooperation has often been most successful in this area. In particular, both churches have tried to promote true Christian community without respect of race, sex, or class. In places that are hostile to Christianity, missionary endeavor has been difficult, and fidelity to the Gospel has proved very costly. The picture in Hebrews of the saints who watch from heaven and encourage us is pertinent here (Heb 12:1).

48. The proclamation of the Gospel by words is an essential task for each generation of believers. Christians also bear witness when they seek to let their light shine before others, so that their conduct as well as their words may bring others to glorify God (Mt 5:16; 1 Pt 2:12). Personal evangelism contributes to the corporate mission and is vitally important in making new believers.

V. The Pattern of Christian Community

49. The real relationships existing within the Godhead, Father, Son, and Holy Spirit, are reflected within the ordered life of creation and still more clearly revealed to the eye of faith in the pattern they establish and make possible for the community life of God's people.

50. Whenever the word of God is truly heard, the church shapes its life in due obedience; the pattern thus brought into being becomes in its turn a means of showing forth the word. As individuals are healed and remade by Christ, so also are the relationships within which their life is brought to fulfillment. When, for example, the community of Christians at Philippi was told to have the mind of Christ, who emptied himself and took the form of a servant, this was not just an instruction to private individuals but an exhortation for the benefit of their common life. Further still, it was not just for their own health and happiness as a community, but for a making known the word to the world: it was a setting forth of the word through an effective embodiment of the servanthood of the incarnate one. One passage in the New Testament—1 John 1:1-3—dares to suggest that the life of the Christian community is a reflection of the life of the Godhead: thus the communal life of Christians has a vertical as well as a horizontal dimension. They do not

merely enjoy fellowship with each other; their life together is a sharing in the life of the Father and his Son Jesus Christ.

51. The Savior rescues us from loneliness and sets us within the infinitely diverse security of his friends. The images used in the Gospels and in the apostolic preaching give indications relating to the ordered life brought into being by Christ. The images are corporate as well as individual. They evoke the bridegroom as well as the bride, the good shepherd's care, the growth and pruning of the vine, the manifold activities and talents of the body, family life in the home, good steward-ship, the tender care of the Samaritan, the touch of the healer, the watchful love of the father. In the light of the Lord's Supper, the image of the body has inspired profound insights and reflections on the church as the body of Christ.

52. It must also be remembered that in the New Testament, the actions that allow the church to grow in strength and ordered life—the setting apart of new ministers or corporate decisions and teaching, for example—are always accompa-nied by the action of the Holy Spirit, who makes it possible for us to live in com-munion and harmony with one another (Acts 13:2; 15:28; 16:6-7; 2 Tm 1:14). The Spirit is the invisible thread running through the work of the church in the world, enabling our minds to hear and receive the word, enlightening them to understand the word, and giving us tongues to speak the word (Jn 14:26; 16:13-14; Acts 4:31). Relating us to one another and to Christ our head, the Holy Spirit gives coherent shape and variety to the people of God. Within that people as they are, and for that people as they shall be, the Holy Spirit invites us all to share in the ser-vice of the one who came to serve.

Part Two: Ministry and Ministries—Serving Within the Apostolic Tradition

53. The life of the church, of the human race as it is gathered together and renewed by Christ, is a life of worship, by which believers share in the exchange of love that is the life of the blessed Trinity, Father, Son, and Holy Spirit. With Christ our head and in the power of his Spirit, we serve God in a variety of ways for God's glory and for making known God's loving purpose.

I. Service of the Word

54. As the apostle sent by God (Heb 3:1), Christ shared his carrying-out of the Father's will with others. These he sent into the world to serve the Gospel, just as he himself had been sent into the world to serve (Jn 20:21-23). They were given the formal title of apostle. Theirs was a ministry of ministries: they were sent out to make him known and to care for his people. The apostles, already joined together

in the public ministry of Christ, continued after the ascension to be his friends and servants, fully aware of their appointed responsibility to tell everyone of what God had done for them in Christ.

55. In the Book of Acts, the apostles are described a "servants of the word" (Acts 6:4; cf. Lk 1:2). This phrase holds a rich meaning, conveying all that is said in Scripture about God's action through his word in creation and in his saving purpose in history. What he says he does. What he does makes him known to us. There is a solidarity between word and deed. This complete interdependence of word and deed in God's action for us culminates in the coming of the person who, in his entire being, is the Word of God. "Service of the Word" implies the service of a living person, whose words are always fruitful and whose deeds make him known. Supremely in Christ, words and actions are one. Through the Spirit these deeds and words culminate in the living presence of Jesus in us. It is in this context that the sermon and the sacrament must be understood. In preaching, the Word of God himself addresses us through the preacher: "Whoever hears you hears me" (Lk 10:16). In the eucharist, our Lord's words, "This is my body," "This is my blood," convey both his meaning and the actual giving of himself.

56. The "servants of the Word" are therefore those who bring the whole of this divine life into the world, enabling all of us, in our turn, to become servants, each one unique and different but all gathered together in perfect harmony.

57. The present disharmony among Christians is crucially reflected in divisions of doctrine and practice concerning this service of the Word. An arrival at a common mind over Christ's purpose for ministry would therefore have a far-reaching effect in the promotion of unity throughout the Christian churches.

II. Gifts of the Spirit

58. The entire Christian community has the responsibility of spreading the Gospel and witnessing to the Lord's work of salvation until he comes. This task has "its origins in the mission of the Son and that of the Holy Spirit according to the purpose of God the Father" (AG, no. 2).

59. Throughout the ages the Holy Spirit has poured out gifts on those who have been baptized in the name of Christ. These gifts are for the building up of the church, which is charged with proclaiming the good news for the salvation of the world, so that all people may come to faith and share in the worship of the triune God (cf. Rom 15:7-16; 2 Cor 4:13-15). Thus, each charism that is given elicits a response that must be lived out in ministry and in service: "And his gifts were that some should be apostles, some prophets, some evangelists, some pastors and teachers, to equip the saints for the work of ministry for the building up of the body of Christ until we all attain to the unity of the faith and of the knowledge of the Son

of God" (Eph 4:11-13). The gifts of the Spirit, therefore, are for communion *(koinonia)*: for the drawing of humanity into communion with the Father and the Son, and for the building up and strengthening of communion among those who believe.

60. Among the gifts bestowed by the Spirit there is the specific charism received by those who are called to the ordained ministry. This charism is directed toward the ordering and harmony which must prevail in the exercise of all the gifts. Properly to understand the relationship between the ministries of the ordained and the nonordained, it is vital to see in both of them the activity of the Spirit who enlivens and unifies the church through the gifts: "Now there are a variety of gifts but the same Spirit; and there are varieties of service, but the same Lord; and there are varieties of working, but it is the same God who activates them all in everyone" (1 Cor 12:47). The same Spirit operates among all the baptized and across all the generations.

61. The New Testament describes the Spirit-filled life in the early Christian communities. The origins of the ordained ministry are found in the commission that Christ gave to his apostles (Mt 28:18-20). While there was at the beginning no single pattern, the ordained ministry was a gift to the church for leadership in its corporate and worshiping life, for the maintenance and deepening of its order and structure, for the organization of its missionary witness, and for discernment in understanding and applying the Gospel. As time passed, the church was led by the Spirit to recognize the threefold ministry of bishop, presbyter, and deacon as normative; some other patterns of ministry that may be discerned in the New Testament became assimilated to the threefold one. While not all the many gifts of the Spirit for ministry have figured equally throughout the history of the church, all have been bestowed afresh at times of crisis and opportunity. Yet the testimony of the New Testament must continue to throw light on the ways in which the ordained ministry has developed and to challenge the ways it functions in our different communions.

III. The Church, a Living Body

62. The community of the faithful is brought into existence by the Holy Spirit. The Spirit relates the faithful to one another, distributing gifts among them. Thus the community receives a living structure. Some of the New Testament images—a body, a household, a people, a vineyard—point to dynamics of growth and to a reality with many aspects and dimensions. Others—the bride, the flock— imply also that it has its own definite identity and is the center of God's attention, called to share the divine love and opened to the Holy Spirit in whom the faithful experience God's love. As it spreads abroad the good news, the community calls all

people to conversion and new life. Led by the Spirit, it extends throughout the many and varied cultures of the world and is sustained through time from year to year, generation after generation. Through the centuries it is rejuvenated as the Gospel strikes the imagination and the Spirit stirs up the love of new and younger members. Like the sap of the vine that brings greenness to all branches and twigs, the church is an overflowing source of life. From the human environment it receives new riches that nurture it and which it in turn transforms, opening up the many cultures of the world to intimations of the kingdom of God. The Holy Spirit directs the course of the Christian community by bringing to it the harvest of love, joy, peace, patience, kindness, goodness, fidelity, gentleness, and self-control (Gal 5:22-25). The community is a living organism, not a collection of individuals; it is a place of meeting where people exchange things old and new, not a museum where things are looked at. What is handed on by its Tradition in the form of memory acts as a leaven among those who receive it, who then enrich it as they cherish it and pass it on again to their successors. There are times, of course, when Christians do not respond as they ought to the Spirit's guidance. They lack fidelity to Christ, they are lukewarm in the worship of God, they do not show love toward one another, they fail in missionary outreach. So, like all living organisms, Christian communities go through periods of dormancy and decline. But even then hope is held out for vigorous and healthy life because the church is sustained by the Spirit of God who never leaves himself without witnesses.

1. The Community of Faith and Baptism

63. The Spirit calls people to this new life, as those who have heard the word come to Christ, the only Savior and Mediator. Baptism is given in the midst of the community to new Christians who, at their baptism, confess the faith they have received. Symbolically they are plunged in the cleansing waters where they receive the Holy Spirit and are given the garment of faith "in the name of the Father, the Son, and the Holy Spirit." United to Christ in his dying and his rising, they bear witness that they are reborn in him. In the administration of baptism, the community testifies to its faith with the words of the traditional creed. For example, the Apostles' Creed had its origin in the candidates' confession of faith. Methodists and Catholics agree that Christians are baptized into the faith that has been received from the apostles and obediently preached by the community and its members. In both our traditions it has been the normal practice for the pastors of the community to preside over the entire process of Christian initiation. Both the Methodist and the Catholic churches consider it right to baptize the infants born to believers. They encourage their members to take the opportunities presented to them to renew the vows that they made, or that were made for them, in baptism.

64. Those who confess their faith, endorsed by the community, are brought through the baptismal waters into the life of God that is communicated through Christ in the Holy Spirit. This life, being the very life of the divine persons, is itself a life of communion and involves participating in the bond of love established by the Spirit between God and creation. The baptized become sisters and brothers in Christ. They are constituted as the family of God, sharing in its privileges and responsibilities.

65. By baptism, the community of the believers shares in the holiness of God, a holiness that is manifested in the Christian life of the faithful. The community feeds on the memory of the Lord, celebrates his abiding presence, and looks forward in hope to the continuing service of God and of neighbor until the end of time, thus affirming its trust in the ultimate victory of Christ over the power of evil. It is itself a sign and instrument of God's kingdom.

66. Thus, the baptized and believing community is a communion. Holding in common the faith in which they are baptized and all the holy things that are God's gifts, they grow into a communion of the people who are made holy by God's grace and power. While all the baptized thus make up "the communion of saints," they also recognize the conspicuous presence of divine grace in specific persons— the saints—whose lives and example testify, even to the shedding of their blood for Jesus, to the transforming action of the Spirit of God in every generation. The "cloud of witnesses" transcends denominational barriers.

2. The Community of Worship

67. The Christian community continues to flourish by virtue of the common baptism and faith of its members. But it is also sustained and nurtured by the celebration of the memorial of the Lord, the service of thanksgiving in which it experiences, as the Spirit is invoked, the presence of the risen Christ. There the word of God is heard in the Scriptures and the proclamation of the Gospel. Through the holy meal of the community, the faithful share "a foretaste of the heavenly banquet prepared for all mankind" (British *Methodist Service Book*, 1975). As they receive the sacrament of his body and blood offered for them, they become the body through which the risen Lord is present on earth in the Holy Spirit (1 Cor 10:16-17). As they share his body and blood that have brought to the sinful world salvation and reconciliation, they proclaim today the past events of the Lord's death and resurrection, and as they do so they present to the world their confidence and hope that Christ who "has died and is risen" will also "come again."

68. This experience of the presence of the Lord in the setting of worship attunes the hearts and minds of the faithful to all other aspects of his presence. They return to him the love they have received from him, when they serve the poor and when they struggle for social justice. In the sick and suffering they see the

sufferings of Christ. In their own pains and sorrows endured for the sake of the Gospel they share in the passion of Christ. In all this the faithful experience the wonderful exchange by which in Christ and the Holy Spirit, all is common to all. And they present to God all that they have and all that they are as their own sacrifice of praise.

69. In the worshiping fellowship, the community confesses Jesus Christ as Lord, shares the peace which Christ gives, and so anticipates the heavenly kingdom where the risen Christ fills all things to the glory of God the Father. The community of the faithful is thus the proclaiming, celebrating, and serving community which gives glory to God in the name of all creatures. By its gatherings on the Lord's day the community shapes the life of its members, helping them to make their weekly and daily tasks expressions of the royal priesthood of the believers gathered together under the high priesthood of the risen Lord. Thus, the community provides for its members a pattern of life consecrated to God and directed towards fulfillment in the final manifestation of Christ.

3. The Ordained Minister in the Community

70. Ever since the time of the apostles, ministers have led the community in the worship of God, in proclaiming Christ and receiving him, in organizing the community's life of service in the Spirit. Worship, witness, and service join hands in word and sacrament: this has served as the central model for what Christian ministers must both be and do.

71. Chosen from among the people, the ordained ministers represent the people before God as they bring together the prayers of the community. Entrusted with the pastoral care of the community, they act in Christ's name and person as they lead the people in prayer, proclaim and explain the word, and administer the sacraments of faith.

72. In each place the pastor gathers the faithful into one, and as all the ministers relate to one another and transmit the same Gospel, they ensure a universality of conviction and communion among all the faithful. They transmit what they have received: the good news as taught from apostolic times, the sacraments as signs and instruments of the Lord's saving presence and action, the call to holiness that the Holy Spirit addresses to all.

73. United around their minister in worship and in witness, and in the carrying out of their vocational tasks, the faithful know themselves to be gathered in Christ by the Holy Spirit. In the pastoral care that is extended to them, the faithful perceive themselves to be led by the Good Shepherd who gave his life for the sheep.

74. As the community is renewed from one Lord's day to the next, it is nourished by the tradition it has received, and responsibility for this is especially

entrusted to those ministers who inherit the apostolic function of oversight in the community. The function of oversight entails on the part of the ministers a solicitude for all the churches: they are charged to ensure that the community remain one, that it grow in holiness, that it preserve its catholicity, and that it be faithful to apostolic teaching and to the commission of evangelization given by Christ himself.

75. These four "marks" of the Christian community should be exemplified at each moment of its existence. They should also be effectively transmitted from one generation to the next. The saints who have passed into the fullness of the mystery of God's grace are forever part of the community: the witness and examples of the past continue to be cherished; the saints in heaven are held as instances of Christ's "closest love" and as present tokens of the ultimate fulfillment of all God's promises.

76. The transmission of the Gospel is the work of the whole assembly of the faithful under the guidance and with the encouragement of their pastors. The living presence of the Lord among his people is the source of the Christian life. The pastors of the community are his servants as he provides grace and spiritual strength to his people and leads them to the goal of their earthly pilgrimage.

77. The transmission of the Gospel in word and sacraments is itself the work of the Spirit. As they urge the faithful to Christian perfection, the ordained ministers obey the call of Christ, and they help the community in its search for the forms of Christian holiness that are appropriate to different periods, ages, and conditions of life. Catholics and Methodists are at one in seeing in a divinely empowered ministry the guidance of the Holy Spirit and are moving in the direction of greater shared understanding of the nature of ordination and of the structure of the ministry in regard to the responsibility to teach and to formulate the faith.

IV. The Ordained Ministry: Call and Empowerment

78. We consider now the call to the ordained ministry, ordination to the ministry, and continuance in it.

1. Call

79. Both Methodists and Catholics recognize the power of God in the enabling of all ministry. During his earthly ministry the Lord Jesus himself in his sovereign freedom appointed twelve. The experience of Paul, who according to his own words received the call to be an apostle direct from the risen Christ, attests to the freedom and movement of the Holy Spirit to call persons at will into ministry. This call may be experienced in several ways: as an internal compulsion that we feel found to obey; through the convergence of several external factors, all of which

indicate its possibility; through the influence of the church and its people, which exercises a claim upon us; or through the indication of a need and the ability under God to fulfill that need. Whichever way the call is experienced, it does not remain an inward compulsion but is tested by the church and finally confirmed before the candidate is ordained. The different ways in which this judgment is made in the Catholic and Methodist contexts reflect the different understanding and experience of being churches that have developed during centuries of independent growth.

2. Ordination

80. Both our traditions retain the practice, attested in the New Testament documents, of setting apart for ministry by the laying on of hands with prayer; prayer is made for the gift of the Holy Spirit appropriate to the particular form of ministry. Ordination takes place in an assembly of the church in which the people give their assent to the candidates, appropriate Scriptures are read, and candidates profess their adherence to the faith of the church. Through the laying on of hands, ordinands are incorporated into the existing body of ministers.

81. In the Catholic understanding and practice of apostolic succession, the bishops through the act of ordination share ministerially the high priesthood of Christ, in one degree or another, with other ministers (bishops, presbyters, and deacons), who are their fellow workers in carrying out the apostolic duties entrusted to them (cf. PO, no. 2).

82. In Methodist understanding and practice, including those Methodist churches that are episcopally ordered, candidates for ordination are accepted by the conference after examination as to the genuineness of their call, their spiritual fitness, and their capacity for ministry. They are then ordained by prayer and the imposition of hands by the bishop, or by the president of the conference, and given the tasks of declaring the Gospel, celebrating the sacraments, and caring pastorally for Christ's flock.

3. Continuance in the Ministry

83. Within the community of the people of God, under the guidance of the Holy Spirit, an authentic ministry, of the ordained as of all the people of God, communicates Christ to persons, edifies them, and builds them up in the faith. In one way or another, it is shown by its fruits.

84. All ministry continues to depend entirely upon God's grace for its exercise. The God who calls crowns his call with gifts for ministry. It is not only the use of the personal gifts of the minister which is at issue here. The minister lives constantly in the grace of God by means of prayer, study of the Scripture, and participation in the sacraments. As an instrument in God's hands, the ordained minister

imparts the word of God to God's people, both by speech and by the sacraments of the church. Both Methodists and Catholics maintain the principle that while the preached word and the acted word call for holiness in the minister, it is not the ministers' worthiness that makes them effective, but the transforming power of the Holy Spirit.

85. The call of God is seen to be a stable and permanent one by both Catholics and Methodists. The ordained person is committed to a lifelong ministry; therefore, just as baptism and confirmation are not repeated, neither is ordination. Both communions are here faithful to the constant practice of the church.

V. Convergences and Divergence

86. Previous paragraphs make it clear that Methodists and Catholics share a fundamentally important perspective on ministry, affirming that the ordained ministry is essentially pastoral in nature. Ordained ministers have the special responsibility of exercising and holding together the functions of proclaiming the Gospel, calling people to faith, feeding the flock with word and sacrament, and making Christ known through the ministry of servanthood to the world. The ordained ministry is a representative one, in the sense expounded in paragraph 71 above.

87. Within this perspective there remain several unresolved issues related to ordained ministry which call for further examination.

1. Sacramentality

88. For Catholics, ordination is a sacrament. Methodists are accustomed to reserve the term sacrament for baptism and the Lord's Supper. They do, however, with Catholics look upon ordination as an effective sign by which the grace of God is given to the recipient for the ministry of word and sacrament.

89. A way forward may lie in deeper common reflection on the nature of sacrament. Christ, "the image of the invisible God" (Col 1:15), may be thought of as the primary sacrament, revealing God's nature and purpose and enabling us to know and serve him. We may also discern within his action on our behalf certain gifts by which our lives are ordered, nourished, and sustained. These have traditionally been classified by Catholics as sacraments in a more specific use of the word.

90. Both Methodists and Catholics see the Holy Spirit as the one who empowers all ministry, both ordained and lay. Further, both Methodists and Catholics would agree that all the people of God must be a sign of Christ in a real sense and that all ministry must be exemplary of Christ and the Gospel. Thus, a life clearly in consonance with Christ is a vocation for all Christians.

91. At Vatican II the Roman Catholic Church referred to the church in terms of a "sacrament of salvation" (AG, no. 5; cf. LG, no. 1). Methodists would prefer the word "sign" to sacrament, but the meaning in each case is essentially the same, because the church obeys the mandate of its founder to preach to all nations the Gospel of salvation it has received.

2. Episkope

92. Methodists and Catholics can acknowledge together the reality of *episkope* (oversight) in the New Testament and can agree that an ordained ministry which exercises *episkope* is vital for the life of the church. Without the exercise of this gift of oversight, disorder and therefore disunity are inevitable. *Koinonia* and *episkope* imply one another. In a Catholic perspective this mutual implication reaches its culmination when the bishop presides over liturgical worship, in which the preaching of the Gospel and the celebration of the Lord's Supper weld together into unity the members of Christ's body.

93. Central to the exercise of *episkope* is the task of maintaining unity in the truth. Thus, teaching is the principal part of the task of *episkope*. In a Catholic understanding the church is united through its unity in faith and sacramental communion. The teaching of a common faith by the college of bishops in union with the successor of Peter ensures unity in the truth. The succession of bishops through the generations serves the continued unity of the church in the faith handed on from the apostles. In the Methodist tradition, Wesley accepted and believed in the reality of *episkope* within the Church of England of which he was a minister. In relation to the Methodist societies, he exercised *episkope* over the whole; all his followers were bound to be in connection with him. He expounded the main teachings of the church by means of his Sermons, Notes on the New Testament, and Conference Minutes, and made available to his people authorized abridgements of doctrinal and spiritual work. His appointment of Francis Asbury and Thomas Coke to the superintendency in America was rooted in his belief that the Holy Spirit wished to bestow the gift of *episkope* at that time and in that place for the sake of maintaining unity of faith with the church of all ages. It was part of a fresh and extraordinary outpouring of the gift of the Spirit who never ceases to enliven and unify the church.

94. As we continue to consider remaining differences over the sacramental nature of ordination and the forms of succession and oversight, we rejoice in the work of the Spirit who has already brought us this far together, recognizing that the ecumenical movement of which we are part is itself a grace of the Holy Spirit for the unity of Christians. When the time comes that Methodists and Catholics declare their readiness for that "full communion in faith, mission, and sacramental life" toward which they are working (*Towards a Statement on the Church*, no. 20),

the mutual recognition of ministry will be achieved not only by their having reached doctrinal consensus, but it will also depend upon a fresh creative act of reconciliation which acknowledges the manifold yet unified activity of the Holy Spirit throughout the ages. It will involve a joint act of obedience to the sovereign Word of God.

3. Who May Be Ordained

95. In the New Testament record there is strong evidence that the pastoral ministry was exercised by both married and unmarried people. By long-standing tradition the Latin rite of the Catholic Church, seeing a positive congruence between celibacy and the ordained priesthood, requires that priests remain unmarried, although exceptions to this practice have been allowed. Methodists, in common with other Protestant churches, ordain both married and unmarried people, but no ultimate doctrinal obstacle divides Methodists and Catholics here.

96. Methodists ordain women because they believe that women also receive the call, evidenced by inward conviction and outward manifestation of the gifts and graces and confirmed by the gathering of the faithful.

97. Catholics do not ordain women, believing that they have no authority to change a practice that belongs to the sacrament of order as received in the Tradition of the church.

98. Our general reflections on the nature of ordained ministry and our treatment of this particular question will need to be mutually illuminating. Further thought will be of benefit to both traditions.

Conclusion

99. Together Catholics and Methodists confess the church as part of the triune God's eternal purpose for the salvation of humankind. The church is the communion of those who have received, receive, and will receive through faith the benefits of the redemptive work of God accomplished in the life, death, and resurrection of the Word made flesh. In the Holy Spirit they acknowledge the lordship of Christ to the glory of the Father. Thus constituted and sustained by the Word and the Spirit, the church is both a sign and an instrument of the Father's good pleasure for the world: it is a sign, because it is the firstfruits of God's gracious purpose and work; it is an instrument because it has the task of further proclaiming the Gospel and doing the works that belong to God's kingdom. By its own communal life it bears witness to that society of love in which the city of God will consist.

100. Catholic and Methodist formularies differ over the concrete location of the church which they both confess. While Wesley and the early Methodists could

recognize the presence of Christian faith in the lives of individual Roman Catholics, it is only more recently that Methodists have become more willing to recognize the Roman Catholic Church as an institution for the divine good of its members. For its part, the Roman Catholic Church since Vatican II certainly includes Methodists among those who, by baptism and faith in Christ, enjoy "a certain though imperfect communion with the Catholic Church"; and it envisages Methodism among those ecclesial communities which are "not devoid of meaning and importance in the mystery of salvation" (UR, no. 3).

101. In the quarter-century since its inception, the Joint Commission between the Roman Catholic Church and the World Methodist Council has contributed to the degree of mutual recognition which now exists. It has done so by the clarification of Methodist and Catholic positions and traditions, especially as these impinge on each other. A large measure of common faith has been brought to light, so that the increase in shared life that has begun may confidently be expected to continue. The need now is to consolidate the measure of agreement so far attained and to press forward with work on those areas in which agreement is still lacking. Continuing doctrinal progress should both encourage and reflect the growth in mutual recognition and in sharing in the life of the triune God.

Participants in the Dialogue

Roman Catholics

Most Rev. James W. Malone, Bishop of Youngstown, USA (cochairman)
Most Rev. John Bathersby, Bishop of Cairns, Australia
Sr. Mary Charles Murray, University of Nottingham, England
Rev. Francis Frost, Ecumenical Institute, Cèligny, Switzerland
Most Rev. John Onaiyekan, Coadjutor Bishop of Abuja, Nigeria
Canon Michael Richards, London, England
Rev. George H. Tavard, Brighton, Massachusetts, USA
Msgr. Kevin McDonald, Pontifical Council for Christian Unity, Vatican City
   (secretary)

Methodists

Rev. Geoffrey Wainwright, Duke University, Durham, North Carolina, USA
   (cochairman)
Rev. David Butler, The Queen's College, Birmingham, England
Most Rev. William R. Cannon, Atlanta, Georgia, USA
Rev. Ireneu Cunha, Oporto, Portugal (1988 meeting)

Rev. Ira Gallaway, Pagosa Springs, Colorado, USA
Mrs. Gillian Kingston, Roscrea, Ireland
Rev. Luis F. Palomo, San José, Costa Rica
Rev. Norman Young, Queen's College, Melbourne, Australia
Rev. Joe Hale, World Methodist Council, Lake Junaluska, North Carolina, USA (secretary)

Staff

Mrs. Linda Greene, World Methodist Council
Miss Josette Kersters, Vatican City

The Word of Life

Sixth Series (1991-1996)

Preface

In every country of the world, men and women, old and young, are found worshiping in churches, cathedrals, chapels, and house groups, confessing in a great variety of cultures and in many tongues "Jesus Christ is Lord." They have discovered the Redeemer of the world to be their own Savior, and their commitment to Christ gives meaning and purpose to their lives.

In Asia and Africa, the number of Christians has doubled in recent years as seeds sown in earlier times come to fruition. Indigenous evangelizers have taken responsibility in the creation and animation of new church communities. New ecclesial communities are also being born in places thought by some to have moved into a "post-Christian" era. In countries of Eastern Europe, believing people have lived their faith with tenacity in the face of atheism and oppression and now bear dynamic witness to the way faith continues to outlive all forces that would destroy it. New signs of life are appearing in western countries where Christians are confessing their faith as a thoughtful alternative to prevailing materialistic values and the full flowering of secularism which had seemed an inevitable trend in the modern world.

Catholics and Methodists participate in this astonishing persistence and explosive growth of Christian presence and witness in the world. Whether in a

Catholic parish in Zaire or in an urban Methodist congregation in Korea, whether at the preaching of the word or in the celebration at the table, the common acclamation rings out: "Christ has died, Christ is risen, Christ will come again." Praise issues in evangelistic testimony and caring service as believing Methodists and Catholics disperse to bear witness to the Lord among their neighbors.

The heart of the faith is common to Catholics and Methodists; but while they sometimes share in prayer and witness together, often they proceed on their own more or less parallel lines. The current situation calls into question the separation that we have inherited and spurs us on to work for our eventual full communion in Christ. The work done by this commission up to now has been directed towards this end. Our previous document, *The Apostolic Tradition*, studied the source of our faith and the means by which it has been communicated to us.

God's Word, revealing God to us, and God's Spirit, enabling us to know God, have led us now to study more closely the ways in which God gives himself to us and the response that we make. God's revelation comes for our reception as the *Word of Life*, to be confessed, propagated, and celebrated. The more we can do these things together, the more we shall be in harmony with the Gospel of reconciliation, and the more credible will be our witness, to the glory of God, Father, Son, and Holy Spirit. Therefore, we seek full communion in faith, mission, and sacramental life. This report is offered as a contribution towards the achievement of the doctrinal agreement necessary to that end.

COCHAIRMEN
Bishop James W. Malone, *Roman Catholic Church*
Dr. Geoffrey Wainwright, *World Methodist Council*

Introduction

1. In the continuing search for the doctrinal agreement necessary to full communion between Catholics and Methodists, the Joint Commission now treats what are usually called, in theological terms, "revelation" and "faith." We are looking for commonly acceptable ways of expounding the historical self-disclosure and indeed self-gift of the triune God, focused in Jesus Christ, the Word made flesh, and brought home to successive generations of believers by the Holy Spirit, released in power at Pentecost. We are seeking a common account of how men, women, and children, opened to the gracious presence of God, are enabled to commit themselves, body and soul, heart and mind and will, to their Maker and Redeemer and, in communion with him, become renewed in the divine image, in the holiness and happiness which is God's intention for humankind. God's revelation and the human response to it constitute the substance of the church's faith, mission, and sacra-

mental life; and the more common the account we can give of these things, the closer we may come to one another in our understanding and practice of them and so be readier for full communion between us.

2. Seeking to place its work under the word of God, the commission heard anew the opening words of the First Letter of St. John:

> That which was from the beginning, which we have heard, which we have seen with our eyes, which we have looked upon and touched with our own hands, concerning the word of life—the life was made manifest, and we saw it, and testify to it, and proclaim to you the eternal life which was with the Father and was made manifest to us—that which we have seen and heard we proclaim also to you, so that you may have fellowship with us; and our fellowship is with the Father and with his Son Jesus Christ. (1 Jn 1:1-3)

This sacred text starts from the particularity of the God of Israel's self-revelation in Christ; the divine Word, who was in the beginning with God and has led the history of the chosen people, has been made flesh in Jesus. That sheer self-gift of God is a word of life to humankind: God so loved the world that he gave his only Son, that whoever believes in him should not perish but have eternal life. In Christ, in his words, his deeds, his entire existence, God has been revealed in audible, visible, palpable form: God has been received by human ears, eyes, and hands. What the first believers have taken in, they then bear witness to and transmit, for the message spreads the offer of a life shared with God. The modes of the announcement will appropriately reflect, echo, and hand on what was seen, heard, and touched in the embodied manifestation of God in Jesus Christ. Accepted in faith, the words, signs, and actions of the Gospel will become the means of communion with the one true God, Father, Son, and Holy Spirit. The divine life into which the Spirit introduces believers will be a common life, as each transmits and receives what is always the gift of God.

3. In this passage from Scripture, we find already indicated all the main themes of the commission's deliberations and report: the gift of the revelation of the triune God; the human response of faith; the proclamation, as missionary message, of what has been received in faith; word and sacrament as the intelligible and tangible means of grace; communion with the triune God as the very life of the church, the community of believers which in God's name offers to the world the salvation that the church already anticipates with joy.

4. The revelation of the triune God is the source of the church's faith, the church's mission, and the church's sacramental life. These are three essential ingre-

dients in the full communion our commission has declared is the final goal of our dialogue (cf. *Towards a Statement on the Church*, no. 20; *The Apostolic Tradition*, no. 94). Revelation, faith, mission, and sacramental life are briefly described below. The main body of the report will go on to look at each in more detail, to outline their connections, and then finally to offer a vision of our goal of full communion.

5. Revelation is God's self-disclosure to human creatures. Having already left a divine mark in all that he has made, God initiated a more direct self-revelation by speaking to Abraham, who was called to the land where his descendants would dwell. The Creator became known as the God of Abraham, Isaac, and Jacob. Abraham and Sarah, who received the promise of God, have been seen as models for all believers. Giving the law through Moses and leading the chosen people through judges, kings, and prophets, God was known to the people of Israel in a unique way among the nations. And this knowledge of God and of our human condition before him has been conveyed to later ages by the Scriptures of the Old Testament.

6. In the midst of this chosen people, at the appointed time, God sent the divine Word, who took flesh from the Virgin Mary as Jesus, the Christ, the Redeemer and Mediator, in whom the divine revelation was fully embodied. The first response to this revelation in Christ is formulated in the Scriptures of the New Testament, which are thus normative for all later ages.

7. The Scriptures attest that it is by the Spirit of God that human beings see God manifest in history. Thus, their response to revelation is more than a mere reaction to extraordinary events; it is "faith," that is, a knowledge that involves complete personal commitment, body and soul, heart and mind, to the divine self-disclosure—of the one whom Jesus called "Abba, Father," of the Word whose presence and action is perceived in the words and acts of Jesus Christ, and of the Spirit, the enabler and supporter of all who believe.

8. Revelation and faith are thus correlative events and moments. What God reveals through Jesus is apprehended in faith through the power of the Holy Spirit. While this faith was, in the Old Testament, an inspired response to God made known as the Creator and the Lawgiver who also spoke through the prophets, it is, in the New Testament, shaped by the fundamental awareness of the tri-unity of God that has been preserved and continues to be experienced in the Christian community. That witness to this trinitarian faith has been handed on in the apostolic tradition. It has been preserved in successive ages by baptism in the threefold name of God, "the Father, the Son, and the Holy Spirit," formulated in the traditional creeds, and reflected in the decisions and exhortations of the great councils of the church. Catholics and Methodists are in full agreement on this christological and trinitarian dimension of revelation and of faith.

9. God's revelation aims to bring about communion between humankind and God. The faithful response to God's gift of himself is fundamentally one of grateful acceptance and loving self-surrender. All who have welcomed the revelation of the Father, Son, and Holy Spirit feel bound to celebrate together the wonderful deeds of God and to declare them in mission to the world:

- Christians have always been ready to give an account of the hope they share (cf. 1 Pt 3:15) and have professed their faith publicly. United with Christ through baptism and the Lord's Supper, they are called to make their own the faith of the whole community of believers. Sunday after Sunday, Methodists and Catholics make the same fundamental affirmations of faith during worship, and this realization impels them to work towards *unity of faith* in every aspect of Christian life.

- From the day of Pentecost, believers have gone out in the power of the Spirit to share what they have seen and heard and handled. They have done so aware that the gift they have received is not for themselves only; that Christ through his Spirit has commissioned them to make disciples of all the nations. Faith flows out in mission. Catholics and Methodists recognize that they have to overcome everything that prevents them from bearing *united witness* to the one God revealed in Jesus Christ.

- The community that professes its faith and reaches out in mission to the world experiences the reality of Christ's promise "I am with you always, yes to the end of time" (Mt 28:20). Its life together, above all its worship, manifests this grace of God. In its prayer, preaching, and sacramental rites it is nourished in communion with God and offers an invitation to humankind to accept the salvation offered in Jesus Christ. Here, too, Christ's Spirit challenges us to be reconciled *at one table* in a unity of worship and praise so that the world may believe.

10. By baptism and the faith in Christ which it signifies, Catholics and Methodists already enjoy a certain measure of ecclesial communion. The purpose of the dialogue between us is to increase and deepen our relationship until we reach sufficient agreement in the Christian truth that our common baptism can without equivocation be completed in our mutual participation in the meal to which the one Lord invites us and all his followers. The unity we seek to promote is not solely for our own enjoyment but for the sake of a credible witness to the reconciliation that God in Christ has wrought for the world and therefore among humankind. Our unity is to allow us to "glorify with one mind and one voice the God and Father of our Lord Jesus Christ" (Rom 15:6), in anticipation of the day

when every knee will bow, and every tongue confess that "Jesus is Lord," to the glory of God the Father (cf. Phil 2:10). As Catholics and Methodists, we are inspired and sustained by a vision of the crowning moment when "there will be a deep, an intimate, an uninterrupted union with God; a constant communion with the Father and his Son Jesus Christ, through the Spirit; a continual enjoyment of the Three-One God, and of all the creatures in him!" (John Wesley, *Sermon 64*, "*The New Creation*," 1785).

Section One: Revelation

I. God's Self-Giving

11. "Canst thou by searching find out God?" (Jb 11:7). The biblical answer is clear: God cannot be found by our efforts to seek him out. The mystery of his being cannot be penetrated by human endeavor alone. Indeed, although human beings have been made in God's image, they have been blind to the light of his mystery in the order of created things. Our knowledge of God is entirely dependent on the Creator's free and gracious choice to make himself known, which he has continued to do in pursuit of his good purpose for us.

12. We call this self-communication of God "revelation" because of the recurrent biblical pictures of one who is hidden taking action to disclose himself, at the same time pointing people in the right direction and opening their eyes so that they may truly see him. Yet in this self-communication not all was revealed. Even Jacob, who wrestled with God, saw him face to face and lived, gaining the new name "Israel" (cf. Gn 32:30), still did not know God in his fullness; God's name was withheld. "I appeared to [them] as God Almighty," Moses is reminded, "but by my name 'the Lord' I did not make myself known to them" (Ex 6:3).

13. Jacob's change of name to Israel, and before him Abram's to Abraham, reminds us that when God is known or seen through revelation, more is gained than information. In biblical thought a name is more than a label; it actually conveys the being and character of the one thus named. So, with knowledge of God in his revelation comes new relationship, new possibility, even in Paul's words, "a new creation" (2 Cor 5:17). When Simon recognizes Jesus as the Son of the living God he becomes Peter on whom the church is to be built. When the light of revelation breaks through to Saul on the Damascus road he becomes Paul, the apostle to the Gentiles. Those who take to themselves God's revelation in Jesus Christ are conformed to his image and receive his name.

II. God's Revelation in History

A. The History of Salvation

14. That God reveals himself in history is a central theme in the church's preaching and teaching, referring as it does to the events which made Israel a people through whom all the nations would be blessed. Some events in particular are emphasized, such as the call of Abraham, the exodus and Sinai events, settling in the promised land, returning from captivity in Babylon. These are seen as paradigmatic manifestations of God as creator, redeemer, sustainer, and liberator.

15. It is important to note, however, two things:

First, that these occurrences by themselves did not necessarily amount to revelation. It was not always clear at the time who this self-revealing God was or what the events implied for the way the participants were to respond. Did the Egyptians acknowledge God's hand in the Exodus? "Is the Lord among us or not?" the people demanded of Moses in the wilderness (Ex 17:7). How could they sing the Lord's song in the alien Babylon? Thus, along with occurrence there was needed the interpreting word—sometimes directly from God, more often through the prophets, and especially in the Torah with its commandments from God revealing his will.

Second, the history in which God is revealed is not limited to these special events. God is present in all history—to Israel as judge even when it seems he has deserted them; Lord over all the nations even if they do not acknowledge him; reflected in creation even if not clearly perceived; imaged in his human creatures even if they have distorted that image.

16. Revelation then has this comprehensive relation to history; for those who have eyes to see and hearts to know, the destiny of all individuals and nations is with the Creator-God, and will be fulfilled when his day comes, unexpected though the terms of such a day may be, as Amos reminds us (cf. 5:18).

B. Jesus Christ, the Decisive Event of Revelation

17. The New Testament writers affirm, in their different ways, that God's self-revelation in history reaches its climax in Jesus Christ. In his life, death, and resurrection he reveals God in a unique way. Jesus does more than announce and point to the coming kingdom; in his powerful deeds and life of loving obedience to the Father, the kingdom is already present (Luke). As proclaimer of the word he is more than the last in a long line of prophets, more even than the prophet whose coming would herald the last days; he conveys the word of God by being its embodiment (John). He is greater than priests and angels, as well as prophets; he is the eternal Son through whom the world was founded and to whom all things are now in subjection (Hebrews).

18. In echoing the same theme Paul continues the image of "uncovering that which has been concealed." In Jesus is unveiled the mystery previously hidden of God's purpose that all nations might be brought to obedience (cf. Rom 16:25). And Jesus does more than simply announce this intention; he reveals God's righteous purpose by fulfilling it, dying so that even the ungodly may be reconciled to God (cf. Rom 5:7-8) and that the reordering of the whole cosmos may begin (cf. Col 1:18-20).

C. Revelation as Word and Act

19. It is obvious enough that it is only because of these earliest witnesses to Jesus that we know him as the self-revelation of God. We are dependent upon those who came to faith in him at the time and spread the word about him, on those who later wrote their accounts not just of what happened but of its meanings and significance, and on those in the community of faith from then until now—lively and faithful interpreters of the tradition.

20. Significantly, this link between event and interpreting word goes back to the actions and speech of Jesus. Reading the Gospels, we see that his words and mighty deeds became witnesses to Jesus himself, inviting people to recognize in him the power and authority of God.

21. So, for example, Jesus' ethical teachings on murder and adultery call not just for renunciation of anger and lust but for decision about who it is that claims authority to go beyond earlier authorities, and hence decision about whether Jesus is to be accepted as authentic revealer of God. In the same way, Jesus' healing miracles come to bear witness to him as they call for faith, not just so that they will work but so that he will be recognized as exercising power and authority from none other than God. Along with the deed, therefore, goes the interpreting word. The casting out of the demon, for example, is linked with Jesus' authority as teacher (cf. Mk 1:21-28); healing the paralytic goes along with his authoritative word of forgiveness (cf. Mk 2:1-12); the implication of his healing on the Sabbath is made clear by his word, "the Son of Man is Lord even of the Sabbath"(Mk 2:28). John too makes it clear that the revelation occurs when deed and word are brought together: the feeding of the multitude with "I am the bread of life" (Jn 6); healing the blind man with "I am the light of the world" (Jn 9); the raising of Lazarus with "I am the resurrection and the life" (Jn 11). Thus the words and the deeds of Jesus alike gain their full significance from their source and power in God.

22. God's purpose was also made known through those who came to have faith in Jesus. As the believing community proclaimed the Gospel of God's love revealed in Jesus the Christ and manifested the gifts of the Spirit in their lives, other people came to believe in Jesus to know his risen presence and to follow his way. This revelation comes not simply through words but also by what believers have

become through their calling by Jesus and empowering by the Holy Spirit. "The light of the knowledge of the glory of God in the face of Christ" that has come to Paul and the others now shines through them, earthen vessels though they are, so that the transcendent power may be known, so that "the life of Jesus may be manifested" (2 Cor 4:5-10; cf 1 Thes 1:5).

23. So it is in the ongoing life of the church. When there is faithful witness to Jesus Christ, people hear through the words of witness the word of God and know through deeds of love the God of love. To such witness in word and deed all the faithful are called, but not in isolation from each other. To be "in Christ" is already to belong not only to him but also to the whole company of believers that lives by his grace. From the beginning of his ministry Jesus called others to be with him in order to embody God's loving purpose for the world. So Paul, after the resurrection, was able to call the church both the body of Christ and the community of the Holy Spirit.

III. Revelation of God: Father, Son, and Holy Spirit

24. From the beginning, the disciples of Jesus recognized that his life and work could not be accounted for in merely human terms. So the questions arose: What was his relation to the Maker of heaven and earth? And to the Spirit who moved over the waters at creation and inspired the words and actions of the prophets? Integrally related to these questions about his person were others about his work: What has he done? How are his death and resurrection God's work for our salvation?

25. The biblical witness has led the church to the conviction that Father and Son and Spirit were giving themselves for the redemption of us all. On the cross Jesus suffered and died, evoking the Father's compassion as his son endured the full extent of human alienation in order to redeem it. Just as we see Jesus' relation to the one he called Father in sharpest focus around his death, so his relation to the Spirit is clearly seen in the witness to his life. It was by the Spirit that he was conceived, anointed at baptism for his vocation as son, and led into the wilderness to face the alternative ways, advocated by the tempter, of being son. In the Spirit he taught; by the Spirit he healed and so revealed the presence of the kingdom; with the Spirit he endowed his followers for their ministry in his name.

26. This testimony to the life of Jesus, as part of the history of Father, Son, and Holy Spirit, is confirmed by the resurrection. For the resurrection testifies both to the victory of the Father, who raised Jesus from darkness and death, and to the power of the Spirit, who conforms believers to the image of Christ. Living in the presence of the risen Lord, we know by faith the transforming power of the Holy

Spirit and are enabled to live as grateful children of the Father. Thus the church gives glory to the one God, Father, Son, and Holy Spirit.

Section Two: Faith

27. God's revelation is received by the faith it prompts; and the act of faith is traditionally styled "the faith by which we believe" (*fides qua creditur*). Correspondingly, believing faith is directed towards God, the story of his revelation, its results, and its expected completion; and the content of faith is styled "the faith which is believed" (*fides quae creditur*). As living response to the living God, faith grows and produces fruits, its authenticity being tested in a process of discernment. These three facets of faith are treated in what follows: the faith by which we believe, the faith which is believed, and the fruitfulness of faith.

I. The Faith by Which We Believe

28. The Gospel invites all human beings to join the first disciples in receiving God's revelation in Jesus Christ. It is in a situation of sin that this revelation is received. All of humanity has been so infected by self-centeredness, self-reliance, and the search for false gods that, facing the total holiness of Jesus, humanity is seen as having sinned in Adam. This basic sinfulness is experienced in many ways, and especially in the insecurity and distress that follow a continual failure to do good and a recurrent choice of what is evil. In the midst of this sinfulness, Jesus comes as the only Savior, God's revelation acquires the dimension of redemption, and faith is offered by the Spirit as saving faith, by which those who believe the Gospel receive forgiveness, justification, sanctification, and all the graces that are needed to persevere in God's ways.

29. Individual believers profess this saving faith as members of a community, the community of those who, like Mary at the annunciation (cf. Lk 1:38), have consented to God's design for their life and who, like Peter, have confessed Jesus to be "the Christ, the Son of the Living God" (Mt 16:16). The church, as the community of salvation, gathers in itself all those who have effectively been called "out of darkness into God's own marvelous light" (1 Pt 2:9). Through sharing the word and participating in the sacraments of faith, the church's members experience the healing hand of Christ when they struggle with the many obstacles that Scripture designates as the world, the flesh, and the devil (cf. 1 Jn 2:13-16); and already they are given a taste of Christ's victory over death (cf. Heb 6:4-5).

30. It is not by human power that the believers perceive the word addressed to them through Christ, believe it, and come to salvation (cf. Mt 16:17). Faith is God's gift, which they accept. Finding in Jesus "the pioneer and perfecter of their

faith, who for the joy that was set before him endured the cross" (Heb 12:2), the faithful undergo conversion, learn fidelity, and witness to the one they trust. They strive to practice a loving and willing obedience. Because they believe in Christ, they obey him. Because they hear and confess the truth of his revelation, they seek to live by it. Because they trust in his promises, they abandon themselves to God and they work towards the perfection to which they are called. In their life of fidelity and obedience, they are led by the promptings of the Holy Spirit.

31. While it is entirely God's gift, faith is inseparably a free act and an attitude of grateful reception of God's grace and revelation and of self-commitment to the living Lord, who from first to last is the guide of the faithful through the action of the Holy Spirit (cf. 1 Cor 12:3). Freely given, it is freely received. As faith transforms human life it enables the mind to discern God's plan of salvation as this is described in the Scriptures and delineated in the creeds in which the church has from time to time formulated its faith in unanimity of hearts and minds (cf. Acts 4:32). In this fidelity, revelation feeds the intellect with heartfelt convictions.

II. The Faith Which Is Believed

32. To speak in the same breath of faith "transforming human life" and "enabling the mind to discern God's plan," of "heartfelt conviction" and "feeding the intellect," of "unanimity of heart and mind" confirms the inseparability of the life of faith and statements of faith. The faith that receives God's revelation, the faith by which we believe, is more than a dimension of human feeling, accompanied though faith may be by experiences of gratitude, assurance, and joy. It is a response that is shaped by the nature and being of God who gives himself in revelation. Thus what is believed is an integral part of faith, and it is this that gives content to that life of fidelity and obedience to which the faithful are led by the promptings of the Holy Spirit.

33. Already in the New Testament there is a clear link between the faith by which we believe, the faith which is believed, and the faithful action consistent with such belief. In the Letter to the Philippians (2:6-8), Paul includes an early hymn about Jesus Christ, "who, though he was in the form of God, did not count equality with God a thing to be grasped, but emptied himself, taking the form of a servant, being born in the likeness of men. And being found in human form he humbled himself and became obedient to death, even death on a cross." This was used, not only to enable Paul and the community to give unified verbal expression to their faith, but also to provide the pattern for their ongoing life as the body of Christ, obedient to the way of their living Lord. Thus, the affirmation of faith is prefaced with the words, "Have this mind among yourselves which you have in

Christ Jesus." The faith by which we believe and the faith which is believed come together in the life of faithful obedience.

34. Historically the church has always expressed this faith in credal form. As noted above, the affirmations in the Letter to the Philippians are made in the context of the giving of life to the believer. That the early church understood its own more formally developed statements of the faith in the same way is shown by its universal use of the name "symbol" for the creed. This reflected a common practice of the time when contracts were made. Each party took a piece of broken clay vessel, later to be fitted together to confirm the identity of the parties to the contract. These interlocked parts were called a symbol (from the Greek *symbolon*, a putting together). So, to call the creed "symbol" was to emphasize the way it brings together God's gift and the church's response, believers too being brought together by affirming the sign of saving faith. Therefore, during the rites of initiation, the bishop gave the creed to persons to be baptized as a symbol of active participation in the believing community, to be reappropriated as the creed was recited thereafter within the context of worship.

35. Thus the creeds are one component, along with sacraments and authority, of what St. Augustine considered the universally recognized ways (*catholica*) of taking to ourselves the self-giving of God in Christ. It is therefore a mistake to view the creeds simply as collections of propositional statements requiring no more than intellectual assent. They convey the gospel message in a way the Catholics and Methodists accept as authoritative and life-giving, as is shown by their being regularly prayed in the liturgy. For both our churches, therefore, what is believed is a matter of glad assurance, leading onto a path of faith to be followed.

36. In his *Letter to a Roman Catholic*, John Wesley affirms the faith to which true Protestants and true Catholics both subscribe, faith which is believed and faith by which we believe, leading on to faithful action. He follows the outline of the Nicene Creed: God the Father of all, who "of his own goodness created heaven and earth, and all that is therein"; Jesus Christ, "conceived by the singular operation of the Holy Ghost and born of the blessed Virgin Mary," joining "the human nature with the divine in one person; dying on the cross, risen and ascended" as "Mediator till the end of the world"; "the infinite and eternal Spirit of God, equal with the Father and the Son, . . . not only perfectly holy in himself but the immediate cause of holiness in us"; the holy catholic church gathered by Christ through his apostles; the forgiveness, justification, and resurrection of the faithful. Then Wesley goes on to insist on the practice of such faith by those who believe. Thus the appeal for unity, that Protestants and Catholics should "help each other on in whatever we are agreed leads to the Kingdom" is based on the conviction that what is believed and affirmed in common must be embodied in the life both of the believer and the community of faith. It is with this conviction that Methodists and Catholics con-

tinue in dialogue, "that we may not fall short of the religion of love, and thus be condemned in what we ourselves approve." Faith is tested by the fruit it bears.

III. The Fruitfulness of Faith

A. The Growth of Faith

37. The living response to the living God revealed in the Bible engages the whole person, and so we may speak of a variety of ways in which the response is lived and expressed within the church. We respond to God's self-disclosure not only by simple assent to what he has done for us in Christ but by a return to our original calling through a life of faith lived in history. Revelation is transmitted by people of flesh and blood in a variety of situations. This brings forth a creative and dynamic fruitfulness so that the church as a living body always develops new expressions of faith, hope, and love.

1. History and Development

38. In the course of its development, the Christian community has gained new insights into the revelation once given. The tradition shows its fruitfulness in the richly varied expression of these insights. Since this is a historical process, we are in a dialogue not only with our contemporaries but with our predecessors in the faith. We must hear what has already been said, and in doing so we recognize the dynamic character of revelation, as the past enters the present and prepares for the future. Coherent development illustrates the fruitfulness of revelation.

39. The church itself, as a seed which grows with the support of the Holy Spirit and in response to God, has an inherent dynamic. There is no way of understanding the fruitfulness of revelation save in the community of faith. Development is an ecclesial process based on the experience and holiness of the faithful. It is seen by both Methodists and Catholics as a more comprehensive phenomenon than the development of doctrine. St. John's Gospel, in speaking of fruitfulness, points to ecclesial perspectives: the Father is the husbandman, Christ is the vine, and we are his branches; and it is the Holy Spirit who will guide the community into the fullness of truth. Since the Holy Spirit shows the way, no limits can be set to God's assistance in this process. Development as the fresh interpretation of faith means allowing our minds in each generation to be formed according to the mind which was in Christ Jesus.

2. The Church and Its Environment

40. Since the church is made up of human beings, its growth in understanding takes place through human interaction. Christians exercise their freedom in creative dialogue with the world. Fruitfulness occurs not only as the result of the

church's own internal pondering on its origin and destiny but also in response to external stimuli. The perception of the truth grows and is tested by the challenges of successive ages.

41. To live the Gospel implies taking up those challenges, in the certainty that Jesus Christ is Lord of history and knowing that the Spirit of God is active in human life, inspiring and leading in the quest for justice, freedom, peace, and human dignity. The church, as it shares in this human endeavor, under the guidance of the Holy Spirit and attentive to the word of God manifested in the Scriptures and in its own historical experience, tries to identify what is good and should be defended and promoted, and to call attention to and resist ideas and courses of action opposed to the Gospel and detrimental to human life. This process, which has always been present in the life of the churches, has been sometimes called "discerning the signs of the times."

42. The church often enters into discussion with different schools of thought as it considers new theories, questions, and discoveries. It listens to friends, rivals, and enemies. But there are times when it must also resist ideas that are opposed to the Gospel. Revelation itself provides the motivation and guidance for this ministry of the word.

B. The Fruits of Faith

43. Faithfulness assumes many forms. They certainly include the following:

1. Confession

People have witnessed to their faith in Jesus Christ, the Incarnate Word, even to the point of martyrdom. In baptism this same faith has been confessed in the midst of the believing community. When necessity arose, the church formulated its belief through the Nicene-Constantinopolitan creed. From time to time in subsequent centuries, synods and councils have again confessed the faith in formulas adapted to new circumstances and in new languages.

44. The developing fruitfulness of the faith has at times led to a refocusing of the understanding of the Gospel. This was notably the case with confessions produced at the time of the Reformation, which centered on the experience of being justified by grace through faith. In them and in the subsequent teaching of the Council of Trent, the Christian and trinitarian heart of the faith was placed in the context of the sovereign action of God alone in bringing sinners to justification and salvation

45. The very fruitfulness of faith means it is also exposed to the diverse influences of the cultures and philosophies it encounters. The desire to increase faith by understanding and to protect it from variations and deviations has led to the formulation of doctrines. Some of these have served in turn as standards of faith and

orthodoxy (as in the traditional creeds), while others have been used to build up theological systems that would be intellectually satisfying and would provide apologetical arguments for the defense and further proclamation of the faith. Different doctrinal emphases and diverse theological syntheses, however, have counted among the many factors that have estranged churches from one another and eventually led to conflicting doctrines and confessions. The attempt to overcome such estrangement ecumenically is itself a fruit of the continuing development of faith.

2. Spiritual Life

46. The manifold fruitfulness of faith has been manifest at the level of thought, in the careful elaboration of doctrine, and also at the level of personal experience. The truths that are implied in the Gospel have been sensed to be living truths leading to newness of life and to deep experiences of God in Christ, present in the heart by the testimony of the Spirit. Ways of spiritual life have been explored and described. The writings of the Syriac, Greek, and Latin fathers, the monastic rules and the theology of the early middle ages, the more scholastic descriptions of ways of ascent to God, the documents of the *devotio moderna* at the time of the Renaissance, are monuments and instruments of the fruitfulness of faith. As they discovered and followed the examples of great saints, the faithful have explored new paths to God and found new evidences of the divine presence in their lives, in the community, and in the world around them. For example, the Virgin Mary, *Theotokos*, has come to be seen, especially by the Orthodox and Catholic tradition, as an icon of the church and of the Christian soul, a model of holiness, and a companion in pilgrimage. Devotion to a disciplined life of prayer and commitment to the works of mercy stood at the origin of the Methodist movement. The untiring efforts of John Wesley to proclaim the Gospel to all, especially the neglected and the poor, and to call them to a life of holiness and a desire for perfection, were themselves a precious evidence of the fruitfulness of faith.

47. Devotion is the form that faith takes in prayer. It inspires new life and manifests the Spirit's enablement of weak human wills to do good. It leads on to discipline, when the desire to follow the Lord organizes personal life, regulates the use of resources, and places personal enthusiasm and passion at the service of the Gospel.

48. In the search for perfection, Christians have found help from outside the Christian tradition, formerly in neoplatonism and recently, for example, in various Asian schools of wisdom. This has not been without its dangers. Yet sources of spiritual life and devotion to counterbalance the danger of deviation have always been available in Scripture, especially in the New Testament and the psalms. Personal life and devotion find their proper setting in the light of the word faithfully preached and of the sacraments administered in accordance with the Gospel. Thus faith,

devotion, and discipline are located within the worship and liturgy of the community.

3. Worship

49. In the presence of the self-revealing God, people feel awe and joy and are moved to express this in praise, prayer, confession, and commitment. They wish to recall the message of grace they have heard; to celebrate the acts of God with words, gestures, and song; to express in prayer their fears, needs, and hopes; and to reenact the story of salvation in liturgy and drama.

50. The Scriptures amply attest the centrality of private and public worship for God's people. When God's revelation of himself came to its fulfillment in Jesus Christ, the people of the new covenant held on to their heritage of worship in a new way. The psalms became a hymnal for the Christian church; the passover meal acquired fuller meaning as a sacrament of salvation in Jesus Christ. Moreover, new hymns were formed (cf. Phil 2:6-11; Col 1:15-20), and baptism in the name of the triune God became the sign of new creation in Christ and incorporation into his body.

51. As the Gospel spreads, entering new cultures, different languages and expressions are used and the church's worship is enriched and diversified. The church welcomes both developments in liturgical traditions and new and spontaneous expressions of faith and worship as signs of the fruitfulness of God's message and the ever-present action of the Holy Spirit. At the same time the church seeks to ensure that they are genuine manifestations of the Spirit and faithfully reflect and proclaim the Gospel.

4. Service

52. The faithful community claims to follow the one who came not to be served but to serve (cf. Mk 10:45). The model for all ministry is found in the Lord himself. In his earthly ministry he proclaimed the coming kingdom and "went about doing good" (Acts 10:38)—healing the sick, calling the dispossessed and marginalized, demanding justice, and restoring life. In a variety of ways the church not only proclaims the message with words but also ministers to the spiritual and material needs of all—in caring for the poor, the stranger, and the neglected. This service of charity has been an essential part of its mission. Having experienced the loving mercy of God, the church also feels bound to denounce injustice and oppression, to work for peace, and to articulate the ethical consequences of God's love for humankind. To all cultures, the church offers the "leaven" of the Gospel.

C. The Discernment of Faith

53. It is the Holy Spirit who makes the revelation given in the very person of Jesus Christ fruitful for building up the church as a whole and for the spiritual journey of each of its members. The Holy Spirit is the source of all authentic discernment. "Do not quench the Spirit, do not despise prophesying, but test everything; hold fast what is good, abstain from every form of evil" (1 Thes 5:19-22). There are several ways and means of "testing" all things, a variety of principles of discernment provided by the Spirit.

i. Criteria for Discernment

1. Fidelity to Scripture

54. Because the Scriptures are the normative witness to the revelation in Christ, they are central to Christian discernment. The Christian believer must become acquainted with their content, reflect on their meaning, and apply their teaching in daily life. "From childhood you have been acquainted with the sacred writings which are able to instruct you for salvation through faith in Christ Jesus. All scripture is inspired by God and profitable for teaching, for reproof, for correction, and for training in righteousness, that the man of God may be complete, equipped for every good work" (2 Tm 3:15-17).

55. Fidelity to the scriptural word is also exercised by those who, in virtue of their ministry, assist the faithful in this scriptural discernment. Thus the Second Vatican Council stated that the "magisterium is not above God's word; it rather serves the word, teaching only what has been transmitted, as by divine mandate and with the Holy Spirit's assistance, it listens to God's word with piety, keeps it in awe and expounds it with fidelity" (DV, no. 10). Wesley was able to spread scriptural holiness throughout the land because he made scriptural truth run with the oil and burn with the fire of the Holy Spirit.

2. Sentire cum Ecclesia

56. This Latin phase is often used in Roman Catholic theology to denote an inner harmony between personal conviction in faith and the teaching of the church. The conviction is designated by a word for *feeling* (*sentire*) rather than for *thinking*, because it is a kind of spiritual instinct, antecedent to any discursive reflection on the truth to which it adheres or on rational proof of that truth. It derives not only from intellectual capacity, but also from moral uprightness and graced spiritual goodness.

57. Wesley was well aware of the paramount importance of such conviction for giving living witness to the basic Christian doctrines handed on from generation to generation by the church. Contemporary divines frequently accused him of irre-

sponsibility in authorizing for preaching men whom they regarded as theological ignoramuses. He retorted that a morally upright tradesman who prayerfully frequents the Scriptures can much more easily attain that level of conviction indispensable for effective witness and preaching than a dissolute clergyman who relies on a purely academic biblical and theological expertise. Wesley knew that, in the mind and the heart of the deeply convinced Christian believer, the Holy Spirit is ever at work, bonding the exercise of particular spiritual gifts into unity with the exercise of complementary gifts in all the other members of the body of Christ, the church.

58. In the perspective of Vatican II, this action of the Spirit brings about an interdependence in communion between the spiritual instinct of the whole body of the faithful and those who are empowered to make normative acts of discernment of what is, or is not, faithful to Christian Tradition. "Thus the remarkable harmony of bishops and faithful comes into being in the preservation, the practice and the confession of the traditional faith" (DV, no. 10). The Latin for "harmony" is *conspiratio*, that is, a "convergence of inspiration," brought about by the Holy Spirit between the *sentire* of the faithful and discernment by the magisterium.

3. Reception

59. One criterion by which new developments in Christian teaching or living may be judged consonant with the Gospel is their long-term reception by the wider church. Such reception sometimes will take place in theological discussion and sometimes in the practical life of the local churches or of the individual believer. In every case reception of what is true is a spiritual process. The deep conviction of gaining the truth, however, can be an occasion for struggle and separation, when conflicting opinions claim to be true. The process of reception, therefore, calls also for a careful listening to the insights of others. Only the truth itself brings about conformity to Christ in the Spirit. To be anointed with scriptural truth by the Spirit of Jesus (cf. 1 Jn 2:20-21) is to let his truth seep into every area of Christian living. It is to assimilate it into the very being of the church and its members, to receive it in the fullest sense of the word. Those who are rooted in the biblical truth by the work of the Spirit not only know the truth, but they know that they know it.

4. By Their Fruits

60. Conformity in deep conviction to Christian doctrinal and moral truth bears fruit in holiness. It produces that spiritual holiness which in his successive descriptions of the character of a Methodist, Wesley so often described as "walking even as Christ walked." This vital link between truth and holiness makes holiness a criterion of the existence of truth in the process of interpretation and development of doctrine. This process involves not just one individual but whole generations in

succession to one another. Towards the end of his life, Wesley attempted several times a history of the Methodist movement. He considered that the truth of the most precious insights of Methodism was demonstrated by the flowering of scriptural holiness in every part of the land. The quality of Methodism's fruits proved the health of the original tree.

61. The Second Vatican Council speaks of a growth in insight into what is passed on by Christian Tradition, coming about through a pondering which unites the heart and the head, in a way characteristic of the *sentire cum ecclesia* referred to earlier. Growth in insight "comes through the contemplation and study of believers who ponder these things in their hearts (cf. Lk 2:19 and 51)" (DV, no. 8). There must be growth in love to achieve more insightful knowledge of the riches of faith. In other words, there must be growth in holiness. Holiness is therefore not only a criterion of the rightness of development in doctrine and ecclesial life; it is a source of such development in its forming of the convictions and insights of believers and their interaction on each other.

ii Agents of Discernment

62. The criteria by which the church discerns the will of God have been applied in several ways and at several levels of the life of the people of God. One may list the following:

1. Discernment by the People of God

63. According to Scripture the discernment of God's will is the task of the whole people of God. The admonition to prove and to approve (*dokimazein*) what is good in the eyes of God is a major theme within the letters of the apostles (cf. Rom 12:2; Eph 5:10-17; Phil 1:9f.; 1 Thes 5:21; 1 Jn 4:1f.). Paul prays for the church in Philippi, "that your love may abound more and more, with knowledge and all discernment, so that you may approve what is excellent, and may be pure and blameless for the day of Christ, filled with the fruits of righteousness which come through Jesus Christ, to the glory and praise of God" (Phil 1:9). The people of God in their daily life have "to learn what is pleasing to the Lord" (Eph 5:10) and what will meet the needs of their neighbors. In this discernment, God's love is the leading power, and the needs of the community of the believers and the sufferings of the people around them are pointers to the right direction. Such active openness in love to the very truth which is Jesus and to the disinherited people of their times drove many of the saints in our two communions to new forms of piety and service in the world. By this kind of discernment, Wesley taught that it was not enough that masters should treat their slaves justly and fairly, but that it was God's will that slavery be abolished.

2. Prophetic Discernment

64. At times in the history of the people of God, shepherds and flock have gone astray. Through the prophets God called his people back to the way. This was not only true for Israel but also for the church of the New Testament. The letters to the seven churches witness to the exalted Lord telling his church what to do and what to abstain from (cf. Rv 1:4–3:22). In the history of the church, prophetic voices of warning and admonition have arisen, some of which were readily listened to and some not. The prophetic call is not based on approval by official authorities or on reception by the whole people of God. It claims to be directly authorized by God.

65. Because there have been cases of false prophecy, St. Paul refers to the necessity of "discerning spirits," distinguishing between spirits (cf. 1 Cor 12:10) and weighing what is said by prophets (cf. 1 Cor 14:29). The gift of prophecy should be exercised according to the analogy of faith (cf. Rom 12:6), in accordance with the basic truth of the apostolic message. Wesley saw such an "analogy of faith" in the basic subjects of biblical preaching: original sin, justification by faith, and present inward salvation. This may be related to the christological criterion: "Every spirit which confesses that Jesus Christ has come in the flesh is from God, and every spirit which does not confess Jesus is not of God" (1 Jn 4:2-3). God's saving and redeeming act has in fact reached human nature and existence in their entirety. This is what links faith in the incarnation of Christ with the message of the justification and sanctification of sinners by faith through God's saving grace. This is the criterion, this is the "analogy of faith," according to which prophecy should be exercised and tested.

66. The difficulty of "weighing" or even "discerning" the words of prophets has to be acknowledged, but this should not diminish the challenge to listen to prophetic voices. This difficulty has sometimes occasioned divisions, and it is only with hindsight that those who have been so divided have been able to begin to distinguish the true from the false in what was at issue.

3. Pastoral Discernment

67. There are times when the church needs a formal decision about whether some doctrines are right or wrong, or which actions are appropriate to the needs of the time as well as to the calling of the church. Already the Acts of the Apostles tells us that the "apostles and the elders gathered together to consider this matter" (15:6). It is the common belief of our churches that there are those who are authorized to speak for the church as a whole and who, after having carefully listened to Scripture and Tradition and the experience of believers trying to live out the Gospel, and after a reasonable and prayerful discussion, may say "It has seemed good to the Holy Spirit and to us" (Acts 15:28a; cf. 1 Cor 7:40b).

68. Both the Roman Catholic Church and the Methodist churches hold that

the first ecumenical councils defined a fundamental, genuine, and valid formulation and interpretation of the apostolic faith.

69. Within the Roman Catholic Church, the teaching office of the bishops in unity with the bishop of Rome is exercised in the name of Jesus Christ. While their teaching office "is not superior to the word of God, but is its servant" (DV, no. 10), the bishops "have received the sure charism of truth," which may authorize them to define the doctrines drawn from the divine revelation.

70. Within Methodism, the teaching office is exercised by the conferences. When Wesley in 1744 first met with some of his preachers for such a conference, he asked them to decide on the following questions: (1) what to teach, (2) how to teach, (3) what to do. Basic for their decision was the testimony of Scripture, but they also looked into the treasures of Christian tradition, especially from the earliest times, and they listened to the experience of those engaged in the work of evangelism and reflected rationally on the questions facing them. On this basis and with these guidelines in mind, Methodist conferences discern what God wants to be preached and done in today's world.

71. The differences between these approaches and their implications for the communion of faith will have to be dealt with at a later stage of the dialogue between Methodists and Catholics.

4. Convergence in Discernment

72. St. Paul himself writes to the Corinthian church with which he is in controversy over the interpretation of the Gospel: "Not that we lord it over your faith; we work with you for your joy, for you stand firm in your faith" (2 Cor 1:24). Every formal expression of pastoral authority, whether the teaching office of the bishops or the power of councils, synods, and conferences, and every expression of prophetic challenge, is to serve the upbuilding of the whole people of God under the lordship of Christ himself. This should lead to a growing interdependence and mutual recognition of those who exercise pastoral authority within the church, those who offer prophetic vision, and all those who, by their response to revelation and their inspiration through the creative love of God, participate in active tradition of the Gospel and compassionate discernment of the will of God for his church and the world.

Section Three: Mission

I. The Mission of the Church Comes from God

A. The Source of Mission

73. The church's missionary activity takes many forms but ultimately has only one source. Mission springs from the triune God's loving design for all humanity.

God's act of creating and his concern for his creatures are expressions of his out-going love. When the Father chose to make himself known, and when he revealed and inaugurated his loving purpose for a world marked by sin, he did this through sending his Son and the Holy Spirit. "When the fullness of time had come, God sent his Son" and "the Spirit of his Son" (Gal 4:4-6). In many places in St. John's Gospel Jesus is designated as the one "the Father has sent" and he himself promises that the Father and he will send the Spirit. It is, therefore, a fundamental Christian convic-tion that the very nature of the church is missionary, and that the church's mission is none other than a sharing in the continuing mission of the Son and the Holy Spirit expressing the Father's love for all humankind.

B. Commissioned by Christ

74. The risen Christ himself calls on those who follow him to share in his mis-sion. Addressing his disciples, he says: "As the Father sent me, so I send you" (Jn 20:21). They are to carry forward his once-for-all redemptive mission in space and time, to all peoples and all ages. He prays also "on behalf of those who will believe in [him] through their word" (Jn 17:20-23). They must all be sanctified by his truth, holding fast to what the Word himself has given them (Jn 17:17; 17:14). As they proclaim Jesus Christ, whose person and mission were totally one, those who follow him spend themselves even to the point of laying down their lives for the Gospel.

C. Mission Empowered by the Holy Spirit

75. Such participation in the mission of Christ is possible only because of the outpouring of the Holy Spirit. The infant church, gathered behind closed doors, was empowered to go out and speak effectively of the mighty deeds God had done through Jesus Christ only after it had received the Holy Spirit at Pentecost (Acts 2; cf. Lk 24:48-49; cf. also Jn 20:22). What happened in Jesus Christ, in a particular time and place, is henceforward communicated to people of every language and cul-ture. In the Spirit, the proclaiming community itself becomes a living Gospel for all to hear.

D. The Baptized and Mission

76. The great commissioning at the end of St. Matthew's Gospel is addressed to the apostles and to all who will share their faith (Mt 28:16-20). All nations are to come to the fullness of life in the triune God in whose name they will be baptized. Those who accept the Gospel will become members of the body of Christ, and a dwelling place of the Holy Spirit, knowing and loving God as their Father. As they are united with Christ, they are also joined to his mission. All aspects of their com-mon life serve to build up the body and its members in holiness. They are thereby enabled to reach out in word and witness to all who have not yet heard the Gospel.

II. Mission: Word and Act

77. Jesus' mission was to proclaim God's saving acts: "The Spirit of the Lord is upon me, because he has anointed me to preach good news to the poor. He has sent me to proclaim release to the captives and recovering of sight to the blind, to set at liberty those who are oppressed, to proclaim the acceptable year of the Lord" (Lk 4:18-19). Jesus was sent to announce that God was coming to release the people from captivity to the powers of evil, sin, and death and to heal their suffering and wounds. What Jesus said, he did. He set those free who were possessed by evil spirits and released those who suffered from guilt and alienation. On the other hand, his preaching reached beyond the present moment. In blessing the poor he gave them the assurance that God was with them and his kingdom would belong to them.

78. Because the ministry of the church derives from the mission of Jesus, his ministry must serve as the paradigm for the mission of the church. The church proclaims what God has done to save humankind through the life, death, and resurrection of Jesus Christ. He is the Word of life, which God has spoken; he is the witness to all human beings that God has come and, from within their limitations, shared the abundance of his love. Taking upon himself the burden and curse of the law, he reconciled us to God and took away our sins, making peace by the blood of his cross. To proclaim God's love in Jesus Christ is more than to remember and tell the story of Jesus and what he has done for us; wherever this story is told, those who hear are empowered by the Holy Spirit to open their hearts to the love of God so that they may live in a community of love, reconciliation, and peace.

79. People who have experienced God's faithfulness and righteousness will share what they have received by deeds of mercy and justice. Moreover, they will seek to shape society according to the pattern of the kingdom of God. Theirs is the fellowship of the new creation, of which they have received a foretaste by the gift of the Holy Spirit. Never claiming to build the kingdom by their own efforts, they will give all the glory to God.

80. Every facet of the church's mission—witness, service, and worship— embraces both word and act:

- Witness requires the public proclamation of the Gospel, telling the story and inviting response and acceptance. It includes testimony from person to person and the silent and yet telling faithfulness of those who suffer and even die for their Lord and his love.
- Service is expressed in care for the sick and needy and all who long for healing; in counseling the troubled; in advocacy for the poor; and in work for peace, justice, and the preservation of creation.

- In worship, the manifold gifts of God's grace are celebrated within the body of Christ. The community that gathers around word and sacrament draws into fellowship people from different backgrounds, with different abilities and gifts, all being made one in Jesus Christ.

All this has been recognized in both our traditions at their best. But we often fall short in practice of what we maintain in principle. This gives a reason for repentance and change of heart, for the integrity of the Gospel demands our full commitment to witness, service, and worship.

III. Mission and Community

81. Since the church is missionary by its very nature, mission is by its very nature ecclesial. Built by the Holy Spirit, the community will be the instrument for the proclamation and acting out of the Gospel, the place where people will grow in faith and holiness, and a paradigm of the new life of joy, peace, solidarity, and service which Jesus Christ offers to all humankind.

82. The church's mission involves prophetic and priestly service. Its message relays God's demand for mercy, justice, and peace in human society, particularly in regard to the weakest and the least privileged. In a world of brokenness and estrangement, the Christian fellowship, as a community of acceptance, forgiveness, freedom, and love, can function as a sacrament of Christ's healing presence.

83. The existence of such a community is the fruit of the Spirit who gathers, sustains, nourishes, and endows the faithful with the diverse gifts which enable them to witness to the Gospel. This requires that the community and its members make constant use of the means of grace God has provided, not least among which are ecumenical sharing, fellowship, and cooperation. Through these means all are called to daily repentance, continual renewal, and the search for holiness. Being thus strengthened by the Spirit, the faithful witness to Christ by word, example, and action, even as they are scattered into the world for their daily life and duties. In turn, their witness, shared in fellowship, prayer, and praise, builds, strengthens, and deepens the community.

IV. The Apostolic Mission

84. The whole people of God has been sent by Christ into the world to witness to the love of the Father in the power of the Holy Spirit. In this sense it is apostolic. All its members are gifted by the Spirit, and there is no gift without its corresponding service. Within that service of the whole there has been, from the beginning, a ministry uniquely called and empowered to build up the body of Christ

in love. This is "apostolic" in the specific sense, because it began with Christ's choosing from among his disciples the twelve "whom he named apostles" (Lk 6:13). It has continued through the ages in those who follow them in that ministry. After his death and resurrection Christ confirmed the commission of the apostles and sent them out as messengers by whom the Gospel, spoken and lived, would be preserved and proclaimed throughout the whole world (cf. Mt 28:19-20). Their consistent witness, in obedience to the Spirit, was to be a sign of the continuing presence of Christ (cf. Acts 1:8). In the mission of the church, their special place has been remembered and acknowledged. The first history of the spread of Christ's teaching is entitled the Acts of the Apostles; the baptismal confession is called the Apostles' Creed; the handing on of that faith from generation to generation is known as the apostolic tradition.

85. In their imperfections, their slowness of understanding, and their waver-ing faith, as well as in their ultimate loyalty, the apostles are representative of the humanity Christ came to save. Their life with him became a model for the life of the church; they began to grasp the revelation; they were held together by a common hearing of the word; they were sent out with a common purpose, to enable all nations to hear, believe, and live the word. Infidelity to the apostolic teaching, the recognizable pattern of their fellowship (Acts 2:41-47), has persisted in the life of the church.

86. The church is like a living cell with Christ as its center; the community, as it grows and multiplies, retains its original pattern. Apostolic communities need people to do for their own time what the apostles did in theirs: to pastor, teach, and minister under the authority of the Good Shepherd and Teacher, the Servant Lord.

87. All those to whom the apostles transmit their faith have a share in their work. All are called to witness. All are called to glorify God and intercede for the world. All are called to serve their neighbor.

88. In the Methodist and Catholic churches some receive by ordination a spe-cial calling and are consecrated and authorized to proclaim and teach the Gospel of God's love in Jesus Christ, to lead the worshiping community to the throne of grace and administer the sacramental gifts of God, and to guide the life of the church, its care for the needy, and its missionary outreach. In the Catholic tradition, these tasks are entrusted to the bishops ordained in the apostolic succession, along with their presbyters and deacons. In the Methodist tradition, following Wesley, ordained ministry is held to be in succession to the apostles, although not dependent in the same way on the succession of bishops.

V. Mission and Ecumenism

89. The Gospel of reconciliation requires a reconciled and reconciling community. The Christian churches are not yet able to carry out God's mission in unity, and this is a serious obstacle to mission. We acknowledge gratefully the fruits that our ecumenical relationships have brought in building up our communities for mission and in the missionary activity of our churches. Our churches should take every opportunity for cooperation and work and pray to overcome the difficulties which stand in the way. We should explore the possibilities for cooperation in service and, whenever possible, in proclamation. The more we overcome differences in doctrine and polity, the stronger will be our witness and the easier it will be to avoid even the suggestion of proselytism. Nearly thirty years of dialogue between Catholics and Methodists have revealed sufficient agreement in faith for our churches to recognize integrity and faithfulness in each other's proclamation of the Gospel. While large areas of agreement between Roman Catholics and Methodists about our responsibilities in society make much common action possible, differences remain concerning some areas of personal and social ethics. A careful and responsible dialogue about those differences would be fruitful, not only for our churches but for our mission in society.

VI. Mission and Cultures

90. According to both Methodists and Catholics, the message of the Gospel is meant for all times. It transcends all cultures. Yet the Gospel—which arose in a Palestinian matrix—has been announced in the languages of many cultures. Since salvation is intended for people where they are, it is relevant to all cultures, and it should be proclaimed in ways that are appropriate to each. Evangelization as proclamation of the Gospel is clearly distinct from interreligious dialogue, in which competent Christians meet with members of other religions in order to reach better mutual understanding. Yet interreligious dialogue itself pertains to the process of mission and the inculturation of the Gospel, since evangelization brings Christians into contact with cultures that have been largely shaped by other religions.

91. One may see a certain analogy between the mystery of the incarnation and the inculturation of the Gospel. The culture that the Gospel ought to enter and transform has, as it were, a body and a soul. The body of a culture includes the web of social, economic, and political structures that provide the stability without which the higher forms of creativity could not develop. These forms—intellectual, artistic, religious—are like the soul of a culture, a response to the attraction of truth, beauty, and goodness for the human spirit. They come from a thirst for a spiritual fullness which no merely human values can provide.

92. Both the Christian evangelist and the converts coming from non-Christian religions are challenged with an unavoidable process of discernment. What in the cultural values, rooted in religious aspirations, are authentic expressions of the movement of transcendence towards the absolute truth and goodness of God? What are deviations from it, imposing limitations on it, or even wounding some of the deepest aspirations of the human heart?

93. The evangelist must never seek to impose the answer to this question. He must have with his hearers the patience which God showed to his people in the Old Testament. Through the prophets, God gave a partial revelation of his saving purpose for the human race before finally communicating the fullness of that purpose in the gift of his only Son (Heb 1:1-2; Jn 3:16). In any case the direct proclamation of the message should not be abandoned. Interreligious dialogue is not a substitute for evangelization, which remains an imperative of the Gospel.

Section Four: Sacramental Life

I. The Mystery of God in Christ and the Church

94. In its 1991 report on *The Apostolic Tradition*, the commission sensed the need for deeper common reflection on the nature of sacrament, starting from the idea of Christ himself as "the primary sacrament" (no. 89). Bearing in mind that one of the oldest names for sacrament is "mystery" (*mysterion*), Christians find a direct scriptural basis for viewing Christ in this way in 1 Timothy 3:16, where Christ is referred to as "the mystery of our religion":

> He was manifested in the flesh,
> vindicated in the spirit,
> seen by angels,
> preached among the nations,
> believed on in the world,
> taken up in glory.

95. The "mystery" of God is God's eternal purpose, which has now been revealed in the person and work of Jesus Christ, a saving design which embraces Jew and Gentile alike in the goodness of God's final kingdom (Mk 4:11; Rom 16:25-27; 1 Cor 2:7-10; Eph 3:1-20; Col 1:25-27; 2:2-3). Christ is "the image of the invisible God" (Col 1:15), the Father's Son upon whom the Holy Spirit always rests (Jn 1:33). Having taken our humanity into his own person, the Son is both the sign of our salvation and the instrument by which it is achieved.

96. As the company of those who have been incorporated into Christ and nourished by the life-giving Holy Spirit (1 Cor 12:13), the church may analogously be thought of in a sacramental way. Precisely as the body of Christ and the community of the Holy Spirit, the church may be spoken of "as a kind of sacrament, both as an outward manifestation of God's grace among us and as signifying in some way the grace and call to salvation addressed by God to the whole human race."[1] Constituted by God's saving grace, the church becomes the instrument for extending the divine offer as widely as the scope of God's eternal purpose for humankind.

97. In such an approach, the sacraments of the church may be considered as particular instances of the divine mystery being revealed and made operative in the lives of the faithful. Instituted by Christ and made effective by the Spirit, sacraments bring the mystery home to those in whom God pleases to dwell.

98. The particular sacraments flow from the sacramental nature of God's self-communication to us in Christ. They are specific ways, in which, by the power of the Holy Spirit, the risen Jesus makes his saving presence and action effective in our midst. Thus, in his public ministry Jesus did not communicate the good news of our salvation in words alone; he addressed himself in signs and actions to those who came to him in faith. Moreover, such signs and actions were addressed to both body and spirit. Thus, he healed the paralytic and forgave him his sins. After Christ's passion, death, and resurrection, the Savior continues his words and actions among us by means of sacramental signs.

99. There is a two-way connection between the church and the sacraments. On the one hand, the sacraments build up the church as the body of Christ until its members come to their full stature; on the other hand, the church is at work through the sacraments by virtue of the mission received from the Holy Spirit.

II. The Sacraments and Other Means of Grace

100. By virtue of their ecclesial nature, the sacraments are organically related to each other. In the celebration of the eucharist, as both word and table, the church is built up as the body of Christ. Into the eucharistic community one is admitted by baptism, which identifies the believer with the death and resurrection of Christ. Methodists and Catholics emphasize this vital connection between ecclesial communion and the sacraments of baptism and eucharist in different but analogous ways. Methodists affirm the full sacramental nature of the rites of baptism and eucharist by attributing to Christ their direct institution. At the same time, they consider other Christian practices, listed by Wesley himself, to be specific means of grace. Catholics attribute primacy to baptism and eucharist among seven sacramental rites which sustain the life of faith.

101. It is our common belief that baptism is an action of God by which the baptized begin their life with Christ the Redeemer and participate in his death and resurrection. As Christ is received in faith, original sin is erased, sins are forgiven, the baptized are justified in the eyes of God and become a new creation; with all believers they share the communion of the Spirit; and they are called to seek perfection in hope and in love through faithful response to God's continuing gifts of grace. Through the ministry of the church, baptism is given with water "in the name of the Father, the Son, and the Holy Spirit." Baptism is irrevocable and is not repeated. While it is received in the context of a local church and in a specific Christian community, it introduces people into the universal church of Christ and the gathering of the saints.

102. With the whole Christian tradition, Methodists and Catholics find in the New Testament the evidence that baptism is the basic sacrament of the Gospel. They also agree that Jesus Christ instituted the eucharist as a holy meal, the memorial of his sacrifice. As the baptized partake of it they share the sacrament of his body given for them and his blood shed for them; they present and plead his sacrifice before God the Father; and they receive the fruits of it in faith. Proclaiming, in his risen presence, the death of the Lord until he comes, the eucharistic assembly anticipates the final advent of Christ and enjoys a foretaste of the heavenly banquet prepared for all peoples. In the words of the Wesleys' *Hymns on the Lord's Supper*:

> He bids us eat and drink
> Imperishable food,
> He gives His flesh to be our meat,
> And bids us drink His blood:
> What'er the Almighty can
> To pardoned sinners give,
> The fullness of our God made man
> We here with Christ receive.[2]

103. Meanwhile, as believers we seek to enact throughout our lives that which we celebrate in the sacraments. Thus prayers of the *Roman Missal* ask that the sacraments received at Easter may "live forever in our minds and hearts," and that "we who have celebrated the Easter ceremonies may hold fast to them in life and conduct."[3]

104. Baptism, received once, and holy communion, received regularly in the church's liturgical festivals, are at the heart of the life of holiness to which the faithful are called. While they are the two biblical sacraments recognized by the Methodist tradition, the Catholic tradition regards other holy actions of the church as also sacraments of the Gospel instituted by the Savior: in them also God's grace

reaches the faithful in keeping with some of the acts and words of Jesus to which the New Testament bears witness.

105. Catholics believe that in confirmation the gift of the Spirit confirms what was done in baptism. The faithful who are aware of sinning and are contrite have access to Christ the healer and forgiver in the sacrament of reconciliation. When they are sick, they also receive in the anointing the touch of Christ the healer. When they marry, they marry in the Lord through a sacrament of mutual communion, in which they are given an image of the communion of all the saints in Christ and a promise of the graces that are needed for the fidelity which they themselves promise. In the sacrament of orders, some of the believers are chosen and empowered to act for Christ in the spiritual guidance of the faithful through the preaching of the word and the administration of the sacraments. In all sacraments the power of the Spirit is at work, inviting the believers to closer union with their Redeemer, to the glory of God the Father.

106. Although Methodists do not recognize these rites as sacraments of the Gospel, they too affirm the active presence of the Holy Spirit in the life of the faithful, the necessity of repentance for sins, the power of prayer for healing, the holiness of marriage, and the enablement by the Spirit of those who are called and ordained for the tasks of the ministry.

107. Catholics and Methodists both recognize other "means of grace" than those they count as sacraments. These include public and private prayer, the reading of Scripture, the singing of hymns, fasting, and what Methodists refer to as "Christian conversation." In the same category one may reckon the traditional works of mercy, such as visiting the sick and serving the poor. As the faithful meet the image of Christ in their neighbor, they acquire and develop a sense of the pervading sacramentality of the life of faith.

Section Five: *Koinonia*–Communion

I. Communion Through the Apostolic Witness

108. The opening passage of St. John's First Letter, already quoted to indicate what is meant by revelation (see Introduction, no. 2), constitutes also the most complete statement of what the New Testament writers understand by the Greek word *koinonia* (communion). The beginning of the passage describes in poignant terms the privilege enjoyed by the apostles of intimate contact with the incarnate Son of God. St. John wants us to grasp, albeit in our limited human perspective, something of the richness of the infinite and life-giving love which the Father has poured out on us in the sending of the Son and the Holy Spirit for our redemption and sanctification. He then addresses directly those whose discipleship of Christ is

to bring them, throughout the ages and in union with the apostles, into an intimate sharing in the communion in love of the three persons of the Trinity: "that which we have seen and heard we proclaim also to you, so that you may have fellowship [koinonia] with us; and our fellowship [koinonia] is with the Father and with his Son Jesus Christ" (1 Jn 1:3).

109. It is of the essence of the church to be a sharing in this communion of love between the three persons of the Trinity. The phrase "communion with us" underlines that our own personal sharing in this love is inseparable from our communion with each other, because it is the nature of this love to bring about a mutual relationship between persons created in the image and likeness of the triune God. The "us" here referred to are those who have the responsibility of bringing the visible Christian community into being through an apostolic preaching which includes word and sacrament. The very existence of the church as a visible institution in this world becomes a manifestation of communion with the persons of the Trinity. Koinonia is thus both invisible and visible communion in love.

110. Entering into this koinonia involves traveling the road of the one whom the apostles heard, saw, and touched. It means, to use other words of St. John's Letter, which John Wesley never tired of repeating in his sermons, abiding in Christ and therefore in the Trinity, by walking even as Christ walked (cf. 1 Jn 2:6). It means entering into the glory of trinitarian love by the way of suffering characteristic of the paschal mystery. We can become, through the Holy Spirit, joint heirs of God with Christ, says St. Paul, "if we suffer with him in order that we may also be glorified with him" (Rom 8:17). In other words, the mystery of trinitarian communion in love, when it touches our lives, changes our way of living into conformity with Christ. The change must penetrate every area of our lives and, in particular, the practicalities of the service of others, by which Christ is still visible to us: "As you did it to one of the least of these my brethren, you did it to me" (Mt 25:40).

II. Basic Expressions of Communion in Our Churches

111. Our life with the triune God and with one another is expressed in various embodiments of communion in our churches. To some extent our living of this communion is restricted to the still separate lives of our Catholic and Methodist communities. Our ultimate goal is that there should be full ecclesial communion between us. As a move in that direction, we should acknowledge some of the vital elements in the partial communion we already enjoy, while also delineating some of the problematic differences on which further work needs to be done.

A. Faith

112. As Roman Catholics and as Methodists we live from the same Gospel, the apostolic message of God's saving acts in Jesus Christ, and we share the same faith. This faith is rooted in the Scriptures, which are the common ground of our preaching and teaching as Christian churches. It is summarized by the creeds of the early church, especially the Apostles' Creed and the Nicene Creed, which we confess regularly in our worship.

113. But we share not only a common root or source of our faith; we recognize in each other the same readiness to respond to the proclamation of the Gospel. In the past, Methodists tended to see the faith of Roman Catholics merely as an assent to what the church teaches, whereas Catholics sometimes thought Methodist belief to be a purely emotional personal conviction. These prejudices have been overcome. Faith is always personal but never private, for faith incorporates the believing individual into the community of faith. Therefore, his or her faith is both a personal conviction and also a sharing of what is held by the "community of the believers." At the same time, to believe in God and the salvation which he has wrought for us is the living response of the whole life of the believer and changes our lives in every respect; it is personal, living faith. Our traditions may stress the corporate and the individual aspects of faith differently, but both are common to us.

114. While we are agreed on the existence of a common faith between us (cf. nos. 32-36), problems arise when we seek to define the distinctive teachings which are necessary to constitute the full communion of faith which would unite our churches.

115. Methodists have learned from John Wesley to discern between, on the one hand, different "opinions" about manners of worship, about ecclesiastical polity, or even about the exposition of certain spiritual truths and, on the other, the essential doctrines of the Gospel. "Opinions" are by no means unimportant and at least within the Methodist connection, there should be as much agreement on them as possible. But for the communion of faith with other Christians, the unity in regard to the "essentials" is decisive and not the differences of "opinions." Such essential doctrines are the three-one God; the divine creation of the world and the vocation of humankind to holiness and happiness; the incarnation and atoning work of God the Son; the work of the Spirit as source of all truth, renewal, and communion; the need of fallen humankind to repent and to believe the Gospel; the divine provision of grace through word and sacrament and the institution and gathering of the church; the summons to love of God and neighbor; and the promise of a final judgment and victory, where all the redeemed will share in glorifying and enjoying God forever. The Methodist churches did not establish a fixed "canon" of these essentials of Christian faith; but whenever the question of the communion of faith with other churches is put, these elements will be vital for the conversation.

116. The Roman Catholic Church is at one with the Methodists over these essential doctrines, but emphasizes that the whole teaching of the church constitutes an organic unity. Its members are therefore called upon to believe the full teaching of the church. But within the ecumenical dialogue also the "'hierarchy of truths' of Catholic doctrine should always be respected; these truths all demand due assent of faith, yet are not all equally central to the mystery revealed in Jesus Christ, since they vary in their connection with the foundation of the Christian faith."[4] This may be helpful when we discuss those doctrines which are important for the teaching and spirituality of the Catholic Church, but which will not be easily accepted by Methodists, e.g., the teaching about Mary in relation to Christ and the church. We will be able to deal with controversial issues without concealing or diminishing what has been already achieved in a common understanding of the Gospel despite some differences which still remain. These should be the subject of further investigation.

B. Worship

117. Communion with God and with one another is lived and experienced by word and sacrament in the worship of the Christian community. In praise and prayer we share the wonderful deeds of God as well as all human joy and the needs which arise among us. Listening to the word of God brings us together as a community of those who look to God's creative and redemptive word for all their needs.

118. The sacramental life of the church expresses this communion with God and with one another in a profound way. The sacraments are at one and the same time effective signs of God's fellowship with his people and of the fellowship of the people of God with one another. Baptism and eucharist, the sacraments which are common to almost all Christian churches, show this most clearly. Those who are baptized receive a share in the death of the one Lord Jesus Christ and in the power of his resurrection; at the same time they are baptized into the one body, the body of Christ with its many members who suffer and rejoice together. At the table of the Lord's Supper, the "cup of blessing" is "a participation in the blood of Christ" and "the bread which we break" is "a participation in the body of Christ"; therefore "we who are many are one body, for we all partake of the one bread" (1 Cor 10:16-17). "Discerning the body" (1 Cor 11:29) means both to recognize the reality of our communion with Christ and to be responsible for the fellowship with brothers and sisters in the Lord.

119. We encourage ongoing discussion at the appointed levels wherever formal mutual recognition of baptism between our churches is still lacking. We are happy that this recognition has already taken place in many regions. Methodists welcome Roman Catholics to their celebration of the Lord's Supper, but they have to respect the fact that participation in communion is still not permissible for

Roman Catholics. In some pastoral circumstances Catholics are able to invite Methodists to take part in their eucharist.[5] The very desire of many people to take part at the Lord's table with Christians of other churches is a sign of a fellowship which looks forward with longing to a full communion not yet attained.

120. Roman Catholics and Methodists are agreed on the provision of an ordained ministry within the communion of the church to safeguard and foster its common life. Together we recognize that Christ the Good Shepherd shares his pastoral care with others. Those who are called to exercise this care in the ordained ministry receive their particular responsibility from him. They are appointed as witnesses to the living truth of the message entrusted to them, guides of the community that responds to the Gospel they proclaim, and providers of the life of worship that should be offered in communion by the whole church. Yet the communion that we seek to establish between Roman Catholics and Methodists finds at this point its most visible obstacle; we cannot share in eucharistic communion because we identify differently the ministers who bear this corporate responsibility in space and time and the kind of teaching authority committed to them. Progress towards full communion depends on the results that can be obtained from the study of this issue.

121. Behind our differences we thankfully confess that we are able to see common ground: all our sacramental life is rooted in Jesus Christ, the "primary sacrament," whose incarnation and death is the deepest sign of God's communion with all the anxieties and needs of humankind and whose life and resurrection is the model and the source of power for our living together in love and mutual compassion.

122. Christian worship is not only constituted by word and sacrament but also by the mutual care of brothers and sisters for one another and for all who are in need. "God's love has been poured into our hearts through the Holy Spirit" (Rom 5:5), and this love binds us together and enables us to love our neighbor as ourselves. This aspect of Christian communion has been especially important for the Methodist movement since the days of John Wesley. Methodists have tried to fulfill this task in small groups gathering regularly for mutual confession, exhortation, encouragement, and prayer. The forms have changed over the years, but the challenge to live this dimension of Christian fellowship is as urgent as ever. We are happy to see that in both our churches this task has been recognized and efforts have been made, sometimes jointly, to meet the need for such a worship in the midst of our daily life.

C. Mission

123. Christian communion as *koinonia* necessarily includes communion in mission. It is communion with God, who sent his Son to reconcile the world and sent his Spirit to restore in human beings the image of God. Communion in mission

is at the same time the fellowship of those who are sent by their risen Lord and who are empowered by his Spirit to be witnesses of God's love and peace throughout the world. Our proclaiming of God's love includes witness of word and deed, by preaching and serving, by struggling for justice and suffering with the oppressed. We draw attention to what we have already said above in section three.

124. We readily admit that in the past we have so often worked without one another or even against one another. This has weakened our witness and has hindered the mission of God. We seek God's forgiveness for our faults and our shortcomings.

125. We have found considerable convergence in our understanding of the church's mission in the world, such that increasingly Methodists and Catholics are able to work together for those they are called to serve. And we hope that communion in mission will also further our communion in worship and in faith. We work and pray for a growing communion between our churches, not because such unity is an end in itself, making life more comfortable and easy for us. Its goals are "that the world may believe" (Jn 17:21) and "that together [we] may with one voice glorify the God and Father of our Lord Jesus Christ" (Rom 15:6).

III. The Church Universal

126. Christian communion is more than the fellowship of the members of the same congregation or the same local community. The church of God has universal dimensions in regard to both time and space. Our Lord's prayer for his disciples, "that they may be one" (Jn 17:11) was not only meant to bring unity to these Christian disciples who lived together at the same time. When Jesus prayed "for those who believe in me through their word" (Jn 17:20), he spoke about the unity and continuity of the church throughout the generations. Communion means therefore also communion with the church of those who preceded us in the faith throughout the ages.

127. Although we may differ in our evaluations about what have been signs of faithfulness and perseverance in the church's history, we certainly agree that God's faithfulness has preserved his church despite the faults, errors, and shortcomings evident in its history.

128. In the same way, we acknowledge the importance of a structure which binds together local churches to testify to the global nature of the Gospel and of the church universal. But we have different perceptions about the nature and the theological weight of those structures.

129. The Roman Catholic Church relies on the promise which it believes to have been given to St. Peter and the apostles (see, e.g., Mt 16:18) and to have been fulfilled throughout history in the apostolic succession and the episcopal college

together with its head, the bishop of Rome as the successor of St. Peter. The hierarchical structure of the church is an important means and guarantee given by God's grace to preserve the continuity and the universality of the Catholic Church.

130. Methodist churches see the continuity of the apostolic tradition preserved by the faithfulness to the apostolic teaching. The teaching office which decides what is faithful and what is not lies in the hands of conciliar bodies, the conferences. All Methodist churches recognize the necessity of a ministry of *episkope*, "oversight," and in many Methodist churches this is expressed in the office of bishop (cf. *Towards a Statement on the Church*, nos. 31-34). Local churches are bound together by connectional structures which have to mediate the needs of local churches and of the church as a whole. Methodists anticipate that more unity and a growing communion between churches of different traditions may be achieved by new conciliary structures. Obviously, Roman Catholics and Methodists share a common concern regarding the church universal as an expression of communion in Christ. But they differ widely in their beliefs about the means which God has given to attain or preserve this goal. These differences may be the greatest hindrances on the way to full communion.

Conclusion

131. The Joint Commission between the Roman Catholic Church and the World Methodist Council has existed for thirty years. Its work has passed through at least two generations. The first need was for mutual acquaintance; and for a decade and more, the commission engaged in this by way of self-introduction and the preliminary tackling together of doctrinal, ethical, and pastoral issues that were being faced on the wider ecumenical scene. A second state developed as the attempt was made to sketch broad theological perspectives, acceptable to both Roman Catholics and Methodists, in which it would eventually become possible to treat the matters which divide us. The commission believes that a considerable commonality of outlook has been established in the areas of pneumatology (1981 report), ecclesiology (1986 report), the apostolic tradition (1991 report), and now revelation and faith (1996 report).

132. The time may have come for concentration, in the directions thus shown, on some of those more detailed questions that have recurrently caused difficulty among us. In particular, future study could address the related topics of pastoral and doctrinal authority, the offices of oversight in the church and succession in them, and the offer made by Rome of a Petrine ministry in the service of unity and communion. We should thus be encouraged to pursue, more immediately and at a deeper level, the understanding that we both have of ourselves and of our part-

ners in respect to the one church of Jesus Christ and the communion which belongs to the body of Christ.

Participants in the Dialogue

Methodists

Rev. Geoffrey Wainwright, Durham, North Carolina, USA (cochairman)
Dr. José Miguez Bonino, Buenos Aires, Argentina
Bishop William R. Cannon, Atlanta, Georgia, USA
Dr. Maxie D. Dunnam, Wilmore, Kentucky, USA
Mrs. Gillian Kingston, Dublin, Ireland
Bishop Walter Klaiber, Frankfurt, Germany
Dr. Norman Young, Melbourne, Australia
Dr. Joe Hale, General Secretary of the World Methodist Council (secretary)

Roman Catholics

Most Rev. James W. Malone, Youngstown, Ohio, USA (cochairman)
Most Rev. John Bathersby, Queensland, Australia
Most Rev. Cornelius Fontem Esua, Cameroon, West Africa
Rev. Francis Frost, Cèligny, Switzerland
Sr. Mary Charles Murray, Nottingham, U.K.
Canon Michael Richards, London, England
Rev. George Tavard, Brighton, Massachusetts, USA
Rev. Timothy Galligan, Pontifical Council for Promoting Christian Unity, Vatican City (secretary)

NOTES

1. *Towards a Statement on the Church*, supra., no. 9, referring to LG, no. 1.

2. John and Charles Wesley, *Hymns on the Lord's Supper* (1745), no. 81.

3. See the Prayer after Communion for the Second Sunday of Easter (*"ut paschalis perceptio sacramenti continua in nostris mentibus perseveret"*), and the Opening Prayer for Saturday in the Seventh Week of Easter (*"ut qui paschalia festa peregimus haec moribus et vita teneamus"*).

4. Pontifical Council for Promoting Christian Unity, *Directory for the Application of Principles and Norms on Ecumenism* (1993), no. 75; cf. UR, no. 11.

5. See the principles and norms which Catholic bishops apply in this matter in Pontifical Council for Promoting Christian Unity, *Directory for the Application of Principles and Norms on Ecumenism* (1993), nos. 104-107, 129-131.

PART FOUR

Christian Church/ Disciples of Christ–Roman Catholic

The Church as Communion in Christ

December 7, 1992

Preface

Begun in 1977, the Disciples of Christ–Roman Catholic International Dialogue has reached a place of maturity among the various bilateral dialogues and within the whole ecumenical movement. While its work has not yet reached the advanced levels of consensus some of the bilaterals have attained, this dialogue has achieved substantial agreements in several areas that give assurance of the unity that is already given to these two traditions and of the fuller unity that will be God's gift someday in the future. This common theological work between Disciples and Roman Catholics also offers unique ecumenical insights that we believe will be helpful to the other dialogues and efforts in the wider search for visible ecclesial unity.

The first report from the International Commission for Dialogue, *Apostolicity and Catholicity*, was published in 1982 and is sometimes referred to as the Ardfert (Ireland) text, the site of the commission's meeting in 1982. This second report, *The Church as Communion in Christ* (1993), is the product of the ten years (1983-1992) of intensive theological work, the building of friendship, and common prayer. This St. Louis (USA) text is offered for study and reception by Roman Catholics and Disciples throughout the world and to our brothers and sisters in other churches who seek to be faithful to Christ's prayer for the unity of the church.

We rejoice in the measure of agreement—however partial—we are able to record. We look forward with promise to the future issues we shall address. We hope and pray this report and the years of dialogue ahead will deepen our communion (*koinonia*), broaden the exchanges between our churches locally and globally, and strengthen our common witness and service to the world in the name of the triune God—Father, Son, and Holy Spirit.

COCHAIRMEN
Samuel E. Carter, SJ, *Bishop of Kingston*
Paul A. Crow Jr., *Disciples of Christ*

Introduction

1. After the completion of the first stage of the dialogue between the Disciples of Christ and the Roman Catholic Church (1977-81) and its agreed account, *Apostolicity and Catholicity* (1982), it was understood that the current state of ecumenism required serious study of the nature of the church. This came from our conviction that the Christian identity in itself and Christian mission in the world are inseparable from a clear and deep understanding of the church.

2. The choice we made to focus on the church coincides with the choice made by many ecumenical dialogues today: the Anglican–Roman Catholic, Orthodox–Roman Catholic, Anglican–Reformed, and Disciples–Reformed International Commissions and the Lutheran–Roman Catholic Commission in the USA. The same focus is found in the Faith and Order Commission of the World Council of Churches and the Joint Working Group of the World Council of Churches and the Roman Catholic Church. This is a sign of our day that reveals the ecumenical movement to be in the midst of a deep probing of the link between ecumenism and the nature of the church.

3. For this second stage of discussions, our dialogue met ten times: in Venice, Italy (1983); Nashville, Tennessee (1984); Mandeville, Jamaica (1985); Cambridge, England (1986); Duxbury, Massachusetts (1987); Gethsemani, Kentucky (1988); Venice, Italy (1989); Toronto, Canada (1990); Rome, Italy (1991) and St. Louis, Missouri (1992). In every meeting we prayed together, we met with members of local congregations, and we studied and discussed together the similarities and differences that characterize our two communities. In our meetings we focused on how the church as communion is linked to the new creation that God wills. We studied the visibility of the church's communion (*koinonia*) as revealed in the celebration of the eucharist and maintained through continuity with the Apostolic Tradition. And we focused on the role of the ministry and the involvement of the whole church in maintaining the faith of the apostles.

I. The Specific Nature of This Dialogue Within the Ecumenical Movement

4. The dialogue between the Disciples of Christ and the Roman Catholic Church has a specific character. This character may be described in sociological categories by saying that it comes not only from an encounter between a Catholic and a Protestant ethos,[1] but more particularly from the ways in which Disciples understand themselves to express a Protestant ethos and Roman Catholics understand themselves to express a Catholic ethos.

5. Generally in a Catholic ethos great emphasis is placed on sacraments and liturgy. The corporate character of the faith in both the definition of doctrine and its continuing affirmation in the life of the church is stressed. Episcopal oversight, rooted in apostolic continuity and succession, is regarded as necessary for the preservation of the Gospel and the life of the church.

6. Generally in a Protestant ethos great emphasis is placed on the proclamation of the word, the necessity of the judgment of each individual's conscience as it is bound by the Gospel, and the individual's responsibility for the appropriation of the word of God. Episcopal oversight may be considered desirable for the well-being of the church but not essential. Sometimes it has been denied that a specific form of oversight originates in the will of Christ for the church. The test of church structures is the extent to which they are faithful to the Gospel and facilitate authentic proclamation and Christian living.

7. These general differences between a Catholic and a Protestant ethos explain important differences between Disciples and Roman Catholics. Not only are their theological traditions and ecclesial structures different, but they have ways of appropriating the Christian mystery in daily life that are not the same. Nevertheless, on some vital issues what they share in common is more determinative for them than their belonging to a Protestant or a Catholic ethos. The customary vocabulary of division between Protestant and Catholic does not apply exactly to the specific priorities of Disciples and Roman Catholics.

8. The Disciples movement emerged out of nineteenth-century Protestantism, but it had nothing to do with a deliberate break from the Roman Catholic Church and lacked the memories of sixteenth- and seventeenth-century controversies. Moreover, some of its most specific concerns were criticisms of the way in which contemporary Protestantism understood and lived out fidelity to the apostolic witness. It came from the desire to lead the church towards a unity rooted in the weekly celebration of the Lord's Supper. Alexander Campbell was convinced that "the union of Christians is essential to the conversion of the world," an insight which has lost none of its force in the twentieth century.[2] The Roman Catholic Church too proclaims that it has a specific mission for the unity of the world, and

affirms that this unity is signified and given by the eucharistic communion. It too teaches that the restoration of unity among all Christians is linked with the salvation of the world. Indeed Disciples and Roman Catholics pursue these goals in ways deeply marked by their different histories. But they have to discern whether all these affirmations and convictions are not in fact the expression of a very profound communion in some of the most fundamental gifts of the grace of God.

9. This is why, after a certain agreement had been expressed in *Apostolicity and Catholicity*, Disciples and Roman Catholics continued their dialogue in order to discover the degree of communion they already share. Their goal is to be together, growing in this communion and fostering it, and to be with all Christians (as the First Letter of Peter puts it) "God's own people, in order that you may proclaim the mighty acts of him who called you out of darkness into his marvelous light" (1 Pt 2:9 NRSV).

10. To be honest and not lead to a "cheap ecumenism," this dialogue required two important and complementary investigations. It was necessary first to discuss clearly the issues on which, because of their history and ethos, Disciples and Roman Catholics are different. But then it was necessary to discern in what measure these differences are really divisive. Are they only two diverse ways of manifesting or living out the same basic conviction? If that should be the case, another question has to be asked: how would it be possible to express visibly this existing communion? More precisely: what kind of changes would be required to enable this existing communion to contribute to the full restoration of Christian unity?

Differences in Christian Faith and Life

11. At first glance the historic differences between the Roman Catholic Church and Disciples of Christ seem to make the division between them irreconcilable. Roman Catholics have understood themselves in the context of the continuous history of the church; Disciples have understood themselves in the context of their origin as a reform movement (developing out of the Presbyterian Church) committed to find a way to overcome denominationalism. Hence, where Roman Catholics have seen the church throughout its history as continuous with the teaching of the apostles, Disciples have considered that some discontinuities in the life of the church have been necessary for the sake of the Gospel. Roman Catholics have found in creeds and doctrinal definitions a sign of the assistance of the Holy Spirit to bind the church into one and to lead it into all truth. Disciples have wanted to remain faithful to the apostolic church of the New Testament with its vision of unity in Christ but have been distrustful of many of the creeds, confessions, and doctrinal teachings within Christian tradition, finding in the way they have been used a threat to unity. This has led them to be suspicious as well of the structure of epis-

copal authority, which Roman Catholics believe is a necessary means for maintaining continuity with the apostles and with their teaching. Roman Catholics have been convinced that the college of bishops in communion with the See of Rome, teaching in conjunction with other ordained ministers and with the whole church, is a necessary means of preserving the church in continuity with the apostles.

12. The celebration of the eucharist (also called the Lord's Supper or Mass) has been central to both Roman Catholics and Disciples, but the eucharist has been understood in different ways.

13. For Disciples the centrality of the Lord's Supper has been highlighted by its celebration every Lord's Day. In obeying the Lord's commandment, "Do this in memory of me," Disciples have understood themselves to be in communion with the faithful in all places and all ages. Hence, they have called all the baptized to the communion table and in particular have eschewed any formal creeds that kept Christians from taking communion together. However, they generally did not recognize the validity of infant baptism until the present century. Understanding themselves as a believers' church after the pattern of the New Testament church, the Disciples have practiced baptism upon confession of faith in Christ and have looked upon faith more as a trusting attitude and a life of witness than as assent to doctrinal formulations. They have emphasized the role of the whole eucharistic congregation in witnessing to the apostolic faith, and they have felt free to designate, as part of their church order, members of the community other than ordained ministers and ordained elders to preside at the eucharist, especially if no regular minister or elder should be present. In the practice of believers' baptism and in the recovery of the weekly celebration of the eucharist, Disciples have claimed to be in continuity with the faith of the apostles.

14. In celebrating the eucharist, Roman Catholics also have claimed to be in continuity with the faith of the apostles. Indeed, they have seen the celebration of the eucharist as a way to enter into communion with the whole body of Christ. They have emphasized that the eucharist signifies the unity of the church and so they have invited to the eucharistic celebration only those in communion with the bishop and through him in communion with all the local churches in communion with the bishop of Rome throughout the world. They have practiced infant baptism and have emphasized the role of the whole community in supporting and nurturing the faith. In using ancient creeds and traditional liturgies, Roman Catholics have understood themselves to be in continuity with the generations of Christians who have gone before them since the apostles. Faith for Roman Catholics is not limited to the assent to such formulations, but it cannot be recognized without such assent. While different members have different gifts in the life of the church, only the bishop or an ordained minister in communion with him is empowered to preside over the celebration of the eucharist.

15. Disciples have been readily critical of some developments in the history of the church, even seeing in these developments errors needing correction, because of their awareness of human finitude. They have been inclined to recognize sin in many aspects of the institutional church. Roman Catholics have recognized sin within individual members of the church but because they believe the church belongs to Christ and has received the gifts of the Spirit that maintain it in holiness and truth, they are slow to find sin and error in the church's actions and teachings and quick to see continuity with the apostolic teaching.

16. Both Disciples and Roman Catholics approach church teachings with appreciative yet critical eyes. Their two different general attitudes about the church as an institution lead Roman Catholics to be more appreciative and Disciples to be more critical. For this reason they differ on the relative weight given, on the one hand, to individual discernment and conscience and, on the other hand, to the communal mind. It can be said that Roman Catholics are convinced that, although they must decide for themselves, they cannot decide by themselves. Disciples, on the other hand, are convinced that, although they cannot decide by themselves, they must decide for themselves.

17. Indeed, Roman Catholics and Disciples appear so different and live in such different ways that for many of their members the proposal that their differences could be overcome is nearly incredible.

A Convergence of Vision?

18. Through our dialogue we nevertheless discovered that, despite these real and continuing differences, our understanding of the church converges on some notable points which both Disciples and Roman Catholics believe necessary for the visible unity of the church. We are convinced that these convergences are important not only for our two traditions but also for all the communities in dialogue to achieve this goal.

19. We had already begun to discover this convergence in the first stage of our dialogue. In *Apostolicity and Catholicity*, we saw that our two traditions had sometimes pursued the same goal using different means. We became convinced that "the Spirit of God has already brought us into Christ and continues to move us toward full visible unity" (no. 4). We recognized that "each Christian's faith is inseparable from the faith of the community" (no. 9), and agreed that "every generation must come to faith anew through the power of the Holy Spirit and hand on this faith to succeeding generations" (no. 10). We were convinced that "there can be only one Church of God" (no. 11) which cannot be destroyed by divisions among Christians. We were able "to affirm the mutual recognition of baptism administered by Roman Catholics and Disciples, convinced that the oneness we received by the grace of

God in baptism must find its completion in visible ecclesial unity" (no. 8). We affirmed a common belief "that the Church takes visible shape in history and that one sign of this visibility is the common profession of the Gospel with reception of baptism" (no. 11). The restoration of "the unique unity of the one Church of God is the goal," we agreed, and "we are already on the way" (no. 11); we sought a renewed fidelity to actions that would intensify and deepen our relationship.

20. In the second stage of our dialogue together we deepened our conviction that we are one on some crucial issues; and the goal of this statement of convergence is to elucidate a shared vision of the church. We do not intend to discuss the extent of communion between Disciples and Roman Catholics. Nor will we focus, one by one, on a number of separate issues that have divided us. Instead, we want to present our shared understanding of the whole plan of God to draw together and redeem the human family, and the essential role of the church in manifesting and bringing about this plan. By beginning with God's offer of salvation to the whole of humanity and the means God gives to remember and announce this offer, we have been able to discover that we share the same understanding of the basic nature of the church.

II. New Creation and Communion

21. Christians confess that the same God who created human beings has also redeemed them. God has not abandoned humanity to its sinfulness but, through the plan of salvation, has given the possibility of forgiveness of sin and new life. This plan of salvation culminates in Christ Jesus. In the Spirit through the Son, the Father gathers into fellowship all those who had been alienated. By drawing people out of isolation and into communion (koinonia) God makes a new creation—a humanity now established as children of God, a people who know themselves to have received forgiveness of sin and to have put away the old and put on the new, even as they await the consummation still to come (Rom 8:18-25).

22. This activity of God—the forgiveness of sins and making a new creation—and the response to it in thanks and praise is fundamental to the experience and understanding of koinonia. Various meaning of koinonia are found in the New Testament. Paul uses koinonia to describe sharing in the eucharist (1 Cor 10:14-20). In breaking the bread and blessing the cup, Christians have koinonia with the body and blood of Christ. The communities which contributed to the collection for the saints in Jerusalem were bound in koinonia (partnership) with them through the sharing of material goods (1 Cor 8:3-4; Rom 15:26-27; Phil 1:5). Yet another use of koinonia stresses the fellowship of those who walk in the light because they are in communion with the Father and the Son and consequently with one another (1 Jn 1:3, 7).

23. To speak of communion *(koinonia)* is to speak of the way human beings come to know God as God's purpose for humanity is revealed. God in Christ through the Holy Spirit calls human beings to share in the fellowship within the divine life, a call to which they respond in faith. Thus, communion refers first to the fellowship with God and subsequently to sharing with one another. Indeed, it is only by virtue of God's gift of grace through Jesus Christ that deep, lasting communion is made possible: by baptism, persons participate in the mystery of Christ's death, burial, and resurrection and are incorporated into the one body of Christ, the church.

24. The new creation is a foretaste of what will come in fullness through the Spirit at the end of time. The Spirit of God, acting in history, is the main agent of that communion which is the church. Persons are brought into living relationship with the Father through the Son by the power of the Spirit. Human relationships are thus set in a new context so that people may recognize one another as equally God's children and come to acknowledge the bonds that link them as a gift from God. People who have come to this new self-understanding see all other human beings as men and women whom God wills also to save. God's redeeming act in Christ demands that all humanity be united.

Eucharist and Continuity with the Apostolic Community

25. To be the communion God wills, the church has to live in the memory of its origin, remembering with thanksgiving what God has done in Christ Jesus. That memory sustains and nourishes its life. The church in fulfillment of its mission proclaims the good news of the gracious, saving acts of God as the word of God is preached, the sacraments are celebrated, and the new life shared with God is given.

26. To live in this memory means for Disciples and Roman Catholics to be in continuity with the witness of the apostolic generation. The New Testament speaks of those called apostles in the earliest period in a variety of ways, and they played a unique and essential role in formulating and communicating the Gospel. The church is founded on their proclamation. They began or nurtured the early communities, and they soon chose collaborators in the first generation of Christians to share the apostolic work of preaching, teaching, and pastoral guidance.

27. Both Disciples and Roman Catholics share an intention to live and teach in such a way that, when the Lord comes again, the church may be found witnessing to the faith of the apostles. By preserving the memory of what the apostles taught, and by proclaiming and living it anew for the present day, both Disciples and Roman Catholics believe that they maintain continuity with the apostolic witness, forming a living tradition that is "built upon the foundation of the apostles and prophets, Christ Jesus himself being the cornerstone" (Eph 2:20).

28. Memory, as in biblical usage, is more than a recalling to mind of the past. It is the work of the Holy Spirit linking the past with the present and maintaining the memory of that on which everything depends—the faith itself and the church which embodies that faith. Through the Spirit, therefore, the power of what is remembered is made present afresh, and succeeding generations appropriate the event commemorated. The Spirit keeps alive the sense of the faith in the whole community and lavishes a variety of charisma that enable it to live in the memory of Jesus Christ. In the eucharist especially, the Spirit makes Christ present to the members of the community.

29. Both Disciples of Christ and Roman Catholics celebrate the eucharist regularly and frequently—at least every Sunday. Although they have differences in the understanding of the eucharist, they are one in the conviction that the communion willed by God takes on a specific reality at the Lord's Supper. In fact, the celebration of the eucharist renews, makes real, and deepens visible fellowship with God. In the eucharistic gathering, they celebrate God's salvation given through Christ as a gift, a gift which empowers for service. To participate in the eucharistic celebration is to be reaffirmed in membership of the people of God, to be empowered by Christ through the Holy Spirit, and so to be made a part of the work of reconciliation in the world.

30. The eucharist is an act through which a divine reality otherwise more or less hidden emerges and is made present. What is revealed is the plan of salvation, the good news that Jesus Christ reconciles humanity to the Father. The eucharist both symbolizes and makes present, together with the gift of Christ himself, the salvation offered through him. In it faith is freshly evoked and is further nourished in the participant; for the community the essential elements of Christian faith and life are expressed.

31. The eucharist is a communal event. In it Christians are bound with Christ and with one another. It is the action that most fully expresses the fellowship that is the church. Here also Christians know more deeply and strengthen the bonds that unite their local community with other local Christian communities. Furthermore, they find themselves impelled by eucharistic communion to extend themselves in care for all those in God's creation, especially those who suffer. Indeed, the eucharist is essential to the being and mission of the church of God in the world. Christians acknowledge that a test of their credibility to the world as a symbol of God's presence can be found in the quality of the communion among themselves and with others.

32. God in Christ invites to the eucharist, and through the Holy Spirit binds together into one body all who break the one loaf and share the one cup. At the Lord's table the unity of the church is accomplished, for believers are joined to Christ and to one another. Thus, precisely because the celebration of the eucharist

is the climax of the church's life, disunity among Christians is felt most keenly at the eucharist; and their inability to celebrate the Lord's Supper together makes them less able to manifest the full catholicity of the church.

Teaching and Continuity with the Apostolic Community

33. Disciples and Roman Catholics are convinced that in their faith they must remain in continuity with the apostles, even if they understand what this demands in different ways. This common conviction challenges them to explore the ways in which each has remained in continuity with the apostolic community, and to explore as well the possibility that each might be enriched by gifts remembered and exercised more fully by the other. As they have come to understand each other better, they have realized that each continues to retain many of the ways in which Apostolic Tradition is maintained.

34. Both receive the Scriptures as a normative witness to the apostolic faith. Both agree as well that the history of the church after the writing and formation of the New Testament canon belongs to the church's continuity in Apostolic Tradition, even though they have different emphases in understanding the significance of that history. Both find within this history many developments which, because they are the work of the Holy Spirit, are normative for the church. Both affirm that the Gospel is embodied in the Tradition[3] of the church.

35. When Roman Catholics and Disciples evaluate earlier formulations of doctrine, both are committed to continuity with the church's history, though in different ways—a significant difference which requires further investigation. Both agree that doctrinal statements never exhaust the meaning of the word of God and that they may need interpretation or completion by further formulations to be clear. Both also agree that fresh doctrinal statements may be needed to preserve the Gospel when it is endangered or to preach it in a new cultural context.

36. Human memory can be deficient and selective because of finitude and sin, and the pilgrim church is affected by these limitations. But both Roman Catholics and Disciples are agreed that the Holy Spirit sustains the church in communion with the apostolic community because Christ promised that the Spirit "will teach you everything and remind you of all that I have said to you" (Jn 14:26 NRSV). The Spirit guides the church to understand its past, to recall what may have been forgotten, and to discern what renewal is needed for the Gospel to be proclaimed effectively in every age and culture. This underlines the importance of reflection and study in the life of the church to keep alive the memory.

37. Continuity with the Apostolic Tradition calls for fresh understandings or practices of discipleship, which the church adopts in order to transmit the same apostolic faith effectively in new times and places. As the church receives the

Apostolic Tradition in different contexts and circumstances, the Spirit enables it to hold fast to the apostolic faith and to discern authentic developments in its thought and practice. The Holy Spirit guarantees that the church shall not in the end fail to witness faithfully to the divine plan.

38. Thus the church not only remembers (in the biblical sense) what was done in the past, the saving act in Jesus Christ. Neither does it only remember what is promised in the age to come (cf. no. 28). At the very heart of the church's memory, God's saving acts in the past provide a foretaste of transformation so that the future breaks in already to the present. Salvation seen from the perspective of the Scriptures reaches out from the past into the future.

The Gifts of the Spirit for the Church

39. The Holy Spirit not only gives the church that memory which enables it to remain in the Apostolic Tradition, but is also present in the church leading Christians and the whole community of the baptized deeper into the mystery of Christ. Both Disciples and Roman Catholics recognize this as a constitutive gift of God to the church. Through the Holy Spirit the believer is drawn into union with the love of Christ for his Father, for humanity, and for the whole of creation. The will of the believer is also led to unite itself with the will of Christ in obedience to the Father. Thus, the individual believer is drawn into deeper communion with the movement of Christ's self-offering, embodied in the eucharist. This in turn becomes the center of a life of witness to Christ.

40. A Christian receives the gift of faith within and for the communion (*koinonia*) which is the church. Hence, the sense of faith (*sensus fidei*) in the life of an individual Christian is a reflection of the extent to which, by the same Spirit, each one shares in the life of the ecclesial body as such; it becomes an expression of the instinct for faith of the whole body. The inner dynamism of the gift of faith—the power of the Holy Spirit which draws believers into spiritual unity—sustains the interaction of the faith of the individual and the faith of the community.

41. The Spirit gives a variety of gifts or charisma which enable the church as a whole to receive and hand on the Apostolic Tradition. At the heart of these are the gifts appropriate to worship, particularly in the celebration of the Lord's Supper. In the act of celebrating the eucharist the whole community of the baptized is drawn together by the Holy Spirit in a visible unity of faith, hope, and love. Together with the charisma of the one who presides at the celebration, many other charisma can be exercised in service of the church in the central action of its life. Then there are charisma of Christian formation, such as the witness to the faith given by parents to their children, and by those who teach in schools and congregations.

42. Moreover, the memory of the apostolic faith is maintained in lives lived according to the Gospel. The faithful have a sense of care for all humankind, responsibility for their well-being, and sharing in their suffering, sorrow, and oppression as well as in their joy, good fortune, and liberation. The charisma which enable the work of mercy—with the poor, the needy, the homeless, the sick, and the aged—recall the whole community to the Gospel imperative of love.

43. In addition there are extraordinary gifts which are found in the lives of people who give vivid witness to the Gospel and capture the imagination of the community of the baptized in such a way that it is recalled to the Gospel and the Apostolic Tradition. These gifts, like all gifts, must be tested in the church for authenticity.

44. Within the mutuality and complementarity of the different charisma which are given to and for the church, there is a particular charisma given to the ordained ministry to maintain the community in the memory of the Apostolic Tradition. Both Disciples and Roman Catholics affirm that the Christian ministry exists to actualize, transmit, and interpret with fidelity the Apostolic Tradition which has its origin in the first generation. It also has a special responsibility in serving and showing forth the unity of the church. The intention of the apostolic community in establishing ministries in other places was initially to establish collaborators rather than to choose successors: what began as an expansion of communion over distance became later on an expansion over time. We have found this a helpful insight in enabling us to affirm a common understanding of the importance of succession.

45. Although historically Disciples came from those traditions which at the Reformation rejected episcopacy as the Reformers knew it in the Roman Catholic Church, Disciples have always recognized that the work of the ministry, shared in the local congregation by ordained ministers and ordained elders, is essential to the being of the church and is a sign of continuity with the Apostolic Tradition. Roman Catholics believe that the bishop, acting in collaboration with presbyters, deacons, and the whole community in the local church, and in communion with the whole college of bishops throughout the world united with the bishop of Rome as its head, keeps alive the apostolic faith in the local church so that it may remain faithful to the Gospel.[4] Both Disciples and Roman Catholics affirm that the whole church shares in the priesthood and ministry of Christ. They also affirm that ordained ministers have the specific charisma of representing Christ to the church and that their ministries are expressions of the ministry of Christ to the whole church. They believe that God has given to the church all the gifts needed for the proclamation of the Gospel, but this does not mean that every member has received every charisma or authority for doing so. Rather, it is the corporate shaping of the whole people of God by the Gospel which enables them to hold fast to "the faith which was once for all delivered to the saints" (Jude 3, RSV). The ordained ministry is specifically given the charisma for discerning, declaring, and fostering what lies in

the authentic memory of the church. In this process this charism of the service of memory is in communion with the instinct for faith of the whole body. Through this communion the Spirit guides the church.

The Church

46. We thus discover that our diversities are real but not all of them are necessarily signs of division. Roman Catholics and Disciples have more in common than might be expected after the exposition of their differences. We are now sure that in confessing together that the church is communion, we are in agreement on a very crucial issue, which is not isolated from many central issues of the faith. We agree—together with many other Christians—on important truths:

- A person is saved by being introduced into this communion of believers, described in the New Testament by images of the body of Christ, the temple of God, the vine, the household of God.
- This communion is never given to the believer without the involvement of other believers, some of them being the ministers of the church, having a specific responsibility for preaching the word of God and presiding at the celebration of the sacraments. Through the word and the sacraments the church is the servant or instrument of God's plan of salvation.
- This communion is ultimately with the apostolic community, whose memory is constantly kept alive and made present, especially thanks to the work of the ordained ministry, the witness of the holy and committed members of the community, and the expression of the mind of the church by all the members trying to be faithful to their vocation.

47. We therefore come to a very important agreement concerning the nature and mission of the church. The church of God is that part of humanity which through faith and in the power of the Holy Spirit responds to God's plan of salvation revealed and actualized in Jesus Christ. Consequently, it becomes the community of all those who in Christ, by the gift of God, are bound into a communion with the Father and with one another. Its members are called to live in such a way that, in spite of their failures and their weakness, this communion becomes visible and is constantly in search of a more perfect realization.

48. This visibility is realized especially in the celebration of the eucharist. There, gathered together and after having confessed their faith, the baptized people receive the body and blood of Christ, the Son of God who reconciled humanity to God in one body through the cross. There they enter into communion with the saints and members of the whole household of God. Moreover, what is celebrated

at the eucharist has to be actualized in a life of common prayer and faith, of faith-fulness to the Gospel, of sharing the spiritual and even material goods of the community, and of commitment to the will of God that the saving work of Christ be extended as offer to all.

49. Participation in this communion begins through baptism and is sustained in continuing eucharistic fellowship. The Holy Spirit uses the church as the servant by which the word of God is kept alive and constantly preached, the sacraments are celebrated, the people of God are served by the ministers with responsibility for oversight, and the authentic evangelical life is manifested through the life of holy and committed members of Christ. This is why Disciples and Roman Catholics agree that the church is the company of all the baptized, the community through which they are constantly kept in the memory of the apostolic witness and nour-ished by the eucharist. The eucharist is never celebrated and received by a member isolated from an ecclesial community gathered around its ministers. The church is therefore at the same time the sign of salvation (to be saved is to be in communion) and the community through which this salvation is offered.

50. By this communion—which is the church—an effective sign is given by God also to the world. This sign stands in contrast to the divisions and hatred within humanity. Even if it is always stamped by the deficiencies of its members, the church of God demonstrates that the division of humanity created by the corrup-tion of the human heart with its egoism and desire for possessions or power has been overcome through the life, death, and resurrection of Christ. A new life is made pos-sible, the life of the children of God whose bonds of relationship are a gift coming from the Father.

51. Moreover, because Christians come to know that God wants all other human beings also to become members of Christ, they are drawn to give themselves in loving witness and service to humanity. This service culminates when they com-mit themselves to the preaching of the Gospel, being obedient to the command of Christ, their Lord. The church is in that way not only a sign of the new humanity God wants but also an instrument the Holy Spirit uses in order to extend salvation to all human situations and needs, in all places until the end of history.

52. Hence, we are able to affirm gladly the traditional conviction that the church is at one and the same time an epiphany of the destiny which God wills for all humanity and a means to achieve that destiny. These inseparable functions of sign and instrument, epiphany and means, are contained in the expression "the church is the sacrament of God's design," as used in the Roman Catholic and Orthodox traditions. This phrase signifies that God realizes the plan of salvation in and through the communion of all those who confess Jesus Christ and live accord-ing to this confession. We know, indeed, that this saving work is not limited to those who confess Christ explicitly, but that the benefits of Christ's work are offered to all

human beings. In hope we expect that these benefits may be accepted by many who do not fully confess the giver of their gifts. Nevertheless, we do believe that the church, by making visible God's reconciling work and being the servant of God in the accomplishment of this work, stands as a light on the mountaintop, awakening the world to a recognition of its true destiny. The communion that is the church allows people to witness what Christian faith confesses: there is salvation and it comes from God through Christ.

Future Work

53. We have not yet, indeed, discussed some of the most important points which continue to divide us. For we believe that these issues can be fairly and deeply treated only on the basis of the kind of agreement we have reached in the document we are now publishing. Moreover we are convinced that they are to be treated in conjunction with the work of other bilateral ecumenical dialogues, which are also struggling with them. They will be proposed for the agenda of our future discussions. Among them four have a very specific meaning for the visible unity of the church:

a. First, our dialogue has made us aware of a point we need to consider more deeply. Even if we agree on the signification and function of the eucharist, we feel that we still have to discuss our traditional teaching and practice concerning the presence of the Lord in the celebration of the Supper, its sacrificial nature, the role of the ordained minister, and the role of the community. This is important, given the emphasis that both Disciples and Roman Catholics put on the weekly celebration of the Lord's Supper and its link with the visible unity of Christians.

b. A second issue is the way we understand the fundamental structure of the church gathered around the eucharist and the Catholic tradition's understanding of episcopacy—given through a sacrament—as the institution necessary for an authentic eucharist to be celebrated.

c. A third issue is the nature of the rule of faith in a changing history. In what sense is "the faith which was once for all delivered to the saints" expressed in the teaching of the church throughout the ages?

d. Lastly, an issue which requires to be explored by all the churches and communities in dialogue with the Roman Catholic Church is the primacy of the bishop of Rome and the affirmation that it is founded in the will of Christ for the church.

54. These are difficult issues. Nevertheless we believe—after these ten years of dialogue on the church—that it will be possible to clarify many misinterpretations

(on both sides) and possibly to discover ways of growing towards the kind of mutual *metanoia* (repentance) and coming together which will allow very profound communion in some of the most important gifts of the grace of God, and make possible important and irreversible steps on our road towards the full unity God intends.

Participants

Disciples of Christ

Dr. Paul A. Crow Jr., Indianapolis, Indiana, USA (cochairman)
Dr. M. Eugene Boring, Fort Worth, Texas, USA (1988-1992)
Rev. Bevis Byfield, Kingston, Jamaica
Dr. Efefe Elonda, Mbandaka, Zaire (1983-1990)
Dr. H. Jackson Forstman, Nashville, Tennessee, USA
Dr. Nadia Lahutsky, Fort Worth, Texas, USA
Dr. Russel D. Legge, Waterloo, Ontario, Canada (1983-1990)
Dr. W. Paulsell, Lexington, Kentucky, USA (1986)
Dr C. Roy Stauffer, Memphis, Tennessee, USA (1987)
Dr. Paul S. Stauffer, Indianapolis, Indiana, USA (1983-1986)
Dr. M. Jack Suggs, Fort Worth, Texas, USA (1983-1987)
Dr. William Tabbernee, Enid, Oklahoma, USA (1989-1992)
Dr. David M. Thompson, Cambridge, England
Dr. Robert K. Welsh, Indianapolis, Indiana, USA (staff, 1983-1987)

Roman Catholics

Most Rev. Samuel E. Carter, SJ, Kingston, Jamaica (cochairman)
Most Rev. Kevin McNamara, Dublin, Ireland (1983-1987)
Most Rev. Basil Meeking, Christchurch, New Zealand
Rev. Michael Jackson, London, England (1988-1992)
Rev. Kilian McDonnell, OSB, Collegeville, Minnesota, USA
Rev. John P. Meier, Washington, D.C., USA
Msgr. John Mutiso-Mbinda, Vatican City (1986-1992)
Dr. Margaret O'Gara, Toronto, Canada
Rev. J. M. R. Tillard, OP, Ottawa, Canada

NOTES

1. By *ethos* is meant the social, mental, religious, and philosophical atmosphere sur-
    rounding a group and influencing its way of life.

2. A. Campbell, "Foundation of Christian Union," *Christianity Restored*, Bethany, Va.,
    1835, 103-104 (more commonly cited in the 2nd ed., *The Christian System*, 1839, 115).
    Alexander Campbell (1788-1866), son of the Rev. Thomas Campbell, a Seceder
    Presbyterian minister from Ahorey, Ireland, who emigrated to the USA in 1807, was
    President of Bethany College, West Virginia, and one of the leading figures in the
    emergence of Disciples of Christ as a distinctive religious movement.

3. The use of a capital T follows the definition agreed at the Montreal Faith and Order
    Conference in 1963: "By the Tradition is meant the Gospel itself, transmitted from
    generation to generation in and by the church, Christ himself present in the life of the
    Church" (*Report of the Fourth World Conference on Faith and Order*, no. 39, p. 50).

4. Cf. LG, no. 22; Norman P. Tanner, ed., *Decrees of the Ecumenical Councils* (1990), ii,
    866.

PART FIVE

Baptist– Roman Catholic

Summons to Witness to Christ in Today's World

July 23, 1988

Preface

This report which we here present is the result of five meetings between Baptists and Roman Catholics in the years 1984-1988. The conversations were sponsored by the Commission on Baptist Doctrine and Interchurch Cooperation of the Baptist World Alliance and the Vatican Secretariat for Promoting Christian Unity. They were the first international conversations between our two bodies.

Our overall theme was "Christian Witness in Today's World." Our primary goal was to come to a mutual understanding of certain convergences and divergences between the Baptist and Roman Catholic world confessional families. Additional goals included:

1. To establish relations and maintain a channel of communication through conversation for mutual as well as self-understanding
2. To identify new possibilities as well as to clarify existing difficulties in regard to a common witness in view of the current world situation and the mandate of Christ to proclaim the Gospel

3. To address existing prejudices between our two world confessional families

During these initial conversations, where we experienced God's presence and God's blessings, these objectives were in large part fulfilled. What we achieved in these conversations is an encouragement to similar efforts at various levels in church life.

At each session the main work was theological discussion. Scholarly papers were presented and discussed by participants. Bible studies related to the selected themes, and visits to local communities in the places where the meetings took place enriched our conversations. In each location, leaders of the Baptist and Roman Catholic communities visited the group and shared with them the support of their good wishes and their prayers.

We offer this report, with thanks, to the bodies that sponsored our conversations. The sixteen of us who have been participants have been conscious of the Spirit of God at work among us, and formed in the course of three years friendships that have been full of encouragement and edification. As this report is completed, we remember fondly one of our members, Rev. Jerome Dollard, OSB, who was suddenly called from this life on December 26, 1985.

Those of us who took part in the conversations regard our experience together as a great gift from God. We hope other Baptists and Roman Catholics will have the grace of a similar experience. In that spirit we offer this report to Baptists, Roman Catholics, and others for their study and their prayerful reflection.

COCHAIRMEN
Bishop Bede Heather, *Roman Catholic Church*
Dr. David Shannon, *Baptist Church*

I. The Conversations in Review

1. Since the Second Vatican Council (1962-1965), Baptists and Roman Catholics have entered into conversations with one another at numerous levels. Only in the past five years, however, have they undertaken a series of conversations at the international level. Jointly sponsored by the Commission on Baptist Doctrine and Interchurch Cooperation of the Baptist World Alliance and the Vatican Secretariat for Promoting Christian Unity, these conversations have focused on a subject of concern to both bodies, namely, "Christian Witness in Today's World."

2. In this series of five conversations, Baptist and Roman Catholic participants, composed of church leaders and scholars, discovered a remarkable amount of consensus on both general and specific issues. Agreement centered on God's saving revelation in Jesus Christ, the necessity of personal commitment to God in Christ,

the ongoing work of the Holy Spirit, and the missionary imperative that emerges from God's redemptive activity on behalf of humankind. There were, of course, some significant differences on both general and specific issues. We often noted that divergences appeared among representatives of the same communion as well as among those of the two communions.

3. The conversations, held annually in various locations, explored the following topics relative to common witness. The first, meeting in West Berlin, July 18-21, 1984, focused on "Evangelism/Evangelization: The Mission of the Church." The second, assembled in Los Angeles, June 24-30, 1985, addressed the issues of "Christology" and "Conversion/Discipleship," aspects of "Witness to Christ." The third, convened in New York City, June 2-7, 1986, explored ecclesiological issues under the title of "The Church as *Koinonia* of the Spirit." The fourth, held in Rome, July 13-18, 1987, directed itself to specific issues standing in the way of improving common Christian witness, that is, proselytism and restrictions on religious freedom. The fifth, located in Atlanta, Georgia, July 18-23, 1988, sought to gather the fruit of the entire series.

II. Common Statement

4. This statement does not offer a summary of the individual sessions. It attempts, rather, to synthesize the discussions over five years and to articulate our shared response to the revelation of God in Jesus Christ as this has been given to us in the Bible and in the faith and practice of our respective communities.

A. Our Witness to Christ

5. Our common witness rests on shared faith in the centrality of Jesus Christ as the revelation of God and the sole mediator between God and humankind (1 Tm 2:5). We come to know Jesus Christ through the Scriptures, especially of the New Testament, which we share in common as the source and sustainer of our faith. That knowledge is experientially confirmed by the internal witness of the Holy Spirit, is handed down by the community of believers, and is certified by the authoritative witness of the church throughout the ages. We are also aware that God set forth in Christ "the mystery of his will" (Eph 1:9). All human language is inadequate to express the mystery of God's grace and love manifested in the life, death, and resurrection of Jesus. We strive, with Paul as our guide, to gain "insight into the mystery of Christ" (Eph 1:4).

6. The distinction between the person and the work of Christ, while helpful to later theology, does not capture the riches of the biblical testimony to Jesus Christ. The christological statements in the New Testament express the faith of

individuals and groups. In their earliest forms, such as we find in Paul's resurrection *paradosis* (1 Cor 15:1-11) and in the "kerygmatic" speeches of Acts (e.g., 2:22-24; 3:14-16; 4:10-12; 10:40-43), Jesus is proclaimed as the one who God raised up (or made Lord and Messiah) for our sins or in whose name we are saved. The doctrine of the person of Christ cannot be separated from the message of the saving work which God accomplished in and through Christ.

7. The New Testament speaks of Jesus in different ways. The synoptic Gospels present Jesus as the one who proclaims the advent of God's reign and enacts it in his ministry (Mk 1:14-15). He calls sinners to repentance (Lk 5:32) and conquers the power of evil (Lk 11:19f.). He takes the side of the sick and the marginal in his society (Lk 4:16-19). He gathers disciples who were to be with him and to be sent by him (Mk 3:13-15). He possesses a unique familiarity with God and teaches those who follow him to pray to God as Father (Mt 6:25-33). He summons those who would follow him to love God and neighbor with whole heart, mind, and soul (Mk 12:28-34) and gives his life as a ransom that others may be free (Mk 10:45).

8. The Gospel of John is a rich source for understanding Christ, and its language and perspective gave shape to the christological formulation of the councils. It was written in order that people might believe that Jesus was the Christ, the Son of God, and that believing they might have life in his name (Jn 20:31). Jesus is presented as the Word who was with God from the beginning and through whom all things were made (Jn 1:1-3). This Word became flesh and dwelt among us so that his glory could be seen. He was full of grace and truth (Jn 1:14). Eternal life was to know the one true God and Jesus Christ whom God had sent (Jn 17:3). Access to this eternal life was by way of faith. The Christian was summoned to confess with Martha, "Lord, I believe that you are the Christ, the Son of God, he who is coming into the world" (Jn 11:27). Through the death and resurrection of Jesus, the Holy Spirit was given for the remission of sin (Jn 20:22-23). Through the witness of the Paraclete, the disciples were made witness to Christ (Jn 15:26-27). Jesus in dying prayed for them that the Father keep them in his name and make them one (Jn 17:11).

9. Jesus is proclaimed as the one who descended from David according to the flesh and is designated Son of God in power according to the Spirit of holiness by his resurrection from the dead (Rom 1:4). He is also the suffering servant and the Son of Man who came not to be served but to serve (Mk 10:45). He is the Savior born for us in the city of David (Lk 2:11) and the one who, though equal to God, emptied himself, taking on the form of a servant, being born in human likeness (Phil 2:7).

10. The work of Christ in presented under a variety of metaphors such as justification (Gal 2:16; Rom 3:26-28; 5:18), salvation (2 Cor 7:10; Rom 1:16; 10:10; 13:11), expiation and redemption (Rom 3:24-25; 8:32), and reconciliation (2 Cor 5:18-20; Rom 5:10-11). These expressions point to the ontological, objective event wherein God has begun the restoration of a fallen humanity to relationship with

himself and has inaugurated a renewal of creation through Christ's death on the cross and resurrection from the dead. The offer of salvation from God in Christ is received in faith, which is a gift of God "who desires all people to be saved and to come to the knowledge of the truth" (1 Tm 2:4).

11. Discussion of our witness to Christ has revealed that our two communions are one in their confessions of Jesus Christ as Son of God, Lord and Savior. The faith in Christ proclaimed in the New Testament and expressed in the first four ecumenical councils is shared by both of our churches. Our discussion uncovered no significant differences with regard to the doctrine of the person and work of Christ, although some did appear with regard to the appropriation of Christ's saving work. We believe that this communion of faith in Christ should be stressed and rejoiced in as a basis for our discussions of other areas of church doctrine and life, where serious differences may remain.

12. While affirming that the Scriptures are our primary source for the revelation of God in Jesus, we give different weight to creeds and confessional statements. Roman Catholics affirm that sacred Scripture and sacred tradition "flow from the same divine wellspring" and that "the church does not draw her certainty about all revealed truths from the Holy Scriptures alone" (DV, no. 9). The faith of the church expressed in its creeds through the ages is normative for Catholics. Baptists, while affirming the creeds of the first four ecumenical confessional statements in their history, do not hold them as normative for the individual believer or for subsequent periods of church life. For Baptists, Scriptures alone are normative.

B. The Call to Conversion

13. Jesus inaugurated his public ministry by announcing the advent of God's reign and by summoning people to be converted and to believe in the Gospel (Mk 1:14-15). He immediately summoned disciples to follow him (Mk 1:16-20). Saul, the persecutor of the early Christians, through a revelation of the Gospel of Jesus becomes Paul, the apostle to the Gentiles (Gal 2:1-10). The mystery of who Jesus is and what he did for us can ultimately be grasped only in faith and in the practice of Christian discipleship through hope and love (1 Thes 1:3).

14. After his resurrection Jesus announced to his disciples that "repentance and forgiveness of sins should be preached in his name to all nations" (Lk 24:47). Before he departed from his disciples, Jesus commissioned them to make disciples of all nations, baptizing them and teaching them to observe all that he commanded them (Mt 28:16-20). After Pentecost the disciples began to proclaim repentance and forgiveness of sins to all nations (Acts 2:5-13). Under the guidance of the same Spirit that was given to the disciples at Pentecost, in its preaching and witness the

church strives to fulfill the mandate of Jesus and through the ages renews this proclamation of conversion and forgiveness.

15. Conversion is turning away from all that is opposed to God, contrary to Christ's teaching, and turning to God, to Christ, the Son, through the work of the Holy Spirit. It entails a turning from the self-centeredness of sin to faith in Christ as Lord and Savior. Conversion is a passing from one way of life to another new one, marked with the newness of Christ. It is a continuing process so that the whole life of a Christian should be a passage from death to life, from error to truth, from sin to grace. Our life in Christ demands continual growth in God's grace. Conversion is personal but not private. Individuals respond in faith to God's call, but faith comes from hearing the proclamation of the word of God and is to be expressed in the life together in Christ that is the church.

16. Conversion and discipleship are related to one another as birth to life. Conversion is manifested in a life of discipleship. In the Gospels Jesus summoned disciples to be with him and to share his ministry of proclaiming the advent of God's reign and bringing the healing power of this reign into human life. He also summoned them to be like him in taking up their crosses and in living in loving service to others. After Easter and Pentecost the early community continued to announce and spread the good news and to witness to the saving power of God. Like Jesus, the disciples were persecuted, but through the gift of the Spirit they remained faithful and continued to proclaim the Gospel.

17. Throughout history God continues to summon people to follow Jesus, and by the gift of the Spirit and the power of faith the risen Lord continues his ministry. Discipleship consists in personal attachment to Jesus and in commitment to proclamation of the Gospel and to those actions which bring the healing and saving power of Jesus to men and women today. The disciple is nurtured by Scriptures, worship, prayer in all its forms, works of mercy towards others, proclamation, instruction, and the witness of daily life. The church, which can be called a community of disciples, is gathered in the name and presence of the risen Christ. This community is summoned to share the gift it has received. The gift is thus a mandate for a tireless effort to call all people to repentance and faith. A community of disciples of Jesus is always a community in mission.

18. As Baptists and Catholics we both strive to "be converted and believe in the good news" (Mk 1:14). Yet, conversion and discipleship are expressed differently in our ecclesial communions. Baptists stress the importance of an initial experience of personal conversion wherein the believer accepts the gift of God's saving and assuring grace. Baptism and entry into the church are testimony to this gift, which is expressed in a life of faithful discipleship. For Catholics baptism is the sacrament by which a person is incorporated into Christ and is reborn so as to share in the divine life. It is always consequent upon faith; in the case of an infant, this faith is

considered to be supplied by the community. Catholics speak of the need for a life of continual conversion expressed in the sacrament of reconciliation (penance), which in the early church was sometimes called a "second baptism." In both of our communions changes in church practice challenge us to consider more deeply our theology of conversion and baptism. In the recently instituted *Rite for the Christian Initiation of Adults*, Roman Catholics affirm that the baptism of adults is the paradigm for a full understanding of baptism. In some areas of the world Baptists receive baptism at a very early age.

C. Our Witness in the Church

19. "*Koinonia* of the Spirit" (Phil 2:1; cf. 2 Cor 13:14) is a helpful description of our common understanding of the church. *Koinonia* suggests more than is implied by English terms used to translate it, such as "fellowship" or "community." Based on the root idea of "sharing in one reality held in common," it was used in a variety of ways by early Christians. According to 1 Corinthians 1:9, Christians are "called into the fellowship of the Son," which means the same as being "in Christ" or being a member of the body of Christ (1 Cor 12:12ff.). As we participate in Christ, we participate in the Gospel (1 Cor 9:23; Phil 1:5) or in faith (Phlm 6) or in the Lord's Supper (1 Cor 10:16ff.). To share in the Supper is to share in Christ's body and blood (v. 21). Fellowship with Christ entails participation in his life (Rom 6:8; 2 Cor 7:3), sufferings (Rom 8:17; 2 Cor 7:3; Gal 2:19-20), resurrection (Col 2:12; 3:1; Eph 2:6), and eternal reign (Rom 8:17; 2 Tm 2:12). For Paul *koinonia* with the risen Christ is the same as *koinonia* with the Spirit (2 Cor 13:14) and with other Christians. This is more than a bond of friendship. All share together in the spiritual blessings of the Spirit and are thus obligated to help one another (Rom 12:13) in their afflictions (Phil 4:14) as well as in their blessings. In 1 John, to be a Christian means to have *koinonia* with God—Father and Son (1:3, 6)—and with other believers (1:3, 7). The accent is placed on active participation—"walking" and "doing"—as an expression of this fellowship.

20. Discussion of the passages cited above led to the following conclusions: (1) that in and through Christ God has laid down the foundation of the church, (2) that *koinonia* both between God and human beings and within the church is a divine gift, and (3) that the Spirit effects the continuity between the church and Jesus. The uniting of a diverse humanity—Jews and Greeks, males and females, slaves and masters (Gal 3:28)—in one body could not have occurred on human initiative. It depended, rather, on God's action through Jesus Christ—dead, buried, and risen. We are now called into communion with God and with one another in the Risen One. God actually binds us together in an intimate fellowship through the

Holy Spirit. God offers the Spirit as a gift to the whole community of faith to guide it and nurture it and bring it to maturity.

21. *Koinonia*, whether between God and humanity or among human beings, must be regarded as a gift of God. Though made "in the image of God," both male and female (Gn 1:27), to dwell in community, Adam, humanity, has ruptured the relationship with God and with one another that would make such community possible. God's long suffering love alone sufficed to salvage a broken humanity, through Israel and above all, through God's Son, Jesus Christ, the new Adam. In the Son God did for us what we could not do for ourselves. The free gift of God in Christ surpassed by far the effects of Adam's transgression (Rom 5:15-17).

22. The Spirit continues in the church the redemptive work God began in the Son. In baptism the Spirit unites the diverse members—Jew and Gentile, slave and freeborn, male and female, and we could add, black and white, rich and poor, etc.—into a single body (1 Cor 12:12-13; Gal 3:28). The Spirit is the ground of every dimension of the church's life—worship, interior growth, witness to an unbelieving world, and proclamation of the Gospel (Acts 2:42-47; 4:32-37). The Spirit apportions different "gifts" with which the members may build up the body of Christ and carry out the mission of the church (1 Cor 12:4-11, 27-30; Rom 12:4-8).

23. *Koinonia*, which is at the heart of the church, is the result of the manifold activity of the Spirit. In the church there are varieties of gifts, but the same Spirit, and varieties of service, but the same Lord, and varieties of working, but the same God, and, though composed of many members, the church is the body of Christ (1 Cor 12:4; Rom 12:5). When Baptists speak of church, they refer primarily to the local congregation gathered by the Spirit in obedience and service to God's word. Catholics by church refer to the community of faith, hope, and charity as a visible structure established and sustained on earth by Christ (LG, no. 8). While both Baptists and Catholics admit the presence of Christ in the church (Mt 18:20; 28:20), they understand this in different ways. Catholics believe that the church is a "society furnished with hierarchical organs and the mystical body of Christ [which] are not to be considered two realities. . . . Rather, they form one interlocked reality which is comprised of a divine and a human element" (ibid.). Baptists affirm that the church is divine as to its origin, mission, and scope; human as to its historical existence and structure.

D. Our Witness in the World

24. The gift of faith we have received is a gift to be shared with others. Jesus was sent by God to proclaim the good news of God (Mk 1:14; cf. Lk 4:18; 7:22). He sent the Twelve (Mt 10:5ff.) and the Seventy (Lk 10:1ff.) to carry the same message. After the resurrection he directed his followers to go into all the world and make

disciples (Mt 28:16-20) and commissioned them to be witness to the ends of the earth (Acts 1:8). The church has engaged in this task throughout its history.

25. Both Baptists and Roman Catholics respond to this summons through a ministry of evangelism or evangelization. Baptists typically emphasize free personal response of individuals to the Gospel, often to the neglect of corporate responsibility. In more recent years, however, some Baptist groups have focused less on the individual and more on the corporate and social implications of evangelism/evangelization.

26. Roman Catholics apply the term "evangelization" to the "first proclamation" of the Gospel to nonbelievers (EN, no. 21) and also in the wider sense of the renewal of humanity, witness, inner adherence, entry in the community, acceptance of signs, and apostolic initiative. These elements are complementary and mutually enriching (ibid., no. 24). Christ is the center and end of missionary effort. Catholic emphasis upon incarnation, however, encourages a greater concern for "inculturation" than does Baptist emphasis upon redemption of fallen humanity from sin. It also opens the way for assigning sacraments a more prominent place in the evangelization task.

27. Recent ecumenical developments have led to increased appreciation by Roman Catholics and Baptists for each other and for other Christian bodies and may open the way to common witness. Documents of the Second Vatican Council and after speak of many factors uniting Catholics and Protestants: faith, baptism, sharing in the life of grace, union in the Holy Spirit, the Christian life, and discipleship. While Vatican II maintained that the church of Christ "constituted and organized in the world as a society, subsists in the Catholic Church" (LG, no. 8), it also acknowledged that "some, even very many, of the most significant elements or endowments which together go to build up and give life to the Church herself can exist outside the visible boundaries of the Catholic Church" (UR, no. 3).

28. Baptists and Roman Catholics differ among themselves about salvation within non-Christian religions. The Second Vatican Council brought to an end the negative attitude toward them that had prevailed in the church and made it possible to enter into dialogue with them about some of the common problems of the present which need global attention. The council expressed its high regard for the manner of life, precept, and doctrines of these religions which "often reflect a ray of truth which enlightens all men" (NA, no. 2). At the same time the council made it clear that the church "proclaims and is in duty bound to proclaim without fail, Christ who is 'the way, the truth and the life' (Jn 14:6), in whom men find the fullness of religious life and in whom God reconciled all things to himself (2 Cor 5:18-19)" (ibid.). Baptists have issued no major statements on salvation through other religions but must construe the biblical pronouncement, "for there is no other name under heaven given among humankind by which we must be saved" (Acts 4:12), in a rather strict fashion. They frequently cite also, "I am the way, and the truth, and

the life; no one comes to the Father, but by me" (Jn 14:6), and apply it in the narrow sense. Some Baptists, nevertheless, have engaged in dialogue or conversations with representatives of the other major world religions. Similarly, they discern the need for cooperation among world religions to solve urgent human problems.

E. Challenges to Common Witness

29. We respond to the summons to be heralds of the good news by proclaiming the name of Jesus to humankind in such a manner that people will be led to believe in Jesus Christ and to live as true Christians. As we strive to make our lives a witness of the faith that sustains us, certain issues emerge which are of common concern.

30. An important area of common concern is the language we use in speaking of our common witness. "Common witness" means that Christians, even though not yet in full communion with one another, bear witness together to many vital aspects of Christian truth and Christian life. We affirm that it embraces the whole of life: divine worship, responsible service, proclamation of the good news with a view to leading men and women, under the power of the Holy Spirit, to salvation and gathering them into the body of Christ.

31. Realizing that "for freedom Christ has set us free" (Gal 5:1), we seek ways that people may respond to the Gospel in freedom and love. We also confess that competition and bitterness among Christian missionaries have often been a stumbling block for those to whom we seek to proclaim the Gospel. Often Christian missionaries are accused of "proselytism," which in both secular and religious circles has taken on the pejorative connotation of the use of methods which compromise rather than enhance the freedom of the believer and of the Gospel.

32. A historical overview shows that the understanding of "proselytism" has changed considerably. In the Bible it was devoid of negative connotations. A "proselyte" was someone who, by belief in Yahweh and acceptance of the law, became a member of the Jewish community. Christianity took over this meaning to describe a person who converted from paganism. Mission work and proselytism were considered equivalent concepts until recent times.

33. More recently the term "proselytism" in its pejorative sense has come to be applied by some to the attempts of various Christian confessions to win members *from each other*. This raises the delicate question regarding the difference between evangelism/evangelization and proselytism.

34. As Baptists and Catholics we agree that evangelization is a primary task of the church and that every Christian has the right and obligation to share and spread the faith. We also agree that faith is the free response by which people, empowered by the grace of God, commit themselves to the Gospel of Christ. It is

contrary to the message of Christ, to the ways of God's grace, and to the personal character of faith that any means be used which would reduce or impede the freedom of a person to make a basic Christian commitment.

35. We believe that there are certain marks which should characterize the witness we bear in the world. We affirm:

- That witness must be given in a spirit of love and humility
- That it leaves the addressee full freedom to make a personal decision
- That it does not prevent either individuals or communities from bearing witness to their own convictions, including religious ones

36. We also admit that there are negative aspects of witness which should be avoided, and we acknowledge in a spirit of repentance that both of us have been guilty of proselytism in its negative sense. We affirm that the following things should be avoided:

- Every kind of physical violence, moral compulsion, and psychological pressure (for example, we noted the use of certain advertising techniques in mass media which might bring undue pressure on readers/viewers)
- Explicit or implicit offers of temporal or material advantages, such as prizes for changing one's religious allegiance
- Improper use of situations of distress, weakness, or lack of education to bring about conversion
- Using political, social, and economic pressure as a means of obtaining conversion or hindering others, especially minorities, in the exercise of their religious freedom
- Casting unjust and uncharitable suspicion on other denominations
- Comparing the strengths and ideals of one community with the weaknesses and practices of another community

37. On the basis of this understanding of proselytism just given, we agree that the freedom of the Gospel and the individual must be respected in any process of evangelism/evangelization. We are aware, however, that often the charge of "proselytism" in a negative sense can be made when one communion comes in contact with the evangelization/evangelism of the other. Every effort must be made to increase mutual knowledge and understanding and to respect the integrity and rights of other individuals and communities to live and proclaim the Gospel according to their own traditions and convictions. In an increasingly secularized world, division and religious strife between Christian bodies can be such a scandal that nonbelievers may not be attracted to the Gospel.

38. From the time of Constantine until the modern period, the Christian church has experienced a wide variety of relationships to secular authority where, by custom, law, and concordat, civil authority and church have been intertwined in many areas of life. Unfortunately, these interrelationships have sometimes led to intolerance and consequent suffering. In some traditionally Roman Catholic countries, Baptists were sometimes deprived of their full civil and religious rights and freedom. On the other hand, in areas where Baptists were a numerical majority or enjoyed greater economic or social power, Roman Catholics, although supposedly enjoying all civil rights, sometimes suffered discrimination, injustice, and intolerance.

39. Baptists were among the first to advocate the separation of church and state. Having taken shape in an age of religious strife and persecution, Baptists have historically advocated freedom of conscience and practice in religious matters, not simply for Baptists but for all persons.

40. Historically, Roman Catholics and Baptists have differed over the relation of the church to civil authority and on the question of religious liberty. With the *Declaration on Religious Liberty* of the Second Vatican Council, Roman Catholicism affirmed strongly that "the human person has the right to religious freedom" (no. 2) and that this freedom means that all men and women "are to be immune from coercion on the part of individuals or of social groups and of any human power, in such wise that in manners religious no one is to be forced to act in a manner contrary to his or her own beliefs" (ibid.). The council states that this freedom is "based on the very dignity of the human person as known through the revealed Word of God and by reason itself" (no. 2). Since religious liberty is a right which flows from the dignity of the person, civil authorities have an obligation to respect and protect this right.

41. Both Baptists and Catholics agree that religious freedom is rooted in the New Testament. Jesus proclaimed God's reign and summoned people to a deep personal conversion (Mk 1:14-15), which demands that a person be able to respond freely to God's offer of grace. The apostle Paul resisted all those who attempted to coerce the churches into practices or beliefs which he felt contrary to the freedom won by the death and resurrection of Christ.

42. In the area of religious freedom Roman Catholics and Baptists can fruitfully explore different forms of common witness. Both groups struggle to exist in situations where religious freedom is not respected. Both are concerned about those who suffer persecution because of their faith.

43. In certain traditionally Roman Catholic countries, civil constitutions and laws enacted prior to the Second Vatican Council have not been changed to reflect the teaching of the council. In some settings with a dominant Baptist majority, the traditional Baptist stress on separation of church and state as a means to assure religious freedom has been weakened. Both groups need to exercise greater vigilance to assure respect for religious liberty.

44. Christians have a right and duty to bring their religious insights and values to the public debate about the structure and direction of a society. This may also include the effort to embody their values in civil law. As they do so, however, they should always be sensitive to and considerate of the rights of individual conscience and of minorities and the welfare of the society as a whole. They should measure their efforts against Jesus' command to love one's neighbor as oneself, his proclamation that both the just and the unjust have the same loving Father, and his own concern for marginal groups in his society.

III. Areas Needing Continued Exploration

A. Theological Authority and Method

45. These conversations between Baptists and Roman Catholics have frequently surfaced different views and uses of theological authority and method. The theoretical reason for that is clear. Baptists rely on Scriptures alone, as interpreted under the guidance of the Holy Spirit, the Reformation principle. Roman Catholics receive God's revelation from the Scriptures interpreted in the light of the tradition under the leadership of the magisterium, in a communal process guided by the Holy Spirit.

46. In fact, however, the differences are not as sharp as this formulation would suggest. At the Second Vatican Council the Roman Catholic Church dealt carefully and in detail with the relationship between Scripture and tradition (DV, no. 2). It endeavored to reach and express an understanding of the relationship between Scripture, tradition, and the teaching office of the church (magisterium). Each of these has its own place in the presentation of the truth of Jesus Christ. The place of one is not identical with that of the other, yet in the Roman Catholic view these three combine together to present divine revelation. On the other hand, Baptists invoke the Baptist heritage as decisively as Roman Catholics cite tradition, usually disclaiming that it bears the same authority as Scripture but holding on to it vigorously nonetheless.

47. Theory and fact need to be brought together in such a way as to alleviate some anxiety on both sides. Roman Catholics often ask how Baptists regard crucial theological statements which the church has issued in its walk through history, e.g., the great christological statements of Nicea and Constantinople. In brief, do they subscribe to orthodoxy of any kind? Baptists, looking at certain dogmas which they regard as grounded in tradition rather than in Scripture, e.g., the immaculate conception and the assumption of Mary, ask whether Roman Catholics set any limits to what can be defined. Can the church simply approve anything it wants as official doctrine? The key issue needing discussion here is that of development of doctrine.

B. The Shape of *Koinonia*

48. Another issue which distinguishes our communions is the different ways in which the *koinonia* of the Spirit is made concrete. Baptists and Catholics obviously conceive of the Spirit working through different structures. For Baptists, *koinonia* is expressed principally in local congregations gathered voluntarily under the lordship of Jesus Christ for worship, fellowship, instruction, evangelism, and mission. In accordance with their heritage they recognize the Spirit's direction through the interdependency of associations, conventions, alliances, and other bodies designed to proclaim the good news and to carry out the world mission of Christ. However, they have sought to avoid development of structures which would threaten the freedom of individuals and the autonomy of local congregations. For Roman Catholics, the *koinonia* which the Spirit effects in the local congregation is simultaneously a *koinonia* with the other local congregations in the one universal church. Correspondingly, they recognize the Spirit's activity in the spiritual and institutional bonds which unite congregations into dioceses presided over by bishops and which unite dioceses into the whole church presided over by the bishop of Rome. Vital to future ecumenical progress would be further discussion of the relationship between the Spirit and structures.

C. Relationship Between Faith, Baptism, and Christian Witness

49. The conversations revealed growing common concern among Baptists and Roman Catholics about authenticity of faith, baptism, and Christian witness. There are, however, obvious divergences. Baptists, viewing faith primarily as the response of the individual to God's free gift of grace, insist that the faith response precede baptism. Baptist congregations, however, vary in the way they receive persons baptized as infants in other congregations. Practices range from rebaptism of all persons who have not received baptism at the hands of a Baptist minister to acceptance of all persons baptized by any mode, whether as infants or as adults. Roman Catholics regard the sacraments, such as baptism, in a context of faith, as an exercise of the power of the risen Christ, comparable to that exercised by Jesus when he cured the sick and freed the possessed. Emphasizing the corporate as well as the individual nature of faith, they baptize infants and catechize them through a process culminating in full participation in the church.

50. Both approaches present some difficulties. Baptists are not one on how children relate to the church prior to baptism. Some churches now have "child dedication" rites, but most have not dealt with the issue at all. Baptist "rebaptisms" (viewed by them as a first baptism) can offend Christians of other communions, because they suggest the others are not really Christian and because they seem to

violate the scriptural call for "one baptism." Roman Catholics and others who practice infant baptism, on the other hand, confront the problem that there is little clear
evidence in the Scriptures for this practice. The baptizing of infants thus seems to
be sustained principally by tradition and a more corporate understanding of faith.

51. The heart of the problem to be addressed here seems to be the nature of
faith and the nature of the sacraments (called "ordinances" by most Baptists), which
raise a number of questions Baptists and Catholics must deal with together. Is faith
solely an individual's response to God's gift? Can the faith of the community supply
for the personal faith of an infant? May one speak of a "community of faith," that
is, of the body of Christ as itself a subject of a common faith in which individual
believers participate? Are the sacraments outward signs of a preceding inner commitment? Are they the means through which Christ himself effects his healing and
saving work? What does it mean to say that baptism is "the sacrament of faith"? The
issues between us are unlikely to be resolved without addressing these questions.

D. Clarification of Key Terms

52. We are aware that religious tension between communities can arise from
different understanding and use of similar terms. A fundamental concept in both
our communities is that of "mission." In its most extensive senses Baptists speak of
the mission of the church to glorify God by making him known through faith in
Jesus Christ. Roman Catholics also speak of "mission" in its broadest sense as everything that the church does in service of the kingdom of God. Baptists understand
missions (plural, in the sense of the outward movement of the church) as one of the
means by which the church accomplishes its mission in the world.

53. Baptists almost never use the term "evangelization" but prefer the term
evangelism to describe how believers, individually or collectively, take the Gospel of
Christ to the world, "going everywhere preaching the word" (Acts 8:4).
"Evangelization" until recent years was not frequently used within Roman
Catholicism. The best working definition can be found in the apostolic exhortation
of Pope Paul VI, *On Evangelization in the Modern World* (1975): ". . . if it had to be
expressed in one sentence the best way of stating it would be to say that the church
evangelizes when she seeks to convert, solely through the Divine Power of the
Message she proclaims, both the personal and collective consciences of people, the
activities in which they engage, and the lives and concrete milieu which are theirs"
(no. 18). Evangelization is, therefore, a broad concept comprising three major activities: (a) *evangelism,* understood as the proclamation of the Gospel to the
unchurched within one's own society or culture; (b) *missionary activity,* which
involves cross-cultural proclamation of the Gospel; and (c) *pastoral activity*—nourishing and deepening the Gospel among those already committed to it.

54. Even with a growing convergence in terminology, evangelism/evangelization assumes different forms within our two communions. The Baptist stress on conversion as an act of personal faith and acceptance of Jesus as Lord and Savior gives precedence to leading people to an explicit confession of faith through proclamation of the Gospel. Roman Catholics stress that by baptism a person is made new in Christ in the church and stress the establishment of Christian community through proclamation of the word and through a ministry of presence and service.

55. Within these different emphases, however, there are strong similarities. Both communions stress the need for unbelievers and the unchurched to hear and live the message of salvation expressed in the Scriptures, and both strive to fulfill Jesus' command to love the neighbor by engaging in works of mercy and charity both at home and in "mission" countries.

E. The Place of Mary in Faith and Practice

56. Devotion to Mary has traditionally been an area of great difference between Roman Catholics and Baptists. It also emerged in our discussions as a challenge to common witness. Baptists in general have two major problems with Marian devotion: (1) It seems to compromise the sole mediatorship of Jesus as Lord and Savior; and (2) Marian doctrines such as the immaculate conception and the assumption, which are proclaimed by Catholics as infallible and hence to be believed in faith, seem to have little explicit grounding in the Bible. According to Roman Catholics, devotion to Mary does not compromise the unique role of Christ, is rooted in her intimate relationship to Jesus, reflects her continuing role in salvation history, and has a solid basis in the New Testament.

57. Because of the long history of misunderstanding and the theological difficulties and subtleties inherent in Marian doctrines, we do not expect consensus in the foreseeable future. In an area such as devotion to Mary, which evokes both strong emotions and strong convictions from both communions, the quest for mutual understanding and respect is put to the test. Roman Catholics must attempt to understand and sympathize with the serious problems Baptists have with Marian devotion and doctrine. Baptists must try to understand not only the biblical and the theological grounds of Marian doctrine and devotion, but its significance in popular piety and religious practice.

F. Concrete Ways to Offer a Common Witness to the Gospel

58. Conversations between Baptists and Roman Catholics will not lead in the near future to full communion between our two bodies. This fact, however, should not prevent the framing of concrete ways to witness together at the present time. It

will be helpful to think of several different levels—international, national, regional, and local—in which Catholics and Baptists could speak or act in concert. Such cooperation is already taking place in a variety of ways: translation of the Scriptures into indigenous languages, theological education, common concern and shared help in confronting famine and other natural disasters, health care for the underprivileged, advocacy of human rights and religious liberty, working for peace and justice, and strengthening of the family. Baptists and Catholics could enhance their common witness by speaking and acting together more in these and other areas. A whole row of issues vital to the survival of humankind lies before us.

The prayer of Jesus, "that they may all be one; even as thou, Father, are in me and I in thee, that they also may be in us, so that the world may believe that thou hast sent me" (Jn 17:21), has given a sense of urgency to our conversations. We testify that in all sessions during the past five years there has been a spirit of mutual respect and growing understanding. We have sought the guidance of the Lord of the church and give honor and glory to him for the presence and guidance of the Holy Spirit. We pray that God, who has begun this good work in us, may bring it to completion (cf. Phil 1:6).

Participants

Baptists

David T. Shannon, Atlanta, Georgia, USA (cochairman)
Pablo Deiros, Buenos Aires, Argentina
Richard W. Harmon, Atlanta, Georgia, USA
E. Glenn Hinson, Louisville, Kentucky, USA
Paolo Spanu, Rome, Italy
G. Noël Vose, Henley, Australia
Michael Zidkov, Moscow, USSR
Glenn A. Iglehart, Syracuse, New York, USA (cosecretary)

Catholics

Most Rev. Bede Vincent Heather, Parramatta, Australia (cochairman)
Rev. Jerome Dollard, OSB, Center City, Minnesota, USA, 1984, 1985 (deceased 1985)
Rev. John R. Donahue, SJ, Berkeley, California, USA
Msgr. Carlo Ghidelli, Milan, Italy
Rev. Karl Müller, SVD, St. Augustine, FRG
Rev. Joseph Komonchak, Washington, D.C., USA (consultant, 1987, 1988)

Rev. Kilian McDonnell, OSB, Collegeville, Minnesota, USA (consultant, 1986)
Msgr. Basil Meeking, Vatican City (cosecretary 1984)
Msgr. John A. Radano, Vatican City (cosecretary 1985ff.)

PART SIX

Pentecostal–Roman Catholic

Introductory Note

Cecil M. Robeck Jr.

On June 28, 1997, participants of the International Roman Catholic–Pentecostal Dialogue were received by His Holiness, John Paul II. This audience marked the twenty-fifth anniversary of the dialogue and brought closure to four rounds of annual discussions between these seemingly disparate traditions. Each of these rounds has led to the publication of a final report at the time of this publication.

The nature of the dialogue between the Vatican and various representatives of the Pentecostal movement is different from any other in which the Catholic Church participates. First, this is not a true bilateral discussion. It is a dialogue between the largest church in the world and certain representatives of the fastest growing Christian movement in the world. This Pentecostal movement is made up of many denominations, congregations, parachurch organizations, and ministries originating throughout the world. While a triennial Pentecostal World Conference exists, its primary purposes include leadership networking and multicultural worship experiences that introduce the participants to the diversity that marks the movement. It conducts no official business on behalf of worldwide Pentecostalism and, therefore, does not function as a genuine "world communion." Second, while the subject of Christian unity is of concern to both parties, the dialogue has explicitly and repeatedly stated that organic or structural unity is not the purpose of these discussions; mutual understanding is.

These are two major concessions which the Vatican has made to Pentecostals in order to facilitate discussion. They have been necessary due to the youth and diversity of the Pentecostal movement. The Pentecostal movement is still less than a century old. But more than that, its various constituents are at many different stages of development. In spite of this, Pentecostals have been encouraged to enter the dialogue at whatever level they are able to do so. Some participants, therefore, are officially delegated by their denominations to speak on their behalf. Others come to the table with the knowledge and blessing of their churches, but without official recognition by their churches. Still others have participated as individuals while under discipline by their churches, or they were under the threat of denominational sanctions because of their ecumenical commitments.

When the dialogue began in 1972, the Rev. David J. du Plessis, who had approached the Vatican about the possibility of opening such a dialogue, was unable to find an adequate number of Pentecostal leaders and/or scholars who were willing or able to join him in the discussion. As a result, du Plessis drew upon his many friends within the charismatic movement in order to supplement the discussion. Some of these partners were members of churches that had also entered into dialogue with the Secretariat (now Pontifical Council) for Promoting Christian Unity. Others came from the Pentecostal movement. Some were scholars who were well prepared to engage in sophisticated theological conversation. There was some unevenness in the composition of the Pentecostal team, although such a mix was clearly representative of the nature of the Pentecostal movement. As a result of this unevenness, not everyone was happy with the outcome. The discussion on baptism, for instance, quickly led to differences of opinion on the Pentecostal team between those who were committed to infant baptism and those who were committed to so-called "believer's baptism."

In spite of their differences, some headway was made with respect to mutual understanding. Catholics were introduced to some of the fine points of Pentecostal spirituality, such as their doctrine of "baptism in the Spirit," as well as discussions on charisms. Pentecostals, on the other hand, were introduced to concerns related to Christian initiation, as well as discernment, and received a brief introduction to the relationship between Scripture and Tradition.

With the second round of discussion, beginning in 1977, a critical decision was made to limit membership on the Pentecostal team to those who were part of the classical Pentecostal movement. This allowed the discussion to become a bit more focused, although the dialogue had not yet found its stride. In the early years of discussion, the teams tended to do a number of short presentations on too many topics. This led to conversations which were less productive than they might otherwise have been, but they provided bite-sized encounters on a range of topics.

Much of the discussion in the second round developed out of the realization that there were substantial differences of opinion on the nature and role which Tradition and traditions held within the Catholic Church. Pentecostals had been unaware of such distinctions. In addition, time was given to discussions on the nature of Scripture, hermeneutics (including the place of faith and reason), and exegesis. The topics of speaking in tongues, healing, and ministry were studied. And under heavy pressure from the Pentecostals, the topic of Mary was taken up.

In one sense, this decision proved to be disastrous. Pentecostal leaders who were not at the dialogue were not pleased with what they believed to be a capitulation to a Catholic agenda. On the other hand, the discussion of Mary made it possible for Pentecostals to begin to think theologically in an area typically left fallow. The dialogue has, therefore, given impetus to wider Pentecostal scholarship.

In 1985, the dialogue pushed ahead to a related topic, the communion of saints. This was particularly profitable, for it led naturally into ecclesiology, primarily by means of the Greek term *koinonia*. Pentecostals were somewhat familiar with that idea, and it was a term that was gaining an increasing value in larger ecumenical discussions. The ecclesiological discussion also allowed the Pentecostal team to reopen the discussion of baptism. In the end, there was a greater degree of agreement than what either team anticipated going into this particular discussion.

In recent years, several dissertations have been published that describe and analyze the results of the dialogue to date. Arnold Bittlinger studies the first quinquennium in *Papst and Pfingstler: Der römisch katholisch-pfingstliche Dialog und seine ökumenische Relevanz* (Peter Lang, 1978). The second quinquennium was the subject of Jerry L. Sandidge's *The Roman Catholic–Pentecostal Dialogue (1977-1982): A Study in Developing Ecumenism* (Peter Lang, 1987). Paul D. Lee has contributed *Pneumatological Ecclesiology in the Roman Catholic–Pentecostal Dialogue: A Catholic Reading of the Third Quinquennium (1985-1989)* (Pontificiam Universitatem S. Thomae in Urbe, 1994). Finally, Terrence Robert Crowe has treated the larger question of Catholic–Pentecostal relations in his *Pentecostal Unity: Recurring Frustration and Enduring Hopes* (Loyola, 1993).

Much remains to be discussed between these two traditions, not the least of which is how they can move beyond their current positions of estrangement from one another. The fourth round of discussions, held from 1990 through 1997, has focused on "Evangelization, Proselytism, and Common Witness." Whether the results will help to alleviate some of the tensions that exist between Catholics and Pentecostals at the grassroots level remains to be seen. In the meantime, both teams have committed themselves to a fifth round of discussions.

Final Report

of the Dialogue Between the Secretariat for Promoting Christian Unity of the Roman Catholic Church and Leaders of Some Pentecostal Churches and Participants in the Charismatic Movement Within Protestant and Anglican Churches

1972-1976

Introduction

1. The series of talks described as the Roman Catholic–Pentecostal Dialogue had its beginning in the contacts made by individual members of the Pentecostal churches with the Vatican Secretariat for Promoting Christian Unity in 1969 and 1970. With the assistance of the Rev. David J. du Plessis, an international Pentecostal leader, noted figure among Pentecostals, and a guest at the Second Vatican Council, and Fr. Kilian McDonnell, OSB, Director of the Institute for Ecumenical and Cultural Research, Collegeville, Minnesota, USA, the initial impulse was clarified and concrete proposals began to emerge.

2. In 1970 the first of two exploratory meetings was held to see if a serious theological discussion between Roman Catholics and Pentecostals on the international level would be possible. The first gathering was largely an occasion for beginning to know one another. At the second meeting in 1971 each side put "hard" questions to the other, a more purposeful conversation resulted, and it became clear that it would be possible to undertake discussions of a more systematic kind.

3. Therefore, later in 1971, a small steering committee with members from both sides worked out a program of topics which could be treated at meetings over a five-year period.

4. The dialogue has a special character. The bilateral conversations which the Roman Catholic Church undertakes with many world communions (e.g., the Anglican Communion, the Lutheran World Federation, etc.) are prepared to consider problems concerning church structures and ecclesiology and have organic unity as a goal or at least envisage some kind of eventual structural unity. This dialogue has not. Before it began it was made clear that its immediate scope was not "to concern itself with the problems of imminent structural union," although of course its object was Christians coming closer together in prayer and common witness. Its purpose has been that "prayer, spirituality, and theological reflection be a shared concern at the international level in the form of a dialogue between the Secretariat for Promoting Christian Unity of the Roman Catholic Church and leaders of some Pentecostal Churches and participants in the charismatic movements within Protestant and Anglican Churches."

5. The dialogue has sought "to explore the life and spiritual experience of Christians and the churches," "to give special attention to the meaning for the Church of fullness of life in the Holy Spirit," attending to "both the experiential and theological dimensions" of that life. "Through such dialogue" those who participate "hope to share in the reality of the mystery of Christ and the Church, to build a united testimony, to indicate in what manner the sharing of truth makes it possible . . . to grow together."

6. Certain areas of doctrinal agreement have been looked at with a view to eliminating mutual misunderstandings. At the same time, there has been no attempt to minimize points of real divergence. One of these, for example, is the importance given to faith and to experience, and their relation in Christian life.

7. The dialogue has been between the Roman Catholic Church and some Pentecostal churches. Here, too, there have been special features. On the Roman Catholic side, it has had the usual authorization given by the Secretariat for Promoting Christian Unity to such meetings on an international scale and the participants were appointed officially by the secretariat. The Pentecostal participants were appointed officially by their individual churches (and in several cases are leaders of these churches) or else came with some kind of approbation of their churches.

Therefore, it has been a dialogue with some Pentecostal churches and with delegates of others. These are churches which came into being over the last fifty or sixty years when some Protestant churches expelled those who made speaking in tongues and other charismatic manifestations an integral part of their spirituality.

8. In addition, there were participants in the charismatic movement who were invited by the Pentecostals. They belong to Anglican or Protestant churches which already have bilateral dialogues in progress with the Roman Catholic Church. Therefore, it is as participants in the charismatic movement and not primarily as members of their own churches that they share in the dialogue.

9. It was also pointed out in the beginning that "this dialogue is not directly concerned with the domestic pastoral question of the relationship of the charismatic movement among Catholics to the Catholic Church. The dialogue may help indirectly to clarify this relationship but this is not the direct concern of our deliberations."

10. At the first meeting of the dialogue in Horgen, Switzerland, June 1972, an exegetical approach was taken in order to study "baptism in the Holy Spirit" in the New Testament, its relation to repentance and the process of sanctification, and the relation of the charismata to it. At Rome in June 1973 the second meeting was devoted to the historic background of the Pentecostal movement, the relation of baptism in the Holy Spirit to the rites of Christian initiation, and the role of the Holy Spirit and the gifts of the Spirit in the mystical tradition. The third meeting, held at Schloss Craheim, West Germany, June 1974, focused on the theology of Christian initiation, the nature of sacramental activity, infant and adult baptism. At the fourth meeting, held in Venice, May 1975, the areas of public worship (especially eucharistic celebration), the human dimension in the exercise of the spiritual gifts, and discerning of spirits were the main concern. In Rome, May 1976, the final session was devoted to the topic of prayer and praise.

Baptism in the Holy Spirit

11. In the New Testament the expression "to baptize in the Holy Spirit" (Mk 1:8) is used to express, in contrast to the baptism of John (Jn 1:33), the baptism by Jesus who gives the Spirit to the new eschatological people of God, the church (Acts 1:5). All men are called to enter into this community through faith in Christ who makes them disciples through baptism and sharers of his Spirit (Acts 2:38-39).

12. In the Pentecostal movement "being baptized in the Spirit," "being filled with the Holy Spirit," and "receiving the Holy Spirit" are understood as occurring in a decisive experience distinct from conversion whereby the Holy Spirit manifests himself, empowers and transforms one's life, and enlightens one as to the whole reality of the Christian mystery (Acts 2:4; 8:17; 10:44; 19:6).

13. It is the Spirit of Christ which makes a Christian (1 Cor 12:13) and that life is "Christian" inasmuch as it is under the Spirit and is characterized by openness to his transforming power. The Spirit is sovereignly free, distributing his gifts to whomsoever he wills, whenever and howsoever he wills (1 Cor 12:11; Jn 3:7-8). There is also the human responsibility to seek after what God has promised (1 Cor 14:1). This full life in the Spirit is growth in Christ (Eph 4:15-16) which must be purified continually. On the other hand, due to one's unfaithfulness to the promptings of the Spirit (Gal 6:7-9; 1 Jn 3:24) this growth can be arrested. But also new ways open up and new crises occur which could be milestones of progress in the Christian life (2 Cor 3:17-18; 2 Cor 4:8-11).

14. The participants are conscious that during the nineteen centuries other terms have been used to express this experience called "baptism in the Holy Spirit." It is one used today by the Pentecostal movement. Other expressions are "being filled with the Holy Spirit," "receiving the Holy Spirit." These expressions should not be used to exclude traditional understandings of the experience of and faith in the reality of Christian initiation.

15. The Holy Spirit gratuitously manifests himself in signs and charisma for the common good (Mk 16:17-18), working in and through but going beyond the believer's natural ability. There is a great variety of ministries in which the Spirit manifests himself. Without minimizing the importance of these experiences or denying the fruitfulness of these gifts for the church, the participants wished to lay stronger stress on faith, hope, and charity as sure guides in responding to God (1 Cor 13:13–14:1; 1 Thes 1:3-5). Precisely out of respect for the Spirit and his gifts, it is necessary to discern between true gifts and their counterfeits (1 Thes 5:22; 1 Jn 4:1-4). In this discernment process the spiritual authority in the church has its own specific ministry (1 Jn 4:6; Acts 20:28-31; 1 Cor 14:37-38) because it has special concern for the common good, the unity of the church, and her mission in the world (Rom 15:17-19; Acts 1:8).

Christian Initiation and the Gifts

16. From the earliest noncanonical texts of the church there is witness to the celebration of Christian initiation (baptism, laying on of hands/chrismation, eucharist) as clearly expressing the request for and the actual reception of the Holy Spirit. The Holy Spirit dwells in all Christians (Rom 8:9), and not just in those "baptized in the Holy Spirit." The difference between a committed Christian without such a Pentecostal experience and one with such an experience is generally not only a matter of theological focus, but also that of expanded openness and expectancy with regard to the Holy Spirit and his gifts. Because the Holy Spirit apportions as he wills in freedom and sovereignty, the religious experiences of per-

sons can differ. He blows where he wills (Jn 3:8). Though the Holy Spirit never ceased manifesting himself throughout the entire history of the church, the manner of the manifestations has differed according to the times and cultures. However, in the Pentecostal movement, the manifestation of tongues has had, and continues to have, particular importance.

17. During times of spiritual renewal when charismatic elements are more manifest, tensions can arise because of prejudice, lack of mutual understanding and communication. Also, at such times as this, the discerning of spirits is more necessary than ever. This necessity should not lead to discernment being misused so as to exclude charismatic manifestations. The true exercise of the charisma takes place in love and leads to a greater fidelity to Christ and his church. The presence of charismatic gifts is not a sign of spiritual maturity, and those who lack experience of such gifts are not considered to be inferior Christians. Love is the context in which all gifts are rightly exercised, love being of a more definitive and primary order than the spiritual gifts (1 Cor 13). In varying degrees all the charisma are ministries directed to the building up of the community and witness in mission. For this reason mystical experiences, which are more generally directed toward personal communion with God, are distinguished from charismatic experiences which, while including personal communion with God, are directed more to ministerial service.

The Giving of the Spirit and Christian Initiation

18. The Holy Spirit, being the agent of regeneration, is given in Christian initiation, not as a commodity but as he who unites us with Christ and the Father in a personal relationship. Being a Christian includes the reception of grace through the Holy Spirit for one's own sanctification as well as gifts to be ministered to others. In some manner all ministry is a demonstration of the power of the Spirit. It is not agreed whether there is a further imparting of the Spirit with a view to charismatic ministry, or whether baptism in the Holy Spirit is, rather, a kind of release of a certain aspect of the Spirit already given. An inconclusive discussion occurred on the question as to how many impartings of the Spirit there were. Within classical Pentecostalism some hold that through regeneration the Holy Spirit comes into us, and that later in the baptism in the Spirit, the Spirit comes upon us and begins to flow from us. Finally, charisma are not personal achievements but are sovereign manifestations of the Holy Spirit.

Baptism

19. Baptism involves a passing over from the kingdom of darkness to Christ's kingdom of light, and always includes a communal dimension of being baptized into the one body of Christ. The implications of this concord were not developed.

20. In regard to baptism, the New Testament reflects the missionary situation of the apostolic generation of the church and does not clearly indicate what may have happened in the second and following generation of believers.

21. In that missionary situation, Christian initiation involved a constellation normally including proclamation of the Gospel, faith, repentance, baptism in water, the receiving of the Spirit. There was disagreement as to the relationship of these items and the order in which they may or should occur. In both the Pentecostal and Roman Catholic tradition, laying on of hands may be used to express the giving of the Spirit. Immersion is the ideal form which most aptly expresses the significance of baptism. Some, however, regard immersion as essential; others do not.

22. In discussing infant baptism, certain convergences were noted: (a) Sacraments are in no sense magical and are effective only in relationship to faith.

23. (b) God's gift precedes and makes possible human receiving. Even though there was disagreement on the application of this principle, there was accord on the assertion that God's grace operates in advance of our conscious awareness.

24. (c) Where paedobaptism is not practiced and the children of believing parents are presented and dedicated to God, the children are thus brought into the care of the Christian community and enjoy the special protection of the Lord.

25. (d) Where paedobaptism is practiced it is fully meaningful only in the context of the faith of the parents and the community. The parents must undertake to nurture the child in the Christian life, in the expectation that, when he or she grows up, the child will personally live and affirm faith in Christ.

26. Representatives of the charismatic movement in the historic churches expressed different views on baptism. Some agreed substantially with the Roman Catholic, others with the classical Pentecostal view.

27. Attention was drawn to the pastoral problem of persons baptized in infancy seeking a new experience of baptism by immersion later in life. It was stated that in a few traditions rites have been devised, involving immersion in water in order to afford such an experience. The Roman Catholics felt there were already sufficient opportunities within the existing liturgy for reaffirming one's baptism. Rebaptism in the strict sense of the word is unacceptable to all. Those participants who reject paedobaptism, however, explained that they do not consider as rebaptism the baptism of a believing adult who has received infant baptism. This serious ecumenical problem requires future study.

Scripture, Tradition, and Developments

28. The church is always subject to Sacred Scripture. There was, however, considerable disagreement as to the role of tradition in interpretation of Scripture.

29. The Pentecostal and charismatic movements have brought to the understanding of Scripture a new relevance and freshness to confirm the conviction that Scripture has a special message, vital to each generation. Moreover, these movements challenge the exegetes to take a new look at the sacred text in the light of the new questions and expectations the movements bring to Scripture.

30. It was agreed that every church has a history and is inevitably affected by its past. Some developments in that past are good, some are questionable; some are enduring, some are only temporary. A discernment must be made on these developments by the churches.

Charismatic Renewal in the Historic Churches

31. The dialogue considered that in the context of the charismatic movement in the historic churches there was justification for new groups and communities within the churches. Though such movements have a legitimate prophetic character, their ultimate purpose is to strengthen the church and to participate fully in her life. Therefore, the charismatic movement is not in competition with the churches, nor is it separate from them. Further, it should recognize the church authorities. In a word the charismatic renewal is a renewal in the body of Christ, the church, and is, therefore, in and of the church.

Public Worship

32. Public worship should safeguard a whole composite of elements: spontaneity, freedom, discipline, objectivity. On the Roman Catholic side, it was noted that the new revised liturgy allows for more opportunities for spontaneous prayer and singing at the eucharist and in the rites of penance. The Pentecostal tradition has come to accept a measure of structure in worship and recognizes the development in its own history toward some liturgy.

33. In the Roman Catholic context the phrase *ex opere operato* was discussed in relation to the celebration of the sacraments. The disquiet of some participants was removed by the explanation of the Roman Catholic doctrine of grace, which stresses that the living faith of the recipient of a sacrament is of fundamental importance.

Public Worship and the Gifts

34. Corporate worship is a focal expression of the worshiper's daily life as he or she speaks to God and to other members of the community in songs of praise and words of thanksgiving (Eph 5:19-20; 1 Cor 14:26). Our Lord is present in the members of his body, manifesting himself in worship by means of a variety of charismatic expressions. He is also present by the power of his Spirit in the eucharist. The participants recognized that there was a growing understanding of the unity which exists between the formal structure of the eucharistic celebration and the spontaneity of the charismatic gifts. This unity was exemplified by the Pauline relationship between chapters eleven to fourteen of 1 Corinthians.

35. There exists both a divine and human aspect to all genuinely charismatic phenomena. So far as concerns the human aspect, the phenomena can rightly be subject to psychological, linguistic, sociological, anthropological, and other investigations which can provide some understanding of the diverse manifestations of the Holy Spirit. But the spiritual aspect of charismatic phenomena ultimately escapes a purely scientific examination. While there is no essential conflict between science and faith, nevertheless, science has inherent limitations, particularly with regard to the dimensions of faith and spiritual experience.

36. A survey of the scientific literature on speaking in tongues was presented. Another presentation outlined a Jungian psychological evaluation of the phenomenology of the Holy Spirit. However, neither of these topics was developed adequately in discussion, and they await more extended consideration. This could be done in the context of a future treatment of the place of speaking in tongues as an essential factor in the Pentecostal experience.

37. The relationship between science and the exercise of the spiritual gifts, including that of healing, was discussed. Classical Pentecostals, as well as other participants, believe that through the ministry of divine healing can come restoration to sound health. Full agreement was not reached in this matter in view of the importance of the therapeutic disciplines, and the participants recommended further in-depth study.

Discernment of Spirits

38. The New Testament witnesses to the charism of the discerning of spirits (1 Cor 12:10) and also to a form of discernment through the resting of the spirits (1 Jn 4:1) and the proving of the will of God (Rom 12:2), each exercised in the power of the Spirit. There are different aspects of discernment of spirits which allow for human experience, wisdom, and reason as a consequence of growth in the Spirit,

while other aspects imply an immediate communication of the Spirit for discernment in a specific situation.

39. Discernment is essential to authentic ministry. The Pentecostal tradition lays stress on the discerning of spirits in order to find "the mind of the Spirit" for ministry and public worship. It is also understood as a diagnostic gift which leads to the further manifestation of other charismata for the edification of the body of Christ and the work of the Gospel. The operation of this gift in dependence upon the Spirit develops both in the believer and community a growth in a mature sensitivity to the Spirit.

40. Normally, but not absolutely, expectancy is a requisite for the manifestations of the Spirit through human acts on the part of the believer and the community, that is, an openness which nevertheless respects the sovereignty of the Spirit in the distribution of his gifts. Because of human frailty, group pressure, and other factors, it is possible for the believer to be mistaken or misled in his awareness of the Spirit's intention and influence in the believer's acts. It is for this reason that criteria are essential to confirm and authenticate the genuine operation of the Spirit of truth (1 Jn 4:1-6). These criteria must be based upon the scriptural foundation of the incarnation, the lordship of Christ, and the building up of his church. The important element of community criteria involves common wisdom of a group of believers, walking and living in the Spirit, when, led by those exercising the ministry of discernment, a mature discipline results and the group is capable of discerning the mind of God.

41. The Roman Catholic tradition understands such community discernment to be exercised by the whole church, of which her leaders receive a special charism for this purpose. All traditions find a confirmatory individual criterion in the extent to which the believer is influenced in his daily life by the Spirit of Christ who produces love, joy, peace: the plenitude of the fruit of the Spirit (Gal 5:22).

Prayer and Praise

42. The relationship between the objective and the subjective aspects of Christian life was raised. Prayer has two main forms: praise and petition. Both have an objective and a subjective aspect.

In the prayer of praise the essential aspect is worship itself, the adoration of the Father in the Spirit and in the truth of Christ (cf. Jn 4:23-24). One of the expressions of this prayer of praise is the gift of tongues, with joy, enthusiasm, etc.

In the prayer of petition, the believer has always to distinguish between God the giver and the gift of God.

43. Also discussed was the relationship between the word of God and our experience of the Spirit. The Bible must always be a control and a guide in the

Christian experience; but on the other hand, the spiritual experience itself constantly invites us to read the Bible spiritually, in order that it become living water in our Christian life.

44. We recognize multiple aspects of the total Christian experience, which embraces the presence of God (joy, enthusiasm, consolation, etc.), and also the experience of our own sin and the experience of the absence of God, with Christ dying on the cross (Mk 15:34; Phil 3:10); desolation, aridity, and the acceptance of our personal death in Christ as an integral part of the authentic Christian life and also of the true praise of God.

Topics for Further Discussion

45. In the course of conversations, a number of areas were touched on which are recommended for further study. Among them were the following: (a) speaking in tongues as a characteristic aspect of the experience in the Pentecostal movement; (b) the subjective dispositions relative to the baptism in the Holy Spirit; (c) the relationship between the faith of the individual and the faith of the community in terms of content; (d) the relationship between faith and experience; (e) the psychological dimension of charismatic experience; (f) an examination of the charismata of healing and the casting out of demons; (g) the relationship between the sacraments and a conscious personal response of God; (h) the nature of the sacramental event and, in this context, the nature of the church; (i) the problem of interpreting Scripture; (j) the ministries and the ministry gifts: their purpose and operation; and (k) the social implications of spiritual renewal.

Character of the Final Report

46. The character of the final report compiled by the steering committee which has served the dialogue does not represent the official position of the classical Pentecostal churches or of the Roman Catholic Church. Rather, it represents the content of the discussion. Though the conclusions are the result of serious study and dialogue by responsible persons, it does not commit any of the churches or traditions to the theological positions here expressed, but is submitted to them for suitable use and reaction.

It has been the consensus of all participants that the dialogue has been an occasion of mutual enrichment and understanding and offers the promise of a continuing relationship.

Editor's note: From its inception the International Roman Catholic–Pentecostal Dialogue has attempted to bring together a group of pastors, teachers, and church leaders from around the world to explore items of mutual concern. In its earliest stages, classical Pentecostals with a vision for the task were difficult to locate and the steering committee believed that it was important to include some members from the burgeoning charismatic renewal to augment their numbers.

Participants in the 1972-1976 Quinquennium

Roman Catholics

Rev. Louis Bouyer, CO, France (1973)
Rev. Juan Miguel Carrigues, OP, France (1972)
Rev. Pierre Duprey, WF, Vatican City (1972-1976)
Msgr. Balthasar Fischer, West Germany (1973-1976)
Canon Jean Giblet, Belgium (1972-1974)
Rev. Boaventura Kloppenburg, OFM, Brazil/Rome (1973)
Rev. Jean Leclercq, OSB, Belgium (1976)
Rev. Joseph Lécuyer, CSSP, Rome (1976)
Rev. Kilian McDonnell, OSB, USA (cochair, 1972-1976)
Rev. John Mahoney, SJ, England (1976)
Rev. Basil Meeking, New Zealand/Vatican City (1972-1976)
Rev. Donatien Mollat, SJ, Rome (1972)
Rev. Albert de Monléon, OP, Jerusalem (1973)
Rev. Heribert Mühlen, West Germany (1972-1976)
Rev. Ignace de la Potteri, SJ, Rome (1976)
Rev. Walter Smet, SJ, Belgium (1976)
Rev. Simon Tugwell, OP, England (1974)

Classical Pentecostals

Rev. Clement le Cossec, Gypsies for Christ, France (1976)
Rev. Richard Fox, Elim, USA (1976)
Rev. Allan Hamilton, Foursquare, USA (1976)
Rev. F. A. Hölscher, Apostolic Faith Mission, South Africa (1972)
Dr. Leonard Lovett, Church of God in Christ, USA (1974)
Rev. W. Robert McAlister, International Evangelical Church, Brazil (1975-1976)
Rev. John McTernan, International Evangelical Church, Italy (1972-1975)
Rev. John Meares, International Evangelical Church, USA (1972)
Dr. François P. Möller, Apostolic Faith Mission, South Africa (1972-1975)
Rev. David J. du Plessis, USA (cochair, 1972-1976)
Rev. Justus T. du Plessis, Apostolic Faith Mission, South Africa (1974-1976)
Rev. Thomas Roberts, Eglise Apostolique, France (1975)

Rev. Carlton Spencer, Elim, USA (1976)
Dr. Russell P. Spittler, Assemblies of God, USA (1972, 1974)
Rev. Leonard Steiner, Swiss Pentecostal Mission, Switzerland (1973)
Dr. Vinson Synan, Pentecostal Holiness, USA (1973, 1976)
Rev. John Tardibono, International Evangelical Church, USA (1976)

Charismatic Renewal

Rev. Arnold Bittlinger, Lutheran, West Germany (1972-1976)
Rev. Larry Christenson, Lutheran, USA (1975)
Rev. David Collins, Episcopal, USA (1975)
Rev. Athanasios Emmert, Orthodox, USA (1972-1973)
Rev. Jean-Daniel Fisher, Reformed, France (1972)
Rev. Michael Harper, Anglican, England (1972-1976)
Dr. Alays von Orelli, nondenominational, USA (1975)
Dr. J. Rodman Williams, Presbyterian, USA (1972-1976)

Final Report

of the Dialogue Between the Secretariat for Promoting Christian Unity of the Roman Catholic Church and Some Classical Pentecostals

1977-1982

Introduction

1. The following is a report of conversations at the international level which represent a second five-year series that had its beginnings in informal talks in 1969 and 1970 between the Vatican Secretariat for Promoting Christian Unity and some members of the classical Pentecostal churches. The cochairmen of this quinquennium were the Rev. David du Plessis of Oakland, California, USA, and the Rev. Kilian McDonnell, OSB, of Collegeville, Minnesota, USA. The conversations took place according to the indications agreed to by the Secretariat for Promoting Christian Unity and the Pentecostal representatives in 1970.

2. This dialogue has its own specific quality. Growth in mutual understanding of classical Pentecostal and Roman Catholic theologies and spiritual practice rather than organic or structural unity is the special object of these bilateral conversations.

3. It is a concern of the dialogue to seek out those areas where classical Pentecostals and Roman Catholics represent divergent theological views and spiritual experiences, and in this way to foster mutual understanding in what distinguishes each partner, such as faith/experience and its role in the Christian life. Without minimizing these differences, the dialogue also seeks common theological ground where "the truth of the Gospel" is shared (Gal 2:14).

4. The Roman Catholic participants were officially appointed by the Secretariat for Promoting Christian Unity. There were various kinds of representation on the classical Pentecostal side. Some were appointed by their individual churches, a few were church officials, others were members who came with the approbation of their churches, and in still other cases they came as members in good standing with their churches.

5. Besides the classical Pentecostals, there were in the first five-year series (1972-1976) participants from the charismatic movement in various Protestant churches. These were members of the Anglican or Protestant communions with whom the Roman Catholic Church was already in formal contact through bilateral dialogues. These Anglican and Protestant participants took part primarily because of their involvement in the charismatic renewal rather than as members of their own churches. The first five-year series of conversations extended from 1972 through 1976. In those meetings the following topics were discussed: "Baptism in the Holy Spirit" in the New Testament and its relation to repentance, sanctification, charisma, rites of initiation; the historic background of the classical Pentecostal movement; the role of the Holy Spirit and the gifts of the Spirit in the mystical tradition; the theology of the rites of initiation; the nature of sacramental activity; infant and adult baptism; public worship, with special attention given to eucharistic worship; discernment of spirits; and the human dimension in the exercise of the spiritual gifts, prayer, and praise.

6. In 1977 a second five-year series was initiated. This second series, 1977-1982 (no session was held in 1978 because of the death of the pope), had a different character than the first series. In order to more clearly focus the conversations, it was decided that this second series should be exclusively a conversation between the classical Pentecostals and the Roman Catholic Church. Therefore, participants in the charismatic renewal who were members of the Anglican and Protestant churches were not included in the dialogue in a systematic way.

7. At the first meeting of the second series of talks, held in Rome, October 1977, the dialogue discussed speaking in tongues and the relation of experience to faith. The second meeting in Rome, October 1979, discussed the relation of

Scripture and tradition, and the ministry of healing in the church. In Venice, October 1980, the meeting focused on church as a worshiping community, and Tradition and traditions. The meeting in Vienna in October 1981 focused on the role of Mary. The last meeting of the series was held at Collegeville, Minnesota, in October 1982, where ministry was the area of concentration.

Speaking in Tongues

8. A personal relationship with Jesus Christ belongs to the definition of a Christian. Classical Pentecostals have never accepted the position or taught that this relationship must necessarily be expressed through speaking in tongues in the sense that one could not be a Christian without speaking in tongues.

9. The manifestation of tongues was never entirely absent in the history of the church and is found in a notable way among Roman Catholics and other Christians involved in charismatic renewal, as well as among classical Pentecostals.

10. It was agreed that every discussion about Christian *glossolalia* should be founded on Scripture. That some New Testament authors saw tongues as playing a role in the Christian life is indicated in various books of the Bible. "And they were all filled with the Holy Spirit and began to speak in other tongues as the Spirit gave them utterance" (Acts 2:4; 10:46; 19:6; Mk 16:17; 1 Cor 12:4, 10, 18; 14:2, 5, 22; Rom 8:26).

11. The teaching of the classical Pentecostals on the charismata seeks to be faithful to the picture of the New Testament church as reflected in 1 Corinthians 12–14. Classical Pentecostals have rendered a service by encouraging the various communions to be open and receptive to those spiritual manifestations to which they claim to have been faithful.

Faith and Experience

12. By experience the dialogue understands the process or event by which one comes to a personal awareness of God. The experience of God's "presence" or "absence" can be a matter of conscious awareness. At the same time, and at a deeper level, there remains the constant abiding faith-conviction that God's loving presence is revealed in the person of his Son, through the Holy Spirit.

13. A Christian is one who experiences not only Easter and Pentecost, but also the cross. The experience of God's "absence" can lead a Christian to a sense of being abandoned, as Jesus himself experienced on the cross. The death of Christ is to be found at the heart of our Christian experience, and therefore we too experience a death: "I have been crucified with Christ; it is no longer I who live but Christ who lives in me" (Gal 2:20).

14. There was no unanimity whether non-Christians may receive the life of the Holy Spirit. According to contemporary Roman Catholic understanding, to which Vatican II gives an authoritative expression, "All must be converted to Jesus Christ as he is made known by the Church's preaching" (AG, no. 7). "The Church . . . is necessary for salvation" (LG, no. 14). But Vatican II also says that all without exception are called by God to faith in Christ and to salvation (LG, nos. 1, 16; NA, nos. 1, 2). This is brought about "in an unseen way . . . known only to God (GS, no. 22; AG, no. 7). This theology is seen as a legitimate development of the total New Testament teaching on God's saving love in Christ. The classical Pentecostal participants do not accept this development but retain their interpretation of the Scripture that non-Christians are excluded from the life of the Spirit: "Truly, truly I say unto you, unless one is born anew, he cannot see the Kingdom of God" (Jn 3:3).

15. In the immediacy of the Holy Spirit's manifestation in persons, he engages the natural faculties. In the exercise of the charisma, human faculties are not set aside, but used. The action of the Spirit is not identical with the forces inherent in nature.

16. Individual spiritual experience is seen as part of the communitarian dimensions of the Gospel. Persons live in community, and the church should be a lived experience of community. There is rich history of community experience in the church.

17. No matter how vivid or powerful the individual's spiritual experience may be, it needs to be discerned and judged by the community. Love, which is the normative bond of community life, is the biblical criterion of all spiritual experience (cf. 1 Cor 13).

Scripture and Tradition

18. Both Pentecostals and Roman Catholics hold that the books of the Old Testament were accepted by the early church as inspired. The primitive church existed for a period without its own Christian Scriptures. Of the early Christian writings, a certain number were accepted by the church, in the light of the Holy Spirit, as inspired.

19. Roman Catholics believe that these Scriptures have been handed down through the centuries in a tradition of living faith, a tradition which has been experienced by the whole church, guided by church leaders, operative in all aspects of Christian life, and on occasion expressed in written form in creeds, councils, etc. This tradition is not a source of revelation separate from Scripture, but Scripture responded to and actualized in the living tradition of the church.

20. Pentecostals maintain that there are not two authorities (i.e., Scripture plus church tradition), but one authority, that of Scripture. However, Scripture

must be read and understood with the illumination of the Holy Spirit. Pentecostals believe that the interpretation of Scripture can only be discerned through the Holy Spirit. In Pentecostal movements there is a broad consensus of what elements are fundamental to the Christian faith. But there is a reluctance to give this consensus a status of tradition, because of a fear that religious tradition operates against the Gospel.

21. Pentecostals feel that further dialogue will be needed to discuss how the Roman Catholic Church can propose, as a matter of faith, doctrines such as the assumption of Mary, which go beyond the letter of Scripture and which Pentecostals believe to be unacceptable tradition.

Exegesis

22. In contemporary Roman Catholic scholarship, the historical-critical method is the accepted framework within which exegesis is done. In this method emphasis is given to understanding an ancient author in his own idiom, cultural context, and religious background.

23. Pentecostals reject the philosophical and theological principles of form and redaction criticism as militating against the plenary inspiration of Scripture. They insist on the necessity of the light given by the Holy Spirit if the reader is to respond with faith and understanding to the word of God. It was a consensus of the participants that this discussion was a valuable contribution to the dialogue.

24. Roman Catholics believe that the light of the Holy Spirit given in and through the church is the ultimate principle of interpretation of Scripture. They reject any exegetical method that would deny this. However, they believe that critical methods are compatible with a Spirit-inspired exegesis and consider them necessary for a proper understanding of the text.

25. The Pentecostal form of exegesis, while having its roots in evangelicalism, is not specifically defined. It is admittedly in a formative stage. Current exegesis would tend to be a pneumatic literal interpretation.

Biblical Interpretation

26. In the event of conflicting interpretation of Scripture texts, Roman Catholics accept the guidance of the Spirit as manifested in the living tradition. While the teaching of the church stands under the word of God, this same teaching serves the authoritative and authentic communication of the word of God to the people (DV, no. 10). While Catholics believe both Scripture and Tradition cohere in each other and thus transmit the word of God, they do accord a priority to Scripture.

27. In the event of conflicting interpretation of Scripture texts, Pentecostals rely on the Holy Spirit's guidance without the developed dogmatic structure found in the Roman Catholic Church. While there may be some danger of subjectivism, God is trusted to provide the guidance of the Spirit within the local body of believers (Jn 14:26; 15:26; 16:13; 2 Jn 2:27).

Faith and Reason

28. In the determination of the limits and validation of religious knowledge, it was agreed that faith and reason cannot be polarized. However, Pentecostals place a greater emphasis upon pneumatic inspiration and supernatural manifestations than on reason for determining the limits and validity of religious knowledge.

29. In spite of the differences mentioned above, it is seen that classical Pentecostals and Roman Catholics agree on the basic elements of the Christian faith, e.g., Trinity, incarnation, resurrection, inspiration of Scripture, the preaching of the Gospel as an integral part of the ministry of the church, and the guidance of the body of Christ by the Holy Spirit.

30. Still needing clarification in this dialogue is the relation between Scripture and tradition. In this relationship, Roman Catholics do grant a priority to Scripture. But according to Vatican Council II, *Decree on Divine Revelation* (no. 10), "Sacred tradition and sacred Scripture make up a single sacred deposit of the word of God. Hence both Scripture and tradition must be accepted and honored with equal feelings of devotion and reverence." Also in need of further discussion is whether the various methods of exegesis—for example, the form-critical method which most Catholic exegetes use—are compatible with classical Pentecostal principles.

Healing in the Church

31. The ministry of healing in the church is practiced in both the Roman Catholic Church and the Pentecostal churches as part of their total ministry. Both Pentecostals and Roman Catholics agree that through prayerful petition they seek the healing of the whole person's physical, spiritual, and emotional needs. Catholics consider the "anointing of the sick" a sacrament. Pentecostals accept anointing with oil as a part of the commission to minister healing with the preaching of the Gospel. (In the Roman Catholic Church, the sacrament of anointing of the sick was formerly named "extreme unction.")

32. In the life of the Roman Catholic Church there have been, and are, those who dedicate their lives to the care of and ministry to the sick. Pentecostals are becoming increasingly involved in this important aspect of ministry to the sick and suffering.

33. There are attitudinal differences with regard to healing. Roman Catholic practice regards healing of the body as one outcome of the ministry to the sick in the church. Pentecostals place more emphasis on the expectation of healing in the afflicted through preaching and praying. There is a basic difference in each approach to healing. Roman Catholics may seek healing in sacramental rites, in healing services, novenas, and similar forms of devotion. They also go on pilgrimage to shrines where healing may take place. At these places many seek and experience a deepening of faith and a spiritual healing. Pentecostals teach people to expect healing anywhere at any time.

34. Both, in their official teaching, recognize and accept that Jesus is the healer and that faith looks to Jesus for this grace. Pentecostals as well as Roman Catholics exercise reserve in making judgments about miraculous manifestations and healings.

35. There is a difference in expectation—that of Catholics being more passive while that of Pentecostals being more aggressive. There is admittedly a new awareness of the reality of the healing in the Roman Catholic Church, both within and outside the sacramental order. On the other hand, the dialogue is aware of the existence of some popular religious expressions that may lack sufficient theological understanding.

36. The place of suffering in this life is looked upon by Roman Catholics and some Pentecostals as a means of grace, as a purifying of the soul, and as an instrument for opening one to God's spiritual strength, which sustains one and causes one to rejoice in affliction. Both Roman Catholics and Pentecostals believe that suffering may lead one to understand and be comforted (Phil 3:10) to the redemptive suffering of Jesus. However, Pentecostals continue to expect healing unless there is a special revelation that God has some other purpose. Both Roman Catholics and Pentecostals accept that the will of God is preeminent in the whole matter of healing.

37. Although there appears to be some similarity in lay participation in the ministry of healing, the discussions revealed that there is still a wide gap between Catholics and Pentecostals. Catholics, singly and in community, pray for the sick and with the sick. However, only the priest may administer the anointing of the sick, which is a sacrament. Pentecostals anoint with oil (Jas 5:14-15) but do not confine the anointing with oil to the ordained ministry. The ministry to the sick, with the laying on of hands by all believers (Mk 16:17-18), is commonly practiced.

38. In contemporary Roman Catholic theology, the necessity for healing is applied to a broader spectrum of social ills. In this application of healing to problems of social injustice, Roman Catholics and classical Pentecostals have widely divergent views. Because of economic and cultural exploitation, many people live in subhuman economic disease. Roman Catholics and Pentecostals have different approaches to the mandate to heal the social conditions which hinder good health.

39. Classical Pentecostals are reluctant to apply divine healing to such a broad range of social injustices. Though they believe exploitative conditions should be rectified, they would emphasize the priority of direct evangelism as the best means of effecting social change.

40. There are a number of areas where there is agreement between Roman Catholics and Pentecostals: the necessity of the cross, healing as a sign of the kingdom, healing of the total person, the involvement of the laity in prayer for healing, the expectation of healing through the eucharist/Lord's Supper, and Christ as the healer.

Community, Worship, and Communion

41. Pentecostals insist on a personal confession of faith in Jesus Christ as the basis of Christian community, rather than on a sacramental and ecclesial approach to the mediating work of Christ. They hold that the believer experiences Christ in every aspect of the worshiping community: singing, praying, testimony, preaching, the ordinance of baptism, the celebration of holy communion, and also in daily living.

42. Roman Catholics insist on conversion to the living God by personal encounter with the living Christ. This conversion often takes place gradually. For Roman Catholics, the church, its ministry and sacraments, are the normal instruments and manifestations of Christ's action and presence and of the gift of his Spirit. The sacraments are acts of Christ which make present and active the saving power of the paschal mystery.

43. For membership in a Pentecostal church, individuals are expected to have experienced a personal confession of faith in Jesus Christ; and then participate in the life, follow the leadership, and be willing to accept responsibility in the church. In some Pentecostal churches, membership is concurrent with one's water baptism by immersion. Membership in the Roman Catholic Church requires baptism, profession of Roman Catholic faith, and active communion with the local community, the bishops, and the successor of St. Peter.

44. Both among Pentecostals and Roman Catholics, members may lose their fellowship in the community for serious deviation in doctrine or practice. This penalty of severance from the church is intended to be remedial, a reminder of one's guilt before God and the need for repentance.

45. Both Pentecostals and Roman Catholics celebrate the Lord's Supper/eucharist with notable difference in doctrine and practice. Roman Catholics regard the eucharist as a sacramental memorial of Christ's sacrifice on Calvary in the biblical sense of the word *anamnesis*. By God's power, in the eucharistic celebration Jesus is present in his death and resurrection. This sacred rite is for Roman Catholics a privileged means of grace and the central act of worship. It is celebrated frequently, even daily. Among Pentecostals, the Lord's Supper does not hold an

equally predominant place in their life of worship. Most Pentecostals celebrate the Lord's Supper as an ordinance in obedience to the command of the Lord. Other Pentecostal churches believe this memorial to be more than a reminder of Jesus' death and resurrection, considering it a means of grace.

46. Generally Pentecostals practice "open communion," that is, anyone may participate in the Lord's Supper provided they acknowledge the lordship of Christ and have examined their own dispositions (1 Cor 11:28). Except in certain cases of spiritual necessity determined by the church, the Roman church admits to communion only its own members provided they are free from serious sin. This is not meant to be a refusal of fellowship with other Christians, but rather expresses the Roman Catholic Church's understanding of the relationship between the church and the eucharist.

47. The justification for this practice by Catholics was contested by Pentecostals. This was found to be painful on both sides, and the dialogue agrees that the subject with regard to admission to communion requires a great deal of further discussion.

48. Both Pentecostals and Roman Catholics agree that a common faith is the basis of communion in the body of Christ. For Roman Catholics, full communion means the collegial unity of the heads of the local churches (namely, the bishops, with the bishop of Rome who exercises the primacy). Pentecostals would not attach the same significance to structural bonds between churches and will welcome fellowship with many autonomous churches. The Roman Catholic Church recognizes the mediation of Christ at work in churches which are not in full communion with it, through the word that is preached and believed, the sacraments that are celebrated, and the ministry that is exercised. If it considers that these gifts are not found in their fullness in a particular church, it does not thereby make any judgment on the actual holiness of the members of that church. The Roman Catholic Church describes the relationship of other Christians with Catholics as that of brothers and sisters in an incomplete communion (UR).

Tradition and Traditions

49. Our views concerning the sacredness and importance of holy Scripture allowed us to sense immediately that we had much more to affirm in one another than to question. Both sides of the dialogue agreed as to the inspired nature of both the Old Testament and the New Testament, thus giving Scripture a privileged place in both churches.

50. The canonicity of the New Testament is agreed upon in terms of selection and the process of its establishment by the church. Both Pentecostals and Roman Catholics recognize the role of the church in the composition of the books of the

New Testament and in the formation of the canon and both acknowledge that the church preceded the written New Testament.

51. The Pentecostal representatives stress that the church itself was created by the calling (election) of Christ and formed by the doctrinal sayings of Jesus and the messianic interpretation of the Scriptures of Jesus himself (Lk 24:45ff.). In this sense, according to Pentecostals, the church itself was formed by the word of God. The church's role in the formation of the New Testament is then essentially that of one who transmits, interprets, and applies the salvific message of Jesus Christ. Roman Catholics emphasize more the role of the church as having an authority recognizing and enunciating the truth of the Gospel in doctrinal pronouncements.

52. Both sides recognize that Scripture is of necessity linked to interpretation. Both agree that scriptural content itself includes interpretation; that it requires interpretation, and thus an authoritative interpreter. There is significant divergence as to the degree of interpretation within Scripture and the kind of interpretation by the church necessary in order to understand Scripture accurately. Disagreement centers around what or who is an authoritative interpreter. To the Pentecostal it is the right interpretation under the illumination of the Holy Spirit leading to consensus. To the Roman Catholic, it is the church interpreting Scripture as understood by the people of God and discerned by the teaching office of the church. Both Pentecostals and Roman Catholics see interpretative authority as an expression of the activity of the Spirit in the church.

53. Both Roman Catholics and Pentecostals recognize the existence of a process of theological discernment in the ongoing life of the church. The Roman Catholics affirm the ministry of discernment by the teaching office of the church and also recognize that a ministry of discernment may exist outside the Roman Catholic Church. The sharpest disagreement arose concerning the irreformable character of some of these discernments. Roman Catholics hold that the faithful will not be led into error when the authority of the church is fully engaged in enunciating the faith. Pentecostals make no such claim.

54. Pentecostals recognize the strength of the Roman Catholic understanding of corporate and collegial interpretation of Scripture. However, Pentecostals would like to share with Roman Catholics their characteristic experience of direct dependence upon the Holy Spirit for illumination and interpretation of Scripture.

55. A major difference was encountered in the understanding of the role of tradition. Roman Catholics in the dialogue explain tradition in a twofold sense, each sense related to the other. Tradition, here spelled with a capital T, stands for everything that is being and has been handed down, the once-for-all revelation made by God in Jesus Christ, the word of God proclaimed in written and oral form, and the whole of the Spirit-filled community's response to the truth of the Gospel. As such, Tradition contains both an active element of handing down by the church

and a passive one of the material handed down. Within Tradition in this sense, the word of God as Scripture has a kind of primacy. In this understanding Tradition is a continuous process.

56. Tradition in this sense is not to be confused with traditions. These are various ways of practice and teaching whereby Tradition is transmitted. These traditions become binding only when they are made the object of a special decision of church authority.

57. Classical Pentecostals would not place the same value upon Tradition (or tradition) as Roman Catholics, unless grounded in the express witness of Scripture. The Pentecostals, while acknowledging the accumulation of traditions in their own history, would say that these traditions apart from Scripture have little authority in the church.

Perspectives on Mary

58. Since Catholic doctrine concerning Mary was perceived as a point of divergence, it was important to classical Pentecostals to discuss this topic. Considerable time was needed to treat the various issues: the doctrine itself, the method by which the doctrine is justified, and the practical consequences at the popular level. The time devoted to the issues is reflected in the space given this topic in the report.

59. Both classical Pentecostals and Roman Catholics agree that the various biblical texts which mention Mary witness to the importance of Mary in the New Testament. The point of divergence was the doctrinal development which took place on the basis of these texts. Classical Pentecostals insist that they cannot go beyond the clear meaning of the text which is normative for all doctrine and experience. Roman Catholics also maintain that Scripture is normative for any and all later doctrinal development. But they further hold that the church, praying and preaching the Scriptures, can, through the guidance of the Holy Spirit who leads into all truth, find in the biblical texts and in complete fidelity to them a meaning which goes beyond the classical Pentecostals' interpretation.

60. Behind the differences between classical Pentecostals and Roman Catholics in interpretation of specific Marian texts in the Scriptures lie doctrinal differences, often implicit and unexpressed. Possibly the most important of these are in the area of Mary's relationship to the church and her role in the communion of saints.

61. Both classical Pentecostals and Roman Catholics were surprised that they had entertained unreal perceptions of the others' views on Mary. Classical Pentecostals were pleased to learn of the concern of authorities in the Roman Catholic Church to be prudent in appraising Marian doctrinal development which

claims a biblical basis. Classical Pentecostals, while recognizing that doctrinal development that is clearly based on scriptural evidence is not entirely absent from Pentecostal history, admit no doctrinal development with regard to Mary.

The Motherhood of Mary

62. Both Roman Catholics and Pentecostals agree that Mary is the mother of Jesus Christ, who is the Son of God, and as such she occupies a unique place. Both Roman Catholics and classical Pentecostals recognize the historical origins of the title "Mother of God" (Theotokos) arising from the christological disputes at the Council of Ephesus (A.D. 431). In order to preserve the unity of the one person having two natures to which the Virgin gave birth, the council approved the title "Theotokos" ("God-bearer" or "Mother of God"). This was not a Marian definition, concerned to give Mary a new title, but a christological definition concerned with the identity of Jesus Christ. It is only at the moment of the incarnation that she becomes the Mother of God. She is not the Mother of God in his eternal triune existence, but the Mother of God the Son in his incarnation.

The Veneration of Mary

63. Roman Catholics and classical Pentecostals concur in the special respect due to Mary as the mother of Jesus. Both view her as the outstanding example or model of faith, humility, and virtue. Both Roman Catholics and Pentecostals share a concern for the necessity of a correct perspective on Mary. However, there are significant differences in the understanding of the veneration to be given to Mary.

64. Pentecostals expressed concern about what they consider to be excesses in contemporary veneration of Mary. For Pentecostals, certain Roman Catholic practices of Marian veneration appear to be superstitious and idolatrous. For Roman Catholics, there is an apparent failure among Pentecostals to take account of the place of Mary in God's design as indicated in holy Scripture.

65. Roman Catholics, while admitting the occurrence of certain excesses in the practice of veneration of Mary, were careful to point out that proper veneration of Mary is always christological. In addition, Roman Catholics gave evidence that practical steps are being taken to correct excesses where they occur, in line with the norms of the Second Vatican Council, LG, no. 8, and Pope Paul VI in his encyclical Marialis Cultus (1974), nos. 24-36.

The Intercession of Mary

66. Both Pentecostals and Roman Catholics teach that Mary in no way substitutes for or replaces the one Savior and Mediator, Jesus Christ. Both believe in direct, immediate contact between the believer and God. Both pray to God the Father, through the Son, in the Holy Spirit. Catholics believe that intercessory prayers directed to Mary do not end in Mary, but in God himself. Pentecostals would not invoke the intercession of Mary or other saints in heaven, because they do not consider it a valid biblical practice.

Catholic Doctrine on the Graces Given to Mary

67. Roman Catholics believe that Mary always remained a virgin, that she was conceived free from all stain of sin, and that at the end of her life she was assumed body and soul into heaven. Pentecostals reject these beliefs.

68. Roman Catholics claim that belief about these graces given to Mary belongs to the tradition of the church in which the word of God is unfolded. Pentecostals can find no warrant for these beliefs in Scripture. As well as questioning the value of tradition as a basis for the doctrines of faith, Pentecostals would suggest that these traditions about perpetual virginity, immaculate conception, and assumption are without scriptural basis.

69. In the "hierarchy of truths" of faith held by the Roman Catholics, these three doctrines are placed among the truths that are integral to the Roman Catholic faith. Roman Catholics do not believe that those outside the Roman Catholic Church who do not hold these truths are, on that account, excluded from salvation.

The Virginity of Mary

70. Both Pentecostals and Roman Catholics agree that Mary was a virgin in the conception of Jesus and see in the texts that state it an important affirmation of the divine sonship of Christ. Roman Catholics believe that Mary remained a virgin after the birth of Jesus and did not have other offspring. Pentecostals commonly maintain that Scripture records she had other offspring and lived as the wife of Joseph in the full sense.

71. Roman Catholics take the evidence of Scripture as being open to the developments concerning the virginity of Mary, which they find expressed in the earliest fathers of the church. They found in Tradition (understood in the total experience and response of the church as she prays and preaches the word of God) evidence of Mary's virginity.

The Immaculate Conception of Mary

72. Roman Catholics hold the doctrine of the immaculate conception to be founded on the church's reflection on the Bible, both the Old and New Testaments. This doctrine is seen to follow upon consideration of her role as the Mother of the Savior and of texts which present her as the perfect fulfillment of Old Testament types, etc., "the virgin daughter of Sion" (Lk 1:26-38; cf. Zep 3:14-20; Zec 2:10; 9:9), the "woman" (Jn 2:1-11; 19:25-27; cf. Gn 3:15). These texts form a biblical theology of Mary, which provides a basis for the development of the doctrine of the immaculate conception. The explicit development of the doctrine in the life of the church led to its definition by Pope Pius IX in 1854.

73. Pentecostals acknowledge Catholic assurances that the special grace claimed for Mary is a redeeming grace that comes from Jesus. She stands among the redeemed and is a member of the church. However, Pentecostals cannot find any basis for the doctrine of Mary's immaculate conception in Scripture. Furthermore, Pentecostals do not see any value for salvation in this doctrine. Roman Catholics see in the Pentecostal attitude a failure to appreciate fully the implications of the incarnation and the power of Christ's saving and sanctifying grace.

74. Further clarification of issues arising from this doctrine would entail a wider discussion by us of pneumatology, christology, and ecclesiology. Roman Catholics believe a basic distortion takes place when this doctrine is considered in isolation.

The Assumption of Mary

75. Roman Catholics see the doctrine of the assumption, which was explicitly affirmed in the fathers of the church as early as the sixth century, to be in accordance with basic biblical doctrines. The Risen Christ is the beginning of the new creation, which is born from above in the death and resurrection of Christ. In Mary, because of her unique relationship with Christ, this new creation by the Spirit was achieved to the point that the life of the Spirit triumphed fully in her. Consequently she is already with her body in the glory of God, with her risen Son.

76. The Pentecostal difficulty rests in the absence of biblical evidence. There is a generally accepted view that Mary, as one of the faithful, awaits the day of resurrection when she, along with all Christians, will be united bodily with her Son in glory. Pentecostals see a parallel between Mary's "assumption" and the Pentecostal understanding of the "bodily resurrection" or the "rapture of the church" (1 Thes 4:13-18, cf. esp. v. 17), but differ as to when this will take place for Mary.

Ministry in the Church

77. While it is recognized that the word *ministry* in the New Testament covers many activities, the focus of the dialogue bears upon how ministry in the church continues the ministry of the apostles.

78. Such ministry includes all that pertains to the preaching and proclamation of God's word on which the churches are founded and all that is required for the building up of the church in Christ.

79. For Roman Catholics, all ministries contribute to these ends, but particular importance is attached to the ministry of bishops, and to that of the presbyters and deacons who collaborate with them. Classical Pentecostals find an exercise of apostolic ministry wherever through the preaching of God's word churches are founded, persons and communities are converted to Jesus Christ, and manifestations of the Holy Spirit are in evidence. Within the variety of polity found in Pentecostal circles, biblical terms such as elder, deacon, bishop, and pastor are used to designate a variety of offices and ministries, and are not always given the same meaning.

80. It is agreed by both sides of the dialogue that order and structure are necessary to the exercise of ministry.

81. In the development and structuring of ministry, there is no single New Testament pattern. The Spirit has many times led churches to adapt their ministries to the needs of place and time.

82. Roman Catholics see evidence of ministerial office in the New Testament and find in such office part of God's design for the early church, but find in the gradual emergence of the threefold ministry of bishop, presbyter, and deacon the way in which God's design is fulfilled and structural and ministerial needs are met in the church.

83. The positions of classical Pentecostals are more varied. Although there is reluctance in some Pentecostal circles to speak of the ministries of apostle and prophet because of the historical abuse sometimes associated with these ministries, they are recognized as existing and important to the life of the church. Even though there is no uniformity in the way that the New Testament depicts ministry, it is the desire of Pentecostals to seek guidelines for ministry and office in the New Testament.

84. Pentecostals appeal primarily to the priesthood of all believers, which connotes access to God and a participation in ministry on the part of all believers. Pentecostals point to a problem of over-institutionalization of ministry. They believe that they find evidence of this in the history and practice of the Roman Catholic Church.

85. Roman Catholics place emphasis on the need for the institution of ecclesial offices as part of the divine plan for the church. They also see such institutions and ministries as related to and aiding the priesthood and ministry of all within the

one body. At the same time they are aware of the dangers of institutionalism. In recent decades, there has been a renewed concern in the Roman Catholic Church for the development of the ministry of all believers. Roman Catholics, furthermore, feel that Pentecostals fail to give due acknowledgment to the visible aspect of the church or to the sacrament of order and the sacramental ministry.

Ordination

86. Pentecostals see ordination as a recognition of spiritual gifts already imparted. For Pentecostals, ministry is always initiated by a divine call and attended by evidence of reception of necessary gifts and graces. Ordination of one who has received appropriate gifts provides denominational authority for his continuing function in the ministry to which he has been called.

87. For Roman Catholics, the ministry of ecclesial office is given by God who calls a candidate and pours out his Spirit upon him and gives him a special share in the priesthood of Christ. This gift must be discerned by the church, in the form laid down by church discipline. Ordination is considered a sacrament, which imparts grace, gifts, and authority for the ministry of the word, sacrament, and pastoral office.

Apostolic Succession

88. Both Roman Catholics and Pentecostals believe that the church lives in continuity with the New Testament apostles and their proclamation, and with the apostolic church. A primary manifestation of this is to be found in fidelity to the apostolic teaching.

89. For Roman Catholics, the succession of bishops in an orderly transmission of ministry through history is both guarantee and manifestation of this fidelity.

90. For Pentecostals, the current dynamic of the Spirit is regarded as a more valid endorsement of apostolic faith and ministry than an unbroken line of episcopal succession. They look to apostolic life and to the power of preaching which leads to conversions to Jesus Christ as an authentication of apostolic ministry. They question Roman Catholics as to whether in their insistence on episcopal succession they have at times ignored the requirements of apostolic life. Roman Catholics hold the necessity of apostolic life for an effective ministry. However, they maintain that the sovereignty of God's act in the transmission of the word and the ministry of sacrament is not nullified by the personal infidelity of the minister.

91. Both partners to the dialogue strongly assert that holiness of life is essential to an effective ministry and recognize that the quality of apostolic life of the minister has an effect on the quality of his ministry. Both, by their respective discipline and practice, seek to provide seriously for the holiness of ministers. Both

recognize that at times, the power and sovereignty of God is operative in the ministry of a weak and sinful minister, although the discipline of both classical Pentecostals and Roman Catholics provides for the removal from office of anyone who is plainly unworthy.

Recognition of Ministries

92. Each partner to the dialogue recognizes that God is at work through the ministry of the other and recognizes that the body of Christ is being built up through it (UR, nos. 3, 22). The issue of recognition depends on ecclesiological questions that still need elucidation. However, serious disagreements still remain.

Topics for Further Discussion

93. During our conversations we touched on a number of topics which could not be discussed adequately and would have to be taken up at a later date. Among them were the following: (a) the personal moment of faith; (b) the communion of saints in relation to mariology and the intercession of the saints; (c) the development of doctrine in its relation to Scripture and Tradition; (d) the inadequacy and limitation in doctrinal formulations marked with the stamp of a certain historical moment; (e) the binding force of the Marian doctrines which have been defined as they relate to salvation within the Roman Catholic Church.

Character of the Final Report

94. This international dialogue with representatives of classical Pentecostals and Roman Catholics has been characterized by the seriousness of the exchange, as participants seek to reflect in all fidelity the doctrine of their church and at the same time to learn from their opposite partners in dialogue what their true faith stance is. These responsibilities have been exercised with candor and earnestness and have resulted in this final report. Clearly, the report does not commit any church or tradition to any theological position but is offered to them for their reflection and evaluation.

Conclusion

95. The members of the dialogue have experienced mutual respect and acceptance, hoping that the major points of difference will provide an occasion for continuing dialogue to our mutual enrichment.

96. It is the consensus of the participants that the dialogue should continue in this same spirit. Every effort will be made to encourage opportunities for similar bilateral theological conversation at the local level.

97. To that end, the dialogue enters into a period of assimilation to digest the results of the first two phases of exchange and to give broader exposure to mutual efforts undertaken to promote better understanding.

98. Finally, the participants wish to affirm the dialogue as an ongoing instrument of communication between the two traditions.

Editor's note: In the first quinquennium, all who attended were considered to be full participants in the dialogue. At the beginning of the second quinquennium, the steering committee decided upon two changes. If this were to be a dialogue representing the classical Pentecostal community, there would no longer be a need to include members of the charismatic renewal. Furthermore, the steering committee decided that it would be advantageous to have a new category of participation. Observer status was introduced to (1) allow some interested parties to attend who, for one reason or another, could not do so as regular participants, (2) provide training for potential participants, and (3) enable the steering committee to bring in interested parties who might be able to represent the goals and the concerns of the dialogue to constituencies who were not yet ready to participate in such discussions.

Participants

The participants and observers in the 1977-1982 quinquennium were:

Roman Catholics

Rev. Barnabas Ahern, CP, USA (1979-1980)
Rev. Laurence R. Bronkiewicz, Rome (1981)
Rev. William J. Dalton, SJ, Rome (1977, 1979, 1981-1982)
Rev. Pierre Duprey, WF, Vatican City (cochair, 1977; participant, 1979-1981)
Rev. Charles W. Gusner, USA (1979)
Rev. Ivan Havener, OSB, USA (1982)
Rev. Joseph Lécuyer, CSSP, Rome (1977)
Rev. Kilian McDonnell, OSB, USA (cochair, 1979-1982)
Msgr. Basil Meeking, Vatican City (cosecretary, 1977, 1979, 1982)
Rev. Anthony Meredith, SJ, England (1980)
Rev. Heribert Mühlen, West Germany (1977)
Rev. David N. Power, OMI, Ireland/USA (1982)
Rev. Jerome Vereb, CP, Vatican City (cosecretary, 1980-1981; participant, 1979, 1982)

Very Rev. Liam G. Walsh, OP, Ireland/Rome (1980-1982)
Rev. Robert J. Wister, USA (1980)
Rev. Joseph W. Witmer, USA (1982)

Pentecostals

Rev. William Carmichael, Assemblies of God, USA (cosecretary, 1980-1982; participant, 1979)
Rev. H. David Edwards, Elim, USA (1981-1982)
Dr. Howard M. Ervin, American Baptist Convention, USA (1979-1982)
Rev. Richard B. Foth, Assemblies of God, USA (1980)
Bishop W. Robert McAlister, International Evangelical Church, Brazil (cosecretary, 1977, 1979; participant, 1982)
Rev. Elias Malki, Middle East Gospel Outreach, Lebanon (1979)
Rev. John L. Meares, International Evangelical Church, USA (1977-1982)
Dr. François P. Moller, Apostolic Faith Mission, South Africa (1977, 1979)
Rev. David J. du Plessis, Assemblies of God, USA (cochair, 1977-1982)
Rev. Justus T. du Plessis, Apostolic Faith Mission, South Africa (1977-1982)
Rev. Thomas Roberts, Eglise Apostolique, France (1977)
Rev. Jerry L. Sandidge, Assemblies of God, USA (1981-1982)

Pentecostal Observers

Rev. James H. Carmichael, Assemblies of God, USA (1981)
Rev. Desmond Evans, Assemblies of God, USA (1980)
Rev. Paul Finkenbinder, USA/Latin America (1977)
Rev. Ronald C. Haus, Assemblies of God, USA (1980)
Rev. David P. Kast, Assemblies of God, USA (1982)
Rev. James Land, International Churches and Missionary Association, USA (1977)
Rev. Terry Law, Living Sound International, Canada/USA (1980)
Rev. Martin Robinson, Church of Christ, England (1981)
Rev. Jerry L. Sandidge, Assemblies of God, USA (1980)
Rev. James Worsfold, Apostolic Church of New Zealand, New Zealand (1977)

Perspectives on *Koinonia*

1989

Introduction

1. This is a report of conversations held on the international level between the Pontifical Council for Promoting Christian Unity[1] and some classical Pentecostal churches and leaders. It contains the results of the third phase of dialogue held 1985-1989.

2. Contacts for the dialogue were initiated in 1969 and 1970. Among the topics discussed during the first quinquennium (1972-1976) were baptism in the Holy Spirit, Christian initiation and the charisms, Scripture and tradition, and the human person and the gifts. In the second quinquennium (1977-1982) consideration was given to faith and religious experience, speaking in tongues, and Mary. The cochairpersons during this third quinquennium, 1985-1989, were the Rev. Kilian McDonnell, OSB, Collegeville, Minnesota, USA, and the Rev. Justus T. du Plessis of the Apostolic Faith Mission of South Africa. The conversations dealt with the subject of the church as *koinonia*.

3. The Rev. David J. du Plessis chaired the Pentecostal delegation during the first two phases of the dialogue. Indeed, the origin of the international Pentecostal–Roman Catholic dialogue, almost twenty years ago, owes much to initiatives he took during and after the Second Vatican Council. David du Plessis continued to take part in the third phase of the dialogue, providing important insights

to our deliberations, until his death in 1987. The dialogue commission acknowledges, with gratitude to God, David du Plessis's important contribution to the origin and continuation of our work.

4. This particular series of discussions has been noted for the growing acceptance of the dialogue by the worldwide Pentecostal community. For the first time several Pentecostal churches authorized the participation of officially appointed representatives to the dialogue. These churches include the Apostolic Church of Mexico (1986); the Apostolic Faith Mission of South Africa (1985-1989); the Church of God (Cleveland, Tennessee), USA (1985-1988); the Church of God of Prophecy, USA (1986-1988); the Independent Assemblies of God International, USA (1987); the International Church of the Foursquare Gospel, USA (1985-1989); the International Communion of Charismatic Churches, USA (1986).

5. Although the unity of the church is a concern of Pentecostals and Roman Catholics alike, the dialogue has not had as its goal or its subject either organic or structural union. These discussions were meant to develop a climate of mutual understanding in matters of faith and practice: to find points of genuine agreement as well as to indicate areas in which further dialogue is required. We hope that further theological convergence will appear as we continue to explore issues together.

6. Building upon the groundwork laid in the previous two series of discussions, this phase of dialogue focused upon the theme of *koinonia*. At its 1985 meeting in Riano, Italy, discussion was directed to the subject of the communion of the saints. In Sierra Madre, California, USA, during 1986, the subject was the Holy Spirit and the New Testament vision of *koinonia*. Discussion was directed toward the relationship of sacraments to *koinonia* in 1987 and 1988. At the meeting in Venice, Italy, in 1987, the dialogue focused upon *koinonia*, church, and sacraments, emphasizing the place of the eucharist, while in its 1988 meeting at Emmetten, Switzerland, the discussion was on *koinonia* and baptism. During the 1989 meeting in Rome we summarized our findings in this report. The presentation of the findings in this report follows a more systematic order than the chronological sequence in which the topics were discussed.

7. The theme of *koinonia* was chosen for several reasons. First, the subject of communion of saints emerged from the portions of the discussions in the second phase of dialogue which had centered on Mary. Participants in the second phase believed that the topic of communion was pregnant with possibilities. Second, they also realized that the larger worldwide ecumenical dialogue was viewing the topic of communion with interest and expectation.

8. *Koinonia* has been an important topic for discussion in a number of international dialogues, for example, in the Orthodox–Roman Catholic dialogue, the second phase of the Anglican–Roman Catholic international dialogue, the

Methodist–Roman Catholic dialogue; the Lutheran–Roman Catholic dialogue; The Baptist–Roman Catholic dialogue; and the Disciples of Christ–Roman Catholic dialogue.

9. The theme of *koinonia* is proving fruitful in the reflection about ecclesiological self-understanding in many Christian churches and communions, as for example in the Anglican Communion and the Lutheran World Federation.[2]

10. During the Second Vatican Council, the Roman Catholic Church emphasized the ecclesiology of communion. The Extraordinary Synod of Bishops, which met in 1985 to celebrate the twentieth anniversary of the closing of the Second Vatican Council, recognized the importance given to the notion of communion by the council. In Pentecostal teaching, *koinonia* is understood as an essential aspect of church life as it relates to the church's ministry to the world and to the relationships of Christians to one another. Both the Roman Catholics and Pentecostals, therefore, have come to appreciate the biblical importance of *koinonia* as portrayed in Acts 2:42: "they [Christians] devoted themselves to the apostles' teaching and fellowship [*koinonia*], to the breaking of bread and the prayers."[3]

11. One of the difficulties we faced in our discussions was the historical difference between the development of the doctrine of the church in Roman Catholicism and in the various Pentecostal traditions. Roman Catholics have a centuries-long tradition of ecclesiological reflection; the Pentecostal movement is less than a century old and has had little opportunity to engage in sustained theological reflection on ecclesiology. Although Pentecostals do not possess a developed ecclesiology, they do embrace a variety of ecclesiological polities, and they hold strongly to certain basic ecclesiological convictions (e.g., the importance of the local congregation). These convictions have been brought to bear on the various issues discussed.

12. While all dialogue participants have sought to represent their church's positions faithfully, the views expressed in this document are those of the joint commission, which now offers its work to the sponsoring bodies.

I. *Koinonia* and the Word of God

13. Though the focus of our dialogue was church as *koinonia*, the question of Scripture and Tradition kept surfacing in all our discussions. We found that much of the agreement and also the disagreement stemmed from the similarities and differences in our understandings of the ultimate bases on which doctrine and practice of the church should rest. Even though we discussed the topic of Scripture and Tradition more extensively in previous phases of the dialogue,[4] we offer the following brief summary of our respective views on Scripture and Tradition because of its link to the topic of this particular dialogue.

A. Jesus Christ, the Perfect Word of God

14. After speaking in many places and in a variety of ways through the prophets, God has now "in these last days . . . spoken to us by a Son" (Heb 1:1-2). He sent his Son, the eternal Word of God, who became flesh (cf. Jn 1:14).

15. Together we believe that our Lord Jesus Christ revealed God in a perfect way through his whole ministry: through his words and deeds, his signs and wonders, but especially through his death and glorious resurrection from the dead, and finally by sending the Spirit of truth (cf. Jn 15:26; 16:7, 12).

16. Jesus Christ is the ultimate and permanent Word of God. The Christian dispensation, as the new and definitive covenant, will never pass away, and we now await no further revelation before the glorious manifestation of our Lord Jesus Christ (1 Tm 6:14; Ti 2:13).

B. The Written Word of God

17. We believe together that the books of both the Old and New Testaments have been written, in their entirety, under the inspiration of the Holy Spirit (cf. Jn 20:31; 2 Tm 3:16; 2 Pt 1:19, 21; 3:15-16). Scripture is the word of God written in human words in history.

18. Without suppressing the humanity of the biblical writers, God used them to express God's perfect will to God's people. The Scripture teaches faithfully and without error that truth which God wanted put into the sacred writings for our salvation (cf. 2 Tm 3:16).

19. We disagree on the limits of the canon of Scriptures. Roman Catholics and Orthodox have the same canon. Pentecostals agree with the Reformation churches in their view of the canon as limited to the sixty-six books of the Old and New Testaments. While Pentecostals do not deny that the books which Roman Catholics treat as deuterocanonical are valuable for the edification of God's people, they do not consider them as normative for faith and practice.

20. Catholics argue that it is significant that the church precedes chronologically the writings of the New Testament. These writings collectively bring together the message transmitted orally by the early apostolic Christian community, filled with the Holy Spirit, and constitute also the witness and response of the people of God to the truth of the Gospel.

21. The Roman Catholic Church sees in the texts of the New Testament—whose authors were inspired—the normative expression of revelation which closed with the death of the last apostle. The writings of the New Testament thus express, in a normative fashion, the Apostolic Tradition. The determination of the canon of Scripture by the church is also an act of that Tradition. The proper interpretation

of Scripture has to be made in the communion of the believers, within the living Tradition which is guided by the Holy Sprit. The same Spirit who inspired the Scriptures also opens the sense of the Scripture to the people of God, so that it nourishes their faith.

22. Both Roman Catholics and Pentecostals recognize that the chosen vessels of God who wrote the New Testament belonged to the church, and they stress that the New Testament biblical authors had a unique place in the history of revelation. Since the church inherited the Scripture from the Old Testament people of God, Israel, and from Jesus himself, and since the church rose out of the proclamation of Christ's chosen apostles, it must be considered the creation of the word of God. The church can live in accordance with the will of God only as it submits itself to the prophetic and apostolic testimony contained in the Scriptures. By accepting the books of the New Testament into the canon of Scriptures, the church recognized the New Testament writings as the word of God addressed to humanity.

23. Pentecostals believe that some traditions express correctly the saving truth to which Scripture testifies (e.g., Apostles' and Nicene Creeds), but they seek to evaluate all traditions in the light of the word of God in Scripture, the ultimate norm of faith and practice in the church.

24. Both Pentecostals and Roman Catholics agree that Scripture, inspired by the Spirit, can be properly interpreted only with the help of the Holy Spirit. "So also no one comprehends the thoughts of God except the Spirit of God" because spiritual things "are spiritually discerned" (1 Cor 2:11, 14).

25. There is, however, a significant divergence as to the nature of interpretation which is necessary to understand Scripture accurately. In Roman Catholicism the interpretation of the Scripture goes on daily in the lives of the faithful at many levels, such as in the family, in the pulpit, and in the classroom. The whole body of the faithful who have an anointing that comes from the Holy One cannot err in matters of belief (cf. 1 Jn 2:20, 27). This characteristic is shown in the supernatural appreciation of the faith (*sensus fidei*) of the whole people, when "from the bishops to the last of the faithful" they manifest a universal consent in matters of faith and morals" (LG, no. 12).[5] Roman Catholics hold that the teaching office of the church "is not above the word of God, but serves it, teaching only what has been handed on, listening to it devoutly, guarding it scrupulously, and explaining it faithfully by divine commission and with the help of the Holy Spirit" (DV, no. 10).

26. Pentecostals appreciate the work of interpretation of Scripture going on in the Catholic Church; however, they look with skepticism on any claim that the whole body of faithful cannot err in matters of belief. Pentecostals also believe that God has given special gifts of teaching to the believing community (1 Cor 12:28; Eph 4:12). But, because Pentecostals hold that Scripture is clear in all essential points, they believe that each Christian can interpret Scripture under the guidance

of the Spirit and with the help of the discerning Christian community. Thus, Christians can make responsible judgments for themselves in matters of faith and practice through their use of Scripture.

27. Roman Catholics encourage Pentecostals to develop greater contact with the wider Christian community's historical interpretation and biblical hermeneutics. Both Roman Catholics and Pentecostals are together growing in respect for the exegetical endeavor and its enriching findings.

28. Since the beginning of this century, Roman Catholics have been according a greater place to Scripture in preaching, liturgy, personal reading, and prayer. Pentecostals in recent years have come to appreciate the importance of the faithful teachers of the word of God through church history. The aspiration of all parties in the dialogue is that, under the guidance of the one Holy Spirit, there will be an increasingly common insight into the meaning of Scripture, which would help overcome the divisions between Christians.

II. The Holy Spirit and the New Testament Vision of *Koinonia*

A. *Koinonia* with the Triune God

29. Both Pentecostals and Roman Catholics believe that the *koinonia* between Christians is rooted in the life of Father, Son, and Holy Spirit.[6] Furthermore, they believe that this trinitarian life is the highest expression of the unity to which we together aspire: "that which we have seen and heard we proclaim also to you, so that you may have fellowship with us; and our fellowship is with the Father and with his Son Jesus Christ"(1 Jn 1:3).

30. Both Roman Catholics and Pentecostals agree that the Holy Spirit is the source of *koinonia*, or communion. The church has been gathered in the Holy Spirit (cf. 2 Cor 13:13). They differ, however, in their points of departure and in their emphases.

31. Roman Catholics, on the one hand, stress the God-givenness of the *koinonia* and its trinitarian character. Their point of departure is the baptismal initiation into the trinitarian *koinonia* by faith, through Christ in his Spirit. Their emphasis is also on the Spirit-given means to sustain this *koinonia* (e.g., word, ministry, sacraments, charisma).

32. Pentecostals, on the other hand, stress that the Holy Spirit convicts people of sin, bringing them through repentance and personal faith into fellowship with Christ and one another (cf. 1 Cor 1:9). As believers continue to be filled with the Spirit (cf. Eph 5:18), they should be led to seek greater unity in the faith with other Christians. The Holy Spirit is the Spirit of unity (cf. Acts 2:1ff.). Just as the Spirit

fell on Gentiles and showed the church to be a universal community, made of both Jews and Gentiles (cf. Acts 10), so also today God is bestowing his Spirit everywhere on Christians from different churches, promoting unity around our common Lord. The common experience of the Holy Spirit challenges us to strive for greater visible unity as we reflect on the shape God wants this unity to take.

33. Our dialogue has helped both partners to discover and appreciate each other's specific emphases. On the one hand, by listening to the Roman Catholic participants, Pentecostals have been reminded of the importance of the communitarian dimension of the New Testament understanding of *koinonia*. Roman Catholics, on the other hand, have been reminded of the importance of the personal dimension of the same *koinonia* with God which comes from the Holy Spirit who convicts persons of sin and brings them to faith in Jesus Christ. We believe that these two emphases are not mutually exclusive but rather that they are complementary.

B. Oneness of the Church

34. Roman Catholics and Pentecostals believe that there is only "one holy catholic apostolic church" made of all believers (cf. Eph 4:4-6). They differ, however, in their understanding of that one church and of the way one belongs to it. Roman Catholics consider the establishment of denominations which result from the lack of love and/or divergence in matters of faith as departures away from the unity of the one church, which in fulfillment of the command of the Lord always remains visibly one and subsists in the Roman Catholic Church (LG, no. 8). Pentecostals tend to view denominations as more or less legitimate manifestations of the one universal church. Their legitimacy depends on the degree of their faithfulness to the fundamental doctrines of the Scripture. We both agree that the Holy Spirit is the Spirit of unity in diversity (cf. 1 Cor 12:13ff.) and not the Spirit of division.

35. By appealing to Jesus' teaching on the wheat and tares (Mt 13:24-30), some Christians distinguish between an invisible church (which is one) and a visible church (which may be divided). While this distinction can be of use in distinguishing between sincere and insincere members of the church, it can cause misunderstanding, since both Pentecostals and Roman Catholics affirm that the church is both a visible and an invisible reality. Neither should the distinction between visible and invisible dimensions of the church be used to justify and reinforce separation between Christians.

36. The essential unity of the church neither implies nor mandates uniformity. "For just as the body is one and has many members, and all the members of the body, though many, are one body, so it is with Christ" (1 Cor 12:12). The diversity is due to the Spirit. "Now there are varieties of gifts, but the same Spirit; and there are varieties of service, but the same Lord; and there are varieties of working, but it

is the same God who inspires them all in every one. To each is given the manifestation of the Spirit for the common good" (1 Cor 12:4-7). The unity which the Spirit forges is resplendent with diversity. The basis of this unity is the lordship of Jesus Christ. No one can confess this lordship except in the Holy Spirit (cf. 1 Cor 12:3). The unity which the Spirit gives must not be identified simply with likemindedness, sociological compatibility, or the felt need for togetherness.

C. *Koinonia* and Gospel Witness

37. The present state of visible separation in Christianity is a contradiction of the unity into which we are called by Christ. Fidelity to the concept of *koinonia* places upon all Christians the obligation of striving to overcome our divisions, especially through dialogue. We need to discern alertly, and in an ongoing way, the character and shape of the visible unity demanded by *koinonia*.

38. Roman Catholics and Pentecostals lament the scandal of disunity between Christians. The lack of agreement on how *koinonia* should be lived out in the church, and our resulting divisions, cloud the world's perception of God's work of reconciliation. Insofar as *koinonia* is obscured, the effectiveness of the witness is impaired. For the sake of giving an effective gospel witness, the issue of Christian unity must be kept before us. For our Lord has prayed for his disciples "that they may all be one; even as thou Father, art in me, and I in thee, that they also may be in us, so that the world may believe that thou has sent me" (Jn 17:21; cf. Jn 13:34).

III. *Koinonia* and Baptism[7]

A. The Meaning of Baptism

39. Pentecostals and Roman Catholics agree that baptism is prefigured in Old Testament symbolism, e.g., in the salvation of Noah and his family (cf. 1 Pt 3:20-21); the Exodus through the Red Sea (cf. 1 Cor 10:1-5); washing as a symbol of the cleansing power of the Holy Spirit (cf. Ez 36:25).

40. They further agree that baptism was instituted by Christ, and that he commanded his disciples to go "and make disciples of all nations, baptizing them in the name of the Father and of the Son and of the Holy Spirit" (Mt 28:19). In accordance with the Lord's commission, his disciples baptized those who were added to the fellowship of believers (cf. Acts 2:41).

41. Pentecostals and Roman Catholics differ in that Roman Catholics understand baptism to be a sacrament, while most Pentecostals understand it in terms of an ordinance (i.e., a rite that the Lord has commanded his church to perform). Some Pentecostals, however, do use the term sacrament to describe baptism. These

differences illustrate the need for further discussion between Roman Catholics and Pentecostals on the meaning of the terms "sacrament" and "ordinance."

42. Most Pentecostals hold that believers' baptism is clearly taught in Scripture (cf. Mk 16:16; Acts 2:38; 8:12, 36-39; 10:34-48) and, therefore, believe that baptism of infants should not be practiced. Roman Catholics admit that there is no incontrovertible evidence for baptism of infants in the New Testament, although some texts (notably the so-called household baptism texts, e.g., Acts 16:15 and 16:31-33) are understood as having a reference in that direction. Roman Catholics note, however, that through a process of discernment during the early centuries of the church, a development took place in which infant baptism became widely practiced within the church; was seen as being of apostolic origin; was approved by many of the fathers of the church; and was received by the church as authentic.

B. Faith and Baptism

43. Pentecostals and Roman Catholics agree that faith precedes and is a precondition of baptism (cf. Mk 16:16) and that faith is necessary for baptism to be authentic. They also agree that the faith of the believing community, its prayer, its instruction, nurture the faith of the candidate.

44. Roman Catholics believe that the faith of an infant is a covenant gift of God given in the grace of baptism, cleansing the child from original sin, and introducing it to new life in the body of Christ. Infant baptism is the beginning of a process towards full maturity of faith in the life of the Spirit, which is nurtured by the believing community.

45. The majority of Pentecostals practice believers' baptism exclusively, rather than infant baptism. They affirm that faith is the gift of God (cf. Eph 2:8), but at the same time stress that it is essentially a personal response of an individual. The Scripture says: "If you confess with your lips that Jesus is Lord and believe in your heart that God raised him from the dead, you will be saved" (Rom 10:9). Because they believe that faith must be personally expressed, Pentecostals maintain that an infant cannot receive the impartation of faith unto salvation (Eph 2:8) or the Holy Spirit. And because they believe that a conscious faith response to the proclamation of the Gospel on the part of the candidate is a necessary precondition for baptism, they do not baptize infants.

46. The general refusal of the Pentecostals to practice infant baptism notwithstanding, Roman Catholics and Pentecostals affirm that the grace of God is operative in the life of an infant. It is God who takes initiative for our salvation, and God does so not only in the life of adults but also in the life of infants. Scripture tells us, for instance, that John the Baptist was filled with the Holy Spirit from his mother's womb (cf. Lk 1:15; cf. also Jer 1:5).

47. Pentecostals and Roman Catholics differ over when one "comes to Christ" and about the significance of baptism itself. For all Pentecostals, there is no coming to Christ apart from a person's turning away from sin in repentance and toward God in faith (cf. 1 Thes 1:9), through which they become a part of the believing community. Baptism is withheld until after a person's conscious conversion. Most Pentecostals regard the act of baptism as a visible symbol of regeneration. Other Pentecostals have a sacramental understanding of baptism.

48. Roman Catholics describe conversion as a process incorporating the individual in the church by baptism. Even in infant baptism, a later personal appropriation or acceptance of one's baptism is an absolute necessity.

49. Roman Catholics and Pentecostals agree that a deep personal relationship to Christ is essential to Christian life. They also see how conversion is not only a personal or individual act, but an act that presupposes a proclaiming community before conversion and requires a nurturing community for growth after conversion. Further discussion is needed, however, on the nature of faith, the sense in which faith precedes baptism, and the meaning of corporate faith in Roman Catholic teaching. What is the nature of the gift of faith given to the infant born into the covenant community by baptism?

50. In the Roman Catholic understanding, one is incorporated into the death and resurrection of Christ through baptism, thereby also entering into the *koinonia* of those saved by Christ. Pentecostals affirm a relationship between baptism and incorporation into the death and resurrection of Christ (Rom 6:3ff.). Even if Pentecostals do not consider baptism, which makes possible incorporation into the *koinonia*, as a sacrament, most of them would not see baptism as an empty church ritual. It serves to strengthen the faith of those who have repented and believed in Christ through the Holy Spirit. Often a person will have a deep spiritual experience at baptism (manifested sometimes, for instance, by speaking in tongues). Provided that the person who is being baptized has experienced conversion, some Pentecostals would even speak of baptism as a "means of grace." Without denying the salvation of the unbaptized, all Pentecostals would consider baptism to be an integral part of the whole experience of becoming Christian.

51. Roman Catholics and Pentecostals agree that faith is indispensable to salvation. Pentecostals disagree with the Roman Catholic teaching that baptism is a constitutive means of salvation accomplished by the life, death, and resurrection of Christ. Nevertheless, Pentecostals do feel the need to investigate further the relationship between baptism and salvation in light of specific passages which appear to make a direct link between baptism and salvation (e.g., Jn 3:5; Mk 16:16; Acts 22:16; 1 Pt 3:21). Further discussion is also needed on the effect of baptism.

C. Baptism and the Church

52. For Roman Catholics, baptism is the sacrament of entry into the church, the koinonia of those saved in Christ and incorporated into his death and resurrection. For Pentecostals, baptism publicly demonstrates their personal identification with the death and resurrection of Christ (cf. Rom 6:3ff.) and their incorporation into the body of Christ. In keeping with the long tradition of the catechumenate, some Pentecostals believe that baptism is a precondition for full church membership to the extent that unbaptized converts are not, strictly speaking, called "brothers and sisters in Christ" but "friends."

53. For both Roman Catholics and Pentecostals, the believing community is important in the preparation for baptism, in the celebration of baptism, and in nurturing the faith of the one baptized. It is essential for the newly baptized believer to continue to grow in faith and love and to participate in the full life of the church.

54. For the Roman Catholic Church, the basis of ecumenical dialogue with Pentecostals, properly speaking, is found in the Catholic recognition of the baptism performed by Pentecostals in the name of the Father, Son, and Holy Spirit. This implies a common faith in the Lord Jesus Christ. This recognition by Roman Catholics of Pentecostal baptism means, in consequence, that Roman Catholics believe that they share with Pentecostals a certain, though imperfect, koinonia (cf. UR, no. 3). The unity of baptism constitutes and requires the unity of the baptized (cf. UR, no. 22). Our agreement on the trinitarian basis of baptism draws and impels us to unity.

55. Pentecostals do not see the unity between Christians as being based in a common water baptism, mainly because they believe that the New Testament does not base it in baptism. Instead, the foundation of unity is a common faith and experience of Jesus Christ as Lord and Savior through the Holy Spirit. This implies that to the extent that Pentecostals recognize that Roman Catholics have this common faith in and experience of Jesus as Lord, they share a real though imperfect koinonia with them. "For just as the body is one and has many members, and all the members of the body, though many, are one body, so it is with Christ. For by one Spirit we were all baptized into one body—Jews or Greeks, slaves or free—and all were made to drink of one Spirit" (1 Cor 12:12, a passage Pentecostals tend to interpret as not referring to water baptism). Insofar as baptism is related to this experience of Christ through the Spirit, it is also significant for the question of unity between Christians.

D. Baptismal Practice

56. Roman Catholics and most Pentecostals agree that a person is to be baptized in water in the name of the Father, Son, and Holy Spirit. Roman Catholics and

most Pentecostals disagree with those Pentecostals who do not baptize according to the trinitarian formula, especially if in baptizing only in Jesus' name (e.g., Acts 2:38) they deny the orthodox understanding of the Trinity.[8]

57. Baptism by immersion is the most effective visible sign to convey the meaning of baptism. Most Pentecostals hold that immersion in water is the only biblical way to baptize. Roman Catholics permit immersion and pouring as legitimate modes of baptism.

58. Pentecostals and Roman Catholics agree that baptism, when it is discerned as properly administered, is not to be repeated.

59. In addition to theological difficulties, Pentecostals perceive certain pastoral difficulties with the practice of infant baptism. These difficulties commonly associated with the practice of infant baptism are significant enough for Pentecostals to suggest that Roman Catholics continue to examine this practice.

60. Roman Catholics freely acknowledge the possible pastoral difficulties (e.g., creation of a body of baptized but unchurched people) inherent in the misuse of the practice of infant baptism. But infant baptism often provides a pastoral opportunity to help those parents weak in faith and practice and is the beginning of a whole process of Christian life for the child. "Conversion" in this sense becomes a series of grace-events throughout life, resulting in a commitment equally as firm as that stemming from a sudden conversion in adulthood.

61. Roman Catholics point out that there is a new emphasis upon adult initiation among Roman Catholics in the post-Vatican II rites, without denying the value of infant baptism. Indeed, because adult baptism is now expressed as the primary theological model, the theology and practice of infant baptism is itself enriched. Not only is faith given to the infant through the sacrament, but the parents themselves are fortified as the ones responsible for the infant's future growth, and so are caught up in the grace-giving event, frequently having their own faith strengthened.

62. Roman Catholics and Pentecostals agree that instruction in the faith necessarily follows upon baptism in order that the life of grace may come to fruition. In this connection a pastor should delay or refuse to baptize an infant if the parents (or guardians) clearly have no intention of bringing up the infant in the practice of faith. To baptize under those circumstances would be to act in a manner contrary to the canon law of the Roman Catholic Church.

63. There are some parallels between the Roman Catholic practice of infant baptism and the common practice of infant dedication in Pentecostal churches in terms of the activity of grace and the role of the Christian community in the life of an infant. In infant dedication, as in infant baptism, the parents of the infant and the believing community publicly covenant together with God to bring the infant up so that he or she will come into a personal relationship with Christ. Though Pentecostals do not believe that dedication mediates salvation to an infant or makes

him/her a member of the Christian Church, they do believe that because of the prayer and the faith of the believing community, a blessing of God rests upon the dedicated infant. Both practices acknowledge in their own way the presence of the grace of God in the infant and are concerned with creating an atmosphere in which the child may grow in the grace and knowledge of the Lord Jesus Christ.

E. Baptism and the Experience of the Spirit

64. Roman Catholics and Pentecostals agree that all of those who belong to Christ "were made to drink of one Spirit" (1 Cor 12:13). We agree that God intends that each follower of Jesus enjoy the indwelling of the Holy Spirit (Rom 8:9). This indwelling of the Spirit is not the fruit or product of human works, but is due to the unmerited, efficacious action of grace by which each person responds to the special initiative of God.

65. We acknowledge that Roman Catholics and Pentecostals have different understandings of the role of the Spirit in Christian initiation and life, but may nonetheless enjoy a similar experience of the Spirit. Our experience of the Holy Spirit, furthermore, heightens our mutual awareness of the need for unity.

66. We agree that the experience of the Holy Spirit belongs to the life of the church. Wherever the Spirit is genuinely present in the Christian community, its fruit will also become evident (cf. Gal 5:22-23). Genuine charismata mentioned in Scripture (e.g. 1 Cor 12:8-10, 28-30; Rom 12:6-8; etc.) also indicate the presence of the Spirit. All such manifestations, however, call for discernment by the community (cf. 1 Thes 5:19-22; 1 Cor 14; 1 Jn 4).

67. Generally, Roman Catholics have tended to be cautious about accepting the more spectacular manifestations of the Spirit such as speaking in tongues and prophecy, although the charismatic renewal has helped them to rediscover ways in which such gifts are rooted in their oldest tradition. Roman Catholics fear that Pentecostals limit the Spirit to specific manifestations. Pentecostals fear that Roman Catholics confine the Spirit's workings to sacraments and church order. Therefore, we share a mutual concern not to confine or to limit the Holy Spirit whom Jesus described by the imagery of the freely blowing wind (cf. Jn 3:8). Each of us seems more worried about the other limiting the Spirit than ourselves. Still, we have learned through our discussions together that there is greater freedom for the Holy Spirit in both of our traditions than we expected to find, and our fears, once shared, have made us more aware of our shortcomings in this regard.

69. Our discussions, too, have made us more aware about the ways in which we use language related to the Holy Spirit. We agree that such ideas as what it means to be "baptized in the Spirit" or "filled with the Spirit" would be fruitful fields for mutual exploration.

IV. *Koinonia* in the Life of the Church

A. *Koinonia* in the Life of God

70. Both Pentecostals and Roman Catholics recognize that believers have a share in the eternal life which is *koinonia* with the Father and with his Son Jesus Christ (cf. 1 Jn 1:2-3), and a communion in the Holy Spirit whom God's Son, Jesus Christ, has given to them (cf. 1 Jn 3:24; 2 Cor 13:14). This, the deepest meaning of *koinonia*, is actualized at various levels. Those who believe and have been baptized into Christ's death (cf. Mk 16:16; Rom 6:3-4) have *koinonia* in his sufferings and become like him in his death and resurrection (cf. Phil 3:10). The next step is the eucharist or the Lord's Supper. "The cup of blessing which we bless, is it not a participation [*koinonia*] in the blood of Christ? The bread which we break, is it not a participation [*koinonia*] in the body of Christ?" (1 Cor 10:16). All believers, furthermore, who have *koinonia* in the eternal life of Father, Son, and Holy Spirit, and who have *koinonia* in Christ's death and resurrection are bound together in a *koinonia* too deep for words. We look forward to the day when we will also have *koinonia* in his body and blood (1 Cor 10:16).

71. While both Roman Catholics and Pentecostals teach the indwelling of the Father, Son, and the Holy Spirit in the believer (cf. Jn 17:21; Rom 8:9), the emphasis on the indwelling of the Trinity in believers is more explicitly articulated in the Roman Catholic faith than in that of the Pentecostals. The nature of the language used to describe it is in need of further exploration together.

72. Together with Roman Catholics, most Pentecostals have a strong commitment to the trinitarian understanding of God. They believe, for instance, that at baptism the trinitarian formula should be used because of Jesus' mandate: "Go therefore and make disciples of all nations, baptizing them in the name of the Father, and of the Son, and of the Holy Spirit" (Mt 28:19).[9] The Pentecostals do, however, feel challenged by Roman Catholics to develop all the implications for faith and piety which their full trinitarian commitment implies.

B. Church as *Koinonia*

73. The importance of an active response to the gifts of God in the service of *koinonia* requires mutuality in its many dimensions. Some of these dimensions are the assumption and sharing of responsibility, and a fuller participation in the life of the local congregation. When church members of whatever rank act arbitrarily without taking into account this sharing, their actions obscure the expression of communion. For Roman Catholics and Pentecostals, *koinonia* in the church is a dynamic concept, implying a dialogical structure of both God-givenness and human

response. Mutuality has to exist on every level of the church, its source being the continuing presence of the Holy Spirit.

74. Roman Catholics must often confess to a lack of mutuality at the local and universal levels, even though mutuality is recognized as a criterion for fellowship. Difficulties surrounding lay participation in decision making processes and the lack of sufficient involvement of women in leadership were examples cited by participants in this dialogue. Roman Catholics, however, would insist that order and hierarchy do not in themselves imply such a defect in mutuality.

75. At the same time, Pentecostals acknowledge both the reluctance that many of their members have in submitting to ecclesial authority and the difficulty which their charismatic leaders have in working through existing ecclesial institutional channels which could protect them from acting irresponsibly or in an authoritarian manner.

76. The difficulties of some Pentecostals with their ecclesial institutions stem in part from frequent emphasis on their direct relation to the Spirit. They forget that the Spirit is given not only to individual Christians, but also to the whole community. An individual Christian is not the only "temple of the Holy Spirit" (1 Cor 6:19). Roman Catholics have rightly challenged Pentecostals to think of the whole community, too, as a "temple of God" in which the Spirit dwells (1 Cor 3:16). If Pentecostals were to take the indwelling of the Spirit in the community more seriously, they would be less inclined to follow the personal "leadings of the Spirit" in disregard of the community. Rather they would strive to imitate the apostles who, at the first church council, justified their decision with the following words: ". . . it has seemed good to the Holy Spirit and to us . . ." (Acts 15:28).

77. In their theology, both Pentecostals and Roman Catholics see themselves standing in a dependent relationship to the Spirit. They acknowledge the need to invoke the Holy Spirit. In accordance with this invocation, they believe in the presence of God whenever two or three are gathered in Christ's name (cf. Mt 18:20).

78. Pentecostals recognize that while there is an emphasis on holiness in the Roman Catholic Church, they observe that it seems possible for some Roman Catholics to live continuously in a state of sin and yet be considered members in the church. This seems to the Pentecostals to undermine the concept of Christian discipleship. Though they are mindful of John's words that if "we say we have not sinned, we make him [God] a liar" (1 Jn 1:10), Pentecostals want to take seriously the warning of the same apostle concerning the unrepentant sinner, namely that "no one who sins has either seen him [the Father] or known him" (1 Jn 3:6).

79. Roman Catholics wonder how Pentecostals deal with the sins of their own members. Do they have an adequate tradition of bringing those who have fallen into sin into a process of repentance and a sense of God's forgiveness? Without such

a tradition how can they avoid harshness when a sinner fails to live up to the congregation's ideal of holiness?

80. Both bodies would do well to recall the scriptural warnings that we must try to see the log in our own eye rather than the speck in our brother's or sister's eye (cf. Mt 7:4). We should reflect, too, on the Lord's caution against trying to have a wheat field from which all tares have been removed (cf. Mt 13:24ff.).

C. *Koinonia,* Sacraments, and Church Order

81. Roman Catholics hold that a basic aspect of *koinonia* between local churches is expressed in the celebration of the sacraments of initiation, namely, by the same baptism, the same confirmation, the same eucharist. Moreover, the celebration of these sacraments requires ordained ministers to preside,[10] ordination being also a sacrament, i.e., an act of Christ in the Spirit celebrated in the communion and for the communion of the church. Furthermore, according to the Catholic tradition, only ordained ministers—principally the bishop—can preside over a local church or diocese.

82. According to Catholic understanding, *koinonia* is rooted in the bonds of faith and sacramental life shared by congregations united in dioceses pastored by bishops. Through their bishops, the local churches are in communion with one another by reason of the common faith, the common sacramental life, and the common episcopacy. Among the fellowship of bishops, the bishop of Rome is recognized as the successor of Peter and presides over the whole Catholic communion. Through their day-to-day teaching, and more specifically through local and universal councils, bishops have responsibility to articulate clearly the faith and discipline of the church. Church order is thus grounded in the *koinonia* of faith and the sacraments; church order is at the same time an active expression of *koinonia*.

83. Roman Catholics hold that some existing ecclesiastical structures (such as the office of a bishop) are "God given," and that they belong to the very essence of church order, rather than serving only its well being.

84. While Pentecostals disagree among themselves concerning how the church should best be ordered (the views range from congregational to episcopal), they accept the full ecclesial status of the churches ordered in various ways. Observing the diversity of the church structures in the New Testament, they believe that the contemporary church should not be narrower in its understanding of the church order than the sacred Scriptures themselves.

85. Although Pentecostals do not limit celebration of the sacraments and leadership in the church to the ordained ministers, they do recognize the need for and the value of ordination for the life of the church. Pentecostals do not consider ordination to be a sacrament. Ordinarily Pentecostals recognize that a charism of

teacher/pastor is recognized or can be given to a person at the laying on of hands, but they do not consider that at ordination the power of the Holy Spirit is bestowed to the person being ordained. Instead, ordination is a public acknowledgment of a God-given charism which a person has received prior to the act of ordination.

86. Some Pentecostals observe what appears to be a "mechanical" or "magical" understanding of the sacraments, especially among Roman Catholic laity, and do not accept the grace-conveying role of the sacraments distinct from their function as a visible word of God. Roman Catholic theology, however, maintains that the sacraments are not "mechanical" or "magical," since they require openness and faith on the part of the recipient. In Catholic understanding, the grace of the sacraments is not bestowed automatically or unconditionally, irrespective of the dispositions of the recipient. What Paul says in 1 Cor 11:27 ("profaning the body and blood of the Lord") is common teaching in the Roman Catholic Church. Sacramental actions can produce "shriveled fruit," as Augustine describes it, when the recipients are not in right relation to the Lord. Furthermore, the efficacy of the sacraments is not dependent upon the personal piety of those who minister them, but rather is ultimately dependent upon the grace of God.

87. Pentecostals believe that church order demanded by *koinonia* is not satisfactorily expressed in some important aspects of Roman Catholic ecclesiology. Even within the context of collegiality, examples which seem to bear this out include those passages where it is stated that "the episcopal order is the subject of this supreme and full power over the universal church," and even more importantly, when it is stated that "the Roman Pontiff has full, supreme, and universal power over the church" which "he can always exercise . . . freely" (LG, no. 22). On the whole, Pentecostals propose that presbyterial and/or congregational ecclesial models express better the mutuality or reciprocity demanded by *koinonia*.

88. Roman Catholics are more inclined to see the Spirit operating through certain ecclesial structures, although Pentecostals, too, recognize that the Spirit may work through ecclesial structures and processes.

89. Both Roman Catholics and Pentecostals are troubled by the discrepancy between the theology and the practice of their own parishes or congregations.

D. The Church and Salvation

90. According to Roman Catholic ecclesiology, the church can be considered both a sign and an instrument of God's work in the world. This formulation from the nineteenth century is still very useful for understanding the role of the church in the world.

91. The church is a sign of the presence of God's saving power in the world. It is also a sign of the eschatological unity to which all peoples are called by God. It

is to be this sign both through its individual members and its gathered communities. Insofar as Christians are divided from one another, they are a countersign, a sign of contradiction to God's reconciling purpose in the world.

92. The church is also an instrument of God for announcing the saving news of grace and the coming of God's kingdom. The church is God's instrument in making disciples of all nations preaching the good news of Jesus' life, death, and resurrection and baptizing them (cf. Mt 28:19).

93. In recent years, Roman Catholics have come to describe the church as "a kind of a sacrament" (LG, no. 1). This new insight is consistent with its past understanding of the sacraments as signs and instruments of God's saving power.

94. Though Pentecostals do not accept the Roman Catholic understanding of sacraments and the Roman Catholic view of the church as "a kind of sacrament," in their own way they do affirm that the church is both a sign and an instrument of salvation. As the new people of God, the church is called both to reflect the reality of God's eschatological kingdom in history and to announce its coming into the world, insofar as people open their lives to the in-breaking of the Holy Spirit. In Pentecostal understanding, the church as a community is an instrument of salvation in the same sense in which each one of its members is both a sign and instrument of salvation. In their own way, both the community as a whole and the individual members that comprise it give witness to God's redeeming grace.

V. *Koinonia* and the Communion of the Saints

A. The Church as *Communio Sanctorum*

95. God calls us into communion with himself (*communio* with the Holy One), into communion in the body and blood of Christ (*communio in sanctis*), and into communion between Christians (fellowship of the saints: *communio sanctorum*). In the Nicene Creed, the phrase *communio sanctorum* has eschatological significance: the saints on earth and those in heaven, marked by the same Spirit, are a single body.

96. In terms of the sharing in holy things (*communio in sanctis*), for Roman Catholics participation in baptism, confirmation, and eucharist is constitutive of the church. For Pentecostals, the central element of worship is the preaching of the word. As persons respond to the proclamation of the word, the Spirit gives them new birth, which is a presacramental experience, thereby making them Christians and in this sense creating the church. Of secondary importance are participation in baptism and the Lord's Supper, spontaneous exercise of the charismata, and the sharing of personal testimonies.

97. Pentecostals would like Catholics to share more among themselves the private devotional reading of the Scriptures. Pentecostals ask Roman Catholics whether they could not deepen the experiential dimension of *koinonia* through spontaneous exercise of the gifts and the sharing of personal testimonies. Convinced that word and sacrament cannot be separated in worship, Catholics ask Pentecostals to reexamine the dynamic relationship between these two in the celebration of baptism and the Lord's Supper.

98. The relation between *koinonia,* sacraments, and church order (see above, nos. 81-89) explains why both the sharing in the same eucharistic faith and also in full communion are normal prerequisites for receiving the eucharist in the Roman Catholic Church. Since for Catholics the eucharist is essential and central in the life of the church, participation in the eucharist means and requires unity of faith. Catholics would like to see Pentecostals express clearly what is required for full communion in their churches.

99. According to the Roman Catholic view, the *communio sanctorum* includes a relationship to all the holy ones of God, the saints on earth and also the saints in heaven. Members of the church are given *koinonia* in the very holiness of God. As a result, they form "a great cloud of witnesses" (Heb 12:1), a "great multitude which no man could number, from every nation, from all tribes and peoples and tongues" (Rv 7:9).

100. In Roman Catholic faith and practice, God alone is the object of worship *(latria)*. However, veneration *(doulia)* is given to saints who have "run the race," "finished the course," and have received "a crown of life." It is also important to realize that no Catholic has an obligation *jure divino* of venerating either relics, icons, or saints. While this kind of devotion is not necessary for salvation, the church recognizes the usefulness of such forms of devotion, recommends them to its members, and resists any condemnation or contempt of such practices (cf. Council of Trent, Session 25).

101. Pentecostals find reassuring the stress in Roman Catholic theology that worship belongs only to God. It is, however, the Pentecostal teaching that the unique mediatorial role of Christ positively excludes veneration of relics, icons, and saints. Pentecostals do, however, affirm that in their worship the earthly saints join in worship with saints in heaven and with them comprise the one, holy, catholic, and apostolic church. As the Scripture says: "we are surrounded by so great a cloud of witnesses" (Heb 12:1) who have lived in history from the beginning of God's dealing with the human race.

B. Holiness, Repentance, and Ministry in History

102. All the baptized are called to be "saints," and indeed, according to Scripture, they called themselves such in the early church (e.g., Acts 9:13; 26:10; Rom 15:25-26; 2 Cor 8:4; 9:1; etc.).

103. We agree that because of sin, the church is always in need of repentance. It is at once holy and in need of purification. The church is a "holy penitent," and is ever in need of renewal both in its persons and in its structures. Both Catholics and Pentecostals recognize the fact that their respective theologies of *koinonia* are all too seldom reflected in the empirical reality of the life in their respective communities.

104. Both sides of this dialogue agree on the fundamental demands for holiness in the minister and agree that the unworthiness of a minister does not invalidate the work of the Holy Spirit. For Roman Catholics, God's acts in the sacraments are effective because they are based on God's faithfulness. They believe that the Holy Spirit works with consistency in ministering to those who come in faith. The church gives serious attention to church discipline because human weakness and sin can become obstacles to the effectiveness of ministry. Pentecostals, too, believe that God can work through the ministers of the word of God in spite of their grave failures and sin in their lives. "Some indeed preach Christ from envy and rivalry, but others from good will . . . What then? Only that in every way, whether in presence or in truth, Christ is proclaimed: in that I rejoice" (Phil 1:15, 18). Pentecostals also believe that the ordinances administered by an unworthy minister are valid (in the sense that, for instance, baptism need not be repeated). Together we believe, however, that the unworthiness of ministers is often a stumbling block that prevents nonbelievers from coming to faith in a true and living God, and it frequently hinders the work of the Spirit in the believing community.

105. Although Pentecostals stress the freedom of the Spirit to act in the community and emphasize the need for active participation of all members of the church, they do acknowledge the necessity of church order. They affirm church order (which can legitimately take different forms) as the will of the Lord for his church, since they observe from the New Testament that the earliest church has not "been without persons holding specific authority and responsibility" (BEM, Ministry, 9) (cf. Acts 14:23; 20:17; Phil 1:1). Since Pentecostals do not reject ecclesial institutions, they recognize that the Spirit operates not only through charismatic individuals, but also through the permanent ministries of the church.

106. There is agreement that the offices and structures of the church, as indeed every aspect of the church, are in a continual need of renewal insofar as they are institutions of men and women here on earth. This presumes that the Spirit can breathe new life into the church's offices and structures when these become "dry bones" (Ez 37). This ongoing effort at renewal has important ecumenical implica-

tions. This is an essential dynamism of "the movement toward unity" of the people of God (UR, no. 6).

107. Pentecostals and Roman Catholics appear to view the history of the church quite differently. The members of this dialogue believe that the differences in these perspectives deserve further mutual exploration. Both Pentecostals and Roman Catholics recognize that continuity in history by itself is no guarantee of spiritual maturity or of doctrinal soundness. Increasingly, both traditions are coming to share a genuine appreciation for the value that church history reveals to them today.

108. Roman Catholics believe that the contemporary church is in continuity with the church in the New Testament. Pentecostals, influenced by restorationist perspectives, have claimed continuity with the church in the New Testament by arguing for discontinuity with much of the historical church. By adopting these two positions, one of continuity, the other of discontinuity, each tradition has attempted to demonstrate its faithfulness to the apostolic faith "once for all delivered to the saints" (Jude 3). The significance of this for the welfare of the whole church urges upon us the need of further common theological reflection on the history of the church.

Conclusion

109. It is hoped that this dialogue might inspire dialogues on national or local levels between Roman Catholics and classical Pentecostals. The participants recommend to their parent bodies that the dialogue continue into a fourth round of discussions.

110. The members of the dialogue during this quinquennium visited worship services representing both traditions. Learning was not confined only to the dialogue table, but also took place in local Catholic parishes and Pentecostal congregations visited during this series of discussions and at informal conversations between sessions.

111. We have explored the subject of *koinonia* and have been richly rewarded as together we affirmed the lordship of Jesus. We felt his pain as we understood our part in the ongoing brokenness of his body. Nonetheless, that we could spend day after day together sharing in great detail and depth our most dearly held Christian convictions, and come away closer to our Risen Lord and to each other, we understand is possible only by the grace and mercy of God.

112. The prayer of Jesus, "that they all may be one" (Jn 17:21) has become increasingly important to us, and the cause for much prayer and repentance still. Nevertheless, we are heartened by the realization that fresh winds of the Spirit are blowing in the church universal, and we are waiting expectantly to see what in the providence of God is yet to come. Our prayer continues to be "Come, Holy Spirit!"

Participants

Roman Catholic

*Rev. Raniero Cantalamessa, OFMCap, Milano, Italy (1987-1989)
*Rev. John C. Haughey, SJ, Charlotte, North Carolina, USA (1985-1989)
*Prof. Hervé Legrand, OP, Paris, France (1985-1989)
s*Rev. Kilian McDonnell, OSB, Collegeville, Minnesota, USA (1985-1989)
   (cochair)
sMost Rev. Basil Meeking, Christchurch, New Zealand (1985-1986)
Prof. Heribert Mühlen, Paderbon, West Germany (1985-1986)
s*Msgr. John A. Radano, Vatican City (1985-1989) (cosecretary)
Rev. John Redford, Kent, England (1985-1989)
*Sr. Helen Rolfson, OSF, Collegeville, Minnesota, USA (1985-1989)

Classical Pentecostal

s*+Rev. Justus du Plessis, Apostolic Faith Mission, Faerie Glen, South Africa
   (1985-1989) (cochair)
sRev. David J. du Plessis, Assemblies of God, Pasadena, California, USA
   (1985–1986) (+1987) (cochair emeritus)
Dr. John L. Amstutz, International Church of the Foursquare Gospel, Los Angeles,
   California, USA (1986)
Rev. Mitchell Belobaba, International Church of the Foursquare Gospel,
   Vancouver, British Columbia, Canada (1985, 1987-1988)
°Rev. Rose Belobaba, International Church of the Foursquare Gospel, Vancouver,
   British Columbia, Canada (1985)
°Dr. Omar Cabrera, Vision de Futuro, Santa Fe, Argentina (1988)
°Mr. Dan Crotty, International Church of the Foursquare Gospel, Ventura,
   California, USA (1985)
°Rev. Edward Czajko, Pentecostal Church, Warsaw, Poland (1988)
°Rev. Olof Djurfeldt, Swedish Pentecostal Movement, Stockholm, Sweden (1986)
Dr. Hugh Edwards, Church of God of Prophecy, Cleveland, Tennessee, USA (1986-
   1988)
*Dr. Howard M. Ervin, American Baptist, Tulsa, Oklahoma, USA (1985-1989)
Dr. James A. Forbes, Original United Holy Church International, New York, New
   York, USA (1986)
Rev. Manuel J. Gaxiola-Gaxiola, Apostolic Church, Mexico City, Mexico (1986)
*Rev. Bernice Gerard, Pentecostal Assemblies of Canada, Vancouver, British
   Columbia, Canada (1986-1989)

Rev. Allan Hamilton, International Church of the Foursquare Gospel, Portland, Oregon, USA (1986)

Dr. James D. Jenkins, Church of God, Cleveland, Tennessee, USA (1985-1988)

Dr. Veroni Kruger, Apostolic Faith Mission, White River, South Africa (1986)

Dr. Peter Kuzmic, Christ's Pentecostal Church, Osijek, Yugoslavia (1985)

°Rev. Silvano Lilli, International Evangelical Church, Rome, Italy (1985)

°Rev. Alfred F. Missen, Assemblies of God, Birmingham, England (1985)

Dr. François Möller, Apostolic Faith Mission, Auckland Park, South Africa (1988)

Dr. Robert Mueller, Independent Assemblies of God International, El Toro, California, USA (1987)

Bishop Earl Paulk, International Communion of Charismatic Churches, Decatur, Georgia, USA (1986)

*Dr. Coleman Phillips, International Church of the Foursquare Gospel, Escondido, California, USA (1988-1989)

s*Dr. Cecil M. Robeck Jr., Assemblies of God, Pasadena, California, USA (1986-1989)

s*Dr. Jerry L. Sandidge, Assemblies of God, Springfield, Missouri, USA (1985-1989) (cosecretary)

°Dr. Vinson Synan, Pentecostal Holiness Church, Oklahoma City, Oklahoma, USA (1986)

°Dr. Del Tarr, Assemblies of God, Fresno, California, USA (1985-1987, 1989)

Rev. H. N. van Amerom, Broedershap van Pinkstengemeenten, Houten, The Netherlands (1987)

°Dr. Miroslav Volf, Christ's Pentecostal Church, Osijek, Yugoslavia (1985-1986, 1988-1989)

NOTES

1. Until 1989, the Pontifical Council was known as the Secretariat for Promoting Christian Unity.

2. At its Eighth General Assembly in February 1990, the Lutheran World Federation voted to change its constitution. It now describes itself as a "communion of churches."

3. Scripture quotations in this text are from the Revised Standard Version of the Bible copyrighted 1946, 1952, 1971, 1973 by the Division of Christian Education of the National Council of the Churches of Christ in the USA.

4. *Final Report* (1972-1976), Document 11 above, nos. 28-30; *Final Report* (1977-1982), Document 12 above, nos. 18-21, 49-57. These reports are published in *Information Service*, the Secretariat for Promoting Christian Unity, Vatican City, 32 (1976/III): 32-37 and 55 (1984/II-III): 72-80. The 1977-1982 reports are also published in Kilian McDonnell, ed., *Presence, Power, Praise* (Collegeville, Minn.: Liturgical Press, 1980), 3:373-395 and in Arnold Bittlinger, *Papst und Pfingstler* (Frankfurt am Main: Peter Lang, 1978). For the report of the 1977-1982 discussions, see Jerry L. Sandidge, *Roman Catholic Pentecostal Dialogue (1977-1982): A Study in Developing Ecumenism* (Frankfurt am Main: Peter Lang, 1987).

5. All quotations from the Second Vatican Council are from Walter M. Abbott, ed., *The Documents of Vatican II* (Piscataway, N.J.: New Century Publishers, Inc., 1966).

6. A segment of Pentecostals known as "Oneness" or "Jesus Name" Pentecostals are opposed to the trinitarian formulation of the faith. Their view of God tends toward modalism, and the baptismal formula which they pronounce is "in the name of Jesus Christ" (Acts 2:38), instead of the traditional trinitarian appeal to Matthew 28:19. Most Pentecostals, however, strongly disagree with this position.

7. We devote a special section to baptism because of the difficulty which baptism and the practice of baptism have in our dialogue.

8. See note 6.

9. See note 6.

10. This relationship between church order and ordained ministry presiding over a community is well illustrated in the celebration of water baptism, although in cases of necessity every Christian is requested to baptize. Until 1923 even the deacons were not allowed to be the ordinary ministers of baptism. Presently bishops retain for themselves the baptism of adults, and parish priests must have their bishop's permission to perform such a baptism.

11. The later distinction made between "fruitful" and "unfruitful""sacraments is another way by which the Roman Catholic teaching asserts the same understanding.

12. Only those who attended the dialogue in 1989 had a part in the drafting and editing of this final report. They are indicated with an asterisk (*). Steering committee members during this quinquennium are indicated with an s, observers with an o.

PART SEVEN

Evangelical–Roman Catholic

Introductory Note

✠ Basil Meeking

Probably most readers of this report will be struck by the comparative nature of much of what it contains. The notable theological divergences between the Evangelical and Roman Catholic participants were examined and discussed and stated with clarity but in a spirit of dialogue. It was a most useful method in view of the short duration of the project, and it probably makes the report of immediate use for particular local discussions.

It ought to be kept in mind also that the use of such a method illustrates an attitude that the participants shared. They saw dialogue as a common approach to revealed truth, not as a negotiation in order to reach agreement. Agreement could come only from unity in faith.

That should not obscure the amount of consensus that the report reflects and states. It is considerable; indeed, it begins with the consensus between Protestants and Catholics that existed at the time of the Reformation but that, in the polemical climate of that time, could not be easily recognized or stated. In the first place there were the three great mysteries: the Trinity, the incarnation, and the redemption.

Then there was the common christocentrism of the dialogue. For all participants, Jesus Christ is the eternal Son of the Father, consubstantial, cocreator of the world, Word of God. Incarnate of the Virgin Mary, he is true God and true man. He suffered and died to redeem us from sin and reconcile us with the Father. He rose again and will come to judge the living and the dead.

Of course, even within such an outline points of divergence began to arise. But it does represent a substantial theological consensus, which was also the basis of a common devotion to Jesus Christ that underwrote the whole dialogue and gave it a tangible spirit.

Here one has also to mention Dr. John Stott, who was the spiritual father of the group each time it met, giving it confidence and a sense of direction. Of course, in the first place it was his stature among Evangelicals that made it possible to bring together Evangelicals from a range of theological backgrounds and church affiliations. It was he who at crucial points kept the discussion on the level of faith so that it never degenerated into polemic.

This dialogue was a beginning. One hopes its fruits will have increasing effect for the mission of Christians in the world. It is a disappointment that as yet more does not seem to have been done with the report from either the Catholic or the Evangelical side. It is surely full of potential for future relationships. In 1993 a conversation was held with the World Evangelical Fellowship and the Pontifical Council for Promoting Christian Unity ("Justification, Scripture, and Tradition: World Evangelical Fellowship–Roman Catholic Dialogue," *Evangelical Review of Theology* 21:2 [April 1997]). A second conversation took place in October 1997.

The Evangelical-Roman Catholic Dialogue on Mission

1977-1984

Introduction

The Evangelical–Roman Catholic Dialogue on Mission (ERCDOM) was a series of three meetings which took place over a period of seven years. The first was held at Venice in 1977, the second at Cambridge in 1982, and the third at Landévennec in France in 1984.

1. The Participants

Those who took part in the dialogue were theologians and missiologists from many parts of the world. Their names are given [below]. Six of us (three from each side) attended all three meetings; others were able to come to only one or two of them.

The Evangelical participants were drawn from a number of churches and Christian organizations. They were not official representatives of any international body, however. For the evangelical movement has a broad spectrum, which includes evangelical denominations (both within and outside the World Council of

Churches), evangelical fellowships (within mainline, comprehensive denomina-tions), and evangelical parachurch agencies (specializing in tasks like Bible transla-tion, evangelism,[1] cross-cultural mission, and Third World relief and development), which accept different degrees of responsibility to the church.[2]

It is not easy to give a brief account of the distinctive beliefs of Evangelical Christians, since different churches and groups emphasize different doctrines. Yet all Evangelicals share a cluster of theological convictions which were recovered and reaffirmed by the sixteenth-century Reformers. These include (in addition to the great affirmations of the Nicene Creed) the inspiration and authority of the Bible, the sufficiency of its teaching for salvation, and its supremacy over the traditions of the church; the justification of sinners (i.e., their acceptance by God as righteous in his sight) on the sole ground of the sin-bearing—often called "substitutionary"—death of Jesus Christ, by God's free grace alone, apprehended by faith alone, without the addition of any human works; the inward work of the Holy Spirit to bring about the new birth and to transform the regenerate into the likeness of Christ; the neces-sity of personal repentance and faith in Christ ("conversion"); the church as the body of Christ, which incorporates all true believers, and all of whose members are called to ministry, some being "evangelists, pastors, and teachers"; the "priesthood of all believers," who (without any priestly mediation except Christ's) all enjoy equal access to God and all offer him their sacrifice of praise and worship; the urgency of the great commission to spread the Gospel throughout the world, both verbally in proclamation and visually in good works of love; and the expectation of the personal, visible, and glorious return of Jesus Christ to save, to reign, and to judge.

The Roman Catholic participants, who spoke from the point of view of the official teaching of their church, were named by the Vatican Secretariat for Promoting Christian Unity. The existence of the secretariat is evidence of the effec-tive renewal of attitude towards other Christians, which has taken place among Roman Catholics as a result of the Second Vatican Council twenty years ago and which is still having its effects. In that council it was acknowledged that "Christ sum-mons the Church, as she goes her pilgrim way, to that continual reformation of which she always has need, insofar as she is an institution of men here on earth."[3] As a result, Roman Catholics have been able to acknowledge joyfully "the riches of Christ and virtuous works in the lives of others who are bearing witness to Christ."[4] This same renewal turned the attention of Roman Catholics to the Scriptures in a new way, exhorting the church "to move ahead daily towards a deeper understanding of the Sacred Scriptures" which "contain the word of God and, since they are inspired, really are that word."[5] And it led to a better expression of the relation between Scripture and tradition in communicating God's word in its full purity. Here indeed are the elements which have enabled Roman Catholics to acknowledge common ground with other Christians, and to assume their own responsibility for overcoming divisions for the sake of the mission of God and the fullness of his glory.

2. The Background

It is the will of God that "all men be saved and come to the knowledge of the truth. For there is one God, and there is one mediator between God and men, the man Christ Jesus, who gave himself as a ransom for all" (1 Tm 2:4-5); "there is salvation in no one else" (Acts 4:12). Mission begins in the activity of God himself who sent his Son, and whose Son sent his Spirit. All who belong to God in Jesus Christ must share in this mission of God.

A dialogue on mission between Evangelicals and Roman Catholics has been possible for two reasons. First, both constituencies have recently been concentrating their attention on evangelism. In July 1974 the evangelical International Congress on World Evangelization took place in Switzerland and issued the *Lausanne Covenant*.[6] A few months later the Third General Assembly of the Roman Catholic Synod of Bishops studied the same topic, and at their request Pope Paul VI issued in December 1975 his apostolic exhortation entitled *Evangelii Nuntiandi*, or *Evangelization in the Modern World*.[7]

Secondly, a study of these two documents reveals a measure of convergence in our understanding of the nature of evangelism, as the following quotations show: "To evangelize is to spread the good news that Jesus Christ died for our sins and was raised from the dead according to the Scriptures. . . . Evangelism itself is the proclamation of the historical, biblical Christ as Savior and Lord."[8] Again, witness must be "made explicit by a clear and unequivocal proclamation of the Lord Jesus. There is no true evangelization if the name, the teaching, the life, the promises, the kingdom, and the mystery of Jesus of Nazareth, the Son of God, are not proclaimed."[9]

3. The Experience

In our time there are many possible forms of dialogue. Some are undertaken with an immediate view to working for organic unity between the bodies which the participants represent. Others do not exclude this purpose but begin from where they are with a more general purpose. Still others begin by stating that they do not envisage organic or structural unity but aim rather at an exchange of theological views in order to increase mutual understanding and to discover what theological ground they hold in common. ERCDOM has been a dialogue of the latter kind. It was not conceived as a step towards church unity negotiations. Rather it has been a search for such common ground as might be discovered between Evangelicals and Roman Catholics as they each try to be more faithful in their obedience to mission.

It was also undertaken quite consciously in the knowledge that there are still both disagreements and misrepresentations between Evangelicals and Roman Catholics which harm our witness to the Gospel, contradict our Lord's prayer for the unity of his followers, and need if possible to be overcome.

During the three meetings friendships were formed and mutual respect and understanding grew, as the participants learned to listen to one another and to grapple with difficult and divisive questions, as well as rejoicing in the discovery of some common understandings.

It was a demanding experience as well as a rewarding one. It was marked by a will to speak the truth, plainly, without equivocation, and in love. Neither compromise nor the quest for lowest common denominators had a place; a patient search for truth and a respect for each other's integrity did.

4. The Report

This report is in no sense an "agreed statement," but rather a faithful record of the ideas shared. It is not exhaustive, for more questions were touched on than could be described in this brief compass. Yet enough has been included to give a substantial idea of how the dialogue developed and to communicate something of it without creating misunderstandings or false expectations.

An effort has been made to convey what went on at all three meetings, bearing in mind that in none was a complete exposé given of most issues. ERCDOM was only a first step, even if not a negligible one.

Our report, as far as it goes, gives a description of some areas in which Evangelicals and Roman Catholics hold similar or common views, which we are able to perceive more clearly as we overcome the stereotypes and prejudiced ideas which we have of each other. In addition, it sets out some of the serious matters on which Evangelicals and Roman Catholics differ, but about which in the last seven years the participants in ERCDOM have begun to learn to speak and listen to each other.

Although all those who participated in the three meetings contributed richly, the responsibility for the final form of the report rests with those who were at Landévennec. Publication is undertaken on the general endorsement of the 1984 participants, although it is not the kind of document to which each was asked to subscribe formally. Nevertheless, it is their express hope that it may be a means of stimulating local encounters in dialogue between Evangelicals and Roman Catholics. Our report is far from being definitive; the dialogue needs to be continued and developed.

The participants in ERCDOM offer this report to other Evangelicals and Roman Catholics as a sign of their conviction that fidelity to Jesus Christ today requires that we take his will for his followers with a new seriousness. He prayed for the truth, holiness, mission, and unity of his people. We believe that these dimensions of the church's renewal belong together. It is with this understanding that we echo his prayer for ourselves and each other:

> Sanctify them in the truth; thy word is truth. As thou didst send me into the world, so I have sent them into the world. I pray . . . that they may all be one; even as thou, Father, art in me, and I in thee, that they also may be in us, so that the world may believe. (Jn 17:17-21)

1. Revelation and Authority

It may well be asked why participants in a dialogue on mission should spend time debating theological questions concerned with divine revelation, the Scriptures, the formulation of truth, principles of biblical interpretation, and the church's magisterium or teaching authority. For these topics may not appear to be directly related to our Christian mission in the world. Yet we judged a discussion of them to be indispensable to our task for two main reasons. The first and historical reason is that the issue of authority in general, and of the relation between Scripture and tradition in particular, was one of the really major points at issue in the sixteenth century. Indeed, the evangelical emphasis on *sola Scriptura* has always been known as the "formal" principle of the Reformation. So Roman Catholics and Evangelicals will not come to closer understanding or agreement on any topic if they cannot do so on this topic. Indeed in every branch of the Christian church the old question "by what authority?" (Mk 11:28) remains fundamental to ecumenical discussion. Our second reason for including this subject on our agenda was that it has a greater relevance to mission than may at first appear. For there can be no mission without a message, no message without a definition of it, and no definition without agreement as to how, or on what basis, it shall be defined.

1. Revelation, the Bible, and the Formulation of Truth

Roman Catholics and Evangelicals are entirely agreed on the necessity of revelation, if human beings are ever to know God. For he is infinite in his perfections, while we are both finite creatures and fallen sinners. His thoughts and ways are as much higher than ours as the heavens are higher than the earth (Is 55:9). He is beyond us, utterly unknowable unless he should choose to make himself known, and utterly unreachable unless he should put himself within our reach. And this is what together we believe he has done. He has revealed the glory of his power in the created universe[10] and the glory of his grace in his Son Jesus Christ, and in the Scriptures which he said bear witness to him (e.g., Jn 5:39).

This process of special revelation began in the Old Testament era. "God spoke of old to our fathers by the prophets" (Heb 1:1). He fashioned Israel to be his people and taught them by his law and prophets. Old Testament Scripture records this history and this teaching. Then the Father sent his Son, who claimed to be the fulfillment of prophecy, himself proclaimed the good news of salvation, chose the twelve apostles to be his special witnesses, and promised them the inspiration of his Spirit. After Pentecost they went everywhere preaching the Gospel. Through their word Christian communities came into being, nourished by the Old Testament and the Gospel. The apostles' teaching was embodied in hymns, confessions of faith, and particularly their letters. In due time the church came to recognize their writings as possessing unique authority and as handing down the authentic Gospel of Jesus Christ. In this way the canon of the New Testament was constituted, which with the Old Testament comprise the Christian Scriptures.

We all recognize that in the Scriptures God has used human words as the vehicle of his communication. The Spirit's work of inspiration is such, however, that what the human authors wrote is what God intended should be revealed, and thus that Scripture is without error. Because it is God's word, its divine authority and unity must be recognized, and because he spoke through human beings, its original human context must also be taken into account in the work of interpretation.

But are human words adequate to describe God fully, even if they are inspired? No. The infinite reality of the living God is a mystery which cannot be fully communicated in words or fully comprehended by human minds. No verbal formulation can be coextensive with the truth as it is in him. Nevertheless, God has condescended to use words as well as deeds as appropriate media of his self-disclosure, and we must struggle to understand them. We do so in the confidence, however, that though they do not reveal God fully, they do reveal him truly.

Roman Catholics and Evangelicals differ slightly in their understanding of the nature of Scripture, and even more on what the proper process of interpreting this word should be. Both groups recognize that God spoke through the human authors, whose words belonged to particular cultures.

Roman Catholics speak of this relationship between the divine and the human in Scripture as being analogous to the divine and the human in Christ. As the Second Vatican Council put it, "Indeed the words of God, expressed in the words of men, are in every way like human language, just as the Word of the eternal Father, when he took on himself the flesh of human weakness, became like man."[11] Thus the written testimony of the biblical authors is inscribed within the logic of the incarnation.

Evangelicals also sometimes use this analogy, but they are not altogether comfortable with it. Although it has some validity, they do not believe it is exact since there is no hypostatic union between the human and the divine in Scripture. They usually emphasize instead the model of God's providence, namely, that he is able even through fallen human beings to accomplish his perfect will. So he has spoken through the human authors of the Bible in such a way that neither did he suppress their personality nor did they distort his revelation.

Thus together we affirm that the written word of God is the work of both God and human beings. The divine and the human elements form a unity which cannot be torn asunder. It excludes all confusion and all separation between them.

With respect to the process of interpretation, Roman Catholics affirm that Scripture must be seen as having been produced by and within the church. It is mediated to us by the inspired witness of the first Christians. The proper process of interpretation is determined by the process of Scripture's creation. We cannot understand it in its truth unless we receive it in the living faith of the church which, assisted by the Holy Spirit, keeps us in obedience to the word of God.

Evangelicals acknowledge the wisdom of listening to the church and its teachers, past and present, as they seek to understand God's word, but they insist that each believer must be free to exercise his or her personal responsibility before God, in hearing and obeying his word. While the church's interpretations are often helpful, they are not finally necessary because Scripture, under the Spirit's illumination, is self-interpreting and perspicuous (clear).

Thus, contemporaneity has come to mean different things in our two communities. Each recognizes that the word of God must be heard for and in our world today. For Roman Catholics God's word is contemporary in the sense that it is heard and interpreted within the living church. For Evangelicals it is contemporary in the sense that its truth has to be applied, by the illumination of the Holy Spirit, to the modern world.

Despite these differences, we are agreed that since the biblical texts have been inspired by God, they remain the ultimate, permanent, and normative reference of the revelation of God. To them the church must continually return, in order to discern more clearly what they mean, and so receive fresh insight, challenge, and reformation. They themselves do not need to be reformed, although they do need constantly to be interpreted, especially in circumstances in which the church encounters new problems or different cultures. Roman Catholics hold that "the task of giving an authentic interpretation of the word of God whether in its written form or in the form of Tradition has been entrusted to the living teaching office of the Church alone."[12] This seems to Evangelicals to derogate from Scripture as "the ultimate, permanent, and normative reference." Nevertheless, both sides strongly affirm the divine inspiration of Scripture.

2. Principles of Biblical Interpretation

Our understanding of the nature of the Bible determines our interpretation of it. Because it is the word of God, we shall approach it in one way; and because it is also the words of men, in another.

A. Humble Dependence on the Holy Spirit

Because the Bible is the word of God we must approach it with reverence and humility. We cannot understand God's revelation by ourselves, because it is "spiritually discerned" (1 Cor 2:14). Only he who spoke through the prophets and apostles can interpret to us his own message. Only the Spirit of truth can open our hearts to understand, to believe, and to obey. This is "wisdom," and the Holy Spirit is the "Spirit of wisdom and of revelation" in our knowledge of God (Eph 1:17). Moreover, the Spirit operates within the body of Christ, as we shall elaborate later.

B. The Unity of Scripture

Because the Bible is the word of God, it has a fundamental unity. This is a unity of origin, since he who has revealed himself does not contradict himself. It is also a unity of message and aim. For our Lord said the Scriptures "bear witness to me" (Jn 5:39; cf. Lk 24:25-27). Similarly we read that "the sacred writings . . . are able to instruct you for salvation through faith in Christ Jesus" (2 Tm 3:15). Thus, God's purpose through Scripture is to bear testimony to Christ as Savior, to persuade all men and women to come to him for salvation, to lead them into maturity in Christ, and to send them into the world with the same good news.

In the midst of great diversity of content, therefore, Scripture has a single meaning, which permeates and illuminates all the partial meanings. We renounce every attempt to impose on Scripture an artificial unity or even to insist on a single overarching concept. Instead, we discover in Scripture a God-given unity, which focuses on the Christ who died and rose again for us and who offers to all his people his own new life, which is the same in every age and culture. This centrality of Christ in the Scriptures is a fundamental hermeneutical key.

C. Biblical Criticism

Since the Bible is God's word through human words, therefore under the guidance of the Holy Spirit, who is the only one who leads us into the understanding of Scripture, we must use scientific critical tools for its elucidation, and we appreciate the positive gains of modern biblical scholarship. Human criticism and the Spirit of God are not mutually exclusive. By "criticism" we do not mean that we stand in judgment upon God's word, but rather that we must investigate the historical, cultural, and literary background of the biblical books.

We must also try to be aware of the presuppositions we bring to our study of the text. For none of us lives in a religion- or culture-free vacuum. What we must seek to ensure is that our presuppositions are Christian rather than secular. Some of the presuppositions of secular philosophy which have vitiated the critical study of the Bible are (a) evolutionary (that religion developed from below instead of being revealed from above), (b) antisupernatural (that miracles cannot happen and that therefore the biblical miracles are legendary), and (c) demythologizing (that the thought-world in which the biblical message was given is entirely incompatible with the modern age and must be discarded). Sociological presuppositions are equally dangerous, as when we read into Scripture the particular economic system we favor, whether capitalist or communist or any other.

One test by which our critical methodology may be assessed is whether or not it enables people to hear the biblical message as good news of God revealing and giving himself in the historic death and resurrection of Christ.

D. The "Literal" Sense

The first task of all critical study is to help us discover the original intention of the authors. What is the literary genre in which they wrote? What did they intend to say? What did they intend us to understand? For this is the "literal" sense of Scripture, and the search for it is one of the most ancient principles which the church affirmed. We must never divorce a text from its biblical or cultural context but rather think ourselves back into the situation in which the word was first spoken and heard.

E. A Contemporary Message

To concentrate entirely on the ancient text, however, would lead us into an unpractical antiquarianism. We have to go beyond the original meaning to the contemporary message. Indeed, there is an urgent need for the church to apply the teaching of Scripture creatively to the complex questions of today. Yet in seeking for relevance, we must not renounce faithfulness. The ancient and the modern, the original and the contemporary, always belong together. A text still means what its writer meant.

In this dialectic between the old and the new, we often become conscious of a clash of cultures, which calls for great spiritual sensitivity. On the one hand, we must be aware of the ancient cultural terms in which God spoke his word, so that we may discern between his eternal truth and its transient setting. On the other, we must be aware of the modern cultures and world views which condition us, some of whose values can make us blind and deaf to what God wants to say to us.

3. The Church's Teaching Authority

It is one thing to have a set of principles for biblical interpretation; it is another to know how to use them. How are these principles to be applied, and who is responsible for applying them?

A. The Individual and the Community

Evangelicals, who since the Reformation have emphasized both "the priesthood of all believers" and "the right of private judgment," insist on the duty and value of personal Bible study. The Second Vatican Council also urged that "easy access to sacred Scripture should be provided for all the Christian faithful."[13]

Both Evangelicals and Roman Catholics, however, recognize the dangers which arise from making Scripture available to all Christian people and from exhorting them to read it. How can they be protected from false interpretations? What safeguards can be found? Whether we are Evangelicals or Roman Catholics, our initial answer to these questions is the same: the major check to individualistic exegesis is the Holy Spirit who dwells and works in the body of Christ which is the church. The Scriptures must be interpreted within the Christian community. It is only "with all the saints" that we can comprehend the full dimensions of God's love (Eph 3:18).

Roman Catholics also say that Scripture is interpreted by the church. Yet the church's task, paradoxically speaking, is at one and the same time to submit totally to the witness of Scripture in order to listen to God's word and to interpret it with authority. The act of authority in interpreting God's word is an act of obedience to it.

But how in practice does the Christian community help us towards truth and restrain us from error? We are agreed that Christ has always intended his church to have gifted and authorized teachers, both scholars and pastors. When Philip asked the Ethiopian whether he understood the Old Testament passage he was reading, he replied, "How can I, unless someone guides me?" (Acts 8:31).

Many of our teachers belong to the past. Both Evangelicals and Roman Catholics have inherited a rich legacy of tradition. We cherish creeds, confessions, and conciliar statements. We peruse the writings of the fathers of the church. We read books and commentaries.

Christ also gives his church teachers in the present (Eph 4:11), and it is the duty of Christian people to listen to them respectfully. The regular context for this is public worship in which the word of God is read and expounded. In addition, we attend church synods and councils, and national, regional, and international conferences at which, after prayer and debate, our Christian understanding increases.

Respectful listening and mutual discussion are healthy; they are quite different from uncritical acquiescence. Both Evangelicals and Roman Catholics are troubled by the authoritarian influence which is being exerted by some strong, charismatic leaders and teachers of different backgrounds. The kind of thoughtless submission which is sometimes given to such was firmly discouraged by the apostles. The people of Beroea were commended because they examined the Scriptures to see whether Paul's preaching was true (Acts 17:11). Paul urged the Thessalonians to "test everything," and John to "test the spirits," i.e., teachers claiming inspiration (1 Thes 5:21; 1 Jn 4:1). Moreover, the criterion by which the apostles exhorted the people to evaluate all teachers was the deposit of faith, the truths which they had heard "from the beginning" (1 Jn 2:24; 2 Jn 9).

B. The Regulation of Christian Belief

We all agree that the fact of revelation brings with it the need for interpretation. We also agree that in the interpretative task both the believing community and the individual believer must have a share. Our emphasis on these varies, however, for the Evangelical fears lest God's word be lost in church traditions, while the Roman Catholic fears it will be lost in a multiplicity of idiosyncratic interpretations.

This is why Roman Catholics emphasize the necessary role of the *magisterium*, although Evangelicals believe that in fact it has not delivered the Roman Catholic Church from a diversity of viewpoints, while admittedly helping to discern between them.

Evangelicals admit that in their case, too, some congregations, denominations, and institutions have a kind of magisterium. For they elevate their particular creed or confession to this level, since they use it as their official interpretation of Scripture and for the exercise of discipline.

Both Roman Catholics and Evangelicals cherish certain creeds and confessions which summarize their beliefs. They also agree that new formulations of faith may be written and affirmed for our times. Other doctrinal statements may be either revised or replaced by better statements, if this seems to be required by a clearer proclamation of the good news. All of us accept responsibility to listen ever more attentively to what the Spirit through the word is saying to the churches, so that we may grow in the knowledge of God in the obedience of faith and in a more faithful and relevant witness.

What, then, Evangelicals have asked, is the status (and the authority for Roman Catholics) of the various kinds of statements made by those with a ministry of official teaching? In reply, Roman Catholics say that the function of the *magisterium* is to regulate the formulations of the faith, so that they remain true to the teaching of Scripture. They also draw a distinction. On the one hand, there are certain privileged formulations, e.g., a formal definition in council by the college of bishops, of which the pope is the presiding member, or a similar definition by the pope himself, in special circumstances and subject to particular conditions, to express the faith of the church. It is conceded that such definitions do not necessarily succeed in conveying all aspects of the truth they seek to express, and while what they express remains valid, the way it is expressed may not have the same relevance for all times and situations. Nevertheless, for Roman Catholics they do give a certainty to faith. Such formulations are very few, but very important. On the other hand, statements made by those who have a special teaching role in the Roman Catholic Church have different levels of authority (e.g., papal encyclicals and other pronouncements, decisions of provincial synods or councils, etc.). These require to be treated with respect, but do not call for assent in the same way as the first category.

We all believe that God will protect his church, for he has promised to do so and has given us both his Scriptures and his Spirit; our disagreement is on the means and the degree of his protection.

Roman Catholics believe that it is the authoritative teaching of the church which has the responsibility for oversight in the interpretation of Scripture, allowing a wide freedom of understanding, but excluding some interpretations as inadmissible because erroneous. Evangelicals, on the other hand, believe that God uses the Christian community as a whole to guard its members from error and evil. Roman Catholics also believe in this *sensus fidelium*. For in the New Testament, church members are urged: "Let the word of Christ dwell in you richly; teach and admonish one another" (Col 3:16). They are also exhorted to "see to it that their brothers and sisters stand firm in truth and righteousness."[14]

4. Can the Church Be Reformed?

A. The Need for Reform

So far in this first section of our report we have concentrated on the church's responsibility to teach. Can it also learn? Can the church that gives instruction receive it? More particularly, can Scripture exercise a reforming role in the church? Is the church itself under the Scripture it expounds?

These are questions which the Roman Catholic Church put to itself anew during the Second Vatican Council and has continued to ask itself since (UR, no. 6).

Evangelicals, however, to whom continuous reformation by the word of God has always been a fundamental concern, wonder whether the reform to which the Roman Catholic Church consented at Vatican II was radical enough. Has it been more than an *aggiornamento* of ecclesiastical institutions and liturgical forms? Has it touched the church's theological life or central structures? Has there been an inner repentance?

At the same time, Roman Catholics have always asked whether Evangelicals, in the discontinuity of the sixteenth-century Reformation, have not lost something essential to the Gospel and the church.

Yet we all agree that the church needs to be reformed, and that its reformation comes from God. The one truth is in God himself. He is the reformer by the power of his Spirit according to the Scriptures. In order to discern what he may be saying, Christian individuals and communities need each other. Individual believers must keep their eyes on the wider community of faith, and churches must be listening to the Spirit, who may bring them correction or insight through an individual believer.

B. Our Response to God's Word

We agree on the objectivity of the truth which God has revealed. Yet it has to be subjectively received, indeed "apprehended," if through it God is to do his reforming work. How then should our response to revelation be described?

We all acknowledge the difficulties we experience in receiving God's word. For as it comes to us, it finds each of us in our own social context and culture. True, it creates a new community, but this community also has its cultural characteristics derived both from the wider society in which it lives and from its own history, which has shaped its understanding of God's revelation. So we have to be on the alert, lest our response to the word of God is distorted by our cultural conditioning.

One response will be intellectual. For God's revelation is a rational revelation, and the Holy Spirit is the Spirit of truth. So the Christian community is always concerned to understand and to formulate the faith, so that it may preserve truth and rebut error. Response to God's truth can never be purely cognitive, however. Truth in the New Testament is to be "done" as well as "known," and so to find its place in the life and experience of individuals and churches. Paul called this full response "the obedience of faith" (Rom 1:5; 16:26). It is a commitment of the whole person.

Understanding, faith, and obedience will in their turn lead to proclamation. For revelation by its very nature demands communication. The believing and obeying community must be a witnessing community. And as it faithfully proclaims what it understands, it will increasingly understand what it proclaims.

Thus reform is a continuous process, a work of the Spirit of God through the agency of the word of God.

2. The Nature of Mission

The very existence of the Evangelical–Roman Catholic Dialogue on Mission testifies to our common commitment to mission. One of the factors which led to its inauguration was the publication of the *Lausanne Covenant* (1974) and of *Evangelii*

Nuntiandi, Pope Paul VI's apostolic exhortation *Evangelization in the Modern World* (1975). These two documents supplied some evidence of a growing convergence in our understanding of mission. Not that Evangelicals or Roman Catholics regard either of these statements as exhaustive, but they consider them valuable summaries and teaching tools.

1. The Basis of Mission

In response to the common criticism that we have no right to evangelize among all peoples, we together affirm the universality of God's purposes. God's creation of the world and of all humankind means that all should be subject to his lordship (Ps 24:1-2; Eph 3:8-11). The call of Abraham and of Israel had the wider purpose that all nations might see God's glory in his people and come to worship him. In the New Testament Jesus sends his disciples out in proclamatory witness, leading to the apostolic mission to all nations. In his Epistle to the Romans, Paul teaches that, since all without distinction have sinned, so all without distinction are offered salvation, Gentiles as well as Jews (3:22f., 10:12).

We are agreed that mission arises from the self-giving life and love of the triune God himself and from his eternal purpose for the whole creation. Its goal is the God-centered kingdom of the Father, exhibited through the building of the body of Christ, and cultivated in the fellowship of the Spirit. Because of Christ's first coming and the outpouring of the Holy Spirit, Christian mission has an eschatological dimension: it invites men and women to enter the kingdom of God through Christ the Son by the work and regeneration of the Spirit.

We all agree that the arrival of the messianic kingdom through Jesus Christ necessitates the announcement of the good news, the summons to repentance and faith, and the gathering together of the people of God. Sometimes Jesus clearly used "the kingdom of God" and "salvation" as synonyms.[15] For to announce the arrival of the kingdom of God is to proclaim its realization in the coming of Jesus Christ. And the church witnesses to the kingdom when it manifests the salvation it has received.

At the same time, long-standing tensions exist between Roman Catholics and Evangelicals. While both sides affirm that the pilgrim church is missionary by its very nature, its missionary activity is differently understood.

Vatican II defines the church for Roman Catholics as "the sacrament of salvation," the sign and promise of redemption to each and every person without exception. For them, therefore, "mission" includes not only evangelization but also the service of human need and the building up and expression of fellowship in the church. It is the mission of the church to anticipate the kingdom of God as liberation from the slavery of sin, from slavery to the law, and from death; by the preaching of the Gospel, by the forgiveness of sins, and by sharing in the Lord's Supper.[16]

But the Spirit of God is always at work throughout human history to bring about the liberating reign of God.

Evangelization is the proclamation (by word and example) of the good news to the nations. The good news is that God's actions in Jesus Christ are the climax of a divine revelation and relationship that has been available to everyone from the beginning. Roman Catholics assert that the whole of humanity is in a collective history which God makes to be a history of salvation. The *mysterion* of the Gospel is the announcement by the church to the world of this merging of the history of salvation with the history of the world.

Evangelicals generally, on the other hand, do not regard the history of salvation as coterminous with the history of the world, although some are struggling with this question. The church is the beginning and anticipation of the new creation, the firstborn among his creatures. Though all in Adam die, not all are automatically in Christ. So life in Christ has to be received by grace with repentance through faith. With yearning Evangelicals plead for a response to the atoning work of Christ in his death and resurrection. But with sorrow they know that not all who are called are chosen. Judgment (both here and hereafter) is the divine reaction of God to sin and to the rejection of the good news. "Rich young rulers" still walk away from the kingdom of grace. Evangelization is therefore the call to those outside to come as children of the Father into the fullness of eternal life in Christ by the Spirit and into the joy of a loving community in the fellowship of the church.

2. Authority and Initiative in Mission

Primary Christian obedience, we agree, is due to the Lord Jesus Christ and is expressed in both our individual and our common life under his authority. Roman Catholics and Evangelicals recognize that the tension between ecclesiastical authority and personal initiative, as also between the institutional and the charismatic, has appeared throughout biblical and church history.

While for Roman Catholics hierarchical structures of teaching and pastoral authority are essential, the servant church, as described by the Second Vatican Council, is called to express herself more fully in the exercise of apostolic collegiality and subsidiarity (the principle that ecclesial decisions are made at the lowest level of responsibility).

Evangelicals have traditionally emphasized the personal right of every believer to enjoy direct access to God and the Scriptures. There is also among them a growing realization of the importance of the church as the body of Christ, which tempers personal initiative through the restraint and direction of the fellowship.

This issue of authority has a bearing on mission. Are missionaries sent, or do they volunteer, or is it a case of both? What is the status of religious orders, mission boards or missionary societies, and parachurch organizations? How do they relate to the churches or other ecclesial bodies? How can a preoccupation with jurisdiction (especially geographical) be reconciled with the needs of subcultures, especially in urban areas, which are often overlooked?

Although our traditions differ in the way we respond to these questions, we all wish to find answers which take account both of church structures and of the liberty of the Spirit outside them.

3. Evangelization and Sociopolitical Responsibility

The controversy over the relationship between evangelization and sociopolitical responsibility is not confined to Roman Catholics and Evangelicals; it causes debate between and among all Christians.

We are agreed that "mission" relates to every area of human need, both spiritual and social. Social responsibility is an integral part of evangelization, and the struggle for justice can be a manifestation of the kingdom of God. Jesus both preached and healed, and sent his disciples out to do likewise. His predilection for those without power and without voice continues God's concern in the Old Testament for the widow, the orphan, the poor, and the defenseless alien. In particular we agree:

a. That serving the spiritual, social, and material needs of our fellow human beings together constitutes love of neighbor and therefore "mission"

b. That an authentic proclamation of the good news must lead to a call for repentance, and that authentic repentance is a turning away from social as well as individual sins

c. That since each Christian community is involved in the reality of the world, it should lovingly identify with the struggle for justice as a suffering community

d. That in this struggle against evil in society, the Christian must be careful to use means which reflect the spirit of the Gospel. The church's responsibility in a situation of injustice will include repentance for any complicity in it, as well as intercessory prayer, practical service, and prophetic teaching which sets forth the standards of God and his kingdom

We recognize that some Roman Catholics and some Evangelicals find it difficult to subscribe to any inseparable unity between evangelization and the kind of sociopolitical involvement which is described above. There is also some tension concerning the allocation of responsibility for social service and action. Roman Catholics accept the legitimacy of involvement by the church as a whole, as well as by groups and individuals. Among Evangelicals, however, there are differences between the Lutheran, Reformed, and Anabaptist traditional understandings of church and society. All would agree that Christian individuals and groups have social responsibilities; the division concerns what responsibility is assigned to the church as a whole.

4. God's Work Outside the Christian Community

We have written about the church and the kingdom. We are agreed that the concept of the church implies a limitation, for we talk about "church members," which infers that there are "nonmembers." But how widely should we understand the kingdom of God? We all agree that God works within the Christian community, for there he rules and dwells. But does he also work outside, and if so, how?

This is a question of major missiological importance. All of us are concerned to avoid an interpretation of the universal saving will of God which makes salvation automatic without the free response of the person.

At least four common convictions have emerged from our discussions. They concern the great doctrines of creation, revelation, salvation, and judgment.

1. *Creation.* God has created all humankind and by right of creation all humankind belongs to God. God also loves the whole human family and gives to them all "life and breath and everything" (Acts 17:25).
2. *Revelation.* There are elements of truth in all religions. These truths are the fruit of a revelatory gift of God. Evangelicals often identify their source in terms of general revelation, common grace, or the remnant image of God in humankind. Roman Catholics more frequently associate them with the work of the *Logos,* the true light coming into the world and giving light to every man (Jn 1:9), and with the work of his Holy Spirit.
3. *Salvation.* There is only one Savior and only one Gospel. There is no other name but Christ's through whom anyone may be saved (Acts 4:12). So all who receive salvation are saved by the free initiative of God through the grace of Christ.
4. *Judgment.* While the biblical concept of judgment refers to both reward and punishment, it is clear that those who remain in sin by resisting God's free grace (whether they are inside or outside the visible boundaries of the church) provoke his judgment, which leads to eternal separation from him. The church itself also stands under the judgment of God whenever it refuses or neglects to proclaim the Gospel of salvation to those who have not heard Christ's name.

The sphere for missionary activity is described differently within each tradition. Roman Catholics would expect God's mercy to be exercised effectively in benevolent action of his grace for the majority of humankind, unless they specifically reject his offer. Such a position gives them cause for confidence. Evangelicals consider that this view has no explicit biblical justification and that it would tend to diminish the evangelistic zeal of the church. Evangelicals are therefore less optimistic about the salvation of those who have no personal relationship to God through Jesus Christ.

We all affirm that the missionary enterprise is a participation in the mission of Jesus and the mission of his church. The urgency to reach all those not yet claimed by his lordship impels our mission.

Whether or not salvation is possible outside the Christian community, what is the motivation for mission work? We agree that the following strong incentives urgently impel Christians to the task of mission:

a. To further the glory of God; the earth should be a mirror to reflect his glory

b. To proclaim the lordship of Jesus Christ; all men and women are called to submit to his authority

c. To proclaim that Christ has struggled with Satan and dethroned him; in baptism and conversion we renounce Satan's rule and turn to Christ and righteousness

d. To proclaim that man does not live by bread alone; the Gospel of salvation is the perfect gift of God's loving grace

e. To hasten the return of the Lord—the eschatological dimension. We look for the day of the Lord when the natural order will be completely redeemed, the whole earth will be filled with the knowledge of the Lord, and people from every nation, people, tribe, and tongue will praise the triune God in perfection

3. The Gospel of Salvation

Roman Catholics and Evangelicals share a deep concern for the content of the good news we proclaim. We are anxious on the one hand to be faithful to the living core of the Christian faith, and on the other to communicate it in contemporary terms. How then shall we define the Gospel?

1. Human Need

Diagnosis must always precede prescription. So, although human need is not strictly part of the good news, it is an essential background to it. If the Gospel is good news of salvation, this is because human beings are sinners who need to be saved.

In our description of the human condition, however, we emphasize the importance of beginning positively. We affirm that all men and women are made by God, for God, and in the image of God, and that sin has defaced but not destroyed this purpose and this image (Gn 9:6; Jas 3:9). Therefore, as the creation of God, human beings have an intrinsic worth and dignity. Also, because of the light which lightens everybody, we all have within us an innate desire for God which nothing else can satisfy. As Christians, we must respect every human being who is seeking God, even when the search is expressed in ignorance (Acts 17:23).

Nevertheless original sin has intervened. We have noted Thomas Aquinas's description of original sin, namely "the loss of original justice" (i.e., a right relationship with God) and such "concupiscence" as constitutes a fundamental disorder in human nature and relationships, so that all our desires are inclined towards the making of decisions displeasing to God.

Evangelicals insist that original sin has distorted every part of human nature, so that it is permeated by self-centeredness. Consequently, the Apostle Paul describes all people as "enslaved," "blind," "dead," and "under God's wrath," and therefore totally unable to save themselves.[17]

Roman Catholics also speak of original sin as an injury and disorder which has weakened—though not destroyed—human free will. Human beings have "lifted themselves up against God and sought to attain their goal apart from him."[18] As a result this has upset the relationship linking man to God and "has broken the right order that should reign within himself as well as between himself and other men and all creatures."[19] Hence human beings find themselves drawn to what is wrong and *of themselves* unable to overcome the assaults of evil successfully, "so that everyone feels as though bound by chains."[20]

Clearly there is some divergence between Roman Catholics and Evangelicals in the way we understand human sin and need, as well as in the language we use to express them. Roman Catholics think Evangelicals overstress the corruption of human beings by affirming their "total depravity" (i.e., that every part of our humanness has been perverted by the fall), while Evangelicals think Roman Catholics underestimate it and are therefore unwisely optimistic about the capacity, ability, and desire of human beings to respond to the grace of God. Yet we agree that all are sinners, and that all stand in need of a radical salvation which includes deliverance from the power of evil, together with reconciliation to God and adoption into his family.

2. The Person of Jesus Christ

The radical salvation which human beings need has been achieved by Jesus Christ. Evangelicals and Roman Catholics are agreed about the centrality of Christ and of what God has done through him for salvation. "The Father has sent his Son as the Savior of the world" (1 Jn 4:14). But who was this Savior Jesus?

Jesus of Nazareth was a man who went about doing good, teaching with authority, proclaiming the kingdom of God, and making friends with sinners to whom he offered pardon. He made himself known to his apostles, whom he had chosen and with whom he lived, as the Messiah (Christ) promised by the Scriptures. He claimed a unique filial relation to God whom in prayer he called his Father ("Abba"). He thus knew himself to be the Son of God and exhibited the power and authority of God over nature, human beings, and demonic powers. He also spoke of himself as the Son of man. He fulfilled the perfect obedience of the servant in going even to death on the cross. Then God raised him from the dead, confirming that he was from the beginning the Son he claimed to be (Ps 2:7). Thus he was both descended from David "according to the flesh" and "designated Son of God in power according to the Spirit of holiness by his resurrection from the dead" (Rom 1:34). This is why his apostles confessed him as Lord and Christ, Son of God, Savior of humankind, sent by the Father, agent through whom God created all things, in whom we have been chosen from before the foundation of the world (Eph 1:4), the Word made flesh.

The incarnation of the Son was an objective event in history, in which the divine Word took upon himself our human nature. Within a single person were joined full divinity and full humanity. Although this understanding of him was not precisely formulated until the theological debates of the early centuries, we all agree that the Chalcedonian definition faithfully expresses the truths to which the New Testament bears witness.

The purposes of the incarnation were to reveal the Father to us, since otherwise our knowledge of God would have been deficient; to assume our nature in order to die for our sins and so accomplish our salvation, since he could redeem only what he had assumed; to establish a living communion between God and human beings, since only the Son of God made human could communicate to human beings the life of God; to apply the basis of the *imitatio*, since it is the incarnate Jesus we are to follow; to reaffirm the value and dignity of humanness, since God was not ashamed to take on himself our humanity; to provide in Jesus the firstfruits of the new humanity, since he is the "firstborn among many brethren" (Rom 8:29); and to effect the redemption of the cosmos in the end.

So then, in fidelity to the Gospel and in accordance with the Scriptures, we together confess the person of Jesus Christ as the eternal Son of God, who was born of the Virgin Mary and became truly man, in order to be the Savior of the world.

In our missionary task, we have not only to confess Christ ourselves, but also to interpret him to others. As we do so, we have to consider, for example, how to reconcile for Jews and Moslems the monotheism of the Bible with the divine sonship of Jesus, how to present to Hindus and Buddhists the transcendent personality of God, and how to proclaim to adherents of traditional religion and of the new religious consciousness the supreme lordship of Christ. Our christology must always be both faithful to Scripture and sensitive to each particular context of evangelization.

3. The Work of Jesus Christ

It was this historic person, Jesus of Nazareth, fully God and fully human, through whom the Father acted for the redemption and reconciliation of the world. Indeed, only a person who was both God and man could have been the mediator between God and human beings. Because he was human he could represent us and identify with us in our weakness. Because he was God he could bear our sin and destroy the power of evil.

This work of redemption was accomplished supremely through the death of Jesus Christ, although we acknowledge the unity of his incarnate life, atoning death, and bodily resurrection. For his death completed the service of his life (Mk 10:45) and his resurrection confirmed the achievement of his death (Rom 4:25).

Christ was without sin, and therefore had no need to die. He died for our sins, and in this sense "in our place." We are agreed about this basic truth and about other aspects of the atonement. But in our discussion two different emphases have emerged, which we have summarized by the words "substitution" and "solidarity," although these concepts are not altogether exclusive.

Evangelicals lay much stress on the truth that Christ's death was "substitutionary." In his death he did something which he did not do during his life. He actually "became sin" for us (2 Cor 5:21) and "became a curse" for us (Gal 3:13). Thus God himself in Christ propitiated his own wrath, in order to avert it from us. In consequence, having taken our sin, he gives us his righteousness. We stand accepted by God in Christ, not because Christ offered the Father our obedience, but because he bore our sin and replaced it with his righteousness.

Roman Catholics express Christ's death more in terms of "solidarity." In their understanding, Jesus Christ in his death made a perfect offering of love and obedience to his Father, which recapitulated his whole life. In consequence, we can enter into the sacrifice of Christ and offer ourselves to the Father in and with him. For he became one with us in order that we might become one with him.

Thus the word "Gospel" has come to have different meanings in our two communities.

For Evangelicals, it is the message of deliverance from sin, death, and condemnation, and the promise of pardon, renewal, and indwelling by Christ's Spirit. These blessings flow from Christ's substitutionary death. They are given by God solely through his grace, without respect to our merit, and are received solely through faith. When we are accepted by Christ, we are part of his people, since all his people are "in" him.

For Roman Catholics the Gospel centers in the person, message, and gracious activity of Christ. His life, death, and resurrection are the foundation of the church, and the church carries the living Gospel to the world. The church is a real sacrament of the Gospel.

So the difference between us concerns the relationship between the Gospel and the church. In the one case, the Gospel reconciles us to God through Christ and thus makes us a part of his people; in the other, the Gospel is found within the life of his people, and thus we find reconciliation with God.

Although pastoral, missionary, and cultural factors may lead us to stress one or other model of Christ's saving work, the full biblical range of words (e.g., victory, redemption, propitiation, justification, reconciliation) must be preserved, and none may be ignored.

The resurrection, we agree, lies at the heart of the Gospel and has many meanings. It takes the incarnation to its glorious consummation, for it is the human Christ Jesus who reigns glorified at the Father's right hand, where he represents us and prays for us. The resurrection was also the Father's vindication of Jesus, reversing the verdict of those who condemned and crucified him, visibly demonstrating his sonship, and giving us the assurance that his atoning sacrifice had been accepted. It is the resurrected and exalted Lord who sent his Spirit to his church and who, claiming universal authority, now sends us into the world as his witnesses. The resurrection was also the beginning of God's new creation, and is his pledge both of our resurrection and of the final regeneration of the universe.

4. The Uniqueness and Universality of Jesus Christ

In a world of increasing religious pluralism, we affirm together the absolute uniqueness of Jesus Christ. He was unique in his person, in his death, and in his resurrection. Since in no other person has God become human, died for the sins of the world, and risen from death, we declare that he is the only way to God (Jn 14:6), the only Savior (Acts 4:12), and the only Mediator (1 Tm 2:5). No one else has his qualifications.

The uniqueness of Jesus Christ implies his universality. The one and only is meant for all. We therefore proclaim him both "the Savior of the world" (Jn 4:12) and "Lord of all" (Acts 10:36).

We have not been able to agree, however, about the implications of his universal salvation and lordship. Together we believe that "God . . . desires all men to be saved and to come to the knowledge of the truth" (1 Tm 2:4), that the offer of salvation in Christ is extended to everybody, that the church has an irreplaceable responsibility to announce the good news of salvation to all peoples, that all who hear the Gospel have an obligation to respond to it, and that those who respond to it are incorporated into God's new worldwide, multiracial, multicultural community which is the Father's family, the body of Christ, and the temple of the Holy Spirit. These aspects of the universality of Christ we gladly affirm together.

Roman Catholics go further, however, and consider that, if human sin is universal, all the more is Christ's salvation universal. If everyone born into the world stands in solidarity with the disobedience of the first Adam, still the human situation as such has been changed by the definitive event of salvation, that is, the incarnation of the Word, his death, his resurrection, and his gift of the Spirit. All are now part of the humanity whose new head has overcome sin and death. For all there is a new possibility of salvation which colors their entire situation, so that it is possible to say: "Every person, without exception, has been redeemed by Christ, and with each person, without any exception, Christ is in some way united, even when that person is not aware of that."[21] To become beneficiaries of the obedience of the Second Adam, men and women must turn to God and be born anew with Christ into the fullness of his life. The mission of the church is to be the instrument to awaken this response by proclaiming the Gospel, itself the gift of salvation for everyone who receives it, and to communicate the truth and grace of Christ to all.[22]

Evangelicals, on the other hand, understand the universality of Christ differently. He is universally present as God (since God is omnipresent) and as potential Savior (since he offers salvation to all) but not as actual Savior (since not all accept his offer). Evangelicals wish to preserve the distinction, which they believe to be apostolic, between those who are in Christ and those who are not (who consequently are in sin and under judgment), and so between the old and new communities. They insist on the reality of the transfer from one community to the other, which can be realized only through the new birth: "if anyone is in Christ, he is a new creation" (2 Cor 5:17).

The relationship between the life, death, and resurrection of Jesus and the whole human race naturally leads Roman Catholics to ask whether there exists a possibility of salvation for those who belong to non-Christian religions and even for atheists. Vatican II was clear on this point: "Those also can attain to everlasting salvation who through no fault of their own do not know the Gospel of Christ or his church." On the one hand, there are those who "sincerely seek God and, moved by his grace, strive by their deeds to do his will." On the other, there are those who "have not yet arrived at an explicit knowledge of God, but who strive to live a good life, thanks to his grace."[23] Both groups are prepared by God's grace to receive his salvation either when they hear the Gospel or even if they do not. They can be saved by Christ, in a mysterious relation to his church.

Evangelicals insist, however, that according to the New Testament, those outside Christ are "perishing" and that they can receive salvation only in and through Christ. They are therefore deeply exercised about the eternal destiny of those who have never heard of Christ. Most Evangelicals believe that, because they reject the light they have received, they condemn themselves to hell. Many are more reluctant to pronounce on their destiny, have no wish to limit the sovereignty of God, and prefer to leave this issue to him. Others go further in expressing their openness to the possibility that God may save some who have not heard of Christ, but immediately add that, if he does so, it will not be because of their religion, sincerity, or actions (there is no possibility of salvation by good works), but only because of his own grace freely given on the ground of the atoning death of Christ. All Evangelicals recognize the urgent need to proclaim the Gospel of salvation to all humankind. Like Paul in his message to the Gentile audience at Athens, they declare that God "commands all men everywhere to repent, because he has fixed a day on which he will judge the world in righteousness by a man whom he has appointed" (Acts 17:30-31).

5. The Meaning of Salvation

In the Old Testament, salvation meant rescue, healing, and restoration for those already related to God within the covenant. In the New Testament, it is directed to those who have not yet entered into the new covenant in Jesus Christ.

Salvation has to be understood in terms of both salvation history (the mighty acts of God through Jesus Christ) and salvation experience (a personal appropriation of what God has done through Christ). Roman Catholics and Evangelicals together strongly emphasize the objectivity of God's work through Christ, but Evangelicals tend to lay more emphasis than Roman Catholics on the necessity of a personal response to, and experience of, God's saving grace. To describe this, again the full New Testament vocabulary is needed (for example, the forgiveness of sins, reconciliation with God, adoption into his family, redemption, the new birth—all of which are gifts brought to us by the Holy Spirit), although Evangelicals still give paramount importance to justification by grace through faith.

We agree that what is offered us through the death and resurrection of Christ is essentially "deliverance," viewed both negatively and positively. Negatively, it is a rescue from the power of Satan, sin, and death, from guilt, alienation (estrange-ment from God), moral corruption, self-centeredness, existential despair, and fear of the future, including death. Positively, it is a deliverance into the freedom of Christ. This freedom brings human fulfillment. It is essentially becoming "sons in the Son" and therefore brothers to each other. The unity of the disciples of Jesus is a sign both that the Father sent the Son and that the kingdom has arrived. Further, the new community expresses itself in eucharistic worship, in serving the needy (especially the poor and disenfranchised), in open fellowship with people of every age, race, and culture, and in conscious continuity with the historic Christ through fidelity to the teaching of his apostles. Is salvation broader than this? Does it include socio-political liberation?

Roman Catholics draw attention to the three dimensions of evangelization which *Evangelii Nuntiandi* links. They are the *anthropological*, in which humanity is seen always within a concrete situation; the *theological*, in which the unified plan of God is seen within both creation and redemption; and the *evangelical*, in which the exercise of charity (refusing to ignore human misery) is seen in the light of the story of the Good Samaritan.

We all agree that the essential meaning of Christ's salvation is the restoration of the broken relationship between sinful humanity and a saving God; it cannot therefore be seen as a temporal or material project, making evangelism unnecessary.

This restoration of humanity is a true "liberation" from enslaving forces; yet this work has taken on an expanded and particular meaning in Latin America. Certainly God's plan of which Scripture speaks includes his reconciliation of human beings to himself and to one another.

The sociopolitical consequences of God's saving action through Christ have been manifest throughout history. They still are. Specific problems (e.g., slavery, urbanization, church-state relations, and popular religiosity) have to be seen both in their particular context and in relation to God's overall plan as revealed in Scripture and experienced in the believing community through the action of the Spirit.

Appendix: The Role of Mary in Salvation

Roman Catholics would rather consider the question of Mary in the context of the church than of salvation. They think of her as a sinless woman, since she was both overshadowed by the Spirit at the incarnation (Lk 1:35) and baptized with the Spirit on the day of Pentecost (Acts 1:14f. and 2:14). She thus represents all Christians who have been made alive by the Spirit, and Roman Catholics speak of her as the "figure" or "model" of the church.

The reason why we have retained this section on Mary within the chapter on "The Gospel of Salvation" (albeit as an appendix) is that it is in the context of salvation that Evangelicals have the greatest difficulty with Marian teaching and that we discussed her role at ERCDOM II.

The place of Mary in the scheme of salvation has always been a sensitive issue between Roman Catholics and Evangelicals. We have tried to face it with integrity.

A. The Interpretation of Scripture

It raises in an acute form the prior question how we use and interpret the Bible. We are agreed that biblical exegesis begins with a search for the "literal" sense of a text, which is what its author meant. We further agree that some texts also have a "spiritual" meaning, which is founded on the literal but goes beyond it because it was intended by the divine—though not necessarily the human—author (e.g., Is 7:14). This is often called the *sensus plenior*. The difference between Roman Catholics and Evangelicals lies in the degree to which the spiritual sense may be separated from the literal. Both sides agree that, whenever Scripture is not explicit, there is need for some check on the extravagances of interpreters. We are also agreed that this check is supplied by the context, both the immediate context and the whole of Scripture, which is a unity. Roman Catholics, however, say that Scripture must be read in the light of the living, developing tradition of the church, and that the church has authority to indicate what the true meaning of Scripture is. Thus, in relation to Mary, Roman Catholics concede that devotion to Mary was a post-apostolic practice but add that it was a legitimate development, whereas Evangelicals believe it has been unwarrantably imported into the Roman Catholic interpretation of Scripture.

B. Mary and Salvation

In one of our ERCDOM II sessions, entitled "The Place of the Virgin Mary in Salvation and Mission," an Evangelical response was made to Pope Paul VI's 1974 apostolic exhortation *Marialis Cultus (To Honor Mary)*. Evangelical members of the dialogue asked for an explanation of two expressions in it which, at least on the surface, appeared to them to ascribe to Mary an active and participatory role in the work of salvation.

The first (I.5) describes the Christmas season as a prolonged commemoration of Mary's "divine, virginal, and salvific Motherhood." In what sense, Evangelicals asked, could Mary's motherhood be called "salvific"? The Roman Catholics replied that the explanation of the term was to be found in the text itself, namely, that she "brought the Savior into the world" by her obedient response to God's call.

The second passage (I.15) refers to "the singular place" that belongs to Mary in Christian worship, not only as "the holy Mother of God" but as "the worthy Associate of the Redeemer." In what sense, Evangelicals asked, could Mary properly be described as the Redeemer's "worthy Associate?" It did not mean, the Roman

Catholics responded, that she was personally without need of redemption, for on the contrary she was herself saved through her Son's death. In her case, however, "salvation" did not signify the forgiveness of sins, but that because of her predestination to be the "Mother of God," she was preserved from original sin ("immaculate conception") and so from sinning. Positively, she could be described as the Redeemer's "associate" because of her unique link with him as his mother. The word should not give offense, for we too are "associates of the Redeemer," both as recipients of his redemption and as agents through whose prayers, example, sacrifice, service, witness, and suffering his redemption is proclaimed to others.

The Evangelicals made a double response to these explanations. First, they still found the language ambiguous and considered this ambiguity particularly unfortunate in the central area of salvation. Secondly, they felt the whole Roman Catholic emphasis on Mary's role in salvation exaggerated, for when the apostles John and Paul unfold the mystery of the incarnation, it is to honor Christ the Son, not Mary the mother. At the same time, they readily agreed that in Luke's infancy narrative, Mary is given the unique privilege of being the Savior's mother and on that account is addressed as both "highly favored" and "blessed among women" (1:28-42). If Evangelicals are to be true to their stance on *sola Scriptura*, they must therefore overcome any inhibitions they may have and faithfully expound such texts.

Our discussion also focussed on the use of the term "cooperation." For example, it is stated in *Lumen Gentium*, chapter VIII, that Mary is rightly seen as "co-operating in the work of human salvation through free faith and obedience" (II, no. 56), and again that "the unique mediation of the Redeemer does not exclude but rather gives rise . . . to a manifold co-operation which is but a sharing in this unique source" (III, no. 62). The Evangelicals agreed that the notion of cooperation with God is biblical (e.g., "workers together with him," 2 Cor 6:1), but pointed out that this refers to a divine-human partnership in which our share lies in the proclaiming—and not in any sense in the procuring—of salvation. The Roman Catholics agreed. The "co-operation" between Christ and us, they said, does not mean that we can add anything to Christ or his work, since he is complete in himself, and his work has been achieved. It means rather that we share in the benefits of what he has done (not in the doing of it) and that (by his gift alone, as in the case of Mary) we offer ourselves to him in gratitude, to spend our lives in his service and to be used by him as instruments of his grace (cf. Gal 1). The Evangelicals were relieved but still felt that the use of the word "co-operation" in this sense was inappropriate.

Another word we considered was "mediatrix," the feminine form of "mediator." The Evangelicals reacted with understandable vehemence against its application to Mary, as did also some Roman Catholics. She must not be designated thus, they insisted, since the work of mediation belongs to Christ alone. In reply, the Roman Catholics were reassuring. Although the word (or rather its Greek equivalent) was used of Mary from the fifth century onwards, and although some bishops were pressing at Vatican II for its inclusion in the text, the council deliberately avoided it. It occurs only once, and then only in a list of Mary's traditional titles. Moreover, in the same section of *Lumen Gentium* (III, nos. 60-62), Christ is twice called "the one Mediator" in accordance with 1 Timothy 2:5-6, and his unique mediation is also referred to twice, which (it is added) Mary's maternal ministry "in no way obscures or diminishes."

The final document of the Puebla Conference of the Evangelization of Latin America (1979), which contains a long section entitled "Mary, Mother and Model of the Church" (nos. 282-303), was cited by Evangelical participants. Number 293 declares that Mary "now lives immersed in the mystery of the Trinity, praising the glory of God and interceding for human beings." Evangelicals find this a disturbing expression, and not all Roman Catholics are happy with it, finding it too ambiguous (if indeed "immersed" is an accurate translation of the Spanish original *immersa;* there has been some controversy about this). Roman Catholics explain that the notion of Mary's "immersion" in the Trinity means that she is the daughter of the Father, the mother of the Son, and the temple of the Holy Spirit (all three expressions being used in no. 53 of *Lumen Gentium*). But they strongly insist that, of course, she cannot be on a level with the three persons of the Trinity, let alone a fourth person. In addition, they point out that Roman Catholics' understanding of the role of Mary should be determined by the whole of chapter VIII of *Lumen Gentium* and other official statements of Roman Catholic belief, rather than by popular expressions of Marian piety.

The fears of Evangelicals were to some extent allayed by these Roman Catholic explanations and assurances. Yet a certain Evangelical uneasiness remained. First, the traditional Catholic emphasis on Mary's role in salvation (e.g., as the "New Eve," the life-giving mother) still seemed to them incompatible with the much more modest place accorded to her in the New Testament. Secondly, the vocabulary used in relation to Mary seemed to them certainly ambiguous and probably misleading. Is it not vitally important, they asked, especially in the central doctrine of salvation through Christ alone, to avoid expressions which require elaborate explanation (however much hallowed by long tradition) and to confine ourselves to language which is plainly and unequivocally Christ-centered?

At the same time Roman Catholics are troubled by what seems to them a notable neglect by Evangelicals of the place given by God to Mary in salvation history and in the life of the church.

4. Our Response in the Holy Spirit to the Gospel

We agree that evangelism is not just a proclamation of Christ's historic work and saving offer. Evangelism also includes a call for response which is often called "conversion."

1. The Work of the Holy Spirit

This response, however, does not depend on the efforts of the human person but on the initiative of the Holy Spirit. As is stated in the Scripture, "for by grace you have been saved through faith; and this is not your own doing, it is the gift of God—not because of works, lest any man should boast" (Eph 2:8-9). There is therefore a trinitarian dimension to the human person's response: it is the Father who gives; his supreme gift is his Son, Jesus Christ, for the life of the world (Jn 6:23); and it is the Holy Spirit who opens our minds and hearts so that we can accept and proclaim that Jesus Christ is Lord (1 Cor 12:3) and live as his disciples. This means that the Holy Spirit guarantees that the salvation which the Father began in Jesus Christ becomes effective in us in a personal way.

When human persons experience conversion, the Holy Spirit illumines their understanding so that Jesus Christ can be confessed as the Truth itself revealed by the Father (Jn 14:6). The Holy Spirit also renders converted persons new creatures who participate in the eternal life of the Father and the Son (Jn 11:25-26). Furthermore, the Holy Spirit, through the gifts of faith, hope, and love, already enables converted persons to have a foretaste of the kingdom which will be totally realized when the Son hands over all things to the Father (1 Cor 15:28).

Thus, the work of the Holy Spirit in Christian conversion has to be seen as the actual continuation of his previous creative and redemptive activity throughout history. Indeed, at the beginning the Holy Spirit was present at the act of creation (Gn 1:2), and he is continually sent forth as the divine breath by whom everything is created and by whom the face of the earth is renewed (Ps 104:29-30). Although all persons are influenced by the life-giving Spirit of God, it is particularly in the Old Testament, which he inspired, that the recreative work of the Holy Spirit after the fall of humankind is concretely manifested. In order to ground the divine plan to recreate humanity, the Holy Spirit first taught the patriarchs to fear God and to practice righteousness. And to assemble his people Israel and to bring it back to the observance of the covenant, the Holy Spirit raised up judges, kings, and wise men. Moreover, the prophets, under the guidance of the Spirit, announced that the Holy Spirit would create a new heart and bestow new life by being poured out in a unique way on Israel and, through it, on all humanity (Ez 36:24-28; Jl 2:28-29).

The recreative work of the Holy Spirit reached its culminating point in the incarnation of Jesus Christ who, as the New Adam, was filled with the Holy Spirit without measure (Jn 3:34). Because Jesus Christ was the privileged bearer of the Holy Spirit, he is the one who gives the Holy Spirit for the regeneration of human beings: "He on whom you see the Spirit descend and remain, this is he who baptizes with the Holy Spirit" (Jn 1:33). Through his death on behalf of sinful humankind and his rising up to glory, Jesus Christ communicates the Holy Spirit to all who are converted to him, that is, receive him by faith as their personal Lord and Savior. This new life in Jesus Christ by the Holy Spirit is signified by baptism and by membership in the body of Christ, the church. Furthermore, through his indwelling in converted persons, the Holy Spirit attests that they are co-heirs with Christ of eternal glory.

2. Conversion and Baptism

We have been agreeably surprised to discover a considerable consensus among us that repentance and faith, conversion and baptism, regeneration and incorporation into the Christian community all belong together, although we have needed to debate their relative positions in the scheme of salvation.

"Conversion" signifies an initial turning to Jesus Christ in repentance and faith, with a view to receiving the forgiveness of sins and the gift of the Spirit, and to being incorporated into the church, all signed to us in baptism (Acts 2:38-39). The expression "continuous conversion" (if used) must therefore be understood as referring to our daily repentance as Christians, our response to new divine challenges, and our gradual transformation into the image of Christ by the Spirit (2 Cor 3:18). Moreover, some who have grown up in a Christian home find themselves to be regenerate Christians without any memory of a conscious conversion.

We agree that baptism must never be isolated, either in theology or in practice, from the context of conversion. It belongs essentially to the whole process of repentance, faith, regeneration by the Holy Spirit, and membership of the covenant community, the church. A large number of Evangelicals (perhaps the majority) practice only "believer's baptism." That is, they baptize only those who have personally accepted Jesus Christ as their Savior and Lord, and they regard baptism both as the convert's public profession of faith and as the dramatization (by immersion in water) of his or her having died and risen with Christ. The practice of infant baptism (practiced by some Evangelicals, rejected by others) assures both that the parents believe and will bring their children up in the Christian faith and that the children will themselves later come to conscious repentance and faith.

We rejoice together that the whole process of salvation is the work of God by the Holy Spirit. And it is in this connection that Roman Catholics understand the expression *ex opere operato* in relation to baptism. It does not mean that the sacraments have a mechanical or automatic efficacy. Its purpose rather is to emphasize that salvation is a sovereign work of Christ, in distinction to a Pelagian or semi-Pelagian confidence in human ability.

There is a further dimension of the work of the Holy Spirit in our response to the Gospel to which we have become increasingly sensitive, and which we believe belongs within our understanding of the work of the Spirit in mission.

In the light of biblical teaching, particularly in the Epistle to the Ephesians,[24] and also in view of the insights gained through Christian missionary experience, we believe that, although the revelation of Jesus Christ as the Truth by the Holy Spirit is in itself complete in the Scriptures, nevertheless he is wanting to lead the church into a yet fuller understanding of this revelation. Hence we rejoice that in the various cultural contexts in which men and women throughout nearly twenty centuries of Christian history have been enabled by the Holy Spirit to respond to the Gospel, we can perceive the many-sidedness of the unique Lord Jesus Christ, the Savior of all humankind.

Accordingly, we hope that the Holy Spirit will make us open to such new and further insights into the meaning of Jesus Christ, as he may wish to communicate by means of various manifestations of Christian life in our Christian communities, as well as in human societies where we earnestly desire that he will create a response to the Gospel in conversion, baptism, and incorporation into Christ's body, the church.

3. Church Membership

Conversion and baptism are the gateway into the new community of God, although Evangelicals distinguish between the visible and invisible aspects of this community. They see conversion as the means of entry into the invisible church, and baptism as the consequently appropriate means of entry into the visible church. Both sides agree that the church should be characterized by learning, worship, fellowship, holiness, service, and evangelism (Acts 2:42-47). Furthermore, life in the church is characterized by hope and love, as a result of the outpouring of the Holy Spirit: "And hope does not disappoint us, because God's love has been poured into our hearts through the Holy Spirit which has been given to us" (Rom 5:5). It is the Holy Spirit who arouses and sustains our response to the living Christ. Through the power of the Holy Spirit, the unity of the human family, which was disrupted by sin, is gradually being recreated as the new humanity emerges (Eph 2:15).

The issue of church membership has raised in our dialogue the delicate and difficult question of the conversion of those already baptized. How are we to think of their baptism? And which church should they join? This practical question can cause grave problems in the relationship between Roman Catholics and Evangelicals.

It is particularly acute in places like Latin America, where large numbers of baptized Roman Catholics have had a minimal relationship with the Roman Catholic Church since their baptism.

When such Roman Catholics have a conversion experience, many Evangelical churches welcome them into membership without rebaptizing them. Some Baptist churches, however, and some others would insist on baptizing such converts, as indeed they baptize Protestant converts who have been baptized in infancy.

Then there is the opposite problem of Protestant Christians wishing to become members of the Roman Catholic Church. Since Vatican II, the Roman Catholic Church has recognized other Christians as being in the first place "brethren," rather than subjects for conversion. Nevertheless, since the Roman Catholic Church believes that the one church of Christ subsists within it in a unique way, it further believes it is legitimate to receive other Christians into its membership. Such membership is not seen as an initial step towards salvation, however, but as a further step towards Christian growth. Considerable care is taken nowadays to ensure that such a step is not taken under wrong pressure and for unworthy motives. In other words, there is an avoidance of "proselytism" in the wrong sense. Then, provided that there is some proof of valid baptism having taken place, there is no question of rebaptism.

Church members need constantly to be strengthened by the grace of God. Roman Catholics and Evangelicals understand grace somewhat differently however; Roman Catholics thinking of it more as divine life and Evangelicals as divine favor. Both sides agree that it is by a totally free gift of the Father that we become joined to Christ and enabled to live like Christ through the power of the Holy Spirit. Both sides also understand the eucharist (or Lord's Supper) as a sacrament (or ordinance) of grace. Roman Catholics affirm the real presence of the body and blood of Jesus Christ and emphasize the mystery of Christ and his salvation becoming present and effective by the working of the Holy Spirit under the sacramental sign,[25] whereas Evangelicals (in different ways according to their different church traditions) view the sacrament as the means by which Christ blesses us by drawing us into fellowship with himself, as we remember his death until he comes again (1 Cor 11:26).

Despite the lack of full accord which we have just described, both Evangelicals and Roman Catholics agree that the eucharist is spiritual food and spiritual drink (1 Cor 10:3-4, 16), because the unifying Spirit is at work in this sacrament. As a memorial of the new covenant, the eucharist is a privileged sign in which Christ's saving grace is especially signified and/or made available to Christians. In the eucharist the Holy Spirit makes the words Jesus spoke at the Last Supper effective in the church and assures Christians that through their faith, they are intimately united to Christ and to each other in the breaking of the bread and the sharing of the cup.

4. Assurance of Salvation

It has always been traditional among Evangelicals to stress not only salvation as a present gift, but also the assurance of salvation enjoyed by those who have received it. They like, for example, to quote 1 John 5:13: "I write this to you who believe in the name of the Son of God, that you may know that you have eternal life." Thus eternal life begins in us now through the Spirit of the risen Christ, because we are "raised with him through faith in the working of God, who raised him from the dead" (Col 2:12). Yet in daily life we live in the tension between what is already given and what is still awaited as a promise, for "your life is hid with Christ in God. When Christ who is our life appears, then you will also appear with him in glory" (Col 3:3-4).

Roman Catholics and Evangelicals are agreed that the only ground for assurance is the objective work of Christ; this ground does not lie in any way in the believer. We speak somewhat differently about the work of Christ, however, and relate it differently in terms of practical piety. Evangelicals refer to the "finished" work of Christ on the cross and rest their confidence wholly upon it. Roman Catholics also speak of Christ's work as having been done "once for all"; they therefore see it as beyond repetition. Nevertheless, they understand that through the eucharist Christ's unique, once-for-all work is made present, and that by this means they maintain a present relationship to it. The relationship to Christ's finished work which Evangelicals enjoy is maintained by faith, but it is faith in what was done, and what was done is never re-presented.

Roman Catholics and Evangelicals both claim an authentic religious experience, which includes an awareness of the presence of God and a taste for spiritual realities. Yet Evangelicals think Roman Catholics sometimes lack a visible joy in Christ, which their assurance has given them, whereas Roman Catholics think Evangelicals are sometimes insufficiently attentive to the New Testament warnings against presumption. Roman Catholics also claim to be more realistic than Evangelicals about the vagaries of religious experience. The actual experience of Evangelicals seldom leads them to doubt their salvation, but Roman Catholics know that the soul may have its dark nights. In summary, Evangelicals appear to Roman Catholics more pessimistic about human nature before conversion but more optimistic about it afterwards, while Evangelicals allege the opposite about Roman Catholics. Roman Catholics and Evangelicals together agree that Christian assurance is more an assurance of faith (Heb 10:22) than of experience, and that perseverance to the end is a gratuitous gift of God.

5. The Church and the Gospel

Evangelicals, because of their emphasis on the value of the individual, have traditionally neglected the doctrine of the church. The topic was not neglected in our dialogue, however. We found ourselves united in certain convictions about the church and in our commitment to it. We were able to agree on a fourfold relationship between the church and the Gospel.

1. The Church Is a Part of the Gospel

The redemptive purpose of God has been from the beginning to call out a people for himself. When he called Abraham, he promised to bless all nations through his posterity and has kept his promise. For all those who are united to Christ, Gentiles as well as Jews, are Abraham's spiritual children and share in the promised blessing.[26]

This wonderful new thing, namely the abolition of the dividing wall between Jews and Gentiles and the creation of a single new humanity, was at the heart of Paul's Gospel (Eph 2:14, 15). He called it "the mystery of Christ," which having been made known to him, he must make known to others (Eph 3:3-9).

Both Evangelicals and Roman Catholics are conscious of past failure in their understanding of the church. Roman Catholics used to concentrate on the church as a hierarchical institution, but now (since Vatican II) see it in new perspective by stressing the important biblical images such as that of the people of God. Evangelicals have sometimes preached an excessively individualistic Gospel, "Christ died for me." This is true (Gal 2:20), but it is far from the whole truth, which is that Christ gave himself for us "to purify for himself a people. . ." (Ti 2:14).

Thus both Roman Catholics and Evangelicals agree that the church as the body of Christ is part of the Gospel. That is to say, the good news includes God's purpose to create for himself through Christ a new, redeemed, united, and international people of his own.

2. The Church Is a Fruit of the Gospel

The first clear proclamation of the good news in the power of the Holy Spirit resulted in the gathered community of God's people—the church (Acts 2:39-42). This was to become the pattern for subsequent apostolic and missionary endeavors with the Gospel. The condition for membership of the community is repentance (chiefly from the sin of unbelief and rejection of Christ) and faith in the Lord Jesus Christ, witnessed to in submission to baptism in his name (Acts 2:38). The benefits of membership include the personal enjoyment of the forgiveness of sins and participation in the new life of the Spirit (Acts 2:38-39; 1 Cor 12:13).

From the beginning, the community of God's people was marked by a devotion to the apostolic teaching, to fellowship (a sharing which extended to practical loving care), to the breaking of bread (the Lord's Supper), and to the prayers or public worship (Acts 2:42). To this believing, worshiping, caring, and witnessing community, "the Lord added to their number day by day those who were being saved" (Acts 2:47).

Evangelicals on the whole have tended to emphasize personal salvation almost to the point of losing sight of the central place of the church. The multiplication of evangelistic organizations and agencies which are not church based has contributed to this distortion. There is, however, a growing desire to correct it. For wherever the Gospel goes, it bears fruit in the spread and growth of the church.

3. The Church Is an Embodiment of the Gospel

The very life of the church as God's new community becomes itself a witness to the Gospel. "The life of the community only acquires its full meaning when it becomes a witness, when it evokes admiration and conversion and when it becomes the preaching and proclamation of the Good News."[27] Thus the church is the sign of the power and the presence of Jesus, the light of Christ shining out visibly to bring all men to that light.[28]

As a fellowship of communities throughout the world, the church is to be "a people brought into unity from the unity of the Father, Son, and Holy Spirit" (Cyprian). This was why Jesus had come into the world and why the living communion of believers between themselves and the Lord of life, and between each other, is to be the proclamation that will move people's hearts to belief (Jn 13:34-35, 17:23).

In every place the believing community speaks to the world by an authentically Christian life given over to God in a communion that nothing should destroy and at the same time given to one's neighbor with limitless zeal (cf. 1 Pt 2:12).

It is also the community of peace which makes Jew and Gentile one, in which by the power of the broken body of Christ, the enmity which stood like a dividing wall between them has been broken down and a single new humanity brought into being (Eph 2:15-16). The church cannot with integrity preach the Gospel of reconciliation unless it is evidently a reconciled community itself.

It is a community that makes present the obedient Lord who underwent death for us. It is founded upon him (Eph 2:20), he is its Lord (Eph 1:22), and its power to speak of him comes from the manner in which it reproduces in all its members and in its common life his obedience to the saving plan of God.

This unity, holiness, love, and obedience are the alternative sign that Christ is not an anonymous or remote Lord. They are the mark of the community given over to God, and they speak about the good news of salvation in Jesus Christ.

4. The Church Is an Agent of the Gospel

That the church must be an agent of the Gospel overflows from its internal life. The church which receives the word must also sound it forth (1 Thes 1:5-8). The church which embodies its message visually must also declare it verbally.

First, the church continues and prolongs the very same mission of Christ.[29]

Secondly, the church received Christ's command to be his witnesses in the power of the Spirit to the end of the earth (Acts 1:8).

Thirdly, the church proclaims the message with the authority of the Lord himself, who gave her the power of the Spirit. As to the qualified subjects of this authority, there are divergences between Evangelicals and Roman Catholics. For Evangelicals, the agent of the proclamation is the whole community of believers, who are equipped for this task by those appointed to the pastoral ministry (Eph 4:11-12). For Roman Catholics also, the evangelistic task belongs to the whole people of God, but they believe bishops have a special role and responsibility both to order the life of the community for this task and, as successors to the ministry of apostolic times, to preach the good news of the kingdom.

To sum up, the church and the Gospel belong indissolubly together. We cannot think of either apart from the other. For God's purpose to create a new community through Christ is itself an important element in the good news. The church is also both the fruit and the agent of the Gospel, since it is through the Gospel that the church spreads, and through the church that the Gospel spreads. Above all, unless the church embodies the Gospel, giving it visible flesh and blood, the Gospel lacks credibility and the church lacks effectiveness in witness.

More and more Christians are recognizing this lack of a fully credible, effective witness because of divisions among themselves. They believe that Christ has called all his disciples in every age to be witnesses to him and his Gospel to the ends of the earth (cf. Acts 1:8). Yet those who profess such discipleship differ about the meaning of the one Gospel and go their different ways as if Christ himself were divided (cf. 1 Cor 1:13). To be sure, Christian separations and divisions have often been due to conscientiously held convictions, and Christian unity must not be sought at the expense of Christian truth. Nevertheless, the divisions and their causes contradict the will of Jesus Christ, who desires his people to be united in truth and love. They also hinder the proclamation of his good news of reconciliation. Therefore the Gospel calls the church to be renewed in truth, holiness, and unity, in order that it may be effectively renewed for mission as well.

6. The Gospel and Culture

The influence of culture on evangelism, conversion, and church formation is increasingly recognized as a topic of major missiological importance. The Willowbank Report *Gospel and Culture* (1978) defines culture as "an integrated system of beliefs (about God or reality or ultimate meaning), of values (about what is true, good, beautiful, and normative), of customs (how to behave, relate to others, talk, pray, dress, work, play, trade, farm, eat, etc.), and of institutions which express these beliefs, values, and customs (government, law courts, temples or churches, family, schools, hospitals, factories, shops, unions, clubs, etc.), which binds a society together and gives it a sense of identity, dignity, security and continuity."[30] Viewed thus, culture pervades the whole of human life, and it is essential for Christians to know how to evaluate it.

It is acknowledged that Evangelicals and Roman Catholics start from a different background. Evangelicals tend to stress the discontinuity, and Roman Catholics the continuity, between man unredeemed and man redeemed. At the same time, both emphases are qualified. Discontinuity is qualified by the Evangelical recognition of the image of God in humankind and continuity by the Roman Catholic recognition that human beings and societies are contaminated by sin. The *Lausanne Covenant* summarized this tension as follows: "Because man is God's creature, some of his culture is rich in beauty and goodness. Because he is fallen, all of it is tainted with sin and some of it is demonic."[31]

We have particularly concentrated on the place of culture in four areas—in the Bible, in cross-cultural evangelism, in conversion, and in church formation.

1. Culture and the Bible

We have already affirmed that the Bible is the word of God through the words of human beings. Realizing that human language and human thought forms reflect human cultures, we saw the need to explore two major questions:

    a.   What was the attitude of the biblical authors to their cultures?
    b.   How should we ourselves react to the cultural conditioning of Scripture?

In answer to the first question, we considered the New Testament. Its message comes to us from the context of the first-century world, with its own images and vocabulary, and is thus set in the context of that world's culture. The culture has become the vehicle of the message.

Yet within that first-century culture there were elements which the Christian and the church were required to resist, out of loyalty to the Lord Jesus. Distinctions between the new community and the surrounding culture were clearly drawn. At the same time, the Christian and the church enjoyed a new freedom in Christ, which enabled them to discern those elements in the culture which must be rejected as hostile to their faith and those which were compatible with it and could on that account be affirmed. Blindness, which leads Christians to tolerate the evil and/or overlook the good in their culture, is a permanent temptation.

Our other question was concerned with how we ourselves should react to the cultural conditioning of Scripture. It breaks down into two subsidiary questions which express the options before us. First, are the biblical formulations (which we have already affirmed to be normative) so intrinsically conditioned by their mode of specific cultural expression that they cannot be changed to suit different cultural settings? Put another way, has biblical inspiration (which Evangelicals and Roman Catholics both acknowledge) made the cultural forms themselves normative? The alternative is to ask whether it is the revealed teaching which is normative, so that this may be re-expressed in other cultural forms. We believe the latter to be the case, and that such re-expression or translation is a responsibility laid both on cross-cultural missionaries and on local Christian leaders.[32]

2. Culture and Evangelism

Christian missionaries find themselves in a challenging cross-cultural, indeed tri-cultural, situation. They come from a particular culture themselves, they travel to people nurtured in another, and they take with them a biblical Gospel which was originally formulated in a third. How will this interplay of cultures affect their evangelism? And how can they be simultaneously faithful to Scripture and relevant to the local culture?

In the history of mission in this century, a progress is discernible. The successive approaches may be summarized as follows:

a. In the first period, the missionary brought along with the gospel message many of the cultural trappings of his or her own situation. Then culture, instead of being (as in the New Testament) a vehicle for the proclamation of the Gospel, became a barrier to it. Accidentals of teaching and practice were taught as if they were essentials, and a culture-Christianity was preached as if it were the Gospel.

b. In the second period, the gospel message was translated into terms (language and thought forms, artistic symbols, and music) appropriate to those to whom it was brought, and the cultural trappings began to be left behind. Now local cultures, instead of being neglected, were respected and where possible, used for the better communication of the Gospel. In a word, the Gospel began to be "contextualized."

c. In the third period, in which we are living, missionaries bring both the biblical Gospel and an experience of life in Christ. They also endeavor to take seriously the people to whom they have come, with their world view and way of life, so that they may find their own authentic way of experiencing and expressing the salvation of Christ. This kind of evangelism tries to be both faithful to the biblical revelation and relevant to the people's culture. In fact it aims at bringing Scripture, context, and experience into a working relationship effective for presenting the Gospel.

3. Culture and Conversion

We are clear that conversion includes repentance and that repentance is a turning away from the old life. But what are the aspects of the old life from which a convert must turn away? Conversion cannot be just turning away from "sin" as this is viewed in any one particular culture. For different cultures have different understandings of sin, and we have to recognize this aspect of pluralism. So missionaries and church leaders in each place need great wisdom, both at the time of a person's conversion and during his or her maturing as a Christian, to distinguish between the moral and the cultural, between what is clearly approved or condemned by the Gospel on the one hand and by custom or convention on the other. The repentance of conversion should be a turning away only from what the Gospel condemns.

4. Culture and Church Formation

In the development of the Christian community in each place, as in the other areas we have mentioned, missionaries must avoid all cultural imperialism; that is, the imposition on the church of alien cultural forms. Just as the Gospel has to be inculturated, so must the church be inculturated also.

We all agree that the aim of "indigenization" or "inculturation" is to make local Christians congenial members of the body of Christ. They must not imagine that to become Christian is to become western and so to repudiate their own cultural and national inheritance. The same principle applies in the West, where too often to become Christian has also meant to become middle-class.

There are a number of spheres in which each church should be allowed to develop its own identity. The first is the question of certain forms of organization, especially as they relate to church leadership. Although Roman Catholics and Evangelicals take a different approach to authority and its exercise, we are agreed that in every Christian community (especially a new one), authority must be exercised in a spirit of service. "I am among you as one who serves," Jesus said (Lk 22:27). Yet the expression given to leadership can vary according to different cultures.

The second sphere is that of artistic creativity—for example, church architecture, painting, symbols, music, and drama. Local churches will want to express their Christian identity in artistic forms which reflect their local culture.

A third area is theology. Every church should encourage theological reflection on the aspirations of its culture and seek to develop a theology which gives expression to these. Yet only in such a way as to apply, not compromise, the biblical revelation.

Two problems confront a church which is seeking to "inculturate" itself, namely, provincialism and syncretism. "Provincialism" asserts the local culture of a particular church to the extent that it cuts itself adrift from, and even repudiates, other churches. We are agreed that new expressions of local church life must in no way break fellowship with the wider Christian community.

Syncretism is the attempt to fuse the biblical Gospel with elements of local culture which, being erroneous or evil, are incompatible with it. But the Gospel's true relation to culture is discriminating, judging some elements and welcoming others. The criteria it applies to different elements or forms include the questions whether they are under the judgment of Christ's lordship and whether they manifest the fruit of the Spirit.

It has to be admitted that every expression of Christian truth is inadequate and may be distorted. Hence the need for mutually respectful dialogue about the relative merits of old and new forms, in the light of both the biblical revelation and the experience of the wider community of faith.

The Second Vatican Council addressed itself to these important matters. It recognized that in every culture there are some elements which may need to be "purged of evil association" and to be restored "to Christ their source, who overthrows the rule of the devil and limits the manifold malice of evil." In this way "the good found in people's minds and hearts, or in particular customs and cultures, is purified, raised to a higher level and reaches its perfection. . . ."[33]

Hence it is not a question of adapting things which come from the world usurped by Satan, but of repossessing them for Christ. To take them over as they are could be syncretism. "Repossession," on the other hand, entails four steps: (a) the selection of certain elements from one's culture; (b) the rejection of other elements which are incompatible with the essence of the biblical faith; (c) the purification from the elements selected and adopted of everything unworthy; (d) the integration of these into the faith and life of the church.

The age to come has broken into this present age in such a way as to touch our lives with both grace and judgment. It cuts through every culture. Vatican II referred to this discontinuity and also emphasized the need for "the spiritual qualities and endowments of every age and nation" to be fortified, completed, and restored in Christ.[34]

For Jesus Christ is Lord of all, and our supreme desire *vis-a-vis* each culture is to "take every thought captive to obey Christ" (2 Cor 10:5).

7. The Possibilities of Common Witness

We turn in our last chapter from theological exploration to practical action. We have indicated where we agree and disagree. We now consider what we can do and cannot do together. Since our discussion on this topic was incomplete, what follows awaits further development.

1. Our Unity and Disunity

We have tried to face with honesty and candor the issues which divide us as Roman Catholics and Evangelicals. We have neither ignored, nor discounted, nor even minimized them. For they are real and, in some cases, serious.

At the same time, we know and have experienced that the walls of our separation do not reach to heaven. There is much that unites us and much in each other's different manifestations of Christian faith and life which we have come to appreciate. Our concern throughout our dialogue has not been with the structural unity of churches, but rather with the possibilities of common witness. So when we write of "unity," it is this that we have in mind.

To begin with, we acknowledge in ourselves and in each other a firm belief in God, Father, Son, and Holy Spirit. This faith is for us more than a conviction; it is a commitment. We have come to the Father through the Son by the Holy Spirit (Eph 2:18).

We also recognize that the Gospel is God's good news about his Son Jesus Christ (Rom 1:1-3), about his godhead and manhood, his life and teaching, his acts and promises, his death and resurrection, and about the salvation he has once accomplished and now offers. Moreover, Jesus Christ is our Savior and our Lord, for he is the object of our personal trust, devotion, and expectation. Indeed, faith, hope, and love are his gifts to us, bestowed on us freely without any merit of our own.

In addition, God's word and Spirit nourish this new life within us. We see in one another "the fruit of the Spirit," which is "love, joy, peace, patience, kindness, goodness, faithfulness, gentleness, self-control" (Gal 5:22-23). No wonder Paul continues in this text with an exhortation that there be among us "no self-conceit, no provoking of one another, no envy of one another" (5:26).

There is therefore between us an initial if incomplete unity. Nevertheless, divisions continue even in some doctrines of importance, as we have made clear in earlier chapters of our report. Our faith has developed in us strong convictions (as it should), some uniting us, others dividing us. The very strength of our convictions has not only drawn us together in mutual respect, but has also been a source of painful tension. This has been the price of our encounter; attempts to conceal or dilute our differences would not have been authentic dialogue but a travesty of it. So would have been any attempt to magnify or distort our difference. We confess that in the past members of both our constituencies have been guilty of misrepresenting each other, on account of either laziness in study, unwillingness to listen, superficial judgments, or pure prejudice. Whenever we have done this, we have borne false witness against our neighbor.

This, then, is the situation. Deep truths already unite us in Christ. Yet real and important convictions still divide us. In the light of this, we ask: what can we do together?

2. Common Witness

"Witness" in the New Testament normally denotes the unique testimony of the apostolic eyewitnesses who could speak of Jesus from what they had seen and heard. It is also used more generally of all Christians who commend Christ to others out of their personal experience of him and in response to his commission. We are using the word here, however, in the even wider sense of any Christian activity which points to Christ, a usage made familiar by the two documents jointly produced by the World Council of Churches and the Roman Catholic Church, which are entitled *Common Witness and Proselytism* (1970) and *Common Witness* (1980).

A. Common Witness in Bible Translation and Publishing

It is extremely important that Roman Catholics and Protestants should have an agreed, common text in each vernacular. Divergent texts breed mutual suspicion; a mutually acceptable text develops confidence and facilitates joint Bible study. The United Bible Societies have rendered valuable service in this area, and the Common Bible (RSV), published in English in 1973, marked a step forward in Roman Catholic–Protestant relationships.

The inclusion of the Old Testament Apocrypha (books written in Greek during the last two centuries before Christ), which the Roman Catholic Church includes as part of the Bible, has proved a problem, and in some countries Evangelicals have for this reason not felt free to use this version. The United Bible Societies and the Secretariat for Promoting Christian Unity have published some guidelines in this matter,[35] which recommend that the Apocrypha be printed "as a separate section before the New Testament" and described as "deutero-canonical."

Many Evangelicals feel able to use a Common Bible in these circumstances, although most would prefer the Apocrypha to be omitted altogether.

B. Common Witness in the Use of Media

Although we have put down the availability of a Common Bible as a priority need, Evangelicals and Roman Catholics are united in recognizing the importance of Christian literature in general and of Christian audiovisual aids. In particular, it is of great value when the Common Bible is supplemented by Common Bible reading aids. In some parts of the world, Bible atlases and handbooks, Bible dictionaries and commentaries, and explanatory notes for daily Bible reading are available in a form which betrays no denominational or ecclesiastical bias. The same is true of some Christian films and filmstrips. So Evangelicals and Roman Catholics may profitably familiarize themselves with each other's materials with a view to using them whenever possible.

In addition, the opportunity is given to the churches in some countries to use the national radio and television service for Christian programs. We suggest, especially in countries where Christians form a small minority of the total population, that the Roman Catholic Church, the Protestant churches, and specialist organizations cooperate rather than compete with one another in the development of suitable programs.

C. Common Witness in Community Service

The availability of welfare varies greatly from country to country. Some governments provide generous social services, although often the spiritual dimension is missing, and then Christians can bring faith, loving compassion, and hope to an otherwise secular service. In other countries the government's provision is inadequate or unevenly distributed. In such a situation the churches have a particular responsibility to discover the biggest gaps and seek to fill them. In many cases the government welcomes the church's contribution.

In the name of Christ, Roman Catholics and Evangelicals can serve human need together providing emergency relief for the victims of flood, famine, and earthquake, and shelter for refugees; promoting urban and rural development; feeding the hungry and healing the sick; caring for the elderly and the dying; providing a marriage guidance, enrichment, and reconciliation service, a pregnancy advisory service, and support for single parent families; arranging educational opportunities for the illiterate and job creation schemes for the unemployed; and rescuing young people from drug addiction and young women from prostitution. There seems to be no justification for organizing separate Roman Catholic and Evangelical projects of a purely humanitarian nature and every reason for undertaking them together. Although faith may still in part divide us, love for neighbor should unite us.

D. Common Witness in Social Thought and Action

There is a pressing need for fresh Christian thinking about the urgent social issues which confront the contemporary world. The Roman Catholic Church has done noteworthy work in this area, not least through the social encyclicals of recent popes. Evangelicals are only now beginning to catch up after some decades of neglect. It should be to our mutual advantage to engage in Christian social debate together. A clear and united Christian witness is needed in face of such challenges as the nuclear arms race, North-South economic inequality, the environmental crisis, and the revolution in sexual mores.

Whether a common mind will lead us to common action will depend largely on how far the government of our countries is democratic or autocratic, influenced by Christian values or imbued with an ideology unfriendly to the Gospel. Where a regime is oppressive, and a Christian prophetic voice needs to be heard, it should be a single voice which speaks for both Roman Catholics and Protestants. Such a united witness could also provide some stimulus to the quest for peace, justice, and disarmament; testify to the sanctity of sex, marriage, and family life; agitate for the reform of permissive abortion legislation; defend human rights and religious freedom; denounce the use of torture and campaign for prisoners of conscience; promote Christian moral values in public life and in the education of children; seek to eliminate racial and sexual discrimination; contribute to the renewal of decayed inner cities; and oppose dishonesty and corruption. There are many such areas in which Roman Catholics and Evangelicals can both think together and take action together. Our witness will be stronger if it is a common witness.

E. Common Witness in Dialogue

The word "dialogue" means different things to different people. Some Christians regard it as inherently compromising, since they believe it expresses an unwillingness to affirm revealed truth, let alone to proclaim it. But to us "dialogue" means a frank and serious conversation between individuals or groups, in which each is prepared to listen respectfully to the other, with a view to increased understanding on the part of both. We see no element of compromise in this. On the contrary, we believe it is essentially Christian to meet one another face to face rather than preserving our isolation from one another and even indifference to one another, and to listen to one another's own statements of position, rather than relying on secondhand reports. In authentic dialogue we struggle to listen carefully not only to what the other person is saying but to the strongly cherished concerns which lie behind his or her words. In this process our caricatures of one another become corrected.

We believe that the most fruitful kind of Evangelical–Roman Catholic dialogue arises out of joint Bible study. For, as this report makes clear, both sides regard the Bible as God's word and acknowledge the need to read, study, believe, and obey it. It is surely through the word of God that, illumined by the Spirit of God, we shall progress towards greater agreement.

We also think that there is need for Evangelical–Roman Catholic dialogue on the great theological and ethical issues which are being debated in all the churches, and that an exchange of visiting scholars in seminaries could be particularly productive.

Honest and charitable dialogue is beneficial to those who take part in it; it enriches our faith, deepens our understanding, and fortifies and clarifies our convictions. It is also a witness in itself, inasmuch as it testifies to the desire for reconciliation and meanwhile expresses a love which encompasses even those who disagree.

Further, theological dialogue can sometimes lead to common affirmation, especially in relation to the unbelieving world and to new theological trends which owe more to contemporary culture than to revelation or Christian tradition. Considered and united declarations by Roman Catholics and Evangelicals could make a powerful contribution to current theological discussion.

F. Common Witness in Worship

The word "worship" is used in a wide range of senses from the spontaneous prayers of the "two or three" met in Christ's name in a home to formal liturgical services in church.

We do not think that either Evangelicals or Roman Catholics should hesitate to join in common prayer when they meet in each other's homes. Indeed, if they have gathered for a Bible study group, it would be most appropriate for them to pray together for illumination before the study and after it for grace to obey. Larger informal meetings should give no difficulty either. Indeed, in many parts of the world Evangelicals and Roman Catholics are already meeting for common praise and prayer, both in charismatic celebrations and in gatherings which would not describe themselves thus. Through such experiences they have been drawn into a deeper experience of God and so into a closer fellowship with one another. Occasional participation in each other's services in church is also natural, especially for the sake of family solidarity and friendship.

It is when the possibility of common participation in the holy communion or eucharist is raised that major problems of conscience arise. Both sides of our dialogue would strongly discourage indiscriminate approaches to common sacramental worship.

The Mass lies at the heart of Roman Catholic doctrine and practice, and it has been emphasized even more in Catholic spirituality since the Second Vatican Council. Anyone is free to attend Mass. Other Christians may not receive communion at it, however, except when they request it in certain limited cases of "spiritual necessity" specified by current Roman Catholic legislation. Roman Catholics may on occasion attend a Protestant communion service as an act of worship. But there is no ruling of the Roman Catholic Church which would permit its members to receive communion in a Protestant church service, even on ecumenical occasions. Nor would Roman Catholics feel in conscience free to do so.

Many Evangelical churches practice an "open" communion policy, in that they announce a welcome to everybody who "is trusting in Jesus Christ for salvation and is in love and charity with all people," whatever their church affiliation. They do not exclude Roman Catholic believers. Most Evangelicals would feel conscientiously unable to present themselves at a Roman Catholic Mass, however, even assuming they were invited. This is because the doctrine of the Mass was one of the chief points at issue during the sixteenth-century Reformation, and Evangelicals are not satisfied with the Roman Catholic explanation of the relation between the sacrifice of Christ on the cross and the sacrifice of the Mass. But this question was not discussed at our meetings.

Since both Roman Catholics and Evangelicals believe that the Lord's Supper was instituted by Jesus as a means of grace[36] and agree that he commanded his disciples to "do this in remembrance" of him, it is a grief to us that we are so deeply divided in an area in which we should be united and that we are therefore unable to obey Christ's command together. Before this becomes possible, some profound and sustained theological study of this topic will be needed; we did not even begin it at ERCDOM.

G. Common Witness in Evangelism

Although there are some differences in our definitions of evangelism, Roman Catholics and Evangelicals are agreed that evangelism involves proclaiming the Gospel, and that therefore any common evangelism necessarily presupposes a common commitment to the same Gospel. In earlier chapters of this report we have drawn attention to certain doctrines in which our understanding is identical or very similar. We desire to affirm these truths together. In other important areas, however, substantial agreement continues to elude us, and therefore common witness in evangelism would seem to be premature, although we are aware of situations in some parts of the world in which Evangelicals and Roman Catholics have felt able to make a common proclamation.

Evangelicals are particularly sensitive in this matter, which is perhaps not surprising, since their very appellation "evangelical" includes in itself the word "evangel" (Gospel). Evangelicals claim to be "Gospel" people, and are usually ready, if asked, to give a summary of their understanding of the Gospel. This would have at its heart what they often call "the finished work of Christ," namely, that by bearing our sins on the cross, Jesus Christ did everything necessary for our salvation and that we have only to put our trust in him in order to be saved. Although many Evangelicals will admit that their presentation of the Gospel is often one-sided or defective, yet they could not contemplate any evangelism in which the good news of God's justification of sinners by his grace in Christ through faith alone is not proclaimed.

Roman Catholics also have their problems of conscience. They would not necessarily want to deny the validity of the message which Evangelicals preach but would say that important aspects of the Gospel are missing from it. In particular, they emphasize the need both to live out the Gospel in the sacramental life of the church and to respect the teaching authority of the church. Indeed, they see evangelism as essentially a church activity done by the church in relation to the church.

So long as each side regards the other's view of the Gospel as defective, there exists a formidable obstacle to be overcome. This causes us particular sorrow in our dialogue on mission, in which we have come to appreciate one another and to discover unexpected agreements. Yet we must respect one another's integrity. We commit ourselves to further prayer, study, and discussion in the hope that a way forward may be found.

3. Unworthy Witness

We feel the need to allude to the practice of seeking to evangelize people who are already church members, since this causes misunderstanding and even resentment, especially when Evangelicals are seeking to "convert" Roman Catholics. It arises from the phenomenon which Evangelicals call "nominal Christianity" and which depends on the rather sharp distinction they draw between the visible church (of professing or "nominal" Christians) and the invisible church (of committed or genuine Christians)—that is, between those who are Christian only in name and those who are Christian in reality. Evangelicals see nominal Christians as needing to be won for Christ. Roman Catholics also speak of "evangelizing" such people, although they refer to them as "lapsed " or "inactive" rather than as "nominal," because they do not make a separation between the visible and invisible church. They are understandably offended whenever Evangelicals appear to regard all Roman Catholics as *ipso facto* unbelievers, and when they base their evangelism on a distorted view of Roman Catholic teaching and practice. On the other hand, since Evangelicals seek to evangelize the nominal members of their own churches, as well as of others, they see this activity as an authentic concern for the Gospel, and not as a reprehensible kind of "sheep-stealing." Roman Catholics do not accept this reasoning.

We recognize that conscientious conviction leads some people to change from Catholic to Evangelical or Evangelical to Catholic allegiance, and leads others to seek to persuade people to do so. If this happens in conscience and without coercion, we would not call it proselytism.

There are other forms of witness, however, which we would all describe as "unworthy," and therefore as being "proselytism" rather than "evangelism." We agree, in general, with the analysis of this given in the study document entitled *Common Witness and Proselytism* (1970), and in particular we emphasize three aspects of it.

First, proselytism takes place when our motive is unworthy, for example when our real concern in witness is not the glory of God through the salvation of human beings but rather the prestige of our own Christian community or indeed our personal prestige.

Secondly, we are guilty of proselytism whenever our methods are unworthy, especially when we resort to any kind of "physical coercion, moral constraint, or psychological pressure," when we seek to induce conversion by the offer of material or political benefits, or when we exploit other people's need, weakness, or lack of education. These practices are an affront both to the freedom and dignity of human beings and to the Holy Spirit whose witness is gentle and not coercive.

Thirdly, we are guilty of proselytism whenever our message includes "unjust or uncharitable reference to the beliefs or practices of other religious communities in the hope of winning adherents." If we find it necessary to make comparisons, we should compare the strengths and weaknesses of one church with those of the other, and not set what is best in the one against what is worst in the other. To descend to deliberate misrepresentation is incompatible with truth and love.

Conclusion

We who have participated in ERCDOM III are agreed that every possible opportunity for common witness should be taken, except where conscience forbids. We cannot make decisions for one another, however, because we recognize that the situation varies in different groups and places. In any case, the sad fact of our divisions on important questions of faith always puts a limit on the common witness which is possible. At one end of the spectrum are those who can contemplate no cooperation of any kind. At the other are those who desire a very full cooperation. In between are many who still find some forms of common witness conscientiously impossible, while they find others to be the natural, positive expression of common concern and conviction. In some Third World situations, for example, the divisions which originated in Europe are felt with less intensity, and mutual trust has grown through united prayer and study of the word of God. Although all Christians should understand the historical origins and theological issues of the Reformation, yet our continuing division is a stumbling block and the Gospel calls us to repentance, renewal, and reconciliation.

We believe that the Evangelical–Roman Catholic Dialogue on Mission has now completed its task. At the same time we hope that dialogue on mission between Roman Catholics and Evangelicals will continue, preferably on a regional or local basis, in order that further progress may be made towards a common understanding, sharing, and proclaiming of "the faith which was once for all delivered to the saints" (Jude 3). We commit these past and future endeavors to God, and pray that by "speaking the truth in love, we are to grow up in every way into him who is the head, into Christ" (Eph 4:15).

Participants

ERCDOM I
Venice, April 1977

Evangelical
Professor Peter Beyerhaus
Most Rev. Donald Cameron
Dr. Orlando Costas
Mr. Martin Goldsmith
Dr. David Hubbard
Rev. Gottfried Osei-Mensah
Rev. Peter Savage
Rev. John Stott

Roman Catholic
Sr. Joan Chatfield
Rev. Pierre Duprey
Msgr. Basil Meeking
Rev. Dionisio Minguez Fernandez
Rev. John Paul Musinsky
Rev. Waly Neven
Rev. Robert Rweyemamu
Rev. Thomas Stransky

ERCDOM II
Cambridge, England, March 1982

Evangelical
Dr. Kwame Bediako
Professor Peter Beyerhaus

Most Rev. Donald Cameron
Mr. Martin Goldsmith
Dr. David Hubbard
Rev. Peter Savage
Rev. John Stott
Dr. David Wells

Roman Catholic
Sr. Joan Chatfield
Rev. Parmananda Divarkar
Rev. Pierre Duprey
Rev. René Girault
Msgr. Basil Meeking
Msgr. Jorge Mejia
Rev. John Mutiso-Mbinda
Rev. John Redford
Msgr. Pietro Rossano
Rev. Thomas Stransky

ERCDOM III
Landévennec, France, April 1984

Evangelical
Dr. Kwame Bediako
Most Rev. Donald Cameron
Dr. Harvie Conn
Mr. Martin Goldsmith
Rev. John Stott
Dr. David Wells

Roman Catholic
Sr. Joan Chatfield
Rev. Matthieu Collin
Sr. Joan Delaney
Rev. Claude Geffré
Msgr. Basil Meeking
Rev. Philip Rosato
Most Rev. Anselme Sanon
Rev. Bernard Sesboué
Rev. Thomas Stransky

NOTES

1. "Evangelism" and "evangelization" are used indiscriminately in this report. The former is commoner among Evangelicals, the latter among Roman Catholics, but both words describe the same activity of spreading the Gospel.

2. Given the diversity of the Evangelical constituency as well as the differences of understanding between Evangelicals and Roman Catholics, the use of the word "church" in this paper inevitably carries some ambiguity. Further conversations would be required before it would be possible to arrive at greater clarity and common terms of ecclesiological discourse.

3. UR, no. 6, in *The Documents of Vatican II*, ed. Walter M. Abbott (Geoffrey Chapman, 1967).

4. Ibid., no. 4.

5. DV, nos. 23, 24.

6. *The Lausanne Covenant:* An Exposition and Commentary by John Stott (World Wide Publications, 1975), Lausanne Occasional Paper No. 3.

7. EN.

8. *Lausanne Covenant,* no. 4.

9. EN, no. 22.

10. E.g., Psalm 19:1-6; Romans 1:19-20.

11. DV, no. 13.

12. Ibid., no. 10.

13. Ibid., no. 22.

14. E.g., 1 Thessalonians 5:14-15; Hebrews 3:12-13; 12:15.

15. E.g., Mark 10:23-27; cf. Isaiah 52:7.

16. In this report we use "the Lord's Supper," "the holy communion," and "the eucharist" indiscriminately; no particular theology is implied by these terms. "The Mass" is limited to Roman Catholic contexts. Similarly we use "sacrament" or "ordinance" in relation to baptism and eucharist without doctrinal implications.

17. E.g., Ephesians 2:1-3; 4:17-19; 2 Corinthians 4:3-4.

18. GS, no. 13.

19. Ibid.

20. Ibid.

21. Pope John Paul II, encyclical *Redemptor Hominis* (Catholic Truth Society, 1979), no. 14.

22. LG, no. 8.

23. LG, no. 16.

24. Cf. Ephesians 3:10; 3:18; 4:13.

25. SC, nos. 7, 47.

26. E.g., Romans 4; Galatians 3.

27. EN.

28. LG, chap. I.

29. John 20:21-22; cf. Matthew 28:16-20; Luke 24:46-49.

30. *The Willowbank Report: Consultation on Gospel and Culture* (Lausanne Committee for World Evangelization, 1978), Lausanne Occasional Paper No. 2, no. 2.

31. *Lausanne Covenant*, no. 10.

32. Here Roman Catholics will want to make reference to the encyclical of Pope John Paul II, *Slavorum Apostoli*, 2nd June 1985.

33. AG, no. 9.

34. GS, no. 58.

35. *Guiding Principles for Interconfessional Cooperation in Translating the Bible* (1968).

36. See Chapter 4 (3).

PART EIGHT

Joint Working Group World Council of Churches– Roman Catholic

Introductory Note

✠ *Basil Meeking*

The Joint Working Group of the World Council of Churches and the Roman Catholic Church is one of the numerous structures that serve some part of the enormous range of activities of the ecumenical movement.

Just before the group came into being in 1965, it was heralded by a photo in *Time* magazine of Dr. Willem Viser't Hooft, first General Secretary of the World Council of Churches, and Rev. Jerome Hamer, OP, soon to become Secretary of the Secretariat for Promoting Christian Unity in Rome. Both were wreathed in smiles in a swimming pool in West Africa. It was part of an account of a meeting of the Central Committee of the World Council of Churches at Enugu in Nigeria that had just mandated the creation of the group.

So it began in sunshine. First contacts, however, of the Roman Catholic Church with the World Council of Churches, when the latter was founded in 1948, had been very slight and were marked by considerable reserve. They flowered after Pope John XXIII announced the Second Vatican Council and with the contacts initiated by Cardinal Bea, President of the Secretariat for Promoting Christian Unity, with the Ecumenical Centre in Geneva. The presence of World Council of Churches observers at the Second Vatican Council did much to create the very positive climate in which the Joint Working Group was founded.

What emerges as one looks over the thirty-two years of its history, its many meetings, its projects, and its publications is a chiaroscuro that mirrors the relationship between its two parent bodies. The fortunate sunny beginning tided it over some more trying times. The outcome today is a well-established, solid relationship with real achievement, sustained by a substratum of considerable mutual trust.

The Joint Working Group, in the words of its *First Report*, "was set up to exam-ine possibilities in the field of dialogue and cooperation. . . . Its business is the joint study of problems and thereafter to report to the competent authorities on both sides." As its mandate said: "The task of the Joint Working Group is to work out the principles to be used in further collaboration." It was not, said the report, "to under-take negotiations between the Roman Catholic Church and the member churches of the World Council of Churches." Moreover, "it has no power to make decisions." In fact, at the outset it had been envisaged that the group would simply be the launching pad for a direct working relationship between the Roman Catholic Church and the World Council of Churches and their own various agencies and departments. The Joint Working Group would be a kind of midwife.

At no point were the relations between the World Council of Churches and the Roman Catholic Church to be a substitute for the bilateral relations of the Catholic Church with individual churches that might be members of the World Council of Churches.

The caution evident in that description of the functions of the group ought not give the impression that the atmosphere in those early days was anything but very warm. Indeed, it had developed rapidly, with a number of close personal friend-ships. And very soon it was possible to raise the question of an even closer struc-tural expression of the relationship.

In the group's *First Report* the question was raised, and it was said, "The mem-bers of the Joint Working Group think that for the moment the common cause of Christian unity would not be furthered if the Roman Catholic Church were to join the World Council of Churches."

However, quite shortly afterward, one of the official Catholic observers at the 1968 Fourth Assembly of the World Council of Churches in a major address raised the possibility. That was done on his own initiative but already, despite the earlier disclaimer, it had begun to be mentioned in the Joint Working Group.

The following year, marking the first visit of a pope to the World Council headquarters in Geneva, Pope Paul VI in his address raised the question but said, however, that he did not consider the possibility mature enough to be able to give a positive answer. At first this displeased some on the side of the World Council, but others interpreted it as putting the question officially on the agenda. In fact, the Joint Working Group had mandated a study on what form the relation of the Roman Catholic Church with the World Council should take and how the collab-oration should go on.

Unfortunately, this raised unduly high hopes in the World Council of Churches. These were shattered in 1972 when the publication of a joint report on Roman Catholic–World Council of Churches collaboration said clearly that

Catholic membership was not to be expected in any immediate future. This was a cloud that hung over the relations for a number of years.

The study had suggested a number of areas of cooperation. In fact the Joint Working Group has since gone ahead with many of them. The overall relationship has grown and matured. In light of that experience, the World Council has been able to see that Catholic membership would indeed mean a World Council of Churches so restructured as to be a different institution.

It was said in the 1972 report that there are no theological reasons against Catholic membership in the World Council. However, at the outset the disparity between the Roman Catholic Church and World Council of Churches had been noted: "On the one hand we have a church, on the other a fellowship of churches." One has to add further that on the one hand there is a fellowship of churches organized on a national or regional basis, and on the other a church for whom its universal dimension is primary. Already that suggests an ecclesiological factor in the hesitation of the Roman Catholic Church to seek World Council membership.

It can, of course, be argued that there is an evident anomaly in the amount and intensity of the collaboration that marks the relationship between the Catholic Church and the World Council. It is greater than that undertaken by many of the council's member churches. Yet it fits the realities of the present situation of the two partners even though the Roman Catholic Church remains a nonmember.

So, against the original intentions, the Joint Working Group has become a necessary fixture and taken on a substantial role, while still acting primarily as a catalyst, bringing together appropriate offices and agencies on each side and working mainly through ad hoc consultations and groups of experts.

While the very substantial Catholic participation in the World Council's Faith and Order Commission accounts for the greatest part of the theological collaboration between the Roman Catholic Church and the World Council of Churches, the Joint Working Group has a significant role in enabling discussion of certain questions not being taken up elsewhere. They are the kind of topics found in the Joint Working Group documents published in the present collection. The Joint Working Group will have to continue to be the forum in which similar questions are worked out. The exchanges between Rome and Geneva in 1997 on the goal of the ecumenical movement might suggest that further work could be done on that question.

As the World Council of Churches prepares for its Eighth Assembly in 1998, the Joint Working Group continues actively to look at the development of the relationship between the Roman Catholic Church and the World Council of Churches and to monitor potential sources of tension and sources of new division as well as promoting a common witness wherever possible.

The group is still a consultative forum to initiate, evaluate, and sustain forms of collaboration between the two partners, reporting to the Assembly of the World Council of Churches and to the Pontifical Council for Promoting Christian Unity. It will try to interpret the major streams of ecumenical thought and action to the Roman Catholic Church and to the member churches of the World Council of Churches and seek to establish collaboration between the various organs and programs of the Catholic Church and the World Council.

The continuing significance of the Joint Working Group can be gauged from what the World Council vision statement, prepared for its Eighth Assembly, says about the World Council of Churches–Roman Catholic relationship:

> We give thanks to God that the Roman Catholic Church is, since the Second Vatican Council, an active participant in the ecumenical movement and a valued partner in various ways with the World Council of Churches (especially through the Joint Working Group and participation in the Commission on Faith and Order). The member churches of the World Council of Churches and the Roman Catholic Church are inspired by the same vision of God's plan to unite all things in Christ. It is inconceivable to us that either the World Council of Churches or the Roman Catholic Church could pursue its ecumenical calling without the collaboration of the other and we firmly hope that both will look for ways to deepen and expand this relationship in the years ahead.

The Fifth Report of the Joint Working Group

June 1982

Introduction

By the time of the Sixth Assembly of the World Council of Churches (1983) there will have been over twenty years of official contacts between the World Council of Churches and the Roman Catholic Church. The Joint Working Group, established in 1965 to serve this relationship, has already submitted four official reports to its respective authorities. The first three had simply recorded what had been done in study and collaboration. The *Fourth Report*, presented to the Fifth Assembly in 1975, also looked ahead to what should and could be done. This *Fifth Report* is presented in the same spirit.

Further, the last seven years have been crowded with church and world events which have deeply influenced the one ecumenical movement and which call for a more widespread and stronger commitment to its goals and its tasks. These events are first outlined here, in order that realism may mark the evaluation of past collaboration between the Roman Catholic Church and the World Council of Churches and the projections for their relationship during the next decade.

I. The Ecumenical Situation

1. Changes in the World Community

Reflection must begin with a vivid consciousness of those changes in the world community which are transforming the cultural, economic, social, and political relations between peoples. The inescapable interdependence of all areas and peoples of the inhabited earth is matched by increasing consciousness of that fact. The human family becomes more aware that it faces either a common future or a common fate. Threats to peace have so critically increased that life itself is at stake. Oppression and violence are destroying the fragile fabric of human communities.

Appalling affluence and consumption of the earth's resources exacerbate growing impatience on the part of the poor and increasing frustration among those not so deprived but who feel themselves powerless to close the gap. New causes of contention continue to arise among nations. Many countries are split within by political and social divisions of great bitterness which lead to confrontation and violence. The precariousness of the economic situation, the breakdown of structures and services, unemployment, and the slowness in finding a new world economic order increase frustration and fear and cynicism. Religion, and its claim to be a source of hope, is questioned and labeled as a way of easy escape from the world's predicament.

Yet, stronger than such events and moods, day by day there is love in the lives of so many people, goodness and selflessness still break through, expectation shines in the eyes of both young and old, the Gospel is shared by hungry hearts, hands are joined in confident prayer. Everywhere people begin to be conscious of their solidarity and to stand together in defense of justice and human dignity, their own and that of others.

2. The Mission of the Church

Such is the context for the mission of the church in the last two decades of this twentieth century. More than ever before, the divisions among Christians appear as a scandal. The lack of full visible unity among Christians weakens the church's mission of reconciling human beings to God and to each other (see 2 Cor 5:18-19), obscures the vision of Christ, the life of the world, and muffles his voice of hope.

More and more, churches are responding by a firm commitment "to the goal of visible unity in one faith and in one eucharistic fellowship expressed in worship and in common life in Christ and to advance towards that unity in order that the world may believe" (Constitution of the WCC, Art. III). They are being drawn together as agents of reconciliation. In many situations they speak and act together as defenders of human dignity and the rights of peoples and individuals, and to offer hope and purpose by pointing toward "the lamb of God who takes away the sin of the world" (Jn 1:29), including the sin which causes and perpetuates Christian divisions.

3. The Common Ground and a Common Goal

Since the Joint Working Group was set up almost two decades ago, far-reaching developments have taken place in relations between the Roman Catholic Church and the Orthodox, Anglican, and Protestant member churches of the World Council. Looking back, one sees the growing awareness of the essential oneness of the people of God in each place and in all places, a oneness based on the real, though imperfect, communion existing between all who believe in Christ and are baptized in his name. Consciousness of this common ground has begun to transform the self-understanding of the churches. Their members are gradually acquiring a new picture of themselves and of their sisters and brothers in other traditions, of the way in which they belong together, of their mutual responsibility and accountability before the world, and of their need "to overcome the obstacles standing in the way to perfect ecclesial communion" (*Fourth Report*, Ia).

This common ground is more fully described in the *Fourth Report* of the Joint Working Group. Acknowledgment of it strengthens the conviction that the Roman Catholic Church and the member churches of the World Council in their bilateral and multilateral relationships share in one and the same ecumenical movement. More and more they are drawn to a common understanding of the goal of unity. This includes unity in one faith and in one visible ecclesial eucharistic fellowship, "built up into a spiritual house to be a holy priesthood, to offer spiritual sacrifices, acceptable to God through Jesus Christ" (1 Pt 2:5). And there is growing understanding that this vision of the one church can be manifested as a conciliar fellowship of local churches which are themselves truly united.

4. Internal Factors Influencing Ecumenical Relationships

The continued relationship between the Roman Catholic Church and the World Council of Churches and its member churches is sustained by this acknowledged common ground and points to a common goal. But during the last two decades both bodies have undergone profound internal developments of their own, which both ease and hinder many areas of collaboration.

Starting from the integration of the International Missionary Council and the entry of the Eastern European Orthodox churches at the New Delhi Assembly (1961), the World Council of Churches has undergone major transformation, growing in membership to more than three hundred churches. More and more it has become a truly worldwide fellowship. At the same time, and building on earlier affir-mations about the ministry of the laity, it has reached out through many programs to make the ecumenical movement a reality among the whole people of God in the whole inhabited earth.

This process of growth and of transformation has faced the World Council with a double task. First, in becoming a truly worldwide fellowship, it had to come to terms with the difficulty of living in a genuine dialogue not only of traditions but also of cultures, with all members participating in each other's lives, sharing burdens and resources, joys and sufferings. Secondly, in addressing itself to the life of its member churches as total communities, it had to respond to the expectations of both women and men, lay and ordained, young and old in their mutual relationships in the ecumenical movement.

In the Roman Catholic Church, the strong call of the Second Vatican Council (1962-1965) for renewal in all areas of personal and communal life has awakened new energies whose potential is still in process of being realized. For instance, renewed awareness of the interrelation of the local church in bonds of communion with the other local churches and with the see of Rome opened up promising possi-bilities for understanding the place of unity and diversity within the church and the nature of ecclesial communion. But the practical implications of this and of the col-legiality it implies are still being worked out in new initiatives and new pastoral struc-tures such as episcopal conferences and other regional and local bodies, and it is these which have primary responsibility for overseeing ecumenical activities.

The patient, unswerving work done under Pope Paul VI to implement the stance of the Second Vatican Council has been followed by the vigorous pastoral leadership of Pope John Paul II; both popes have expressed a strong, clear, ecu-menical commitment.

The dramatic and often enthusiastic first steps of Roman Catholic ecumenical involvement were followed by difficulties, some expected, some unforeseen. The scope and complexity of the task is being accepted more realistically, and the differ-ences in structure, history, and approach to problems are more honestly taken into account, not least in the relations with the World Council and its member churches.

5. A New "Tradition" of Ecumenical Common Witness

It is a cause for joy that some quite notable convergences are emerging in the-ological understanding of those very issues which had been so divisive: for example, on the nature of the mission of Christ, on the church and its unity, on baptism, eucharist, and ministry. Especially there has been a striking convergence in the appreciation of the centrality of the word of God and the eucharist in liturgical worship, and this is being expressed in the similarity of forms used in eucharistic worship. Convergence in forms of social action and common witness has been evident regionally and locally, as churches have become more seriously engaged in trying to do everything together, save what the conviction of faith forbids. There is at present a strong convergence in concern for prayer and spiritual life. This is marked by a number of new movements among laity and clergy which have spread across all traditions.

Indeed one can speak of a new "tradition" of ecumenical understanding, shared concerns, and common witness. At the same time, this new heritage is being challenged, because new voices are trying to be integrated into it. Strong accents from the experiences of Christian life and witness in Africa, Asia, Latin America, and Oceania join those from Europe and North America. The various ecumenical agendas, which these different Christian traditions work out in their search for an authentic confession of Christ in each place and situation, are not always identical and can cause tensions in the common exploration of the unfathomable riches of the word of God for our times. In face of Christian renewal, there are different judgments about those cherished customs and practices which are so woven into the life of a church that they risk becoming identified with the substance of faith itself. Even the real convergences in theological understanding of faith and order are a strong challenge to churches to find the right ways to enable them to be received by all members. In fact, the remaining causes of division, theological or otherwise, are thrown into starker relief by those very convergences.

So the convergences, which some joyfully welcome as signs of the Spirit's patient work, are questioned by others as inimical to what they believe to be their Christian identity. The dialogue within each church about dialogue between the churches is a constant pastoral necessity.

It is a deep concern that there are groups and whole communities within the structured life of the parent bodies of the Joint Working Group, as well as outside it, which stand apart from the explicit dialogue and from the binding relationship of collaboration. Many of them are distant from both the process and the conclusions of ecumenical reflection, which thus become difficult to communicate in face of an attitude of estrangement.

Many churches, organizations, and communities have learned to see the concerns for proclaiming the explicit Gospel of Jesus Christ, commitment to social justice, and spiritual renewal as inseparable elements of their total life, mutually nourishing and a part of fidelity to their calling. Yet others want to separate one aspect at the expense of the others, a separation which goes across traditional confessional lines in a way that creates new divisions.

So both the Roman Catholic Church and the member churches of the World Council find in their ecumenical fellowship new kinds of potential divisions, even beyond the confrontation and polarization which mark many societies and the world as a whole. Both face the task of holding together the different elements of Christian witness and of keeping them vitally present in the one ecumenical movement. The common problems they face become a kind of new bond between the council's member churches and the Roman Catholic Church as they seek to build communion among their own membership and to overcome new kinds of tension and division. With this goes the need for a continued effort of ecumenical awareness-building and formation of a new generation of young church members, who are less aware of the scandal of the divisions which remain, of the goal of unity, and the urgency of the task.

6. Shared Concerns and Common Responses

So in the last decade, the World Council and its member churches and the Roman Catholic Church have found themselves with similar experiences. Under the shock of some of them, they have sometimes been driven inwards to concentrate on their own concerns. Yet in many cases their response to the challenges has been parallel, almost identical.

The reports of the 1973 Bangkok and the 1980 Melbourne Conferences, together with the Nairobi Section I report on "Confessing Christ Today," and Pope Paul VI's apostolic exhortation *Evangelii Nuntiandi (Evangelization of the Modern World)* affirm the inseparable relationship between proclamation of the Gospel and action for justice in all Christian witness. Several papal statements and some WCC programs, such as those on Faith, Science, and Technology, and on Good News to the Poor, show a convergence in understanding of the witness of the churches and the priorities of mission.

This new perspective on contemporary ways of confessing Christ in word and life has been strengthened through the studies of the WCC Commission on Faith and Order on "Giving Account of the Hope That Is in Us," and through the "Common Witness" study of the Joint Working Group, which bring together the search for a common expression of the apostolic faith and the practice of common life and witness among the churches.

There are also similarities in the concern for the role of the laity and the meaning and direction of laity formation in terms of the responsibility of the whole people of God to share the mission of Christ in and to the world.

New insights which women are making known about themselves and their awakened expectations of full participation in the life of church and society pose theological and pastoral challenges and open up new possibilities. These have to be addressed together within the framework of a genuine community of men and women in church and society.

There is the challenge to the churches arising both from the remarkable progress in the multilateral studies of the Faith and Order Commission of the World Council and at the same time from the proliferation and intensification of bilateral theological dialogues. Some of the latter, in which the Roman Catholic Church is engaged, have reached a stage that is of considerable significance for the partners and the ecumenical movement as a whole. How the further steps are to be taken will be inevitably a matter affecting all churches and will be of significance for the Faith and Order work where there is active Roman Catholic participation.

7. Acknowledging Continuing Differences

This brief survey of the relationship since the Joint Working Group came into being indicates progressive growth and convergence as well as the emergence of new problems.

As the JWG moves into a new phase of its work, there is a more realistic assessment of the differences between the two parent bodies, particularly on the international level, which still justify the answer given when the possibility of Roman Catholic membership in the council was raised in the early 1970s—"not in the immediate future." Nor is it a question which is yet ready to be taken up again.

Among the reasons given are the way in which authority is considered in the Roman Catholic Church. It believes itself to be constituted as a "universal fellowship with a universal mission and structure as an essential element of its identity" (*Fourth Report*, II). Thus it gives importance to the differences of structure between itself and the WCC member churches and the differences of operation on a world level. Acknowledging this condition, a sense of realism has developed in the relationship which combines mutual respect and a practical attitude in face of the differences and the convergences achieved by two decades of experience.

The Roman Catholic Church acknowledges its responsibility within the one ecumenical movement and accepts the challenge of undertaking increased collaboration with the World Council of Churches and its member churches, despite its own nonmember status.

The question asked in the *Fourth Report* remains valid: "How can the Roman Catholic Church and the World Council of Churches, without forming one structured fellowship, intensify their joint activities and thereby strengthen the unity, the common witness, and the renewal of the churches?" The guidelines for the Joint Working Group as formulated in the *Fourth Report* have provided a clear orientation and framework and are here reaffirmed. If they are fully implemented, the Joint Working Group can be a more visible sign and expression of the relationship, in its role of servant to the two partners.

II. Functions and Operations of the Joint Working Group

The description of the function of the JWG given in the *Fourth Report* continues to be an adequate indication of what it is and the way it works. It is intended to enable the Roman Catholic Church and the World Council of Churches to evaluate together the development of the ecumenical movement. As before, it will be a joint group with continuity of membership and sufficient breadth of representation from both sides. As an instrument of the parent bodies, it is in close contact with them and accountable to them.

1. Functions

The Joint Working Group aims primarily at discovering and assessing promising new possibilities for ecumenical development. It has the task of stimulating the discussion on the ecumenical movement and of being a challenge to the parent bodies by proposing new steps and programs.

The Joint Working Group endeavors to interpret the major streams of ecumenical thought and action in the Roman Catholic Church and in the member churches of the World Council of Churches. It facilitates the exchange of information about the progress of the ecumenical movement, especially at the local level.

The Joint Working Group seeks to establish collaboration between the various organs and programs of the Roman Catholic Church and of the World Council of Churches. In accordance with the principles and procedures of its parent bodies, it encourages the genuine development of a relation which will facilitate such collaboration. To do so it draws upon the insights gained from local experience. As in the past, it remains a consultative group, not an operative agency. It may be empowered by the parent bodies to develop and administer programs it has proposed when this is called for.

As the Joint Working Group seeks to initiate and help keep alive the discussion on the implications of the ecumenical movement in the Roman Catholic Church and in member churches of the World Council of Churches, it also seeks the best means of communicating its findings and recommendations. An essential aspect of its task is to share its findings with its parent bodies.

2. Collaborators

The Joint Working Group seeks to be in contact with a large number and range of ecumenical organizations and programs, especially on the local level. It may call upon various offices and programs of the parent bodies for assistance when special help is needed in certain areas in the process of collaboration. It also seeks information and advice from individuals and organizations which have particular ecumenical experience and competence.

3. Style of Operation

As the Joint Working Group seeks to meet the needs of the churches, the style of collaboration must be kept flexible. It must be adaptable to the various and changing needs. Therefore, it seeks to keep new structures to a minimum, while concentrating on ad hoc initiatives, as they are required by the actual developments within the ecumenical movement. On occasion, of course, particular projects may call for some structural organization, which will be set up after due authorization. Flexibility of style does not mean unplanned activity or lack of accountability. Rather it means more careful attention to the setting of priorities and to the use of resources.

III. Activities of the Joint Working Group, 1975-1983

In its *Fourth Report* the Joint Working Group gave a prospective outline of priorities for collaboration and joint action in the years following 1975. Three of them have engaged the Joint Working Group in a major degree and call for description in this section.

A. Priorities for Collaboration

1. The Unity of the Church—the Goal and the Way

This question had featured prominently in the initial reflections of the Joint Working Group when it was in process of formation. It was introduced again in order to look at new common perspectives coming out of theological discussions involving the Roman Catholic Church and member churches of the World Council of Churches over the preceding decade. For since the Joint Working Group had come into being, a number of old questions concerning unity had been clarified. A study so wide in its implications would need to go on over a number of years and it was to be structured in three parts:

1. Identification of the convergences beginning to appear between the Roman Catholic Church and WCC member churches
2. Studies and consultations on the goal of unity, with mention of (a) elements of unity; (b) the church as sign and instrument
3. Consideration of the way to unity, i.e., the visible interim steps that lead to the goal

The Joint Working Group itself took up the first of these in its meeting in 1977 as it looked at work already done and especially at the convergences in basic areas of faith and order. It had before it this material:

- Draft notes on convergences between the Roman Catholic Church and the WCC
- Reactions to the Faith and Order report, "One Baptism, One Eucharist, and a Mutually Recognized Ministry"
- Reactions to a survey on the extent to which churches have agreed on the mutual recognition of baptism as administered by each other (the survey was published as Faith and Order Paper No. 90)

The Joint Working Group felt its work on this first part of the topic was only an initial step which would have to be developed in the future, and this task still remains to be done.

Since the Joint Working Group is not itself an organ of study, it sought the help of the Faith and Order Commission in organizing the second part of the study. Using the plans developed by the Joint Working Group, the Commission organized a consultation at Venice in 1978 on the issue of unity in faith. From this came a report which, after revision by the JWG and by a number of theologians from various traditions, was published as the Faith and Order Study Paper No. 100 with the title, "Towards a Common Profession of Faith." It makes these points:

- Ecumenical growth will require agreement on a common profession of faith
- The essential elements of such a profession are known to us through the witness of the apostolic community transmitted in the Scriptures
- The ancient professions of faith were developed in response to particular challenges and tensions
- The needs of the contemporary world could lead the churches to give new emphasis to different aspects of the apostolic texts
- Diversity of doctrinal expressions in the divided churches is not always a sign of dividedness in faith

The significance of this phase of the study is that a first step has been taken to speak together of the one apostolic faith and of the convergences in theological understanding which can help Christians to move towards professing it together. Thus the study has started with a crucial point from which it can now move to the questions raised originally by the Joint Working Group.

The significance for the study of the other work being done in the Faith and Order Commission (where twelve Catholic theologians are members) ought to be noted. Since its 1978 meeting at Bangalore, the commission has had its own long-term study project, "Towards the Common Expression of the Apostolic Faith Today." It had already identified this as one of the requirements for unity, along with the need for agreement on baptism, eucharist, and ministry. The study is being continued; preliminary reports have been published and are now being put to WCC member churches and the Roman Catholic Church for response. This is a new and important step for the growth in theological convergence and has implications for the Roman Catholic relation with the WCC, as member churches and the Roman Catholic Church are invited to look at the implications of this work.

The third part of the study has concentrated on current forms of ecumenical collaboration, especially councils of churches, as illustrating ways to unity. At its meeting in 1979 the Joint Working Group outlined a proposal for developing this theme, and an exploratory consultation was held in Venice in 1982 focusing on the role of councils of churches and "preconciliar structures" in promoting visible interim steps towards unity. The consultation reflected on the role of councils of churches as a means of meeting and mutual recognition and of growing together towards full communion. It also looked at the importance of Roman Catholic involvement in councils for fulfilling this role.

There are other elements which relate to the study. One was mentioned by the JWG in its *Fourth Report* when it spoke of the need "for an evaluation of the relation of bilateral confessional dialogues to one another and to multilateral conversations." Something was done towards this when, between 1978 and 1980, the secretaries of Christian World Communions, the Secretariat for Promoting Christian Unity, and the Faith and Order Commission organized three sessions of a forum on bilateral dialogues, which has enabled an exchange of information and some reflection on the necessary interaction between multilateral and bilateral approaches to unity within the one ecumenical movement.

2. Common Witness

This was the second of the principal questions to engage the Joint Working Group in the period after Nairobi, and it was a major topic for discussion in its meeting in 1977. In the late 1960s, the JWG had already done a study which was published in 1970 under the title "Common Witness and Proselytism." Meanwhile, common witness at all levels had increased greatly and took many new forms. Together with the rapid changes in society and in human relations, this seemed to warrant a new look at the topic. It was decided to begin with actual experience, and the Ecumenical and Missiological Institute of Leiden generously enabled a survey to be made with a reflective analysis of the data obtained. This was the starting point for further work done in small groups and then in a larger consultation at Venice in 1979. The text produced was submitted to the JWG, which authorized its publication at the beginning of 1981 with an appendix which contains examples from several countries of various kinds of common witness. It has been published, not as a definitive document but as a working paper which can stimulate discussion and obtain reactions.

To appreciate the development to which the new study testifies, it may be useful to compare the two studies commissioned by the Joint Working Group. That of 1970 began as an attempt to confront the problem of proselytism. While remaining somewhat marked by its problem-orientation, it was able to move forward to an effort at articulating the value of common Christian witness. This study remains a valuable point of departure and a resource for further work, but it needed to be reviewed in light of what has happened since 1970.

The 1981 study takes up parts of the previous document that had not been sufficiently utilized and expands others that require development. Its major thrust is an attempt to develop the notion of common witness on the basis of a new understanding of unity and mission. The genuine practice of common witness on the local level in so many places has put the problem of proselytism in a different light, even if it is still a difficulty in new ways in some places. The study, in trying to reflect on and evaluate the new rich heritage of common witness, aims at drawing the attention of the churches to the importance of such witness for the unity that is sought and for the ecumenical movement as a whole. It also takes into consideration the factors which have stimulated common witness since 1971 and the difficulties which have impeded it. Here one sees the relevance of the examples which are attached as an appendix.

The timeliness of the new study and the need for such an instrument of sensitization may be seen by looking at two recent major statements on common witness. The first is taken from the report of the World Missionary Conference held at Melbourne in May 1980:

> In celebrating, we witness to the power of the Gospel to set us free. We can only celebrate in honesty if the churches realize the damage done to their common witness by the scandal of their comfortable life in division—we believe that unless the pilgrimage route leads the churches to visible unity, in the one God we preach and worship, the one Christ crucified for us all, the one Holy Spirit who creates us anew, and the kingdom, the mission entrusted to us in this world will always be rightly questioned. (*Your Kingdom Come*, p. 201)

The second is from an address given by Pope John Paul II:

... Yes, the urgent duty of Catholics is to understand what this witness must be, what it implies and requires in the life of the Church. . . . In all situations, according to circumstances, it would be necessary to endeavor, with great pastoral wisdom, to discover the possibilities of joint witness of Christians. Doing so, we will come up against the limits that our divergences still impose on this witness and this painful experience will stimulate us to intensify the effort towards a real agreement in faith. . . . It is necessary to advance in this direction with prudence and courage. (Address to the Plenary of the Secretariat for Promoting Christian Unity, Feb. 8, 1980, *Information Service*, no. 43/1980/II)

3. Social Collaboration

From the time of the Second Vatican Council, there has been quite a range of collaboration in the social field between the Roman Catholic Church and the World Council of Churches. It took place in the context of the whole relationship between the two bodies and of the activity of the Joint Working Group, which concerned itself with this field from the beginning. Hence there was exchange of information, regular consultation, and various contacts and efforts of collaboration between the agencies on each side.

a) A common effort was launched in 1968 with the setting up of SODEPAX as a joint venture of the Pontifical Commission, Justice and Peace, and the World Council of Churches. Described as "an ecumenical experiment," it was given a three-year mandate to awaken the Christian churches and their members to a realization of their obligations to promote social justice, human development, and peace. With a competent staff, SODEPAX made a widespread response to local initiatives and began to work in six program areas—social communications, education for development, mobilization for peace, development research, theological reflection, work with peoples of other faiths.

After thorough reassessment, SODEPAX continued with a much smaller staff and program for three further mandates until 1980. In this period it concentrated on its program of education for development in the sense of awareness building. It served as a liaison between the Pontifical Commission Justice and Peace and the Unit of Justice and Service of the World Council of Churches, stimulating them to extend and intensify the already existing collaboration. In more recent times it issued a regular bulletin, *Church Alert*. SODEPAX maintained its local contacts and continued to act as a catalyst for some initiatives. It has been in making study and information resources for joint initiatives available to local situations that SODEPAX perhaps rendered the greatest service.

However, as a joint venture, SODEPAX continually came up against problems concerning its own structure and function, as well as the limits of the whole relation between the Roman Catholic Church and the World Council of Churches. And this rendered its operation at times unduly difficult. It also happened that the whole wide range of social collaboration tended to become limited to what SODEPAX itself was doing. As a consequence, initiatives that might have been taken up by the various responsible bodies on each side were neglected. Hence in 1980 it was decided that SODEPAX be discontinued.

b) Meanwhile, both within the churches and between them, differences on social ethics became acute in new ways. Different ecclesial presuppositions, divergent attitudes to the role of ideologies, different approaches to methods of social and political changes, different stands on questions of sexual ethics, different understandings of the relation of church and society are some examples. So in 1975 while mapping out its program for the period after the World Council's Nairobi Assembly, the Joint Working Group listed collaboration in social thought and action among its priorities.

The present report deals only with activities between the Roman Catholic Church and the World Council of Churches on the international level. But the ecumenical effort affected concrete situations and attitudes and brought about collaboration at all levels. Hence it is clear that although they are not mentioned in this report, all initiatives at the local, national, and regional levels have a special importance. The Joint Working Group, insofar as it is within its competence, wants to promote and sustain them in their development and wider diffusion.

A new discussion began at the JWG meeting at Le Louverain in 1979, when an outline was formulated for a study on collaboration in social thought and action. Three areas for the work were pointed up: (a) the respective characteristics of the two partners as they act in the social field—this would be an attempt to take seriously the difference in nature between them and the different styles of operation it implies; (b) the areas of apparent convergence on issues of social ethics and those of obvious divergence; (c) points on which it is desirable to deepen and enrich the joint reflection of the Roman Catholic Church and the WCC. In specifying this plan further, the JWG in 1980 gave its opinion that the differences in structure and operation need to be taken fully into account if progress is to be made, emphasizing at the same time that "the differences in almost every case are not such as to prevent collaboration but rather call for sensitivity and careful planning to achieve coordination of efforts, participation in each other's studies and programs, or common action according to the circumstances. For what ultimately matters and indeed determines whether structures and styles of operation are experienced as helps or hindrances is the will to work together effectively" (Minutes of the JWG, 1980, Marseilles).

The JWG was aware both that new means of expressing the collaboration would have to be sought and that it was also necessary to find better instruments for the whole relation in this field. Therefore the JWG proposed a consultation to look at the structures and styles of operation on both sides and to find flexible intermediate instruments to reinforce the collaboration and develop new forms to express it. The consultation took place in March 1981 and the *aidenmémoire* it produced was given to the relevant organisms on each side in the hope that it might enable further steps to be taken together.

c) Until the present, this study has been an effort to respond to the facts of the situation and to find ways to move ahead in developing the partnership between the bodies on each side. Because both the Roman Catholic Church and the WCC wished to find a concrete visible means to foster further collaboration, the JWG developed the idea of a new flexible body, which would assist it in planning, perform a liaison function, and serve as a sign of the ecumenical will to work together. After the conversations of the Joint Working Group on social collaboration at Le Louverain and Marseilles, the executive of the JWG advocated the setting up of a joint consultative group for social thought and action.

The constituent members of this joint consultative group are the subunits of Unit II: i.e., the Commission on Inter-Church Aid, Refugee, and World Service (CICARWS), the Commission of the Churches on International Affairs (CCIA), the Commission on the Churches' Participation in Development (CCPD), the Christian Medical Commission (CMC), the Program to Combat Racism (PCR), as well as one representative of each of the program units: Faith and Witness, and Education and Renewal. On the Catholic side they are: the Pontifical Commission Justice and Peace, the Pontifical Council Cor Unum, the Pontifical Council for the Laity, the Secretariat for Promoting Christian Unity. It is an interim structure to give visibility to the collaboration between the staffs on each side. It does not make decisions but is to help orientate the collaboration in the social field, to facilitate its coordination, and advise the Joint Working Group, where appropriate, suggesting initiatives to the JWG and to its participating bodies as well as receiving suggestions from them. It is to hold three meetings and then its role and continued existence will be reviewed.

The Joint Consultative Group considers its experience to date a positive one. It has allowed a general exchange of information and has proposed areas to be pursued, notably an effort of catechesis in the field of peace and disarmament and joint reflection on social involvement and proclamation of the Gospel. The Joint Consultative Group can also provide a framework within which questions of immediate collaboration between the various commissions concerned with issues of justice and service in the WCC and the corresponding bodies of the Roman Catholic Church can be stimulated, further clarified, and organized on a more regular and organic basis. It seems it may be expected to play a modest but useful role in an area where more needs to be done. It feels that its initial period will help in finding more long-term forms of collaboration and foresees the possibility of its own continuance.

d) Relations between individual offices of the Holy See and subunits of the World Council continued and intensified in the period 1975-1983:

- CICARWS, CCPD, and CMC carried on various kinds of collaboration with the Pontifical Commission Justice and Peace and the Pontifical Council Cor Unum. This included participation in each other's meetings, work groups, and study groups as well as providing information and expertise for one another's works. It was helped by means of joint staff meetings between some dicasteries and some of the subunits, which clarified positions and mutually enriched outlook and programs. One result of these joint staff meetings is the recent joint publication by CCIA/PCJP of the volume *Peace and Disarmament: Documents of the World Council of Churches and of the Roman Catholic Church*.

- There has been a special relationship between the Christian Medical Commission, the Secretariat for Promoting Christian Unity (since 1971), and Cor Unum. Among other things, this made it possible to have a Roman Catholic consultant with the CMC staff until summer 1979. Since then the position has not been filled. CMC invites Cor Unum, together with other Roman Catholic participants, to all its meetings. CMC has participated in Cor Unum study groups on health. There is cooperation at national and local levels, which focuses especially on primary health care and is expressed through more than twenty national coordinating offices for health and through joint efforts in the procurement of pharmaceutical supplies.

- The Commission Justice and Peace has developed a relationship with the Church and Society subunit through the latter's study, "Faith, Science, and Technology."

B. Ongoing Collaboration

The mandate of the JWG requires it to initiate and promote collaboration between the organs and programs of the Roman Catholic Church and the World Council of Churches. Throughout this past period it has supported many forms of collaboration which give significant expression to the relation between the two parent bodies. In addition to what has already been mentioned in preceding sections, the following are worthy of note.

1. Commission on Faith and Order

For almost fifteen years the Commission on Faith and Order has had a number of Roman Catholic theologians among its official members. This has enabled the Commission to draw increasingly on Roman Catholic participation of agreed statements on *Baptism, Eucharist, and Ministry* and in the broader effort to explore the conditions of a common confession of the apostolic faith today which incorporates the results of the study initiated by the Joint Working Group.

2. Week of Prayer for Christian Unity

The Secretariat of the Commission on Faith and Order and the Secretariat for Promoting Christian Unity have continued to convene an international group to prepare the common material for the celebration of this week, based on proposals coming each year from an ecumenical group in a particular country. The Week of Prayer continues to be of great significance in stimulating local ecumenical initiatives. The prayer cycle "For All God's People" offers a means of developing a new pattern of mutual intercession.

3. Relationships with Commission on World Mission and Evangelism (CWME)

For several years, a number of Roman Catholic missionary orders which work with the Congregation for the Evangelization of Peoples have established a consultative relationship with the Conference on World Mission and Evangelism of the WCC. They have also sent observer-consultants to attend the meetings of the Commission on World Mission and Evangelism. This collaboration has been particularly important for Roman Catholic participation in the World Missionary Conference of CWME at Melbourne in 1980, as well as for the study on Common Witness, initiated by the Joint Working Group.

4. Dialogue with People of Living Faiths

Though not structured in ways comparable to the collaboration in the areas of Faith and Order and World Mission and Evangelism, a very fruitful cooperation has developed between the WCC Working Group on Dialogue with People of Living Faiths and Ideologies and the Vatican Secretariat for Non-Christians. In recent years attention has focused on dialogue with Muslims, and both sides attach great importance to the continuation of this relationship.

5. Ecumenical Institute, Bossey

A new field of collaboration has opened up around the program of the Ecumenical Institute with the presence of some Roman Catholic students, a Roman Catholic board member, and the visit of the Graduate School to Rome each year at the end of its course.

For some time the Secretariat for Promoting Christian Unity has endeavored to ensure an effective Roman Catholic presence with the teaching staff of the Ecumenical Institute both for the period of the Graduate School and the major courses sponsored by the Institute.

6. The Sixth Assembly of the World Council of Churches, Vancouver, July/August 1983

Since the time of the Second Vatican Council, it has become increasingly possible for the Roman Catholic Church and the World Council of Churches to participate and in some way share in each other's great events. The Assembly of Vancouver offers also to the Roman Catholic Church the occasion to celebrate the ecumenical movement and renew its ecumenical commitment, even though it will be less directly involved in those aspects of the assembly which make it the highest legislative body of the council. There will be twenty Roman Catholic delegated observers at the assembly, as well as some advisers and guests. There is a considerable effort being made to inform Roman Catholics on various levels of the assembly and to awaken an intelligent interest in it and to invite them to support it by prayer. By means of reports from several study consultations, a Roman Catholic contribution is also being made to the study process in the assembly.

IV. Proposals for Future Work

Before submitting proposals for its future work, the Joint Working Group wants to draw attention to a concern which applies equally to all areas of its activities. In the mandate of the JWG, given in the *Fourth Report* and reaffirmed here, hope is expressed that the JWG will "draw upon insights gained from local experience to foster . . . collaboration." Already in its interim account, published with the agreement of the parent bodies in 1980 (cf. "Deepening Communion: An Account of Current Work," in *Ecumenical Review* XXXII/2, April 1980, pp. 179ff.), the JWG expressed its conviction "that it needs to receive greater visibility in order to stimulate local collaboration" (ibid., p. 185). Examples were given there of how this objective could be achieved. They included the sharing of results of its deliberations with the constituencies on both sides, even at an interim stage, the sharing of study documents, visible gestures to highlight aspects of collaboration, visits, special meetings, using the Week of Prayer, and highlighting the Joint Working Group meeting itself.

1. The Way Towards Unity

Were a reminder needed, the experience of the past decade would demonstrate that the necessary process of mutual clarification, study, and negotiation is not itself enough to achieve unity. The ecumenical movement is an integral part of the whole reconciling work of Christ in which we participate most fruitfully by that holiness of life which is an identification with God's will. Essential to it is a conversion of heart and life both corporate and individual. This must vivify and motivate the necessary renewal of present structures and provide the impulse not only to bring Christians together and enable them to accept each other, but to arrive at a common confession of the one faith and reconciliation in one ministry. It is, in short, the conversion to that which God wills for the church. This is the condition which is indispensable for all the other efforts to be fruitful.

Significant progress has been made in recent years through bilateral and multilateral dialogues, in cooperation between the JWG and Faith and Order, as well as through the forum on bilateral conversations, in sharpening the common understanding of the goal of unity, as well as discerning essential elements and conditions of unity. While the JWG is not itself the place for dialogue as such, it does have to concern itself with the whole relations between the Roman Catholic Church and the member churches of the World Council and must therefore interest itself in the results of the dialogues and their meaning for unity. The JWG should maintain close contact with the work of the Commission on Faith and Order, especially in the area of a common expression of the apostolic faith and in the deepening of agreement on the understanding and practice of baptism, eucharist, and the ministry. The publication of the convergence statement *Baptism, Eucharist, and Ministry* presents a considerable challenge also for the Catholic side as it becomes necessary to determine how far this work does represent a convergence in faith.

In continuing the earlier joint program on the "Unity of the Church, the Goal, and the Way," outlined in 1976, the Joint Working Group proposes to focus attention on those parts which have not been sufficiently taken up, i.e., (1) a renewed reflection on the church as sign and sacrament, coming back after more than a decade to its earlier ecclesiological study on "Catholicity and Apostolicity"; (2) a continuation of the review of ecumenical structures of collaboration, specifically councils of churches and the other interim structures which already express a unity *in via*. In pursuing this study, attention should be given to the themes proposed by the exploratory consultation organized by the Faith and Order Commission and the Secretariat for Promoting Christian Unity in 1982 on the significance of councils of churches in the ecumenical movement. These include the following:

- The ecclesial importance of the "recognition" and "fellowship" experienced in a council of churches
- The place of councils on the way towards visible unity and their role in promoting movement from one stage to another
- The interaction of local, national, regional, and world "levels" as these affect the life of councils and their member churches
- The relation of councils of churches to other forms of ecumenical collaboration

Further, to emphasize the search for "visible interim steps," the JWG sees potential value in a reflection on the possibilities of common worship, including the sharing of liturgical and devotional resources, the ecumenical significance of the veneration of saints, and the encouragement of informed, mutual intercession (see "For All of God's People," Geneva, 1978).

Finally, in line with the effort of recent years to face together the pastoral care of mixed marriages, it would be valuable to reflect on what has been happening. It might be possible to see how this pastoral collaboration could intensify and become more widespread, so that a better witness be given to the growing unity between churches.

2. Common Witness

Work for the visible unity of the church and common witness in the world are intimately related. The two studies published by the Joint Working Group— "Common Witness and Proselytism" (1970), and "Common Witness" (1981)— bring evidence to show that common witness is one of the essential ways of discovering and deepening the unity which is given in Christ, while the strongest form of common witness is the will of the churches to give visible expression to the communion which already exists among them. This communion is not yet complete, but common witness serves to show in striking ways how it is growing and is a means of deepening it. Inevitably in giving witness together, divided Christians are brought in new and painful ways to face the divisions which remain, yet this very experience becomes, through witness given together, an impelling motive to work for the fullness of visible communion. Common witness does not confuse or hide the issue of division but helps the churches live and act together before the world in the name of Jesus Christ as Lord and Savior. It is thus a test and condition for the ecumenical movement.

Therefore, the JWG affirms common witness as one of its priorities. It will explore ways in which the relationship between the Roman Catholic Church and the WCC may give evidence of it. It has also to work out the implications of the

1981 document for possible action at the world level by the Roman Catholic Church and the WCC. The document is translated into several languages, and it must continue to be the task of the JWG to ensure that it is brought in an adequate way to the attention of the Roman Catholic Church and the WCC member churches for reflection, reaction, and implementation, so that they may renew their commitment to witness in unity and may explore fuller possibilities of common witness in their respective situations.

Part of the task is also an articulation of the import of the theological perspectives on common witness, outlined in the study document, for the other studies on the unity of the church, for the reception of the doctrinal convergences being reached by the churches, and ultimately for the achievement of a sharing in eucharistic communion.

In view of the desire expressed at the time of the Second Vatican Council for a common declaration on religious freedom, and giving account to the present situation in the world which elicited the recent statement of the World Council of Churches on religious liberty, it becomes desirable to explore the possibility of working together on the question of religious liberty to secure a common witness.

Recently the Joint Working Group has stressed the need to stimulate ecumenical awareness and to give a new ecumenical formation on regional and local levels by various endeavors of common witness. One means of doing this may be through a series of joint regional consultations over the next few years to explore in a practical way opportunities for common witness.

3. Social Collaboration

Common witness includes the efforts of the churches to act together in the defense and promoting of human dignity, the relief of human need, and the affirmation of justice and peace which must be expressed in human relationships and in the structures of society. The concern for Christian social responsibility is an integral part of the apostolic mission of the church. Missionary perspectives necessarily open on to solidarity with the poor, justice, peace, and respect for human rights, while the social responsibility of the church has its context in the proclamation of the word and the opening of the human spirit to the transcendent.

This area, however, has also an integrity of its own, and should continue to be seen by the JWG as belonging to its proper field of concern. Recognizing that social collaboration will continue to be conditioned by the differences in structure and method of working in the Roman Catholic Church and the WCC, the Joint Working Group should not cease to encourage the development of flexible forms of collaboration on the international as well as on national and local levels.

Despite the doctrinal differences among the churches, in recent years an ecumenical convergence has been growing in the understanding of several issues in
social ethics. Recognizing this convergence, the JWG should look for ways which
could help to make visible to a wider audience the joint commitment to these elementary affirmations about Christian social responsibility, which are in conformity
with the common Christian faith. In accordance with its earlier discussion at Le
Louverain (1979), the JWG sees value in exploring possibilities of common pastoral
and catechetical guidance and common work in the following areas:

a. *Development:* There is, for example, agreement that structural changes
   are required in the international economic order to correct inequities
   and spread the use of resources and the benefits of technology among all
   peoples.
b. *Peace:* Agreement exists, among other points, that the madness of the
   arms race diverts resources from development, increases the threat of
   force in international dispute, and creates the conditions for the destruc-
   tion of the human race.
c. *Human Rights:* Based on inherent human dignity, the "image of God" in
   us, and on our common redemption in Christ, the rights *(inter alia)* to
   life, to access to health care, to work, to a decent standard of living, to
   cultural identity, to education, to participation in public life, to dissent
   for conscience's sake, to physical and psychological integrity, to freedom
   from torture, and to religious liberty must be safeguarded by international
   agreement (see Minutes of the JWG, Le Louverain, 1979).

Attention should also be given to the possibility of encouraging initiatives in
the area of racism and concerning the role of women.

In addition, the Joint Working Group had noted in 1979 that there are areas
on which convergence is lacking and which need to be explored further before common action could be possible. These differences appear among the member
churches of the WCC as well as between some of them and the Roman Catholic
Church: the pattern of difference changes with the issues include: aspects of the
roles of women and men in the life of the community; patterns of family life, birth
control, and sexual ethics; forms and means of responding to the need for social
change; and methodological approaches to ethics.

Finally, the Joint Working Group should look for ways to enrich and deepen
the joint reflection of the WCC and the Roman Catholic Church on basic theological and ecclesiological themes which constitute the necessary background for
deeper mutual understanding of ecumenical social responsibilities. Such themes are
the relation of the kingdom of God to this world, the role of faith in social problems,

the relation between evangelism and struggle for justice in society, the action of the churches and the role of laity, the modes of intervention of the church in the secular realm of society.

On a more practical level, the JWG should encourage appropriate initiatives to come to a closer and more effective coordination between the network of Roman Catholic Church and WCC related service agencies at various levels in the area of aid and relief, in order to avoid the possibilities of divisive effects of separate programs for local communities.

It is important to find ways of sharing information about the considerable volume of ecumenical work going on in local situations and to evaluate this, so that a fruitful interaction may be achieved between initiatives at various levels.

4. Ecumenical Formation

The JWG insists on the present urgency of the task of ecumenical formation. It stresses that the improved relations between still separated Christians are not enough. The scandal of Christian division and their deleterious effect on Christian witness continues to obscure the saving power of Christ's grace. God's plan to sum up all things in Christ requires to be shown forth in the common proclamation of the one apostolic faith and in the communion of the one visible eucharistic fellowship, and to be an active power in drawing the human community into reconciliation and oneness. Hence the need to deepen an understanding of the mystery of the church.

Ecumenical formation is a process which includes several elements. It means imparting information about what God is doing through the ecumenical movement to draw his people into one. It entails learning about existing differences between Christians and their churches and about the new convergences being achieved. Such learning comes both from obtaining the relevant information and from involvement in the deeper levels of experience in the life of the Christian community at worship, in service, and in witness. It comes, too, in the acknowledgment and practice of responsibility toward each other by communities of separated Christians, as well as by their engagement in various forms of ecumenical dialogue.

The ecumenical dimension is an indispensable part of all processes of Christian formation and nurture, be it the formation of laity, youth work, programs of catechesis and religious education, or theological training.

Today many people, especially those participating in programs of laity formation, receive their most significant experience of the ecumenical dimension in the common effort for justice, peace, and development. Such initiatives touch on urgent problems and bring Christians together in the exercise of responsibility for building the whole human community, as well as relating global issues to daily action.

Reflection on the nurturing character of all these experiences is needed. It is clear that further ways have to be found of bringing together the different processes of learning, relating formal teaching processes to informal methods of learning (such as conscientization). This can also help Christians to appreciate the necessary relation between the goal of the unity of the church and the concern for the unity of mankind.

Much has to be done if ecumenical formation is to become a full part of the whole Christian ministry. The impact of ecumenical initiatives among educators often remains on the professional level and insufficiently communicates with or benefits from the experience of parish and local communities. Promising new forms of Christian formation at various levels still often do not take sufficient account of the ecumenical movement and its role in the mission of the church. More attention could be given to the ecumenical process found in frequent local and spontaneous efforts of local and spontaneous joint study and action (e.g., during Lent, etc.).

The formal catechetical programs of various churches often take the ecumenical dimension for granted. It is necessary to spell it out sufficiently and to exploit the new theological convergences. Opportunities of joining in common action with regard to catechetical materials or syllabuses, where this is possible (see the apostolic exhortation of Pope John Paul II, *Catechesi Tradendae*), must not be missed.

Young people have a new experience and often relate to events in the world with a special sensitivity. Better ways must be found of alerting them to the ecumenical dimension and its place in the total responsibility of Christians to and for each other and for the world. As they face life, they need help to discern and to use those living situations where ecumenical learning takes place. In this they will need the wisdom and support of those who have pastoral and teaching roles in the church. Likewise those who have leadership in the churches have to show confidence in young people and react with sensitivity to the contribution which they will make.

Another crucial area is that of theological education and particularly the education of pastors, perhaps the most influential point in ecumenical sensitization. There is a great range of possibilities, but even where there are joint or collaborative faculties and programs more could be done to draw out their potential with the support and guidance of those responsible in the various churches. In some seminaries homage is paid to ecumenical ideals, while there is an absence of any formal teaching about the ecumenical movement or its history and its theological, spiritual, and pastoral significance for the Christian community. As well as trying to include the ecumenical dimension in the courses on theology, it seems still necessary to have also courses which give explicit information and reflection on the ecumenical movement.

At this point in the history of the ecumenical movement and of the relations between the Roman Catholic Church and the WCC and its member churches, a new effort has to be made to assess and use more effectively the resources for this basic task of ecumenical formation.

5. Continuing Collaboration

It will be the task of the Joint Working Group to look carefully at what can be done to develop and extend the regular pattern of collaboration and common effort with the various subunits of the World Council of Churches. In several instances it is substantial and has its own rhythm and style, in others it is still necessary to be on the watch for possibilities of deepening what are as yet only initial contacts. There are several areas where immediate work has to be done.

A. Faith and Order

With completion of the study *Baptism, Eucharist, and a Mutually Recognized Ministry*, it is now important to find the right ways of obtaining reactions. First steps were taken at an earlier stage in the work, and these did involve some Catholic theological faculties. Now the effort has to be made on a wider scale to have the document known and to test its conclusions so that the convergence in faith which it represents may become part of the consciousness of Christian people. Further necessary progress can take place only if discussion is aroused on all levels, especially on the implications of the convergences for the relationship between the churches.

A similar task has to be done with the study *Toward a Common Expression of the One Apostolic Faith Today*, although this is not yet in its final stages.

B. Dialogue with Other Faiths and Ideologies

The pattern of contact and exchange of collaboration now seems to have developed to the point where one or other initiative of common program could be undertaken and ways of giving visible and structured expression to the relationship be explored.

C. Community of Women and Men in Church and Society

Work on this theme has been done on the Roman Catholic side and is actively being pursued in the World Council of Churches. It involves many of the major issues of today seen from the angle of the involvement and responsible participation of men and women in the life of society. It seems desirable to do more towards a sharing of information and resources and, if possible, coordination of work with consideration given eventually to common efforts in evaluation and follow-up. It could be interesting also, and not only in connection with this question, to look together at the changes on each side in the understanding of the role of the laity over the last thirty years.

D. Joint Staff Meetings

Meetings between the staff of the individual responsible Roman dicasteries and the corresponding subunit of the World Council of Churches have proved their usefulness for exchange of information, mutual sharing of resources, and discovering ways of developing the partnership. They already take place regularly between the Pontifical Commission Justice and Peace with the Churches' Commission on International Affairs and with the Churches' Commission for Participation in Development, between the Dialogue with Living Faiths and Ideologies and the Secretariat for Non-Christians, between the Program for Theological Education and the Congregation for Catholic Education, between the Pontifical Council for the Laity and the Unit on Education and Renewal. It is important to be alert to new possibilities for bringing other partners from each side into such a regular contact.

V. The Future of the Joint Working Group in the Ecumenical Movement

1. The Joint Working Group was set up in 1965 by the Roman Catholic Church and the WCC as a manifestation of their need to work together in the ecumenical movement.

Its task was described as being to clarify the principles and methods of ecumenical collaboration while giving due account to the differences between its parent bodies, one a worldwide church, the other a council of churches. It has continued to emphasize, as was evident in the *Fourth Report* in 1975, the common ground between the churches engaged in the ecumenical movement and affirmed the real though imperfect communion that already exists between the Roman Catholic Church and the churches in the fellowship of the World Council of Churches.

So the JWG expresses the will of member churches of the WCC and the Roman Catholic Church to meet, to grow in mutual recognition, and to find new ways to be together in the service of unity and mission. Its structure is modest, but with the confidence and support of its parent bodies, it acts as a continuing reminder to the churches engaged in the ecumenical movement that dialogue and action, the restoration of communion, and the commitment to common witness, to the unity of the church, and the renewal of the human community belong together. So it attends to both the theological and the social and pastoral dimensions and tries to stimulate the interaction between all levels of ecumenical work. It is an instrument of its parent bodies with the task of keeping prominently before them and before all Christian churches the urgent need to grow in communion and to manifest the existing fellowship of churches through common witness.

2. In the period which lies ahead, the JWG must review the contacts and collaboration taking place between the subunits of the WCC and partners on the Roman Catholic side and try to find appropriate ways to expressing them. It must continue to be a vantage point from which the whole relationship and its place in the ecumenical movement is surveyed. It will address itself anew to its priorities for the next period—the unity of the church, common witness, and social collaboration. Most challenging is the attention it must give to ecumenical formation. This theme reflects a new perspective and is a response to an urgent need in the current ecumenical situation, which calls for the deepening of ecumenical consciousness and the identification of realistic and visible steps which can be taken together.

In all of this, it becomes always more necessary that the JWG draw insights from what is happening locally. Here case studies of ecumenical initiatives will have a larger role to play, and special attention will need to be given to the aspirations and experiences of the major regions, with all their diversity and new promise. In turn the JWG has to make an increasing effort to communicate what it is doing and the significance of this—in the first place always to its parent bodies as it interprets major streams of ecumenical thought and action in the Roman Catholic Church and in member churches of the WCC. Increasingly it must find effective ways to communicate this also to all who have ecumenical and pastoral responsibility, as it discovers and assesses promising new possibilities for ecumenical development. The JWG is in many ways in a unique position both to stimulate its parent bodies by proposing new steps and programs and to respond to some of the major streams of ecumenical thought and action, surveying, interpreting, encouraging, and challenging. This will meet the demand that the JWG be more and more a point to reflect on and analyze important events which affect the unity willed by Christ for the church and the renewal of the human community. Only so can it have resources to contribute to a new ecumenical mentality among Christians.

3. The Joint Working Group is a small body and its immediate aims necessarily limited, but the bodies it serves have a wide constituency and broad responsibilities. The time in which we live needs the ecumenical hope which it promotes. It is a sign that new obstacles to ecumenical advances must also be faced without hesitation. With its vivid memories of the past two decades of the ecumenical movement, it can keep Christians from the Roman Catholic Church and the member churches of the WCC aware of the great change that has taken place, helping them to consolidate these gains in the life of the Christian fellowship and to go along joyfully with what God is doing to bring his people into one.

The Sixth Report of the Joint Working Group

1990

Foreword

The Joint Working Group (JWG) for relationships between the Roman Catholic Church and the World Council of Churches (WCC) has just become twenty-five years old—an opportunity for it to take stock of what it has achieved.

The JWG came into existence immediately after Vatican II and the opportunity the latter opened up and endorsed for the Roman Catholic Church. The group was entrusted with studying the conditions for cooperation between the WCC and the Roman Catholic Church and even—in the first few years—with considering the possibility of the latter becoming a member of the WCC. When that prospect proved premature, the WCC turned its attention to furthering relations and practical cooperation between the two partners as far as possible.

In submitting the *Sixth Report* of JWG we wish, first of all, to say how grateful we have been for the experience we have had since it was given its present membership following the 1983 Assembly of the World Council of Churches at Vancouver.

Fraternal cooperation among its members has indeed been gradually consolidated till it has become a real fellowship characterized by natural trust and respect.

We have learned to talk to each other and listen to each other with real openness. And our awareness of the common mission of our churches in the world has deepened to the point where that mission is seen as the urgent priority.

Reading this *Sixth Report* will in itself show the extent to which the productive relations between the WCC and the Roman Catholic Church have multiplied and developed. Setting aside the places in which they have found institutional expression, especially in the Commission on Faith and Order, most of the subunits of the WCC and their Roman Catholic partners have worked out a process of mutual consultation and sometimes common action which must be taken fully into account. The JWG has constantly applied itself to following this process through and expanding it. It has nevertheless not confined itself to this but has also sought to contribute its own bricks to the common structure. The JWG decided to publish as an appendix to this report two documents—on "The Church: Local and Universal" and on the "Hierarchy of Truths"—which it had ordered and officially received and which demonstrate this. We hope they will make a useful contribution to opening up new stages of fruitful reflection on the journey towards Christian unity.

It is true that we have also had to face certain difficulties—especially as the report shows in the field of social thinking and action. And in the last few years, Roman Catholic participation in the World Convocation on Justice, Peace, and the Integrity of Creation was subject to a variety of ups and downs on which there is no occasion to go into detail here. We would mention only that this enabled us to realize that as Cardinal Willebrands put it, "the difference in nature between the WCC and the Roman Catholic Church" represents a continuing obstacle to the full development of their relations. This obstacle must be analyzed more thoroughly. That must be one of the priority tasks of the next JWG.

Above all, however, we wish in submitting this report to state jointly our firm conviction that whatever may be the hazards of the day-to-day history of ecumenism, the search for unity must never cease. We have to be completely and constantly obedient to our Lord's command: "That they may all be one." We cannot play fast and loose with that prayer and take up our stance in some status quo. On the contrary we must gratefully appraise the whole way along which the Lord has already brought us over the last fifty years and go forward yet more boldly and hopefully on the path he himself has opened up and in which he constantly walks ahead of us and awaits us!

JOINT PRESIDENTS OF THE JOINT WORKING GROUP
Bishop Alan Clark
Pastor Jacques Maury

Introduction

The Joint Working Group of the Roman Catholic Church and the World Council of Churches joyfully celebrates its twenty-five years of ecumenical endeavor. Its mandate to serve the Roman Catholic Church–WCC relationships was given by the Central Committee of the WCC at Enugu, Nigeria, in 1965 and by the authorities of the Roman Catholic Church in the same year.

Since then the group has made five reports. They reflect the steady growth and maturing in the relations between the Roman Catholic Church and the WCC. The *Sixth Report* is prepared in a spirit of gratitude for these fruitful years. It gives an account of the activities of the group since the last assembly of the WCC at Vancouver in 1983. It also looks to the future with hope as the relationships continue and develop.

I. The Ecumenical Situation

1. Current Development

The life of the churches and the thrust of the ecumenical movement are affected by the situation of our world. Today there are many signs of hope for the human family, not least in places where spiritual forces have helped to break down the forces of tyranny. But we also face many grave problems which threaten the well-being of humanity and call for the concern and solidarity of all people of good-will. The followers of Jesus Christ have a special duty to be fully present in the world in this time of promise and difficulty. It is a time when the ecumenical movement is more than ever necessary if the churches and Christian communities are to be a sign and seed of the unity, peace, and hope which the human family needs.

There is much room for encouragement. An increasing number of Christian communities and ecumenical organizations are active in working for unity among Christians. A number of the essential issues dividing Christians have still to be resolved, but suspicion and hostility have in large part given way to goodwill and mutual respect. Churches and Christians of different confessions often engage in common witness and in projects of interchurch aid which respond to urgent human need. In a world so often marked by despair, the ecumenical movement itself, as a historic effort to achieve full reconciliation among Christians, is a source of hope. The movement reaches back to the deepest spiritual roots that all Christians share and can be an answer to the spirit of secularism which marks our modern world.

The WCC and the Roman Catholic Church have played an important part in the ecumenical process, not least through their Joint Working Group. The official visit of Pope John Paul II in 1984 to the WCC, as well as the visit of Dr. Emilio

Castro, General Secretary of the WCC, to the Holy See in 1986, have helped con-solidate the relationships and the cooperation. In its letter to the Extraordinary Synod in 1985, the Central Committee of the WCC could speak of the bonds of "fraternal solidarity" that exist between the two partners. On important ecumenical occasions, each has shared in the initiatives and events of the other. The Assisi Day of Prayer for Peace, called by Pope John Paul II in 1986, was supported by the pres-ence of a high-level delegation from the WCC. There has been notable Roman Catholic presence in the WCC assemblies and conferences.

So the ecumenical task has continued well. However, it has yet to reach its goal of full visible unity. The JWG still has substantial work to do. It is more than ever called to help the Roman Catholic Church and the WCC to strive for the unity of Christians and for the unity and solidarity of all human beings.

2. Patterns of Relationships Between the WCC and the Roman Catholic Church

Twelve Roman Catholic theologians are full members of the Faith and Order Commission.

Seven others participate as consultants in the Commission on World Mission and Evangelism (CWME). A Roman Catholic representative is on the Bossey Board. For a number of years now, three Roman Catholics have worked on the WCC program staff: in CWME, Bossey, and JPIC. Various forms of contact and working relationships have developed also between other WCC subunits and Vatican offices and missionary societies. There has been useful and continual mutual exchange of information, of newly published documents, and of staff visits.

Catholic consultants and observers have participated in a series of WCC con-ferences, meetings, consultations, and seminars.

Many member churches of the WCC and the Roman Catholic Church have close relationships on regional and national levels in taking part in and contribut-ing to ecumenical organizations.

3. Factors That Influence the Relationships

The above-mentioned patterns are positive factors which promote ecumeni-cal collaboration and strengthen relations not only between WCC subunits and Vatican departments, but also between WCC member churches and the Roman Catholic Church throughout the world. Encouraging statements about the results of this collaboration and achievement of the JWG have been made by Pope John Paul II, representatives of the WCC, and leaders of local churches.

Through the agenda of the JWG and other ecumenical endeavors, the Roman Catholic Church and the churches in the WCC fellowship have faced the challenges of division. They have shared in some basic theological reflections on visible unity and contributed to the process of reconciliation, renewal, and growing communion. The WCC and the Roman Catholic Church have increased awareness of the need for mission and dialogue, for promoting the values of the Gospel in secularized societies, for Christian stewardship of creation, for furthering justice and peace, for the protection of human rights and dignity.

The WCC member churches belong to almost all Christian traditions. They bring a variety of theological streams into the WCC, which has implications for ecumenical dialogue and collaboration.

The diverse understandings of the ecumenical goal and of the means of achieving visible unity may affect ecumenical progress. Acts of proselytism, excessive concern for "confessional identity," lack of awareness about common problems, and ecumenical tasks also affect dialogue and rapprochement. Divergences on basic doctrinal questions, ethical, social, and political issues further limit the process of advancing towards full communion and effective common action. The WCC and the Roman Catholic Church differ in their nature, their structure, their style of operation, their exercise of authority. Sometimes these differences are a hindrance to cooperation. The Roman Catholic Church is a universal church with a strong hierarchical structure fostering unity in diversity. The WCC is a fellowship of autonomous churches bound together in the search for visible unity and common witness. They are not held together by canonical/structural form, but see themselves as belonging to an ecumenical fellowship which enables them to grow together.

The ecumenical partners need to be sufficiently attentive to the use of their own press and other media in portraying the image of the "other." Likewise, more care needs to be taken in the ways the partners speak of some events in the life of the churches and their ecumenical significance.

II. Functions and Operations of the JWG

In its first official report, the JWG stated that "its task, both spiritual and pastoral, is to be undertaken in a spirit of prayer and in the conviction that God is guiding his people. . . . The group is . . . called on to discern the will of God in the contemporary ecumenical situation" (*First Report*, 1). This has been a guiding principle for the members of the group.

The JWG is a consultative body. It explores new forms of cooperation between the WCC and the Roman Catholic Church and prepares projects but does not make or monitor policy.

At present the JWG consists of twelve members from each side, some of whom are involved in pastoral work in different parts of the world, others are from departments of the Roman Curia and units of the WCC. Consultants are co-opted for particular tasks. The JWG normally meets once a year.

A small executive committee is responsible for the ongoing work between annual meetings and prepares the agenda and material for the plenary meetings. At the end of its normal seven-year mandate, the JWG presents an official report to the parent bodies.

Members may also discuss questions and ideas arising from JWG work with their own churches so as to foster dialogue and ecumenical relations.

The JWG is called to help in assessing the ecumenical situation and stimulating the search for visible unity and common witness. It should select those ecumenical issues which require particular care and promote development of relationships between the WCC and the Roman Catholic Church. This means giving attention, support, and encouragement to whatever contributes to wider ecumenical progress and discerning differences which hinder WCC–Roman Catholic Church relations. By keeping itself informed and stimulating the spread and exchange of information, and sponsoring particular studies, the JWG serves as an instrument of cooperation between the WCC and the Roman Catholic Church. When its findings commend themselves to the parent bodies, the JWG offers its services in helping to present ideas and proposals to the appropriate departments on either side and to such concerned bodies as theological faculties and ecumenical institutes.

III. Activities of the JWG During the Period of 1983-1990

A. Priorities of This Period

Since the Sixth Assembly of the WCC (1983), the JWG has concentrated on four areas: "Unity of the Church—the Goal and the Way," "Ecumenical Formation," "Common Witness," and "Social Thought and Action." Some of these themes, of course, overlap.

1. Unity of the Church—The Goal and the Way

The JWG has kept high on its agenda the goal of visible unity of Christians and has regularly undertaken studies of specific importance for this task. A significant role in this work has been carried out by the Faith and Order Commission and the Pontifical Council for Promoting Christian Unity. The JWG hopes that by such studies it can be of service in complementing and supporting the ongoing work of bilateral and multilateral dialogues.

In the period 1983-1990 five areas of studies relating to unity have been undertaken by the JWG. Two are primarily theological: "The Church: Local and Universal" and "The Hierarchy of Truths." The impetus for work on these two themes came during the visit of Pope John Paul II to the WCC (1984). A third area of study concerns new potential sources of division, especially ethical issues. A fourth relates to the impact of councils of churches on the ecumenical movement. A fifth is concerned with a particular pastoral issue: Christian mixed marriages.

a. The Local and Universal Church

This study document deals with fundamental aspects of the mystery of the church: its local and universal expressions. There is first of all a discussion of the ecclesiology of communion. It is presented as a framework within which the study of the church local and universal takes place. It emphasizes that these two dimensions of the church are not two alternative aspects of the church from which to choose, but must be understood in relationship and seen simultaneously. A second part looks at the church local and universal in ecumenical perspective, presenting the view of Orthodox, Roman Catholic, and Protestant positions on this theme. A third section indicates ecclesial elements required for full communion with a visibly united church, which is the goal of the ecumenical movement. This discussion includes a presentation of the way the notion of ecclesial communion has been interpreted by the Roman Catholic Church in the Second Vatican Council (1962-1965) and by the New Delhi (1961) and Nairobi (1975) Assemblies of the WCC. A fourth section describes the ways in which the different Christian world communions understand and use canonical structures to express and safeguard communion within their churches.

The JWG commissioned and received this study document and presents it with the hope of stimulating further ecumenical reflection on this theme.

b. Hierarchy of Truths

The purpose of this study was "an ecumenical attempt to understand and interpret the intention of the Second Vatican Council in speaking of a 'hierarchy of truths,' and to examine some implications for ecumenical dialogue and common Christian witness" (no. 3). The result of this work is a study document [Document 17 below]. It analyses the conciliar statement, indicates examples of a "hierarchy of truths" in Christian history and in different Christian traditions (even though the expression is not used there), and draws out implications for ecumenical dialogue and for the goal of full communion, as well as for mission, common witness, and theological method. It is noteworthy that this study document is the first ecumenical text on this subject.

The JWG commissioned and received this study document and hopes that it will render a service to the wider ecumenical discussion.

c. Ethical Issues as New Sources of Potential Divisions

The past twenty-five years have seen more and better multilateral and bilateral dialogues on those doctrinal differences which helped to cause and perpetuate divisions among the churches. In many of these dialogues the Roman Catholic Church has been an active partner with member churches of the WCC. Convergence and common affirmations are beginning to form on such classical divisive doctrinal issues as Scripture and Tradition, baptism, eucharist, and ministry.

But during the same period, personal and social ethical questions have appeared, causing disputes and even threatening new divisions within and among churches. All Christian traditions recognize that ethics cannot be separated from revealed doctrine: faith does have ethical consequences. Yet the JWG notes that in fact there is not enough serious, mature, and sustained ecumenical discussion on many of these ethical issues and positions, personal and social; for example, nuclear armaments and deterrence, abortion and euthanasia, permanent married love and procreation, genetic engineering and artificial insemination.

The JWG has taken the first steps in exploring the new sources of potential ecumenical divisions. It first asked a few interchurch groups to investigate and illustrate this development in local contexts, and then it convened a small group of specialists to review these studies. The JWG proposes that the subject be a priority for the post-Canberra period. The JWG's intention is not to examine the substance of each of the potentially or actually divisive issues, but to see how they may best be approached in dialogue. Such issues can offer new opportunities for the increase of mutual understanding and respect and, we may hope, for common witness without compromise of a church's convictions or of Christian conscience. The JWG emphasizes the following questions:

1. Why are some ethical issues so emotionally and intellectually divisive that often mature dialogue about them is inhibited, even avoided?
2. In what ways do churches formulate ethical principles and decide on specific issues?
3. Do churches help their members to enlighten and form consciences?
4. In what ways do the churches understand and use their authority to decide on specific issues for all their members?
5. What are the ways in which the churches should humbly enter into public debate, where peoples of other world faiths or of secular persuasions also desire to live together peacefully and justly; how should Christian convictions be presented as a contribution to the common good?

6. When does an ethical issue on which Christians disagree become an obstacle to full ecclesial communion?

In discussing these questions, Christians can rediscover the resources which our church traditions provide for ethical analysis and decision making. We can better learn to respect the convictions of others who are rooted in their traditions and commitments and to continue dialogue even in disagreement, without demanding that anyone should compromise convictions "for the sake of unity."

d. Councils of Churches

On several occasions the JWG has discussed what councils of churches can do to foster unity and to follow up its own work. A very important contribution during the period under review was the Second World Consultation for National Councils of Churches (NCCs), held in Geneva in 1986. This meeting brought together 120 leaders from some seventy NCCs and regional ecumenical bodies:

a. To share their experience and expertise
b. To encourage the "reception" of recent developments, such as the increased participation of the Roman Catholic Church in NCCs (thirty-five NCCs and three regional councils of churches with Roman Catholic membership) and
c. To continue reflecting on their ecumenical role and ecclesiological significance.

There were major papers on councils as instruments of unity and in relation to justice, peace, and service. One workshop explored specific ecclesiological issues, following on from the theological consultation on "The Significance and Contribution of Councils of Churches in the Ecumenical Movement," which was held in Venice in 1982. Other workshops dealt with the role of NCCs in ecumenism, aspects of mission and dialogue, issues of finance and resource sharing, and councils in their social and political context.

The papers, responses, and workshop reports have been published by the WCC in *Instruments of Unity: National Councils of Churches Within the One Ecumenical Movement* (ed. Thomas F. Best; Geneva: WCC, 1988).

The vitality and development of NCCs affect the ecumenical movement as a whole. Of particular interest to the JWG are the cases where the Roman Catholic Church is moving to official membership; this at times promotes reflection on crucial ecclesiological and practical issues.

The Geneva Consultation touched upon a number of important matters of common concern in the community of national councils. Examples include:

1. The emergence of *koinonia* as an expression of self-understanding of the councils, affirming unity, diversity, and creative interaction.
2. Shared life and commitment prompt shared reflection on the nature of the church.
3. People learn more about ecumenism as they take part in the work of NCCs.
4. Churches in a council learn together what it means to be "the church in that place."
5. They begin to understand "the instrumental" character of it, but also to appreciate that times have a germinal unity, a certain "ecclesial density" (*Instruments*, pp. 42-43).
6. Churches in a council will be brought up against the problem of the local and the universal and the relation between authority and autonomy.

e. Christian Mixed Marriages[1]

In the course of the first years of its existence, the JWG on many occasions considered the pastoral challenges which mixed marriages pose. Its work certainly contributed to the progress represented by Pope Paul VI's *Matrimonia Mixta* (1970), which has been developed in the new *Code of Canon Law* (1983). Churches normally encourage marriages between persons of the same communion. However, churches and society no longer view mixed marriages as the object of reproach but now consider them with greater appreciation and understanding. The churches still seek more effective pastoral means to assist couples and their children in such marriages—both in preparation for marriage and continuing Christian counseling during the marriage itself. Those couples who take seriously their vocation in marriage as a union in Christ have found it to be an enriching ecumenical experience. Nevertheless, because of the divisions in Christianity, they and their children reflect the sufferings of Christ; with hope and prayer they travel together the road of conversion towards the goal of unity.

Conscious of the increase in mixed marriages and their significance for the ecumenical movement, the JWG held a consultation on this question in 1989. Its report pointed to the rich experience offered by mixed marriages but also to persisting problems such as (1) the mutual recognition by churches of such marriages, (2) differing baptismal practice, (3) the education of children, (4) intercommunion.

The consultation stressed the need for common pastoral care before and during marriage, especially during the early years. It recommended more study of the ecclesiological implications of mixed marriages. Finally, it asked that the next JWG should study the report.

2. Ecumenical Formation

The *Fifth Report* of the JWG emphasized the urgency of the task of ecumenical formation. It stressed that the ecumenical dimension must be an indispensable part of all processes of Christian formation, whether of laity, of youth, in catechesis, in religious education, in theological training.

The subject has been a priority in the subsequent sessions of the JWG. Following discussion and reflection at the Riano meeting (Rome), 1985, a first draft of a possible study document on the subject was prepared. This went through a series of revisions, with texts being prepared for discussion in Bossey, 1987; Venice, 1988; and St. Prix (Paris), 1989. But a primary task remains: to adapt the content, length, and style of the draft document to the audience it addresses. After a small consultation in 1990, the executive of the JWG will hand over the unfinished task to the next JWG in the hope that the new group will give the topic priority on its agenda.

3. Common Witness

Collaboration between Christians in the search for new ways of rendering common witness has been consistently encouraged by the Roman Catholic Church and the WCC. Pope John Paul II has emphasized that common witness among Christians is a stimulus to the search for full unity. In the joint statement issued by the then General Secretary Dr. Philip Potter and by Cardinal Willebrands on the occasion of the visit of Pope John Paul II to the WCC (1984), mutual commitment to collaboration in the social field and the need to strengthen cooperation in several other areas was stressed. Pope John Paul II has expressed his conviction that "common witness among Christians is possible in various fields. It is founded on the common faith which exists among them and which the comparison in the dialogue in process has shown in a new light. . . . The common witness which can be given today is a stimulus for the search for full unity" (*L'Osservatore Romano*, 23 January 1986).

The JWG is pleased to note that in many countries important work of common Bible studies, use of the Ecumenical Prayer Cycle, joint Bible translations, publication, and distribution is carried out. Very important is also the collaboration between churches in the area of press, radio, television, and other means of communication, as well as the training of personnel in specific fields. In some places, the celebration of local, national, regional, and international events, the common struggle for human rights, justice, and peace (e.g., Basel Assembly on Peace with Justice, 1989), and the sharing of resources have also contributed to unity, renewal, and common Christian witness.

a. Common Witness, Mission, and Unity

Following the publication of the *Common Witness* document by the JWG in 1982, steps were taken to distribute it widely and to emphasize its importance both to the visitors to the WCC and to Roman Catholic groups. The presence of Roman Catholic consultants in the CWME and their participation in the WCC Mission Conference in Melbourne (1980) led to the appointment of a Roman Catholic consultant to the staff of CWME in 1984.

During the period under review, there has been a renewal of CWME staff visits to Rome as well as a visit of Catholics from Rome to Geneva. Members of the staff participated in three Roman Catholic mission seminars. An invitation to the Missiological Congress at the Urbaniana University (Rome) was also extended to CWME.

A series of visits was made by the Roman Catholic consultant to both Roman Catholic and Protestant missionary organizations in order to discuss common witness as practiced at both national and local levels. An important part of the consultant's work during recent years has involved promoting and organizing Roman Catholic involvement in work arising from the WCC Mission Conference in San Antonio, Texas (May 22–June 1, 1989). This included a seminar on the conference theme held in Rome with representatives of the WCC, some departments of the Roman Curia, and Roman Catholic missionary organizations. A Vatican delegation of twenty observers was present at the conference itself. The local committee for the conference was chaired by the ecumenical officer of the Roman Catholic diocese of San Antonio.

Roman Catholic representatives contributed to the discussion on the mission/unity issue both at Faith and Order and CWME meetings.

The question of proselytism has been raised at various meetings and has made the need to promote common witness more urgent. It will be for the next JWG to suggest ways in which common witness, mission, and unity can be further promoted. It is important to involve those organizations and groups who share the concern for a common witness to Jesus as Lord and Savior in today's world. There is also need to continue ecumenical reflection on the challenge of new religious movements.

b. The Week of Prayer for Christian Unity

The Week of Prayer is one of the oldest ways of expressing and celebrating the spiritual communion that binds the churches together in listening to the word of God, in praise, and intercession. The eightieth anniversary of the Week of Prayer, 1987-1988, was marked by gratitude for this form of ecumenical fellowship and "spiritual ecumenism," which is generally regarded as an indispensable basis for all other ecumenical endeavors.

Christians are convinced that their efforts to overcome their divisions can only be fruitful through the Lord's blessing. Therefore, prayer should be at the very center of the ecumenical movement. The various other ecumenical activities that may be occasioned by the Week of Prayer are important, but they should not "obscure" the significance of praying together for unity. In thousands of places all over the world, Christians gather together to pray for Christian unity and the needs of all people. In many places and circumstances this week remains, for various reasons, the main expression of local ecumenism. The material for the Week of Prayer is prepared each year through joint consultations of the Pontifical Council for Promoting Christian Unity (PCPCU) and the Faith and Order Secretariat (WCC). Local churches of different traditions prepare draft texts for these consultations.

At all its meetings, the JWG has heard reports about the Week of Prayer for Christian Unity. It has noted that in several countries, observance of the week is expanding, while there is a certain stagnation in others. An inquiry undertaken by the PCPCU in 1984 regarding the Week of Prayer showed how vital is the practice of ecumenical prayer for education and renewal, unity and common witness. The considerations and suggestions of the JWG point in the same direction. Churches must be reminded that the week is not just a prayer for unity once a year, but is an integral part of continuous ecumenical formation and collaboration; that material and proposals for the week should reflect a wider range of context and opportunities; that more preparation/adaptation should be done at the local level; and that more thought should be given to the relationship between prayer, ecumenical formation, and shared activities.

The JWG is convinced that the Week of Prayer can provide one of the most fundamental ecumenical experiences and inspirations and that therefore it deserves the active participation and commitment of all churches.

c. Collaboration in Justice, Peace, and Integrity of Creation (JPIC)
The initiative for the JPIC program and convocation came from the Sixth Assembly at Vancouver (1983). At the 1985 JWG meeting, the PCPCU was asked to investigate the possibility of Roman Catholic participation in JPIC. In January 1987 the WCC Central Committee officially invited the Roman Catholic Church to be a "co-inviter" with the member churches of the WCC, nonmember churches, and CWCs for the World Convocation on JPIC (Seoul, 1990). In December 1987, Cardinal Willebrands informed Dr. E. Castro that although the Roman Catholic Church would not be a "co-inviter" because of some unresolved difficulties (for example, "the different nature of the two bodies"), it would collaborate in the project because of the common Christian concerns for justice, peace, and integrity of creation. The Roman Catholic Church sent participants to the preliminary consultations (Geneva, 1986; Glion, 1986; Granvollen, 1988), appointed a staff person to

work full-time in Geneva with the JPIC desk, and designated five official representatives on the thirty-member preparatory group.

In September 1988, the WCC general secretary invited Cardinal Willebrands to arrange for the Roman Catholic Church to appoint fifty participants to the Seoul Convocation. Cardinal Willebrands and Cardinal Etchegaray (Pontifical Council for Justice and Peace) responded to Dr. Castro in November 1989: the Roman Catholic Church would appoint twenty experts to Seoul in the capacity of advisers—the type of participation now customary in WCC assemblies and other major meetings. Meanwhile, the Roman Catholic staff assigned to JPIC remained; Roman Catholics continued to serve on the local planning committee in Seoul; and the Roman Catholic Church assured financial support for the convocation. Furthermore, local Roman Catholic churches have fully participated, together with other Christians, in the development of national or regional JPIC programs, and their representatives attended the convocation in Seoul as members of delegations either of NCCs or of regional ecumenical bodies of which the Roman Catholic Church is a member.

At its January 1990 meeting, the JWG discussed the process that led to the official Roman Catholic decision. The common preparatory group work and the presence of Roman Catholic official advisers and others at Seoul, as well as the urgency of common Christian witness in confronting the world's survival issues, will lead the JWG to follow attentively this post-Seoul process and to be alert to the ways of possible cooperation in the period which leads to the Canberra Assembly and thereafter.

4. Social Thought and Action

At its meetings in Le Louverain (1979) and Marseilles (1980), the JWG accepted a proposal to form a Joint Consultative Group on Social Thought and Action (JCG) that would undertake a study on collaboration in the field of social thought and action. When the mandate of SODEPAX came to an end in 1981, the JCG continued work in this field, focusing first on development, peace, and human rights. Later, attention was specifically given to the issues of racism and apartheid (1985-1987). At its meeting in Venice (1988), the JWG, with the agreement of the parent bodies, decided not to renew the mandate of the JCG, which ended the same year. The work formerly done by this group is now to be carried out by the JWG itself, with the help of small ad hoc study groups, on basic issues such as development and debt crisis, racism and apartheid, armaments and arms transfers, human rights and religious liberty. At its 1989 meeting, the JWG strongly recommended that it was now time to explore the possibilities of common witness against racism. The Pontifical Council on Justice and Peace (PCJP) and the WCC Program to

Combat Racism (PCR) are working together on a common reflection on the issues of racism and apartheid.

B. Ecumenical Collaboration in Other Areas Between WCC and Roman Catholic Church Partners

1. Major Studies and Other Activities in the Field of Faith and Order

Since 1968, the Roman Catholic Church has been officially represented in the Commission on Faith and Order; so have several other nonmember churches of the WCC. This is the basis for continuing and extensive cooperation, which has enabled Faith and Order to include in its work Roman Catholic theological perspectives and contributions. Thus, the wider dimensions of current ecumenical endeavors have always been present in this work. In recent years this cooperation and the consequent wider outlook has deepened and led to remarkable results.

The 1982 Lima document on *Baptism, Eucharist, and Ministry* was a major result of this cooperation. The document was elaborated with the help of Roman Catholic theologians and led to convergences on issues that had long been divisive. In the broad discussion process on BEM from 1987 to 1990, the Roman Catholic Church was actively involved at international, national, and local levels. Roman Catholics have discussed BEM in ecumenical groups, seminars, commissions, seminaries, theological faculties, publications, etc.

Most importantly, the Roman Catholic Church accepted the invitation of Faith and Order to send a response to BEM at the highest appropriate level. This involved several steps. First, the document was sent to Roman Catholic bishops' conferences, theological faculties, and others, asking them to study it and send their reports to the PCPCU. These reports were analyzed and taken into account by the PCPCU, which then, with the help of a team of theological consultants, prepared a draft response to BEM. The response was brought to its final form as a result of collaboration between the PCPCU and the Congregation for the Doctrine of the Faith. In August 1987, it was sent by the PCPCU to the Faith and Order Secretariat in Geneva.

The Roman Catholic Church has thus, for the first time, given an official response to an ecumenical document. The response affirms the ecumenical achievement represented by BEM. It contains a positive evaluation of large sections of BEM, points to areas that from a Roman Catholic point of view need further study, and raises ecclesiological questions which, according to the Roman Catholic Church, need to be faced if ecumenical progress is to be made. It reaffirms the commitment of the Roman Catholic Church to continuing multilateral dialogue.

Pope John Paul II and other Roman Catholic leaders have repeatedly underlined the importance of BEM in the movement toward visible unity. The BEM process is probably the most significant instance for many years of ecumenical rapprochement between Roman Catholics and Christians of other traditions.

Roman Catholic theologians have participated in all meetings, consultations, and drafting groups of Faith and Order in recent years. They have thus made theological contributions to the major study programs on *Towards the Common Expression of Apostolic Faith Today* and *The Unity of the Church and the Renewal of Human Community.*

The meeting of the Faith and Order Commission in Budapest in August 1989 received the results of these studies, which will determine the future direction of the work of Faith and Order. This will include more comprehensive work on ecclesiology, especially a reconsideration of the "unity we seek," for which Roman Catholic contributions and cooperation are of crucial importance. The same applies to the plan to hold the Fifth World Conference of Faith and Order in 1993.

2. Bilateral and Multilateral Dialogues

While the WCC and the Roman Catholic Church cooperate directly through multilateral dialogue in Faith and Order, many member churches of the WCC have been engaged for a long time in bilateral dialogue with the Roman Catholic Church, either through their respective CWCs at the world level or directly at the national level. During the last eight years, both the number and range of bilateral dialogues have increased. They represent an important element of the present ecumenical movement and have led to significant results.

There is common agreement that multilateral and bilateral dialogues have complementary purposes and possibilities. Ways have been developed to further their complementary character and to help to give them common purpose. Thus, the work of Faith and Order has profited from the insights and results of bilateral dialogues, and these in turn have focused attention on the developments and achievements in multilateral dialogues. For example, several bilateral dialogues and many responses of the churches to BEM have seen the BEM document as providing a wider framework within which dialogues can find common aims. The *Fourth Forum on Bilateral Conversations*, sponsored in 1985 by the CWCs and organized by Faith and Order, has confirmed the complementary character of multilateral and bilateral dialogues by evaluating and comparing main elements of multilateral convergence on BEM and the results of bilateral dialogues on the same issues (*Report of the Fourth Forum on Bilateral Conversations*, Faith and Order Paper No. 125, Geneva, 1985). The Fifth Forum was held in 1990 and focused on the question of consistent ecclesiology in bilateral and multilateral dialogues.

It will also be a task of the next JWG to follow developments in bilateral and multilateral dialogues and help to ensure that they together serve the one ecumenical movement. This corresponds to a request by the WCC Central Committee in 1988 which was addressed to the JWG and Faith and Order.

3. Dialogue and Witness

Cooperation between the WCC Dialogue Subunit and the Pontifical Council for Interreligious Dialogue (PCID) has continued regularly. There have been yearly joint staff meetings held alternately in Rome and Geneva. Conversations during the past three years have been concerned with

1. The role of dialogue in relation to religious fundamentalism
2. Dialogue and mission
3. The place of dialogue in a religiously plural society

In 1988 a joint meeting was held to discuss the possibilities and problems of tripartite dialogue: Christians, Jews, and Muslims. The WCC and its Roman Catholic partners have also been jointly in contact with Islamic and other organizations.

Roman Catholic groups have participated in the study of the Dialogue Subunit on "My Neighbor's Faith and Mine," which makes Christians more aware and informed about religious pluralism. Interreligious dialogue is growing in importance. WCC and Roman Catholic Church partners should discuss the questions it raises and share information, studies, and publications.

4. Faith, Science, and Ethics

There are moves towards collaboration on these topics: (1) faith and science, (2) technology and environment, and (3) the theology of creation. For example, Cardinal Sin addressed a Church and Society meeting on technology and its effects on the poor, held in Manila. Roman Catholic observers attended the working committee meetings of the Subunit on Church and Society in 1988 and 1989. Further, Roman Catholic theologians attended consultations on "A Theology of Nature and Theocentric Ethic" (Annecy, September 1988) and on "God, People, and Nature—One Community" (Sao Paulo, June/July 1988). Valuable Roman Catholic contributions on these themes were made.

5. Health Care, Healing, and Medicine

Since 1982 collaboration in this field has found expression in the presence of Roman Catholic observers/consultants at the WCC Christian Medical Commission (CMC) meetings. They are appointed jointly by the PCPCU and the Pontifical Council for Health Care Workers. The partners have undertaken joint activities in the field of health care, healing, and medicine. For some years there have been mutual invitations to meetings. The exchange of visits between CMC and the Vatican staff have helped further collaboration. One proposal that would augment this cooperation in the future is the appointment of Roman Catholic consultants to work with the CMC.

6. Diaconal Service, Peace, and Refugee Work

The WCC–CICARWS Emergencies Desk maintains good relations with Caritas Internationalis on disasters and often works closely with national organizations related to Caritas Internationalis, such as Caritas Germany, Caritas Switzerland, Catholic Relief Services, and Secours Catholique in France. Effective joint relief work has been done in Ethiopia, and there are plans to support actively long-term reconstruction by the Armenian Apostolic Church. A protocol has been signed by the Armenian Soviet Republic, by WCC–Caritas Internationalis, and by the Armenian Apostolic Church. In the wider context of coordinating agency response to disaster, CICARWS and Caritas Internationalis are members of the LICROSS-Volags Steering Committee in which six members are engaged, the others being the League of the Red Cross Societies, Oxfam, Catholic Relief Services, and the Lutheran World Federation. It, too, should be noted that there was important coordination through the CCDA in 1983-1986.

In June 1989 CICARWS visited Rome and met Bishop Alois Wagner, the vice-president of Cor Unum. A number of areas of mutual interest were identified, and an agreement to encourage dialogue on world developments, refugee service, and relief operation was warmly welcomed. Sharing information on the position of the two organizations, in the Vatican and the WCC, will help the two bodies in meeting the challenge ahead.

In many parts of the world (Africa, Latin America, Europe), CICARWS partners and networks collaborate with Roman Catholic colleagues. In Africa there are many NCCs in which Catholics are full members, e.g., Sudan, Botswana, Namibia, Swaziland, Lesotho, and Liberia. In these countries there are ongoing refugee programs in which CICARWS and the Roman Catholic Church participate fully in leadership and funding.

The Roman Catholic Church and the WCC member churches together address issues relating to peace, e.g., in Sudan, and make joint statements. In 1988 a visit to Europe by Sudan church leaders was organized in which Roman Catholics participated. In 1989 a journey was made to North America to explain to churches and human rights movements the difficult situation in Sudan and its people's deep need for peace. The Namibia Repatriation Program, handled by CICARWS, received funds from Roman Catholic funding agencies. These brief examples— refugee aid, joint projects, peace action, repatriation programs—indicate that some African Christian Councils are active in coordinating essential programs and need direct funding to be able to offer to their societies leadership and resources. An equitable way must be found by all partners to support ecumenical enterprises.

In 1984 CICARWS Refugee Service held a consultation of church-related partners in western countries which had significant Roman Catholic Church participation to examine the situation of asylum and refugee protection.

In 1986 a global Consultation on Protection and Asylum in Zurich was jointly organized by CICARWS, Swiss Inter-Church Aid (HEKS), and Caritas Switzerland. The consultation brought together representatives of the various Catholic and WCC-related networks. It called for greater collaboration between Roman Catholic and WCC-related groups serving refugees. An international Ecumenical Committee on Refugee Protection was established, to be convened alternately by the WCC and Caritas Internationalis with the participation of other global bodies, such as the LWF, International Catholic Migration Commission, etc.

After this initiative on the international level, efforts have been made to foster collaboration between WCC and Roman Catholic agencies at the regional levels. The Zurich consultation called for the establishment of joint committees or working groups in each of the regions.

The North American Continuation Committee for Refugee Protection is composed of both Roman Catholic and WCC-related bodies (Canadian Bishops' Conference, Canadian Council of Churches, NCCC-USA, U.S. Catholic Conference) and meets regularly. In Europe, a joint CEC-CICARWS European Churches' Working Group on Asylum and Refugees was set up and has met every two years since 1988. Catholic participation has been continuous, represented by an observer from the Council of European Bishops' Conferences.

7. International Issues and Human Rights

Member churches of the WCC in Latin America and the Caribbean have taken wide-ranging initiatives on human rights, with Roman Catholic participation at the local level. These are seen as ministries of assistance to victims of human rights violations, as well as pastoral help. Human Rights Resources on Latin America (HRROLA) has spread ecumenical groups which have Roman Catholic leadership. It has sought funds from churches and agencies related to CICARWS–WCC for work in which most, if not all, membership in a given ecumenical committee belongs to the Roman Catholic Church.

Examples of cooperation dot the landscape of Latin and Central America. Representatives from El Salvador have, with the help of CCIA, appeared before the UN Human Rights Commission. Chilean experience includes the work of the Committee of Cooperation for Peace in Chile. This committee, made up of Lutherans, Methodists, Orthodox, Roman Catholics, and Evangelicals, has carried out ministries with political prisoners, exiles, and families of those who have disappeared.

In Brazil the NCC, constituted by the Roman Catholc Church and Protestant churches, has closely followed the situation on human rights, especially in relation to land rights involving several indigenous nations. The Ludigenist Missionary Council is developing sections and programs in this connection which are appreciated by the different ethnic groups. The participation of leaders of some Protestant churches in the Pastoral Commission on Land has opened up this section of the National Bishops' Conference of Brazil to ecumenical dialogue and greater commitment. This progress was confirmed at the seventh Inter-Ecclesial Meeting of Basic Ecclesial Communities in July 1989, where Roman Catholic, Orthodox, and Methodist bishops were present.

WCC and Roman Catholic-related organizations jointly sponsored a meeting in Brussels, May 16-20, 1988, on the European Community and the Debt Crisis of African, Caribbean, and Pacific (A.C.P.) countries.

Representatives of the Vatican PCJP have attended the Commission on Churches' Participation in Development (CCPD) Advisory Group and Economic Advisory Group meetings. CCPD is a member of the Advisory Board of the Swiss Roman Catholic–Protestant initiative regarding the international debt crisis.

8. Education (General Education, Theological Education, Family Education)

Collaboration in these areas during most of the period under review was limited to those situations in which the WCC and Roman Catholic partners in education participated in jointly planned activities with NCCs and regional ecumenical bodies to which local Roman Catholic churches belong. Examples of this were a workshop held in the Pacific on Ecumenical Learning for JPIC, in September 1988, and the Consultation on the Church and Persons with Disabilities held in Bangkok in March 1989.

Another area of indirect collaboration is in relation to "street children." Following the International Year of the Child (1979), a three-year Inter-NGO Program on Street Children and Street Youth was started on the initiative of the International Catholic Child Bureau (ICCB) in 1982. The WCC and ICCB among others founded a new organization in 1986, called CHILDHOPE, in order to continue the work. The headquarters are in Rio de Janeiro.

Since the beginning of 1988, the scope for joint collaboration, particularly in the field of adult education, increased significantly when a Roman Catholic priest from Mauritius joined the WCC staff. Because of his previous involvement in ecumenical adult education work in Asia and the Pacific, he has brought the WCC into contact with a new network of Roman Catholic or Roman Catholic-related organizations that are open to ecumenical collaboration on justice, peace, and development education.

In eastern and southern Africa, Training for Transformation programs, which were originally started by the Roman Catholic Church, are now being planned ecumenically by NCCs (e.g., Zambia, Zimbabwe) and the All-Africa Conference of Churches, with significant Roman Catholic involvement. The WCC Adult Education Program is actively participating in this development.

Catholic educators are involved in the work of the Program on Theological Education (PTE) through the Association of Theological Institutions. Roman Catholic representatives have attended some consultations sponsored by PTE and other ecumenical partners.

9. Renewal and Spirituality

Since 1983, "spirituality" has figured largely in the life and the programs of the WCC and in cooperation between the WCC and the Roman Catholic Church.

A first step towards "A Spirituality for Our Times" was a consultation held in Annecy (France) in December 1984, in which the Roman Catholic contribution was substantial. Because of need for further study and reflection on some aspects of spirituality, the Subunit on Renewal and Congregational Life (RCL), as well as other subunits of the WCC, have organized a series of seminars and consultations. In all of these the Roman Catholic participants shared their specific experiences and understanding, making possible creative dialogues between various traditions and cultures of the ecumenical community.

In the period 1985-1988, a series of workshops have been held for renewal of worship in Europe, Africa, Asia, Latin America, Caribbean, North America, and Australia. Roman Catholics participated in these meetings and, in some cases, shared in the leadership.

10. The Role of the Laity in Church and Society

A good deal of common work in this field has been done on the one hand by the RCL and other subunits in Program Unit III "Education and Renewal" and, on the other, by the Pontifical Council for the Laity (PCL).

The Subunit on RCL has a desk for Lay Centers. In Asia, Africa, North America, Caribbean, and Europe, networks of ecumenical centers and lay academies include Roman Catholic centers and staff. RCL and other subunits in Education and Renewal sent their comments on the *Lineamenta* document prior to the Synod of Bishops in October 1987 to the Synod Secretariat in the Vatican. Moreover, WCC Unit III engaged in a meeting in Geneva on 26-27 February 1987 with representatives of the PCL on the questions raised by the subject of the synod of bishops in 1987.

In November 1988, WCC staff visited the PCL in Rome and discussed the present dialogue and the promotion of this topic. In February 1990, this discussion was carried further in the seminar on "Merging Ecumenical Trends Regarding Laity" organized by Unit III with Roman Catholic participation. As part of future cooperation between the WCC and the PCL, the RCL has proposed to continue this ecumenical reflection on "The Role of the Laity in Church and Society."

11. Ecumenical Institute at Bossey

During recent years, the dynamic WCC–Roman Catholic Church collaboration at Bossey has continued. It has been strengthened by the appointment, this time for three years, of a Roman Catholic professor to the annual graduate school. The participation of a Roman Catholic observer on the Bossey Board, the continued interest of the PCPCU in the graduate school, and the invitation to Bossey staff and students to visit annually various departments of the Roman Curia, the Unions of Superiors General, the missiology Department of the Gregorian University, the Dominican House of Studies, the Focolare Movement, and the St. Egidio parish community have made a positive impact on WCC–Roman Catholic Church relationships and on youth commitment to the ecumenical movement.

12. Preparation for the Seventh Assembly of the WCC

Roman Catholic theologians and others have been involved in the preparations for the Canberra Assembly through consultations on the theme and subthemes, several regional meetings, visitors programs, and ecumenical team visits. Twenty Roman Catholic observers will attend the assembly and contribute to its deliberations. Others are serving on the local committees, and many Roman Catholic parishes throughout Australia are participating in the preparatory process of study and prayer.

IV. Prospects for the Future (1991-1998)

1. Towards a More Effective Role for the JWG

The JWG is dedicated to its mandate. In a happy atmosphere, it has fulfilled difficult tasks and tried to meet vital priorities. But its status, its heavy agenda, the sensitive nature of the issues it deals with, short annual meetings, and limited financial resources do not allow it to cover the whole pattern of relationships between the Roman Catholic Church and the WCC.

Further work is needed to strengthen its role. This could be done. Composition, working methods, financial resources, and staffing could be improved. Possibilities should be explored of holding some meetings in different countries. This could stimulate local contacts and make the JWG more effective.

Better communications, through publications, special visits, and meetings, could help the work of the JWG to be better known within its constituencies.

Given the limited time and resources available to the JWG, its agenda should be more limited in scope, and better use could be made of the time spent together. While continuing to devote part of its agenda to reviewing cooperation between various programs of the WCC and the departments of the Roman Catholic Church, the JWG should in future give greater attention to assessing both the ecumenical situation and important developments in various regions of the world, particularly at the local level. In some cases these reviews could be done through written reports. The JWG should concentrate on developing topics of crucial importance for church unity and common Christian witness.

The signs of the times continue to be a challenge to all churches and a call to renewal and unity. The demands of WCC–Roman Catholic Church relationships call for renewed joint efforts to achieve the goal of visible unity of the church and the renewal of human community. Credible Christian witness, mutual respect, and growth in truth and love must be sustained and further developed.

2. Proposals for Future Work

After assessing its activities over the past seven years, as well as the development in the ecumenical situation, the JWG proposes the following priorities for the next period:

a. Ecclesiological dimensions of ecumenical work
b. Ecumenical education and formation
c. Common witness and mission

The first area provides continuity on the central and ongoing concern for the unity of the church—the goal and the way, and places emphasis on ecclesiological issues, such as the ecclesiology of communion and the unity we seek.

The second and the third areas also focus on major ecumenical fields, where joint effort is urgently needed.

a) There are many indications that both in bilateral and multilateral ecumenical dialogues, the understanding of the nature and mission of the church is becoming a central topic. This is so because ecumenical conversations so far have led to the recognition that many of the remaining difficulties in the theological dialogue have their roots in different ecclesiologies, especially in different concepts of the place and mission of the church in God's saving and transforming action. Closely connected with this are (1) the question of authority in the church, (2) the relations between church and humanity, (3) the ecclesiological basis of a common

Christian witness and service in a broken world crying out for reconciliation and renewal. "The ecclesiology of communion" integrates a number of basic ecclesiological concerns within a coherent vision.

Through its work on *The Church—Local and Universal* and other topics, the JWG has already been involved in the new ecclesiological debate. This debate will continue, and the JWG should be an active partner in it. The group may again choose a specific aspect of ecclesiology for its own contribution.

The question of "the unity we seek" remains important on the ecumenical agenda. There has been an emerging ecumenical consensus on the conditions and expression of the goal of visible unity, as witness the statements of the WCC Assemblies from New Delhi (1961) up to Nairobi (1975). However, since 1975, developments in bilateral dialogues and Faith and Order studies, new relationships between the Roman Catholic Church and other churches, experiences in church union negotiations, changes in ecumenical perspective have all made necessary a restatement of "the unity we seek," which should build on the New Delhi and Nairobi statements.

The 1991 Canberra Assembly is expected to take up this task. It will be a major responsibility of the JWG to evaluate such a restatement, to assist in its interpretation and application, and to monitor and support further steps towards this goal.

Among matters needing specific attention are

- The continuing impact and implication of the BEM process
- The continuing development of the Faith and Order studies on "Towards the Common Expression of the Apostolic Faith Today" and "The Unity of the Church and the Renewal of Human Community"
- The ecumenical significance and contribution of councils of churches (cf. chapter III, A.1.D. above)
- The possibility of a more comprehensive ecumenical movement and its structures (especially with regard to evangelical and charismatic/Pentecostal movements)
- Developments of and input from bilateral multilateral dialogues

During the next period the JWG should further deepen the study of New Sources of Division: Ethical Issues (cf. chapter III, A.1.C.).

The report and the recommendations of the consultation (1989) on mixed marriages (cf. chapter III, A.1.E.) should be studied particularly for its ecumenical and ecclesiological implications.

Major demographic changes, refugees, and migrant workers make more urgent problems of interreligious marriages. A new study on this question should be undertaken in cooperation with the Pontifical Council for Interreligious Dialogue and the WCC Subunit on Dialogue with People of Living Faiths.

b) Further study on ecumenical formation (see chapter III, A.2.) should embrace the wide field of ecumenical education. Promoting work for unity, transforming the life of Christians so as to bring about deeper conversion of heart and renewal of the church, should extend to the education of priests, pastors, theologians, and laity.

c) During the 1990s the call for common Christian witness in missionary endeavors "so that the world may believe" (cf. Jn 17:21) should continue to be a major task for the JWG (cf. above, chapter III, A.3. and 3a).

The JWG should further explore ecumenical approaches to "Dialogue and Proclamation of the Gospel." This could be done in collaboration between the WCC subunits (CWME, Dialogue) and Roman Catholic partners.

The JWG should also go on moving towards common perspectives on social thought and action. During the past period there have been difficulties in tackling some social issues, such as apartheid, JPIC, and with some of the instruments used, e.g., SODEPAX and the JCG. The JWG has called a special meeting to examine these problems, to discern successes and failures, and to make recommendations for the future. Its report will be given to the executive committee of the JWG for consideration in the next steps of collaboration.

The JWG recognized that throughout the world, ecumenical cooperation at local, national, and regional levels between WCC member churches and the Roman Catholic Church often flourishes, with fruitful results in common witness and mission. The JWG recommends that in the future more account be taken of such ecumenical collaboration and its significance evaluated.

d) Further, the JWG recognized that new issues are arising in the world which may call for ecumenical collaboration. These include the considerable spiritual and ideological challenges for the whole world coming from the events in central and eastern Europe and in other regions. The response of churches to these theological, economic, political, and social issues could be strengthened through ecumenical cooperation. The role of the churches and their life together in such changing societies, and the kinds of solidarity and fellowship they may need from churches elsewhere, could be part of the JWG's future concern. Likewise, the global ecological crisis, newly recognized as an urgent matter of survival, may well call for joint responses. Future decisions about official WCC–Roman Catholic Church cooperation in any of these areas should be carefully considered in the light of the recommendations to come from the meetings on these subjects.

e) Besides these aims, the JWG could continue to monitor collaboration on matters which may arise from major ecumenical events. The need to give attention to the results of the JPIC World Convocation has already been mentioned. The

Seventh Assembly of the WCC at Canberra in February 1991 will certainly provide new ecumenical impetus. The theme of the assembly, "Come Holy Spirit—Renew the Whole Creation," can open up fresh dimensions in theological exploration, spiritual understanding, and hope for God's presence and action in the world. Likewise, Roman Catholic events, such as the General Synod of Bishops in 1990, and the Special Synod of African Bishops, the centenary of the first social encyclical, *Rerum Novarum* (1991), can open new paths to explore in this relationship. The JWG encourages openness to the Spirit as we consider the ecumenical implications of these events. They could provide room for increased collaboration between the WCC and Roman Catholic Church.

f) *Churches and Christians Towards the Year 2000.* As we approach the end of a millennium, the attention of churches and peoples throughout the world will be focused upon hope for the future. This historical turning point will provide a natural occasion for all Christians to reflect on the state of their ecumenical relationships, recommit themselves to unity, and strengthen their common witness for the sake of the world's salvation. The next JWG to serve after the Canberra Assembly could take the responsibility of coordinating the responses to the assembly made by the WCC member churches, the Roman Catholic Church, and if possible, other nonmember churches. It may be hoped that the churches might offer together to the world a Christian vision of unity and renewal, of social, economic, and spiritual life which can contribute to the work for a stable and just world as we enter a new millennium. This goal might be considered by the newly established JWG.

The JWG renews its hope that it will continue to serve as an instrument of unity and ecumenical collaboration between the two partners. It will try to open hearts and minds to the gifts of the Holy Spirit who leads all Christians to unity (cf. Gal 5:22-23).

Members of the Joint Working Group

Representatives of the World Council of Churches

Rev. Jacques Blanc, France (cosecretary, 1984-1985)
Rev. Jacques Maury, France (comoderator)
Rev. Donald Anderson, Great Britain
Dr. Julio De Santa Ana, Brazil
Ms. Marie Assad, Egypt (1984-1986)
Rev. Arie R. Brouwer, USA (1984-1985)
Rev. Günther Gassmann, Switzerland
Ms. Gloria R. Guzman, Philippines
Most Rev. John of Karelia and all Finland, Finland

Rt. Rev. Misaeri Kauma, Uganda
Ms. Mercy Oduyoye, Switzerland (since 1987)
Dr. Todor Sabev, Switzerland (cosecretary since 1985)
Ms. Jean Skuse, Australia
Ms. Ruth Sovik, Switzerland (since 1986)

Consultants
Rev. Ion Bria
Dr. John Pobee

Representatives of the Roman Catholic Church

Most Rev. Basil Meeking, New Zealand (cosecretary, 1984-1986)
Msgr. John Mutiso-Mbinda, Vatican City (cosecretary since 1986)
Most Rev. Alan Clark, England (comoderator)
Most Rev. Pierre Duprey, Vatican City
Most Rev. Jan Schotte, CICM, Vatican City
Most Rev. Jorge Mejia, Vatican City
Most Rev. Donald J. Reece, West Indies
Most Rev. Anselme T. Sanon, Burkina Faso
Msgr. Peter Coughlan, Vatican City
Rev. Thomas F. Stransky, CSP, Israel
Rev. Frans Bouwen, M.Afr., Israel
Ms. Madeleine Ramaholimihaso, Madagascar
Sr. Joan Delaney, MM, Switzerland (1984-1990)
Sr. Monica Cooney, SMSM, Switzerland (since 1990)

Consultants
Most Rev. Francesco Marchisano
Msgr. John A. Radano

NOTE

1. "Mixed marriages" is used simply to describe the union of spouses of different Christian churches or communions. In more recent times the term "interchurch marriages" is used in some areas to indicate that both parties are clearly committed to their respective churches.

The Church: Local and Universal

A Study Document Commissioned and Received by the Joint Working Group

1990

Preface

One of the ways in which the Joint Working Group of the Roman Catholic Church and the World Council of Churches has attempted over the years to fulfill its purpose of fostering closer relations between the two has been to sponsor the joint study of issues that are of great significance in the quest for Christian unity. The theme of "The Church: Local and Universal" is one of these challenging issues.

The JWG has given attention to this theme in the period since the Sixth Assembly of the World Council of Churches in Vancouver, 1983. The Central Committee of the WCC asked in 1984 that this theme be studied. The JWG meeting at Riano (Rome), September-October 1985, made plans for "The Church: Local and Universal" to be an important topic for the subsequent meeting in 1987. It asked for three papers to introduce the theme with Catholic, Protestant, and Orthodox perspectives, and suggested that these include some consideration of an ecclesiology of communion and also the organization of this communion at the local and universal levels, taking account of diversity within the unity of the church and of cultures. At Bossey, April-May 1987, the JWG heard and discussed these papers which were prepared by Pierre Duprey, Günther Gassmann, and Ion Bria. As the process continued, the perspectives of other scholars were collected for continued discussion of the theme at the 1988 meeting. Contributions came from Emmanuel Lanne, OSB, Jean Tillard, OP, Margaret O'Gara, and Patrick Granfield, OSB, who had in hand, as they wrote, the three papers mentioned above, as well as the list of questions raised at the discussion at Bossey. These contributions were discussed by the JWG in Venice, April-May 1988, which decided that a consultation on the theme should be held later in 1988. Since all of the contributions for 1988 were from Catholic sources, it asked that theologians belonging to the Orthodox and the Protestant traditions be part of this consultation.

The consultation was convened in Rome during December 1988 by the Secretariat for Promoting Christian Unity and the Commission on Faith and Order. Members included Nicholas Losky, Geoffrey Wainright, Günther Gassmann, Emmanuel Lanne, OSB, Patrick Granfield, OSB, and John A. Radano. The work of the group was facilitated by a draft text prepared beforehand by Patrick Granfield who made use of the papers previously prepared for the JWG meetings of 1987 and 1988. His text was the basis for discussion. The draft resulting was discussed by the JWG in St. Prix (Paris) in February 1989. It was further revised by a small committee in September 1989, reviewed by the JWG at its meeting in Rome, January-February 1990, and received there in its present form as a study document.

The Joint Working Group does not intend this study to be an exhaustive presentation on this theme. Rather it is intended to point to some factors which may help to give support and direction to the continuing ecumenical exploration of this theme. It highlights, for example, the necessity of both the local and the universal expressions of the church, their interdependence, the healthy tension that exists between them, and some aspects of the ecumenical convergence seen today on these notions of the church. It also explores the ecclesiology of communion and its usefulness as a framework for discussing the relationship between the local and universal church, not only within each Christian communion but also in terms of the ecumenical relationship between divided Christian communions. It points to different expressions of ecclesial communion and helps us to see aspects of ecumenical convergence here as well.

This report was prepared with the conviction that the ecclesiology of communion can be a way of expressing and especially of building on the real although imperfect communion already existing between churches despite their continuing division.

Introduction: The Church as Local and Universal Communion

1. The church is the icon of the Trinity, and the Trinity is the interior principle of ecclesial communion. From the resurrection to the parousia, communion is willed by the Father, realized in the Son, and caused by the Spirit in and through a community. Every authentic Christian community shares in this communion and is part of the mystery of God unfolded in Christ and the Spirit. Thus, the eschatological reality is already present, and ecclesial communion expresses the "fellowship of the Holy Spirit." At the same time, the church has an inner dynamism toward that unity that rests in the Holy Spirit. In the words of Cyprian, "The Church is a people made one with the unity of the Father, the Son, and the Holy Spirit."[1]

2. Different views of the church as local and universal are found among the various Christian communions (cf. below, nos.12-24). Common perspectives on the theological understanding of the local and universal church are therefore critically important for the restoration of Christian unity and have been frequently considered in ecumenical documents.[2] There is only one church in God's plan of salvation. This one church is present and manifested in the local churches throughout the world. It is the same unique church of Jesus Christ, his body, which is thus present in every local church. It is also the same Spirit who from the day of Pentecost gathers together the faithful in the one church and in the individual local churches.

3. Any ecclesiological investigation of the local and universal church must recognize both its christological and pneumatological dimensions, which are reflected in the holy Scriptures and the early creeds. The christological dimensions of the church are realized in and through the activity of the Holy Spirit. Thus Ignatius of Antioch could affirm that "where Jesus Christ is, there is the Church Catholic" (*To the Smyrnaens* viii, 2) and Irenaeus that "where the Church is there is the Spirit, and where the Spirit is, there is the Church" (*Adversus haereses* III, 24, 1). The church is the people of God, the body of Christ, and the temple of the Holy Spirit.

4. This paper will explore in four sections the local and universal aspects of the one church. First, the concept of the ecclesiology of communion as a theological basis and framework for the unity of the church as universal and local; second, the local and universal communion in ecumenical perspective; third, the ecclesial elements of communion; and fourth, the structuring of communion.

I. The Ecclesiology of Communion

5. More and more, the concept of *koinonia*[3] or communion is seen as having great value for understanding the multiplicity of local churches in the unity of the

one church. *Koinonia* refers to the source and nature of the life of the church as body of Christ, people of God, and temple of the Holy Spirit. In particular, this concept allows us to hold two dimensions of the church—its locality and universality—not as separate entities, but as two integrated dimensions of one reality.

6. The theological meaning of *koinonia* is rich. Used nineteen times in the New Testament, the term *koinonia* in its primary sense means participation in the life of God through Christ in the Holy Spirit. *Koinonia* is the gift of the Holy Spirit: we share in the "fellowship of the Holy Spirit" (2 Cor 13:14). *Koinonia* refers to a profound, personal relationship between God and humanity (Acts 2:42 and Jn 1:3). The Old Testament themes of inheritance and covenant convey similar ideas.[4] Israel is the inheritance of the Lord (Ex 34:9), and a covenant exists between God and his people (Jer 24:7). *Koinonia* rests on God's free choice to communicate himself to us: "We are called into the communion of his [God's] Son, Jesus Christ our Lord" (1 Cor 1:9). Through baptism believers are called into the fellowship of the Spirit. As a result we share in the passion and consolation of Christ (2 Cor 1:7; Phil 3:10); and we participate in the divine nature (2 Pt 1:4). For St. Paul, the sharing of possessions and the financial help for needy churches (*koinonia* in Rom 15:26 and 2 Cor 9:13) are signs of our communion in the life of God.

7. Because it is the result of our union (*koinonia*) with God, the Christian community can also be called *koinonia*. The *koinonia* or bond of union between believers and God establishes a new relationship among believers themselves. It is realized by participating in the life of the triune God through word and sacrament. The church is *koinonia* precisely because of the fellowship that its members have in the life of the Spirit.[5] Our vertical relationship with God makes possible our horizontal unity with our fellow believers.[6] *Koinonia* is a dynamic reality that binds us together within the one body of Christ. Our communion with the triune God and with one another develops throughout history and will never be completely realized until we are ultimately united with God in glory. According to Irenaeus, the history of salvation is a progressive introduction of humanity into communion with God (*Adversus haereses* IV, 14, 2).

8. Does communion relate only to the church? Can it also extend to the world and operate in society? Communion refers primarily to the church, since communion is based on participation in the life of the Trinity. The absence of communion among churches affects the world and society, because it is a negative sign of the gospel message of unity. But growing communion among the churches presents even now a positive sign of Christian unity and an effective way to encourage common Christian witness. Division among Christians is a scandal, but the church's mission to announce the Gospel to the world is strengthened as communion grows.

9. In a broader sense a notion of communion can also be related to the whole of humanity. All human beings are created in the image of God and are thus called

into communion with God. Because it is God's plan of salvation to reconcile broken humanity and to bring it to fulfillment in the kingdom of God, there is a dynamic in history towards solidarity and constructive interdependence. The church is called by God to serve this movement of reconciliation and to help break down barriers which prevent that renewed community among human beings willed by God. "By her relationship with Christ, the church is a kind of sacrament or sign and instrument of intimate union with God and of the unity of all humanity"(LG, no. 1). "The Church is bold in speaking of itself as the sign of the coming unity of mankind" (Uppsala Assembly of the WCC, Section I).

10. The notion of the ecclesiology of communion has been found helpful in various bilateral conversations. *The Final Report* of ARCIC-I noted that *koinonia* is the term "that most aptly expresses the mystery underlying the various New Testament images of the Church."[7] The Lutheran–Roman Catholic Commission described the church as "a communion subsisting in a network of local churches."[8] According to the Nairobi Report of the Joint Commission between the Roman Catholic Church and the World Methodist Council, *koinonia* "includes participation in God through Christ in the Spirit, by which believers become adopted children of the same Father and members of the one body of Christ sharing in the same Spirit. And it includes deep fellowship among participants, a fellowship which is both visible and invisible, finding expression in faith and order, in prayer and sacrament, in mission and service" (no. 23).[9] The *First Report* of the Catholic–Orthodox Joint Commission, issued at Munich in 1982 and entitled "The Mystery of the Church and of the Eucharist in the Light of the Mystery of the Holy Trinity," spoke of the way in which "the unfolding of the eucharistic celebration of the local church shows how the *koinonia* takes shape in the Church celebrating the eucharist." It went on to describe aspects of that *koinonia*, including that "the *koinonia* is eschatological . . . kerygmatic . . . [and] at once ministerial and pneumatological."[10] The Reformed–Catholic dialogue spoke of the church, indicating that ". . . it comes together for the purpose of adoration and prayer, to receive ever new instruction and consolation and to celebrate the presence of Christ in the sacrament; around this centre, and with the multiplicity of gifts granted by the Spirit . . . it lives as a *koinonia* of those who need and help each other" (*The Presence of Christ in Church and World*, 1977).[11]

11. Various Christian world communions have also recognized the importance of the ecclesiology of communion. Within the Roman Catholic Church, for example, Cardinal Willebrands said that "the deepening . . . of an ecclesiology of communion is . . . perhaps the greatest possibility for tomorrow's ecumenism,"[12] and the 1985 Synod of Bishops called by the pope on the twentieth anniversary of the closing of the Second Vatican Council recalled that "the ecclesioiogy of communion is the central and fundamental idea of the council's documents."[13] In its "Statement

on the Self-Understanding and Task of the Lutheran World Federation," the Seventh Assembly of the LWF (1984) stated that "We give witness and affirm the communion in which the Lutheran churches of the whole world are bound together."[14] The ecclesiology of communion was also a major consideration of the Anglican Communion within the Lambeth Conference in 1988.

II. Local and Universal Communion in Ecumenical Perspective

12. Any discussion of the *koinonia* in the local and universal church must be first placed in the broader context of the one, holy, catholic, and apostolic church, the *una sancta* of the early Christian creeds.[15] The *una sancta* in the plan of God is God's creation—an eschatological reality existing throughout history from the earliest days (*ecclesia ab Abel*) to the return of Christ in glory. The local and universal church are historical manifestations of the *una sancta*, even though they should not be purely and simply identified with it. They have their unity in the *una sancta*. There is only one church of God, whether it is expressed locally or universally.

1. The Local Church

13. The local church is truly church. It has everything it needs to be church in its own situation: it confesses the apostolic faith (with special reference to belief in the Trinity and the lordship of Jesus); it proclaims the word of God in Scripture, baptizes its members, celebrates the eucharist and other sacraments; it affirms and responds to the presence of the Holy Spirit and his gifts; announces and looks forward to the kingdom; and recognizes the ministry of authority within the community. All these various features must exist together in order for there to be a local church within the communion of the church of God. The local church is not a free-standing, self-sufficient reality. As part of a network of communion, the local church maintains its reality as church by relating to other local churches. In the words of Vatican II: "The Church of Christ is truly present (*vere adest*) in all legitimate local congregations of the faithful which, united with their pastors, are themselves called churches in the New Testament" (LG, no. 26).[16]

14. The local church is not an administrative or juridical subsection or part of the universal church. In the local church the one, holy, catholic, and apostolic church is truly present and active (CD, no. 11). The local church is the place where the church of God becomes concretely realized. It is a gathering of believers that is seized by the spirit of the risen Christ and becomes *koinonia* by participating in the life of God.

15. All Christian world communions can, in general, agree with the definition of the local church as a community of baptized believers in which the word of God is preached, the apostolic faith confessed, the sacraments are celebrated, the redemptive work of Christ for the world is witnessed to, and a ministry of *episkope* exercised by bishops or other ministers is serving the community. Differences between world communions are connected with the role and place of the bishop in relation to the local church.

16. For churches of the "catholic" tradition, the bishop is essential for the understanding and structure of a local church. Bishops, as successors of the apostles, are "the visible principle and foundation of unity in their own particular churches" (LG, no. 23). According to the *First Report* of the Catholic–Orthodox Joint Commission (Munich, 1982), "the bishop stands at the heart of the local church as minister of the Spirit to discern the charisma, and take care that they are exercised in harmony, for the good of all, in faithfulness to the apostolic tradition" (II/3). The Anglican–Roman Catholic International Commission defined the local church as "the unity of local communities under one bishop" (ARCIC-I, *Final Report*, p. 92). Accordingly, the church is most fully revealed/realized when God's people are united at the eucharistic assembly with the bishop. Consequently, the local church in these traditions is primarily the diocese, but it may also refer to several dioceses.

17. For churches of the Reformation and free church traditions, which have developed a great variety of institutional structures and forms of self-understanding, the term "local church" is not so common and therefore also not defined by referring to the office of the bishop. For these churches it is the local Christian community (parish, congregation) for which the above definition would apply and which could, therefore, be called a local church.

18. Yet in addition to the common elements mentioned above in no. 15, there are also certain convergences concerning the differences just mentioned within churches characterized by an episcopal concept of the local church. The local congregation or parish is recognized as the local expression of the diocese and the entire church (cf. SC, no. 42). Such communities must, however, be related to the local church, i.e., diocese, and be in communion with it.[17] Reformation and free churches, on the other hand, which put special emphasis on the local congregation, have developed structures which serve a larger community of congregations (e.g., districts, dioceses, circuits) and have developed ministries (e.g., bishops, superintendents, regional pastors) which carry special responsibilities (together with presbyterial-synodical organs) for such larger units. In the past such larger geographical structures were seen mainly under practical aspects. In the present, however, such wider expressions of a local church are seen in a number of churches also in pastoral and ecclesiological terms: as communions of communities.

2. The Universal Church

19. The universal church is the communion of all the local churches united in faith and worship around the world. However, the universal church is not the sum, federation, or juxtaposition of the local churches, but all together are the same church of God present and acting in this world. The issue here is fundamentally ecclesiological and not organizational.[18] The communion of local churches gathered by and around the celebration of word and sacrament manifests the church of God. The concept of the universal church recognizes the diversity of cultural and social conditions. "While preserving unity in essentials," Christians have "a proper freedom in the various forms of spiritual life and discipline, in the variety of liturgical rites, and even in the theological elaborations of revealed truth" (UR, no. 4). Catholicity enters into the very concept of church and refers not simply to geographic extension but also to the manifold variety of local churches and their participation in the one *koinonia*. Each local church contributes its unique gifts for the good of the whole church.

20. The Roman Catholic Church and the Orthodox Church understand themselves as representing the church universal. Reformation and free churches, because they had to organize themselves on the national level, often had difficulties in grasping and experiencing the universal dimension of the church. However, through their involvement in the ecumenical movement and their experience within the Christian world communions and the fellowship of the World Council of Churches, they have developed a stronger sense of the universal character of Christ's church, which transcends their own reality as churches organized on a national or regional level. This experience and insight find expression also in the development of Christian world communions, which according to the WCC Assembly at Uppsala (1968) provide "some real experience of universality."[19] It is the task of the ecumenical movement to lead the churches to that unity which enables them to confess and express together the universal communion of the church of Jesus Christ.

3. The Question of Priority

21. In the past, biblical scholars generally held that the term *eklesia* was first used to designate the local church of a city or region and only later the universal church. Contemporary biblical study, however, raises questions about the earlier view of priority. It presents evidence that suggests a more complex picture of the early Christian community than that indicated by the axiom "first particular, then universal."[20]

22. One way of looking at the question of priority is by using an eschatological and pneumatological ecclesiology. This approach does not assign a priority exclusively to either the local or the universal church, but suggests a simultaneity of both. Both are essential. Thus it must be said, on the one hand, that in God's general plan of salvation the universal has an absolute priority over the local. For Christ came to gather together the dispersed children of God; at Pentecost the Spirit of God was poured out upon all flesh (cf. Acts 2:17). God created the church in the framework of universal reconciliation and unity. The Pentecostal experience and the word and grace of Christ have continual and universal relevance. The Gospel of salvation is addressed to humankind as a whole without exception. In this sense the universal has priority and will keep it forever.

23. At the same time, the church began and came into existence at a determined place. "When the day of Pentecost had come, they were all together in one place" (Acts 2:1). From this place the apostles began to preach the Gospel to all the nations (cf. Mt 28:19). In the concrete historical situation of the foundation of the church, the local had priority and will keep it until the second coming of Christ, because the Gospel is preached each time in a determined place; the faithful receive baptism and celebrate eucharist in this determined place, even though it is always and necessarily in communion with all the other local churches in the world. There is no local church that is not centered on the Gospel and not in communion with all other churches.[21]

24. Since Pentecost, the church celebrates the eucharist as the one, holy, catholic, and apostolic church. The eucharistic celebration, therefore, embraces the church both in its local and universal dimension. It thus affirms a mutual presence of all the churches in Christ and in the Spirit[22] for the salvation of the world.

III. The Ecclesial Elements of Communion

25. The ecclesial elements required for full communion within a visibly united church—the goal of the ecumenical movement—are communion in the fullness of the apostolic faith; in sacramental life; in a truly one and mutually recognized ministry; in structures of conciliar relations and decision making; and in common witness and service in the world. This goal is still to be achieved, and on the way to this goal, it is important to note how the notion of ecclesial communion has been interpreted by the Roman Catholic Church in the Second Vatican Council and the way in which it has been interpreted within the World Council of Churches.

1. Interpretations of Ecclesial Communion

26. The Second Vatican Council described two types of ecclesial communion. The first is full and complete ecclesial communion in which the ecclesial elements of the one, holy, catholic, and apostolic church are integrally present. Accordingly the council taught that the unique church of Christ "subsists" in the Catholic Church, ". . . although many elements of sanctification and of truth can be found outside her visible structure"(LG, no. 8). This leads to the second type, which is partial and incomplete, but nonetheless real ecclesial communion. The essential elements are present in some way in other Christian churches: the written word of God; faith in Christ and in the Trinity; baptism; the sacraments; the life of grace; faith, hope, and charity; the interior gifts of the Holy Spirit; and prayer and other spiritual benefits (UR, nos. 3, 20-23; LG, no. 15). By their nature these elements tend toward full realization of catholic unity (LG, nos. 8, 15). Although a non-Catholic community may not have the "institutional" fullness of the ecclesial elements, this does not mean that it does not have an authentic "pneumatic" response to the presence and grace and form a vital communion of faith, hope, and charity.[23] The ecclesiology of communion offers a promising way to explain and express the incomplete but real communion that already exists between the Catholic Church and the other churches. It allows us to speak of a growing communion.

27. Vatican II, in its teaching on "subsists" and the presence of ecclesial elements outside its visible boundaries, provided sound theological basis for genuine ecumenical commitment. Although it did not resolve the problems, it nevertheless with courage and consistency laid the foundation for further progress. The ecumenical bilateral and multilateral conversations since the council have continued to examine in detail the thorny questions connected with a common profession of faith, the sacramental life, and the role of authority.

28. Elements of communion among the churches have been discussed and clarified in the World Council of Churches in the perspective of "the unity we seek." The results of these reflections are formulated in statements of the 1961 New Delhi and 1975 Nairobi Assemblies of the WCC.

29. The New Delhi statement said: "We believe that the unity which is both God's will and his gift to his church is being made visible as all in each place who are baptized into Jesus Christ and confess him as Lord and Savior are brought by the Holy Spirit into one fully committed fellowship, holding the one apostolic faith, preaching the one Gospel, breaking the one bread, joining in common prayer, and having a corporate life reaching out in witness and service to all and who at the same time are united with the whole Christian fellowship in all places and all ages in such wise that ministry and members are accepted by all, and that all can act and speak together as occasion requires for the tasks to which God calls his people."[24]

30. Taking up the report of a Faith and Order consultation in Salamanca, the Nairobi Assembly stated its vision of unity in the following way: "The one Church is to be envisioned as a conciliar fellowship of local churches which are themselves truly united. In this conciliar fellowship, each local church possesses, in communion with the others, the fullness of catholicity, witnesses to the same apostolic faith, and therefore recognizes the others as belonging to the same Church of Christ and guided by the same Spirit. As the New Delhi Assembly pointed out, they are bound together because they have received the same baptism and share in the same eucharist; they recognize each other's members and ministries. They are in their common commitment to confess the gospel of Christ by proclamation and service to the world. To this end, each church aims at maintaining sustained and sustaining relationships with her sister churches, expressed in conciliar gatherings, whenever required for the fulfilment of their common calling."[25]

31. The two statements from New Delhi and Nairobi refer to ecclesial elements that are generally recognized as being indispensable for any realization of visible church unity both on the local and universal level. These include the common confession of the apostolic faith; mutual recognition of the apostolicity and catholicity of the other churches and of each other's members, sacraments, and ministries; fellowship in the eucharist, in spiritual life, and in mission and service in the world; and the achievement of mutual fellowship, also in conciliar meetings and decisions. Both statements emphasize local unity, but this is interrelated especially in the Nairobi statement, with the universal dimension of unity in the form of a conciliar fellowship (or as a Faith and Order consultation in November 1988 stated: "conciliar communion of common faith and life in the service of God's world"). The descriptions of New Delhi and Nairobi are not limited solely to the goal of visible unity. They express at the same time basic elements of the faith and life of the church, both in its local and universal dimensions.

32. It is obvious that the essential elements of communion or unity stated in these two texts of the WCC correspond to the elements mentioned earlier in this paper. The different Christian traditions believe that these elements, in different forms, are present within their traditions and that, accordingly, full ecclesial communion exists within them. Also between member churches of the WCC different degrees of communion have developed, including, for many, eucharistic hospitality, interim eucharistic sharing, altar and pulpit fellowship understood as full communion. The question then arises as to how the communion can be described between churches which are not yet able to enter into forms of eucharistic fellowship.

33. All churches which participate actively in the ecumenical movement agree that even where eucharistic fellowship and full communion are not yet achieved between churches, nevertheless forms of communion do exist. The churches are no longer living in isolation from each other. They have developed

mutual understanding and respect. They pray together and share in each other's spiritual experience and theological insights. They collaborate in addressing the needs of humanity. Through bilateral and multilateral dialogues, they have achieved remarkable convergences with regard to previously divisive issues of doctrine and church order. They share, in different degrees, in the basic elements of communion. It is, therefore, possible to speak of an existing real though imperfect communion among the churches—with the understanding that the degrees and expressions of such communion may vary according to the relationships between individual churches.

34. This recognition of an already existing though imperfect communion is a significant result of ecumenical efforts and a radically new element in twentieth-century church history. It provides a basis for renewal, common witness, and service of the churches for the sake of God's saving and reconciling activity for all humanity. And it provides a basis and encouragement for further efforts to overcome those barriers which still prevent the recognition and implementation of full communion between the churches.

2. The Interdependence of Local and Universal in the Communion of Churches

35. Elements of communion at the local level correspond to and interact with their expression at the universal level, because the Holy Spirit is the same source at both levels. Different churches, however, may have different ways of manifesting the same ecclesial elements. Ecclesial communion is lived and experienced in eucharistic communion. The eucharistic synaxis celebrates both the communion with the eternal life of the triune God, and the link with all worshiping communities, as members of the one body of Christ (cf. 1 Cor 10:17).

36. "The local church is wholly church, but it is not the whole Church."[26] This applies already in the case of existing world communions, even though they may understand "local church" differently. It will continue to apply when full unity among Christians has been realized. The local church should never be seen in isolation but always in a dynamic relationship with other local churches. It has to express its faith in relation to other churches, and in so doing it manifests communion. The catholicity of the church implies an interrelatedness and interdependence among local churches. Once a local church turns in on itself and seeks to function completely independently from other local churches, it distorts a primary aspect of its ecclesial character. The local church is not a freestanding, self-sufficient reality. As part of a network of communion, the local church maintains its reality as church by relating to other local churches.[27]

37. Mutual solicitude, support, recognition, and communication are essential qualities among local churches. Even from earliest times, the local churches felt themselves linked to one another. This *koinonia* was expressed in a variety of ways: exchange of confessions of faith, letters of communion as a kind of "ecclesiastical passport," hospitality, reciprocal visits, mutual material help, councils, and synods.[28]

38. Interrelatedness is now more evident among local churches of the same world communion. The unity we seek prompts us all to find ways of restoring such *koinonia* at the local and universal levels with Christian communities from whom we are at present divided. Ecumenism in its local and universal expression, with its emphasis on dialogue and mutual concern, has already opened up many avenues of collaboration, spiritual and theological exchange, and convergence on essential issues of faith and order.

39. At the same time, however, the growth in the *koinonia* is especially tested when, locally or universally, the churches are called upon to act together on pressing social issues. Ethical issues can become factors of division, as witnessed in the ongoing discussion on abortion, birth control, divorce, and homosexuality. The old slogan that "doctrine divides, service unites" is no longer axiomatic. The impact of sociocultural challenges and the need for common responses to them is of immense importance for the future of ecumenism.

40. Each Christian world communion has to face specific challenges regarding universality and particularity. The Protestant churches have stressed the importance of the local church, but they face the problem of concretely manifesting universality among their own churches. Participation in the World Council of Churches has heightened the experience of universality among the member churches. In the Roman Catholic Church today dialectical tension between local authority and central authority remains a critical issue.[29]

IV. The Structuring of Communion

41. The very nature of the church of God, the elements of ecclesial community already discussed, and the lived experience of individual Christian communities all form the basis on which the canonical expression of communion has to be developed. Here are meant questions of polity, order, law, authority, and constitution which all refer to the structure of the church and of communion. What has been said above about the nature of communion and its many qualities is presupposed here. The canonical dimension of communion applies to the local and universal framework of one particular tradition as well as to the already partially existing communion among different churches.

1. Canonical Structures

42. Communion, as we have seen, refers to a dynamic, spiritual, objective reality which is embodied in ecclesial structures. The gift of communion from God is not an amorphous reality but an organic unity that requires a canonical form of expression. The purpose of such canonical structuring is to ensure that the local churches (and their members), in their communion with each other, can live in harmony and fidelity to "the faith which has been once and for all entrusted to the saints" (Jude 3).

43. In the Roman Catholic Church, communion with the bishop of Rome is necessary. Vatican II referred on several occasions to "hierarchical communion."[30] It taught that one becomes a member of the college of bishops through sacramental ordination and hierarchical communion with the head and members of the college. At his ordination a bishop receives the office (munus) of sanctifying, teaching, and governing. But these tasks can be exercised only in hierarchical communion with the head and members of the college of bishops. Furthermore, although bishops possess the threefold munera through their ordination, they cannot exercise them in a particular place without a specific determination, a "canonical mission" by the pope. The college of bishops cannot act independently of the pope, since the collegial character of the body would be inoperative without its head.

44. Despite certain differences in the life and the practice of Orthodox churches, they believe on the basis of a common canonical tradition that episcopal ordination confers the functions of sanctifying, teaching, and ruling. They have comparable practices dealing with the designation and assignment of bishops. Moreover they agree that the bishops must be in hierarchical communion with the head of the synod. In this context, Canon 34 of the "Apostolic Canons" is an appropriate expression of the Orthodox understanding of communion.[31]

45. The Reformation and free churches have developed their canonical structures of expressing and safeguarding communion within their churches. According to their particular heritage, they employ presbyterial and synodical structures for this purpose and, in many cases, integrate into them episcopal ministries under different titles, including the office of bishop. In their respective Christian world communions these churches have also developed canonical structures which enable consultation, cooperation, and common witness, but which do not allow for decisions which are binding for the individual member churches of that communion. However, there is a general tendency to strengthen ways in which these communions can express their common faith, life, and service on a universal level.

46. The ministry of the bishop of Rome as the minister of universal unity is essential to Roman Catholicism. According to Catholic faith, Peter and his successors, the bishops of Rome, have been entrusted by God to confirm the brethren in

the faith "which has been once and for all entrusted to the saints" and in the unity of the one, holy, catholic, and apostolic church (cf. LG, no. 25; CD, no. 2). The bishop of Rome is seen as the sign and guarantee of the communion of local churches with each other and with the church of Peter and Paul. His ministry is multiple: to protect both unity and legitimate diversity; to offer support and solicitude; to facilitate communication between churches; and to arbitrate differences.

47. The office of the papacy remains a controversial issue in ecumenism, but there are signs of better mutual understanding.[32] On the Orthodox side, the Ecumenical Patriarch Dimitrios I, following a deliberation and resolution of his synod, and convinced that it expressed the mind of the early church, stated that the bishop of Rome is marked out as the one who has the presidency of charity and is the first bishop in rank and honor in the whole body of the Lord.[33] The pope can be called *primus inter pares* (first among equals), because this apostolic see has exercised a primacy of love from earliest times.[34] In bilateral dialogues, Lutherans speak of the value of the "Petrine function,"[35] and Anglicans have agreed that "a universal primacy will be needed in a reunited church and should appropriately be the primacy of the bishop of Rome."[36] The Joint Roman Catholic–World Methodist Council Commission noted: "Discernment of the various factors in Scripture and history might contribute to an agreed perception of what functions the see of Rome might properly exercise in a ministry of universal unity, by what authority, and on what conditions" (no. 40).[37] Despite these positive statements, the problems of *ius divinum* (divine right), primacy of jurisdiction, infallibility, and the papal teaching authority remain subjects of intense ecumenical dialogue.

2. The Shape of Future Unity

48. If all local churches are to be united to form one *communio ecclesiarum* (communion of churches), there must be an acceptance of the basic ecclesial elements of communion: common profession of the same apostolic faith; proclamation of the word of God; mutual recognition of the sacraments, especially baptism and eucharist; and agreement on the nature and exercise of pastoral leadership. Such agreements and recognitions are necessary for the achievement of visible unity in legitimate diversity.

49. Several models of structured Christian communion have been proposed and critically analyzed within the ecumenical movement. Some of the models of comprehensive union that have been suggested include the following: organic union, corporate union, church fellowship through agreement (concord), conciliar fellowship, communion of communions, and unity in reconciled diversity.[38] Nevertheless, the precise shape the united church of the future should take and the

forms of diversity it could embrace is an important but still unresolved question for all Christian communities.

50. Furthermore, the different understandings of the Christian world communions concerning the relationship between the church local and universal clearly affect our approach toward future unity. Questions are raised if ecumenical relations develop rapidly on the local level between traditions which have not achieved full communion on the universal level. For example, what degree of communion can local churches of different traditions achieve in these cases, without breaking communion with churches of their own tradition?

51. In conclusion, it can be said that although canonical communion does not yet exist among local churches of different traditions, the churches are in communion in a profoundly spiritual way. Our churches share the common Gospel in the Christian heritage. Because ecclesial communion is a fellowship inspired by the indwelling Spirit, we can say that the barriers of our divisions do not reach to heaven. Christian unity is both a gift and a task. Christians of all communities pray for the unity of all in each place and look forward to that "one visible church of God, truly universal and sent forth to the whole world so that the world may be converted to the Gospel and so be saved, to the glory of God" (UR, no. 1).

NOTES

1. Cyprian, *De Orat. Dom.* 23, PL 4, 553 and cited in LG, no. 4.

2. For example, see Faith and Order Paper No. 59, report of Joint Working Group on "Catholicity and Apostolicity," 133-158 and 216-217. The individual papers of the group can be found in *One in Christ* 6 (1970), 242-483. Note especially paper by E. Lanne, "The Local Church: Its Catholicity and Apostolicity," 288-313; Secretariat for Promoting Christian Unity [now the Pontifical Council for Promoting Christian Unity], "Ecumenical Collaboration at the Regional, National, and Local Levels," SPCU *Information Service* 26 (1975): 8-31, esp. Part 2; Paul VI, Address During the 1973 Week of Prayer for Christian Unity, SPCU *Information Service* 21 (1973): 3-4; World Council of Churches, *In Each Place. Towards a Fellowship of Local Churches Truly United* (Geneva: WCC, 1977); and Roman Catholic–Lutheran Joint Commission, *Facing Unity*, Document 2 above.

3. *Koinonia* comes from *koinos*, common, the opposite of *idios*: proper, particular, private. *Koinoo* means to put together or to pool. *Koinonia*, then, refers to the action of having something in common, sharing in, participating in. It is often rendered in Latin by *communio* or *communicatio*.

   For studies on *koinonia* consult P. C. Bori, *Koinonia* (Brescia: Paideia, 1972); J. M. McDermott, "The Biblical Doctrine of *Koinonia*," *Biblische Zeitschrift* 19 (1975), 64-77 and 219-233; H. J. Sieben, "*Koinonia*, communauté-communion," *Dictionnaire de Spiritualité* (Paris, 1975), col. 1743-1745; S. Brown, "*Koinonia* as the Basis of New Testament Ecclesiology?" *One in Christ* 12 (1976), 157-167; and J. M. R. Tillard, *Eglise d'Eglises. L'ecclésiologie de communion* (Paris: Cerf, 1987).

4. See "Héritage et alliance," in *Vocabulaire de Théologie Biblique* (Paris, 1970).

5. The *communio sanctorum* in the creed may refer both to the "communion of the saints or holy people" and to "communion in holy things"—sharing the sacraments of baptism and the eucharist. See S. Benko, *The Meaning of Sanctorum Communio: Studies in Historical Theology* (London: SCM, 1964), 3.

6. John Paul II has used the terms "vertical" and "horizontal." He noted that the vertical dimension of *communio* with God is primary. If it is not deeply experienced, it can weaken the possibility of the horizontal dimension reaching its full potential. Address at the Meeting of the U.S. Bishops in Los Angeles, 16 September 1987, *Origins* 17:16 (1 October 1987): 257.

7. *The Final Report*, in GA 65.

8. FU 9.

9. *Towards a Statement on the Church:* Report of the Joint Commission Between the Roman Catholic Church and the World Methodist Council, Document 5 above.

10. SPCU *Information Service* 49 (1982): 109.

11. GA 447.

12. "The Future of Ecumenism," *One in Christ* 11 (1975): 323.

13. Extraordinary Synod of Bishops, 1985, *A Message to the People of God and the Final Report* (Washington: NCCB, 1986).

14. Eugene L. Brand, *Toward a Lutheran Communion: Pulpit and Altar Fellowship*, LWF Report, 26 (Geneva: The Lutheran World Federation, 1988), 9. This report shows that the ecclesiology of communion has long been a subject of discussion within the Lutheran World Federation.

15. See Ion Bria, ed., *Jesus Christ—The Life of the World: An Orthodox Contribution to the Vancouver Theme* (Geneva: WCC, 1982), 12-13.

16. For a discussion of the theology of the local church in Vatican II, see the following: P. Granfield, "The Local Church as a Center of Communication and Control," *Proceedings of the Catholic Theological Society of America*, 35 (1980), 256-263; H. Legrand, "La réalisation de l'Eglise en un lieu," in *Initiation a la pratique de la théologie*, B. Lauret and F. Refoulé, eds., Tome III, *Dogmatique 2* (Paris: Cerf, 1983), 143-345; and J. A. Komonchak, "The Local Realization of the Church," in *The Reception of Vatican II*, G. Alberigo et al., eds. (Washington: Catholic University of America Press, 1987), 77-90.

17. A problem in some parts of the Catholic world is the decrease in the number of ordained ministers. As a consequence there are many parishes where the liturgy of the word is becoming more common than the eucharistic liturgy. When a priest is not available, appointed lay members and religious lead the congregation in prayers and readings and distribute the eucharist. There is great concern that the practice of infrequent eucharistic liturgies could adversely affect the doctrine that the eucharist is central to the Catholic concept of the church.

18. In the words of J. D. Zizioulas: "There is one church, as there is one God. But the expression of this one church is the communion of the many local churches." See Zizioulas, *Being as Communion* (London: Darton, Longman and Todd, 1985), 134-135.

19. *The Uppsala Report, 1968*, ed. Norman Goodall (Geneva: WCC, 1968), 17.

20. For further discussion on this point, see R. E. Brown, "The New Testament Background for the Concept of the Local Church," *Proceedings of the Catholic Theological Society of America* 36 (1981), 1-14, here 4.

21. For the New Testament communities of St. Paul, the church of the saints of Jerusalem was a reference for communion (cf. 2 Cor 8–9). This local church was also the test for apostolic faith (cf. Gal 2:1ff.).

22. Cf. J. D. Zizioulas, *Being as Communion*, 132-133.

23. It should be noted that the expression "full and complete communion" and "partial and incomplete communion" are not found as such in Vatican II. They are intended to correspond to *"plena communio"* (UR, no. 3) and *"quaedam communio, etsi non perfecta"* (UR, no. 3). Some authors prefer to speak of "full and perfect communion," an expression used by Paul VI. This expression assumes the possibility of "incomplete and imperfect communion." Obviously, the use of "perfect" and "imperfect" relates to wholeness or completeness and not to the moral qualities of holiness or goodness.

24. Lukas Vischer, ed., *A Documentary History of the Faith and Order Movement, 1927-1963* (St. Louis: The Bethany Press, 1963), 144-145.

25. Davis M. Paton, ed., *Breaking Barriers, Nairobi, 1975, The Official Report of the Fifth Assembly of the World Council of Churches*, Nairobi, 23 November-10 December 1975 (London: SPCK, and Grand Rapids: Wm. B. Eerdmans, 1976), 60.

26. J. J. von Allmen, "L'Église locale parmi les autres Eglises locales," *Irénikon* 43 (1970), 512.

27. See J. Ratzinger, "The Pastoral Implications of Episcopal Collegiality," *Concilium* (American edition), Vol. 1, 45.

28. See L. Hertling, *Communio: Church and Papacy in Early Christianity* (Chicago: Loyola University Press, 1972) and B. P. Prusak, "Hospitality Extended or Denied: *Koinonia* from Jesus to Augustine," *The Jurist* 36 (1976): 89-126.

29. On this issue, see P. Granfield, *The Limits of the Papacy: Authority and Autonomy in the Church* (New York: Crossroad, 1987).

30. LG, nos. 21 and 22; *Nota praevia*, 2 and 4; and CD, no. 5.

31. Canon 34: "The bishops of every region ought to know who is the first one (*protos*) among them, and to esteem him as their head, and not to do any great thing without the consent; but every one ought to manage only the affairs that belong to his own diocese and the territory subject to it. But let him (i.e., the first one) not do anything without the consent of all the other (bishops); for it is by this means that there will be unanimity, and God will be glorified through Christ in the Holy Spirit." Text in F. X. Funk, *Didascalia et constitutiones apostolorum*, 1905, 572-574.

32. See V. von Aristi et al., *Das Papstramt: Dienst oder Hindernis für die Oekumene?* (Regensburg: F. Pustet, 1985).

33. "Letter of Dimitrios I to Pope Paul VI on the Tenth Anniversary of the Lifting of the Anathemas," 14 December 1975, in E. J. Stormon, SJ, ed., *Towards the Healing of Schism, The Sees of Rome and Constantinople. Public Statements and Correspondence Between the Holy See and the Ecumenical Patriarchate 1958-1984* (New York/Mahwah: The Paulist Press, 1987), no. 331, 279-281.

34. Ignatius to the Romans I. Also, see J. Meyendorff, et al., *The Primacy of Peter in the Orthodox Church* (Leighton Buzzard: Faith Press, 1963). Also P. Duprey, "Brief Reflections on the Title 'Primus inter Pares,'" *One in Christ* 10 (1974), 7-12.

35. P. C. Empie and T. A. Murphy, eds., *Papal Primacy and the Universal Church: Lutherans and Catholics in Dialogue V* (Minneapolis: Augsburg, 1974).

36. ARCIC, *The Final Report*, in GA 108.

37. *Towards a Statement on the Church*, Document 5 above.

38. Briefly summarized in FU 8-20, with appropriate bibliographical references.

The Notion of Hierarchy of Truths— An Ecumenical Interpretation

A Study Document Commissioned and Received by the Joint Working Group

1990

Introduction

1. During Pope John Paul II's visit to the World Council of Churches' offices in Geneva (12 June 1984), Dr. Willem A. Visser't Hooft, former WCC General Secretary, suggested a study on the "hierarchy of truths." The expression is in the Second Vatican Council's *Decree on Ecumenism* (1964). The concept has aroused ecumenical hopes, but the expression still needs clarification of its use in the decree and of its implications for the ecumenical dialogue. The pope immediately favored the suggestion.

2. The Joint Working Group of the Roman Catholic Church and the World Council of Churches commissioned two consultations on "the hierarchy of truths." The first took place at Bossey, Switzerland, September 1985. After the JWG had

commented on the initial report (October 1985), the second consultation met in Rome, March 1987. The draft returned to the JWG meeting in May 1987. A small editorial group incorporated the comments from the JWG and from other consultors. The JWG again reviewed the text in April-May 1988 and in February 1989, and received this present version in January 1990 as a study document to help further reflection on the theme.

3. This report is an ecumenical attempt to understand and interpret the intention of the Second Vatican Council in speaking of a "hierarchy of truths," and to offer some implications for ecumenical dialogue and common Christian witness. The report also relates "hierarchy of truths" to other Christian traditions, although it can do so only in an approximate way. These traditions do not normally use the expression, although they appreciate the insights it contains or they may express them in different terms.

Chapter One: The Conciliar Statement and Its Contents

4. "In ecumenical dialogue, when Catholic theologians join with separated brethren in common study of the divine mysteries, they should, while standing fast by the teaching of the Church, pursue the work with love for the truth, with charity, and with humility. When comparing doctrines, they should remember that there exists an order or 'hierarchy' of truths in Catholic doctrine, since they vary in their relation to the foundation of the Christian faith. Thus the way will be open whereby this kind of 'fraternal emulation' will incite all to a deeper awareness and a clearer expression of the unfathomable riches of Christ (cf. Eph 3:8)" (UR, no. 11).

5. The paragraph is in the decree's second chapter, which deals with the practice of ecumenism in the Roman Catholic Church (nos. 5-12). This practice includes the continual examination of our "own faithfulness to Christ's will for the Church," and our efforts "to undertake with vigor, wherever necessary, the task of renewal and reform" (no. 4). Essential in such ecumenical practice is doctrinal dialogue which is carried out "with love for the truth, with charity, and with humility" (no. 11). Therefore, the concept of "the hierarchy of truths" relates directly to the task of ecumenical dialogue.

6. The decree emphasizes the necessity for a clear, full, and understandable explanation of Catholic doctrine (no. 11) as a presupposition to "dialogue with our brethren." Then in conversation Christian communions explain their doctrine more profoundly and express it more clearly, in order to achieve a more adequate understanding and accurate judgment about each other's teaching and life (cf. no. 9). Then in the same number 11, the decree broadens this understanding of dialogue: it is a search together into the divine mysteries to incite "a deeper realization and a clearer expression of the unfathomable riches of Christ." One thus has to

understand the statement on a "hierarchy of truths" within this broader, never-ceasing investigatory concept of dialogue.

7. Two immediate sources for the teaching about the "hierarchy of truths" indicate its meaning. Archbishop Andrea Pangrazio (Italy) first presented the idea to the council (November 1963). He noted that "to arrive at a fair estimate of both the unity which now exists among Christians and the divergences which still remain, it seems very important to pay close attention to the hierarchical order of revealed truths which express the mystery of Christ and those elements which make up the Church." Later (October 1964), in a written modus or proposed amendment to the decree, Cardinal Franz König (Vienna) proposed the exact phrase, "hierarchy of truths." He emphasized that the truths of faith do not add up in a quantitative way, but that there is a qualitative order among them according to their respective relation to the center or foundation of the Christian faith (Modus 49).

8. The decree is silent about the meaning of "the foundation of Christian faith." According to the official reason (ratio) in Modus 49 for the introduction of the phrase, the importance and the "weight" of truths differ because of their specific links with the mystery of Christ and the history of salvation.

9. Thus by using the words "order" or "hierarchy" the council intended to affirm the organic nature of faith. Truths are articulated around a center or foundation; they are not placed side by side.

Chapter Two: Hierarchy of Truths in Christian History

10. "Hierarchy of truths" was a new concept at the Second Vatican Council. But the phrase expresses an insight into a reality which has had different forms in the history of the church. The following serve as examples.

11. Even though the Scriptures are divinely inspired as a whole and in all its parts, many have seen an order or "hierarchy" insofar as some biblical sections or passages bear witness more directly to the fulfillment of God's promise and revelation in Jesus Christ through the Holy Spirit in the church.

12. One sees several kinds of "hierarchies" in relation to the authority of the church councils and to their contents. Most Christian traditions give special priority to the seven ecumenical councils of the early church. Some see also a "hierarchy" among these seven councils, inasmuch as those which have formulated the doctrine of the mystery of Christ and of the Spirit within the communion of the Holy Trinity should as such hold a preeminent position in comparison with the other councils.

13. The sacraments could provide another example of a "hierarchy" within the same order which directly concerns the faith. Baptism (which for some includes chrismation) as incorporation into the church, and the eucharist as the center of

the life of the church, are regarded as primary, while all other sacramental acts are related to these major sacraments.

14. The mystery of Jesus Christ, particularly seen in his death and resurrection, is at the center of the liturgical year. All the celebrations during the year, such as Christmas and Epiphany, Easter and Pentecost, and feasts of the saints, highlight a different aspect of the one mystery which is always fully present. Thus the various festivals of the liturgical year with their particular emphases are related in different ways (*diversus nexus*) to the center or foundation—the mystery of Jesus Christ.

15. The churches of the Reformation observe also a kind of "hierarchy" in dealing with the truths of the Christian faith. These churches hold that the Gospel of God's saving action in Jesus Christ, witnessed to normatively by Holy Scripture, is the supreme authority to which all Christian truths should refer. It is in relation to the Gospel as the center of the faith that these churches have summarized the truths of the faith in catechisms meant for the edification of the people of God in their faith, in new liturgical formularies and books, and in confessions of faith which are to guide the pastors in their preaching and the synods in their decisions. All this implies a "hierarchy of truths."

16. The Orthodox tradition refers to the fullness of truth, the totality of the revelation of God. The revealed divine truths constitute an indivisible unity, the coherent apostolic tradition. This holy tradition, on which the Church bases its unity, represents the entire content of the divinely revealed faith. There is no distinction between principal and secondary truths, between essential and nonessential doctrines. This position does not mean that within Orthodox theological reflection and formulations, there is no room for differentiation or distinctions. Orthodox theologians suggest that the concept of "hierarchy of truths" could help to distinguish permanent and common teachings of faith, such as the declared symbols (creeds) of the seven ecumenical councils and other credal statements, from those teachings which have not been formulated and sanctioned with the authority of those councils. Here may be room for differentiation. This raises, on the other hand, the problem of the nature of the teaching authority in the church.

Ecumenical discussions on "hierarchy of truths" are thus inseparable from the ways in which the church formulates authoritatively the truths and insights of its faith.

Chapter Three: Interpretation

A. Hierarchy

17. The *Decree on Ecumenism* uses "hierarchy of truths" as a metaphor (and places "hierarchy" between quotation marks). This indicates an order of importance

(a) which implies a graded structure (b) in which the different decrees serve different functions. The decree applies this to Christian doctrine in two ways. First, there is an order between propositional truths of doctrine and the realities which are known by means of the propositions. Propositional truths of doctrine which articulate the faith, such as the Marian dogmas, refer ultimately to the divine mystery and guide the life of the people of God. Secondly, "neither in the life nor the teaching of the whole church is everything presented on the same level. Certainly all revealed truths demand the same acceptance of faith, but according to the greater or lesser proximity that they have to the basis of the revealed mystery, they are variously placed with regard to one another and have varying connections among themselves" (The Secretariat for Promoting Christian Unity, "Reflections and Suggestions Concerning Ecumenical Dialogue" [1970], IV, 4 b). Some truths lean on more principal truths and are illumined by them (cf. Congregation for the Clergy, *General Catechetical Directory* [11 April 1971], no. 43; Congregation for the Doctrine of the Faith, *Mysterium Ecclesiae* [24 June 1973], no. 4).

18. Some Christian traditions upon reflection perceive two dimensions of a "hierarchy of truths." On the one hand, God's revelation itself exhibits an order, such as the transition from the old covenant to the new covenant. On the other hand, in the continuing response of faith to revelation by God's pilgrim people, one sees an ordering of truth which has been influenced by the historical and cultural contexts of time and place. These varied responses in faith to revelation have resulted in different orderings and emphases in the doctrinal expressions of various churches in their various historical periods, and of groups and even of individuals within churches. The Second Vatican Council recognizes that in the investigation of revealed truth, East and West have used different methods and approaches in understanding and proclaiming divine things, and that sometimes one tradition has come nearer than the other to an appropriate appreciation of certain aspects of a revealed mystery or has expressed them in a clearer manner (UR, no. 17).

19. In the ecumenical dialogue, churches may become more aware of existing hierarchies or orderings of truths in their tradition and life. Through dialogue, changes can result also in the ordering of a church's own teachings, and this can facilitate rapprochement. The Reformation churches, for example, increasingly acknowledge the significance of the episcopal ministry in their order of truths; and the Roman Catholic Church is finding a new appreciation of the doctrine of justification by faith. These are signs of convergence.

B. Foundation

20. The *Decree on Ecumenism* states that "the foundation of Christian faith" determines the different ordering of doctrinal truths (no. 11). What does this term

"foundation" mean? The council's deliberations hint at the meaning by reference to the "mystery of Christ" (Pangrazio) and to the "mystery of Christ and the history of salvation" (Modus 49). This context clearly indicates that the "foundation" refers primarily to the living and life-giving center or foundation of the Christian faith itself and not to any of the formulations which express it. Although many different formulas have witnessed to this center or foundation, e.g., the Nicene-Constantinopolitan Creed and the Apostles' Creed, no one formula can fully grasp or express its reality.

21. This foundation is primarily that reality on which the entire Christian faith and life rests, and by which the community of Christ's disciples is constituted as his body. It establishes the true nature of the church and sustains it on its pilgrim way. The central place where this foundation is proclaimed, confessed, and celebrated is the worship of the church.

22. Any attempt to describe this foundation on a conceptual level should refer to the person and mystery of Jesus Christ, true God and true human being. He is the one who said "I am the way, and the truth, and the life" (Jn 14:6). In the life, death, and resurrection of the Son of the Father, God has come into our midst for our salvation, and the Holy Spirit has been poured out into our hearts. In the Spirit's power God has established his one church, enables its members to experience Christ in faith and to be witnesses to him, and empowers the church to reach out to all humankind until all have been gathered up in God's kingdom.

23. This foundation is normatively witnessed to by the prophets, apostles, and the apostolic communities in the Old and New Testaments. In faithfulness to the original apostolic witness, it is confessed in the ecumenical creeds and handed on by the church through the ages.

C. Nexus

24. The decree bases its affirmation of a "hierarchy of truths" on the fact that these truths have different links (*diversus nexus*) with the foundation of the Christian faith. What is "different"? How do different affirmations of truth relate in different ways to the same foundation?

25. First of all, the council's sentence does not mean that there is only a more or less incidental relationship between these truths and the foundation, so that a merely relative character stamps them and one can consider them optional in the life of faith. Still less does the decree's sentence consider truths of faith as more or less necessary for salvation or suggest degrees in our obligation to believe in all that God has revealed. When one fully responds to God's self-evaluation in faith, one accepts that revelation as a whole. There is no picking and choosing of what God has revealed,

because there is no picking or choosing of what revelation is—our salvation. Hence, there are no degrees in the obligation to believe all that God has revealed.

26. The difference of the link of each truth is in its wider or closer proximity to the foundation of faith. This proximity does not ask us to fit each one of these truths into a static system of ordered concepts. Rather, we are to perceive the dynamic relationship which a given truth entertains with the foundation in the communal and personal faith as it is lived by each member of the body of Christ. We are to see the importance or the proximity or the "weight" which each truth has with the foundation of faith in the existential relationship of Christians and their communities.

27. This presupposes that those truths which serve to explain and protect other more fundamental truths have only an indirect link with the foundation of faith, or at least a link which is less direct than that of other truths. This is important in the search for unity among churches, because each Christian communion establishes a more or less immediate link between this or that truth and the foundation.

Chapter Four: Ecumenical and Theological Implications

28. The concept of "hierarchy of truths" has implications for the relations between churches as they seek full communion with one another through such means as the ecumenical dialogue. It can help to improve mutual understanding and to provide a criterion which would help to distinguish those differences in the understanding of the truths of faith which are areas of conflict from other differences which need not be.

A. Implication for the Search for Full Communion

29. The notion of "hierarchy of truths" acknowledges that all revealed truths are related to and can be articulated around the "foundation"—the "mystery of Christ"—through which the love of God is manifested in the Holy Spirit. All those who accept and confess this mystery and are baptized are brought into union with Christ with each other and with the church of every time and place. This fellowship is based upon the communion of the Holy Spirit, who distributes various kinds of spiritual gifts and ministries and binds the members together in one body which is the church. Thus "the mystery of Christ," "the center," "the foundation," is not only that which Christians believe but also a life which they share and experience.

30. Those who accept and confess the mystery of Christ and the Holy Trinity and are baptized and thereby share in the fellowship of the Holy Spirit are challenged to manifest that fellowship in shared life, in common witness, in common confession of faith and service to humanity, in shared worship, in joint pastoral care,

and in commitment to ecumenical dialogue. Such living out the degree of communion that already exists excites desire for greater communion.

31. While the common "foundation" and baptism unite Christians with one another in the communion of the Holy Spirit, they have not yet been able in a perfect way to make this communion fully visible. This is due to human weakness and sin, to theological and doctrinal disagreements, to historical factors, and in part also to differences about the ordering of truths around the central mystery.

32. In their common acknowledgment of the "foundation," divided Christians are led to view their differences of ordering the truths around this foundation in a more positive and constructive way; for example, the place in different churches of the doctrine of justification in relation to the "foundation." They understand some differences to be instances of that legitimate diversity of expression of common truth which may always characterize the communion of the Church; for example, those differences in theological reflection and devotional practice which may have arisen on account of historical and cultural factors are not necessarily differences with regard to the foundation of the faith. The communion of a visibly united church will certainly include a diversity which is a proper expression of its catholic, apostolic faith.

33. However, there are doctrinal differences which are still decisive obstacles that Christians have to overcome before they can manifest full communion in a shared sacramental and ordered life. These differences vary in importance according to their relation to the central mystery of Christ. Ecumenical dialogue is one of the principal means by which Christians better understand the weight and importance of these differences and their relation to the "foundation" of our common faith. In such dialogue Christians can gain new perspective on their common task to reorder priorities in faith and practice and to take appropriate steps and stages on the way to fuller communion.

34. An appreciation of "hierarchy of truths" could mean that the ecumenical agenda will be based upon a communion in the "foundation" that already exists and will point the way to that ordering of priorities which makes possible a gradual growth into full communion.

B. Implications for Ecumenical Dialogue

35. If rightly used, the concept of "hierarchy of truths" can help those Roman Catholics who are responsible for teaching the faith eagerly to become more open to fuller communion in the faith of Christ when they are "comparing doctrines" (UR, no. 11) in ecumenical dialogue. Those of other Christian confessions also make use of such an ordering of truths and emphasize this method especially in their ecumenical initiatives. For Protestants, the Gospel has a more immediate link with

the foundation than does the ministry which serves the Gospel. This different link also brings about differences in what we have in common. That there is only partial communion among churches is due not only to their disagreement about certain doctrines but also to the different links they establish between the truths and the foundation of faith. The progress made in ecumenical dialogue leads to convergences which tend to attenuate the differences which the Christian communions have established between the links of certain truths with the foundation of faith. Several churches, by recognizing this in their involvement in bilateral and multilateral dialogues, are experiencing the beginnings of such convergences.

36. By better understanding the ways in which other Christians hold, express, and live the faith, each confessional tradition is often led to a better understanding also of itself, and can begin to see its own formulations of doctrine in a broader perspective. This experience and discernment of each other is mutually enriching. The process respectfully approaches the mystery of salvation and its various formulations with no intent to "reduce" the mystery by any or all formulations. The process is a means of more adequately assessing expressions of the truth of revelation, their interrelation, their necessity, and the possible diversity of formulations. Refocusing on the "foundation," a "hierarchy of truths" may therefore be an instrument of that theological and spiritual renewal which the ecumenical movement requires.

37. The notion of "hierarchy of truths" could be helpful in the area of *mission and common witness*. Especially in secularized and highly complex societies, it is important to proclaim in word and life those foundational truths of the Gospel in a way that speaks to the needs of the human spirit. The common discernment of these needs is imperative, and the common use of a "hierarchy of truths" may facilitate an ecumenical discernment of the "foundation" and thus lead to convergence in theological understanding which may clarify the content of a common witness.

38. The contemporary understanding of the missionary task has to respect and take into account the richness, complexity, and diversity of cultures. The process by which the Christian faith is interpreted and welcomed in various cultures requires sensitivity to this diversity. A "hierarchy of truths" may also be a means of ensuring that the necessary expressions of the faith in various cultures do not result in any loss of its content or in a separation of Christian truths from the foundation. Both in relating content of faith and culture and in making a distinction between them, the notion of "hierarchy of truths" may play an important part.

39. The notion of "hierarchy of truths" could also be a useful principle in *theological methodology and hermeneutics*. It could provide a way for ordering theological work by acknowledging both the organic wholeness and coherence of the truths of the faith and their different places in relation to the "foundation." It is *dialogical* in spirit inasmuch as it envisages "comparing doctrines" within the specific traditions and within a broader ecumenical context. In directing primary attention to the per-

son and mystery of Jesus Christ, "the one who is, who was, and who is to come" (Rv 1:8), the concept may help theology to respect the historical dimension of our search for, and witness to, the truth.

40. By focusing on the "foundation"—the mystery of Christ—the notion of "hierarchy of truths" contains an orientation towards the full realization of the kingdom of God and thereby already now evokes a sense of urgency and responsibility. This can highlight the dynamic character of the Christian faith, its relevance for every time and age, and therefore serve the pilgrim churches in their task of "discerning the signs of the times" and to give an account of their faith and hope in their concrete situations. In responding to the challenges of the present with an awareness of a "hierarchy of truths," Christians are encouraged both to draw gratefully on the wisdom of their traditions and to be creative by seeking fresh responses in the light of God's coming kingdom.

Participants

The work on the study document *The Notion of "Hierarchy and Truths"* was organized by the Pontifical Council for Promoting Christian Unity and the Secretariat of the Commission on Faith and Order of the World Council of Churches.

The following persons participated in one or several meetings at which the study document was prepared:

Pontifical Council for Promoting Christian Unity

Most Rev. Basil Meeking (secretary, 1985-1987)
Msgr. John Radano (secretary, 1987-1990)
Prof. Georges Bavaud
Prof. William Henn, OFM
Rev. Emmanuel Lanne, OSB
Prof. René Marlé, SJ
Rev. John Mutiso-Mbinda
Dr. Hendrik Witte

Faith and Order Communion, WCC

Dr. Günther Gassmann (secretary, 1985-1990)
Very Rev. George Dragas
Prof. Jan Lochman
Prof. Nicolas Lossky
Dr. Mary Tanner
Rev. Max Thurian

Ecumenical Formation: Ecumenical Reflections and Suggestions

A Study Document of the Joint Working Group Between the Roman Catholic Church and the World Council of Churches

May 20, 1993

Preface

It is well accepted that there is an ecumenical imperative in the Gospel. However, there is also the indisputable fact that the goal of unity is far from realized. In that context of contradiction, the Joint Working Group of the Roman Catholic Church and the World Council of Churches decided in 1985 to focus on ecumenical formation as a contribution towards conscientizing people with regard to ecumenism. The minutes for that particular meeting of the JWG report:

> It might aim at a more popular readership. The pamphlet should be part of a wider process of promoting the idea of ecumenical formation. It should include an explanation of why ecumenical for-

mation is a priority, along with documentation. Anything produced on ecumenical formation ought to be subtitled "ecumenical reflections and suggestions," to make clear there is no intention of giving directives in a field in which each church has its proper responsibility.

The document is designed to be educational, aimed at stimulating ongoing reflection as an integral part of a process of ecumenical formation. It is rooted in a conviction that there must be a deep spirituality at the heart of ecumenical formation.

With these words, we are happy to recommend this document for study.

COMODERATORS
Most Rev. Alan Clark
His Eminence Metropolitan Elias Audi

I. The Ecumenical Imperative

1. In his high priestly prayer Jesus prayed for all those who will believe in him, "that they may all be one; as you, Father, are in me and I am in you, may they also be in us, so that the world may believe that you have sent me. The glory that you have given me I have given them, so that they may be one, as we are one" (Jn 17:21-22).

The unity to which the followers of Jesus Christ are called is not something created by them. Rather, it is Christ's will for them that they manifest their unity, given in Christ, before the world so that the world may believe. It is a unity which is grounded in and reflects the communion which exists between the Father and the Son and the Holy Spirit. Thus, the ecumenical imperative and the mission of the church are inextricably intertwined, and this for the sake of the salvation of all. The eschatological vision of the transformation and unity of humankind is the fundamental inspiration of ecumenical action.

Disobedience to the Imperative

2. However, from very early in her history, the church has suffered from tensions. The earliest Christian community in Corinth experienced tensions and factions (1 Cor 1:10-17). After the Councils of Ephesus (in 431) and Chalcedon (in 451), an important part of the church in the East was no more in communion with the rest of the church.

In 1054 there was the great break between the church of the East and the church of the West. As if those were not enough, the western church was unhappily divided further at the time of the Reformation. Today we continue to have not only the persistence of those divisions but also new ones.

Whatever the reasons, such divisions contradict the Lord's high priestly prayer, and Paul considers such divisions sinful and appeals "that all of you be in agreement and that there be no divisions among you, but that you be united in the same mind and the same purpose" (1 Cor 1:10).

3. Against that background, ecumenical formation is a matter of urgency because it is part of the struggle to overcome the divisions of Christians which are sinful and scandalous and challenge the credibility of the church and her mission.

Some Significant Responses to the Ecumenical Imperative

4. If there is a tragic history of disobedience to the ecumenical imperative, there is also heartwarming evidence that time and again the churches, conscious of their call to unity, have been challenged to confront the implications of their divisions. For instance, attempts at reconciliation between the East and the West have taken place in the thirteenth and fifteenth centuries. Also in the centuries that followed, there were voices and efforts calling the churches away from divisions and enmity. At the beginning of this century, the modern ecumenical history received significant impulses from the 1910 World Missionary Conference at Edinburgh. In 1920 the Ecumenical Patriarchate published an encyclical proposing the establishment of a "*koinonia* of churches," in spite of the doctrinal differences between the churches. The encyclical was an urgent and timely reminder that "world Christendom would be disobedient to the will of the Lord and Savior if it did not seek to manifest in the world the unity of the people of God and of the body of Christ." Around the same time, Anglicans and Catholics engaged in theological dialogue at the Malines Conversations, and the first World Conferences on Life and Work (Stockholm, 1925) and Faith and Order (Lausanne, 1927) were held.

5. Another recall to the ecumenical imperative in modern times was the meeting held in 1948 at Amsterdam, at which the WCC was formally constituted. The theme of this meeting was very significant: "Man's Disorder and God's Design." The long process which culminated in the birth of the WCC represents a multilateral response to the ecumenical imperative, in which a renewed commitment to the *una sancta* (the one, holy, catholic, and apostolic church) and to making our own the prayer of Jesus that "your will be done on earth as it is in heaven," were openly declared to be on the agenda of the churches.

6. A further important landmark on the ecumenical road was the announcement made by Pope John XXIII, on 25 January 1959, the feast of the conversion of

St. Paul, to convene the Catholic bishops for the Second Vatican Council, which Pope John XXIII opened in October 1962. This council, which has been highly significant for ecumenical advance, definitely accelerated the possibilities for the Catholic Church to take part in the multilateral dialogue in Faith and Order, and to engage in a range of bilateral dialogues which are now an important expression of the one ecumenical scene. Various bilateral conversations between various churches attest to growing fruitful relations between churches and traditions which for centuries were at variance.

7. There have also been historic and symbolic actions which are very significant efforts to overcome the old divisions. For example, on the 7th of December 1960, Pope Paul VI and Patriarch Athenagoras, in solemn ceremonies in Rome and Constantinople, took steps to take away from the memory and the midst of the churches the sentences of excommunication which had been the immediate cause of the great schism between the church of Rome and the church of Constantinople in 1054. Moreover, the icon of the Apostles Peter and Andrew in embrace—Peter being the patron of the church of Rome and Andrew the patron of the church of Constantinople—presented by the ecumenical patriarch to the pope, illustrates in graphic and religious form the reconciliation between the churches of the East and the West. The responses of many churches to the Faith and Order document on *Baptism, Eucharist, and Ministry*, which was the result of multilateral ecumenical dialogue, is a further illustration of ecumenical advance.

The Imperative, A Permanent Call

8. The foregoing historical moments in the life of the church stand like promontories in the ecumenical landscape and attest to the fact that in spite of persisting divisions, of which there is need for repentance, churches are experiencing a reawakening to the necessity of unity that stands in holy writ and in the Lord's will for the church. Indeed, many have observed that relationships between churches have radically changed from isolation and enmity to mutual respect, cooperation, dialogue, and between several churches from the Reformation, also eucharistic fellowship. The people of God are hearing anew the call "to lead a life worthy of the calling to which you have been called . . . bearing with one another in love, making every effort to maintain the unity of the Spirit in the bond of peace" (Eph 4:13). These and other developments are steps towards that visible unity, which is a *koinonia* given and expressed in the common confession of the one apostolic faith; mutual recognition and sharing of baptism, eucharist, and ministries; common prayer; witness and service in the world; and conciliar forms of deliberation and decision making.

II. Ecumenical Formation: What Is Meant by It?

9. That for long periods we have been disobedient to the ecumenical imperative is a reminder that the spirit of ecumenism needs nurturing. Ecumenical formation is an ongoing process of learning within the various local churches and world communions, aimed at informing and guiding people in the movement which—inspired by the Holy Spirit—seeks the visible unity of Christians.

This pilgrimage towards unity enables mutual sharing and mutual critique through which we grow. Such an approach to unity thus involves at once rootedness in Christ and in one's tradition, while endeavoring to discover and participate in the richness of other Christian and human traditions.

A Process of Exploration

10. Such a response to the ecumenical imperative demands patient, humble, and persistent exploration, together with people of other traditions, of the pain of our situation of separation, taking us to both the depths of our divisions and the heights of our already existing unity in the triune God, and of the unity we hope to attain. Thus, ecumenical formation is also a process of education by which we seek to orient ourselves towards God, all Christians, and indeed all human beings in a spirit of renewed faithfulness to our Christian mission.

A Process of Learning

11. As a process of learning, ecumenical formation is concerned with engaging the experience, knowledge, skills, talents, and the religious memory of the Christian community for mutual enrichment and reconciliation. The process may be initiated through formal courses on the history and main issues of ecumenism, as well as be integrated into the curriculum at every level of the education in which the church is involved. Ecumenical formation is meant to help set the tone and perspective of every instruction and, therefore, may demand a change in the orientation of our educational institutions, systems, and curricula.

12. The language of formation and learning refers to some degree to a body of knowledge to be absorbed. That is important: but formation and learning require a certain bold openness to living ecumenically as well. In 1952 the Fourth Faith and Order Conference took place in Lund, Sweden. The statement that came from it may be read as a representative text:

> A faith in the one Church of Christ which is not implemented by acts of obedience is dead. There are truths about the nature of

God and His Church which will remain forever closed to us unless we act together in obedience to the unity which is already ours. We would, therefore, earnestly request our Churches to consider whether they are doing all they ought to do to manifest the one-ness of the people of God. Should not our Churches ask them-selves whether they are showing sufficient eagerness to enter into conversation with other Churches and whether they should not act together in all matters except those in which deep differences of conviction compel them to act separately? . . . Obedience to God demands also that the Churches seek unity in their mission to the world.

A Process for All

13. Thus in pursuit of the goal of Christian unity, ecumenical formation takes place not only in formal educational programs but also in the daily life of the church and people. While the formation of the whole people of God is desired, indeed is a necessity, we also insist on the strategic importance of giving priority to the ecu-menical formation of those who have special responsibility for ministry and leader-ship in the churches. To that extent, theologians, pastors, and others who bear responsibility in the church have both a particular need and responsibility for ecumenical formation.

14. The ecumenical formation of those with particular responsibility for form-ing and animating future church leaders could involve the study of ecumenical his-tory and documents resulting from the ongoing bilateral and multilateral dialogues. In addition, ecumenical gatherings and organizations, particularly of scholars, can provide a useful climate for it. Exchange visits among seminary students in the course of their training may also help this process of deepening the appreciation of other traditions as well as their own.

An Expression of Ecumenical Spirituality

15. It follows from the ecumenical imperative that the process of formation in ecumenism has to be undergirded by and should indeed be an expression of ecu-menical spirituality.

It is spiritual in the sense that it should be open to the prayer of Jesus for unity and to the promptings of the Holy Spirit, who reconciles and binds all Christians together.

It is spiritual in yet another sense, of leading to repentance for the past dis-obedience to the ecumenical imperative, which disobedience was manifested as contentiousness and hostility among Christians at every level. Having ecumenical spirituality in common prayer and other forms as the underpinning of ecumenical formation invites all to conversion and change of heart, which is the very soul of the work for restoring unity.

Furthermore, it is spiritual in the sense of seeking a renewed lifestyle, which is characterized by sacrificial love, compassion, patience with one another, and tolerance. The search for such lifestyle may include exposing students to the spiritual texts, prayers, and songs of other churches with the goal and hope that such familiarity will contribute towards effecting change of heart and attitude towards others, which itself is a gift of the Holy Spirit. Such efforts will help deepen mutual trust, making it possible to learn together the positive aspects of each other's tradition, and thus live constructively with the awareness of the reality and pain of divisions.

16. Ecumenical formation is part of the process of building community in the one household of God, which must be built on trust, centered on Jesus Christ the Lord and Savior. This demands a spirituality of trust which, among other things, helps to overcome the fear to be exposed to different traditions, for the sake of Christ.

III. Ecumenical Formation: How to Realize It?

Pedagogy Built on Communion

17. The renewed emphasis on understanding the church as communion, like the image of the church as the body of Christ, implies differentiation within the one body, which has nevertheless been created for unity. Thus, the very dynamic of ecumenism is relational in character. We respond in faith and hope to God who relates to us first. God relates to us in love, commanding us to love one another (Mk 12:29-31). This response ought to be wholehearted. Therefore, in order to help Christians to respond wholeheartedly to the ecumenical imperative, we must seek ways to relate the prayer of Jesus (Jn 17:20-24) to all our hearts and minds, to the affective as well as to the cognitive dimensions in them. Christians must be helped to understand that to love Jesus necessarily means to love everything Jesus prayed, lived, died, and was raised for, namely, "to gather into one the children of God who are scattered abroad" (Jn 11:52), the unity of his disciples as an effective sign of the unity of all peoples.

18. The *koinonia* or communion as the basic understanding of the church demands attempting to develop common ecumenical perspectives on ecclesiology. Unity is not uniformity but a communion of much diversity. Therefore, it is necessary to explore with others the limits of legitimate diversity. In this regard special cognizance must also be taken of the religious and sociocultural context in which

the process of ecumenical formation takes place. Where there is a predominant majority church, ecumenical sensitivity is all the more required.

Going Out to Each and Every One

19. The effectiveness of Christian unity in the midst of a broken world ultimately depends on the work of God's Spirit who wishes each one of us to participate. God speaks to us today the words which were addressed to Adam and Eve, "Where are you?" (Gn 3:9) as also the words to Cain, "Where is your brother?"(Gn 4:9). All Christians should become aware, and make each other aware, of who and where their sisters and brothers are and where they stand in regard to them, whether near or far (Eph 2:17). They should be helped to go out to meet them, to get involved with them. Involvement and participation in the whole ecumenical formation process is crucial.

20. In a Christian response to God and the ecumenical imperative which comes from God, there is no such thing as "the few for the many." The response to the prayer of Jesus must be the response of each and every one. Therefore, the growth into an ecumenical mind and heart is essential for each and for all, and the introduction of, and care for, ecumenical formation are absolutely necessary at every level of the church community, church life, action, and activities; at *all* educational levels (schools, colleges, universities; theological schools, seminaries, religious/ monastic communities, pastoral and lay formation centers; Sunday liturgies, homilies, and catechesis).

Commitment to Learning in Community

21. While ecumenical formation must be an essential feature in every curriculum in theological training, care must be taken that it does not become something intended for individuals only. There must be commitment of learning in community. This has several components: (a) learning about, from, and with others of different traditions; (b) praying for Christian unity, and wherever and whenever possible, together, as well as praying for one another; (c) offering common Christian witness by acting together, and (d) struggling together with the pain of our divisions. In this regard the participation of different institutions for theological education in a common program of formation is to be encouraged. Working ecumenically in joint projects becomes another important aspect of ecumenical formation. The reason for such joint action must always be related to the search for Christian unity.

22. Seeking a renewed commitment for ecumenical formation does not imply to gloss over existing differences and to deny the specific profiles of our respective

ecclesial traditions. But it may involve a common rereading of our histories and especially of those events that led to divisions among Christians. It is not enough to regret that our histories have been tainted through the polemics of the past; ecumenical formation must endeavor to eliminate polemic and to further mutual understanding, reconciliation, and the healing of memories. No longer shall we be strangers to one another but members of the one household of God (Eph 2:19).

Open to Other Religions

23. In this world, people are also divided along religious lines. Thus, ecumenical formation must also address the matter of religious plurality and secularism and inform about interreligious dialogue, which aims at deeper mutual understanding in the search for world community. It must be clear, however, that interreligious dialogue—with other world religions such as Islam, Buddhism, Hinduism, etc.—has goals that are specifically different from the goals of ecumenical dialogue among Christians. In giving serious attention to this important activity, Christians must carefully distinguish it from ecumenical dialogue.

24. That spirt of tolerance and dialogue must get to the pews and marketplaces where people feel the strains of the different heritages which encounter each other. The faith that God is the Creator and Sustainer of all also requires Christians to do everything in their power to promote the cause of freedom, human rights, justice, and peace everywhere, and thus actively to contribute to a renewed movement towards human solidarity in obedience to God's will.

Using the Instruments of Communication

25. In today's search for unity, there is a relatively new factor which must be taken seriously—the scientific technological advances, particularly the communications revolution. The world has become a global village in which peoples, cultures and religions, and Christian denominations which were once far off are now next door one to another. The sense of the "other" is being pressed on us, and we need to relate to one another for mutual survival and peace. Thus, the possibilities of mass communication can be an asset for communicating the ecumenical spirit.

The media can be an extremely important resource for ecumenical formation, and the many possibilities which they offer to promote the ecumenical formation process should be made use of. However, the world of the media has its own logic and values; it is not an unambivalent resource. Critical caution must, therefore, be exercised in availing ourselves of the media for the ecumenical task.

Conclusion: Ecumenical Formation and Common Witness

26. Ecumenism is not an option for the churches. In obedience to Christ and for the sake of the world, the churches are called to be an effective sign of God's presence and compassion before all the nations. For the churches to come divided to a broken world is to undermine their credibility when they claim to have a ministry of universal unity and reconciliation. The ecumenical imperative must be heard and responded to everywhere. This response necessarily requires ecumenical formation, which will help the people of God to render a common witness to all humankind by pointing to the vision of the new heaven and a new earth (Rv 21:1).

The Challenge of Proselytism and the Calling to Common Witness

A Study Document of the Joint Working Group Between the World Council of Churches and the Roman Catholic Church

September 25, 1995

Foreword

We would like to present the document *The Challenge of Proselytism and the Calling to Common Witness*, which has been prepared by the Joint Working Group between the World Council of Churches and the Roman Catholic Church, in response to concerns expressed by some of our churches in regard to the missionary outreach of other churches that would seem to bear some of the characteristics of proselytism.

It is within the concern for full Christian unity and common Christian witness that the question of proselytism is looked at in this document. There is the common conviction that central to the work of Christian unity is an urgent need for all Christians to be able to give a truly common witness to the whole Christian faith.

In this spirit, the document may help Christian communities to reflect on their own motivation for mission and also on their methods of evangelizing. Dialogue in a truly ecumenical spirit with those considered to be proselytizing is highlighted.

It is our hope, therefore, that this document will be shared at different levels of church life and reflected on by churches, so that it can contribute towards breaking down mistrust, suspicion, misunderstanding, or ignorance of the other, where any of these may exist, as well as encourage persevering effort to seek new ways and means of closer collaboration in evangelization, according to the different circumstances of time, place, and culture.

All such efforts will mean a deeper commitment to the goal of full communion among Christ's disciples in the certitude that our fellowship is with the Father, through the Son, in the Holy Spirit. This document is meant as a contribution to that goal.

COMODERATORS
Metropolitan Elias of Beirut
Most Rev. Alan C. Clark

I. Introduction

1. This document is the result of discussions in the Joint Working Group (JWG) and is presented with the conviction that it is timely and with the hope that it may serve as an impulse for further reflection and action in the churches. The conversations in the JWG were marked both by the grateful recognition of the increase of common witness of Christians from different traditions and serious concerns about tensions and conflicts created by proselytism in nearly all parts of the world. It is the new reality of common witness and a growth in *koinonia* which forms the backdrop for a critical consideration of proselytism, which has been described as conscious efforts with the intention to win members of another church.[1]

2. Even though the JWG has addressed the questions of common witness and proselytism on two previous occasions, recent dramatic events have led it to study these issues once again. Over the past few years, we have become more aware of the concern being expressed in new situations and contexts in which people tend to be vulnerable in one way or another, and where proselytizing activity is alleged to be taking place. Some situations invite urgent ecumenical attention, such as:

- Within the climate of newly found religious freedom, e.g., in Central and Eastern Europe, where there is a threat felt by some churches that their members are under pressure from other churches to change their allegiance

- Instances in the "developing world" (often easily identified with nations in the southern hemisphere, though also found elsewhere), in which proselytizing efforts take advantage of people's misfortunes—e.g., in situations of poverty in villages, or in the mass migration to the cities where new arrivals have a sense of being lost in anonymity or marginalized, and are frequently outside the pastoral structures of their own church—to induce them to change their church affiliation

- Where people of a particular ethnic group, traditionally members of one church, are said to be encouraged by unfair means to become members of other churches

- The activity of some new missionary movements, groups or individuals, both within our churches and outside them, especially those originating in the newly industrialized nations, which enter countries often uninvited by any church and begin missionary activity among the local people in competition with the local churches

- In various places the arrival of evangelizing groups making extensive use of the mass media and causing confusion and division among local churches

- In many parts of the world the churches are experiencing proselytism activities of sects and new religious movements

3. The purpose of this document is to encourage all Christians to pursue their calling to render a common witness to God's saving and reconciling purpose in today's world and to help them to avoid all competition in mission that contradicts their common calling. With this aim the document seeks to facilitate a pastoral response to the continuing challenge of proselytism, which not only endangers existing ecumenical relations but is also an additional barrier to our growing together in reciprocal love and trust as brothers and sisters in Christ.

4. Today, we thank God for the achievements of ecumenical theological dialogues during recent decades and for a new climate of understanding and friendship in which ecumenical relations are being developed. We are also grateful for all the recent encouraging signs of better mutual understanding and joint perspectives in the area of common witness and proselytism.[2] These are recorded in bilateral and multilateral dialogues among churches and can be seen in significant initiatives of common witness at different levels of church life. These agreements and joint actions provide a basis and encouragement to intensify our efforts to bear together a credible witness to the Gospel in the contemporary world.

5. In this study process we wish to affirm what continues to be valid in the two previous WCC–Roman Catholic Church Joint Working Group documents: *Common Witness and Proselytism*,[3] and *Common Witness*.[4] We also want to take into account relevant material on evangelism and proselytism from some of the afore-

mentioned dialogues. In addition, this study process will be linked with another possible study on proselytism in the World Council of Churches by Unit II.[5]

6. We acknowledge with appreciation similar studies being undertaken by ecumenical bodies like, e.g., the Conference of European Churches[6] and the Middle East Council of Churches.[7] Our desire is to invite reflection and action on the part of churches of different traditions in a task to which all are called on our pilgrimage to a fuller expression and experience of visible Christian unity.

II. Mission and Unity: The Context of Common Witness

7. An essential element of the church is to participate in the mission of God in Jesus Christ to the world by proclaiming through word and action God's revelation and salvation to all people (1 Jn 1:1-5). Indeed, God's mission towards a "reconciled humanity and a renewed creation" (cf. Eph 1:9-10) is the essential content and impulse for the missionary witness of the church.

8. Mission in this sense of being sent with a message that is addressed to the spiritual and also material needs of people is thus an inescapable mandate for the church. This imperative is affirmed today by many churches and is expressed through their regular activities as well as special efforts (New Evangelization, Decades of Evangelism, Mission 2000). Sent to a world in need of unity and greater interdependence amidst the competition and fragmentation of the human community, the church is called to be sign and instrument of God's reconciling love.[8]

9. Ecumenical relationships, however, have from the beginning of the modern ecumenical movement been shaped by the insight that the search for the visible unity of Christ's church must include the commitment to and the practice of a common missionary witness. In the prayer of Jesus "that they all may be one so that the world may believe" (Jn 17:21), we are reminded that the unity of Christians and the mission of the church are intrinsically related. Divisions among Christians are a counterwitness to Christ and contradict their witness to reconciliation in Christ.

10. In responding to the appeal for the unity of Christians in effective missionary witness, we need to be aware of the reality of diversity rooted in theological traditions and in various geographical, historical, and cultural contexts. We recognize, therefore, that the unity we seek is a unity that embraces a legitimate diversity of spiritual, disciplinary, liturgical, and theological expressions that enrich common witness. It will include the discovery and appreciation of the many diverse gifts of Christ which we share already now as Christians in "real but imperfect communion," gifts given for the upbuilding of the church (cf. Rom 12:4-8). Even when churches are not in full communion with each other, they are called to be truthful to each other and show respect for each other. Such an attitude does not subvert their self-

understanding and their conviction to have received the truth, but rather facilitates the common search for unity and common witness to God's love for the world.

11. In the growing ecumenical *koinonia*, there must also be a way of witnessing to the Gospel to each other in faithfulness to one's own tradition and convictions. Such mutual witness could enrich and challenge us to renew our thinking and life, and could do so without being polemical towards those who do not share the same tradition. "To speak the truth in love" (Eph 4:15) is a challenge and an experience long accepted within the ecumenical movement.

12. The recognition of an already existing, though imperfect, communion among churches is a significant result of ecumenical efforts and a new element in twentieth-century church history. This existing communion should be an encouragement for further efforts to overcome the barriers that still prevent churches from reaching full communion. It should provide a basis for the renewal, common witness, and service of the churches for the sake of God's saving and reconciling activity for all humanity and all creation. It should also provide a basis for avoiding all rivalry and antagonistic competition in mission because "the use of coercive or manipulative methods in evangelism distort *koinonia*."[9]

13. When Christians by means of efforts towards common witness struggle to overcome such lack of reciprocal love, of mutual understanding, and of trust, they will be open to the call for repentance and for the renewal of their efforts. This is the way "to come to the unity of the faith and of the knowledge of the Son of God, to maturity, to the measure of the full stature of Christ" (Eph 4:13).

14. These efforts include self-critical reflection on our relationships with other churches, openness to appreciate authentically evangelical expressions of life in them and to be mutually enriched. They will also include engaging in a more authentic dialogue where we can speak meaningfully and honestly to one another, discussing difficulties as they arise and trying to build up relationships (cf. Eph 4:15).

III. Some Basic Principles of Religious Freedom

15. We acknowledge the right of every person "alone or in community with others and in public or in private"[10] to live in accordance with the principles of religious freedom.[11] Religious freedom affirms the right of all persons to pursue the truth and to witness to that truth according to their conscience. It includes the freedom to acknowledge Jesus Christ as Lord and Savior and the freedom of Christians to witness to their faith in him by word and deed.

Religious freedom involves the right to freely adopt or change one's religion and to "manifest it in teaching, practice, worship, and observance"[12] without any coercion which would impair such freedom.

We reject all violations of religious freedom and all forms of religious intolerance as well as every attempt to impose belief and practices on others or to manipulate or coerce others in the name of religion.

16. Freedom of religion touches on "one of the fundamental elements of the conception of life of the person." The promotion of religious freedom contributes also to the harmonious relations between religious communities and is therefore an essential contribution to social harmony and peace. For these reasons, international instruments and the constitutions and laws of almost all nations recognize the right to religious freedom.[13] Proselytism can violate or manipulate the right of the individual and can exacerbate tense and delicate relations between communities and thus destabilize societies.

17. The responsibility of fostering religious freedom and the harmonious relations between religious communities is a primary concern of the churches. Where principles of religious freedom are not being respected and lived in church relations, we need, through dialogue in mutual respect, to encourage deeper consideration and appreciation of these principles and of their practical applications for the churches.

IV. Nature and Characteristics of Proselytism

18. In the history of the church, the term "proselytism" has been used as a positive term and even as an equivalent concept for missionary activity.[14] More recently, especially in the context of the modern ecumenical movement, it has taken on a negative connotation when applied to activities of Christians to win adherents from other Christian communities. These activities may be more obvious or more subtle. They may be for unworthy motives or by unjust means that violate the conscience of the human person; or even if proceeding with good intentions, their approach ignores the Christian reality of other churches or their particular approaches to pastoral practice.

19. Proselytism as described in this document stands in opposition to all ecumenical effort. It includes certain activities which often aim at having people change their church affiliation and which we believe must be avoided, such as the following:[15]

- Making unjust or uncharitable references to other churches' beliefs and practices and even ridiculing them
- Comparing two Christian communities by emphasizing the achievements and ideals of one and the weaknesses and practical problems of the other
- Employing any kind of physical violence, moral compulsion, and psychological pressure, e.g., the use of certain advertising techniques in mass media that might bring undue pressure on readers/viewers[16]

- Using political, social, and economic power as a means of winning new members for one's own church
- Extending explicit or implicit offers of education, health care, or material inducements or using financial resources with the intent of making converts[17]
- Manipulative attitudes and practices that exploit people's needs, weaknesses, or lack of education especially in situations of distress and fail to respect their freedom and human dignity[18]

20. While our focus in this document is on relationships between Christians, it is important to seek the mutual application of these principles also in interfaith relations. Both Christians and communities of other faiths complain about unworthy and unacceptable methods of seeking converts from their respective communities. The increased cooperation and dialogue among people of different faiths could result in witness offered to one another that would respect human freedom and dignity and be free of the negative activities described above.

V. Sources of Tension in Church Relationships

21. We need to look at some of the sources of tension in church relationships which could lead to proselytism in order to ground some of this concern. One is the holding of distorted views of another church's teaching or doctrine and even attacking or caricaturing them, e.g., denouncing prayer for the dead as a denial of the need for personal acceptance of Christ as Lord and Savior; discrediting the veneration of icons as signs of crude idolatry; interpreting the use of art in church buildings as a transgression of the first commandment.

22. Different understandings of missiology and different concepts of evangelization also underlie some interchurch tensions, e.g., seeing God's gift of salvation as coming exclusively through one's own church, seeing the task of mission as exclusively concerned with social matters or exclusively with spiritual matters, rather than in a holistic way. They can lead to competition or even conflict in missionary practice among the churches rather than a common approach to mission.

23. Different theological and pastoral understandings of the meaning of certain concepts can also contribute to tension in relationships. For example, some aim at the reevangelization of baptized but nonpracticing members of other churches. But there are different interpretations of who is "unchurched" or a "true" Christian believer. Efforts to understand the perspectives of other Christian communities on these matters are therefore necessary.

24. The varieties of understanding of membership existing among churches can also be an unnecessary source of tension. There are theological issues involved.

The way of becoming a member and even the way of terminating membership in particular churches can be understood very differently. The duties and responsibilities of members also differ from church to church. This diversity of understanding influences the way we see changes in church affiliation.

25. Unfortunately, there are occasions when the personal and cultural confusion of people, their social-political resentments, the tensions within a church, or their hurtful experiences in their own church can be played upon to persuade them to be converted.

26. Sometimes, evangelizers can be tempted to take advantage of the spiritual and material needs of people or their lack of instruction in the faith in order to make them change their church affiliation, because they may interpret this as a lack of pastoral care and attention to these people on the part of churches to which they belong. But in fact, pastoral care, even if it could be more adequate, may be available to the person in his/her own church. Here again there may be different perceptions as to what is adequate and what is inadequate in the field of pastoral care. However, the churches must always look for ways to improve the pastoral care they give to their people, especially the quality of instruction in the faith.

27. Tensions also arise on occasion because of the unjust interference on the part of the state in church matters in order to influence people to change church membership.

28. In other situations, where a church identifies with the government or works in collusion with it to the extent that it fails to exercise its prophetic role, tensions can arise within the Christian community from what may be seen as preferential treatment by the government for that particular church.

29. Tensions can result in evangelizing activity when there is a lack of sufficient regard for people's culture and religious traditions. There can also be dangers if we lose sight of the fact that the Gospel must take root in the soil of different cultures, while it cannot be limited to any culture.

30. Finally, there can be a lack of respect for the beliefs and practices of minority groups in contexts dominated by a majority church and an inability to see them as full and equal partners in society that causes tensions in relationships. In some cases, a dominant Christian tradition has allowed restrictive laws to be framed by the state which disfavor Christians of another tradition.

VI. Steps Forward

31. Despite all efforts to combat it, the problem of proselytism is still with us, causing painful tensions in church relationships and undermining the credibility of the church's witness to God's universal love. Ultimately, proselytism is a sign of the real scandal which is division. By placing the issue of proselytism in the context of

church unity and of common witness, we suggest a perspective which makes it possible to approach the problem within an adequate theological framework.

32. As responsible ecumenical relationships in many different contexts are a complex reality requiring study and theological dialogue, prayer, and practical collaboration, we would like to recommend the following to the churches, keeping in mind that the movement for Christian unity can also contribute to breaking down barriers between people in the wider society as well:

- To encourage churches to pray for one another and for Christian unity in response to the prayer of our Lord, that his disciples "may all be one . . . so that the world may believe" (Jn 17:21)

- To prepare more adequate Christian formation programs within our churches so that people are better equipped to share their own faith, as well as ecumenical programs that will foster respect for the integrity of other Christian churches and openness to receive from them

- To develop a sensitivity to existing ecclesial realities in a given area so that when providing the required pastoral care for one's own church members, it can be done in an atmosphere of communication and appropriate consultation[19]

- To condemn publication of unverified alleged events or incidents concerning church activities that only fan feelings of fear and prejudice, and of one-sided or prejudicial reports on religious developments which can undercut efforts towards cooperation[20]

- To try to understand history from the perspective of other churches in order to arrive at a shared common understanding of it and, where necessary, at reconciliation, mutual forgiveness, and healing of memories

- To study together the nature of *diakonia* in order that the characteristics of Christian service be made clear and transparent; that is, that it may be truly inspired by the love of Christ and that it may not be a reason for tension, nor a means of proselytism

- To help people to a greater awareness of the phenomenon of sects and new religious movements, through collaborative efforts, and also to consider the question of how to respond pastorally but firmly to coercive religious practices by persons and groups that are not in keeping with the principles of religious liberty

- To include in any future study of proselytism the significant participation of Christians, both within and outside WCC–Roman Catholic Church circles of influence, especially those accused of these practices and those who have changed church affiliation through the efforts of another church[21]

33. These efforts will be effective and successful to the extent that relationships of reciprocal trust are built between the churches.

VII. Conclusion

34. Knowing that our common faith in Jesus, Lord and Savior, unites us and that baptism is an effective sign of unity, we are called to live our Christian vocation in unity and to give visible witness to it.

35. Therefore, it is not enough to denounce proselytism. We need to continue to prepare ourselves for genuine common Christian witness through common prayer, common retreats, Bible courses, Bible sharing, study and action groups, religious education jointly or in collaboration, joint or coordinated pastoral and missionary activity,[22] a common service (*diakonia*) in humanitarian matters, and theological dialogue. The immensely rich Christian spiritual patrimony of contemplative prayer can be a resource for all. We acknowledge that our current divisions limit the extent to which we can engage in common witness. We recall and make our own the principle cited in the Third World Conference on Faith and Order at Lund, Sweden, 1952:

> We earnestly request our churches to consider whether they are doing all they ought to do to manifest the oneness of the people of God. Should not our churches ask themselves whether they are showing sufficient eagerness to enter into conversation with other churches and whether they should not act together in all matters except those in which deep differences of conviction compel them to act separately? . . . Obedience to God demands also that the churches seek unity in their mission to the world.[23]

36. There is also an urgent need to continue to work collaboratively in order to transcend the lines that society draws between those at the center and those on the peripheries, between those who have an abundance of resources and those marginalized because of race, economics, gender, or for other reasons. These societal divisions often provide the context for proselytism and therefore challenge our divided churches to closer collaboration that will be a common Christian witness.[24]

37. In all of these reflections we take our inspiration from the Gospel itself:

> This is my commandment: love one another, as I have loved you. No one can have greater love than to lay down his life for his friends. . . . You did not choose me, no, I chose you; and I commissioned you to go out and to bear fruit, fruit that will last; so

that the Father will give you anything you ask him in my name. My command to you is to love one another. (Jn 15:12-13, 16-17)

Note on this Study Document

As proselytism is a reality that obliges churches to seek a solution and a question that continues to surface at different meetings, including the WCC Central Committee and the Assembly in Canberra, the Joint Working Group, at its meeting in Wennigsen, Germany, in March 1992, decided to work on a new study document on proselytism, as this would be a broader forum to gather some of the findings from various meetings, including the bilateral dialogues, and to make a synthesis of solutions proposed.

At subsequent JWG executive meetings, decisions were made to base the new study on the 1970 document *Common Witness and Proselytism* and the 1982 document *Common Witness*. Mr. Georges Lemopoulos and Sr. Monica Cooney were asked to prepare an outline for the work. Consultations were held with various people both within the WCC and outside. A draft outline, prepared with the help of Fr. Karl Müller, SFD, and Prof. Dr. Reinhard Frieling, was then submitted to the JWG executive meetings, and a first draft was presented to the JWG plenary meeting in Crete, June 1994.

Dr. Günther Gassmann and Msgr. John Radano were then appointed as drafters. They presented an amended draft to the JWG Executive in Geneva in October 1994, after which both WCC Program Unit II and Program Unit III (CCIA) were consulted (the latter on the question of religious freedom).

A final draft was discussed at the JWG plenary in Bose, Italy, May 1995, and finalized at the executive, Geneva, September 1995.

This document points out the problem of proselytism, noting the different realities in a variety of contexts, as it is not a problem of any two churches in a particular area. It is prepared in the conviction that while we continue to proselytize and to accuse one another of proselytism, instead of speaking the truth in love, we cannot respond to the call to common witness, nor can we live the command to love one another as God has first loved us.

NOTES

1. Cf. also the more detailed description of proselytism in nos. 18-19.

2. Among many other examples which could be added here cf. (a) ERCDOM, Document 14 above; (b) Baptist–Catholic Dialogue, Document 10 above; (c) Letter of Pope John Paul II to Bishops of Europe on Relations Between Catholics and Orthodox in the New Situation of Central and Eastern Europe (May 31, 1991), in *Information Service* 81 (1992), 101-103; (d) *General Principles and Practical Norms for Coordinating the Evangelizing Activity and Ecumenical Commitment of the Catholic Church in Russia and in the Other Countries of the CIS*, Pontifical Commission for Russia (from the Vatican, June 1, 1992); (e) "Uniatism: Method of Union of the Past, and the Present Search for Full Communion," Report of the Joint International Commission for the Theological Dialogue Between the Roman Catholic Church and the Orthodox Church, Balamand, June 17-24, 1993, in *Information Service* 83 (1993), 96-99; (f) U.S. Orthodox–Roman Catholic Consultation at the Holy Cross Orthodox School of Theology, Brookline, Mass., May 26-28, 1992, in *Origins* 22:5 (June 11, 1992): 79-80; (g) Santiago.

3. CWP, no. 1.

4. CW.

5. Cf. also Santiago, pp. 256-257 (Report of Section IV: Called to Common Witness for a Renewed World, no. 14).

6. Cf. *At Thy Word: Mission and Evangelization in Europe Today*. Message of the Fifth European Ecumenical Encounter. Santiago de Compostela, November 13-17, 1991, *Catholic International* 3:2, pp. 88-92. *God Unites: In Christ a New Creation*, Report of the Tenth Assembly of CEC, Prague, September 1-11, 1992, pp. 182-183 (Final Report of the Policy Reference Committee, Appendix 18).

7. *Proselytism, Sects and Pastoral Challenges—Working Document of the Commission of Faith and Unity*, MECC, 1989; *Signs of Hope in the Middle East*, MECC/EMEU Consultation, Cyprus, 1992; *History of the Dialogue Between the MECC and Western Evangelicals*.

8. This perspective is expressed, e.g., in LG, no. 1, and in the Faith and Order Study Document *Church and World, The Unity of the Church and the Renewal of Human Community*, Faith and Order Paper No. 151 (Geneva: WCC Publications, 1990).

9. Santiago, p. 56 (Report of Section IV: Called to Common Witness for a Renewed World, no. 14).

10. *Declaration on the Elimination of All Forms of Intolerance and of Discrimination Based on Religion or Belief*, 25 November 1981, art. 1,1.

11. Cf. DH; UR; "Christian Witness, Proselytism and Religious Liberty in the Setting of the World Council of Churches," *The Ecumenical Review* 13 (1960): 79-89; WCC Executive Committee Statement on Religious Liberty, Geneva, September 1979; *Study Paper on Religious Liberty*, CCIA–WCC Background Information 1980/1; *Religious Liberty—Some Major Considerations in the Current Debate*, CCIA–WCC Background Information 1987/1.

12. *Declaration on the Elimination of All Forms of Intolerance and of Discrimination Based on Religion or Belief*, art. 7, 7 and 7, 2.

13. *Universal Declaration of Human Rights*, art. 18. Cf. also *Conference on Cooperation and Security in Europe: Helsinki Final Agreement.*

14. "A historical overview shows that the understanding of 'proselytism' has changed considerably. In the Bible it was devoid of negative connotations. A 'proselyte' was someone who, by belief in Yahweh and acceptance of the law, became a member of the Jewish community. Christianity took over this meaning to describe a person who converted from paganism. Mission work and proselytism were considered equivalent concepts until recent times." Cf. Document 9 above.

15. Cf. CWP.

16. Document 9 above, no. 36.

17. Cf. Balamand, no. 24.

18. Cf. ERCDOM, Document 13 above (Section 7.3: Unworthy Witness).

19. Cf. Balamand, no. 22.

20. U.S. Orthodox–Roman Catholic Consultation at the Holy Cross Orthodox School of Theology, Brookline, Mass., May 26-28, 1992, *Origins* 22:5 (June 11, 1992).

21. Santiago, pp. 256-257 (Report of Section IV: Called to Common Witness for a Renewed World, no. 14).

22. CW, no. 44.

23. Oliver S. Tomkins, ed., *The Third World Conference on Faith and Order* (Lund, August 15-25, 1952) (London, SCM Press Ltd., 1953), 16.

24. The theological basis for this common witness and further suggestions may be found in CW, *passim.*

The Ecumenical Dialogue on Moral Issues: Potential Sources of Common Witness or of Divisions

A Study Document of the Joint Working Group Between the Roman Catholic Church and the World Council of Churches

September 25, 1995

Foreword

Already in 1987, the Joint Working Group (JWG) began to discuss new potential and actual sources of divisions within and between the churches, and it gradually focused on personal and social ethical issues and positions as potential sources of discord or of common witness.

The JWG summarized its reflections in its 1990 *Sixth Report*. The report noted that "in fact there is not enough serious, mature, and sustained ecumenical discussion on many ethical issues and positions, personal and social: for example, nuclear armaments and deterrence, abortion and euthanasia, permanent married love and procreation, genetic engineering and artificial insemination" (III.A.1.c.).

The JWG submitted the *Sixth Report* to the Roman Catholic authorities and to the Seventh Assembly of the World Council of Churches (Canberra, February 1991). Both mandated that the JWG should deepen the study as one of the priorities during its next period. It was not to examine the substance of the potentially or actually divisive issues, but it was to describe them and outline how they may best be approached in dialogue, in the hope that such issues can offer new opportunities for the increase of mutual understanding and respect and for common witness, without compromise of a church's convictions or of Christian conscience.

The JWG commissioned consultations, codirected by Dr. Anna-Marie Aagaard (University of Aarhus), one of the WCC presidents, and by Fr. Thomas Stransky, CSP (Tantur Ecumenical Institute, Jerusalem), a Roman Catholic member of the JWG. The report of the first consultation, held in October 1993 (Rome), was submitted to the JWG plenary in June 1994 (Crete, Greece) for decisions on future procedures. Tantur hosted the second, larger consultation in November 1994. A draft received the reactions of the JWG Executive (February 1995) and of the Tantur participants. The JWG plenary in May 1995 (Bose, Italy) corrected a new draft and accepted the text as a study document of the JWG itself.

The study is in two parts:

1. "The Ecumenical Dialogue on Moral Issues: Potential Sources of Common Witness or of Divisions"
2. "Guidelines for Ecumenical Dialogue on Moral Issues"

The study is intended primarily for those dialogues at local, national, and regional levels where Roman Catholics are partners. It may be useful for other bilateral or multilateral discussions.

It is important to understand that the study does not analyze specific controversial issues as such in an attempt to arrive at norms. Rather, it describes present situations and illustrates some underlying contexts which help to place the issues. It suggests possible ways and not the results of dialogue.

The JWG places this study within its general concentration on "The Unity of the Church—the Goal and the Way" (cf. *Sixth Report*, III.A.1.), and more specifically, on new Christian ways of rendering common witness in society at large. Furthermore, the JWG is aware of the study in progress within the WCC (Units I and III) on "Ecclesiology and Ethics" and suggests that it may be complemented by the JWG study document.

COMODERATORS

His Eminence Metropolitan Elias of Beirut

Most Rev. Alan C. Clark

I. Ethics and the Ecumenical Movement

Of increasing urgency in the ecumenical movement, in the relationships between the churches called to give common witness, is their need to address those moral issues which all persons face and to communicate moral guidance to church members and to society at large.

I.1. Cultural and social transformations, conflicting basic values, and scientific and technological advances are fraying the moral fabric of many societies. This context not only provokes questioning of traditional moral values and positions, but it also raises new complex ethical issues for the consciousness and conscience of all human beings.

I.2. At the same time, renewed expectations rise in and beyond the churches that religious communities can and should offer moral guidance in the public arena. Christians and those of other faiths or of secular persuasions desire to live peacefully and justly in a humane society. Can the churches together already offer moral guidance as their contribution to the common good, amidst experienced confusion and controversy?

I.3. Pressing personal and social moral issues, however, are prompting discord among Christians themselves and even threatening new divisions within and between churches. This increases the urgent need for the churches together to find ways of dealing with their controversial ethical issues. By taking the time and care to listen patiently to other Christians, we may understand the pathways by which they arrive at moral convictions and ethical positions, especially if they differ from our own. Otherwise, Christians will continue often to caricature one another's motives, reasoning, and ways of behavior, even with abusive language and acts. Dialogue should replace diatribe.

Other Christians or other churches holding diverging moral convictions can threaten us. They can question our own moral integrity and the foundations of our religious and ethical beliefs. They can demean the authority, credibility, and even integrity of our own church. Whenever an individual or a community selects a moral position or practice to be the litmus test of authentic faith and the sole criterion of the fundamental unity of the church, emotions rise high so that it becomes difficult to hear one another.

Christians, while "speaking the truth in charity" (Eph 4:15), are called upon, as far as possible, "to maintain the unity of the Spirit in the bond of peace" (Eph 4:3) and avoid wounding further the *koinonia* which already exists, although imperfectly, among Christians.

I.4. Therefore, if some ethical issues arouse passionate emotions and create awkward ecumenical relations, the churches should not shun dialogue, for these moral issues also can become church-reconciling means of common witness. A variety of issues are woven into the moral positions of communities. In a prayerful, non-threatening atmosphere, dialogue can locate more precisely where the agreements, disagreements, and contradictions occur. Dialogue can affirm those shared convictions to which the churches should bear common witness to the world at large. Furthermore, the dialogue can discern how ethical beliefs and practices relate to that unity in moral life which is Christ's will.

I.5. Attentive concern for the complexities of the moral life should not cause Christians to lose sight of what is most fundamental for them all: the starting and ending point is the grace of God in Jesus Christ and the Spirit as mediated in the church and in creation. Our life in God is the fundamental continuing source of our movement towards deeper *koinonia*. Only God's initiating and sustaining grace enables Christians to transcend moral differences, overcome divisions, and live their unity in faith.

II. The Church as Moral Environment for Discipleship

Included in the call to the church to be the sign and instrument of salvation in a transformed world is the call to create a moral environment which helps disciples of Christ to shape their personal and communal ethical lives through formation and deliberation.

II.1. The church has the enduring task to be a community of "the Way" (cf. Acts 9:2; 22:4), the home, the family which provides the moral environment of right living and conduct "in Christ," who in the Spirit makes known "the paths of life" to his disciples (Acts 2:28; Ps 16:11).

Discipleship holds together what Christians believe, how believing Christians act, and how they give to fellow Christians and to others an account of why they so believe and so act. Discipleship is the way of believing and acting in the daily struggle to be a faithful witness of Jesus Christ, who commissions his community of disciples to proclaim, teach, and live "all that I have commanded you" (Acts 1:8; Mt 28:20).

II.2. Within the *koinonia* the disciple of Christ is not alone in the process of discerning how to incarnate in one's life the ethical message of the Gospel. Faithful discipleship arises out of private prayer and public worship, of fellowship in sharing each other's joys and bearing each other's burdens. It is nourished by the examples of the saints, the wisdom of teachers, the prophetic vision of the inspired, and the guidance of ministerial leaders.

In real but imperfect communion with one another, each church expects itself and other churches to provide a moral environment through formation and deliberation.

II.3. Formation and deliberation describe the shaping of human character and conduct, the kinds of Christian persons we are and become, and the kinds of actions we decide to do. The scope of Christian morality comprises both our "being" and our "doing." Useful for showing the inseparable dimensions of moral life are the distinctions between moral vision, virtue, value, and obligation.

- Moral vision is a person's, a community's, or a society's "basic script" of the moral realm, the vision of what belongs to the good, the right, and the fitting. A moral vision encompasses, informs, and organizes virtues, values, and obligations. In the Christian moral life, various summaries of teaching and different images express the gospel vision itself: the commandments of love of God and of neighbor, the prophetic teachings on justice and mercy, the beatitudes, the fruits of the Spirit, ascetic ascent and pilgrimage, costly discipleship and the imitation of Christ, stewarding a good land. These and other biblical images suggest pathways which bring definition and coherence to the moral landscape.
- Moral virtues are desirable traits of a person's moral character, such as integrity, humility, and patience; compassion and forgiveness; or prudence, justice, temperance, and fortitude. In an analogous way one can predicate these virtues to communities and societies.
- Moral values are not so much these internalized qualities of character but those moral goods which individuals and society prize, such as respect for the dignity of the human person, freedom and responsibility, friendship, equality and solidarity, and social justice.
- Moral obligations are those duties which persons owe one another in mutual responsibility, in order to live together in harmony and integrity, such as telling the truth and keeping one's word; or those imperatives of a biblical moral vision, such as loving and forgiving the neighbor, including enemies.

II.4. This way of describing the scope of morality (vision, virtue, value, obligation) can provide interrelated criteria for the church's moral task: to be ever the witness to "our great God and Savior Jesus Christ who sacrificed himself for us in order to set us free from all wickedness and to purify a people so that it could be his very own and would have no ambition except to do good" (Ti 2:13-14). A Christian ethic is reductionistic and deficient if it addresses only one or another of these four elements; all of them interact and modify one another. Even when it does address all four, different configurations may characterize its response.

II.5. The task of moral formation and deliberation is one which the churches share. All churches seek to enhance the moral responsibility of their members for living a righteous life and to influence positively the moral standards and well-being of the societies in which they live.

This identifies an ecumenical objective: the quality of the moral environment that churches create together in and through worship, education and nurture, and social witness. Reverence for the dignity of each person created "in the image of God" (Gn 1:37), the affirmation of the fundamental equality of women and men, the pursuit of creative nonviolent strategies for resolving conduct in human relationships, and the responsible stewardship of creation—these are positive contributions of churches through the moral environment they foster. On the other hand, churches can also distort character and malform conscience. They have at times undergirded national chauvinism and ethnocentrism and actively discriminated against persons on the basis of race or nationality, class or gender.

III. Common Sources and Different Pathways of Moral Deliberation

For those pathways of moral reflection and deliberation which churches use in coming to ethical decisions, the churches share the Scriptures and have at their disposal such resources as liturgy and moral traditions, catechisms and sermons, sustained pastoral practices, the wisdom distilled from past and present experiences, and the arts of reflection and spiritual discernment. Yet church traditions configure these common resources in different ways.

III.1. The biblical vision by itself does not provide Christians with all the clear moral principles and practical norms they need. Nor do the Scriptures resolve every ethical case. Narratives join many instructions about proper conduct—general commandments and prohibitions, prophetic exhortations and accusations, counsels of wisdom, legal and ritual prescriptions, and so forth. What moral theology names universal moral principles or norms are in the biblical texts mixed with specific but ever valid commandments and particular provisional prescriptions. The Scriptures' use of images in provocative, often paradoxical ways further makes interpretations of biblical moral teaching difficult.

Nevertheless, there is general consensus that by prayerfully studying the Scriptures and the developing traditions of biblical interpretations, by reflecting on human experiences, and by sharing insights within a community, Christians can reach reasonable judgments and decisions in many cases of ethical conduct.

III.2. Within the history of the church, Christians have developed ways of reflecting systematically on the moral life by the ordering of biblical concepts and images and by rational argument. Such methods intend to introduce clarity and consistency where divergences of discernment threaten to foster confusion and chaos.

For example, one tradition suggests different levels of moral insight and distinguishes between first-order (and unchanging) principles and second-order (and possibly changing) rules. Or more recently, the language of "hierarchy of values" distinguishes between those core values at the heart of Christian discipleship and those other values which are less central yet integral to Christian morality. By emphasizing the "first-order principles" or the "core values," Christians can discover how much they already share, without reducing moral truth or searching for a least common denominator.

III.3. Christian traditions, however, have different estimates of human nature and of the capacity of human reason. Some believe that sin has so corrupted human nature that reason cannot arrive at moral truths. Others maintain that sin has only wounded human nature, and that with divine grace and human discipline, reason can still reach many universally applicable truths about moral living.

For example, by appealing to Scripture and Tradition, to reason and experience, the Roman Catholic Church has developed its understanding of human person and human dignity, of human acts and their goals, and of human rights and responsibilities. In its tradition of moral reflection and teaching, the supreme norm of human life is that universal divine law by which God, in wisdom and love, orders, directs, and governs the whole world and all ways of the human community. By nature and through grace, God enables every person intelligently to grasp this divine law, so that all men and women can come to perceive unchangeable truth more fully. Thus, the revealed law of God and what one calls "natural law" together express that undivided will of God which obliges human beings to seek and to know it as best they can and to live as conscience dictates.

III.4. The tracing of the different pathways which link vision with judgment and decision may help Christians to locate and evaluate some of their differences. For example, Christians who adopt the language of human rights have an effective way of highlighting concern for the powerless, the poor, and the marginalized. While different parties may agree on certain fundamental rights, they can reach different, even contradictory, applications; for example, rights to religious freedom. Moreover, formulations and extensions of rights have become the subject of much dispute, especially in addressing such ethical issues as human reproduction and abortion.

One Christian vision of the integrity of sexual life links sexual relationship with procreation by an interpretation of natural law and of the biblical accounts of creation. Some churches, such as the Roman Catholic Church, hold this position. Other churches judge it most difficult, even impossible to affirm such a link. Those which find the appeal to natural law inconclusive accept the possible separation of the good of procreation from the good of sexual relationship and use this argument to approve contraceptive means in marriage.

III.5. The Christian stance towards war is another example of different pathways which lead to different conclusions. Every tradition accepts the biblical vision of peace between neighbors and, more specifically, the New Testament witness to nonviolent attitudes and acts. A major division has arisen, however, from different judgments concerning the church's collaboration with civic powers as a means of influencing human history. Those churches which have opted for collaboration accept some versions of the "just war" theory; they tolerate, even encourage, the active participation of patriotic Christians in some wars between nations and in armed revolutions within a country. But groups within these same churches agree with those other churches which choose to witness within the political order as noncompromising opponents to all use of military force, because it is contrary to the nonviolent, peacemaking way of Christ. These Christians abstain from bearing arms, even if that be civil disobedience.

Here one can identify the precise point of difference in major theological options which have fundamental consequences for the policy of a church towards war and the conduct of its members.

IV. Different Authoritative Means of Moral Discernment

Different understandings and exercise of church polities and structures of authority mean that moral formation and concrete ethical positions are themselves developed in different ways, even when similar attitudes and outcomes often emerge.

IV.1. The formation of conscience and the development of connected positions on specific ethical issues follow various pathways among different traditions, such as the Orthodox or Roman Catholic, Reformed or Lutheran, Baptist or Friends (Quaker). Every church believes that its members have the task of rightly applying their faith more fully to daily life. All traditions have their own ways of beginning, moving through, and concluding their moral deliberations and of acting upon them. There are different ways of discussion, consulting and arriving at decisions, and of transmitting and receiving them.

Influencing this process are the different ways in which they understand the action of the Holy Spirit and the exercise of the specific role of ministerial leadership in moral discernment and guidance.

In the Roman Catholic Church, bishops, according to the gift received from the Holy Spirit and under his guidance in their ministry of oversight (episkope), are the authoritative guardians and interpreters of the whole moral law, that is, both the law of the Gospel and the natural law. Bishops have the pastoral responsibility and duty of offering moral guidance, even sometimes definitive judgment that a specific action is right or wrong. Moral theologians provide ethical discernment within the community. Confessors, pastoral counselors, and spiritual directors seek to take account of the unique needs of the individual person.

In the Orthodox Church, decisions on ethical issues rest with the hierarchy, whether a synod of bishops or an individual bishop, who are inspired by the Scriptures and the long tradition of the church's pastoral care and moral guidance. The main concern is the spiritual welfare of the person in his or her relationship to God and to fellow human beings. The prudential application of church law and general norms (*oikonomia*) sometimes temper strictness, sometimes increase severity. It is a principal means for both spiritual growth and moral guidance. Orthodox tradition cherishes also the role of experienced spiritual fathers and mothers, and in the process of moral reflection, it stresses prayer among both laity and ordained.

Other churches do not ascribe to ministerial leadership this competency in interpretation or such authority of judgment. They arrive at certain ethical judgments by different polities of consulting and decision making which involve clergy and laity. The Reformed traditions, for example, hold that the living word of the sovereign God is always reforming the church in faith and life. Doctrinal and ethical judgments should be based on the Holy Scripture and informed by the whole tradition of the church, catholic and ecumenical. But no church body has the final authority in defining of word of God. Redeemed and fallible human beings within the church faithfully rely on the process, inspired by the Holy Spirit, whereby they select their ordained and lay leaders and reach authoritative but reformable expressions of faith and positions on personal and social ethics.

IV.2. Thus, ecumenical dialogue on moral issues should include the nature, mission, and structures of the church, the role of ministerial authority and its use of resources in offering moral guidance, and the response to the exercise of such authority within the church. These subjects will in turn help to locate ecumenical gifts and opportunities for common witness, as well as tensions and conflicts.

First, the tensions and conflicts. Is there anxiety and unease because many fear the erosion of the foundational sources of Scripture and Tradition, and of church authority which they believe to be most reliable in guiding Christian conscience and conduct? Or are the ways in which particular church traditions understand, accept, and use the sources and authorities themselves the source of tension and divisiveness? Does deliberation of ethical issues generate anxiety and anger because some persons negatively experience these sources and their use? For example, the interpretation of Scripture and Tradition in such ways that they present the oppressive face of social and theological patriarchy?

One often best understands persistent unchanging stands on a specific issue not by focusing narrowly on it, but by considering what people sense is at stake for life together in society if certain sources, structures, and authorities are ignored or even ridiculed. For example, in some settings, questions about the beginning and ending of life—abortion and euthanasia—carry such moral freight.

Furthermore, some churches stress more than others the structures of authority and formal detailed statements on belief and morality. This can create an imbalance and lack of realism in the dialogue, if one easily compares the official teachings of some churches with the more diffuse estimates of the general belief and practice of others.

Thus, awareness of the moral volatility which surround the sources and authorities used—which they are, by whom and how they are interpreted, and with what kinds of concerns they are associated—is critical for understanding why some moral issues are difficult and potentially divisive among Christians.

IV.3. Second, gifts and opportunities. Discerning the gifts in church traditions that may lie unnoticed as treasures for the moral life poses another set of questions for the ecumenical dialogue:

- What do inherited understandings and forms of *koinonia* (communion or fellowship), *diakonia* (service), and *martyria* (witness) mean for moral formation today?
- Which visions, virtues, values, and obligations are nurtured by the *lex orandi, lex credendi, lex vivendi* (the rule of praying, of believing, of living) as particular traditions and structures embody them?
- Which practices in the varied traditions contribute to the legitimate difference and authentic diversity of the moral life of the one church? How can both common and distinctive practices contribute to the moral richness of the *koinonia*?

In dialogue Christians thus need both to recognize the rich resources they share for moral formation and to ask critically how these in fact function in a variety of contexts, cultures, and peoples.

V. Ecumenical Challenges to Moral Formation and Deliberation

Churches which share real but imperfect *koinonia* face new challenges as communities of moral formation and deliberation: the pluralism of moral positions, the crisis of moral authority, changing moral judgments on traditional issues, and positions on new ones.

V.1. Christians agree that there is a moral universe which is grounded in the wisdom and will of God, but they may have different interpretations of God's wisdom, of the nature of that universe, and of the degree to which human beings are called to fashion it as cocreators with God.

We cannot deny three facts:

- First, Christians do share a long history of extensive unity in moral teaching and practice, flowing in part from a shared reflection on common sources, such as the ten commandments and the beatitudes.
- Second, divided Christian communities eventually did acquire some differences in ways of determining moral principles and acting upon them.
- Third, these differences have led today to such a pluralism of moral frameworks and positions within and between the ecclesial traditions that some positions appear to be in sharp tension, even in contradiction. The same constellation of basic moral principles may admit of a diversity of rules which intends to express a faithful response to biblical vision and to these principles. Even the explicit divine commandment "Thou shalt not kill" receives conflicting applications: for example, yes or no to the death penalty as such or for certain crimes.

V.2. The crisis of moral authority within the churches further complicates effective moral formation and deliberation. Even where a church has an established moral tradition, some members strongly propose alternative positions. In fact, church members are becoming more vocal and persistent in sharp criticism of authoritative moral teaching and practice, and they use the same sources as the basis for differing ethical positions. The fashioning of effective moral formation and deliberation in these settings is an urgent ecumenical task.

V.3. The process of the formulation and reception of ethical decisions also poses a major challenge of participation: who forms and formulates the churches' moral decisions, using which powers of influence and action, and which instruments of consultation? How do church members and the society at large assess, appropriate, and respond to official church pronouncements? What are the channels of such a response, and what kinds of response are encouraged or discouraged?

V.4. Are not the conditions and structures of dialogue themselves prime ethical issues for churches? They are potentially either divisive or reconciling. They can either enhance or undermine koinonia in faith, life, and witness. One starting point is simply to acknowledge that the way in which a church (or churches together) orders and structures its decision making and then publicly communicates its decisions already embodies a social ethic and influences moral teaching and practice. Structures, offices, and roles express moral values or disvalues. Ways of exercising power, governance, and access have moral dimensions. To ignore this is to fail to understand why moral issues and the ways in which they are addressed can be so divisive, even within the same church.

V.5. The extent to which moral judgments can change needs candid dialogue. For example, until the middle of the eighteenth century, historical churches even in their official statements acquiesced in the practice of slavery; some leaders even pro-posed biblical and theological arguments to sanction it. Today all churches judge slavery to be an intrinsic evil everywhere and always wrong. What does this kind of change of a former established teaching of the churches mean for understanding that degree of unity in faithful moral teaching which full communion requires?

Christians in dialogue should not ignore or hide evidence of change in moral teaching or practice. Churches do not always welcome such openness, despite their emphasis on human finitude and sin in the historical development of teachings and practices. Moreover, the interpretation of change in moral teaching is itself a source of disagreement and tension. While some may interpret the change as positive growth in faithful moral understanding, others may judge it as easy compromise or rank failure.

Apartheid is a particular example, where after long deliberation some families of churches went beyond the rejection of apartheid as inconsistent with the Gospel to judge that those who maintained apartheid to be Christian as placing themselves outside the fellowship of the church.

Hence, an ecumenical approach to morality requires the awareness of differ-ent evaluations of changing moral traditions.

V.6. Several new ethical issues especially challenge ecumenical collaboration when the churches have no clear and detailed precedents, much less experience and consensus. Only to begin a long list of examples: economic policies in a world of "haves" and "have-nots"; immigration and refugee regulations within and between nations; industrialization and the environment; women's rights in society and in the churches; *in vitro* fertilization, genetic engineering, and other biomedical developments. Christians and others experience the urgency of these unavoidable, complex ethical issues. They expect the churches to offer moral guidance on them.

Even the experts in the empirical sciences may offer contradicting data or dis-agree on the implications of scientific findings. The ways in which the churches together seek out, gather, and order the facts with the best knowledge available from the empirical scientists is already an ecumenical challenge. In the light of this, Christians can responsibly address the moral implications of issues and offer guidance.

VI. Christian Moral Witness in a Pluralistic Society

Christians are called to witness in the public forum to their common moral convictions with humility and with respect for others and their convictions. They should seek dialogue and collaboration with those of other faith communities, indeed with all persons of good will who are committed to the well-being of humanity.

VI.1. In the political process of legislation and judicial decision, churches may rightly raise their prophetic voice in support or in protest. In common witness they can take a firm stand when they believe that public decisions or laws affirm or contradict God's purposes for the dignity of persons or the integrity of creation.

One can highlight the example of common witness of Christians in the struggle against apartheid and "ethnic cleansing." In fact, such moral issues of human rights and equality have been community-building experiences of *koinonia* in faith and witness, which some perceive as profound experiences of "church."

VI.2. Sometimes churches and Christian advocacy groups may agree on the basic values which they should promote, yet they disagree about the means that should be used, especially in the political arena. In such situations, they should seek collaboration as much as their agreement allows and at the same time articulate the reasons for their disagreement. Disagreement over some particular points or means to an end should not rule out all collaboration. In these cases, however, it is all the more important to be open and explicit about the areas of disagreement so as to avoid confusion in common witness.

VI.3. In the public arena, the churches are one family of moral community among others, whether religious or secular. Moral discernment is not the exclusive preserve of Christians. Christian moral understandings and approaches to ethical issues should be open to evaluate carefully the moral insights and judgments of others. Often moral traditions overlap, even when the approaches and idioms of language may be different.

In any case, the manner and the methods by which the churches publicly commend their own moral convictions must respect the integrity of others and their civic rights and liberties. For the authority of the churches in the public moral debate of pluralistic societies is the authority of their moral wisdom, insights, and judgments as these commend themselves to the intelligence and conscience of others.

Guidelines for the Ecumenical Dialogue on Moral Issues

The acceptance and practice of these suggested guidelines for dialogue can promote the goal of the ecumenical movement: the visible unity of Christians in one faith and one eucharistic fellowship, expressed in worship, common life, and service, in order that the world may believe.

We assume that churches are seeking to be faithful to God in Christ, to be led by the Holy Spirit, and to be a moral environment which helps all members in the formation of Christian conscience and practice. We affirm the responsibility of every church to provide moral guidance for its members and for society at large.

God, who through the Spirit leads Christians to manifest the unity of the church, calls the churches, while still divided, to common witness: that is, together in Christian discipleship they are to manifest whatever divine gifts of truth and life they already share and experience.

A lack of ecumenical dialogue on personal and social moral issues and a weak will to overcome whatever divisiveness they may prompt place yet another stumbling block in the proclamation of the one Gospel of Jesus Christ, who is "the Way, the Truth, and the Life" (Jn 14:6).

Guidelines

1. In fostering the *koinonia* or communion between the churches, we should as much as possible consult and exchange information with one another, in a spirit of mutual understanding and respect, always "speaking the truth in charity" (Eph 4:15).

2. In dialogue we should try first to understand the moral positions and practices of others as they understand them, so that each one recognizes oneself in the descriptions. Only then can we evaluate them out of our own tradition and experience.

3. In comparing the good qualities and moral ideals or the weaknesses and practices of various Christian communities, one should compare ideals with ideals and practice with practice. We should understand what others want to be and to do in order to be faithful disciples of Christ, even though those others—as we ourselves—are burdened with weakness and sin.

4. We recognize that Christians enjoy a history of substantial unity in moral teaching and practice. By placing ethical issues within this inheritance of moral unity, we can more carefully understand the origin and nature of any present disagreement or division.

5. We trust that Christians can discover the bases for their moral vision, values, and conduct in the Scriptures and in other resources: moral traditions (including specific church and interchurch statements), liturgies, preaching and catechetics, pastoral practices, common human experiences, and methods of reflection.

6. We should seek from the empirical sciences the best available knowledge on specific issues and, if possible, agree on the data and their ethical implications before offering moral guidance.

7. We should acknowledge that various church traditions in fact sometimes agree, sometimes differ in the ways they:

- Use Scriptures and other common resources, as well as the data of empirical sciences
- Relate moral vision, ethical norms, and prudential judgments
- Identify a specific moral issue and formulate the problems
- Communicate within a church those values and disciplines which help to develop its own moral environment in the shaping of Christian character
- Understand and exercise ministerial leadership and oversight in moral guidance

8. We should be ever alert to affirm whatever is shared in common and to admit where there are serious divergent, even contrary, stances. We should never demand that fellow Christians with whom we disagree compromise their integrity and convictions.

9. In the public arena of pluralistic societies, we should be in dialogue also with others, whether religious or secular. We try to understand and evaluate their moral insights and judgments and to find a common language to express our agreements and differences.

10. When the dialogue continues to reveal sincere but apparently irreconcilable moral positions, we affirm in faith that the fact of our belonging together in Christ is more fundamental than the fact of our moral differences. The deep desire to find an honest and faithful resolution of our disagreements is itself evidence that God continues to grace the *koinonia* among disciples of Christ.

Participants

October 1993 Consultation

Prof. Anna Marie Aagaard, University of Aarhus, Denmark
Rev. Peter Baelz, United Kingdom
Rev. Brian V. Johnstone, CSSR, Academia Alfonsiana, Rome
Msgr. John A. Radano, Pontifical Council for Promoting Christian Unity
Dr. Teodora Rossi, Rome
Prof. Alexander Stavropoulos, Athens University
Rev. Thomas Stransky, CSP, Tantur Ecumenical Institute, Jerusalem
Rev. Elizabeth S. Tapia, Union Theological Seminary, New York

November 1994 Consultation

Prof. Anna Marie Aagaard, University of Aarhus
Rev. Peter Baelz, United Kingdom

Rev. Bénézet Bujo, Moraltheologisches Institut, Universität Fribourg
Rev. Brian V. Johnstone, CSSR, Academia Alfonsiana, Rome
Rev. William Henn, OFMCap, Collegio S. Lorenzo, Rome
Dr. Donna Orsuto, Gregorian University/The Lay Centre at Foyer Unitas, Rome
Msgr. John A. Radano, Pontifical Council for Promoting Christian Unity
Prof. Larry Rasmussen, Union Theological Seminary, New York
Dr. Martin Robra, WCC/Unit III ECOS, Theology of Life Program
Prof. Alexander Stavropoulos, Athens University
Rev. Thomas Stransky, CSP, Tantur Ecumenical Institute, Jerusalem
Rev. Elizabeth S. Tapia, Union Theological Seminary, New York

Index

speaking in tongues, 365, 369, 371, 374,
381, 408, 411
spiritual life, 297-298
nurturing of, 267-268
and renewal, 533
"spiritual" unity, 19
Stafford, J. Francis, *as contributor*, 236
Stewart, Richard, 236
Stott, John, 426
*Summons to Witness to Christ in Today's
World*, 343-360
syncretism, 466
synod of Lutheran Church, as authoritative
teacher, 35

Tanner, Mary, foreword, xiii-xvi
teaching the Gospel
and apostolic faith, 258-259
authoritative teaching, 250-251, 436-
438
bishops' responsibility, 134
continuity with apostolic community,
332-333
ordained ministry and, 133-138
priests and, 136
revelation and authority, 431-439
within Methodism, 303
within Roman Catholic Church, 303
Theological Declaration of Barmen, 185
*The Theology of Marriage and the Problem of
Mixed Marriages*, 180, 224
Thomas Aquinas, Saint, 12, 97, 136
Thomas, Saint, 209
Tillard, Jean-Marie, 234, 542
*Toward a Common Expression of the One
Apostolic Faith*, 509
Towards an Agreed Statement on Holy Spirit,
233
*Towards the Common Expression of the
Apostolic Faith Today*, 495, 528
Towards a Common Profession of Faith, 494
*Towards a Common Understanding of the
Church*, 179-229
Towards a Statement on the Church, 235-253,
255, 256, 278-279, 286, 318
tradition, and Holy Scripture, 33, 355, 373,
382-383, 387-389, 401-404, 431
Trinity
apostolic faith and, 258
and the Church, 90-106
and communion, 95
justification and church, 77-78

koinonia with, 404-405
and revelation of God, 291-292
and work of Jesus Christ, 201-202
Triune God. *See* Trinity
"two kingdoms" doctrine, 11, 149-151

Unitatis Redintegratio. See Decree on
Ecumenism
United Bible Societies, 468
United Reformed Church in the United
Kingdom, 185
unity of Church. *See* church fellowship;
models of union/unity
*The Unity of the Church and the Renewal of
Human Community*, 528
The Unity We Seek, 91, 102
universal church. *See* church universal
Ut Unum Sint, x, xvii

Vatican Council II. *See* Second Vatican
Council
Vatican Secretariat for Non-Christians,
501, 510
Vatican Secretariat for Promoting Christian
Unity, 3, 7, 196, 235, 343, 344, 367,
368, 379, 380, 428, 481, 500, 501, 503,
542, 565
See also under its later name Pontifical
Council for Promoting Christian
Unity
Vischer, Lucas, 3

Wagner, Alois, 530
Wainwright, Geoffrey, 542
as contributor, 256, 284
introductory note, 233-234
Ways to Community, 3, 16, 17, 74, 75
WCC. *See* World Council of Churches
Week of Prayer for Christian Unity, 195,
501, 524-525
Wesley, John, 241, 244, 251, 264, 265, 266,
278, 279, 288, 294, 297, 299, 301-303
and discernment, 314
on the Lord's Supper, 311
sermons of, 313
Wicks, Jared, 234
Willebrands, Cardinal, 12, 13, 514, 523,
525, 526, 545
witnessing, 305
challenges to common witness, 352-355
to Christ, 345-347
in the Church, 349-350